The Most
Scenic Drives
In America

The Most Scenic Drives In America

120 Spectacular Road Trips

Reader's Digest

The Readers Digest Association, Inc.
Pleasantville, New York/Montreal

A Reader's Digest Book

Copyright © 2005 The Reader's Digest Association, Inc.

All rights reserved.
Unauthorized reproduction, in any manner, is prohibited.

Reader's Digest is a registered trademark of
The Reader's Digest Association, Inc.

Published by arrangement with Dolezal & Associates

For Reader's Digest

Project Editor: Barbara Booth

Associate Art Director: George McKeon

Cover Designer: Jennifer Tokarski

Executive Editor, Trade Publishing: Dolores York

Director of Production: Michael Braunschweiger

Associate Publisher, Trade Publishing: Christopher T. Reggio

President & Publisher, Trade Publishing: Harold Clarke

ISBN: 10:0-7621-0871-1
ISBN: 13: 978-0-7621-0871-8

For Dolezal & Associates

Project Manager: Robert J. Dolezal

Photoshop Artist: Jerry Bates

Layout Artist: Barbara Dolezal

Writer: Robert J. Dolezal

Researchers: Jerry Bates, Robert J. Dolezal

Prior Edition Contributors:

Writers: Chris Bohjalian, John L. Cobbs, Justin Cronin, Martha Fay, Catherine Fredman, Carole Jacobs, Barbara A. Noe, Donald S. Olson, William G. Scheller, Mel White

Researchers: David J. Fleischmann, Margie Rynn, John Sellers, Joel Stein

Copy Editor: Mel Minter

Indexer: Rose Bernal

Maps: Ortelius Design, Inc., Madison, Wisconsin

Endpaper map: Copyright © GeoNova LLC

A Note to our Readers
Researchers and editors gathered and carefully fact-checked all of the information in this book. Since site information is always subject to change, you are urged to check the facts presented before you begin your trip to avoid any inconvenience.

Address any comments about *Most Scenic Drives* to:

The Reader's Digest Association, Inc.
Adult Trade Publishing
Reader's Digest Road
Pleasantville, NY 10570-7000

rd.com For more Reader's Digest products and information, visit our website.

Printed in China
1 3 5 7 9 10 8 6 4 2

About This Book

One of America's most popular pastimes is, quite simply, going for long, leisurely drives in the country—and that's what this book is all about. Making its way through each of our 50 states—from Alaska to Florida and Maine to California—this completely revised edition of THE MOST SCENIC DRIVES IN AMERICA serves as your personal guide to the most colorful, breathtaking, intriguing, dramatic, and eye-pleasing stretches of road in the U.S.A. Divided into four regions—the Western States, the Rocky Mountain States, the Central States, and the Eastern States—the 120 tours in THE MOST SCENIC DRIVES IN AMERICA will take you on an unforgettable visit to America's scenic splendors, celebrating its natural wonders, man-made marvels, and gloriously varied landscapes.

The drives were selected with assistance from state tourism offices, the National Forest Service, the National Park Service, chambers of commerce, and countless travel experts in every part of the country. Each drive route (shown in red on a specially designed map) follows a numbered sequence of points of interest—towns and cities, canyons and caverns, mountains and meadows, parks and historic sites—with each of these places described in the text and pinpointed on the map.

To help you plan and better enjoy the tours, each drive is accompanied by a fact-filled Trip Tips box that provides information on mileage, the best travel seasons, nearby attractions, special events, and whom to contact for more details. Star Routes—22 in all—offer thumbnail sketches of shorter but especially scenic roads that are located in the same vicinity as the main tours. Additional boxes highlight distinctive characteristics of the areas, whether they are local plants, animals, customs, foods, or a variety of historical events.

Both out on the road and in the comfort of your home, you'll find that THE MOST SCENIC DRIVES IN AMERICA will be a welcome companion. It not only helps motorists plan trips filled with beauty and diversity but also fascinates the armchair traveler with hundreds of colorful photographs that bring the scenery to life. Whether you plan to take a drive in some far corner of the country or one that's virtually in your own backyard, THE MOST SCENIC DRIVES IN AMERICA will guide you to a host of beautiful byways—the roads that driving was made for.

—The Editors

The
Western
States

Page 10

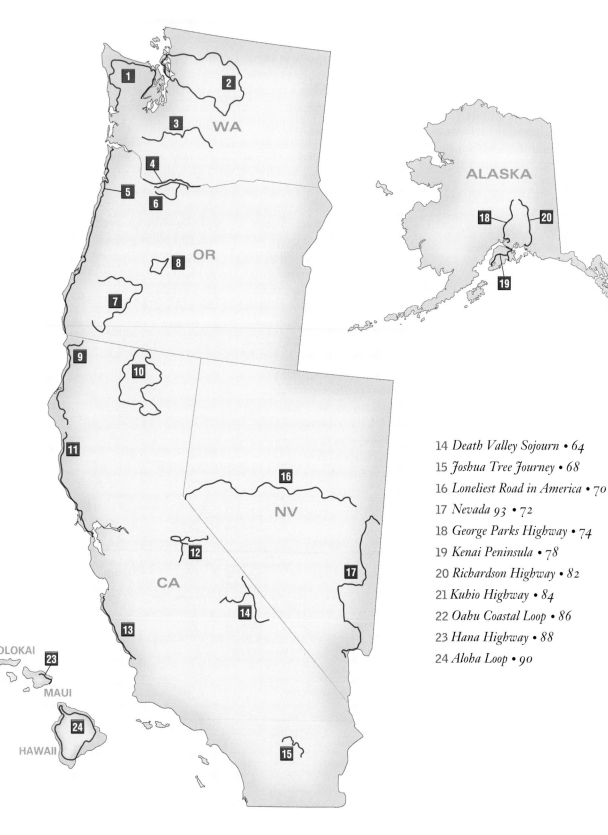

PART 2

The Rocky Mountain States

Page 94

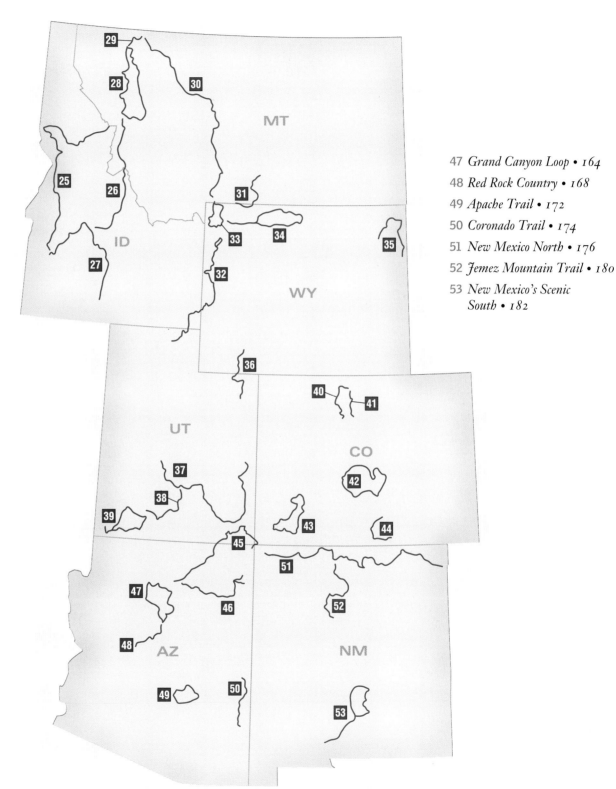

PART 3

The Central States

Page 184

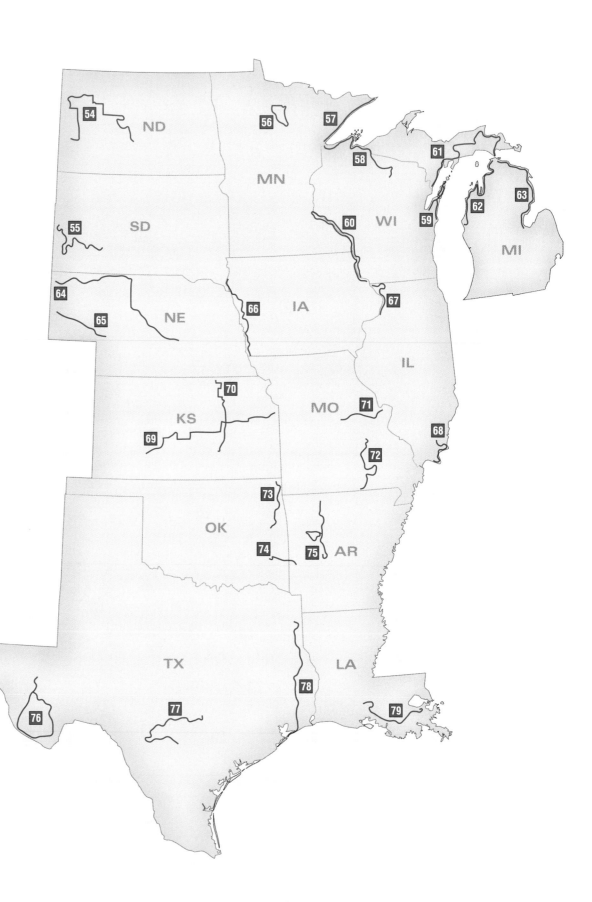

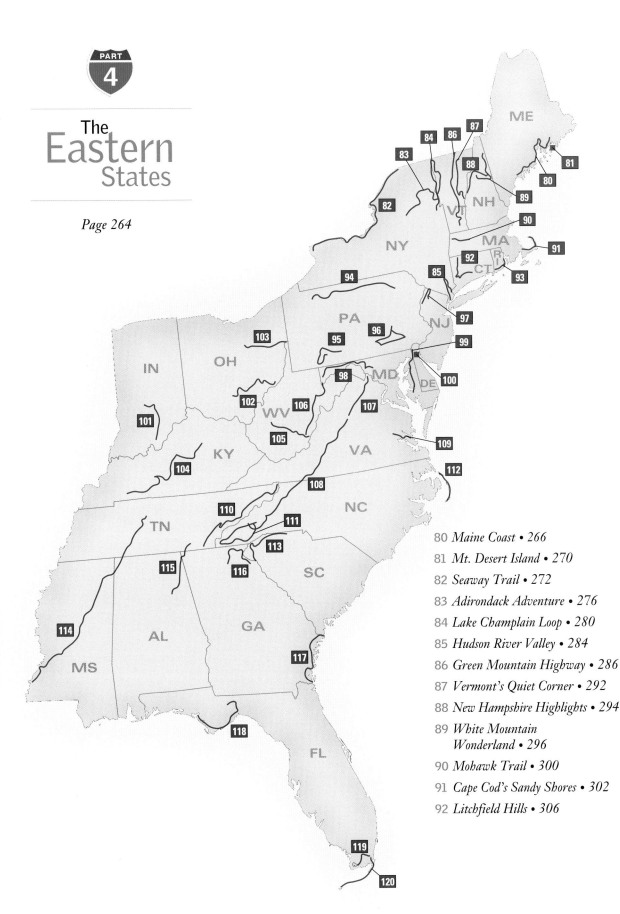

PART 4

The Eastern States

Page 264

PART 1

The Western States

Olympic Loop

Three wildly different worlds in one, the Olympic Peninsula embraces misty rain forests, snowcapped summits, and rocky shores—all within a single drive.

Mountains and fog drape Hurricane Ridge in Olympic National Park.

For an American locale, the names sound vaguely exotic, distinctly different: Dosewallips, Elwha, Queets, Hoquiam. And how fitting, for the territory they share, Washington's Olympic Peninsula, makes up a moody, remote, and richly varied corner of the continental United States.

▮ Potlatch State Park

Nearly surrounded by water (the Pacific Ocean to the west, the Strait of Juan de Fuca to the north, and Puget Sound to the east), the Olympic Peninsula abounds with scenic waterside views. The vistas unfold right at the start of this dramatic drive: for some 30 miles between Potlatch and Brinnon, Rte. 101 hugs the wooded western bank of the Hood Canal, a long, narrow arm of Puget Sound. On the great bend of the canal sits Potlatch State Park, an ideal place for digging clams and picking oysters (a license is required). The 57-acre park, named for the feast local Indians held to celebrate the birth of an heir or other special event, is a good place to have a little feast of your own, since numerous spots are available for picnicking.

▮ Lake Cushman State Park

As the drive continues north along the lower canal, fishing resorts dot the shore, while to the west the Olympic Mountains beckon with their snowy peaks. Closer to the highway, the route is studded with showy rhododendrons, reddish madrona trees, and roadside stands offering fresh shellfish. At Hoodsport a spur road leads north to Lake Cushman State Park and then on to Olympic National Park, where a nearby attraction is the Staircase Rapids Nature Trail. The four-mile path gets its name from the coursing cascades created by the steep terrain traversed by the Skokomish River.

▮ Dosewallips State Park

Straddling Rte. 101, this 425-acre park provides the best of two worlds—the fresh water of the Dosewallips River and the salt water of the Hood Canal. The mild currents of the canal make it an ideal habitat for clams and Quilcene oysters (named for a nearby town that boasts one of the largest oyster hatcheries in the world). The best time to harvest these oysters is at low tide, but first call the shellfish hotline at 800-562-5632 to find out which areas to avoid (some may have unsafe levels of bacteria).

▮ Mt. Walker Viewpoint

A few miles north of Brinnon, turn east on a steep gravel road leading to the summit of Mt. Walker, where the view takes in more than 5 million acres of surrounding territory—an area nearly as large as New Hampshire.

Poised 2,750 feet above sea level, a scenic overlook affords sweeping panoramas of the Olympic Mountains, Puget Sound, and the Cascade Range. From the northern viewpoint you can see Quilcene Canyon, Quilcene Bay, and several distant pinnacles. The southern viewpoint takes in the Hood Canal Floating Bridge, the longest one of its kind in the world that is built over tidal waters; the city of Seattle, some 30 miles away; and 14,411-foot Mt. Rainier, the highest peak in Washington.

Mt. Walker can also be reached by foot. About a quarter mile past the entrance to the gravel road, a two-mile trail meanders up the mountainside through a forest of Douglas firs.

▮ Port Townsend

Continuing north on Rte. 101, take Rte. 20 (just before Discovery Bay) to Port Townsend. Located at the entrance to Puget Sound, this quaint coastal town was once a hectic seaport cluttered with high-masted riggers from around the world. Nowadays the town's main attraction is its wealth of

∷∷∷ Trip Tips ∷∷∷

Length: About 250 miles, plus side trips.

When to go: Drive is popular year-round, but best from April through October.

Lodging: Available at Port Angeles, La Push, Forks, Kalaloch, and (during summer) at Lake Crescent and Sol Duc Hot Springs.

Words to the wise: Bring adequate rain gear for hiking and camping. When beach walking, consult a tide table.

Nearby attractions: The Space Needle (offering dramatic views of Puget Sound, the Olympic Range, and Mt. Rainier), Seattle. Victoria, British Columbia (ferry departs from Port Angeles).

Further information: Olympic National Park, 600 E. Park Ave., Port Angeles, WA 98362; tel. 206-452-0330; www.nps.gov/olym/

lovingly preserved 19th-century buildings, some of them converted into bed-and-breakfast inns and most of them reminiscent of San Francisco's gabled Victorian charm. A number of picturesque private homes can be visited during special tours held in May and September.

At nearby Fort Worden State Park, a 430-acre estate on a former naval base, a parade ground serves as the stage for summer arts festivals. Stroll along the park's beach for a view of the Cascades and nearby islands.

6 Sequim

Visitors to Sequim (pronounced Skwim) might wonder why it is that the region surrounding this sunny little town gets fewer than 17 inches of rain per year, while the western slopes of the Olympic Mountains receive well over 100 inches annually. The fact is that the Olympic Peninsula has both the driest and the wettest climates in all of the Pacific Northwest. And the key to this phenomenon is the mountains themselves. Though not high compared to other ranges, the peaks are so close to the sea that they manage to wring most of the moisture from rising air masses as they move inland from the Pacific. The result is a drenched rain forest to the west of the mountains and a dry rain shadow to the east.

7 Dungeness National Wildlife Refuge

Curving 5½ miles out into the Strait of Juan de Fuca, Dungeness Spit tames the strait's wild waves within a calm saltwater lagoon. The refuge here—founded as a sanctuary for black brant, one of many migrating waterfowl that feed and rest in the area—is also home to deer, seals, shellfish (most notably, the delicious Dungeness crab), and more than 275 kinds of birds. A half-mile trail from an adjacent campground leads through woodlands to the base of the spit and then continues beyond a bluff to the tip, where lighthouse lovers can visit an 1857 beacon.

8 Port Angeles

Port Angeles is not only the largest city on the Olympic Peninsula, but also the gateway to Olympic National Park, which dominates the peninsula like a great, gorgeous centerpiece. The park owes its existence to one of its inhabitants: the Roosevelt elk. Much of the nearly 1 million acres that now make up the sprawling park were declared a forest reserve in 1897 by Congress. In 1909 President Theodore Roosevelt designated the area a national monument to protect a local treasure—a subspecies of elk (renamed the Roosevelt elk in his honor). Some 30 years later, his cousin, President Franklin D. Roosevelt, made the monument our 28th national park.

At the park's main visitor center, located on Mt. Angeles Road, visitors can learn about its natural history and receive information on camping, hiking, fishing, and accommodations. Skirted by Rte. 101, the park is accessible by numerous spur roads, but none of them extend into its core. More than 600 miles of trails pick up where the roads end, helping to keep this enchanted realm as unspoiled as ever.

9 Hurricane Ridge Road

Just beyond the park's visitor center, a 17-mile drive on Hurricane Ridge Road leads south to Hurricane Ridge, so named because winter storms can whip up 100-mile-per-hour winds. As it climbs to an elevation of one mile, the road slices through a dense forest of Douglas firs where deer, marmots, and black bears may be spotted. Turnouts along the way offer dramatic vistas of the Strait of Juan de Fuca, Dungeness Spit,

Vancouver Island, and on clear days, the northern Cascades on the far side of Puget Sound. The views from the ridge itself are even more dramatic: the San Juan

At low tide, tidepools abound at the Point of Arches on Shi Shi Beach, south of Neah Bay. Follow the cardinal rule of tidepooling: look but don't touch or take—leave them for others to see.

The rain forest of the Olympic Peninsula receives moisture nearly every day of the year and requires nearly a half inch per day just to keep up its rainfall average. For safety, use the boardwalks found on major hiking trails through the forest.

Islands and the Canadian coast lie to the north, while to the south soar jagged peaks of the Olympic Range, with 7,965-foot-tall Mt. Olympus rising above them all.

From Hurricane Ridge, hike along the Big Meadow Nature Trail or take Obstruction Point Road, an eight-mile stretch of unpaved road, to Obstruction Point, where several hiking trails originate. In winter, when the snow gets as deep as 20 feet, it often lasts through June), Hurricane Ridge becomes a mecca for skiing, sledding, and snowshoeing.

10 Elwha River Valley

Once you are back on Rte. 101, the drive continues west toward Elwha, where a paved road heads south along the Elwha River, a prime fly-fishing stream. The forest of hemlocks, firs, and big-leaf maples obscures all but the occasional glimpse of the Elwha River, but scenic turnouts provide plenty of opportunities for picture taking. The route takes you past two campgrounds, a lake, and a scenic overlook before reaching a two-mile trail that leads to Olympic Hot Springs.

11 Lake Crescent

According to Indian lore, Lake Crescent was formed when nearby Storm King Mountain became so furious at two warring tribes that it broke off a piece of itself and hurled it at them, inadvertently damming a stream. But science offers another explanation, holding that the lake was carved by glaciers during the Ice Age, some 10,000 years ago. However it was born, Lake Crescent is a beauty—a sparkling, deep-blue gem whose fresh waters mirror the surrounding wooded hillsides. About 10 miles long and more than 600 feet deep, the lake is one of the largest bodies of water in Olympic National Park. Among the activities to be enjoyed here are swimming, boating, camping, paddle-wheeler cruises, and fishing (anglers are especially fond of the rare Beardslee trout found about 80 feet below the surface). Near the visitor center, a short trail leads across a single-log bridge to 90-foot-high Marymere Falls.

12 Sol Duc Hot Springs

If miles of hiking or hours of sitting behind the wheel have made you tired or sore, the warm mineral waters of Sol Duc Hot Springs may be just the tonic you need. Long cherished by Indians for their therapeutic value, the springs were discovered by a pioneer in 1880 and have been soothing aching muscles ever since.

The resort, which is tucked away in a valley of old-growth Douglas firs, has three hot tubs (temperatures range from 98°F to 104°F), a heated swimming pool, and rustic cabins. Sol Duc is also a major trailhead for hikes into the park's interior.

13 La Push

Continuing westward on Rte. 101, the drive leaves Olympic National Park and heads toward the village of Forks. One mile north of town, take a 15-mile detour west to La Push, an old Indian fishing village that is home to the Quileute Indian Reservation. The town's charcoal-gray beaches are noted for their ever-changing collection of driftwood and their fine views of offshore whales and sea stacks.

14 Bogachiel State Park

Situated on the banks of the Bogachiel River, this 125-acre park makes an ideal base camp for exploring the western side of the Olympic Peninsula. Two short

Star Route

★ Coastal Route 112

A few miles west of Port Angeles, Rte. 112 veers off from Rte. 101 for a 62-mile side trip to Neah Bay. After crossing the Elwha River, the drive weaves past wooded hills, then hugs the shore as it approaches Neah Bay, where the Makah Museum houses thousands of prehistoric Indian artifacts. A short, treacherous trail nearby leads to Cape Flattery (the north-westernmost point in the lower 48 states), where a bluff overlooks Tatoosh Island and the entrance to the Strait of Juan de Fuca.

trails wind through a densely forested valley where red alders and cottonwoods suddenly give way to spruces and hemlocks. During fall, salmon and steel-head attract anglers from all over. Continuing south, follow Hoh River Road east into the heart of the Hoh Rain Forest.

15 Hoh Rain Forest

Take some soil—earth so rich and deep that it can support just about any form of vegetation. Add a dash of heat, but just the right amount—a bit too much and the plants will wither, too little and they could freeze. Then let the mixture sim-mer in moisture—plenty of rain, fog, and humidity. Such is the recipe for a rain forest.

One of the best examples of a temperate-zone rain forest in the world, and one of the few conifer-ous ones in existence, the Hoh is nourished by a continuous stream of warm, moist air from the Pacific, yielding some 140 inches of rain-fall per year. The result is a land-scape of extraordinary lushness. Perhaps a dozen different shades of green, all of them suffused

with soft sunlight, soothe the eyes with a glorious glow. Feathery ferns, verdant vines, lime-colored lichen—these are but a few of the 300-odd kinds of plants that thrive within this great natural greenhouse.

The forest is also alive with animals, and every now and then they make their presence known to visitors, piercing the eerie still-ness with some startling sight or sound—the unmistakable shriek of a bald eagle, perhaps, or the sudden leap of a Douglas squirrel. Countless deer, elk, cougars, and black bears inhabit the Hoh, and you may even catch a glimpse of one of these critters along the two short trails that loop from the visitor center, located at the end of Hoh River Road. For a more ambitious hike, obtain a free back-packing permit for the Hoh River Trail, which meanders some 17 miles through the river valley to the base of Mt. Olympus.

16 Ruby Beach

After leaving the misty, mystical rain forest, the drive heads toward Ruby Beach, part of the Kalaloch Strip, which is accessible over short paths from the highway. Though vastly different from the rain forest, this 11-mile-long

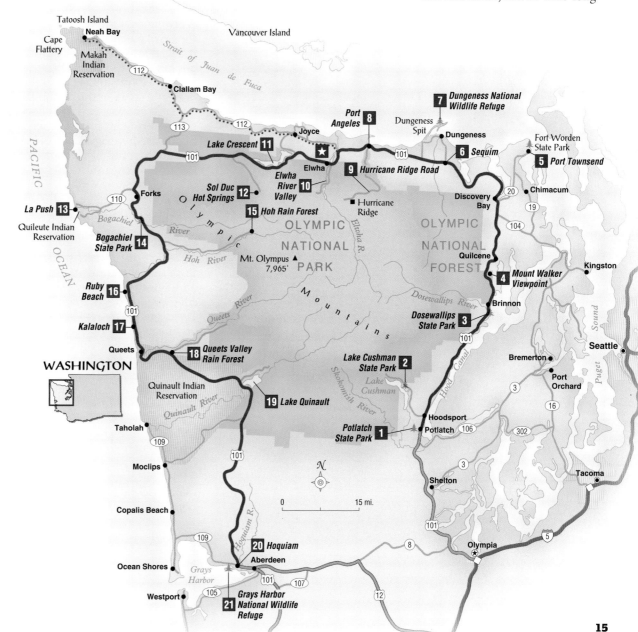

Crossed by a hiking bridge, Rainforest River on the Olympic Peninsula cascades its tumultuous water down steep-sided ravines of verdant green moss-covered rocks on its way to the Pacific Ocean.

coastal strip—part of Olympic National Park's 57 miles of wild seashore—is equally untouched by time. One of the few changes that have occurred can be seen from Ruby Beach, which is named for the glistening garnet crystals that give the sand its pinkish hue. Offshore sea stacks bear witness to a time long ago when these massive blocks of basalt and volcanic rock were still a part of the mainland.

17 Kalaloch

A few miles south of Ruby Beach, the drive reaches Kalaloch, where the largest coastal beach campground on the Olympic Peninsula is perched on a bluff that offers dramatic views of the ocean, particularly on stormy days. Clamming, surf fishing, and beach hiking are popular activities here, but the best fun of all comes at low tide, when visitors can explore tidepools teeming with sea urchins, hermit crabs, anemones, and other creatures of the sea.

18 Queets Valley Rain Forest

Imagine a place where you can feel both the salty spray of an ocean and, only a short drive away, the fragrant drizzle of a rain forest. Welcome to Queets Valley, where an unpaved 14-mile road along the Queets River connects one watery wonderland with another. Like the park's other rain forests— Hoh and Quinault—Queets is a place of emerald splendor, a gigantic garden where nearly every square inch of ground is graced with greenery—club moss, licorice ferns, sorrel, and the like. But while Queets may be crowded with plants, people are less abundant here. As a result, shy-natured Roosevelt elk (some 5,000 of which live in the park) can occasionally be seen grazing in the meadows beside three-mile-long Sam's River Loop Trail, which has its trailhead at the campground.

19 Lake Quinault

Surrounded by a dark, dense rain forest, Lake Quinault—a glacier-fed lake four miles long and two miles wide—is one of the most popular recreation spots on the Olympic Peninsula. At Quinault Lodge, one of the few large, old-fashioned lodges left in the Pacific Northwest, you can get information on rafting and nearby nature trails and hiking trails. Take a short walk from the lodge to the Quinault loop trail, which leads to one of the largest known stands of Douglas firs in America. After arriving at the lake, drop by the forest station on South Shore Road to check out road conditions and inquire about permits and regulations for fishing, boating, and other water activities.

20 Hoquiam

Logging is a chief industry in the Pacific Northwest, and it has given rise not only to this deepwater port city, but to one of the town's main attractions—Hoquiam's Castle. When it was built in 1897 by a timber tycoon named Robert Lytle, this elegant 20-room mansion must have seemed curiously out of place amid sawmills and saloons. But lusty townfolk came to appreciate its stately presence, fondly dubbing it "the castle." Among the antique furnishings on display in this grand showplace are Tiffany-style lamps, a huge hand-carved dining room set, and an ornate turn-of-the-century bar. It gives a fascinating glimpse of extravagance nearly beyond imagination.

21 Grays Harbor National Wildlife Refuge

The same glorious spectacle takes place here each and every spring: arctic-bound shorebirds—up to 300,000 at a time—come from as far away as Argentina to feed and rest at Bowerman Basin before

A buck mule deer, its antlers cloaked in velvet, stands in a meadow near Port Angeles below Hurricane Ridge.

heading north to their traditional breeding grounds in subarctic and arctic Alaska and Canada. Because the basin is the last spot in Grays Harbor that is flooded at high tide and the first to be exposed at low tide, it provides maximum feeding time for the hungry migrants. Swarming over mudflats, the birds feast on small, shrimplike crustacean animals that are found here in profusion. Western sandpipers, dunlins, and semipalmated plovers are just a few of the two dozen or so shorebird and migratory waterfowl species that comprise this unique coastal community—the largest concentration of shorebirds anywhere on the U.S. mainland's West Coast.

A Seafood Sampler

Whether you like to savor seafood prepared by a master chef or prefer to catch and cook your own, the Olympic Peninsula offers unrivaled quality, variety, and abundance. Local restaurants pride themselves on such favorites as halibut, snapper, rockfish, flounder, albacore tuna, Columbia River sturgeon, and salmon (sometimes cooked Indian-style: on a cedar board over an open alder fire).

For those who derive just as much enjoyment from the hunt itself, several sumptuous varieties of shellfish—including large Pacific and tiny Olympia oysters, razor and geoduck (pronounced gooey-duck) clams, and Dungeness crabs—can be found along the shores of Puget Sound, the Strait of Juan de Fuca, and the Pacific Ocean. Perhaps nowhere can you sample a greater selection of seafood than at the annual Washington State Seafood Festival, or OysterFest. Held during the first weekend in October in Shelton (about 15 miles south of Potlatch State Park), the extravaganza features more than 100 vendors serving up dozens of local delicacies.

Along with crashing waves, you'll find scenic offshore islands and rocks of basalt and conglomerate called sea stacks on the beaches near La Push, a waypoint on the Olympic Pennisula.

17

North Cascades Loop

A spin around the northwest corner of Washington takes travelers from volcanic peaks to glacial lakes, from sun-drenched farm fields to misty coastal islands.

Lake Chelan is encircled by mountains near the Chelan Butte Wildlife Area.

The route traced here was impossible until 1972, when the rugged northern Cascade Mountains were finally breached by a highway. Now the mountains serve as the first leg of a remarkably diverse loop that embraces serene wilderness preserves, charming towns, bountiful orchards, and gleaming waterways—all blending harmoniously over the course of an impressive 400-mile journey.

1 Sedro-Woolley

This logging town, whose enigmatic name combines the Spanish word for cedar *(cedro)* with the surname of one of its early settlers, serves as the gateway to the North Cascades. Known as America's Alps, the mountain range is beautifully preserved in North Cascades National Park—505,000 acres of fragrant forests, flower-strewn meadows, imposing mountain peaks, intriguing wildlife (bears, wolves, cougars, deer, ptarmigan—a subarctic grouse—and more), and 318 glaciers (about half the total to be found in all of the lower 48 states). A park information center on the western edge of Sedro-Woolley helps visitors get off to an informed start in their explorations of the region.

2 Baker Lake

At Concrete head north off the North Cascades Highway (Rte. 20) and follow a U.S. Forest Service spur to 9-mile-long Baker Lake. A recreational reservoir east of snow-capped Mt. Baker—a 10,778-foot volcano that on occasion still spews out clouds of steam—the lake is a popular place for hiking, sailing, canoeing, and angling for trout, salmon, and whitefish. In spring Baker Lake attracts the state's largest gathering of ospreys, which return every year to nest.

3 Rockport State Park

A mecca for hikers, campers, and picnickers, Rockport State Park contains groves of old-growth Douglas fir up to 300 feet tall. More than five miles of trails crisscross the park, some allowing close-up views of wetlands and the forest understory, and others leading to sunny overlooks.

4 Skagit River Bald Eagle Natural Area

Between Rockport and Marblemount, Rte. 20 passes the Skagit River Bald Eagle Natural Area—some 1,500 acres that have been set aside as a sanctuary for the hundreds of bald eagles that arrive in late fall. From their perches in cottonwood trees along the banks of the river, the birds eye the water, then dive for salmon and steelhead. Visitors can view the birds from river rafts (launched from Marblemount) or from various turnouts along the route.

5 Gorge Creek Falls

Emerging from a 500-foot-long tunnel, Rte. 20 rejoins the Skagit River and soon arrives at Gorge Creek, which cascades hundreds of feet over ledges and boulders. For a thrilling perspective on the stream, stand on the steel bridge and peer through the grating into the turbulent water 900 feet below.

6 Diablo Lake

The lake is remarkable for its jade-green color, which is caused by glacial flour (suspended rock sediments that refract the light). Visitors can cruise the man-made lake by motor launch—part of a tour of the hydroelectric facilities offered by Seattle City Light. The trip includes a ride on an incline railway that inches up steep Sourdough Mountain. For magnificent views of the gemlike lake, the dam, and the glacier-honed peaks that encircle them, drive to the overlook on the southeastern shore of the lake. For a hiker's perspective, take the Thunder Creek Trail, which begins at the Colonial Creek Campground and weaves through miles of dense forest.

7 Ross Lake Overlook

A few miles to the east of Diablo Lake, one can see the southern arm of Ross Lake—an immense, 12,000-acre body of water that snakes some 25 miles through the mountains to the Canadian border. From here Rte. 20 swings south through Okanogan National Forest, where visitors can ride horses and burros on backcountry trails.

8 Rainy Pass

Rte. 20 climbs gradually toward Rainy Pass, which at 4,855 feet is one of the finest lookout points in the area. Here the highway crosses the Pacific Crest National Scenic Trail—a hiker's paradise that extends from Canada to Mexico. A paved trail leads to deep blue Rainy Lake, where visitors can gaze at a waterfall, a glacier, and the surrounding peaks. In fall the bright golden leaves of mountain ash are mirrored in the lake.

9 Whistler Basin Overlook

In spring the melting snow on Whistler Mountain feeds waterfalls that cascade down steep slopes into Whistler Basin. In summer

:::::: Trip Tips ::::::

Length: About 400 miles, plus side trips.

When to go: April through October. (The North Cascades Highway is closed between Ross Dam Trailhead and Mazama in winter.)

Not to be missed: Skagit Valley Tulip Festival (April): Burlington, LaConner, and Mount Vernon.

Nearby attractions: Boeing aircraft assembly plant, Everett. San Juan Islands (via ferry from Anacortes). Space Needle, Seattle.

Words to the wise: No fuel is available on the 70-mile stretch of highway between Marblemount and Mazama.

Further information: Cascade Loop Association, Box 3245, Wenatchee, WA 98801; tel. 509-662-3888; www.cascadeloop.com.

Rafting on Skykomish River near Index on the Stevens Pass Highway.

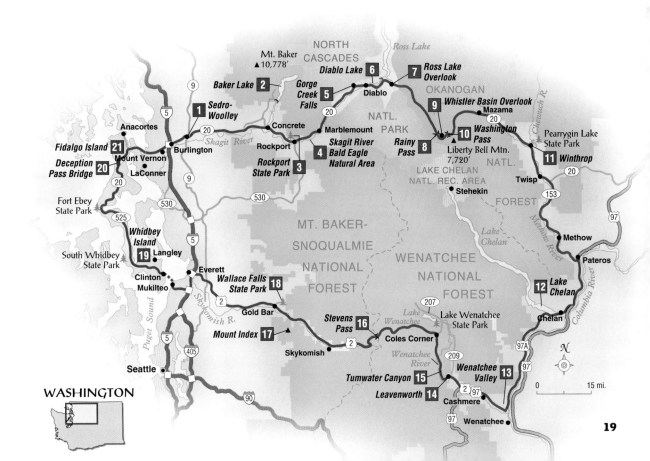

the nearby alpine meadow is thickly quilted with wildflowers. Be on the lookout for deer, marmots, and pikas—especially in the early morning hours and at dusk.

10 Washington Pass

From an overlook just off this 5,477-foot pass—the highest on the North Cascades Highway— the view to the south is dominated by the crags of Liberty Bell Mountain, which towers to a height of 7,720 feet. Here too, travelers can review the damp, forested mountains they've left behind and anticipate the sunny slopes and dry valleys that lie ahead, east of the mountains. The road descends in a series of hairpin turns, with avalanche chutes visible along the highway.

Roozengaarde tulips and daffodils near Mt. Vernon.

11 Winthrop

Poised at the fork of the Methow and Chewuch rivers, this tiny town was founded in the late 1800s and—complete with boardwalks and hitching posts—seems to have retained its frontier appearance. The old-fashioned facades, however, are actually false fronts erected in 1972 to promote tourism. The allure here owes as much to the weather as to the architecture: the valley basks in sunshine some 300 days a year, and so it is a mecca for all manner of outdoor activity— from camping and hiking to mountain biking, snowmobiling, and cross-country skiing. Wildflowers and wildlife—countless acres of lupine, larkspur, and mariposa lilies, along with mule deer, songbirds, and waterfowl—thrive in this climate too. Nearby are 578-acre Pearrygin Lake State Park, which flanks a spring-fed lake with a bright sandy beach, and Big Valley Ranch, a former cattle ranch that is now a wildlife preserve.

12 Lake Chelan

The loop leads southward now, meandering down Rte.153 through the fruit orchards, horse ranches, and hayfields of the Methow River valley toward Lake Chelan. Cradled in a narrow glacial trough between the Chelan Mountains and Sawtooth Ridge, the long, narrow, sapphire-blue lake is up to 1,500 feet deep. At the southern end the resort town of Chelan serves as the launch point for excursion boats and seaplanes to Stehekin, a 19th-century mining community 55 miles uplake and inaccessible by road. Private farms along the lower shoreline yield at midlake, becoming a mix of forest and rugged bluffs scaled by mountain goats. At the northern tip lies the Lake Chelan National Recreation Area, a wilderness laced with hiking trails.

13 Wenatchee Valley

The Wenatchee area calls itself the Apple Capital of the World, and the claim makes sense: its enormous annual crop of apples is greater than the number produced by any other apple-growing locale. In spring, mile after mile of orchards are suffused with delicate white-pink blooms; in fall, the trees hang heavy with red and golden globes.

Beautiful Ohme Gardens, in the town of Wenatchee, was begun by an orchardist in 1929 as a family retreat. Situated on nine acres of rock outcroppings high above the valley, the gardens are a harmonious blend of evergreens, alpine flowers, stone paths, and tranquil pools—all enlivened by chirping birds and scampering rabbits.

In nearby Cashmere visitors can tour an authentically restored 19th-century pioneer village or stop by a popular candy factory to witness how Aplets and Cotlets, renowned local confections, are fashioned from apples, apricots, and nuts.

14 Leavenworth

On the verge of becoming a ghost town a few decades ago due to a loss of industry, Leavenworth reinvented itself as a village embodying all the charm and flavor of the Bavarian Alps. Half-timbered and balconied chalets and frescoed facades line the flower-bedecked streets, and merchants in traditional lederhosen or dirndls proffer frosty steins of *Bier* and steaming plates of *Wurst*. Leavenworth is also a prime location for whitewater rafters and kayakers, who shoot the challenging Wenatchee River rapids found along the river's course between the towns of Leavenworth and Cashmere.

15 Tumwater Canyon

For several miles the drive parallels the Wenatchee River as it passes through Tumwater Canyon. Although the trees here are usually resplendent with fall color, about one-third of them were consumed by fires in the summer of 1994.

At Coles Corner Rte. 207 leads to five-mile-long Lake Wenatchee, a pristine gem fringed with beaches, boat launches, and picnic spots.

16 Stevens Pass

Though rare and elusive, mountain goats can sometimes be seen from the highway at 4,061-foot Stevens Pass, an area popular with skiers in winter. For an unusual hike that combines glorious scenery with a glimpse into railroading's past, visit the Iron Goat Trail, which traces the route of the old Great Northern Railway for several miles below Stevens Pass. You can reach the trail by turning north onto the Old Cascade Highway and then taking Rte. 6710 to the trailhead. A few miles to the west, near Skykomish, Deception Falls thunders down the mountainside and under the highway bridge.

17 Mt. Index

Jagged and forbidding, 5,979-foot Mt. Index is graced by high waterfalls that appear as silvery threads from the highway. In the mountain's shadow, the turbulent Skykomish River (known locally as "the Sky") poses challenges to whitewater rafters, and a gentle invitation to anglers casting for salmon and steelhead.

18 Wallace Falls State Park

In the timbered foothills outside of Gold Bar (a name that recalls the town's past as a mecca for prospectors) lies Wallace Falls State Park. A trail here winds to the brink of a tumbling 265-foot waterfall, rewarding hikers with stunning views of both the Skykomish

Valley and nearby Mt. Baker–Snoqualmie National Forest.

As Rte. 2 follows the Skykomish River downstream towards the ocean, the rugged highlands of the Cascade Range gradually give way to the rocky coastline typical of the coast along the inland waters of Puget Sound. At the port town of Everett, visitors can glimpse the swarms of ferries mixed with pleasure craft that ply the waterway, and hear the plaintive dog-like barks of the many Steller sea lions that bask on the beaches and many offshore rocks of Everett Jetty Island.

19 Whidbey Island

The turn-of-the-century lighthouse at Mukilteo recedes from view as the ferry chugs across Possession Sound to Whidbey Island, with its charming towns and cliff-backed coves. The bayside village of Langley is a favorite weekend getaway for local urbanites, who come to stroll streets lined with boutiques, antique shops, and galleries. For a somewhat "wilder" environment, head to South Whidbey State Park, a 340-acre habitat for old-growth Douglas firs and red cedars, as well as eagles and black-tailed deer.

Farther up-island, at Fort Ebey State Park, a fortification dating from World War II surrounds what many locals consider the prettiest beach on Whidbey Island: Partridge Point. For views of the Olympic Mountains and Mt. Rainier framed by boughs of pine and fir, you can take the Ebey's Landing Loop Trail, which traverses windblown bluffs and paths lined alternately with driftwood and wild roses.

20 Deception Pass Bridge

Linking Whidbey with its northern neighbor, Fidalgo, this 1,487-foot steel cantilever bridge stands above a narrow neck of water where tides swirl and surge around the rocks. Below, a state park embraces some 4,067 acres of forests, marshlands, freshwater lakes, and beaches on the sound. Both the bridge and park offer stunning views of Puget Sound—populated by porpoises and otters and dotted with some 200 enchanting islands.

21 Fidalgo Island

At the northern end of Fidalgo Island, the port town of Anacortes bustles with ferries, charter fleets, and pleasure boats—it's a favorite spot for salmon fishermen in summer. From the top of 1,270-foot Mt. Erie, the highest point on the island, the busy maritime scene reminds one of toy boats on a gleaming blue pond.

Continuing on Rte. 20 to the mainland, the Cascade loop ends where it began—in the fertile Skagit Valley. Here the moist lowlands abound with truck and dairy farms and are abloom each spring with whole fields of daffodils, irises, and—most famously—the world's largest crop of tulips.

Overlook Washington Pass and Liberty Bell in North Cascades National Park.

Magnificent Mt. Rainier

Forged by fire and crowned by ice, this gleaming colossus in the heart of Washington presides over miles of deep snowfields, flower-filled meadows, pristine streams, and lush evergreen forest.

Mt. Rainier is studded with glaciers and crevasses above Paradise.

Like jewels on a necklace, the premier attractions at Mt. Rainier National Park—Longmire, Paradise, the Grove of the Patriarchs, Sunrise, and other locales—are linked by a single winding road that enters the park at its southwestern corner, zigzags up and down canyons and forested slopes, and swings around to the northeastern side of the mountain. Among the sights you'll see along the way are massive glaciers, subalpine meadows, thundering waterfalls, ancient stands of first-growth timber, and—reigning over all—the sleeping giant volcanic peak that Washingtonians affectionately refer to simply as "the mountain."

◻ Mayfield Lake

Heading east through the farm country between I-5 and Mayfield Lake, Rte. 12 affords views of three lofty and nearby Cascade peaks: Mt. Rainier to the northeast, Mt. Adams to the southeast, and Mt. St. Helens to the south. Picturesque Mayfield Lake, bordered by two lovely parks, is home to bass and trout.

◻ Elbe

The drive turns north onto Rte.7 at Morton and leads to the little town of Elbe, home base for the Mt. Rainier Scenic Railroad. Steam-powered, with open cars and restored coaches, the train chugs through forests on a 14-mile round-trip to Mineral Lake. Visible along part of the route is Mt. Rainier's icy summit, some 25 miles to the northeast.

◻ Nisqually Entrance

Viewed from a few miles away, Mt. Rainier appears to hover in the sky like a massive mirage. The 14,411-foot-high dormant volcano, the loftiest in the Cascades, is the majestic centerpiece of Mt. Rainier National Park. From the Nisqually Entrance on Rte. 706—the park's main access point—the road winds through towering Douglas firs and beautiful stands of red cedars to Longmire, where a museum and the well-marked Trail of the Shadows introduce visitors to the history and natural wonders of the lowland forest.

◻ Cougar Rock

From Longmire the road climbs through lush mountain growth to Cougar Rock, one of the park's major campgrounds. About a mile and a half farther on, pause to look at graceful Christine Falls. To see the 60-foot cascade from the most pleasing angle, walk down the short path leading to a viewpoint below the stone bridge.

◻ Narada Falls

Here the Paradise River hurtles off an old eroded lava flow, plunging 168 feet to the valley floor. On sunny days visitors who take the short hike from the parking area to the base of the falls, where the air is suffused with spray, are likely to catch sight of a glorious rainbow.

◻ Paradise

As the road climbs ever higher, the forest thins out, yielding to subalpine meadows and clear views of Mt. Rainier's upper slopes. Inspired by these mountain vistas and by the stunning array of wildflowers (Indian paintbrush, pearly everlasting, lupines, phlox, and more) that carpet the meadows in summer, an 1885 visitor dubbed the area Paradise. Beauty and accessibility have since made Paradise the most popular destination in the park. The legions of travelers who hike its trails and enjoy its views are welcomed at the rustic Paradise Inn and the flying-saucer-shaped Jackson visitor cen-

::::: Trip Tips :::::

Length: About 220 miles.

When to go: Best in summer (for wildflowers) and early fall (for foliage and fewer crowds). From November through April all park roads except the Nisqually–Paradise road are usually closed.

Lodging: Paradise Inn, Paradise (open summer only). National Park Inn, Longmire (open year-round).

Supplies: Longmire.

Visitor centers: Longmire; Paradise; Ohanapecosh; Sunrise.

Further information: Superintendent, Mount Rainier National Park, Ashford, WA 98304; tel. 206-569-2211; www.guest services.com/rainier.

Star Route

⭐ Spirit Lake Memorial Highway

For a close encounter with Mt. St. Helens, the explosive neighbor of Mt. Rainier that blew its top in 1980 and began erupting again in 2004, head south on I-5 to the exit at Castle Rock and turn east onto Rte. 504. This 48-mile spur —Spirit Lake Memorial Highway— leads past the Mt. St. Helens Visitor Center at Silver Lake, where you can walk through a model volcano. Farther along are the blasted remains of trees and examples of regenerating forest. The road culminates at the Coldwater Ridge Visitor Center, where visitors are close enough to look into the awesome crater.

ter, which contains an intriguing array of mountain-related exhibits.

7 Stevens Canyon Road

Beginning at Inspiration Point, an overlook that affords an impressive view of Mt. Rainier, this beautiful road scales canyon walls, skirts lakes and waterfalls, winds south and then north again along Backbone Ridge, and ends in the park's southeastern corner. Along the way are the glacier-gouged Reflection Lakes, so named because their still surfaces provide clear mirror images of Rainier's gleaming summit. Where Stevens Canyon Road crosses the Cowlitz River, churning water has etched a deep chasm in the volcanic rock. A bridge spans the narrow gorge, which is known as Box Canyon. From the top of the bridge, visitors can gaze at the roiling river some 180 feet below.

8 Ohanapecosh

Near the Stevens Canyon entrance to the park, two trails invite visitors to stroll through the stately old-growth forest of the Ohanapecosh River valley. The Grove of the Patriarchs Trail winds for a mile and a half through stands of enormous Douglas fir, western hemlock, and western red cedar that are believed to be some 1,000 years old. Another rewarding trail is the three-mile loop to Silver Falls, where the waters of the Ohanapecosh River gush through a slot in ancient volcanic rock and then plunge into a deep, turbulent pool.

9 Sunrise

Much of the road between Ohanapecosh and Sunrise runs steadily north along the banks of creeks, with Rainier's gleaming icecap looming to the west. Beyond the park's White River entrance, an especially scenic spur zigzags upward and emerges on subalpine meadows at Sunrise, the highest point in the park accessible by car. Although more remote than Paradise, its sister attraction on the other side of the mountain, Sunrise is less crowded and has more spectacular views of Mt. Rainier and the neighboring Cascades. Its most prominent vista takes in nearly four-mile-long Emmons Glacier, the largest glacier in the lower 48 states. Botanical exhibits and a scale model of Mt. Rainier are featured at the Sunrise visitor center.

10 Mather Memorial Parkway

After twisting and turning downhill from Sunrise, the drive reconnects with Rte. 410, known as

Deer at Mt. St. Helens National Volcanic Monument near Toutle.

Mather Memorial Parkway. Following this route south and turning east at lofty Cayuse Pass, the drive eases along hairpin turns to Tipsoo Lake, a gemlike, glacier-carved basin near Chinook Pass. From there, the route heads east out of the park, through the Naches Valley (prime apple-growing country), and on to Yakima.

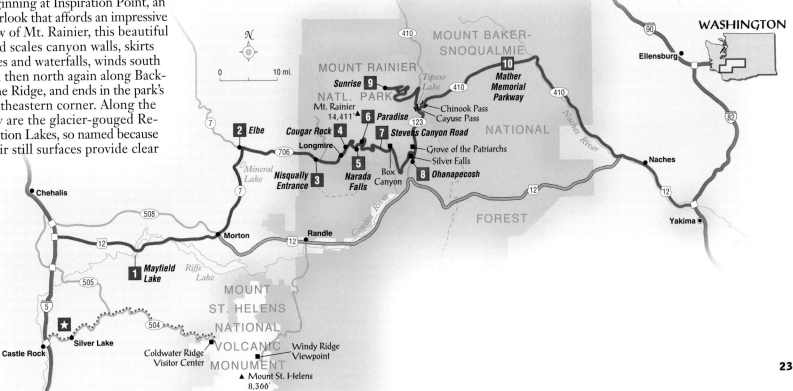

Columbia River Gorge Road

Paralleling the river traveled by the Lewis and Clark expedition on the last leg of its journey to the Pacific Ocean, the Columbia River Road snakes along the Washington side of the river's awesome gorge.

A raft passes under the Husum bridge as it flows through white water on the White Salmon river.

::::: **Trip Tips** :::::

Length: About 140 miles.

When to go: Popular year-round.

Nearby attractions: Fort Vancouver National Historic Site, Vancouver. Pearson Air Museum, Vancouver. Spring Creek National Fish Hatchery, Underwood.

Further information: Columbia River Gorge National Scenic Area, Wacoma Center, 902 Wasco Ave., Hood River, OR 97301; tel. 503-386-2333; www.crgva.org.

Etched across the Cascade Range by the mighty Columbia River, the gorge delights travelers with memorable vistas: ancient Indian fishing grounds, panoramic views first noted in the diaries of Lewis and Clark, historic steamboat towns, modern dams, basaltic cliffs, and—ever looming in the distance—snowcapped volcanic peaks.

1 Cape Horn Viewpoint

Overlooking a striking panorama at the western gateway to the Columbia River Gorge, the viewpoint provides a fine introduction to the beauties of this breathtaking natural boundary between Washington and Oregon. Hundreds of feet below, at the foot of massive vertical cliffs, lies the river itself, and rising from the opposite bank are the steep wooded hills of Oregon.

2 Beacon Rock

Described by Lewis and Clark as a "remarkable, high detached rock," this enormous monolith—nearly 850 feet tall and second only to Gibraltar in size—is the core of a vanished volcano. Climb the steep, zigzagging trail to the top, and you'll be rewarded with views of the gorge and its cliffs, the islands dotting the Columbia River, Oregon's Mt. Hood, and the snow-covered cone of Washington's Mt. Adams. Across the road are the trails and campgrounds of Beacon Rock State Park, a 4,500-acre sanctuary where woodpeckers and thrushes punctuate the stillness in extensive stands of Douglas firs, incense cedars, red alders, and western hemlocks.

3 Bonneville Dam

This huge dam, built in the 1930s, created a 48-mile-long lake on the Columbia River. Visitors who stop in at the Northshore visitor center can get a look at a massive, humming hydroelectric generator that is as big as a house. Fish ladders and underwater fish-viewing windows permit close-up glimpses of migrating salmon swimming up the river to spawn, and exhibits that display local Indian artifacts, Lewis and Clark memorabilia, and the history of the dam.

4 Stevenson

Early rivermen used to stop at this lumbering town to load the cordwood that fueled their steamships. You can recall the flavor of those days by taking a two-hour cruise on a 600-passenger stern-wheeler. You can also visit the Columbia Gorge Interpretive Center, where models of early steamships are on display, along with relics of frontier life and exhibits that highlight the geological features of the gorge. Nearby Rock Creek Park is a pleasant spot for viewing the gorge and mountains.

5 Home Valley Park

Looking east from the park at Home Valley, campers and picnickers can see an imposing pair of mountains—Wind Mountain in Washington and Shellrock Mountain in Oregon—known locally as the Guardians of the

Gorge. Fishermen launch their boats here to angle for salmon and trout, and windsurfers take advantage of brisk breezes to skim over whitecaps on the river.

6 Cook–Underwood Road Loop

At the little town of Cook turn onto the Cook–Underwood Road for a scenic detour north to Willard and then south again to Underwood, where the White Salmon River joins the Columbia. The road winds up and down through lovely countryside, and an overlook along the way affords a spectacular view of the Columbia River Gorge, the Hood River Bridge, and, rising in the distance, majestic 11,285-foot Mt. Hood.

7 Trout Lake

For another scenic side trip, head north on Rte. 141, which follows the turbulent White Salmon River to Trout Lake. Pausing at the river towns of Husum and BZ Corners, you can view white-water rafters riding the rapids. Trout Lake itself, a tranquil and unspoiled little community, serves as the gateway to Mt. Adams, the snowy giant that dominates all views to the north. A few miles west of Trout Lake, you can explore natural ice caves, where frigid drafts greet all who enter and lanterns illuminate the natural sculptures within.

8 Roadside Park

To the east of the White Salmon River, the landscape, no longer rugged and lushly forested, consists instead of dry, nearly treeless

rolling hills. The mountains themselves account for this remarkable change: the tall peaks of the Cascade Range force the moist, east-moving Pacific air masses upward, where the moisture cools and condenses as rain or snow that falls on the western slopes. By the time the air gets east of the mountains, it has been wrung dry, leaving a relatively arid zone below.

On the nine-mile stretch of road between Bingen and Lyle, with cliffs to the left and railroad tracks to the right, there are few safe places to stop and admire the view. One exception is Roadside Park, which offers an excellent view of the gorge.

9 The Dalles Lock and Dam

Visitors can tour the navigation locks and take a shuttle train to the powerhouse, fish ladders, and petroglyphs (Indian stone carvings) that were moved here for display. The shoreline of Lake Celilo, the 24-mile reservoir formed by the dam, is frequented by bald eagles and nesting Canada geese. A few miles east of the dam, at Horsethief Lake State Park, petroglyphs are etched on the basalt cliffs that face the river. Farther along, near Wishram, the Celilo Falls Monument overlooks the flooded site of a historic fishing ground where the Indians used to spear salmon

Windsurfers in the waves at Doug's Beach in the Columbia River Gorge at Lyle.

from wooden scaffolds anchored to the cliffs, then smoked the fish for consumption throughout the coming year.

10 Maryhill Museum of Art

Looking oddly out of place amid barren hills at the eastern end of the gorge is this French-style chateau. Surrounded by landscaped lawns where peacocks strut, it is filled with works of art, many of which are by Rodin and other European masters. The inspiration of turn-of-the-century capitalist Sam Hill, the chateau was constructed of concrete, a material that Hill, a road builder, particularly favored. Nearby, topping a bluff beside the Columbia River, is another concrete structure: a replica of Stonehenge, which Hill built as a memorial to Washingtonians who fought in World War I.

25

Oregon Coast Highway

Unspoiled in rugged beauty and unsurpassed in natural drama, the Oregon coast reminds us that where land and water meet, scenic treasures often abound.

1 Brookings

Fish and flowers are the hallmarks of this town near the southern end of the Oregon Coast Highway. The fish in question are such favorites as salmon and steelhead, which are taken from the Chetco River. The flowers—azaleas—flourish at Azalea Park. Featuring 25 acres of the shrubs, some of them 20 feet tall and over 400 years old, the park delivers amply on the promise of its name. (Brookings also supplies a large share of America's commercially grown lilies.)

At the north end of town, Rte. 101 passes Harris Beach State Park and, farther to the north, Samuel H. Boardman State Park, where a 10-mile trail affords panoramic

Human figures are dwarfed by wave-beaten rocks, the sea, and the endless vistas at Shore Acres State Park.

Think of Oregon and you probably think of trees, for the state is America's leading source of timber. But Oregon is notable for its coastline as well. This 360-mile fringe, paralleled by Rte. 101, is dotted with lagoons, lakes, and lighthouses; coves and canyons; sand dunes and seaports.

What makes it truly special, however, is a landmark law that designates all beaches free and open to the public.

With their large brightly hued beaks, tufted puffins are easy to spot along Oregon's coastal cliffs.

clifftop views. The next few miles leading to Cape Sebastian are particularly beautiful, with unobstructed views of offshore rocks.

2 Cape Sebastian State Park

About 22 miles north of Brookings, a steep road off the Coast Highway leads to the Cape Sebastian headland, which offers stunning views of craggy cliffs and rocky coves. At 1,100-acre Cape Sebastian State Park, tall ever- greens form a verdant backdrop for the colorful azaleas and rhododendrons that carpet the cape.

3 Port Orford

This major fishing center is one of the oldest settlements on the Oregon coast. Among its attractions are the Sixes and Elk rivers, the Thousand Island Coast (a series of offshore rocks that are favored by harbor seals and sea lions), and Battle Rock City Park, where you can survey the coastline from atop an oceanfront monolith.

4 Cape Blanco State Park

Perched on a cliff overlooking the Pacific, the park occupies 1,900 acres of windswept land that once served as a pasture. The scenic views here encompass offshore rocks and reefs, as well as the Cape Blanco Lighthouse, the state's westernmost beacon. A three-mile trail leads down to a black sand beach (not uncommon along the Oregon coast).

5 Bandon-by-the-Sea

The drive from Cape Blanco to the coastal village of Bandon passes through a kaleidoscope of splendid scenery—dense fir forests

Despite clearing skies, a storm over Shore Acres State Park continues to whip up the waters of the Pacific.

and wide-open plains, lush green farmland and barren beige shores. At the waterfront begins a five-mile scenic drive that heads south past large sea stacks. These fantastic rock formations are especially impressive when silhouetted against blazing sunsets, as they often are at Face Rock Wayside, located along the loop. The town's biggest annual event is the Cranberry Festival, held in late September, when Bandon celebrates its status as the Cranberry Capital of Oregon.

6 Cape Arago

For a short side trip that loops past a wildlife preserve and three coastal parks, go 12 miles north of Bandon and take the Beaver Hill–Seven Devils Road to the South Slough National Estuarine Research Reserve. Covering some 5,200 acres of coastal wetlands, South Slough is home to black bears, black-tailed deer, salmon, and more than 150 kinds of birds.

Driving west on Cape Arago Highway, visitors next encounter a trio of state parks, each one offering something special. The first stop, Sunset Bay State Park—true to its name—is dazzling at day's end. The park's calm, warm bay, hemmed in by high cliffs and Douglas firs, is one of the safest swimming spots on the coast, as well as a good place to cast for rockfish and sea trout.

Shore Acres State Park—once the estate of Louis J. Simpson, a timber baron—is truly a feast for the eyes, with some seven acres of award-winning English and Japanese gardens that explode with a riot of color. Irises, azaleas, rhododendrons, dahlias, and roses seem to spring from every corner

A lush river valley and the rock formation known locally as the Nob, seen from atop Cascade Head.

of this 743-acre park, which features plants from around the world. At Christmastime, Shore Acres takes on an extra-special glow, with more than 100,000 miniature lights sparkling on its trees, bushes, and buildings.

Cape Arago State Park, the last one on the loop drive, is a good place to stop for a quiet picnic. Set on a rugged headland, the secluded park overlooks the Pacific, offering fine views of passing whales. During low tide, wander down to the coastal coves and look for sea urchins, sea stars, hermit crabs, and other animals that thrive in the tidepools.

7 Oregon Dunes National Recreation Area

The Coast Highway reaches one of its highlights just north of Coos Bay, where some 32,000 acres of sand dunes begin their 41-mile northward stretch. These massive mounds of fine, cream-colored sand were formed in a process that began millions of years ago, when sedimentary rock from nearby mountains started to erode into particles that rivers carried to the ocean. Over time, countless grains of sand were moved inland by tides, waves, and currents, and then sculpted by the wind. Some of the best views of these ever-shifting, ever-undulating dunes are available at the Eel Creek Campground (about 13 miles north of Coos Bay), where a short trail from the parking lot leads to dunes that extend both north and south for as far as the eye can see. A film about the dunes is featured at the visitor center in nearby Reedsport.

8 Umpqua Lighthouse State Park

The dunes that are visible from this park are as much as 500 feet tall—the highest of any coastal dunes in the United States. Bordering Winchester Bay, the park occupies 450 acres dominated by Sitka spruce, shore pine, and western hemlock. Lake Marie, framed by trees, is a good spot for swimming and rowboating.

The nearby Umpqua River Lighthouse, on a bluff overlooking the bay, was built in 1892 to replace the first lighthouse in the Oregon Territory (the original was destroyed by a storm some 30 years earlier). At the whale-watching station across the road, visitors can get a panoramic view of the shore and dunes. Just a few miles north of the lighthouse, the Oregon Dunes Overlook provides equally impressive views.

9 Jessie Honeyman State Park

Seeing dunes from a car window is nice, but for a real thrill, try crisscrossing them in a motorized dune buggy. Rides of varying lengths are available both north and south of Jessie Honeyman State Park, which also features dense evergreen forests, a splendid array of wildflowers, two freshwater lakes, and 241 campsites (all equipped with fireplaces and picnic tables).

Trip Tips

Length: About 360 miles.

When to go: Popular year-round, but best in summer (because of water activities) and during fall (when less crowded).

Lodging: Reservations recommended during June, July, and August.

Words to the wise: In peak seasons allow plenty of time, since traffic is heavy and the road is narrow and winding.

Nearby attractions: Tillamook County Creamery (Oregon's largest cheese-making plant), Tillamook Naval Air Museum, and Tillamook County Pioneer Museum, Tillamook. Columbia River Maritime Museum, Astoria. Latimer Quilt & Textile Center, Latimer.

Further information: Oregon Tourism Commission, 775 Summer St. NE, Salem, OR 97301, tel. 800-547-7842, www.travel oregon.com.
Oregon Coast Visitor's Ass'n., P.O. Box 74, Newport, OR, 97365, 888-628-2101, www.visittheoregoncoast.com

10 Florence

As the drive continues north on Rte. 101, acres of sand give way to lush greenery. At the northern boundary of the Oregon Dunes National Recreation Area, you'll come to Florence, billed as the City of Rhododendrons. In late May the whole town is festooned with blossoms in purple, pink, and white. Located at the mouth of the Siuslaw River, Florence has a recently restored historic district, a small artists colony, a park overlooking the waterfront, and 17 lakes filled with bass, crappies, perch, and bluegills.

11 Sea Lion Caves

Eleven miles north of Florence the drive reaches Sea Lion Caves, a popular attraction on the coast. Discovered in 1880 by a local ship captain, the grotto is one of the world's largest sea caves (despite its name, it has a single cavern). It is also one of the few places where wild sea lions live year-round on the U.S. mainland.

From the top of a cliff, a high-speed elevator transports visitors down 208 feet to an observation window that looks in on a vast, vaulted chamber at sea level. Inside this multihued cavern—12 stories high and a hundred yards long—hundreds of sea lions, some as heavy as 1,200 pounds, delight spectators with their playful antics. On warm, sunny days they often move outdoors to bask on rocks. Two species can be seen here: the golden brown Steller sea lion and the darker California sea lion.

Framed by the cave's natural window is Heceta Head Lighthouse, Oregon's most powerful beacon, which sits on a bluff across the water. Just south of the lighthouse, Devils Elbow State Park offers fabulous views of the coast.

12 Cape Perpetua

Finding refuge on this headland during a dangerous storm, Capt. James Cook, the British explorer, christened it Cape Perpetua because he felt as if he had been delayed here forever. But far worse fates could befall a visitor. Towering more than 800 feet above the Pacific Ocean, Cape Perpetua is a place of natural, scenic, and historic wonders. Tidepools teem with sea stars, barnacles, limpets, and hermit crabs. In an ancient rain forest, giant spruces bear witness to the past. Piles of discarded clam shells—some measuring 40 feet in height—provide the only remaining evidence of Indian habitation along the entire Oregon coast.

At Devils Churn far-off whales can be glimpsed through a telescope, while spectacular views can be enjoyed nearer at hand. Three

miles north of the cape, the drive passes through Yachats, one of the few places in the world where sardinelike silver smelts come close to the shore to spawn.

13 Oregon Coast Aquarium

About 28 miles north of Yachats, the excitement moves into the Oregon Coast Aquarium. At this state-of-the-art facility, you'll delight in the antics of sea otters and sea lions as they play along the aquarium's rocky shores, while tufted puffins frolic in the pools of one of the largest outdoor sea bird aviaries in North America. Encounter sharks and other deep-sea denizens in Passages of the Deep—a 200-foot undersea tunnel snaking its way through three marine habitats. Next door is the Hatfield Marine Science Center, which further explores and explains the mysteries of the sea.

14 Newport

This picturesque port is a good place to get out of the car and take a stroll. Amble along the old bayfront to glimpse fishing fleets and admire fresh fish displayed by some of the best seafood markets on the coast. Saunter along the seashore in search of semiprecious agates washed in by waves. Or wander to the south end of town to the Yaquina Bay Lighthouse, the only one remaining in Oregon that combines a tower and keeper's quarters. Gulls, puffins, and cormorants nest on a nearby island, and whales cruise by offshore.

15 Otter Crest Loop

For a short but especially scenic side trip, take Otter Crest Loop west to Devils Punchbowl State Park, so named because a collapsed cavern here churns with seawater at high tide. The drive continues to Cape Foulweather, where the visitor center—perched nearly 500 feet above the pounding surf—

The Fine Art of Whale Watching

More than 20 species of whales parade past the Oregon coast, but only a few come close enough to shore to be seen. The most common of these, gray whales, migrate 6,000 miles to the nutrient-rich waters of the Arctic between February and June and then return, from November until January, to the warm lagoons off the coast of Mexico to breed. About 400 "resident whales"—gray whales that do not migrate—can be seen offshore year-round. But the best chance of spotting these 40-ton mammals is from mid-December through mid-January, when as many as 30 whales per hour cruise by the coast.

To spot whales from the shore, wait for a calm, overcast day and perch yourself on a tall, outlying cliff during the early-morning hours. Scan the horizon for a "blow" (a white puff of water vapor), then look for periodic spouts. If you're lucky, you may even see a whale breach—spring above the surface before splash diving—like the humpback shown above.

commands marvelous views of the nearby tiny hilltop towns.

16 Depoe Bay

Home of one of the world's smallest navigable harbors (only six acres), this cozy seaside village is a major port for sightseeing and whale-watching excursions. In stormy weather nature stages a spectacular show here, as seawater spouts skyward through crevices in the rocks along the waterfront.

17 Cascade Head

Like the silverspot butterfly that makes its home here, this 280-acre, privately owned preserve is ever so lovely—but all too fragile. The ecosystems found in this sanctuary are diverse yet delicate,

Nearby Lincoln City, a popular shopping and entertainment center, claims another miniature marvel—the world's shortest river, only 120 feet long.

so some areas are off limits and in others visitors must stay on designated trails to prevent damage to the landscape. Some of the trails meander through cathedral-like forests of Sitka spruce and red alder; others lead past wide-open fields rippling with goldenrod, wild rye, and Indian paintbrush; and a few end at a grassy headland with striking views of nearby shores and far-off hills. A variety of wildlife can be seen here, including black-tailed deer, great horned owls, snowshoe hares, Pacific giant salamanders (among the largest in the world), and two rare plants, the Cascade Head catchfly and the hairy checkermallow.

18 Three Capes Scenic Loop

About nine miles north of Neskowin, travel west on the first turn-off in Pacific City to Cape Kiwanda State Park. Photographers love the place for its gorgeous red-and-yellow sandstone cliffs; hang-gliding enthusiasts come to launch from its massive dunes; and surf watchers thrill at the sight of magnificent waves crashing against cliffs and caves. At nearby Pacific City—one of the only places on the coast where dories (flat-bottom fishing boats with high sides) are launched directly into the surf; fishermen sell just-caught seasonal fish all year long.

Cape Lookout, the second stop on the loop, was formed by several ancient lava flows and truly lives up to its name; it juts so far out into the ocean that it affords views of Tillamook Head, 42 miles to the north, and Cape Foulweather, 39 miles to the south. Atop this rocky headland you'll find Cape Lookout State Park, its 2,000 acres laced with miles of trails that meander through coastal rain forest and along sandy shores. One of the beaches runs along Netarts Spit, a five-mile finger of sand pointing north. A stopover on the Pacific flyway, the cape and adjoining waters attract more than 150 species of birds, including blue herons, murres, and oystercatchers.

The last stop on the loop is Cape Meares State Park, where a lighthouse over 100 years old (surrounded in spring and summer by wild roses) offers clifftop views of a sea lion rookery below and offshore rocks and reefs. But perhaps the most unforgettable sight here is a giant Sitka spruce that is located near the lighthouse parking lot. Nicknamed the Octopus Tree, this odd-looking creation of nature has six candelabra-like limbs (the product of furious coastal winds and abundant rainfall) that reach out horizontally as far as 30 feet before turning skyward.

19 Oswald West State Park

Legend has it that a fortune in Spanish doubloons is buried somewhere in the side of Neahkahnie Mountain, a former volcano that erupted under the ocean over 13 million years ago. But the greatest treasure to be found here lies at the mountain's base—a 2,500-acre park in a rain forest of soaring spruce and cedar trees. The park offers 12 miles of hiking trails and exhilarating ocean views.

20 Cannon Beach

On the way to Cannon Beach, take time out to enjoy the dazzling ocean views visible from lookout points along the road. One mile east of town you can see a replica of the ship cannon that washed ashore here in 1896 and gave this tiny artists colony its name.

Towering over the beach is 235-foot-tall Haystack Rock, a bullet-shaped monolith that is one of the most-photographed sights on the coast. Nearby are two recreation areas: Ecola State Park, which offers glorious views of the coast through fog-shrouded firs, and

less-crowded Indian Beach, one of the state's few rocky beaches.

As you leave Cannon Beach and continue north on Rte. 101, you'll pass Seaside, Oregon. It is the oldest coastal destination resort community in Oregon, the Pacific endpoint of the Lewis and Clark Trail, and the site of a 1.8-mile-long oceanfront promenade with outstanding views of the ocean. Visit its historic aquarium.

21 Fort Clatsop National Memorial

"Great joy…we are in view of the ocean…which we [have] been so long anxious to see." So wrote the explorers Meriwether Lewis and William Clark in their journal on November 7, 1805—19 months and 4,000 miles after their party of 33 had begun its epic journey from St. Louis, Missouri, to the Pacific Ocean. But before long a taste of winter in the Northwest turned their glee into gloom. "O! How horriable is the day…waves brakeing with great violence against the shore…all wet and confined to our shelters."

Lewis and Clark built their log cabins and stockade, known as Fort Clatsop, beside a river that now bears their names. In 1955 these structures were faithfully re-created near the original site—a damp, sun-dappled forest of spruce and hemlock. Also re-created here are the daily crafts that were practiced in the early 19th century. On summer days, interpreters dressed in period garb demonstrate such skills as candle making, canoe building, and firing a muzzle-loader musket.

22 Astoria

It seems only fitting that the drive should end at the bustling seaport of Astoria, for it was here, in 1811, that John Jacob Astor's fur-trading company established a post that became the first permanent

Ancient yet pristine, this forest in northern Oregon seems, almost magically, to have escaped the tyranny of time.

American settlement in the Pacific Northwest. There are over 600 historic homes in Astoria. The most famous is Flavel House, a splendid Victorian mansion erected in 1885 by Captain George Flavel, who is believed to have been Astoria's first millionaire.

On Coxcomb Hill, 12-story-high Astoria Column provides a panoramic view of the town below, Saddle Mountain to the south, and to the north, the graceful span of the Astoria Bridge, which crosses the Columbia River between Oregon and Washington.

Mt. Hood–
Columbia River Gorge Loop

Once part of a nearly impenetrable wilderness that tested the mettle of even the most determined pioneer, the dramatic volcanic peaks and river gorges of northern Oregon today are delightfully accessible.

The waters in Multopor Fen Preserve in Oregon's Mt. Hood territory provides serene reflections of Mt. Hood.

Few landscapes can equal the magnificence and variety of the one encircling Mt. Hood. Mountaintops under a continuous cover of snow, verdant forests laced with rushing streams and waterfalls, fertile farmlands, and the awesome gorge of one of America's great rivers—these are among the treasures waiting to be discovered here.

1 Sandy

Miles of farmland skirt Rte. 26 on the drive up to the town of Sandy, where visitors can tour historic sites and swim in the close-by Sandy River. As the highway continues to the east, the landscape changes rapidly, with the foothills of the Cascade Range beginning their relentless ascent. Towering Douglas firs, some of them centuries old, cover the slopes, and growing nearby, rhododendrons and oaks add eye-pleasing splashes of color in the spring and fall. Soon, too, the Salmon River briefly comes into view, running to the Sandy River.

2 Wildwood Recreation Area

Situated on the banks of the Salmon River, picturesque Wildwood is one of many places to pause and sample the countryside. Take advantage of its picnic areas and hiking trails or, in the spring and fall, join the anglers who come in pursuit of trout and salmon. Visit Streamwatch, an underwater viewing port that lets you see life inside the river from a unique angle.

3 Mt. Hood National Forest

Mountain lions and black bears lurking near alpine lakes, butterflies sipping the nectar from colorful wildflowers, waterfalls leaping over ledges—the splendors of nature are the star attractions throughout Mt. Hood National Forest. Encompassing more than a million acres, the wilderness is best known for its namesake, majestic Mt. Hood. The highest point in Oregon at 11,235 feet, the mountain's conical dome is a dormant volcano that hasn't had a major eruption for probably a thousand years or more. Nowadays, its treeless upper slopes are blanketed not with fiery lava flows but with immense glaciers that glisten in the sunlight.

In April, most of Hood River County's many acres of fruit orchards are in full blossom.

Between mile markers 45 and 46, past Rhododendron, note the reconstruction of the West Barlow tollgate. It marks a portal of the historic Barlow Road Drive extending from Mt. Hood to Oregon City. Blazed in 1845, this overland route was a lifesaver to pioneers heading west on the Oregon Trail; before the trail was opened, they had to convert their covered wagons into rafts and float down the risky and tumultuous Columbia River rapids.

4 Laurel Hill

Laurel Hill—its steep slopes are a challenge just to walk on, let alone descend in a covered wagon—was the last major obstacle faced by pioneers traveling toward the valleys and coasts to the west. In a task that could take days, the can-do pioneers used ropes to slowly lower their wagons down the hill. Today, historical markers relate their ordeal, and rhododendrons decorate the slopes.

5 Timberline Lodge

A six-mile turnoff climbs past vast forests and seasonal waterfalls to Timberline Lodge, a masterpiece of craftsmanship built by the WPA during the Great Depression. Constructed of stone and timber, the hotel is filled with handsome details, including huge fireplaces and fine examples of woodworking.

Outside, alpine gardens thrive in the warmer months. You can also explore the surrounding countryside on a network of hiking trails that meander through flower-filled meadows. For a bird's-eye view, sightseers can ride the mile-long chairlift that traverses the upper reaches of Mt. Hood.

6 Trillium Lake

Named for the three-petaled wildflower that flourishes in these woodlands, Trillium Lake lies two miles south of Rte. 26. Stands of evergreens surround the lake, whose surface forms a mirror for reflections of snowcapped Mt. Hood. Visitors come to this pleasant alpine retreat to hike, swim, fish, and boat.

7 Bennett Pass

The next leg of the journey through the Cascades follows Rte. 35, which soon climbs to 4,674 feet at Bennett Pass. Once over the crest, the road curves alongside the rushing Hood River, hemmed in by canyon cliffs that rise steeply from its banks. The descent continues through forests

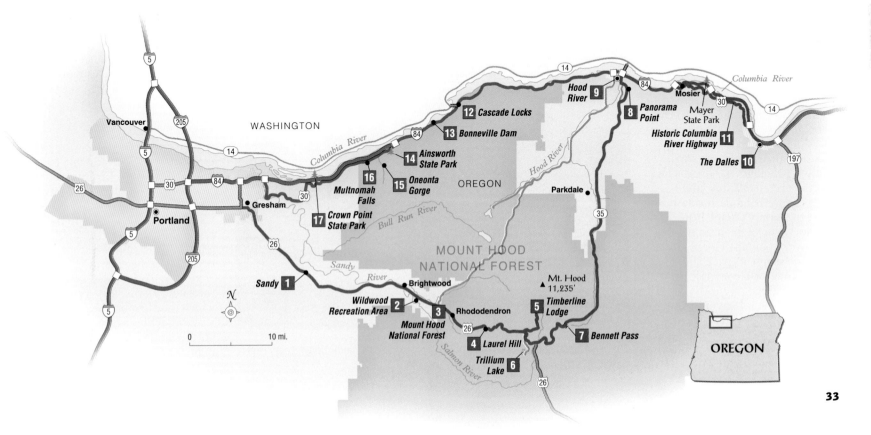

of birches and pines to the fields and orchards that spread like a quilt across the lower Hood River valley.

8 Panorama Point

Panorama Point offers one of the most startling views to be found along the drive to the Columbia River Gorge. A short detour on East Side Road leads to the lookout, where the panorama takes in the high volcanic peaks found to the north in Washington, the river valley, the forest-covered foothills, and the omnipresent crown of Mt. Hood.

9 Hood River

The city of Hood River grew from and around the timber industry. After much of the area's old-growth forests had been felled, however, the land was given over to farming, and thousands of fruit trees were planted. Today the harvest includes apples, pears, and cherries. Besides the orchards, many neighborhoods are also bedecked with roses, petunias, forsythias, and other flowers.

In recent years the area has become a magnet for windsurfers, who find ideal conditions for their sport in the Columbia River Gorge. Winds often whip steadily through the gorge, and small waves on the river add to the excitement. For a glimpse of the windsurfers' colorful sails, stop at Columbia Gorge Sailpark, where a small sandy beach abuts the river. The sport—a relatively new one—lends a jauntily modern counterpoint to the city's many historic buildings, one of the most notable being the Columbia Gorge Hotel.

For a change of pace and a chance to let someone else drive, take a relaxing trip on the Mt. Hood Railroad. Leaving from the town's historic district, the train makes a scenic 44-mile tour through the Hood River valley, with ample picture opportunities.

10 The Dalles

An interstate highway, I-84, parallels the Columbia River to The Dalles, which was named by French explorers who thought the area's basaltic rocks resembled flagstones, or *les dalles*. As the interstate follows the generally widening gorge to the east, the road leads past tall pinnacles of volcanic rock deposited in ancient eruptions, floodplains, tablelands, and on the opposite bank, hills covered with mosses and an abundance of majestic conifers.

When Lewis and Clark came to the region on their epic journey in 1805, they found it to be a center for Indian trade. Their glowing descriptions—and the discovery of gold—inspired others to follow, and the town was established in 1838. Today wheat fields and cherry orchards edge The Dalles, and the historic district contains numerous fine examples of 19th-century homes and government buildings.

11 Historic Columbia River Highway

On the return trip west, leave the interstate for the eastern section of the Historic Columbia River Highway (Rte. 30). Constructed between 1913 and 1920, the road remains to this day a testament to the skills of its builders. Switching back and forth in search of the most scenic route, the highway is a marvel of design, with panoramic viewpoints, arched bridges, and beautifully designed stonework.

To the west of The Dalles, the historic highway soon enters a region of barren hillsides. These areas became scablands about 13,000 years ago, when they were ravaged by huge floods caused by melting ice-age glaciers. The growth that occurs today finds its nourishment in the ashes deposited by eruptions in the area.

Traversing the dells and bluffs that rise above the Columbia River, the old highway between Rowena and Mosier passes into a

transition zone—the dividing line between the arid prairies to the east and the moister forests to the west. Here too you will find one of the most astonishing segments of the drive—the Rowena Loops, where the road zigzags wildly up and down hillsides. The highway also passes two natural areas, the Tom McCall Preserve and Mayer State Park, both of which showcase flowers and wildlife.

12 Cascade Locks

Back on the interstate the drive heads west past farmlands, commercial centers, and miles of forest before entering Cascade Locks. Over the years the town's name has become a bit of a misnomer, for its cascade was submerged after the completion of the Bonneville Dam and, since its locks were built to circumvent the cascade, they too are no longer a distinguishing feature. Nevertheless, a park overlooks the unused passageway, and a museum depicts the area's colorful history.

To get an entirely different perspective on the region, you can board the *Columbia Gorge*, a grand old stern-wheeler that makes daily excursions in the summer. Travelers can also view the river from the Bridge of the Gods, which crosses over to Washington.

13 Bonneville Dam

The Bonneville Dam was the first of many dams built to tame and tap the Columbia River torrents. A series of fish ladders, or water-filled terraces, are on view at the visitor center. Salmon leap from pool to pool on a remarkable journey to the upper reaches of the river, where they spawn. The fish come from as far away as Alaska, returning to the very waters in which they first hatched.

Another viewing area looks out on the underwater world of the huge bottom-dwelling white sturgeon. Sometimes weighing more

The north slope of Mt. Hood is an imposing presence that looms above Lost Lake, conifer forests, and the colorful autumn leaves.

⠿⠿⠿ Trip Tips ⠿⠿⠿

Length: About 200 miles.

When to go: Popular year-round.

Words to the wise: Roads are sometimes closed in winter because of fallen trees and ice- and snowstorms.

Nearby attractions: Hood River and Flerchinger vineyards and Pheasant Valley Winery, Hood River. Washington Garden, rose and Japanese gardens, Portland.

Further information: Oregon's Mt. Hood Territory, 65000 E. Hwy. 26, Welches, OR 97067, 888-622-4822, www.mthood territory.com

than 1,500 pounds, the ancient fish, with bony plates instead of scales, have been prowling the rivers and seas since the time of the dinosaurs.

14 Ainsworth State Park

At exit 35 leave the interstate for the 22-mile western sector of the Historic Columbia River Highway, which skirts a lush forest of birch, maple, and fir trees on its way to Ainsworth State Park. Perched atop steeply rising bluffs, the park sits back from the smooth-coursing Columbia River. Of the area's many hiking trails, one standout leads to nearby Horsetail Waterfall, where the hiking path actually passes behind the falling water.

15 Oneonta Gorge

Traveling two miles farther west through the dense forest, you'll come to Oneonta Gorge, a botanical area maintained by the U.S. Forest Service. The narrow cleft of this gorge—shady, moist, and cool—shelters a verdant array of lichens, mosses, and shrubs. A fairly difficult hike (especially in the wetter winter months) climbs 900 feet to Oneonta Falls, and other trails loop through the area.

16 Multnomah Falls

The Historic Columbia River Highway passes more than a dozen waterfalls, but most people consider Multnomah Falls to be the grandest of them all. Divided into upper and lower cascades, the falls plunge a total of 620 feet. The icy stream resounds with a roar as it leaps and lands, while clouds of mist envelop the mosses and ferns clinging to the cliffsides.

Plenty of parking is provided for the area's many sightseers, and a nature center and 1920s stone lodge have fine views of the falls above. Trails—paved, but on the steep side—explore the hillsides; one crosses an arched footbridge above the lower falls.

Back on the scenic highway, more waterfalls come into sight, tumbling down the steep ridges that line the road. From east to west, the major cascades visible from the highway are Wahkeena, Bridal Veil, Shepperds Dell, and Latourell falls.

17 Crown Point State Park

A winding drive on the Historic Columbia River Highway climbs upward to Crown Point State Park, a well-maintained preserve that sits perched atop an enormous volcanic rock—the park's namesake—that rises more than 700 feet above sea level. The preserve, with unobstructed views extending both east and west, is an excellent place to observe the breathtaking beauty of the mighty Columbia river, its awesome gorge cut through the volcanic bedrock, and its abundant wildlife. Almost certain to catch your eye from here is Beacon Rock—an even larger monolith towering nearly 850 feet on the opposite side of the river—beckoning travelers to come explore the companion scenic drive to be found on the scenic northern bank, a fitting close to your visit to the Columbia River.

Twice airborne, Multnomah Falls slices down the slopes of Larch Mountain.

Rogue–Umpqua Scenic Byway

A full measure of natural splendors awaits in southwestern Oregon, where myriad creeks and rivers race down forested slopes to golden valleys and finally the sea.

The twin spires of Old Man Rock looms high above the North Umpqua River.

The Rogue-Umpqua Scenic Byway arcs across the western slopes of the Cascade Range—a serene countryside where fingers of fog gather in fir-scented valleys, and ancient volcanoes brood overhead. Crowning this memorable drive, side trips climb through a pristine parkland to Crater Lake, one of the world's most awesome scenic wonders and, further south, to beautiful Applegate Lake.

1 Colliding Rivers Viewpoint

Passing grass-covered hills, scrubland, and small stands of oaks and pines, Rte.138 makes a leisurely ascent—about 18 miles in length—from Roseburg to Glide. Once in town, be sure to visit the Colliding Rivers Viewpoint, which overlooks the confluence of the North Umpqua and Little rivers. An exhilarating sight in the wetter months, their waters churn every which way before settling down as one. Across the road, the Colliding Rivers Information Center offers helpful information on local camping, hiking, and watersports.

For still more views of the North Umpqua River, as well as the kayakers and rafters who brave its currents, consider a walk along the North Umpqua Trail, which runs alongside the waterway for some 75 miles. Beginning about six miles east of Glide at the Swiftwater Trailhead, the path—often in the shade of maple, alder, and Douglas fir trees—can be accessed from many points along the drive.

2 Susan Creek Falls

Many of the numerous creeks that empty into the North Umpqua River finish their downhill courses as sparkling waterfalls. Susan Creek, one of them, can be reached by a short hike from mile marker 29. Although the terrain is challenging, the sound of the 50-foot falls—a steady rumble heard through the trees—is an added incentive to make the trek.

3 Fall Creek Falls

As the drive continues upriver toward the Umpqua National Forest, the vegetation grows markedly denser than in the foothills below. The vast woodland—nearly a million acres—is a medley of rivers, creeks, lakes, volcanic formations, and stands of Douglas fir mixed with many other hardwood species.

Of the many footpaths that wend through the area, the Fall Creek Falls Trail is especially dramatic. About a mile long, it begins two miles beyond the entrance sign for the national forest. The hike slips through a crevice, past numerous columns of volcanic rocks, and ends with theatrical flair at Fall Creek Falls and its punchbowl-shaped basin.

4 Steamboat

Hemmed in by cliffs and forested peaks, the scenic byway curves beside the North Umpqua River —icy cold and glassy clear—to the small community of Steamboat. The waterway here is famed for its summer runs of steelhead trout, a vigorous fish that can weigh up to 15 pounds. The area also serves as a gateway to the surrounding woodlands. One side trip, a six-mile drive on Steamboat Creek Road (Rte.38), weaves through Black Gorge to Steamboat Falls.

Once back in Steamboat, the drive continues east on Rte.138, arriving some 10 miles later at Weeping Rocks (near Marsters Bridge), one of several places to stop and observe spawning chinook salmon. Fighting the often powerful current, the fish swim upriver in late summer and early fall. After finding suitable spots, they make their nests—depressions in the riverbed called redds—with thrusts of their tails, a motion that displaces sand and gravel.

5 Toketee Falls

Thousands of years ago, a massive volcano called Mt. Mazama rained a thick layer of fiery debris across much of this region. Many centuries of erosion, however, have worked their magic, washing away and reforming the volcanic deposits. Several of these rock formations are likely to catch your eye on the way to Toketee Falls.

Large outcrops of porous, sand-colored pumice shine at intervals on the riverbanks, and Eagle Rock, composed of tightly packed pillars of basalt, stands just past Eagle Rock Campground. Also visible from the road are Old Man and Old Woman rocks—two stony peaks that rise above the surroundings.

Farther on, follow Rte.34, a forest road that leads to the parking lot at the start of the Toketee Falls Trail. Tracing the North Umpqua River through a narrow chasm, the hike ends at an observation platform. The view overlooks the two-tiered waterfall. The first cascade plummets 40 feet into a pool, and the second makes an 80-foot drop to the North Umpqua River Canyon below.

Farther east, the Toketee Reservoir makes an ideal camping spot, with some waterside sites. For those who fish, the catch might include brook, rainbow, and brown trout—tempting campfire fare.

6 Watson Falls

Not far from the highway, Watson Falls plunges 272 feet, making it one of the tallest waterfalls in Oregon. A half-mile trail leads to the thunderous marvel. Still more

cascades, Clearwater and White-horse falls, lie to the east.

7 Lemolo Lake

Rte. 2610, a side trip to the north, traverses the forest to Lemolo Lake, a picturesque locale with deep coves and sandy beaches. Located some 4,000 feet above sea level, the lake is usually chilly, but water-skiers are undeterred, chancing a frigid dip in its waters for an exhilarating ride behind a speeding boat. Those unwilling to brave getting wet might try fishing; landlocked kokanee salmon and German brown trout are among the potential prizes for anglers. In winter the area becomes a sports haven for cross-country skiers and snowmobilers, who follow trails through the snowy pines.

8 Diamond Lake

After swinging to the south, Rte. 138 passes fragrant fields of summer wildflowers on the way to Diamond Lake. Filling part of a glacial basin, the watery jewel is flanked by mountains. To the west is 8,363-foot Mt. Bailey, its icy face sometimes shimmering in the

A must-see Star Route leads to Crater Lake National Park, where the sky and the sapphire-blue water thrills the eye.

morning sun. Mt. Thielsen—a steep, narrow peak cresting nearly a thousand feet higher in the east—has earned the nickname Lightning Rod of the Cascades.

9 Hamaker Campground

South of Diamond Lake, the drive forks west onto Rte. 230, descending past now-hardened lava flows and a forest of lodgepole pines. The byway then meets the Wild and Scenic Upper Rogue River, which carves a 200-mile course on its way to the Pacific Ocean.

Eagle Rock is a monument of note in the Umpqua National Forest.

Two excellent trails let visitors explore the waterway. The Upper Rogue River National Recreation Trail, easily accessed from Hamaker Campground, shadows the river for 48 miles, passing old-growth Douglas firs, some 500 years old and 200 feet tall. Leading from Rte. 6560 to the Rogue-Umpqua Divide Wilderness, the Hummingbird Meadow Trail guides hikers across aromatic fields of wildflowers—and may offer a glimpse of a hummingbird sipping nectar.

10 Rabbit Ears

These massive twin peaks—once part of a volcano's interior—seem to some wondrously alive, as if cocked to the murmurings of the wilderness. For a close-up view, secondary routes loop around the ears and lead to Hershberger Lookout. Mts. Bailey and Thielsen dominate the northern skyline, and to the south the Cascades roll like waves toward California.

Star Route

★ Crater Lake National Park

Turn east on Rte. 62 to reach Crater Lake National Park. When an ancient volcano known as Mt. Mazama erupted 7,700 years ago, the pumice and ash it expelled covered much of the Northwest. After the discharge the mountain collapsed; today Crater Lake is filled with water, and the mirrored expanse, six miles wide, lies encircled by green forests and steep-sided mountains, which take on an extra sparkle—a profound contrast to the lake—when covered by the snows of winter. From the entrance station, follow the access road to 33-mile-long Rim drive, and circle the lake—it's the deepest body of fresh water in the United States, with depths of more than 1,900 feet. Daybreak, when a remarkable shade of blue reflects from the water's surface, is the best time to see the lake; no wonder Klamath Indians felt the lake was a sacred passageway to a world below.

Mt. Thielsen's spire dusted with snow is a lonely sentinel in the Umpqua National Forest.

11 Rogue Gorge

After exploring the national park, backtrack on Rte. 62 to the town of Union Creek, which was once a base camp for the Civilian Conservation Corps. Like the government workers before them, today's sightseers are bound to be impressed by the local landscape.

While in the area, visit the Rogue Gorge Viewpoint, where it is easy to see why the Rogue River is so aptly named. Churning wildly—unbridled and uncontrolled—the Rogue roars through a narrow basalt cut. Farther south at Natural Bridge Viewpoint, the waterway ducks out of sight,

flowing through an underground channel; still tumultuous, it reappears from the ground about 200 yards farther downstream. The route follows the river south and west, crossing the stream repeatedly on numerous bridges.

12 Stewart State Park

A popular spot for camping, an easy day hike, or a picnic beneath the comforting shade of pines, Stewart State Park makes an inviting stop. While away an afternoon fishing for trout and bass, or sunbathe on the park's lawn, which slopes gently to the shores of Lost Creek Reservoir.

Table Rocks are reminiscent of a western movie as they frame Mt. McLoughlin.

13 Table Rocks

This pair of volcanic remnants, while shadows of their former selves, still manage to impress. Short but fairly difficult hikes climb each of the rocks, which are separated by several miles. The views from the flat, rocky summits take in countryside that was once teamed with Takelma Indians. In spring, the grasslands of this area is strewn with varied arrays of wildflowers.

14 Jacksonville

The official Rogue-Umpqua Scenic Byway route ends at Gold Hill, but there are jewels to be found to the south. Once in Gold

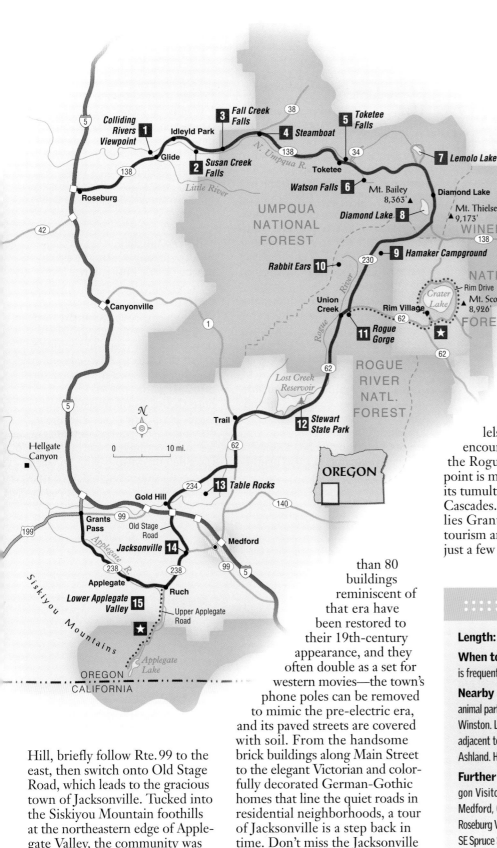

The map labels:

- Colliding Rivers Viewpoint **1**
- **3** Fall Creek Falls
- Idleyld Park
- **4** Steamboat
- **5** Toketee Falls
- Glide
- **2** Susan Creek Falls
- Toketee
- **7** Lemolo Lake
- Roseburg
- Little River
- Watson Falls **6**
- Mt. Bailey 8,363'
- Diamond Lake
- Mt. Thielsen 9,173'
- Diamond Lake **8**
- WINEMA
- UMPQUA NATIONAL FOREST
- **9** Hamaker Campground
- NATL.
- Rabbit Ears **10**
- Canyonville
- Union Creek
- Rim Village
- Crater Lake
- Rim Drive
- Mt. Scott 8,926'
- FOREST
- **11** Rogue Gorge
- Hellgate Canyon
- Lost Creek Reservoir
- ROGUE RIVER NATL. FOREST
- Trail
- **12** Stewart State Park
- OREGON
- Gold Hill
- **13** Table Rocks
- Grants Pass
- Old Stage Road
- Medford
- Jacksonville **14**
- Applegate
- Ruch
- Lower Applegate Valley **15**
- Upper Applegate Road
- OREGON / CALIFORNIA
- Siskiyou Mountains
- Applegate Lake
- 0   10 mi.

The Rogue Gorge is a cauldron of steaming white water.

15 Lower Applegate Valley

From Jacksonville, head west through the Lower Applegate Valley. A soothing counterpoint to the rugged Cascades, the area exudes a mellow grace—a rural mix of small towns, vineyards, and farms with golden fields and horses. The Applegate River, like an attentive escort, parallels the road, whispering encouragements all the way to the Rogue River, which by this point is much tamer than during its tumultuous descent down the Cascades. Beyond the Applegate lies Grants Pass, a center for tourism and trade. Gold Hill is just a few miles south on Rte. 5.

Hill, briefly follow Rte. 99 to the east, then switch onto Old Stage Road, which leads to the gracious town of Jacksonville. Tucked into the Siskiyou Mountain foothills at the northeastern edge of Applegate Valley, the community was established in the high-spirited days of a local gold rush. More than 80 buildings reminiscent of that era have been restored to their 19th-century appearance, and they often double as a set for western movies—the town's phone poles can be removed to mimic the pre-electric era, and its paved streets are covered with soil. From the handsome brick buildings along Main Street to the elegant Victorian and colorfully decorated German-Gothic homes that line the quiet roads in residential neighborhoods, a tour of Jacksonville is a step back in time. Don't miss the Jacksonville Museum, with exhibits that document the growth of the valley.

::::: Trip Tips :::::

Length: About 190 miles, plus side trips.

When to go: Popular year-round; snow is frequent in winter above 3,000 ft.

Nearby attractions: Wildlife Safari, animal park with petting zoo and auto tour, Winston. Lithia Park, landscaped grounds adjacent to Oregon Shakespeare Festival, Ashland. Hellgate Canyon, east of Galice.

Further information: Southern Oregon Visitors Association, P.O. Box 1645, Medford, OR 97501; tel. 800-448-4856. Roseburg Visitors & Convention Bureau, 410 SE Spruce St., Roseburg, OR 97470; tel. 800-444-9584, www.visitroseburg.com

Star Route

★ Applegate Lake

For a detour within a detour, head south on Rte. 238 where the drive drops into a ravine and the roadside is lined with poplars and cottonwoods turning into an area of intermittent grasslands. From Ruch, follow Upper Applegate Road to Applegate Lake, passing at about the midway point the McKee Covered Bridge—a structure built in 1917. The lake, bordered by the steep, evergreen-clad slopes of the Siskiyou Mountains, forms a sparkling oasis. Visitors can swim in the lake or explore one of the many well-kept trails. Stop by Swayne Viewpoint for a glimpse of the region to the south. You'll see the Red Buttes Wilderness, with thousands of acres of rich and varied terrain—old-growth forests, meadows, and sawtooth ridges marked by horns and arêtes.

Cascade Lakes Highway

A range of dormant volcanoes presides over a land of living splendors: pine-packed forests, fish-filled lakes, and meadows festooned with flowers.

Dawn paints the sky over Sparks Lake, one of many along the drive.

Forged by fiery volcanoes and cut by ice-age glaciers, the Cascade Range lends its name to this route (it used to be known as Century Drive because it traverses nearly 100 miles). But these majestic peaks, which prevent the Pacific Ocean's moist air from moving east, endow central Oregon with far greater gifts than a name: some 250 days of sunshine per year and countless scenic wonders.

1 Bend

"Farewell, Bend!" a westward-bound pioneer once cried out wistfully as he left this idyllic spot on a curve of the Deschutes River, giving rise to Farewell Bend (later shortened to Bend by the poetry-spurning U.S. Post Office). But today this rapidly expanding ski-resort town might more aptly be called Welcome Bend, for its pleasant climate and lovely scenery have made it a magnet for tourists and big city refugees alike. Among the town's attractions are Drake Park, a riverside haven, and Pilot Butte, a volcanic cinder cone whose 500-foot summit takes in a view of up to nine Cascade peaks.

2 Mt. Bachelor

Heading westward from central Oregon's high desert, Cascade Lakes Highway climbs through airy stands of pine, fir, and mountain hemlock to the base of 9,065-foot-tall Mt. Bachelor. Home of a first-rate ski resort, the mountain has long served as a training site for the U.S. Ski Team. The Summit chairlift rewards passengers with a panorama that encompasses parts of California, Washington, and Oregon.

Far below, you can spot evidence of the fierce volcanic activity that shaped this landscape thousands of years ago: dark lava flows and pale pumice fields, lofty domes and deep chasms. Gleaming snowfields now cap the summits of four dormant volcanoes: Broken Top and the Three Sisters.

Continuing west, the road cuts across Dutchman Flat, a small desert of volcanic pumice brightened by pink pussy-paws, sulfur flowers, and other hardy plants. A few miles ahead, richer soil nourishes such wildflowers as Indian paintbrush, columbine, elephant-head, and alpine stars, all of which ring picturesque Todd Lake. At nearby Sparks Lake, listen for the boisterous calls of yellow-headed blackbirds.

3 Devils Garden

Before turning south, the drive passes Devils Hill, a large lava flow, and Devils Garden, a small meadow at its base. Indians have inhabited this region for the past 10,000 years, and traces of their presence can be seen in the pictograph that adorns a large boulder. Another local rock of historic significance is the one taken from here to the moon by astronaut James Irwin, one of several Apollo crewmen who trained in this area for lunar landings. Nearby Devils Lake delights visitors with an eerie optical illusion: crystal-clear water

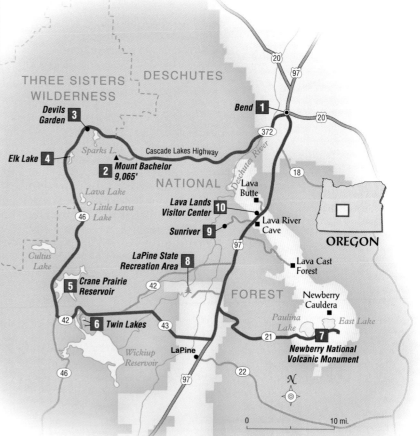

and a shallow white pumice bottom make it seem as if boats on the surface are floating in midair.

4 Elk Lake

One lovely lake after another unfolds along this stretch of the drive, and all of these sparkling gems swarm with rainbow and brown trout as well as kokanee salmon. Elk Lake boasts a picture-perfect setting, with Mt. Bachelor and South Sister rising above the surrounding forest, and the bright canvas of sailboards skimming across the lake's breezy surface.

Little Lava Lake, farther to the south, is the source of the fast-flowing Deschutes River, which can be seen from the road as it rushes through great green meadows. An historic Forest Service guard station offers information to summer visitors.

Just west of the route sprawls the Three Sisters Wilderness, nearly 287,000 acres of unspoiled beauty accessible by numerous trails. (Black bears, deer, and golden-mantled ground squirrels are only a few of the creatures you may spot along the way.) Cultus Lake, which is doubly blessed with gently sloped, sandy beaches and warm waters, is ideal for swimming, windsurfing, and waterskiing.

5 Crane Prairie Reservoir

Many anglers rate this 4,000-acre man-made lake as the best fishing spot in the state and one of the best in the country. Osprey Point, on the southwest bank of the reservoir, is a good place for spotting wood ducks, Canada geese, and the great fish hawks that give the point its name.

For sheer drama few sights in nature can match that of an osprey in pursuit of prey. Diving from 100 feet or more above the water, this master hunter zeroes in on a fish and plunges toward it like a guided missile, thrusting out its taloned feet just before hitting the water. More often than not, it emerges with a prize—sometimes stolen in midair by a brazen bald eagle.

6 Twin Lakes

Of all the evergreens seen along Rte. 42, which heads east toward Twin Lakes, the tall, long-needled ponderosa pine is perhaps the loveliest. Its glorious scent fills the air around these two looking-glass lakes, whose near-perfect roundness reflects their origin as volcanic craters.

7 Newberry National Volcanic Monument

At Rte. 97, drive north to the turnoff for a side trip to Newberry Crater. Now dormant, this huge volcano partially collapsed, forming a five-mile-wide caldera at its peak. Inside the caldera lie such unexpected wonders as two sparkling lakes, a 100-foot waterfall, and an obsidian lava flow (a river of black volcanic glass).

8 LaPine State Recreation Area

The largest ponderosa pine in Oregon, a sky-scraping specimen 191 feet tall, resides in this 2,300-acre park. Known for its scenic views of the Deschutes River, the area serves as an ideal base camp for exploring nearby lava fields and the Cascade Mountains.

9 Sunriver

On the way to Sunriver, a popular resort community, the drive rolls through vast Ponderosa pine

At Newberry National Volcanic Monument, see rivers of glasslike obsidian on the hillsides, a source worked into Native American arrowheads.

forests. Settled on the site of an old military base, the town boasts two championship golf courses, a marina, and a nature center complete with live animals, a botanical garden, and, for sky gazers, an astronomical observatory.

10 Lava Lands Visitor Center

Pull in to the Lava Lands Visitor Center, just off the road, for a good introduction to the surrounding 50,000 acres of Newberry National Volcanic Monument. A steep road winds up and around Lava Butte, a cinder cone jutting 500 feet above a sea of lava. From its summit you can gaze into the cone's crater and look out over a high desert plateau dotted with desert shrubs, cinder cones, and ponderosa pine. In the distance you can see the Cascade Range's crest to the west and north, including Mt. Bachelor, Three Sisters, Broken Top, and—on a clear day—even Mt. Hood. Lava River Cave, a nearby lava tube more than a mile long, can be explored by those willing to hike, lantern in hand, through its chilly corridors. A few miles south lies Lava Cast Forest, a collection of stone tree molds formed when molten lava engulfed a forest 7,000 years ago.

Redwood Highway

In a realm where rugged cliffs meet the sea and giant trees seem to scrape the sky, this one-of-a-kind highway unfurls amid the wonders of California's northern coast.

The redwoods of Jedediah Smith State Park, located near Crescent City, California, is a well-marked byway that parallels U.S. Highway 199. Thousands of giant coast redwood trees line the roadway's margins, dimly lit by shafts of sunlight from above.

Giving its name to this glorious ribbon of road just four hours north of San Francisco, the redwood is a marvel to behold—the tallest of living things and a stately remnant from the age of dinosaurs. These ambassadors from another time grow only in a narrow coastal strip that extends northward to Oregon, overlooking steep ocean cliffs, marshy lagoons, and seaside villages replete with picturesque Victorian homes.

1 Leggett

The town of Leggett, where the Pacific Coast Highway meets Rte. 101, provides an excellent introduction to the world of the old-growth redwoods. Drive-Thru Tree Park features the remarkable Chandelier Tree, a 315-foot giant with a tunnel carved through its massive trunk. Visitors can enjoy a picnic or hike the manicured trails that wind through portions of this 200-acre grove of awe-inspiring trees. In this unique world a misty silence holds sway and only occasional shafts of sunlight penetrate the broad canopy overhead.

2 Standish-Hickey State Recreation Area

Heading north from Leggett, Rte. 101 follows deep and winding canyons along the meandering south fork of the Eel River into the region known as the Redwood Empire. To the west lie the King Mountain Range and the "Lost Coast" of California, a virtually uninhabited wilderness where up to 80 inches of rain drench the highlands each year and beaches are strewn with numerous historic shipwrecks; to the east dense forests and lush meadowlands roll by mile after mile.

Parks abound along the route. The Standish-Hickey State Recreation Area, just two miles north of Leggett, occupies 1,000 acres of mostly second-growth redwoods, maples, oaks, and Douglas firs, and one spectacular redwood, named for *Mayflower* colonist Miles Standish. The Eel River, though, is the main attraction here, offering one of the best deep swimming holes in the valley, and excellent fishing for salmon and steelhead trout. In winter, run-off from the neighboring mountains transforms this placid river of clean emerald waters into a raging torrent.

3 Richardson Grove State Park

The redwoods are hard to miss at this 1,000-acre park—the highway passes right through the heart of an old-growth forest. For a closer

During the summer, salmon fishermen moor their boats in the calm waters behind the rocky Trinidad headland, sheltering them from the Pacific Ocean.

look, investigate the 10 miles of inviting trails that loop through the cathedral-like groves and along the rocky banks of the Eel.

4 Avenue of the Giants

Past the little town of Garberville, this 33-mile stretch of road parallels and crisscrosses Rte. 101 as it passes through one of the state's largest and most venerable redwood forests. A self-guiding auto tour (instructions are available at either the north or south ends of the scenic drive) suggests nine stops, but abundant turnouts offer the chance to pause and marvel unassisted at these giants. Reaching heights of 300 feet and more, many stand taller than the Statue of Liberty and have been growing since the days of ancient Rome.

5 Humboldt Redwoods State Park

Occupying some 50,000 acres along the avenue's most scenic stretches, Humboldt Redwoods ranks as the largest state park in

northern California and is home to one of the largest remaining old-growth redwood forests. Along the riverside flats, great stands of ancient trees darken the fern-carpeted forest floor; in the rolling uplands, mixed hardwoods and gentle grasslands bloom in spring with orchids, lilies, and huckleberries. Scattered along the route, more than 100 memorial groves bear the names of men and women who helped to save the redwoods. The Dyerville Giant, once honored as the champion of coastal redwoods, toppled in 1991. The sight of this 362-foot Goliath in repose is one of the park's main attractions; with a little imagination you can hear the echo of its thundering crash to the forest floor.

6 Humboldt Bay National Wildlife Refuge

Continuing north, the highway moves from forest to ocean, and the second-largest natural harbor in California (after San Francisco). Though guarded by treacherous

waters, Humboldt Bay itself is calm and can be safely explored by tour boat or kayak. Along this 15-mile stretch of protected waters, porpoises, sea lions, and playful harbor seals reward those with a watchful eye. Extensive wetlands and broad tidal flats make the Humboldt Bay National Wildlife Refuge one of northern California's premier spots for bird-watching. More than 200 species of water-fowl, raptors, and shorebirds reside here year-round or visit during spring migrations. For the most rewarding glimpses of avian life, take the Hookton Slough Trail, the Shorebird Loop Trail, or South Jetty Road.

7 Eureka

Lovers of period architecture will delight in this charming bayside city, once a rough-and-tumble frontier town, whose whimsical name (meaning "I have found it") recalls California's gold rush days. More than 10,000 Victorian homes line Eureka's picturesque streets, with styles ranging from the under-stated to the opulent: Carson Mansion (now a privately owned club) surely ranks among the most ornate homes in America.

Fronting Humboldt Bay and Eureka's busy harbor, the Old Town section is steeped in the flavor of frontier life. Once a seedy neighborhood of bordellos and saloons, the area was transformed by city planners into an inviting commercial district of museums, shops, and eateries, all housed in vintage buildings.

8 Azalea State Reserve

Named for President William McKinley after his assassination in 1901, the town of McKinleyville becomes a fragrant paradise each April, when the 30-acre Azalea State Reserve bursts into bloom. Well-marked trails guide visitors through this unique natural gar-den, where the pink and white blossoms of western azaleas enliven the banks of quiet forest creeks.

9 Trinidad

Near the old fishing village of Trinidad is a foggy promontory called Trinidad Head, where sitka spruce tower over ocean cliffs and, in winter and spring, hikers can glimpse migrating whales. A white granite cross at the summit marks the spot where the region was first claimed by Spanish ex-plorers in 1775. Memorial Light-house, a replica of the 1871 original, stands at the edge of town, overlooking offshore rocks where sea lions doze and, to the north, Trinidad State Beach, a windswept stretch of tidepools and driftwood.

10 Patricks Point State Park

Five miles north of Trinidad, the headland called Patricks Point juts seaward from the coast. Its 650-acre forested park includes a reconstructed Yurok Indian village as well as flowering meadows, sandy beaches, and dramatic cliffs carved by the pounding surf. A broken wall of sea stacks—portions of the mainland orphaned by erosion—frames the ocean view.

Humboldt Bay's small boat harbor borders Eureka's Old Town district.

11 Humboldt Lagoons State Park

Comprising several inland bodies of water, Humboldt Lagoons State Park is a naturalist's delight, with several distinct habitats coexisting in harmony. Salt- and freshwater marshes support numerous birds migrating along the Pacific Fly-way, including herons, egrets, pelicans, and many species of ducks and geese. To the west a 15-mile-long barrier beach protects the lagoons from the raging sea.

12 Redwood National Park

Signed into being by President Lyndon Johnson, and later expand-ed to 106,000 acres by President Jimmy Carter, this wilderness of giants that also includes several California state parks, hugs the Pacific coastline from Orick all the way to Crescent City, a distance of some 40 miles. To get oriented, begin with a stop at the Redwood Information Center, located off Rte. 101 just north of Freshwater Lagoon near the town of Orick. Here one can view maps, publica-tions, and exhibits, as well as sched-ule a visit to the Tall Trees Grove.

Not to be missed is a side trip to the park's interior via Bald Hills Road. On the way, take time for the Lady Bird Johnson Grove Trail (ironically, a former logging road), an easy one-mile loop that takes hikers through the stately grove. Farther along Bald Hills Road, a six-mile access road descends to the Tall Trees Trailhead (a free permit is required), where a three-mile loop skirts the 361-foot Howard Libby Tree. Before losing six feet of its top in a windstorm, it was the tallest tree in the world. The record is now held by the Mendocino Tree, 367.5 feet, near Ukiah, California.

13 Prairie Creek Redwoods State Park

The first of three state parks within the Redwood National and State Parks World Heritage Location, Prairie Creek draws campers and hikers from around the country to enjoy its inviting blend of forests, prairies, creeks, fern canyons, and hidden beaches. The park has an unusual welcoming committee: herds of Roosevelt elk, some with three-foot antlers, graze with serene indifference on the tall-grass prairie bordering the scenic parkway that threads through the area. The park is well-known for its wildlife, including black bears, bobcats, foxes, and such endangered bird species as the famously controversial spotted owl and the somewhat less well-known marbled murrelet, which nests in old-growth trees.

14 Del Norte Coast Redwoods State Park

North of Prairie Creek, the scenic parkway rejoins Rte. 101 and then jogs inland, crosses the broad Klamath River—famed for its autumn migrations of Chinook salmon—and returns to the coast at False Klamath Cove and the next great stand of trees at Del Norte Coast Redwoods State Park. Shrouded in fog, this primeval forest of redwood, alder, and spruce stretches to the water's edge; each spring a sumptuous understory of rhododendrons, azaleas, and wildflowers blazes with brilliant color. Although nature has long since restaked its claim, the area was once heavily logged—as you hike the trails, look for huge, fern-covered stumps and the crumbling trestles of the old logging railroad.

15 Lake Earl Wildlife Area

Crescent City's C-shaped harbor is known for its chilly sea breezes and breathtaking mountain vistas, and the region nearby is famous for its Easter lily farms, which produce the vast majority of the nation's bulbs. Aptly, the city celebrates Easter twice—once in spring and again in summer, when revelers toast the harvest at its Easter-in-July festival.

North of Crescent City, the Lake Earl Wildlife Area offers a fitting finale to the coastal portion of the drive. Unlike the rugged cliffs to the south, the coastline here consists of wind-sculpted sand dunes that run inland as much as half a mile. In August the first wave of migrating Arctic birds arrives, and by October this 5,000-acre reserve of pastures, lakes, and marshland is host to huge, honking parliaments of canvasbacks, mergansers, tundra swans, and the world's population of the Aleutian Canada goose, a rare variety numbering just 6,000 or so.

16 Jedediah Smith Redwoods State Park

Named for a mountain man and fur trapper who was the first white to travel overland from the Mississippi to California, 10,000-acre "Jed Smith," as it is known locally, is one of the state's oldest and most beautiful parks. Tempera-

The Carson mansion in Eureka, home of the private Ingomar club, is the archetype of Victorian splendor. It was built by a lumber magnate in the 1880s.

tures run a bit higher here than to the west, nurturing a harmonious blend of interior and coastal plant-life, including fragrant cedars, ponderosa pines, and the ever-familiar redwoods, which flourish in the ferny lowlands of the Smith River basin. For an especially scenic detour, take Howland Hil Road, which follows Mill Creek's winding course and provides easy access to the Mill Creek Trail and many of the park's stately groves of tall trees. Northern-most of the great redwood parks, Jedediah Smith is also one of the least visited, making it a perfect spot to enjoy the warm sunshine that comes as a welcome contrast to the chilly coastal fogs just 10 miles away.

17 Smith River National Scenic Byway

Stretching from Crescent City to the Oregon border, this 33-mile scenic drive along Rte. 199 offers spectacular mountain scenery. The highway follows the nationally designated Wild and Scenic Smith River through the Siskiyou Mountains and Six Rivers National Forest. Along the way you can behold a sublime, uninterrupted wilderness of deep gorges, broad canyons, and lofty peaks.

Mt. Shasta–Cascade Loop

Circling the southern limit of the Cascade Range—a wonderland shaped by titanic natural forces—
this drive visits sky-shearing volcanoes, flourishing forests and wetlands that teem with life,
and even otherworldly underground chambers.

Shasta Lake, a reservoir of the Sacramento River, is known as the Houseboat Capital of the World.

Although relatively few people live in northeast California—some call it one of the state's best-kept secrets—the region boasts a bounty of scenic riches. This long-distance loop tour, filled with variety and novelty, offers an ideal introduction, wending among the most dazzling treasures of a dramatic land.

1 Redding

Nestled in the northern reaches of the Sacramento Valley, Redding boomed in 1872, when the railroad was built. The city serves today as a gateway to the surrounding wilderness. Its streets offer hotels, restaurants, shopping, museums, Turtle Bay Exploration Park, and the all-glass pedestrian Sundial bridge.

Preview the area's wildlife and enjoy quiet strolls on the Sacramento River Trail. A leisurely 9.5-mile loop through riverside oak groves, the pathway is full of the sights and sounds of many species of colorful songbirds.

2 Shasta Lake

The drive heads due north on I-5 to Shasta Lake, a favorite of both boaters and water-skiers. Shaped like an oddly fingered hand, with each digit stretching toward an incoming river, the lake was created by Shasta Dam. Massive and imposing—its spillway rises 487 feet—the dam ranks as one of the nation's largest concrete structures. The lake's zigzagging shoreline is a mix of red-clay cliffs and foothills cloaked with pines and manzanita. To visit the dam, take Shasta Dam exit 7 miles north of Redding on I-5, and continue through the city of Shasta Lake. Shasta Dam Blvd. will lead you to a panoramic view of the region.

3 Lake Shasta Caverns

Five miles beyond the turnoff to Shasta Dam lies the small community of O'Brien, the jumping-off point for tours of these caverns—a cache of hidden beauty that rivals the area's more conspicuous wonders. The trip begins with a 15-minute ferry ride across Shasta Lake, followed by a short hop on a bus that climbs to a simple, nondescript door. Behind it, though, lies a surreal display of geologic art: an interior adorned with fluted columns, white spires, and crystallized stalagmites—all built slowly, drip by drip.

4 Castle Crags State Park

With the Trinity Mountains to the west, the interstate leads to Castle Crags State Park, where huge dome-topped granite spires rise more than 4,000 feet above the Sacramento River. Hoping to strike it rich, gold diggers once prospected here, but today the treasures are strictly scenic. Trails lead sightseers to the foot of the impressive peaks and weave through the area's forest, overgrown with Douglas firs and incense cedars.

5 Dunsmuir

On the way to Dunsmuir, I-5 continues alongside the Sacramento River, which courses through brush-covered canyons beside the Southern Pacific Railroad. The trains that steamed through here were instrumental in the town's growth, and an old railroading center offers visitors a glimpse of those earlier days.

Dunsmuir is also known for its drinking water, which comes from an underground spring and is bottled for nationwide export. Take a sip at one of the public fountains, then decide whether or not the town's nickname, Home of the Best Water on Earth, is truly deserved.

6 Mt. Shasta

Shasta's great peak—visible from more than a hundred miles away—beckons travelers along much of this drive. By day it appears as a proud monarch topped with a crown of snow, but its slopes, smoldering in the glow of the evening's last light, have also been likened to a giant ember. From all angles and in all guises, though, Mt. Shasta, cresting at 14,162 feet, is a delight to behold and an inspiring monument to the volcanic past. For a closer look and an eagle's-eye view of the region, follow Everitt Memorial Highway (Rte. A-10), which makes a relatively easy climb nearly halfway to the glacier-clad summit.

The Modoc Indians, inhabitants of this area when pioneers arrived, had a rich folklore to explain the natural world. According to one of their legends, the Chief of the Sky Spirits grew weary with the ice and snow in heaven, so he opened a hole in the sky with a rock and in doing so formed a cone-shaped pile below. Seeing that the work was good, the god moved his wife and children to the mountain's inner core. When the volcano rumbled, hurtling sparks high into the air, the natives claimed that meant the Chief of the Sky Spirits was tossing a log on the family fire.

With a lot less mythic dash, scientists explain that Mt. Shasta's great bulk—its base spans a distance of 17 miles—has contained within it at least four separate volcanic cones. The mountain's fairly symmetrical shape was formed over the centuries—some speculate 100,000 years were required —as one eruption after another discharged lava, with later flows coming to rest atop earlier ones.

7 Klamath National Forest

After passing a steep-sided volcanic cone called Black Butte, I-5 enters the welcoming town of Weed, once a busy lumbering center notorious for its brawling inhabitants. The drive then heads northeast on Rte. 97, making a gradual climb into the Cascades and the Klamath National Forest. Visit the Living Memorial Sculpture Garden, 13 miles east of Weed, or simply enjoy the route's natural attractions. Vast and diverse, the forest includes juniper, ponderosa pine, incense cedar, and shrubs such as sagebrush and rabbitbrush.

Trip Tips

Length: About 500 miles, plus side trips.

When to go: Much of the area can be enjoyed year-round, but temperatures, especially in the mountains, are most comfortable from June to October. Many alpine routes are closed during winter.

Nearby attractions: Shasta State Historic Park, ruins of gold-mining boomtown Shasta City, Rte. 299, west of Redding. Shasta-Trinity National Forest, three wilderness areas and more than 2 million acres laced with trails and rivers, west and north of Redding.
Eagle Lake, resort area, with swimming, fishing, and campgrounds, Rte. A1, near Susanville.

Further information: Shasta Cascade Wonderland Association, 1699 Hwy. 273, Anderson CA 96007; tel. 800-474-2782, www.shastacascade.com.

After topping out at Mt. Hebron Summit, the road descends between volcanic mountains. On the way, you'll cross old lava flows, then eventually enter Butte Valley, a sweeping expanse that was once all lake; today it is a huge depression, spotted with marshes and farms and encircled by sage-covered hills and high peaks.

8 Lower Klamath Lake

Just a bit south of Oregon, the drive turns east, following Rte. 161 to Lower Klamath Lake, part of Lower Klamath National Wildlife Refuge, among the world's best sites for viewing bald eagles. One of the world's greatest nature-watching locales, the area teems with literally millions of birds—some 400 species in all. Although each season offers something special, spring and fall get the highest concentrations of birds, with huge flocks of waterfowl filling the sky.

Unpaved roads (bird-watchers can use their cars as blinds) loop through the refuge, offering views

Limestone formations abound in Shasta Caverns.

Thin veils of water cascade from fractured layers of rock at picturesque Burney Falls.

of the display, which includes ducks, geese, swans, grebes, pelicans, herons, hawks, and eagles. To the east Tule Lake National Wildlife Refuge offers more of the same, so be sure to bring your camera and binoculars.

9 Lava Beds National Monument

Switch onto Rte. 139 south, which passes through Tule Lake, then leads to the well-marked turnoff to Lava Beds National Monument, one of the stops on the Volcanic Legacy Scenic Byway, an All-American Road that continues down Rte. 49. After skirting the southern shores of Tule Lake, the road passes through a region that was once scorched under sinuous rivers of lava, which cooled into an array of formations, including bluffs and caves. On the area's younger rocks—some about a thousand years old—lichens have gained a toehold, the first step in transforming the stones into soil. Further along in this lengthy

process, other parts of the once-fiery land now support tufts of grass, sagebrush, and stands of western junipers.

Where plants grow, animals are almost certain to follow. Eagles and hawks—their aeries safely hidden among the cliffs—might be seen soaring above. On land deer and pronghorns share living space with stealthier animals such as marmots and foxes. Stop by the national monument's visitor center, complete with interpretive displays, for helpful information.

10 Ash Creek Wildlife Area

After returning to Rte. 139, the drive passes through an isolated wilderness, where the facilities are few and scattered. To the east of this area lie the vast high deserts of California and Nevada. Before the town of Adin, the highway again climbs into the mountains and crests at 5,188 feet. Black basalt and gray ash—more reminders of past volcanism—can be seen along the way.

Grazing grounds and alfalfa fields then come into view, and just off the highway at Ash Creek Wildlife Area, some 14,000 acres offer yet another bird-watcher's haven. The boggy banks along the seasonal streams and pools are the haunts of diving ducks, terns, and sandhill cranes. The last, often arriving during their mating season, put on an extravagant show, bowing and leaping in ritual dances.

11 Fall River Mills

Fly-fishing connoisseurs rave about the spring-fed brooks outside Fall River Mills, a mountain town perched at an elevation of about 3,400 feet. In the mid-1800s a pair of mills operated here, one a sawmill for processing lumber, the other a gristmill for making flour. Exploring the local streets, visitors can take in an old blacksmith shop and jail at Fort Crook Museum, which also houses exhibits of the pioneers and native American artifacts.

Mt. Shasta–Cascade Loop

12 Burney Falls

Eleven miles beyond Fall River Mills, turn north onto Rte. 89 for the start of a six-mile journey to Burney Falls. Trails lead to the 129-foot cascades, which in the wetter months are watery plumes that burst from a cliffside. When the conditions are right, rainbows color the rising clouds of mist. For that very reason, perhaps, the local Ilmawi Indians allowed other tribes to camp beside the falls, the only part of their territory where such an intrusion was permitted.

13 Lassen National Scenic Byway

After a quick turnaround, head south on Rte. 89, which runs through the Hat Creek valley and Lassen National Forest. A lengthy, steep rim—visible evidence of a fault in the earth's crust—juts up just to the east.

At the junction with Rte. 44, turn toward the east on the first leg of the scenic byway. This superb route passes myriad volcanic remnants and provides access to many trails, which lead to lakes and fine views of the forest.

The soil in this region supports a variety of different trees. A list of the various species includes ponderosa pine, lodgepole pine, red fir, white fir, and Douglas fir. Aspens also grow here, surviving in areas that have relatively high amounts of moisture, such as creek banks and along the fringes of open meadows. Scattered about the forest floor, an array of colorful wildflowers sprout late in the spring, chasing the melting snows up the slopes.

At Rte. 36, a turn to the west leads to Lake Almanor, a restful vacation spot. The dome of nearby Lassen Peak reflects on the water's often mirrorlike surface. Since lake temperatures are fairly mild in the summer, swimmers delight

Mt. Shasta, seen at moonrise from the mirrored waters of Lake Siskiyou.

in turning the mountain's image into unrecognizable ripples.

14 Lassen Volcanic National Park

Few national parks can illustrate with as much clarity the fact that the earth's surface is forever changing. Rte. 89—which leads to the visitor center and viewing areas—snakes through skirting steam vents, boiling mudpots, gaseous fumaroles, and cone-shaped mountains of cinder and ash.

Boardwalks lead to many of the sites, and visitors are advised to stay on the trail, for parts of this region where the earth's molten interior escapes to the surface have been known to collapse. A shining example of nature's power is Lassen Peak, which last erupted for seven years beginning in 1914 and is the park's tallest volcano, cresting at 10,457 feet—yet another showstopper in a national park that, despite its unsettled volcanic past, offers a relaxing escape at one of the national park system's best-kept secrets.

49

Pacific Coast Highway

From the roller-coaster hills of San Francisco to the dazzling seascapes of the North Coast, this California highway is paved with scenic riches.

Trails lead visitors through glades of mixed Douglas fir and redwood forest in the Pacific Coast's many parks.

Majestic cliffs rising over an endless, churning sea; workaday fishing towns set in tidy coves; ancient forests nourished by moist ocean air; and ridged hills that parade toward the shimmering blue waters of the Pacific—these are but a few of the sights to be savored along California's North Coast. No wonder residents, who are never far from nature's bounties, consider this coastal strip one of the state's most prized possessions and regard its main thoroughfare —Rte.1, known simply as the One— as a highway to heaven.

1 Marin Headlands

Imagine the dilemma of its creators: how do you build a bridge worthy of San Francisco Bay? To the south lies the gemlike city itself, a compact, colorful cluster of buildings piled high like bright packages; to the north, the Marin Headlands, a pastoral promontory rising with easy grace from the boisterous bay.

Yet, despite such competition, the Golden Gate Bridge achieves a complementary beauty all its own. Indeed, it would be hard to imagine San Francisco Bay without this heroic, ruddy marvel.

North across the bridge, the Marin Headlands—part of the vast Golden Gate National Recreation Area—offer exhilarating city and ocean views. From here, north of the Golden Gate, the city is framed by the bridge's twin towers. Beyond, urban bustle gives way to natural splendor: the rounded hills, gray-sand beaches, and soaring seaside cliffs that characterize the North Coast. (Traffic lights will be few and far between for the next 150 miles, but the road's many curves do a splendid job of governing the traffic flow.) A few miles north of San Francisco, take the Panoramic Highway west toward Muir Woods National Monument.

2 Muir Woods National Monument

They are nature's tallest trees, a living link to the age of dinosaurs. They are the redwoods of coastal California, and while specimens here are dwarfed by their siblings to the north, the redwoods of Muir's Cathedral Grove—the last such remaining stand in the Bay Area—are awesome by any measure, soaring 250 feet above the ferny forest floor. The oldest among them, at 1,000 years, was a mere sapling when Vikings first set foot in the New World. Six miles of trails guide visitors along the banks of Redwood Creek and into the heart of the grove, which the naturalist John Muir, exaggerating only slightly, called "the best tree-lover's monument in all the forests of the world."

3 Point Reyes National Seashore

Back on the Panoramic Highway, follow the steep, tortuous road through Mt. Tamalpais State Park. At Stinson Beach the road regains the shoreline and there parallels the notorious San Andreas Fault, following it north up Olema Valley and Tomales Bay. Extending some 650 miles from the Mexican border to Cape Mendocino, the fault marks the junction of the Pacific and North American crustal plates. As these huge landmasses grind past each other at a speed of two inches per year, pressure builds up and is then suddenly released when the plates jump. A well-marked trail offers a first-hand glimpse of some of the damage caused by one such memorable jolt, the great San Francisco earthquake of 1906.

Just north of Olema, a turnoff leads to 70,000-acre Point Reyes National Seashore, which extends some 70 miles around the Point Reyes Peninsula, a craggy triangle that juts out into the Pacific. Eons ago, this orphaned hunk of southern California granite was dragged

about 350 miles northward by the San Andreas Fault. Along the beach, mountain and seaside habitats meet and mingle, producing a potpourri of dunes and estuaries, hills and forests, marshes and pastures. Wildlife far outnumbers people here. Bobcats, elk, mountain lions, and several endemic and exotic, introduced species of deer roam freely within the park's borders, while offshore a lucky visitor may spot the cruising bulk of a gray whale, an orca, or the occasional fin of a great white shark.

4 Tomales Bay State Park

Tomales Bay, a 13-mile-long inlet that separates Point Reyes from the mainland, is tranquil, protected, and uneventful—everything the Pacific is not. Along these restful shores, the ocean's rages are quickly forgotten and every sense is tickled by a different delight: the sweet scent of Bishop pine, the whir of countless waterfowl alighting on vast marshlands, the succulence of a freshly gathered oyster, the soothing warmth of the waters along Hearts Desire Beach, and the breathtaking beauty of the bay itself, backed by the green and golden hills of the Bolinas Ridge.

5 Bodega Bay

Movie buffs may be struck by a sense of déjà vu when they enter the village of Bodega Bay, for it was here that Alfred Hitchcock filmed *The Birds*, his classic tale of nature run amok. Today the town is more notable for its splendid seafood and harborside views than for its brief brush with fame. Spend an afternoon strolling along its anchorage or hiking the trail from Spuds Point Marina around Bodega Head, a rocky promontory that protects the tranquil waters of the bay from the swells and surf of the open sea.

CALIFORNIA

Bodega Head also marks the beginning of Sonoma Coast State Beach, a chain of parks that parallels the drive for the next 14 miles. No seaside pleasure is absent here. Climb the dunes or look for underwater treasures in the tidepools of Salmon Creek. Picnic beneath the cliffs of Schoolhouse Beach. Marvel at the pounding force of the Pacific along the rocks of Duncans Landing. Or stand at Goat Rock, near the point where the wide Russian River empties into the sea.

Warrior for the Wilderness

Through all the wonderful centuries since Christ's time, God has cared for these trees... but He cannot save them from fools—only Uncle Sam can do that." So wrote naturalist John Muir in 1901, only a few years after first being awed by California's mighty redwoods, whose durable, versatile wood made them a prime target for timber barons. Muir's campaign to persuade Uncle Sam to set aside precious public land was so successful that he became a leading champion of our national park system. His contributions are honored at both Muir Woods National Monument and the John Muir National Historic Site in nearby Martinez, California.

6 Armstrong Redwoods State Reserve

In tribute to the very trees he harvested, timber tycoon James Armstrong set aside this 750-acre redwood forest in the 1870s, making it one of the first virgin redwood preserves. The shade cast by these ancient giants is so deep that, according to lore, local Indians refused to enter this "dark hole." Today the forest is accessible to all; there's even a trail for visually impaired hikers.

Though camping is not permitted within the grounds of the park, it's available right next door at the Austin Creek State Recreation Area, where many of the hiking trails offer fine, sweeping views of the surrounding Russian River countryside. Twenty miles of trails, ranging from a gentle creekside saunter to a vigorous scramble up the slopes of McCray Mountain, lead you through dense forests of pine and oak and fields carpeted with assorted wildflowers.

7 Fort Ross State Historic Park

Visitors to this windswept coastal terrace invariably wonder what an Imperial Russian outpost is doing here. The explanation dates back to 1742, when Russian fur-trappers first crossed the Bering Strait, the body of water separating Siberia from Alaska. The trade in sea-otter pelts drew them deep into California, and by 1812, representatives of the Russian-American Fur Company waded ashore to establish a fortified supply depot.

The Russian presence at Fort Rossiya, or Russia (later trimmed to Ross), was short-lived, however. By 1820 hunting had decimated the sea-otter population, and the foggy coastal climate made farming maddeningly difficult. In 1841 the Russians sold the whole kit and kaboodle to John Sutter, who stripped it bare and hauled its livestock and arsenal to the

Waves splash against the rocky headlands of Gerstle Cove at Salt Point State Park.

Sacramento Valley. Some of the settlers dispersed into the hills, giving the interior towns their distinct Russian flavor.

Today's Fort Ross is largely a reconstruction—though faithful to the original. Carefully re-created are the weathered redwood stockade, the comparatively lavish commander's headquarters, and a Russian Orthodox chapel crowned by two towers. Perhaps most authentic of all is the mood of the place, for no visitor can stand on

this isolated bluff, whipped relentlessly by wind and waves, and not imagine the loneliness felt by a transplanted settler who found himself in a beautiful land so far from home.

8 Salt Point State Park

Giant toadstools, abstract sculptures, delicate honeycombs—sandstone formations like these, nestled among the headlands of Salt Point State Park, took some 50 million years to create. But

these fanciful forms, carved by the wind and the sea, are surely worth the wait. The park also contains one of California's first underwater preserves, a natural metropolis of anemones, nudibranchs, sea stars, chitons, abalone, and other marine life.

9 Kruse Rhododendron State Reserve

A short hop inland from the stony wonders of Salt Point, this 317-acre forest preserve offers a more delicate—and seasonal—variety of beauty. Reclaiming a hillside once devastated by fire, 20-foot-high banks of rhododendrons burst with pink blossoms every spring. Bit by bit, the flowers are yielding to the encroaching woods—part of natural patterns of plant succession—but in the meantime they continue to paint a lovely scene.

10 Point Arena

Hugging the coast, the drive takes in some of northern California's most cherished countryside—verdant pastures, dreamy ocean vistas, and hills of tall grasses that ripple with every briny breeze. One of the region's few towns is Point Arena. Once a busy logging port, the village was nearly obliterated by the 1906 earthquake. The Point Arena Light Station fared no better, but it was subsequently rebuilt and today is open to the public. Climb its 147 steps to arresting views of sea and coastline, which is so treacherous that 10 ships foundered on these rocks in a single night in 1865.

11 Van Damme State Park

Proving that trees don't necessarily have to be tall to have presence, this park's pygmy forest—mature pines and cypresses stunted by the combined effects of highly acidic soil, poor drainage, and wicked, salt-laden winds—barely reach the knee in some locations (elsewhere they achieve a more respectable, though still anemic, height of eight feet). Still, not everything here is pint-size. A network of trails and old logging roads along the Little River leads into the heart of a mature, second-growth forest, featuring Douglas firs, Pacific hemlocks, and redwoods. Fern Canyon, as its name implies, is especially lush, upholstered with a generous growth of ferns, rhododendrons, assorted wildflowers, and a waterfall.

12 Mendocino

Gracious, picturesque, and charming in every way, this hamlet of 1,100 residents seems to have been imported from the coast of Maine. Saltbox houses, Victorian gingerbread mansions, and weathered picket fences embroidered with roses grace its tidy streets.

The East Coast ambience is no accident: the town's settlers, lured west by the logging boom, were homesick New Englanders. Hollywood has used this Cape Cod look-alike as a stand-in for numerous movie and television locales. Fans of the television show *Murder She Wrote*, set in fictional Cabot Cove, Maine, are sure to recognize Jessica Fletcher's cottage when they pass by the Elisha Blair House, built in 1888.

13 Russian Gulch State Park

The next headland to the north marks the starting point for this small but diverse natural reserve, among the coast's most picturesque and remarkable. The park's main attraction is Devil's Punch Bowl, a 200-foot-long sea-cut tunnel that has collapsed at its inland end, forming a blowhole that becomes active during winter storms. The route crosses an arched bridge over Russian Gulch and shadows the creek through woodlands of maple, alder, laurel, and pine.

14 Jug Handle State Reserve

At this unusual oceanside park, it is possible to climb the stairs of history, one eon at a time. Thanks to coastal erosion and shifting landmasses, five discrete terraces stairstep from the sea, each about 100 feet higher and 100,000 years older than the one below it. With each step the ecology matures, ascending from tidal pools at the first level to pygmy forest at the top. A well-marked tour explains the flora and fauna at each level, as well as the mighty forces that built this living time machine.

15 Fort Bragg

Flower fans will rejoice at the dazzling displays at the Mendocino Coast Botanical Gardens, two miles south of Fort Bragg. Not a single square inch of this 47-acre preserve is wasted, and each season brings a new riot of color, from blooming dahlias, foxgloves, and roses to blazing Japanese maples.

There's nothing flashy about Fort Bragg (even the town's best eatery is named, simply, The Restaurant). But the village is not without its attractions, including a trip through the region's history at the Guest House Museum and a ride on the Skunk Train, an old-time logging railway that chugs through redwood forest to the town of Willits, 40 miles inland.

16 MacKerricher State Park

After hours of driving ever so slowly on this long, serpentine road, what could be more thrilling than to gallop freely along a wide crescent of sandy beach? For equestrians MacKerricher State Park is a rider's paradise, but you need not be on horseback to enjoy the beauty of this 2,200-acre preserve, the largest

The rocky coast near Mendocino has inviting sandy beaches as well as crashing waves.

of Mendocino County's coastal parks and home to more than 90 species of birds. Along 10 miles of ocean frontage, cliffs, beach, and headland vie for control of the shore but never hold it for long. From the playful seals that bask on the rocks below Laguna Point to upland fields of tall grass, poppy, and huckleberry, all the gifts of the Pacific Coast are gathered here in one splendid package. Make the most of your visit: pack a picnic basket and spread a cloth on the grass overlooking the coves and bridges.

Yosemite and Beyond

Bejeweled with cliffs, domes, meadows, lakes, and waterfalls—the legacy of bygone glaciers— Yosemite National Park offers visitors a degree of beauty and variety that is truly mesmerizing.

The Merced River threads swiftly through Yosemite National Park's glacially carved valley floor, with Glacier Point on one hand and Upper Yosemite falls on the other.

Near the eastern border of California, in the heart of the Sierra Nevada, lies the wondrous dominion known as Yosemite. Beginning near the park's southwest corner, the drive heads north to Yosemite Valley, the most-visited section of the park, where El Capitan, Bridalveil Fall, and other famed attractions predominate. The route then winds northeast across an expanse of subalpine wilderness—replete with meadows, ponds, and granite domes—before leaving the park and descending steep slopes to an eerily beautiful lake.

1 Yosemite National Park

Heading north from Oakhurst, Rte. 41 meanders into the ever-green-scented Sierra National Forest, a vast domain that abuts Yosemite National Park and is dominated by ponderosa pine, oak, and incense cedar. For a unique way to sample the forest, take the 45-minute ride on the Yosemite Mountain Sugar Pine Railroad, which hauled timber out of the woods beginning in 1899 but now restricts its load to visitors. About seven miles north of the railroad, the southern entrance to Yosemite National Park beckons like the gates of Eden. In the words of its early champion John Muir, Yosemite "is surely the brightest and the best of all the Lord has built." Native Americans must have thought so too, for they lived in the area for nearly 4,000 years before pioneers discovered it in the mid-1800s. First declared a national park in 1890, thanks in large part to the efforts of John Muir, Yosemite has attracted more and more visitors with the passage of time, and they now number many millions each year.

2 Mariposa Grove

Just beyond the park's entrance, a two-mile spur winds east to the Mariposa Grove of giant sequoias. No ordinary trees, these noble giants—among the largest of living things—can grow more than 300 feet tall, with trunks that measure up to 27 feet across. The venerable Grizzly Giant, about 2,700 years old, was in its youth when Socrates dispensed his wisdom to students in ancient Greece. Another Goliath, the Wawona Tunnel Tree, was made famous when, in 1881, an opening was cut in its base to allow stagecoaches and, in later years, cars to pass through—until the tree toppled in 1969. A tram tour and museum inform visitors about the magnificent trees.

3 Wawona

Located in a broad, pleasant valley on the south fork of the Merced River, the village of Wawona was once a favorite stop on the old stagecoach route to Yosemite.

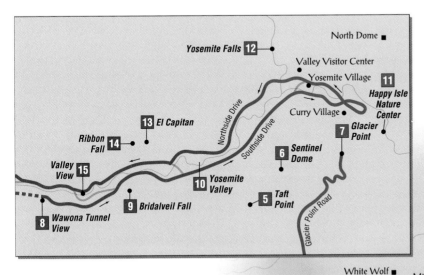

The era is recalled by the elegant 1870s-vintage Wawona Hotel, while the Pioneer Yosemite History Center re-creates the park's early days with a stage-coach ride, period buildings, a covered bridge, and a variety of exhibits.

4 Badger Pass

Beyond Wawona the drive winds north through hilly forests and across shallow creeks to Chinquapin (named for the glossy ever-green shrub that grows nearby). Here Rte. 41 meets Glacier Point Road, a 16-mile spur that en-compasses some of Yosemite's most stunning vistas. In winter Badger Pass, the first stop along the way, attracts thousands of downhill and cross-country skiers to its powdery trails and slopes. During the snow season Glacier Point Road is closed east of Badger Pass, but in spring and summer the road descends to bloom-sprinkled meadows where deer graze and insects buzz.

5 Taft Point

Following Glacier Point Road a few miles to the east, the drive reaches the trail to Taft Point. After walking about a mile, hikers arrive at the lofty rim that over-looks Yosemite Valley. From an isolated lookout they have a breathtaking preview of three-tiered Yosemite Falls, monumen-tal El Capitan, and many other world-famous wonders that can be viewed from a closer perspective when the drive continues through the valley below.

6 Sentinel Dome

Exceptional vistas await those who walk the nearby one-mile trail to Sentinel Dome, the last leg of which takes hikers up the curved side of this massive mound of granite to its 8,122-foot summit. Tenacious Jeffrey pines, gnarled and stunted by strong winds, grow from openings in the rock. In spring Sentinel Fall cascades down cliffs to the west of the dome.

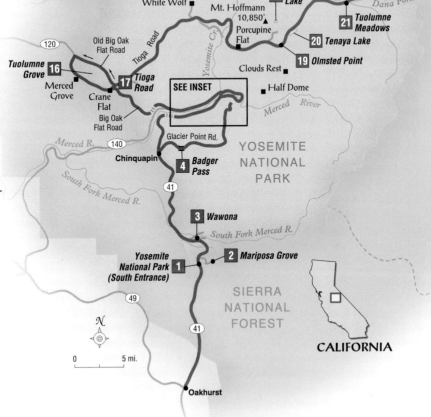

7 Glacier Point

For its last two miles, Glacier Point Road leads steeply down a series of switchbacks to its terminus, Glacier Point, where the vistas are among the park's most spectacular. From a dizzying granite precipice a short walk from the parking lot, the overlook takes in the floor of the Yosemite Valley some 3,200 feet below, Half Dome (from this angle resembling the head of a bird), numerous waterfalls (Vernal, Nevada, Yosemite), and the High Sierra in the background, with its limitless expanse of domes, ridges, and snow-covered peaks.

8 Wawona Tunnel View

Backtracking to Chinquapin and heading north, the drive winds through forests of ponderosa pine, incense cedar, and black oak to Wawona Tunnel, a passageway nearly a mile long that was dynamited through solid granite in 1933. Emerging from the tunnel, visitors are treated to a classic panorama as they enter Yosemite Valley. An interpretive sign in the parking area identifies by outline the valley's major features: Sentinel Dome, Half Dome (from this angle resembling the nose of a dolphin), Bridalveil Fall (tumbling from a hanging valley between Cathedral Rocks and the Leaning Tower), and astonishing El Capitan.

9 Bridalveil Fall

Plunging more than 600 feet down a sheer rock face, the waters of Bridalveil Fall are blown by breezes into a fine mist that descends as a gentle, rainbow-forming shower on spectators below. Native Americans called the fall Pohono, "spirit of the puffing wind."

Sunset's last rays color the peaks of the Yosemite Valley.

10 Yosemite Valley

Just past the Bridalveil Fall parking area is Southside Drive, a one-way road that ushers visitors into awesome Yosemite Valley. Formed about a million years ago, the U-shaped valley was scooped from the Sierra Nevada by massive glaciers, whose retreat left a monumental legacy—sheer granite cliffs and domes that rise thousands of feet from the bottom of the valley. Following the swift Merced River, the route leads through the valley to the Curry Village parking area, where visitors can board free shuttle buses that tour the valley floor, including stops at several places in the park where cars are not allowed—among them the Happy Isle Nature Center.

11 Happy Isle Nature Center

Here the Merced River branches into several channels, creating small islands in the river that are linked by footbridges. The nature center, which features exhibits on ecology and natural history, also serves as the trailhead for hikes to a number of Yosemite treasures. A 1½-mile trail leads to Vernal Fall and continues another two miles to the top of 594-foot Nevada Fall. Happy Isle became a distinctly unhappy place in 2001, when a massive quarter-mile-long rockfall decimated its forest and structures. Fallen boulders and trees can be seen there where they came to rest.

12 Yosemite Falls

Whether by car or shuttle bus, be sure to stop at Yosemite Village (located on Northside Drive, the westward-running part of the one-way road that loops through the valley), where a visitor center offers information and exhibits. From the visitor center one can hike (about ¾ mile) or drive to Yosemite Falls, the highest waterfall in North America. At 2,425

Half Dome may be the most recognizable landmark found in Yosemite National Park. Rounded by natural forces expanding its granite into a dome, a glacier carved away one side thousands of years ago, leaving a knifelike edge.

feet, this regal ribbon of white water (actually three waterfalls in one, with upper, middle, and lower tiers) is more than a dozen times higher than Niagara Falls and twice the height of the Empire State Building. A footbridge at the base of the falls, often showered with a fine spray, leads to a seldom-traveled path through the forest that skirts the site of John Muir's cabin.

13 El Capitan

Among the best known and most revered of Yosemite's wonders, this sheer granite monolith rises to a height of 3,593 feet above El Capitan Meadow. As you gaze up at its sleek, striated surface, look for the intriguing patterns of light and shadow caused by passing clouds. Look also—perhaps with the aid of binoculars—for tiny insectlike dots moving across the upper portions of El Capitan's cliffs: they are, of course, human rock climbers, and they are—to say the very least—intrepid.

14 Ribbon Fall

Just to the west of El Capitan, Ribbon Fall plummets some 1,612 feet to the valley floor. The park's highest single waterfall (that is, the longest uninterrupted stream of water), Ribbon Fall is also the first to dry up in the summer. The

reason: it drains only four square miles of land. Nevada Fall, in contrast, drains 118 square miles and flows year-round.

15 Valley View

A sister site to the Wawona Tunnel View to the south, Valley View (sometimes called Gates of the Valley) encompasses stunning panoramas of Yosemite's great stone monuments, the Merced River, and Bridalveil Fall. Unless one stops at the turnout, it is also a good-bye view over the shoulder, because the drive now continues west out of Yosemite Valley. After passing through a tunnel, the route heads north on Big Oak Flat Road,

57

With Lembert Dome looming in the distance, midsummer wildflowers such as Lemmon's paintbrush brighten the grassy carpet of Tuolumne Meadows.

winding through valleys and crossing creeks, until it approaches the Crane Flat area, where visitors are able to hike in to explore two groves of giant trees.

16 Tuolumne Grove
Although not as large as the Mariposa Grove, Yosemite's other two groves of giant sequoias—the Tuolumne and nearby Merced—invoke in onlookers the same sense of reverence for the ancient trees, remnants of a lineage dating to

the dinosaurs. Curiously enough, park rangers and lightning storms set fires in the groves that are allowed to burn—not to destroy the sequoias but to protect them. Fires burn off competing species and bare the soil, permitting the trees' seeds to germinate. In 1878 a vehicle tunnel was cut into the stump of one of the larger trees in the Tuolumne Grove. Dubbed the Dead Giant, the stump—tunnel and all—endures to this day, but is no longer drivable.

17 Tioga Road
Threading through an unpeopled expanse of wilderness—the "other" Yosemite—Tioga Road traverses some 45 miles and climbs almost 4,000 feet between the meadows of Crane Flat and lofty Tioga Pass to the east. As the road ascends, the dense forest of mixed evergreens gives way to stands dominated by handsome, 100-foot California red firs. At various spots along the way, such as the camping areas at White Wolf, Yosemite

Creek, and Porcupine Flat, backpackers begin their treks through pristine forest, discovering hidden lakes, rocky chasms, and remote mountain peaks. Even those who stay close to the car will learn about the natural history of the area from numerous roadside exhibits. Keep in mind, though, that snows close Tioga Pass and the road during the winter. It usually opens in late June.

18 May Lake
About midway along Tioga Road's meander across the park's high country, a two-mile spur turns north toward May Lake. This side route winds past a meadow called Snow Flat, where deep snows accumulate in winter. The spur terminates at the May Lake Trail, where a mile-plus hike leads to the lake, one of Yosemite's five High Sierra campsites. Here visitors will find backcountry trails that afford commanding views of nearby Mt. Hoffmann.

19 Olmsted Point
About two miles farther along Tioga Road, Olmsted Point provides some of the park's most stunning panoramas. To the south is the glacier-polished granite expanse of Tenaya Canyon, 9,926-foot Clouds Rest (a rocky peak often wreathed in mist), and in the distance a relatively unfamiliar back view of Half Dome's enormous rounded bulk. The view to the east encompasses beautiful Tenaya Lake and, looming above it, 9,800-foot Polly Dome.

20 Tenaya Lake
Its clear alpine waters surrounded by massive domes of polished granite, Tenaya Lake was named Pywiak—"lake of the shining rocks"—by the native Americans who once lived there. Lovely picnic spots dot the road along the lake's northern shore, and

fishermen angle for trout from motorless boats. Many visitors, lured by some of the finest rock climbing available anywhere in the country, scale nearby Pywiak Dome, Stately Pleasure Dome, and other rounded peaks.

21 Tuolumne Meadows

As Tioga Road ascends from Tenaya Lake, it heads east past Medlicott Dome, Fairview Dome, and other granite peaks that boldly protrude from forests of hemlock and pine. At about 8,600 feet above sea level, the drive reaches Tuolumne Meadows, the largest subalpine meadow in the Sierra Nevada, where rolling grassland provides a pleasing contrast to the greatest concentration of granite domes in the world. In summer the gray domes act as a backdrop for the blazing palette of wildflowers that carpets the meadows. Numerous ponds and streams attract mule deer, black bears, coyotes, and other wildlife, including the water ouzel, a wrenlike bird that walks underwater on the bottoms of streams to look for food. In late October, the mating season of bighorn sheep, the serenity of the Tuolumne landscape is occasionally pierced by the cracking sound of rams butting their heads together in competition for mates. The area's natural wonders are best appreciated along the network of trails—such as the Pacific Crest Trail, the trail to Elizabeth Lake, and the John Muir Trail to Cathedral Lakes—that lead from the visitor center into the depths of this remarkable wilderness.

22 Tioga Pass

With Lembert Dome visible to the north, the route runs alongside the Dana Fork of the Tuolumne River and climbs through forests of lodgepole pine toward Dana Meadows and Tioga Pass. At 9,945 feet, Tioga Pass is the

Tufa towers stand sentinel at the shoreline of Mono Lake, an ancient saltwater lake at Yosemite's eastern boundary.

loftiest highway pass in all of the Sierra Nevada. At its summit sits the eastern entrance to Yosemite National Park. A mile-long trail leads through forests of whitebark pine (a high-altitude tree common in these mountains) to sparkling Gaylor Lakes to the west.

23 Lee Vining Canyon

From Tioga Pass the drive descends eastward past meandering creeks that attract trout fishermen and damp meadows that offer occasional views of rock wrens, bobcats, and yellow-bellied marmots. The road skirts Tioga and Ellery lakes, then spirals down the dizzying slopes of Lee Vining Canyon. Between lofty Tioga Pass and the desert town of Lee Vining, the road drops some 3,000 feet in about 14 miles. To the east an impressive panorama takes in the arid landscape below, including the Mono Craters, a chain of dormant volcanoes, and the snowcapped White Mountains in the distance.

24 Mono Lake

Just northeast of Lee Vining lies a natural wonder unlike any other on the drive: ancient and mysterious Mono Lake. Nestled in a basin of sagebrush, with volcanic hills rising around its borders, the salty, million-year-old body of water is bedecked with bizarre natural statues, called tufa towers. Exposed by turns to view as the lake's water level dropped, then hidden as the waters rose again, the exquisite calcite sculptures were formed under the surface when carbonates in the water combined with calcium from freshwater springs feeding into the lake. Over time the hardened minerals piled up inch by inch, forming hundreds of knobs, spires, and minarets. Tufa formations can also be created by groundwater that percolates through briny sand.

This surreal moonscape is a wonderland for birds. Attracted by brine shrimp and alkali flies, legions of gulls (California's largest nesting population), phalaropes, eared grebes, snowy plovers, and other birds come to feast on the lake's tiny denizens. The salty water, much denser than seawater, affords swimmers a delightful sensation of buoyancy. Concluding the drive with a potpourri of eerie marvels, Mono Lake serves as an intriguing coda to the splendor and spectacle of California's Yosemite National Park.

Big Sur Coast

With absolutely striking results, the age-old conflict between sea and shore is repeated endlessly along the central coast of California.

The hulking dome of Morro Rock is a landmark for fishermen returning to the nearly landlocked Morro harbor, site of many different wildlife habitats.

After 14 years of backbreaking construction, this stretch of Rte. 1 was opened to traffic in 1934, eventually gaining fame as one of the world's outstanding scenic highways. As the drive snakes down the Big Sur coast—an area defined, more or less, as lying between Monterey and San Luis Obispo—it passes pristine beaches, wave-battered cliffs, shadowy forests that fill the valleys of the Santa Lucia Range, and offshore waters that are filled with life.

1 Monterey
Once under the crown of Spain, whose ships landed here in 1602, Monterey was claimed for America in 1846, when the Stars and Stripes was run up the flagpole at the Custom House. The area was a lonely outpost then, a haven for smugglers and a few farmers and ranchers. The abundance and grandeur of the peninsula, though, would in time attract many, and today tourists flock to Monterey to share in the riches.

To learn about the town's colorful past, sample the well-marked walking tour that leads through Monterey's historic district. On the shore of the bay lies Cannery Row, once a factory-filled hub for fish processing. The canneries —as well as the odd lot that worked and lived in the area— were immortalized by novelist John Steinbeck.

No longer a rough-and-tumble, foul-smelling industrial center, Cannery Row has been spruced up and nowadays offers a wax museum, restaurants, shops, and the top-notch Monterey Bay Aquarium. The seaside marine park is full of surprises, with creative displays that allow close-up viewing of many marine denizens, including wolf eels, sea otters, sharks, bat rays, and jellyfish.

2 Pacific Grove
Although it was settled just up the peninsula from Monterey in 1875, Pacific Grove was in many ways light-years away. Its Methodist founders, seeking a seaside retreat for religious contemplation, shunned their rowdy, often bawdy neighbors. Today, however, the boundaries between the two towns have blurred, as parks, stores, offices, museums, and homes have spread across the peninsula.

For spectacular vistas follow Ocean View Boulevard along the shores of Monterey Bay, stopping off at Lovers Point Park and Point Pinos Lighthouse. Sunset Drive, another road with fine views, parallels the Pacific side of the peninsula and leads to Asilomar State Beach, where the wide swath of sand is perfect for strolling, beachcombing, or—reminiscent of the town's early inhabitants—soul-searching reflection.

True to its nickname, Butterfly Town USA, Pacific Grove enjoys another distinction. It is the winter home to hordes of monarch butterflies. Lured by mild weather, the insects fly in from as far away as Canada and congregate in dense clusters on eucalyptus and Monterey pine trees. They are usually best observed in George Washington Park and in a grove on Lighthouse Avenue. (Don't disturb them, though: the town imposes penalties on anyone who does.)

3 17-Mile Drive
Sunset Drive swings inland after Asilomar State Beach, passes the well-landscaped grounds of a conference center, then intersects with 17-Mile Drive. Monterey cypresses, gnarled by the wind and ocean spray, are among the highlights along the toll road, which loops through part of the Monterey Peninsula. Other roadside delights include 1920s mansions, world-class golf courses, rocky headlands, and—of course—the Pacific Ocean. Tour maps are provided at all five of the entrance tollgates.

4 Carmel-by-the-Sea
After touring 17-Mile Drive, exit at the Carmel gate, avoiding the traffic bottlenecks that sometimes occur on Rte. 1, and head into charming Carmel-by-the-Sea. Once in the upscale community, you'll find a patchwork of cottages, shops, galleries, sandy beaches, and a restored 18th-century Spanish mission. Long a haven for artists, the town has counted renowned poets, novelists, and painters among its inhabitants. But no matter what one's line of work, it's easy to be inspired by the area's scenic beauty.

Follow Scenic Road, which skirts the Pacific, to its end at Carmel River State Beach, one of the less-crowded spots to enjoy the seashore. Although the ocean is quite chilly and the currents are strong, the sandy beach is a quiet escape.

5 Point Lobos State Reserve
The storm and stir of the earth's largest ocean have left a dramatic, indelible mark on the wild head-

lands at Point Lobos State Reserve. Take the trails that wend along the craggy fingers of rock, their crests capped with gnarled Monterey cypresses, to land's end. In the inlets below, the large, surging waves crash and tides come and go.

Sea lions—the barks of the males barely audible above the roaring surf—dot the small islands that fringe the mainland. To observe sea otters, bring along binoculars and look to the area just beyond the surf line; lolling belly-up in the kelp beds, the frolicsome animals use stones to smash open abalone shells. Much more awaits you here, but to enjoy the many sights, try to arrive early, since the refuge sets a daily limit on the number of visitors given access.

6 Garrapata State Park

The bad news is that *garrapata* means "tick" in Spanish, and in the wilds along the central coast, the little bloodsuckers are fairly common, especially in the spring and fall. Check your clothing after walks. Now the good news: Garrapata State Park comprises a diverse, pristine seaside, with steep, rocky headlands in the north and sandy beaches in the south.

Rte. 1 passes for some four miles within the borders of the park, which has no headquarters and no large parking lots, just turnouts where numbered gates mark trailheads. Some of the best scenery can be reached from gates 13, 15, and 16. The trails from these access points cross Soberanes Point, a verdant ledge above the sea.

Moonstone Beach in Cambria, south of Hearst Castle, was named for rare translucent agates with milky markings that resemble the celestial orb of the nighttime sky.

7 Point Sur State Historic Park

Slicing a thin line between the sea and the spines of foothills, Rte. 1 continues down the coast, then leaps across the famed Bixby Bridge. Like many spots on the highway, turnouts here allow sightseers to stop and enjoy dramatic overlooks. Pull over at the bridge's northern end, where the view includes not only the meeting of land and sea but the bridge itself. Arched high above a gorge, the concrete span hurtles across Bixby Creek, which empties into the sea some 265 feet below.

About five miles to the south, the drive nears a massive dome-shaped volcanic rock, which is crowned by Point Sur State Historic Park. The lighthouse here—its powerful beam can be seen for more than 20 miles—has warned sailors away from the treacherous point for over a century. Before its construction was completed, shipwrecks were common here on the coast.

Offered on most weekends, volunteer-led tours teach about the past keepers and their families. Isolated on the lonely promontory (before the highway was built, a horse trail was the only route down the coast), they had to be resupplied every four months or so by boat. Nowadays, automation has made caretakers unnecessary, but the old buildings that made their existence possible, including a barn and a blacksmith shop, are still standing.

8 Andrew Molera State Park

A study in variety, the park's terrain encompasses wind-sheltered beaches, sea-cut cliffs, flower-filled meadows, free-flowing rivers, and a 3,450-foot mountain.

Coloring the slopes of a valley, a river of calla lilies cascade through Garrapata State Park.

After exploring the area's hiking trails, consider settling in for the night at one of the primitive camp-sites, letting the rhythmic rumble of the sea lull you to sleep.

9 Pfeiffer Big Sur State Park

South of the park Rte. 1 swings inland—one of the few places where it does so—then passes through the sparsely populated town of Big Sur, which lies scattered along the valley of the Big Sur River. One of the best ways to explore the wilderness in the area is to visit Pfeiffer Big Sur State Park. A hike up its narrow river canyon takes you to refreshing pools edged with smooth boulders. Trails also lead through a redwood grove, to waterfalls, and to fishing spots where you can try for trout.

About a mile south of the entrance to Big Sur State Park, Sycamore Canyon Road exits Rte. 1 for Pfeiffer Beach. This quiet oceanside stretch, where small patches of beach are wedged among the rocks, is pitted with caves and blowholes that were carved out by the sea's surge.

10 Julia Pfeiffer Burns State Park

After Rte. 1 descends from a climb that takes it nearly 1,000 feet above the sea, the drive enters Julia Pfeiffer Burns State Park. A must here is the Overlook Trail, which traverses the clifftops above the ocean. For a special treat, look down on McWay Cove, where a creek finishes its short journey with a fine flourish—an 80-foot waterfall tumbling down at the seaside.

CALIFORNIA

Among the many birds that flock to these wilds are brown pelicans. Watch them sail across the sky, then dive head-first for fish. An added plus, as on most of the California coast, are the gray whales; the huge marine mammals can be seen migrating back and forth between Alaskan and Mexican seas.

A different kind of graceful giant, the redwood tree, grows in the park's interior. Hiking trails— sometimes steep but always rewarding—weave through the creek-laced area. Trailside sights include wildflowers and chaparral (a low, dense covering of shrubs).

Basking sea lions are commonly seen on the Pacific Coast wherever rocks are found.

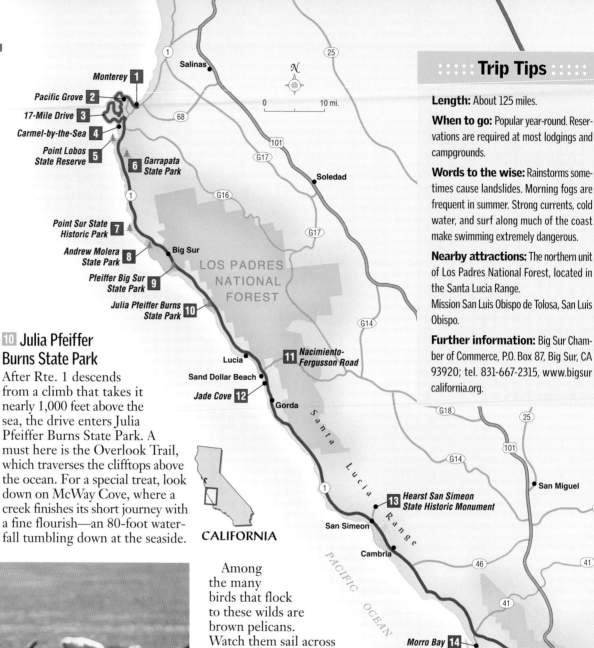

Monterey 1
Pacific Grove 2
17-Mile Drive 3
Carmel-by-the-Sea 4
Point Lobos State Reserve 5
Garrapata State Park 6
Point Sur State Historic Park 7
Andrew Molera State Park 8
Pfeiffer Big Sur State Park 9
Julia Pfeiffer Burns State Park 10
Nacimiento-Fergusson Road 11
Jade Cove 12
Hearst San Simeon State Historic Monument 13
Morro Bay 14

Salinas
Big Sur
LOS PADRES NATIONAL FOREST
Soledad
Lucia
Sand Dollar Beach
Gorda
San Simeon
Cambria
Santa Lucia Range
PACIFIC OCEAN
Montana de Oro State Park
Los Osos Oaks State Reserve
San Luis Obispo
San Miguel
Pismo Beach
LOS PADRES NATIONAL FOREST

0   10 mi.

Trip Tips

Length: About 125 miles.

When to go: Popular year-round. Reservations are required at most lodgings and campgrounds.

Words to the wise: Rainstorms sometimes cause landslides. Morning fogs are frequent in summer. Strong currents, cold water, and surf along much of the coast make swimming extremely dangerous.

Nearby attractions: The northern unit of Los Padres National Forest, located in the Santa Lucia Range.
Mission San Luis Obispo de Tolosa, San Luis Obispo.

Further information: Big Sur Chamber of Commerce, P.O. Box 87, Big Sur, CA 93920; tel. 831-667-2315, www.bigsurcalifornia.org.

11 Nacimiento-Fergusson Road

Just south of Kirk Creek, the highway intersects with Nacimiento-Fergusson Road. This paved 25-mile byway—a white-knuckle side trip with hairpin curves and panoramic views—traverses the Santa Lucia Range and ends at an army base not far from Rte. 101.

12 Jade Cove

Farther down the coast, Rte. 1 skirts Sand Dollar Beach—an excellent spot for seaside picnics—then comes to the signs and turnouts at Jade Cove. Take the short walk to the area's pebbled beaches, which are hemmed in by sea-carved cliffs, and search for the semiprecious bits of jade.

13 Hearst Castle

About one mile north of San Simeon, Piedras Blancas is a year-round gathering spot for elephant seals. Stop for a while and admire these grotesque creatures.

Officially known as Hearst San Simeon State Historic Monument, the castle was built by publisher William Randolph Hearst on a hill overlooking the coast. The palatial estate took nearly 30 years to complete and contains a museum-quality collection of art—antique furniture, sculptures, paintings, mosaics, and tapestries—to complement the Mediterranean Revival architecture.

In the 1930s and 1940s, floods of famous guests—movie stars,

Nearly every region of California has its own wine country. Paso Robles is no exception, with numerous wineries found on the highway between Rte. 1 and the city.

politicians, athletes—were invited to the estate. Departing from the visitor center in San Simeon, shuttle buses climb to Hearst's paradise, one of the state's most popular tourist destinations. Four guided tours are offered each day to the public. Visitors can also enjoy the movie, *Hearst Castle: Building the Dream*, which is shown in the home's own theater.

14 Morro Bay

Morro Rock, created by an ancient volcano, towers about 575 feet above the Pacific Ocean just north of Morro Bay's inlet. It guards a nearly landlocked harbor with a variety of natural habitats—from mud flats and tidal wetlands to estuaries—protected from the sea by a long sandspit. The area is home to more than 250 species of

birds, including peregrine falcons on Morrow Rock. Other area birds include black oystercatchers and great blue herons. Morro Bay State Park, midway down the bayshore, is crossed by trails and has a natural history museum. It's a great spot to get an overview of the natural attractions of the area.

Drive south of Morro Bay to enjoy Los Osos Oaks State Reserve, which contains stands of 700-year-old oak trees. On the shoreline of the Pacific Ocean, Montaña de Oro State Park is named for the nearby mountains, which turn gold when fields of mustard and poppies bloom across their slopes. Walkers on the park's trails can explore beaches, dunes, and cliffs.

Finish the drive by visiting Mission San Luis Obispo de Tolosa in the city of San Luis Obispo, founded in 1772 by Junipero Serra. Your visit to the Big Sur coast ends as Rte. 1 rejoins U.S. 101, midway between San Francisco and Los Angeles.

Whether on a life-size board or a tabletop, chess is a fascinating way to pass time in Morro Bay.

Death Valley Sojourn

Austere and hauntingly beautiful, this arid realm—
punctuated by dunes, craters, canyons, and mountains—
is an ancient yet ever-changing geological wonderland.

What moved the rock? Ghostly grooves on the dry lake beds of Death Valley reveal that, in times of rainfall, winds are strong enough to slide boulders.

Death Valley National Park, located mostly in California but extending slightly across the border into Nevada, is a land of stunning beauty and startling contrasts: crusty salt flats and towering, snow-dusted mountain peaks; colorful hills and craggy canyons; parched deserts and spring-fed oases. Exploring this challenging landscape, which embraces the hottest, driest, and lowest places found anywhere in North America, visitors can read of earth history in the ancient landforms, and of human history in the artifacts and lore left by 19th-century prospectors, mule skinners, and westward-moving pioneers.

1 Panamint Springs and Dunes
Approaching Death Valley National Park from the west, Rte. 190, the main access road on that side of the park, passes through Panamint Springs, a privately owned resort. Mountains loom ahead on the horizon—the rugged Panamint Range, which forms the western rampart of Death Valley. (Telescope Peak, 11,049 feet high and often covered with snow, is the tallest in the range.)

Nearer at hand—just to the east of Panamint Springs but somewhat off the beaten path—are the lovely Panamint Dunes. An unpaved mining road leads partway to the rolling sandhills. Park where the road veers to the right up a steep slope toward the mine and, if the heat is not too merciless, hike the final four cross-country miles to the dunes, which are visible in the distance.

Star-shaped, with surfaces patterned by shifting winds, some of the dunes are as tall as 250 feet. Climb one and your reward will be fine views of the Panamint Valley and surrounding mountains. You may also see unexpected signs of life: although seemingly inhospitable, the dunes are home to Mojave fringe-toed lizards, kangaroo rats, tumblebugs, and other creatures whose tracks can sometimes be found crisscrossing the sand. In spring, a variety of wildflowers enhance the sandy scene with their cheerful splashes of color.

2 Stovepipe Wells Village
At Towne Pass the highway climbs the heights of the Panamint Mountains and descends to the flat glimmering expanse that is Death Valley. Before long it arrives at Stovepipe Wells Village, a modest oasis named for a historic site located a few miles to the northeast. There, long ago, an old stovepipe was sunk into the sand to form the shaft for a much-used well.

Also nearby is Mosaic Canyon, a fine spot for hiking. In the canyon, walls of finely polished marble contrast with other surfaces composed of angular rock fragments that have been cemented into patterns resembling mosaics. The scattered shrubs growing in the canyon include desert holly, creosote bush, ocotilla, and Mormon tea.

3 Sand Dunes
Some 14 square miles of dunes lie to the east of Stovepipe Wells Village. The highest, most dramatic of them are found right along Rte. 190. There are no trails to follow; hikers are free to roam at random. The best time to see the dunes is in the morning or late afternoon, when the air is cool, the light is gentle, and the shadows are long, accentuating the dunes' intricate, wind-sculpted forms.

4 Devils Cornfield
As Rte. 190 continues eastward across Death Valley, a sandy plain appears to the south, dotted with

::::: Trip Tips :::::

Length: About 310 miles.

When to go: Best from October to April, when temperatures are moderate. Daytime highs between May and September often reach the triple digits.

Lodging: Stovepipe Wells Village. Furnace Creek.

Supplies: Food and fuel are available at Stovepipe Wells Village, Scottys Castle, and Furnace Creek.

Words to the wise: Be sure your car is in good mechanical condition and begin each day with an ample supply of gas. In summer carry at least two gallons of drinking water per person and check your gauges frequently. Radiator water is stored in tanks along park roads. If your car breaks down, stay with it until help arrives. Use extreme caution when walking near abandoned mines, due to danger of collapse and rattlesnakes.

Nearby attractions: Sequoia and Kings Canyon National Parks, Three Rivers, CA.

Visitor center: Furnace Creek.

Further information: Death Valley National Park, Death Valley, CA 92328; tel. 760-786-3200, www.nps.gov/deva/.

When one thinks of the desert, thoughts turn to the graceful arcs of sand dunes. These giants are at Panamint.

odd-looking clumps that bear a distant resemblance to corn shucks. They are actually arrowwood plants, perched atop pedestals of soil that were formed by the scouring forces of wind and water.

5 Scottys Castle

A spur trip of some 30 miles to the north, with desert stretching out on the west and mountains rising to the east, leads to Grapevine Canyon, where a plush Spanish provincial mansion surpisingly looms like a desert mirage. The structure was begun in 1922 by Chicago businessman Albert Johnson, whose doctors had advised him to spend time in a warm, dry climate. The showy hacienda, known as Scottys Castle, takes its name from Johnson's friend Walter Scott, also known as Death Valley Scotty. An ex-cowboy, prospector, and teller of tall tales, Scotty helped Johnson conceive the project and lived there after Johnson's death. Replete with costly antiques, a giant pipe organ, an indoor waterfall, and a chandelier weighing half a ton, this elegant, unexpected extravaganza is set amid soothing, spring-fed, manicured grounds.

A few miles to the west of Scottys Castle, the ground is gouged by a giant hole known as Ubehebe Crater. Formed by volcanic explosions, the crater measures half a mile across and 750 feet deep. Hundreds of layers of multicolored rock are visible along the trail that descends into the crater's depths.

6 Salt Creek Nature Trail

Returning to Rte. 190, head south. The drive comes to Salt Creek, a wash that flows from springs year-round and is the home of one of nature's anomalies: inch-long pupfish left over from the Ice Age. Through the centuries, as water in the area became scarcer and more salty, the pupfish managed to survive by gradually adapting to their changing habitat.

As you follow the dirt path and boardwalk that form a loop trail through the area, notice the vegetation, including pickleweed and salt grass, and look for the tracks of night visitors such as bobcats, foxes, and coyotes. Salt Creek is a choice area for birding too; be on the alert for ravens, spotted sandpipers, killdeers, common snipes, as well as birds of prey.

7 Harmony Borax Works

In the 1880s, borax "cottonballs" were gathered from the valley floor and then processed here by pioneering entrepreneurs and their Chinese laborers. The borax was then loaded, as much as 20 tons at a time, onto massive wagons that were hauled by the famous 20-mule teams for 165 miles across the desert to the railroad town of Mojave. Though borax is no longer mined in Death Valley, it was called the white gold of the desert and still is quite valuable. It is used to make soaps, disinfectants, and food preservatives and serves a variety of industrial purposes as well. Among the sights at the Harmony Borax Works are a 20-mule-team wagon and the ruins of adobe buildings. Original mining machinery and other displays can be seen at the Borax Museum two miles to the south.

8 Furnace Creek

A verdant oasis situated near the heart of Death Valley, Furnace Creek is one of the few sites in the area with enough water to support a flourishing human community. A visitor center and museum provide information on the history and natural wonders of Death Valley. Mesquite and palm trees, some towering to a height of 50 feet, lend ample shade to the Furnace Creek Ranch, a modern resort offering golf and tennis. It evolved from an 1880s ranch where gritty, exhausted mule-team drivers recuperated from grueling treks hauling borax across the blazing desert to Mojave. About a mile south of the visitor's center is the elegant establishment known as the Furnace Creek Inn.

9 Zabriskie Point

From the valley floor Rte. 190 ascends to this 710-foot overlook that was named in honor of a pioneering borax miner. The view

Spring in the desert means wildflowers, such as Indian paintbrush.

when accented by long shadows, Zabriskie Point is best visited early in the morning or late in the afternoon.

10 Dantes View

The road to Dantes View climbs, steeply at times, to a lofty perch at more than 5,000 feet, where the temperatures average some 20° cooler than on the valley floor. The view encompasses Death Valley's lowest and highest points (Badwater and Telescope Peak), the shimmering

11 Golden Canyon

You'll have to backtrack to Rte. 178 and then head south to reach Golden Canyon, the first mile of which has a well-marked nature trail. The narrow canyon, wedged between eroded cliffs and the slopes of badlands, displays rocks of varying hues, from bright red to brown, yellow, and green. Looming above the trail are the fluted cliffs of Red Cathedral. Visible too is Manly Beacon, a golden peak named for William Lewis Manly, a courageous pioneer who hiked all the way to Los Angeles to bring back help for travelers stranded in Death Valley in 1849.

expanse of salt flats, alluvial fans spreading out from the mouths of canyons, and the Panamint Mountains in the distance.

from the point is breathtaking—a medley of rugged, wrinkled badlands, mustard- and cinnamon-colored hills, remnants of lava flows, and distant peaks. Because the terrain appears most dramatic

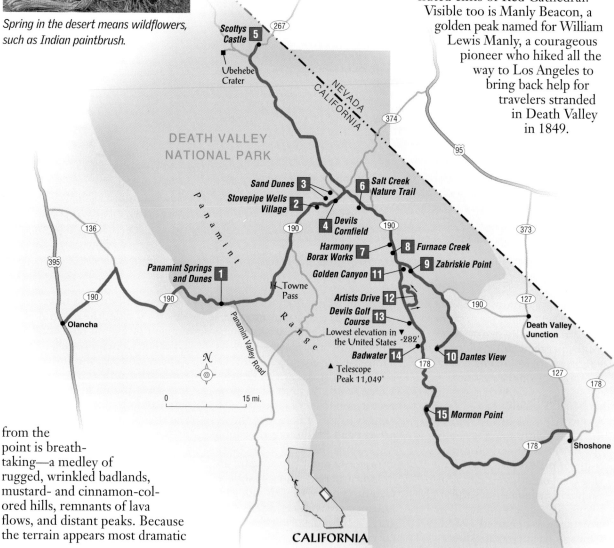

Scottys Castle 5

Ubehebe Crater

NEVADA / CALIFORNIA

DEATH VALLEY NATIONAL PARK

Sand Dunes 3
Stovepipe Wells Village 2
Salt Creek Nature Trail 6
Devils Cornfield 4
Harmony Borax Works 7
Furnace Creek 8
Zabriskie Point 9
Golden Canyon 11
Panamint Springs and Dunes 1
Towne Pass
Artists Drive 12
Devils Golf Course 13
Lowest elevation in the United States -282'
Badwater 14
Dantes View 10
▲ Telescope Peak 11,049'
Mormon Point 15
Olancha
Death Valley Junction
Shoshone

CALIFORNIA

0   15 mi.

12 Artists Drive

This nine-mile, one-way loop drive winds through hilly badlands imbued with such a patchwork of colors that it looks as though one of the titans had dropped his paintbox. Tinted by the interaction of various minerals, sediments, and volcanic debris with the elements, the landscape is truly rainbow-hued. Artists Palette, in particular, about midway through the loop, mixes bright colors such as yellow, red, green, and orange with pastel pinks and lavenders.

13 Devils Golf Course

A gravel road leads to this odd and forbidding landscape, where an expanse of what seem like miniature mountains up to two feet high are bedecked with white, fanglike crystals of sodium chloride (chemically identical to table salt). Forty-niners heading for the California goldfields had an especially difficult time making their way across this jagged terrain.

14 Badwater Basin

The lowest point in Death Valley reachable by car, Badwater Basin seems especially low when contrasted with the high peaks that rise nearby. Supposedly, the brackish pool here got its name from a surveyor who labeled it "Bad Water" when his mule refused to drink. While the water is not poisonous, its composition is similar to a solution of Epsom salts—and just about as appetizing. Even so, the tiny Badwater snail manages to survive in the salty water, and a few plants—pickleweed, salt grass, iodine bush, and others—live along the fringes of the pool.

Baked by temperatures that can reach 120°F or higher, Zabriski Point marks the midpoint of Death Valley.

High on a mountainside above the pool is a sign that reads "Sea Level." Simply but dramatically, it reminds visitors that the entire Badwater Basin is very low indeed —in fact, about four miles to the northwest of the pool is the lowest point in the United States, at 282 feet below sea level. Above the sign, high in the Black Mountains, is Dantes View, the loftiest point you can reach by car. To the west is Death Valley's loftiest mountain, Telescope Peak, whose snowy summit hovers upside down in the still water of the pool.

15 Mormon Point

Here Death Valley's most ancient rock is exposed to view. Through the millennia, as younger layers of rock were eroded away by wind and water, a rounded black core called a turtleback—some 2 billion years old—became visible at the surface. As you continue along

Rte. 178 toward the eastern border of Death Valley National Park, watch for the colorful displays of wildflowers that adorn Jubilee Pass in spring.

Thermal springs deposited the colorful minerals of Artists Drive. After the springs dried and the land was uplifted into hills, erosion exposed mineral salts of many hues.

Joshua Tree Journey

The high Mojave and low Colorado deserts join together
in this southern California landscape, where
serene solitude is tempered by an unearthly beauty.

:::::: **Trip Tips** :::::

Length: About 140 miles.

When to go: Popular year-round.

Supplies: Food and fuel are available in nearby towns, but not in Joshua Tree National Park.

Words to the wise: Be on the alert for flash floods from thunderstorms.

Nearby attractions: Anza-Borrego State Park, Borrego Springs. Palm Springs. Salton Sea.

Visitor centers: Twentynine Palms, Cottonwood Spring.

Further information: Joshua Tree National Park, 74485 National Park Drive, Twentynine Palms, CA 92277; tel. 760-367-5500, www.nps.gov/jotr/.

Twisted and spiky as those in a Dr. Seuss book, Joshua trees are unlikely members of the lily family.

According to lore, it was Mormon pioneers in the 1850s who first likened the upstretched limbs of the short-leaved desert yucca to the raised arms of the prophet Joshua, beckoning them to a promised land. Today that promise is fulfilled in Joshua Tree National Park, where some 800,000 acres of sublime desert landscape provide a refuge for the human spirit.

1 Big Morongo Canyon Preserve

Before entering the park itself, stop at this 3,900-acre refuge, which is nourished by one of the few creeks in the region that flows all year long. This oasis, lined with willows and cottonwoods, attracts desert wildlife from miles around. On summer evenings bighorn sheep descend the steep canyon walls to drink, and hosts of birds visit on their spring and fall migrations.

2 Twentynine Palms

Some 30 miles east of Morongo Valley, the town of Twentynine Palms makes an inviting stop. First inhabited by Chemehuevi and Serrano Indians, the oasis here later served as a jumping-off point for prospectors and cattle-men on their way into the desert. Today the town is home to the park's main visitor center, where displays and a well-marked nature trail inform visitors about the region's history and wildlife. A few Joshua trees can be seen at the center, but most are located at the park's higher elevations (between 3,500 and 6,000 feet), where they thrive on cool temperatures and the occasional hard winter freeze. Here and elsewhere in the park, look for the hammocklike nest of the rare Scott's oriole slung between the Joshua trees' branches.

3 Fortynine Palms Oasis

After a steep, 1½-mile hike up a ridge where barrel cacti grow, the sight of this jewel of an oasis stirs and refreshes the soul: from the overlook, craggy canyon walls descend 300 feet to a serene pool surrounded by tall fan palms. As at Morongo Valley, bighorn sheep often visit here (look for them at dawn and dusk), and ancient Indian petroglyphs can be seen on the canyon walls above the oasis.

4 Hidden Valley

At the town of Joshua Tree, the drive leaves Twentynine Palms Highway and heads south by way of Park Boulevard, a 17-mile paved road that takes you to the heart of the high desert. Hidden Valley, named by cattle and horse rustlers who used it to graze their stolen livestock, is no secret to the rock climbers who flock to its shapely granite domes. They can be seen inching their way up these massive rocks, whose names (Trojan Head, Old Woman, the Blob) bespeak their intriguing shapes.

5 Keys View

From this overlook atop the Little San Bernardino Mountains, the panoramic view of the Coachella Valley and the mountains beyond can take your breath away. Let your gaze travel south to the Salton Sea, then west to the snowcapped heights of San Jacinto Peak (look for Palm Springs at the base) and San Gorgonio Mountain, the highest point in southern California.

6 Ryan Mountain

Heading east from Cap Rock junction, the next section of the drive skirts the mountains separating Queen and Lost Horse valleys and leads to a strenuous 1½-mile climb that affords some of the best views inside the park. From the top of Ryan Mountain, Joshua Tree's central geography stands revealed, its maze of valleys, mountains, and narrow gorges laid out like a vast topographic map. The mountain is named for Jeb and Thomas Ryan, who were onetime proprietors of the Lost Horse Mine. Nearby are the remains of the Ryan brothers' turn-of-the-century homestead, along with eight marked gravesites.

7 Queen Valley

Unfolding serenely beneath blue desert skies, Queen Valley invites the traveler to linger and gaze. Vast groves of Joshua trees (many up to 700 years old) stretch to the horizon, and in springtime their white blossoms are beautifully balanced by the crimson flowers of Mojave mound cacti. For travelers equipped with four-wheel-drive vehicles, Queen Valley is also the beginning of the Geology Tour Road, an 18-mile route that leads through some of the park's most distinctive formations, including the scorched basalt remnant of an unborn volcano.

8 Jumbo Rocks

A wide plateau of boulders, buttes, and domes, Jumbo Rocks looks as if it were tossed together by playful giants. At sunrise and sunset the rocks glow with fiery hues—orange, pink, and gold—and the entire area seems to tremble with color. A well-marked 1¾-mile trail leads to Skull Rock, one of the site's most eerie monuments.

9 Arch Rock Trail

Accessible by a short trail from the White Tank Campground, Arch Rock is one of nature's more graceful creations: a granite bridge that was sculpted over the centuries by wind and water. The "tank" itself, a man-made catchment for rain and run-off, was built and used a hundred years ago by cattlemen to water their livestock. Finding it requires some scrambling over boulders to the south of the arch, where shady recesses provide inviting spots to take a picnic or a brief catnap.

10 Cholla Cactus Garden

South of White Tank, Pinto Basin Road begins its gentle descent down the western slope of the Pinto Basin, offering mile after mile of spectacular vistas. In this transition zone between the Mojave and the Colorado, the ecosystems of the high and low deserts merge, and Joshua trees give way to cacti and creosote bushes. Daytime temperatures in the summer can reach 110°F, so few plants can survive here. One of the hardiest can be found at the Cholla Cactus Garden. The Bigelow cholla, nicknamed the teddy bear cholla or jumping cholla, is covered with a thick mat of furlike barbs. The cholla cactus "jumps" by shedding its spiny joints, which attach themselves to unwary passersby. The plant commands respect, and it is best observed from the safe distance of the garden's nature trail.

11 Cottonwood Spring

Crossing the Pinto Basin and the craggy ridges of the Hexie Mountain foothills, the drive eases into Cottonwood Spring. A modest

Star Route

★ Palms to Pines Highway

Beginning at Palm Desert, the drive follows Rtes. 74 and 243 from palm-studded lowlands to the lofty pine woods of San Bernardino National Forest. At first, hairpin turns lead up the dizzying slopes of the Santa Rosa Mountains, followed by a smooth cruise through the grasslands of Garner Valley. Inviting trailheads await hikers at Idyllwild, and the last leg of the drive winds through the lushly forested San Jacinto Mountains, descending to the austere, boulder-strewn hills near Banning.

visitor center nearby offers displays and information. The spring itself, which gushed profusely at the turn of the century, now trickles gently through a grove of cottonwoods and palms. Indian bedrock mortars invoke the spring's distant past, while present-day travelers find it a fitting spot to bid farewell to Joshua Tree National Park.

Loneliest Road in America

The desert of central Nevada—for the most part unforgiving and remote—has a silent grace that remains unbroken but for historic sites and a two-lane highway.

Sand Harbor State Park at Lake Tahoe presents endless contrasts of blue.

Galloping at a tear, brave riders of the Pony Express once carried mail to the West Coast along the very course now followed by Rte. 50. Often traveling for long stretches with not another living soul in sight, their journeys led them through an inhospitable land of sand and peaks—the Great Basin. The region, however, has changed since those early times, today offering travelers friendly towns and conveniences. So when Rte. 50 is called the Loneliest Road in America, take it with a grain of salt and enjoy an area as rich in lore as the hills once were in ore.

1 Lake Tahoe

Deep blue and surrounded by evergreen forests and snowy peaks, Lake Tahoe offers one last lush treat before you set off on this trek through mostly stark terrain. The views from Rte. 50, which wends along the eastern shore, occasionally open up to reveal the vastness of the lake. Perched at an altitude of more than a mile, Tahoe has sparkling clear water, with depths of up to 1,645 feet. For a fine panorama, take a ride to the top of the mountain on the Heavenly Gondola in South Lake Tahoe—site of Nevada's largest ski resort.

2 Carson City

With the High Sierra in the rear-view mirror, the drive leads to Carson City, the state's capital, which was named for frontiersman Kit Carson. While much of the land seems barren, looks are deceiving; the region has great biodiversity and yields a wealth of precious minerals. In fact, one of the richest veins of silver and gold ever discovered, the famed Comstock Lode, was unearthed in nearby Virginia City, luring miners by the thousands in the mid-1800s.

A small city sprang up almost overnight, and as area mines began to pay off, tycoons set about building impressive mansions. One of the earliest, the Bowers estate, still stands some 10 miles north of town; made of granite, it cost $200,000 to build and furnish in 1864, then a staggering sum.

3 Dayton

Like a carpet rolled out for royalty, Rte. 50 runs on one long strip to the northeast, crossing a sagebrush plateau on the way to Dayton. In earlier times the town was a Pony Express station and the site of Nevada's first gold strike.

Virginia City, about seven miles to the north via Rte. 341, was nicknamed the Queen of the Comstock. Historical tours are available of the former boomtown, once home in the mid-1800s to some 25,000 people, including a young reporter with the pen name Mark Twain. Among the many restored buildings are mansions, churches, banks, saloons, and an opera house.

4 Fort Churchill State Historic Park

With the silence of the desert intensifying, sagebrush and sand are constant companions as the road continues on toward Fort Churchill, reached by a short side trip to the south. The old adobe army post was built in 1860, then abandoned nine years later. A visitor center tells the fort's story, but it is among the crumbling walls that sightseers can most palpably feel the isolation of the place, especially when the wind whips by.

The Lahontan State Recreation Area, with boating and swimming, lies to the east. Its lake, an improbable oasis in a land that averages less than six inches of rain per year, owes its existence not to the forces of nature, but to the ingenuity of man.

5 Fallon

Silver and gold may have inspired the settlement of towns such as Dayton, but it was water—thanks to the Lahontan Reservoir—that gave Fallon its start. Fields of alfalfa ring this island of greenery,

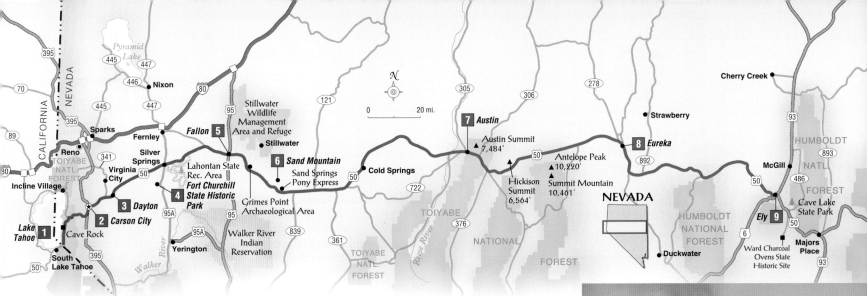

and its quiet neighborhoods boast manicured lawns and shady streets. To the northeast Stillwater Wildlife Management Area and Refuge, with more than 224,000 acres, offers sanctuary to hosts of birds, including cinnamon teal, redheads, and whistling swans.

Grimes Point Archaeological Area, about eight miles to the east, holds several hundred boulders carved with prehistoric designs. Although archaeologists have yet to decipher the images, most speculate that the petroglyphs tell of hunts and seasonal variations.

Civilization, of course, has undergone a whirlwind of change since those ancient days, and one of its greatest inventions—the airplane—can be seen in the skies here. Taking off from the Fallon Naval Air Station are some of our country's newest and fastest jets.

Sand Mountain

As the highway leads east, it dips into the dry bed of an ancient sea; then 15 miles farther, Sand Mountain, a large dune, looms above the flatlands. The sculptural formation, about two miles long, rises an abrupt 600 feet. At one end of its base lie dilapidated stone walls, the ruins of a Pony Express station.

The Pony Express, though long on legend, was short on life. No matter how fast the horses ran and how hard the riders pushed themselves, together they could never match the speed of the transcontinental telegraph. Virtually overnight, what had taken days by pony could be sent in seconds by wire. On October 24, 1861, a scant 18 months after start-up, the Pony Express was dissolved.

7 Austin

Bare, bold mountains and sagebrush desert characterize the remote stretch of Rte. 50 that leads onward to Austin. Although this area may appear lifeless, the relative stillness is broken by such animals as snakes, lizards, coyotes, and jackrabbits—all more active by night than during the day. Flying above, however, are some of the more conspicuous denizens of the desert, including ravens, hawks, eagles, and occasionally, flocks of horned larks.

Historic Austin, with views of the steep-sided Toiyabe Range, was another of Nevada's silver mining boomtowns. It sprang up in 1862 and quickly became one of the state's most populated areas. Unlike many mining towns that went bust before soundly constructed buildings could be erected, Austin offers a number of surviving structures, including lovely early churches. Three pioneer sanctuaries, their bricks stacked

high against the sweep of sky, make the town a welcoming, historical sight. And just outside town, down a twisting canyon road, lies a huge stone fortress, Stokes Castle, the fanciful creation of a mining baron.

8 Eureka

The road out of Austin soon climbs to Austin Summit, a pass perched at an elevation of 7,484 feet. To the southeast rises Hickison Summit, where visitors can picnic on the lower slopes and enjoy far-off views and petroglyphs. Antelope Peak and Summit Mountain punctuate the eastern horizon, both more than 10,000 feet high. Continuing on to Eureka, you'll feel your engine alternately strain and sigh as Rte. 50 crosses ridge after ridge.

Eureka itself, nestled in a valley among these peaks, is one of the state's best-preserved mining towns. Its buildings, made with bricks to avoid the fires that had ravaged earlier wooden structures, include an old newspaper office (now a museum), an 1880s opera house, and a well-restored courthouse that is still in use.

The historic Ghost Train at Ely's Nevada Northern Railway Museum tours the rugged high desert.

9 Ely

After a 77-mile drive past grazing grounds—more peaks and sage-covered valleys—the drive enters Ely, a onetime mining center. Here, though, copper was the treasure, and an amazing 22,000 tons of ore per day were scooped from the ground. Like the silver lodes to the west, however, copper is no longer mined here.

Stop at the Nevada Northern Railway Museum, one of the most complete of its kind. Antique locomotives, passenger cars, and offices are on display. The trains set out on regularly scheduled tours—a pleasant way to conclude a visit to the Loneliest Road in America.

Nevada 93

In a land of bewitching beauty, a mix of crinkled mountains and parched valleys contrasts with chilly caverns and a mammoth man-made lake.

Red Rock Canyon offers formations in every breathtaking hue found under the sun.

Far off the beaten path, this desert drive embraces a host of unexpected treasures. Beginning with the watery playground at Lake Mead, it winds past eroded rock formations, multihued canyons, and old mining towns and ends with ancient trees that grow near a glacier.

1 Lake Mead National Recreation Area

For millions of years, the 1,400-mile-long Colorado River snaked its way untrammeled from the Rocky Mountains to the Gulf of California. To tame the river and create what was once the world's largest reservoir took nothing less than the construction of the dam that, at its completion in 1935, ranked as the world's largest.

The Herculean task of building Hoover Dam took 18 months of excavation and tunneling to divert the river, 24 months to block the canyon with nearly 7 million tons of concrete, and up to 5,000 workers on the job around the clock.

Statistics are one thing, but seeing is believing. The guided tour, which begins at the Hoover Dam visitor center, allows visitors to appreciate the combined efforts of thousands of workers that was required to construct the 528-foot dam one sees today.

The crystalline waters of 110-mile-long Lake Mead—the vast reservoir that was created by the dam—are a mecca for swimmers, boaters, windsurfers, divers, anglers, and sightseers. As large as it is, though, the lake is just a small part of the 1.5-million-acre recreation area that surrounds the Colorado River as it flows from the show-stopping Grand Canyon all the way south through the seared desert surrounding Lake Mojave.

2 Valley of Fire State Park

Like a fanciful mirage, the many peaks, spires, and pillars in Nevada's largest state park shimmer in jewel-toned hues. Wind and water over the course of millions of years sculpted the landscape here into a masterpiece of haunting beauty. Interpretive trails lead visitors past raspy red rocks where desert tortoises linger in cool recesses and beside smooth cliff faces where, a thousand years ago, Anasazi artists etched mysterious petroglyphs. North toward Overton, the Lost City Museum holds yet more remnants of the long-vanished Anasazi civilization that flourished in the region until A.D. 1200.

3 Pahranagat National Wildlife Refuge

The desert stretches long and lonely as Rte. 93 runs north between the gaunt hills of the Sheep Range to the west and the sun-baked Delamar Mountains to the east. But underground water, in true oasis fashion, feeds Lower Pahranagat Lake and, 4½ miles beyond, Upper Pahranagat Lake. Lush meadowlands and stands of cottonwoods crowd the narrow valley, which serves as a stop for

Star Route

★ **Red Rock Canyon Scenic Drive**
Located west of Las Vegas, this 13-mile, one-way, horseshoe-shaped drive takes visitors past spectacular sandstone cliffs and towering peaks. Turnouts along the way lead to stunning vistas and inviting trails, such as the short hikes to Lost Creek and Pine Creek Canyon. Bighorn sheep and wild burros sometimes meander across barren hillsides and come to drink at lush, leafy oases.

migrating waterfowl and a nesting area for great blue herons, swans, and dozens of smaller species.

4 Caliente

Local wildlife—wary coyotes, browsing deer, and prowling bobcats—border the ambitious lobby mural of the mission-style train depot, Caliente's trademark building. South of town, the gentle Meadow Valley Wash is hemmed in by majestic Rainbow Canyon, where sheer rock walls have been stained by minerals into a kaleidoscope of color, and the valley floor is dotted with postcard-perfect farms and ranches.

North of town a 28-mile detour along a steep gravel road leads to Beaver Dam State Park. Short interpretive walks and longer hiking trails corkscrew through the park's pine-scented canyons at nearly a mile above sea level.

5 Cathedral Gorge State Park

Rte. 93 hugs Meadow Valley Wash on its way to Cathedral Gorge, a strikingly eroded landscape spiked with steep-sided buttes. Hike on superb nature trails or take in the views of the gorge at Miller's Point Overlook, about a mile from the park entrance.

6 Pioche

In the mid-1870s Pioche reveled in its reputation as the bawdiest, most lawless town in Nevada. Feverish with dreams of wealth, prospectors poured into the settlement, swelling the population to 7,000. So reckless was life there, legend tells us, that while about four dozen men died "with their boots on," only two were brought to justice. The pioneer cemetery records some of the shootings and shenanigans that earned Pioche its special place in frontier history.

Meanwhile, the city fathers were swept away with boomtown optimism, floating bonds in 1871 for a new courthouse that the county didn't manage to pay off until 1938. By then, with accrued interest, the debacle had been dubbed the Million-Dollar Courthouse.

Southeast of Pioche, through Eagle Valley (where golden eagles swoop with effortless grace), is Echo Canyon State Park. A reservoir that's well-stocked with rainbow trout abuts a steep rock wall —the perfect acoustical setup for echoes. Nine miles beyond is Spring Valley, another state park favored by anglers. A number of

Wheeler Peak looms over the highway Great Basin National Park.

homesteaders' cabins are perched among the soaring, cinnamon-colored rocks.

7 Great Basin National Park

Continuing 100 miles or so beyond Pioche, the drive ventures deep into Nevada's only national park, where the trove of scenic riches includes caves, a glacier, some of the world's oldest trees, and hushed groves of white-barked aspen. An outstanding example of a mountain island in the vast Great Basin desert, the park is an unexpected ark that brims with life.

At the visitor center schedules are posted for 90-minute ranger-led tours of Lehman Caves. The tours follow a short paved trail through caverns where the temperature averages a chilly 50°F and the walls and ceilings are covered with lavish decorations.

The park's 12-mile Wheeler Peak Scenic Drive passes scrubby mountain mahogany and broad forests of spruce and limber pine

on its 3,400-foot climb from the visitor center to the Wheeler Peak Campground. At the road's end, trails fan out to the 13,063-foot summit, to Nevada's only glacier, and to placid, tree-rimmed alpine lakes. On the higher reaches of the Snake Range, near the end of the scenic drive, twisted bristlecone pines cling tenaciously to the rock-strewn soil; some of these patriarchs, especially those nearest the tree line, are up to 3,000 years old.

Trip Tips

Length: About 360 miles.

When to go: Popular year-round.

Words to the wise: Information on hiking and camping is available at the Bureau of Land Management in Caliente. Ranger-led tours of Great Basin National Park are given only in summer.

Nearby attractions: Las Vegas. Ward Charcoal Ovens State Historic Site, near Ely.

Further information: Nevada Commission on Tourism, 401 N. Carson St., Carson City, NV 89710; tel. 800-638-2328, www.travelnevada.com.

George Parks Highway

Threading through the land of the midnight sun, this wilderness ramble reveals
the many facets of Mt. McKinley, the icy jewel in Alaska's craggy crown.

Denali, the Great One, was the name Alaska's native people gave to Mt. McKinley, North America's highest peak.

To explorer George Vancouver, who sailed into the upper Cook Inlet in 1794, the crests of Mt. McKinley and its attendant peaks were "distant stupendous mountains." These wonders remain as awesome as ever, but thanks to the George Parks Highway, completed in 1971, they are now within easy reach of their admirers.

1 Palmer

Ice sculpted the face of Alaska, and the chisel marks are visible in the very first leg of this dramatic drive. Heading northeast from Anchorage, the Glenn Highway (Rte. 1) crosses two ice-fed rivers—the Knik and the Matanuska—en route to Palmer, gateway to the glacier-gouged Matanuska and Susitna valleys.

The colossal sheet of ice that covered this region some 12,000 years ago has long since retreated, but the silt and soil it left behind make the Mat-Su Valley (as the two valleys are jointly called) a veritable 15,000-acre vegetable garden. With daylight stretching to 19 hours and 21 minutes at the summer solstice, local farms turn out radishes the size of softballs and cabbages weighing as much as 90 pounds. You can find this prodigious produce at roadside stands throughout the summer or at the annual Alaska State Fair, which is held in Palmer during the 10 days before Labor Day.

The area north and east of town is laced with hiking trails that afford good views of snow-capped Pioneer Peak, named to honor some early emigrants from the Lower 48. In 1935, 202 families moved here from Depression-ravaged farms in Minnesota, Michigan, and Wisconsin to form the Matanuska Colony, a New Deal agricultural collective believed to be the first and only one of its kind in America. Hence the area's gabled barns are more reminiscent of Midwestern dairy farm architecture than they are of north-country homesteads.

2 Hatcher Pass

Just north of Palmer, the drive jogs west for a wilderness detour to Hatcher Pass. About 10 miles up Palmer–Fishhook Road, where the pavement gives way to gravel, the route enters a gorge and begins climbing through stands of willow, spruce, and birch that border the Little Susitna River. This stream once yielded gold but now is prized instead for its silver—silver salmon, that is. Grub-stakers picked the river clean of gold by the early 1900s, but its modern riches swim upstream on their spawning runs from late July through August.

Farther up the road is Independence Mine State Historical Park, where exhibits recall the heyday of drill-and-blast gold mining. Hiking trails thread the 1,000-acre park and overlook the lake-pocked floor of the Mat-Su Valley below.

Two miles west of the park, the side trip reaches its scenic high-light: 3,886-foot-high Hatcher Pass, which serves as the cross-country training center for the U.S. Ski Team. Situated 1,500 feet above the tree line, this alpine enclave features hanging valleys, scooped-out cirques, and meadows carpeted in the summer

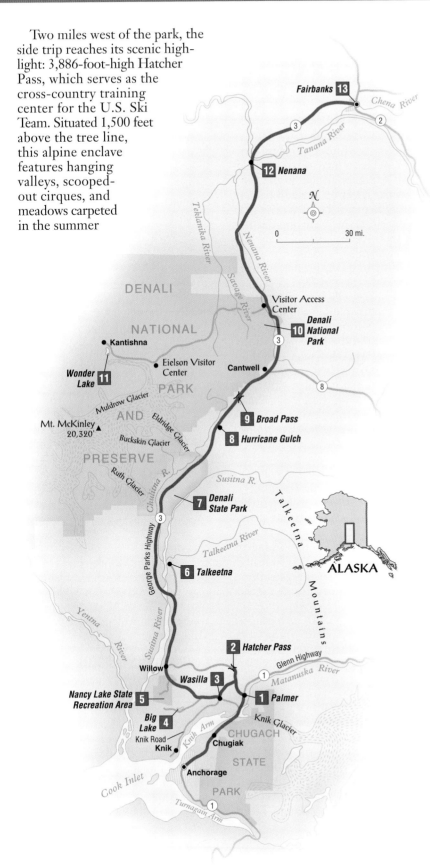

months with bluebells, chocolate lilies, low-bush cranberries, and forget-me-nots. Sweeping vistas take in Summit Lake, to the west, and the surrounding Talkeetna Mountain range.

3 Wasilla

From Hatcher Pass the drive does an about-face and retraces part of its path to Wasilla, a hamlet that hugs the shores of two long, narrow lakes. Turn off the highway near the center of town for a picnic at Lakeshore Park, which offers winter skating, summer swimming, and year-round views of the crenelated Chugach Mountains.

Founded in 1917 as a station on the Alaska Railroad, which links Anchorage and Fairbanks, Wasilla is now the biggest town between those two cities. About 10 miles east of Wasilla, the George Parks Highway (Rte. 3) intersects with the Glenn Highway. Named for the man who governed the Alaska Territory from 1925 to 1933, this paved artery runs north into the rugged heart of the state.

Wasilla is also along the route of a different sort of scenic drive —the annual Iditarod Trail Sled Dog Race, sometimes referred to by locals as the Last Great Race on Earth. In early March solo mushers drive dog teams about 1,100 miles from Anchorage to Nome. Visitors who miss the race can catch it on video at the Iditarod Headquarters, a log cabin museum located two miles south of town on Knik Road. This museum chronicles the colorful history of the event, which commemorates a race against disaster: in 1925 a relay of heroic dog teams traveled 674 miles in about 127 hours to deliver serum to diptheria-threatened Nome on the Arctic Ocean. Dog racing is also the theme of the Knik Museum and Sled Dog Mushers Hall of Fame, located at mile 13.7 on the Knik Road.

4 Big Lake

From Wasilla the drive proceeds due west, snaking through low, level terrain all the way to the turnoff for Big Lake. A short side trip leads to three state recreation areas (Big Lake North, Big Lake South, and Rocky Lake) supplied with campgrounds and picnic sites.

Beware of the Bears

Bear attacks are rare (more people are injured by moose than bears), but you should still take precautions in bear country. When camping, choose a site well away from salmon streams or berry patches, store food in airtight containers, and do all cooking and eating at least 100 yards from your tent. When hiking, travel in a group, leave dogs in the camper or car, announce your presence by making noise, and above all, move away if you spot any cubs. If you do encounter a bear, stay calm. While waving your arms over your head, talk to the animal in a normal tone. You may try to back away diagonally very slowly, but don't run. If the bear charges (usually a bluff), drop to the ground, curl up into a fetal position, and remain still until the bear is far away.

Although Big Lake is just five miles long, it is the largest of the dozen or so ponds that glaciers created in the lower Mat-Su Valley. Man picked up where the ice left off, dredging waterways that connect Big Lake to several of its smaller siblings. You can explore this network's 53-mile shoreline by powerboat, paddle-wheeler, or canoe. Tranquil waterside views are available from restaurants that front the lake.

5 Nancy Lake State Recreation Area

Back on Rte. 3, the drive curves northwest toward Willow. Shortly after crossing the train tracks at mile 66.5 (the Parks Highway parallels the Alaska Railroad),

---

⠿⠿⠿⠿⠿ Trip Tips ⠿⠿⠿⠿⠿

Length: About 360 miles plus side trips.

When to go: Best from June through August.

Supplies: Visitors to Denali National Park should bring rain gear, warm clothing, sturdy footwear, binoculars, and insect repellent.

Words to the wise: During summer, reservations for campsites and shuttle buses in Denali National Park must be made in person several days in advance.

Not to be missed: The Iditarod Trail Sled Dog Race from Anchorage to Nome, held in early March. Summer Solstice celebrations, featuring all-night events—even cookouts—in late June.

Nearby attractions: Alaskaland, a 44-acre historical theme park, Fairbanks. Creamer's Field Migratory Waterfowl Refuge, Fairbanks.

Further information: Alaska Public Lands Information Center, 605 West 4th Ave., Anchorage, AK 99501; tel. 907-271-2737, www.nps.gov/aplic/.

Rte. 3 intersects a spur road leading into Nancy Lake State Recreation Area. This swampy but scenic domain, covering nearly 23,000 acres, is studded with some 130 lakes.

Nancy Lake Parkway, the area's gravel access road, meanders through forests of spruce, birch, and aspen inhabited by moose, black bears, and coyotes. Sandhill cranes have been known to perform their elaborate springtime courtship ritual within view of the road, and common loons often can be glimpsed on the canoe trail that stitches together 22 of the area's lakes (canoes can be rented at the South Rolly Lake Campground).

Returning to the highway, the drive passes through Willow, a lazy little town that almost became Alaska's state capital during the 1970s, when a move from Juneau was considered but never carried out. Willow lost its shot at glory but held on to a more eternal claim to fame: it is here that travelers heading north on the Parks Highway often catch their first glimpse of mighty Mt. McKinley, which reigns supreme over the 600-mile-long Alaska Range.

6 Talkeetna

During climbing season—May and June—mountain fever reaches its peak in Talkeetna, a colorful town that serves as a springboard for expeditions to Mt. McKinley, some 60 miles to the northwest. Weather permitting, one of the best views of the mountain comes at mile 13 on the Talkeetna spur road, which branches northeast from the highway at mile 98.7.

At 20,320 feet high, Mt. McKinley is North America's loftiest pinnacle. But what makes the mountain so daunting to scale is not its height but its climate. Thin air, frigid temperatures (even in summer), and winds gusting up to 150 miles per hour make McKinley's upper reaches one of the

most-forbidding places on earth. In spite of such danger, about a thousand people per year try to reach its summit; in a good year, half of them succeed.

7 Denali State Park

Back on Rte. 3, the drive passes through a white-and-green grove of birch trees intermixed with ferns that stretches all the way to the Susitna River bridge and beyond. From here north, the terrain gradually shifts from the open valleys of south-central Alaska to the icy escarpments of the interior.

Nowhere is this change more dramatic than in Denali State Park, a 324,000-acre wilderness preserve that lies in the shadow of Denali National Park. Turnouts throughout the state park afford views of Mt. McKinley and the mammoth glaciers—notably Ruth, Buckskin, and Eldridge—that inch their way down the southern flanks of the McKinley group, sometimes coming within five miles of the road.

8 Hurricane Gulch

With so many natural wonders at every turn, it's easy to forget that Alaska also harbors its fair share of man-made marvels. A prime example of these is the bridge at Hurricane Gulch, a 260-foot-high, 558-foot-long span across the widest and deepest gorge on the George Parks Highway. Built in 1971, the bridge is in turn eclipsed by the railway trestle to the west, which is 36 feet higher, 360 feet longer, and 50 years older.

9 Broad Pass

After vaulting Honolulu Creek, the drive takes aim for a breach in the wall of the Alaska Range and enters Broad Pass, the pivot point for a panorama of peaks that soar nearly 12,000 feet skyward. Broad Pass divides the east and west segments of the Alaska Range. Form-

Alaska's Biggest Guessing Game

The place: Nenana. The time: it's anybody's guess. Each spring when the frozen Tanana River begins to thaw, Alaskans try to predict the precise day, hour, and minute when the ice will finally break up. The event, known as the Nenana Ice Classic, has been a tradition since 1917, when surveyors working on the Alaskan Railroad decided to relieve their boredom with an offbeat lottery.

The excitement begins in February, when a flagpole, connected by cable to a clock on shore, is set up on the river ice. Contestants have until early April to place their two-dollar bets, which pour in by the thousands from all over America. Sometime in April or May, at a moment known only to Mother Nature, the ice shifts and some lucky soul—or souls, if more than one person chooses the same day and time—wins the jackpot, usually about $100,000.

ing part of the Continental Divide, these majestic mountains segregate rivers to the south, which flow into the Gulf of Alaska, from those to the north, which empty into the Yukon River.

10 Denali National Park

Some call it the Denali dilemma: in spite of its size (6 million acres—an area larger than the state of Massachusetts), the park has so many visitors (about 600,000 per year—nearly equal to the population of Alaska) that it must limit access to protect its fragile wilderness. This spirit of preservation has been a hallmark of Denali

National Park since its inception. In 1906 hunters in the foothills of Mt. McKinley were eradicating the Dall sheep, shaggy white critters with curlicue horns, at an alarming rate. Outraged, conservationist Charles Sheldon launched a campaign to save the animals. On February 26, 1917, his efforts finally paid off; President Woodrow Wilson signed a law that brought Mt. McKinley National Park into existence, saving it for perpetuity.

Three boundary expansions and one name change later, Denali National Park remains a pristine wildlife sanctuary that is home to 38 kinds of mammals—including grizzly bears, moose, wolves, and caribou—and 158 species of birds, which migrate here from several continents. To protect the preserve, the park prohibits cars beyond the Savage River, 15 miles west of Rte. 3 on the park road. Shuttle buses departing from the visitor center cover the final 70 miles to Wonder Lake.

If you can't spare the two or three days it may take to get a bus pass during the summer, try to catch a glimpse of Mt. McKinley between miles 9 and 11 of the park road. Even from 70 miles away, you'll easily see why Alaskan natives dubbed the peak Denali, "The Great One." The mountain towers more than 18,000 feet above the surrounding lowlands, making it, when measured from base to summit, even higher than Mt. Everest. Yet McKinley's majesty is often veiled by a mist of its own making: warm, moist air from the Gulf of Alaska condenses on the mountain's southern face, creating a steady drizzle that obscures it from view two days out of three.

Wonder Lake is found at the end of the park road in Denali National Park; it is accessible only by park buses.

11 Wonder Lake

At the visitor center sightseers board a bus to Wonder Lake. Although the road never rises above 4,000 feet, it offers a wealth of scenic high points. Sable Pass, at mile 39, is the surest place to spot grizzly bears, which are so fond of the wildflowers and berries here that a mile-wide zone on either side of the road has been closed to hikers since 1952.

Continuing west, the route clambers up Polychrome Pass, named for its rainbow of mineral-rich rocks. Tinged pink, red, orange, yellow, rust, and purple by exposure to the air, these stony outcroppings frame a southerly view of glacial handiwork: kettle lakes, erratics (isolated boulders), and the braided East Toklat River.

You can get off the bus and start hiking almost anywhere, but the best place is the Eielson visitor center (mile 66). In the summer a naturalist leads a "tundra trek"—a chance to identify some of the park's 430-plus kinds of flowering plants. The visitor center also affords prime views of Mt. McKinley and Muldrow glacier, extending 32 miles and almost three miles of elevation. Save film for Wonder Lake—sunrise and sunset bathe Mt. McKinley in haunting hues of pink and purple.

12 Nenana

After returning from the Eielson visitor center (an eight-hour round-trip bus ride) or Wonder Lake (11 hours round-trip), resume the drive behind the wheel of your own vehicle. Grip it tight, though, because the next 65-mile stretch, which meets the scenic gorge of the Nenana River, is riddled with sharp turns, windy passes, canyon crossings, and frost heaves (dips and blips in the pavement caused by moisture freezing in the soil beneath the road surface).

Nenana means "a good place to camp between two rivers," and the name is certainly apt. The town's setting is the confluence of the Tanana and Nenana rivers. About 20 miles north, the route reaches Skyline Drive, running along the ridgetops with spectacular views.

13 Fairbanks

As the drive crosses the Chena River, the land levels out and Fairbanks spreads out along eight miles of the river's banks. A boisterous bit of civilization amidst Alaska's wilderness, birch-blanketed hills surround the town; climb those to the north and west for good views of the Tanana River valley.

One such vantage point is the 2,250-acre campus of the University of Alaska, which perches on a grassy ridge four miles west of Fairbanks. In addition to its cultural museum, botanical garden, and musk-ox farm, the university affords one last look at Mt. McKinley, now a distant vision on the far horizon, if your luck is good and its ever-present clouds part, giving you a clear view.

Kenai Peninsula

On this grand peninsula, where forests, mountains, and glaciers meet the Gulf of Alaska, land and sea meld gracefully into one.

In autumn, creeks near Portage Glacier teem with spawning salmon.

Start with a wildly irregular coastline, its rocky headlands gouged into fjords by glacial ice. Add jagged, snow-dusted peaks, scraping the sky like sawteeth in every direction. Mix in massive glaciers and rivers teeming with salmon. Then link this astonishing scenery together with two beautifully maintained highways, and you have the Kenai Peninsula, regarded by Alaskans as a priceless jewel.

1 Anchorage

Home to about half of Alaska's population, Anchorage is wedged like an arrowhead between the Knik and Turnagain arms of Cook Inlet and sprawls eastward to the steepening foothills of the Chugach Mountains. With this prosperous city as its starting point, the drive heads along the Seward Highway, a two-lane road winding south for

127 miles to its terminus at Seward on Resurrection Bay. From its very first mile, the highway offers scenic views: the Chugach Mountains dominate the eastern horizon, while the snowcapped summits of the Alaska Range seem to rise from the chilly blue waters of Cook Inlet to the west. Numerous moose live in the greater Anchorage area, as do a number of bears. These creatures are sometimes visible from the road heading out of town, as are bald eagles soaring overhead. Gazing skyward, you may notice that the eagles share the air with pontoon-fitted seaplanes, based at Anchorage's Lake Hood, the busiest seaplane port in the world.

2 Potter Point State Game Refuge

On the outskirts of Anchorage, the highway passes through a prime locale for bird-watching. Potter Marsh, as it is known hereabouts, attracts waterfowl from early spring through fall. A boardwalk winds across one section of the marsh, affording close encounters with Canada geese, arctic terns, green-winged teal, and pintails.

3 Chugach State Park

Nearly half the size of Delaware, Chugach State Park encompasses a half-million acres of forest, mountains, and glaciers. Visit the Potter Section House, a restored building once occupied by railroad workers who maintained tracks here during the days of steam locomotives. Declared a state historic site, the structure contains memorabilia about the Alaska Railroad.

Continuing east, the road follows the north coast of Turnagain Arm, so named by Captain James Cook, who sailed with his expedition up this narrowing extension of Cook Inlet in an unsuccessful hunt for the fabled Northwest Passage in 1778. When he hit a dead end, Cook was forced to "turn again."

A sled dog rests before the start at Fur Rondy, held in Anchorage in February.

4 Beluga Point

Nearing Beluga Point, you may see a number of cars slowing down or pulling off the road at the viewing area overlooking Turnagain Arm. The seasonal tie-up, caused by the sight of white beluga whales, is known locally as a "whale jam." To facilitate viewing, the area is equipped with telescopes and interpretive displays. When a pod of whales swims by, thin puffs of mist can be seen suspended in the air over their spouts, and their white bodies contrast beautifully with the dark waters of Turnagain Arm.

Competing with whales for visitors' attention near Beluga Point are the unusual "bore tides" created when incoming tides from Cook Inlet are squeezed into Turnagain Arm's narrow channel. These walls of water can be eight feet high and travel about 10 miles an hour. Announcing its approach with an eerie roar, the bore arrives about two hours after low tide.

5 Alyeska Resort

As you continue along the highway, look for roadside waterfalls, bluebells in bloom, and Dall sheep climbing the nearby slopes. For a bird's-eye view of the area, turn north at Girdwood, where a three-mile spur leads to the Alyeska

Chugach State Park, minutes from Anchorage, is a favorite summer hiking spot for city dwellers and visitors to Alaska.

Resort, the largest in the state. A 60-passenger aerial tram glides partway up Mt. Alyeska, offering panoramic vistas of Turnagain Arm and the Alyeska Glacier.

6 Twenty-Mile River

Just north of Portage, the Twenty-Mile River empties into Turnagain Arm. A roadside turnout offers a striking view up the river's long, verdant valley, where locals use long-handled nets to land smelt in May. Nestled at the valley's far end is Twenty-Mile Glacier, where the river begins its journey.

7 Portage Glacier

Linked to the Seward Highway by a five-mile paved road that begins just south of Portage, this much-visited tourist attraction offers visitors a vivid introduction to the power of glaciers. You'll see frigid blue water at lovely Portage Lake near the parking area; the imposing face of the receding glacier is a stout hike away. The Begich, Boggs visitor center offers a number of displays, including relief maps of the surrounding icefields and vials filled with ice worms—tiny black creatures that live atop and below glacial ice. Visitors cannot hike to Portage Glacier, but they can view it up close from a tour boat on Portage Lake or take the trail to nearby Byron Glacier.

8 Summit Lakes

The views of Turnagain Arm fade to the rear as the drive cuts south through Chugach National Forest. Among the many lakes dotting Chugach's millions of acres are Lower Summit Lake, on the east side of the road, and then Summit Lake, a bit to the south. Lower Summit Lake lures nature photographers seeking exemplary shots of wildflowers.

9 Kenai Lake

For five miles or so, the Seward Highway cruises along the easternmost shoreline of blue-green Kenai Lake. Its unusual color is produced by rock particles suspended in the glacial meltwater that feeds the lake. Ground by glaciers into a fine powder, the particles reflect blue-green from the spectrum of sunlight, lending a turquoise cast to the snowy peaks mirrored in the water. At the lake's south end, a lovely trail leads from Primrose Campground to Lost Lake.

10 Exit Glacier

Two miles north of Seward, turn west onto a gravel road that parallels the Resurrection River for nine miles. The road ends at the Exit Glacier Ranger Station in Kenai Fjords National Park. A three-mile-long river of ice flowing from massive Harding Icefield, Exit Glacier looms like a blue monolith over the surrounding landscape. Visitors can approach the glacier's base by walking about a half-mile on an easy trail from the ranger station. A longer, more strenuous trail leads hikers up the flank of the glacier to a spot overlooking the Harding Icefield itself.

Nimble Climbers

Smaller cousins of the bighorn (or mountain) sheep of the western United States and Canada, Dall sheep are a familiar sight on Turnagain Arm near Beluga Point. Named for turn-of-the cenury naturalist William H. Dall, these agile climbers have concave, elastic hooves that give them a sure-footed edge on steep, rugged slopes, where, beyond the reach of enemies, they munch on mountain grasses. Dall sheep range from Alaska, where they are white, to British Columbia, where they are nearly black.

Radiating glaciers in every direction, this mantle of ice measures an imposing 35 miles by 20 miles. Buried within its frigid bulk are all but the tallest peaks to be found in the Kenai Mountains.

11 Seward

Tucked between Resurrection Bay and the foot of Mt. Marathon, the city of Seward serves as the gateway to Kenai Fjords National Park, a 580,000-acre mosaic of glaciers, fjords, icefields, and mountainous coastline. At a National Park Service visitor center at Seward harbor, exhibits explain how the local fjords were created by glaciers thousands of years ago. Today, these flooded valleys are home to legions of sea otters, sea lions, whales, and other marine creatures. To view them, observers can board the Seward-based tour boats that cruise up and down the coastline. The boats also provide close-up views of glaciers giving birth to mammoth icebergs, accompanied by ear-shattering crashes and thunderous plunges into the icy sea.

12 Kenai River

After backtracking north to tiny Tern Lake Junction, turn onto the Sterling Highway, a 142-mile road heading west toward Cook Inlet and then south along the inlet to Homer. The Sterling Highway first skirts the northern tip of Kenai Lake and then parallels the Kenai River for about 10 miles. Summer anglers, fishing from the shore and from rafts along this stretch of river, dream of catching a king salmon akin to the 97-pounder caught here in 1985, which set a world record for the species; fish up to 50 pounds are more commonly caught. Moose, eagles, bears, and Dall sheep can be seen from the highway and on wildlife float trips along the river.

13 Skilak Lake Loop Road

Branching off the Sterling Highway, this rough gravel road meanders 19 miles through magnificent high country before rejoining the highway near Sterling. Motorists pass a number of picturesque lakes dotted with canoes and fishing boats, including 15-mile-long Skilak Lake. Look for moose wandering the roadside and be prepared for flat tires.

14 Kenai National Wildlife Refuge

This enormous tract of forests and lakes—nearly 2 million acres —occupies much of the Kenai Peninsula. It was originally set aside to preserve the populations of moose, but it provides a home for a number of other wild creatures as well.

Throughout the summer, motorists commonly see moose cows and calves feeding in roadside woods and wetlands within the refuge. The visitor center near the town of Soldotna offers daily slide shows, wildlife displays, and information about the refuge's 200 miles of hiking trails.

15 Clam Gulch

Turning south at Soldotna, the Sterling Highway reaches Cook Inlet at Clam Gulch. The restaurants in this aptly named town serve clam chowder, steamers, and razor clams, and motels rent buckets and shovels for clamming. During the low tides, on the flats

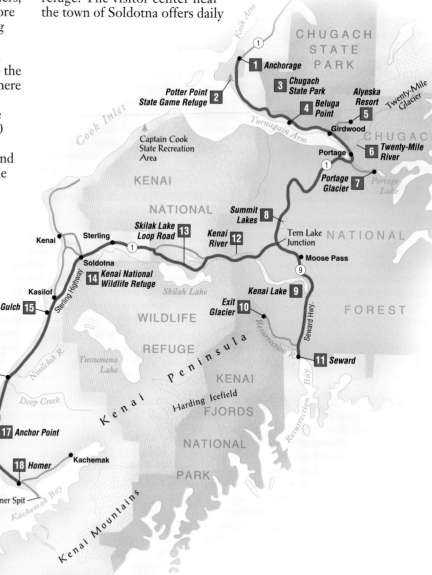

between Cape Kasilof (north of Clam Gulch) and Anchor Point (to the south), clammers dig into the cold sand to extract razor clams, the main attraction here.

To the west, across Cook Inlet from the Clam Gulch tidal flats, a perpetually snowcapped array of tall peaks greets the eye. Mt. Redoubt stands 10,197 feet high, and to its left, 30 miles down the coast, Mt. Iliamna tops off at an impressive 10,016 feet.

16 Ninilchik

Just before entering Ninilchik, take a side road to the town's original site, where it stood from its founding in the 1820s until its mid-20th-century relocation about a half-mile away. At the site of the old village, weathered log buildings still stand in the beach grass, and a Russian Orthodox church built in 1901 overlooks the sea. In present-day Ninilchik a favorite preoccupation is clamming, but when the king salmon begin their summer spawning runs up Deep Creek and the Ninilchik River, the town is overtaken by a frenzied fishing fever, and anglers crowd every bit of the bank.

This Russian Orthodox church and its cemetery are a reminder of Ninilchik's past as a Russian fur-trading community.

Trip Tips

Length: About 330 miles, plus side trips.

When to go: Popular year-round, but best in summer.

Words to the wise: Be alert for sudden changes in weather.

Nearby attractions: Resurrection Pass Trail, Hope. Kenai Historical Museum, Kenai. Small boat harbors, Seward and Homer.

Further information: Kenai Peninsula Tourism Marketing Council, 10819 Kenai Spur Highway, Suite 103-D, Kenai, Alaska 99611; tel. 800-535-3624, www.kenai peninsula.org.

17 Anchor Point

With high peaks rising to the west across Cook Inlet, the highway hugs the shoreline as it approaches the town of Anchor Point. A short side road leads to the Anchor River Recreation Area, a mecca for anglers. There, too, a plaque notes the spot as "the most westerly point on the North American continent accessible by a continuous road system.

18 Homer

Most of Homer lies on the shore of Kachemak Bay, but part of it—a 4½-mile-long needle of sand, rock, and gravel known as Homer Spit—juts into the bay itself. Surrounded by snowy peaks and icy waters, the spit pulsates with an inviting variety of sights, smells, and sounds. Charter boats chug out of the spit's small boat harbor, their customers hoping to snag one of the regal-size halibut that abound in the waters of Cook Inlet. Heady-smelling shops on the boardwalk dispense fresh seafood of all kinds, both cooked and raw. (If you have a camp stove and a large pot, you can buy shrimp or

clams, fill the pot with half seawater and half fresh, and enjoy an open-air seafood cookout.)

Before leaving Homer, cruise along Skyline Drive, which runs atop high bluffs overlooking the town, and gaze down at Kachemak Bay, the rugged Kenai Mountains beyond it, and the glaciers that ooze from the vast Harding Icefield. As eagles soar overhead and fireweed brightens the slopes that frame this Alaskan panorama, you'll come to see why many residents regard Homer as one of the most beautiful places on earth.

Richardson Highway

Far from the hustle and bustle of city life, this scenic drive explores a land of snowy mountains, dense forests, and life-sustaining rivers in the wilds of Alaska.

Creeks lined with deep moss and lichen flow to the nearby Gulf of Alaska.

Linking Fairbanks and Valdez, Rtes. 2 and 4—the Richardson Highway —have played a vital role in local history. Originally a footpath, then a wagon trail, the route was a vital corridor for early prospectors. Even though today's travelers aren't seeking gold, they are nonetheless rewarded with treasures, from glacier-clad peaks to alpine wildflowers and peaceful little towns.

1 Tanana River

A few miles out of Fairbanks, the hub of Alaska's interior, Rte. 2 meets with and then, for the most part, parallels the Tanana River. The waterway springs high in the Wrangell Mountains, where the summer meltwater trickles from beneath glaciers. Here the Tanana flows for long stretches in a braided channel, with interweaving stream-lets of silver-gray, till-laden water coursing down the gravel bed.

One of the state's few agricultural regions, this broad and level land is bordered by mountain ranges. The snowy peaks—white summits pointing skyward along the southern horizon—may appear small but in fact are among the highest in North America.

Sharing the sweeping farmland are military bases, recreation areas, campsites, and small towns, one of which calls itself North Pole. Managing to outlast the six-month long winters, many wild animals— moose, bears, and caribou, to name just a few—can be spotted through-out the area.

2 Big Delta

As it spans the Tanana River at the farming community of Big Delta, Rte. 2 parallels the Trans-Alaska Pipeline, a companion since the outskirts of Fairbanks. Carrying about one-fourth of America's domestically produced supply of crude oil, the steel tube runs from the petroleum-rich fields above the Arctic Circle to the port of Valdez —an 800-mile trip. The pipeline, four feet in diameter, was completed in 1977 and is in many places visible from the highway. Visit the viewing area at the south end of the bridge, where interpretive signs relate key information.

About a half-mile later, turn to the northeast on Rika's Road for a visit to Big Delta State Historical Park, which recalls the early days when gold fever was luring prospectors into unexplored territory. Costumed guides are on hand to lead tours through a re-created 1910 roadhouse.

3 Delta Junction

Creeks, lakes, spruce groves, home-steads, campgrounds, and fields of barley form a pleasing mosaic in the Delta Junction area. A couple of roads wend through the town, and a visitor center lies just south of the intersection of Rtes. 2 and 4. From this point onward, Rte. 2 is known as the Alaska Highway, a rugged, often unpaved road that leads southeast for more than 1,400 spectacular miles to Dawson Creek, British Columbia, Canada.

As for the Richardson Highway, it heads south along Rte. 4, climbing beside the Delta River into the Alaska Range. The road is well supplied with scenic turnoffs, and binoculars often prove helpful, especially when observing bison— transplanted to the area in the 1920s—and herds of caribou.

4 Isabel Pass

After passing colorful wildflowers, a peak called Donnelly Dome, and a retreating glacier that once nearly engulfed the road, the Richardson Highway peaks its highest point— 3,000 feet—at Isabel Pass. As it descends from the pass, the route skirts picturesque wildlands with campsites, lodgings, lakes, and free-flowing rivers. The Wrangell Mountains, with three peaks over 16,000 feet, rise to the southeast.

::::: **Trip Tips** :::::

Length: About 370 miles, with mile markers (roadside signs) beginning 4 miles outside Valdez and ending with 364 in Fairbanks.

When to go: Summer; July is the warmest month, with daytime highs about 60° to 70°F. Road is usually open in winter.

Words to the wise: Roads can be damaged by frost heaves.

Nearby attractions: Fielding Lake State Recreation Site, Rte. 8, west of Paxson. Chitina, southeast of Copper Center.

Further information: Valdez Convention and Visitors Bureau, P.O. Box 1603-MP, Valdez, AK 99686; tel. 800-770-5954, www.valdezalaska.org.

Bridal Veil Falls near Valdez tumbles in six distinct tiers.

5 Wrangell–St. Elias National Park and Preserve

Several mountain ranges converge here in our largest national park, where glaciers—one of them larger than Rhode Island—engulf alpine summits and valleys. Park headquarters and a visitor center lie near mile marker 105, just north of Copper Center. Only two roads, both of them dirt, lead into the park's interior. They dead-end at the tiny towns of McCarthy and Nebesna, the limits of civilization.

A real challenge to the hiker, who must be self-sufficient, the park offers few services or facilities. Those adventuring away from the towns find themselves crossing vast untrodden tracts—the realm of Dall sheep, mountain goats, bears, and caribou.

6 Worthington Glacier

Crossing paths with the pipeline several times, Rte. 4 climbs into the Chugach Mountains for a tour of forests, tundra, and peaks. One notable sight along the way, the Worthington Glacier, is visible at mile marker 30. A turnout allows for easy viewing, and a spur route at mile 28.7 leads even closer to the frozen giant, its blue ice blemished with glacial debris and crevasses.

The drive then continues to Thompson Pass, where one winter, snow piled up to an incredible depth of 974 inches, a record for the state. The views—at first mere glimpses through narrow chasms—open up to reveal snowfields and jagged slopes. Take some time to explore the region, an alpine Eden laced with creeks and abloom with flowers and foliage plants.

7 Keystone Canyon

After a 7½-mile descent from the pass, Rte. 4 swings into Keystone Canyon, then snakes for some four miles through the sheer-sided gap. The canyon walls hem in the Lowe River, whose waters, slate-gray with glacial debris, give life to streamside stands of cottonwoods. Bridal Veil and Horse Tail falls plummet at roadside, lending a lovely grace note.

8 Valdez

Spread on a ledge dramatically wedged between mountains and the sea, today's Valdez was rebuilt four miles west of its original site, devastated by a tsunami in 1964. The community dates to the late 1890s, when gold seekers flooded the area.

Today the emphasis is on black gold, for in Valdez the oil flowing down the Trans-Alaska Pipeline is pumped aboard ships. The well-protected harbor also accesses the Alaska Marine Highway, a National Scenic Byway. Ferries cruise to the nearby retreating Columbia Glacier, where sightseers watch in awe as huge blocks of ice tumble to the sea, and as far south as Prince Rupert, Canada.

Kuhio Highway

Known as the Paradise of the Pacific, the Hawaiian Islands, with their abundant sunshine, idyllic beaches, and vibrant greenery, never fail to charm all comers.

Hanalei Pier on Kauai is near the northernmost point of land in the Hawaiian islands.

Kauai, lushest of the major islands, has been called the Garden Isle. Blessed also with many moods and splendors, it best reveals itself when seen from the Kuhio Highway. The road, with signs marking points of interest along the way, starts in the sunny south, skirts the rainy mountains of the interior, and ends at the impassable wilds that form Kauai's unforgettable northern shore.

1 Lihue

Isolated from the rest of the world by the Pacific Ocean, Hawaii developed not only a unique culture but also became colonized by many plants and animals found nowhere else. To discover some of its one-of-a-kind treasures, visit the small but superb Kauai Museum on Rice Street (Rte. 51). On exhibit are examples of the feathery capes once worn by native royalty, vintage photographs of plantation life, and a video of the island as seen from the air.

Once versed in local history, it is time for some in-person sightseeing. Continue along Rice Street, which rolls down to Kalapaki Beach and Nawiliwili Bay, a frequent port of call for cruise ships. At the harbor pick up Niumalu Road to Alekoko, which is also known as the Menehune Fish Pond. A thousand years ago the natives raised mullet, a food fish, in its waters. The pond, according to legend, was built in a single night by the Menehune, leprechaun-like creatures that were said to inhabit Hawaiian forests.

Double back to the bay and Rte. 56 out of Lihue. Heading northward, the road twists through a countryside where emerald fields of sugarcane give way to cloud-shrouded volcanic peaks, the tallest one climbing to 5,243 feet.

2 Wailua Falls

A side trip leading inland on Rte. 583, Maalo Road, leads to Wailua Falls, a pair of side-by-side cascades that leap off a verdant ledge into a shimmering pool. The higher of the two makes an 80-foot plunge, a dramatic sight that has often been filmed for television and motion-picture productions.

3 Lydgate State Park

After returning to Rte. 56, you might find it hard to stay on the road, for the island's tempting scenery and beaches are nearly irresistible invitations to stop and explore. Hanamaulu Beach, with its white sand and tropical setting, is a favorite with locals. Better yet, perhaps, are the natural pools at Lydgate. Ideal for swimming, the water holes are edged with volcanic rocks, the benign end-products of the fury that shaped Kauai.

The region of Lydgate, known to early inhabitants as Wailua Nui Hoano, or "Great Sacred Two Waters," was the island's ancient hub, both politically and economically. Parts of it were held so holy that only royalty and priests were allowed entry. Several early temples still stand amid towering coconut palms. One was dedicated to the rising sun; another offered refuge to any lawbreaker who could reach its sanctuary before his pursuers caught him.

4 Fern Grotto

For a change of pace, head to the Wailua Marina for a 1½-hour round-trip cruise—accompanied by musicians and dancers just as the kings of old were—along the Wailua River to Fern Grotto. Considered to be Hawaii's only navigable waterway, the Wailua streams down from the green peak of Waialeale, drenched by rains and with rainfall measured at many feet per year. Once at Fern Grotto, a romantic setting with a drapery of enormous ferns, you'll see why so many newlyweds come to the cave to have their pictures taken.

5 Wailua River State Park

The Wailua River runs between grassy banks through this park, where Kauai's oldest temple, Holo Holo Ku Heiau, lends a grim historical touch: the ancient site was once the setting for human sacrifices. By way of contrast, the nearby birthing stones were used by royal mothers when giving birth to future kings.

To reach the ancient religious sites, follow Rte. 580, which winds beside the river's northern banks. Farther on, the highway leads to Opaekaa Falls, where powerful plumes spill down from a plateau cloaked with lush vegetation.

Back on Rte. 56, the drive skirts popular tourist destinations, then enters the bustling little town of Kapaa, which offers a variety of shops and restaurants. From Kapaa you'll see the mountain peaks that form a silhouette known as the Sleeping Giant. Up ahead lies stunning stretches of the Coconut Coast, which can be reached by side roads that branch away from the Kuhio Highway. At land's end, secluded, beach-lined coves await, including the ones at Kealia and

Trip Tips

Length: About 40 miles.

When to go: Popular year-round.

Words to the wise: Since the roads in places are winding, rent a car you can comfortably handle. Powerful surf, especially in winter along the north shore, can make swimming dangerous.

Nearby attraction: Waimea Canyon State Park, north of Waimea, known as the Miniature Grand Canyon of the Pacific.

Further information: Hawaii Visitors Bureau, 4334 Rice St, #101, Lihue, HI 96766; tel. 808-245-3971, www.kauaidiscovery.com.

Anahola. Be aware, however, that the sandy oceanfronts have one daunting drawback: powerful undertows.

6 Kilauea National Wildlife Refuge

As the mountains begin to grow craggier—hints of the drama to come—the drive eventually intersects with Kolo Road. Make the turn, continue to Kilauea Road, and follow the signs to this wildlife haven.

Among the delights here are the black-footed albatrosses, or gooneys, gull-like birds with wingspans up to seven feet. You might also catch sight of rare Hawaiian monk seals; they come to nap on the rocks below the refuge's green thumb of land topped with a lighthouse.

Rte. 56 continues beside steep green peaks, lush meadows, and frequent waterfalls. Stop at Hanalei Valley Overlook for a panoramic sight, especially dazzling when sunbeams shoot through clouds and the arches of rainbows.

Farther on, Hawaiian coots, stilts, ducks, and moorhens frequent the refuge. The road to the refuge passes into the valley and, at one point, hops across a one-lane bridge. You may not think much of the bridge—it is rather ordinary-looking—but to residents the span is a special treasure: it is too narrow for the big tour buses to pass across, sparing the area from the crowds of visitors that are sometimes found milling about other attractions; native Hawaiians reserve it for themselves.

7 Hanalei

Expect the unexpected in Hanalei—from an eclectic mix of inhabitants to a herd of bison—but most of all be sure to note the meeting of razor-edge peaks and the blue Pacific. Historic sites in town include the Waioli Huiia Church, where Sunday hymns are sung in Hawaiian, and the Waioli Mission House, little changed since 1837.

The Waioli Huiia Church in Hanalei, Kauai, holds traditional Hawaiian services.

Once you're back on the road, cross more one-lane bridges and the drive leads through a fertile, stream-fed valley. The crop with the huge heart-shaped leaves is taro, the Hawaiian staff of life.

Beyond, you'll find two of the better spots to stop and enjoy the views: the pier at Hanalei Bay, with views of the sea and the surrounding mountains, and Lumahai Beach, the setting for scenes in the movie *South Pacific*.

8 Caves of Haena

Caverns are the highlight here. Dry Cave, just across from Haena Park, is the opening of a lava tube that, according to legend, snakes all the way to an inland summit. Native lore also explains the nearby Wet Cave. Pele, the goddess of volcanoes, is said to have created the caverns while she searched for buried fires. When she struck crystal-clear waters here instead of flames, the tempestuous goddess fled the island—much to the relief of all.

9 Kee Beach

The drive finishes its remarkable journey in Kee Beach, a haven for snorkelers and tropical fish of just about every imaginable hue. Visitors can also explore the Kalalau Trail, a footpath that rambles for 11 miles along the miraculous meetings of land and sea known as the Napali Coast.

Some spectacular scenery, fortunately, lies on the first mile of trail. Hikers cross clifftops about 100 feet above the sea and can feel the ground tremble underfoot even as the surf below seethes with some of the earth's most powerful waves.

Oahu Coastal Loop

Venturing along the windward coast of Oahu, the drive explores fortresslike cliffs, emerald gardens that conjure the dawn of time, and some of the most-celebrated ocean waves in all the world.

The sheltered waters of Kaneohe Bay are a favorite spot for viewing the underwater reefs and sandy sea bottoms filled with colorful tropical fish.

Long ago Oahu was nicknamed "the gathering place," and the name has proved prophetic: today Oahu hosts three-fourths of Hawaii's population and the largest share of its visitors. But this drive, traveling beyond the bustle of Honolulu and Waikiki, calls attention to another Oahu. Following the narrow shoreline at the windward base of the Koolau Range, Rtes. 72, 61, and 83 trace a journey from one Oahu icon, Diamond Head, to another, Waimea Bay.

1 Diamond Head

An ancient crater towering over Oahu's southern tip, Diamond Head was named by early British sailors who spied the sparkle of diamond-like crystals on its seaward flanks. Visitors can begin exploring this dormant volcano by skirting the manicured estates along its southern shoulder, then following an old military tunnel into the heart of the crater. Here a short but steep path leads up stairways and through pedestrian tunnels to the 760-foot summit. The view takes in Waikiki and Honolulu to the northwest, the wooded foothills of the Koolau Range to the north, and Koko Head to the east.

2 Koko Head Regional Park

The rugged volcanic rock formations here contrast beautifully with sandy, palm-fringed beaches. One can hike up the lofty promontory called Koko Head, then snorkel amidst lovely corals and the darting, inquisitive fish of Hanauma Bay, a surf-eroded crater that is now a marine preserve. At Halona Blowhole, seawater compressed within an underwater lava tube spews geyserlike into the air. Rising above the blowhole are the slopes of 1,208-foot Koko Crater.

3 Nuuanu Pali State Wayside

Rte. 72 arcs around Oahu's easternmost reach at Makapuu Point, where bodysurfers ride the waves that roll in past Rabbit and Turtle islands, and marine-life enthusiasts seek close encounters with the seals and dolphins on display at Sea Life Park. Heading northwest between Waimanalo Bay and the steep side of the Koolau Range, the drive climbs Rte. 61 to Nuuanu Pali Lookout, a spectacular cliff-top vista that spans the coast from Makapuu to Kaneohe Bay, taking in verdant forest at the base of the cliffs and an infinity of ocean. Nuuanu Pali is also the scene of one of old Hawaii's bloodiest episodes. Here, in 1795, King Kamehameha I cemented his hold on much of the archipelago by driving his enemies off the 1,200-foot cliffs.

4 Hoomaluhia Botanical Gardens

Off Rte. 83 to the south of Kaneohe, tucked against the base of the Koolau Range's monumental cliffs, lie 400 acres of gardens known as Hoomaluhia, where botanists nurture a dizzying array of native Hawaiian flora. Visitors can hike on well-marked trails or stroll the shores of the garden's placid lake.

5 Kahekili Highway

Known as the Kahekili Highway, this stretch of Rte. 83 between Kaneohe and Kahaluu embraces a series of lovely stopping-off points. At the 19th-century estate called Haiku Gardens, breadfruit trees, lily ponds, and a great sheltering banyan are the backdrops for a restaurant and secluded thatched huts that attract local wedding parties. The Byodo-In Temple, two miles farther north, is a detailed replica of a 900-year-old Kyoto shrine, set against the lofty cliffs of the Koolau Range. Here colorful carp drift though a placid pool, and peacocks strut past a great statue of Buddha. Two miles farther down the road is Senator

Seldom seen from Waikiki is Diamond Head's scenic lighthouse.

a peerless Pacific sunrise (for campsites, use the area's southern entrance, near milepost 17). At low tide, you can wade out to Goat Island, a seabird sanctuary with two exquisite beaches.

9 Waimea Bay

At Sunset Beach and Banzai Pipeline, enormous tubular waves challenge the world's most daring surfers. Just ahead lie the creamy sands of Waimea Bay, where in winter the stout of heart ride thunderous 30-foot waves. A more serene venue can be reached by following Pupukea Road to the ruins of Puu O Mahuka Heiau, the largest of Oahu's sacred sites. Just south of Rte. 83 and the town of Waimea, follow the banks of the Kamananui Stream on Waimea Valley Road to the lush green landscapes of 1,800-acre Waimea Valley Audubon Center. Well-marked hiking paths at the center wind through botanical gardens. Long ago a Hawaiian village stood on these grounds, and the heritage of that time is recalled in displays of archaeological artifacts and the opportunity to view rare and endangered Hawaiian flora and fauna, providing a lively link to Oahu's storied past.

Trip Tips

Length: About 60 miles.

When to go: Popular year-round.

Nearby attractions: Dole Pineapple Plantation, Wahiawa. Polynesian Cultural Center, Laie. Honolulu. Pearl Harbor. Waikiki Beach.

Further information: Hawaii Visitors Bureau, 2270 Kalakaua Ave., Suite 801, Honolulu, HI 96815; tel. 877-525-6248, www.visit-oahu.com.

Fong's Plantation and Gardens, named for the first U.S. senator of Asian descent. Some 725 bougainvillea-drenched acres represent Oahu in miniature, with sugarcane fields, nearly 100 varieties of edible fruits and nuts, and 27,000 orchid plants.

6 Kualoa Regional Park

Rte. 83 hugs Kaneohe Bay along a four-mile stretch north of Kahaluu, and side roads lead inland to the farm country of the Waiahole and Waikane valleys, where tree-ripened papayas are offered at roadside stands. North of Kaneohe Bay are the sugary sands and nodding palms of Kualoa Regional Park. From this windswept point visitors can hike, at low tide, about 500 yards to the cone-shaped island whimsically dubbed Chinaman's Hat. As you gaze back at the beach and distant cliffs, look for shorebirds flitting overhead.

7 Kahana Valley State Park

Like a stony sentinel, a natural rock formation called the Crouching Lion signals the approach to

Kahana Valley State Park, where a lightly traveled five-mile path meanders through more than 5,000 acres of ironwoods, coconut palms, and other trees. On the ocean side of the road, a county park offers a glimpse of the Huilua Fish Pond, a watery enclosure used long ago by Hawaiians to corral fish.

8 Malaekahana State Recreation Area

Remote from Waikiki both in spirit and in miles, serene Malaekahana appears just as the drive begins its gentle westward curve around northernmost Oahu. The park invokes an older, simpler Hawaii, where sea breezes stir the fronds of coconut palms along a sunny crescent of sand. You can rent a campsite or rustic cabin and enjoy

Hana Highway

Although harrowing for those behind the wheel, this tortuous Hawaiian highway, clinging to the coast of Maui, has been hailed as a world-class scenic drive.

The twisty coastal road to Maui's town of Hana is a drive you'll never forget.

The road to Hana is, to say the least, less than ideal: narrow hairpin turns are more the norm than the exception, and tiny towns along the way remain throwbacks to an earlier era of simplicity and isolation. Yet the difficulties of this winding coastal route are at the same time one of its great virtues, for they force drivers to slow down. And slowing down, one local likes to point out, leaves you time to "smell the flowers"—not at all a bad idea in this pretty corner of paradise.

1 Hookipa Beach Park

Though the beach here is beautiful in its own right, the big attraction is the opportunity to watch some of the world's best windsurfers in action. Jumping, tacking, and even cartwheeling across the blue waters off Hookipa Beach, athletes by the hundred perform acrobatic feats in an idyllic setting. The combination of steady surf and robust winds make the area such an ideal locale for windsurfing that even international championship competitions are held here.

2 Twin Falls

About two miles beyond the point where Rte. 36 becomes Rte. 360, a short trail leads to a pool fed by this pair of waterfalls. It is in this area, too, that the highway begins to curve crazily, snaking along the lower slopes of the sleeping giant Haleakala, a volcano whose highest point crests at 10,023 feet.

The course the Hana Highway follows was originally a footpath, a narrow trail blazed by ancient Hawaiians. Later, convicts used shovels to widen the route, and some decades after that, it was finally paved. Despite these steady improvements, the road retains a well-deserved reputation for being difficult—indeed, about three hours are required to navigate its 52 serpentine miles.

From Twin Falls onward, a Technicolor world lines the highway, which enters an enchanted realm adorned with vibrant greenery, misty waterfalls, and pristine pools. More than 50 bridges—many just one lane wide—span the terrain's many gorges, and the views occasionally open to reveal seascapes of the blue Pacific Ocean and dark sand beaches that lie below. Wild orchids and fragrant yellow ginger blossoms are among the plants that emblazon the roadside. The jungle—a maze of bamboo, African tulip, breadfruit, and paperbark trees—grows so dense that in places a green canopy arches above the roadway.

3 Huelo

Serene save for a few squawking roosters, the small community of Huelo, with its tiny Kaulanapueo Church, stands brightly against the blue backdrop of the Pacific Ocean. Constructed of coral in 1853, the New England–style church features an austere interior, complete with the original pews.

Farther along, look for stands of rainbow eucalyptus trees around the old plantation town of Kailua. The Hana Highway then leads to Waikomoi Ridge, where a nature trail zigzags through a forest of

:::::: **Trip Tips** ::::

Length: About 50 miles.

Words to the wise: Paia is the last place to get fuel before Hana, where the only service station closes at 6 p.m. Companies renting cars usually do not pay for damages incurred by drivers on unpaved roads, only paved ones.

Nearby attraction: Haleakala National Park, more than 28,000 acres of volcanic wilderness, including a craterlike valley, rain forest, and waterfalls, located in southeastern Maui.

Further information: Maui Visitors Bureau, 1727 Wili Pa Loop, Wailuku, HI 96793; tel. 808-244-3530, www.visitmaui.com.

bamboo. Just down the road at Puohokamoa Falls, you can picnic beside a 30-foot cascade that tumbles into a rock-lined pool. Yet another waterfall and swimming hole lie nearby, but the unmarked trail that leads to them is fairly treacherous and often slippery.

4 Kaumahina State Wayside Park

This wayside park is not only practical, offering restrooms and picnic tables, but also beautiful, with a lush tangle of native plants. Dazzling, too, is the overlook, which provides a panorama of the rugged coastline and Honomanu Bay.

Once back on the road, you'll come to the largest valley on the north side of Haleakala, about a mile or so farther on. Carved by erosion during the volcano's first period of dormancy, it stretches inland for more than five miles.

5 Keanae

If you're not sure of the names of the many flowers and trees alongside the road, Keanae Arboretum is the place to find out. Trails weave through the large park, and one well-tended garden thrives with yellow plumeria, banyan trees, and other native and exotic plants—all of them clearly identified.

To enjoy another of the island's rustic villages, follow the side road that rambles down the windswept Keanae Peninsula to Keanae. Snug in a nook along the jagged coast, it looks out on the relentless surf and ebony volcanic rocks that glisten in the sunshine.

6 Wailua

Water-logged taro patches—a signature sight in Hawaii—carpet the lonely Wailua Valley, a green expanse best viewed from the Keanae Valley Wailua Overlook. After taking in the view, follow the spur road that leads to the village of Wailua. Along the way, you may see the locals pounding the starchy taro root with boards and stones, one step in the recipe for poi.

Wailua's St. Gabriel's, better known as the Miracle Church, is wrapped in legend. When the community decided to build the tiny heart-decorated chapel in 1870, the story goes, a storm washed ashore all the coral and sand necessary for the job. Then, just as advantageously, when the work was done, another storm came and swept the excess back to sea.

7 Nahiku

As the history of the village of Nahiku reveals, this quiet coastal community was not always so serene. In 1912 entrepreneurs arrived to start a rubber plantation and, after ripping up large tracts of rain forest, planted hundreds of rubber trees. What the planters did not bargain for was the fact that the trees, drenched by Nahiku's frequent rains, would yield but little rubber. Today the failed venture is recalled by the rubber trees that remain along Nahiku Road.

8 Waianapanapa State Park

Just past Hana Airport, Rte. 360 comes to this park, a verdant area perched on a lava flow beside the sea. A black sand beach, created where molten lava met the ocean, features a stone arch and a blow-hole that you may be lucky enough to see and hear in action. One trail wends through the area's dense jungle—a tangle of leaves and vines—to two lava tubes filled not with fire but with water.

Hawaiians tell the tale of a beautiful princess who fled her enraged husband and hid on a cave ledge. After a diligent search the husband discovered his wife and, in a raging fury, killed her. Every April red water now flows from the caves—supposedly a reminder of her fate. Scientists, however, have another explanation, saying that the likely cause of the color change is an explosion of millions of tiny red shrimp in the water.

9 Hana

After a seemingly endless succession of tortuous turns, fern-filled gulches, and splashing waterfalls, the highway comes to the hills and pastures of Hana, a quiet town with a few shops and cottages. Despite its present-day rural charm, the area was once the site of fierce fighting. Since Hana lies just across the Alenuihaha Channel from Hawaii, the Big Island, it was very important to rival kings. One of the battle sites, Kaukiki, a cliff above Hana Bay,

Along Maui's Hana Highway, numerous coves invite visitors to take alfresco swims.

was captured by Hawaiian invaders. Peace was not established throughout the realm until the great King Kamehameha I united all of the islands early in the 19th century.

10 Kipahulu District of Haleakala National Park

A word of warning is in order before heading out on the 10 miles past Hana: the road is so crooked and narrow that drivers are jostled to their very bones. The grueling trip, however, is richly rewarded, especially in this sector of Haleakala National Park, where sparkling water holes form a staircase of cascades. Some 24 pools and many feet of elevation later, the water flows into the Pacific. After the hard ride, be sure to take a dip, the perfect remedy.

Farther down the road in Kipahulu lies Palapala Hoomau Church and the clifftop grave of Charles Lindbergh, who spent his last years in Kipahulu. The pavement ends about three miles past the church. Only the truly adventurous—in four-wheel-drive vehicles—should attempt to tackle the untamed route that lies ahead.

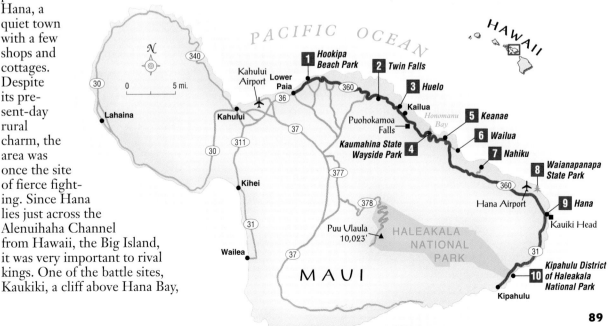

Aloha Loop

A wondrous work in progress, this idyllic, incredibly diverse island—embracing snowy peaks and sandy shores, lush valleys, and barren lava deserts—is easily explored on a richly rewarding loop tour.

Fire-tinged steam rises from the sea as molten lava flows into the Pacific. The lava was ejected from the Kilauea Volcano in Hawaii Volcanoes National Park.

At 1 million years of age, Hawaii's Big Island is the youngest of the islands that constitute our 50th state. But its size more than makes up for its youth. The Big Island, as locals call it, is nearly twice as large as all the others combined—and it's growing bigger every year. Since 1986, volcanic activity has added several hundred acres to this truly living landscape.

1 Hilo

Despite the fact that it's the second-largest city in Hawaii, Hilo paces itself to a slow beat. Its once-raffish waterfront has been transformed into a genteel park, and the old neighborhoods are now dotted with cappuccino shops. But vintage clapboard buildings and weathered Chinese storefronts still adorn this tropical town.

With over 120 inches of rainfall per year, Hilo is not only the wettest city in America, but a virtual greenhouse for such botanical beauties as torch gingers, garde-

Banyan trees abound at the Hawaii Tropical Botanical Garden.

nias, and orchids (some 30,000 types of which flourish on this part of the island). Many of the town's gardens and nurseries are open to the public, including the Nani Mau Gardens, which boasts the island's largest collection of orchids, and the Hawaii Tropical Botanical Garden.

Banyan Drive—named for the multi-trunked trees that line the road, each one of them planted by a different American celebrity during the 1930s—skirts the edge of Waiakea Peninsula before reaching Liliuokalani Gardens. A footbridge leads from this serene Japanese-style haven to Coconut Island, a palm-fringed hideaway that is perfect for picnicking. You can take a dip here too, but the best place for swimming and surfing is at the black sand beach in Richardson's Ocean Park, just to the east of town.

Traveling north on Rte. 19 (the Bayfront Highway), turn inland—mauka, as the locals say—on Waianuenue Avenue for a detour to Wailuku River State Park. The park's main draw is Rainbow Falls, a sight that becomes downright dazzling after heavy rains, when the spray shimmers with vivid hues. Farther upstream, the water pours into a series of pools with such turbulence that they have been dubbed the Boiling Pots.

Nuts About Macadamias

Named for Dr. John Macadam, a friend of the man who first recognized their virtues, macadamia nuts have been hailed for their perfection. Cooks are crazy about these sweet nuggets because they're tasty and versatile. Nutritionists are nuts about them because they're healthy. But Hawaiians are wild about them for a different reason: they're a leading source of income on the Big Island.

2 Hawaii Tropical Botanical Garden

Back on Rte. 19 (now known as the Mamalahoa Highway), continue north along the Hamakua Coast. At the town of Papaikou, turn east toward the sea—*makai*, in common parlance—and follow Onomea Scenic Drive to the Hawaii Tropical Botanical Garden. This 17-acre preserve features more than 2,000 species of plants—a collection that is believed to be the world's largest assortment of tropical plants growing in a natural environ-

ment. Numerous trails throughout the garden invite visitors to meander past preening parrots, squawking cockatoos, hidden waterfalls, and hushed lily ponds.

3 Akaka Falls State Park

At Honomu follow Rte. 220 inland past dense fields of sugarcane to Akaka Falls State Park, 66 acres of ferns, orchids, and bamboo groves. A short nature trail overhung with verdant, sweetly scented vegetation circles past cascading Kahuna Falls and the astonishing Akaka Falls.

4 Laupahoehoe Beach Park

Located on a small peninsula, this grassy park is shaded by spreading ironwood trees and tall coconut palms—an ideal setting for a relaxing picnic. The park takes its name from *pahoehoe*, the smooth, ropey type of lava found here. Inky black, the lava contrasts vividly with the frothy, white-tipped waves that pound against the shore.

5 Kalopa State Recreation Area

A few miles past Paauilo, an old plantation town dating back to Hawaii's sugarcane era, a turnoff leads to Kalopa State Recreation Area. Nestled on the lower slopes of Mauna Kea, this lush 615-acre forest reserve is laced with several well-marked hiking trails.

6 Waipo Valley Lookout

To visit Waipo Valley is to get a glimpse of the Garden of Eden. One mile wide and six miles long, this singularly beautiful spot was so favored by Hawaiian royalty that it is nicknamed the Valley of the Kings. Its splendor is indeed regal: perpetually green, thanks to numerous streams, waterfalls, and ancient fish ponds, the enchanted rain forest here is so productive that in times of famine its prodigious produce—bananas,

guavas, noni apples, and a host of other fruits—sustained the island's entire population in ancient times.

Since the road down into the valley resembles a zigzagging roller coaster, motorists without four-wheel drive should take a tour instead. Shuttles depart hourly from the Waipo Valley Lookout at the end of Rte. 240, but advance reservations are advised.

7 Waimea

From the gorgeous greens of Waipo, backtrack to Rte. 19 and head inland past sweeping high-country pastures and, to the south, 13,796-foot-tall Mauna Kea. Measured from its base on the floor of the sea, this dormant volcano, at some 32,000 feet, ranks as the world's highest peak. Because it is surrounded by ocean, Mauna Kea is blessed with pollution-free air so crystal-clear that its summit is the best spot on earth for stargazing. (No fewer than 13 observatories crown the peak's summit.)

As the drive heads west to Waimea, you might find it hard to believe you're still in the tropics. In far-off meadows fringed by hardwood trees, cowboys on horseback tend grazing cattle. These colorful Hawaiian cowpokes are called *paniolo*, and many of them work for the 225,000-acre Parker Ranch, said to be among the largest farmsteads in the United States. The ranch's history is detailed at a

The gossamer plume of Akaka Falls tumbles 442 feet down a moss-covered cliff. Visitors often see long-tailed tropical birds looping through the waterfall's mists.

visitor center, which also features a video on ranching and a tour of the ranch's historic homes. *Paniolo* can be seen in action at rodeos held in Waimea all summer long.

8 Mookini Luakini Heiau

Rte. 250 (the Kohala Mountain Road) breezes past green volcanic pastures that are knee-high in sweet grasses and outlined by rows

of stately Norfolk Island pines and fragrant eucalyptus trees. Vistas are wide and handsome, as hills ripple one into another on their way to the sea.

The most famous of Hawaii's warrior kings, King Kamehameha I, who united all of the islands by 1810, launched his military campaign from North Kohala. This little-visited region is awash with

Gentle waves lap the shore of Hapuna Beach State Park.

sacred and historic sites, including many stone temples *(heiaus)*. One of the oldest is Mookini Luakini, built in A.D. 480; it stands along the same dirt road as King Kamehameha's birthplace, just beyond the turnoff to Upolu Airport as you head farther west on Rte. 270.

9 Lapakahi State Historical Park

Tucked above a flawless beach, this 260-acre park chronicles early Hawaiian village life through reenactments of daily activities. Paths wander past the stone walls and foundations of a partially restored 600-year-old coastal settlement where people lived off the land, the sea, and their own wits. Some of the plants they depended on—hau wood for canoes, hala leaves for woven baskets, and medicinal noni fruits—still flourish here.

10 Puukohola Heiau National Historic Site

Just south of Kawaihae, the reef-protected shore at Samuel M. Spencer Beach Park offers the best swimming and snorkeling in the area. A path from the beach leads to the Puukohola National Historic Site, where King Kamehameha I, acting on the advice of a prophet, erected a temple in honor of a war god to ensure victory over his adversaries. Measuring 224 feet by 100 feet, the *heiau* was built from rocks and boulders that were fitted together without mortar. On the day it was dedicated, the man who would be king helped fulfill the prophecy by having his principal rival slain as he arrived for the ceremony.

11 Puako Petroglyphs

Rejoin Rte. 19 (now known as the Queen Kaahumanu Highway) as it speeds southward. Just beyond the turnoff for Hapuna Beach State Park is the entrance to the Mauna Lani Resort, where a sign shows the way to the Puako Petroglyphs. A half-mile trail winds past lava boulders incised with mysterious markings from the past: turtles, warriors, fish, and enigmatic spirals. The 3,000 petroglyphs in and near Puako are some of the oldest and best rock carvings in Hawaii.

12 Kaloko-Honokohau National Historical Park

Continuing south, you'll find an intriguing waypoint. Designated as a National Historical Landmark in 1962, then a National Park in 1978, there are more than 200 archaeological sites to be found in this 1,160-acre park. Its resources hold the secrets to Hawaii's historic culture and its unique wildlife. Remember that half the park is oceanfront—take time to swim, hike, and bird-watch.

13 Kona Coast

As Rte. 19 continues south, bougainvilleas brighten miles of the monochromatic lava moonscape beside the highway. Inland are the steep slopes of long-dormant Mt. Hualalai; on the seaward side the lava cascades to the water's edge. In the resort town of Kailua-Kona, Rte. 19 becomes Rte. 11.

Napoopoo Road, branching off at the town of Captain Cook, careers through plots of coffee trees—the only gourmet coffee crop in the United States—on its way to Kealakekua Bay. Divers and snorkelers converge at the park here, a Marine Life Conservation District where tropical fish prowl the coral reefs. In 1779 Capt. James Cook, the British explorer, sailed into this bay shortly before he was killed by natives. An obelisk on a spit of land across the bay commemorates his death.

14 Puuhonua O Honaunau National Historical Park

Rte. 160, a narrow coastal route, crosses the crusty lava of the Keei plain as it heads south toward

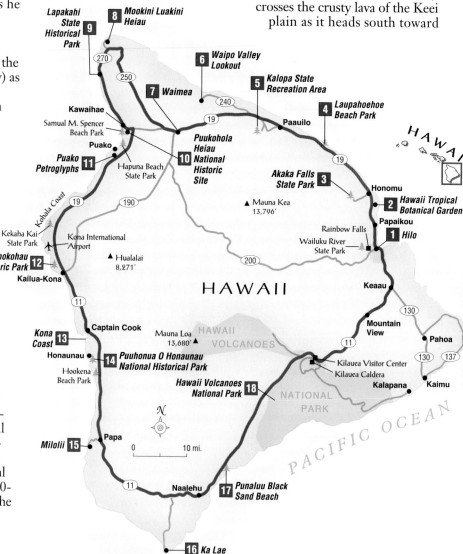

Trip Tips

Length: About 225 miles.

When to go: Thanks to its idyllic tropical setting, Hawaii is a popular destination year-round.

Words to the wise: Set aside at least three days for the trip.

Not to be missed: Snorkeling off the coast provides close-up views of coral and brightly colored fish.

Nearby attractions: Mauna Loa Macadamia Nut Corporation, Hilo. The Laurance S. Rockefeller Collection of Asian and Pacific Art, Kohala Coast. The Lyman House Memorial Museum, Hilo.

Further information: Big Island Visitors Bureau, 250 Keawe St., Hilo, HI 96720; tel. 800-648-2441, www.bigisland.org.

Honaunau Bay and Puuhonua, the island's only remaining ancient place of refuge. Until 1819 the protocol of daily life in Hawaii was governed by kapu, a sacred code of rules and prohibitions. Sanctuaries like the one here were set aside for defeated warriors and transgressors, who were spared execution and reinstated into society if they managed to reach one of these havens.

Highlights at the 180-acre historical park include ancient royal fish ponds, a wall fitted with jagged lava, a *heiau* that once held the remains of 23 chiefs, and countless wide-eyed tiki idols.

From Puuhonua Rte. 160 winds through groves of macadamia nut trees. A side road leads to St. Benedict's Church. Its interior is embellished with folksy biblical murals—the handiwork of a priest.

Kilauea's lava flows to the sea like a river. Visit at night, when you'll see fire and brimstone worthy of Dante.

15 Milolii

A paved spur off Rte. 11 descends to the black sands of Hookena Beach Park, a good spot for surfing. Farther south, a narrow road weaves across sterile lava flows toward Milolii, where fishermen ply the waters in motorized outriggers, one of Hawaii's last fishing villages.

16 Ka Lae

As the drive rounds the southern tip of the island, take the turnoff at South Point Road for a visit to Ka Lae, the southernmost point in the United States—nearly 500 miles farther south than Key West. Some historians believe that Hawaii's first settlers landed here, perhaps as early as A.D. 150.

17 Punaluu Beach Park

Rte. 11 passes through Naalehu—the southernmost town in America—before angling north to squeeze between the coastline and Mauna Loa's massive shoulder. Up ahead is one of the region's best recreation spots, Punaluu Black Sand Beach, made popular by its black-sand beach and sea turtles.

18 Hawaii Volcanoes National Park

As Rte. 11 climbs between Mauna Loa, the world's most massive mountain, and Kilauea, the world's most active volcano, the drama mounts with every passing mile. The Hawaiian islands grew over millions of years as rivers of lava poured from their volcanoes, and the spurts of glowing red lava that Kilauea coughs up remind us that the process continues today. Local lore attributes such outbursts to Pele, the goddess of fire, who is said to dwell in Kilauea Caldera and is given to sudden fits of rage. But geologists tell a more scientific, if less colorful, tale for the fires on view at Hawaii Volcanoes National Park—one of the few places on earth where visitors can drive right up to the rim of an active volcano. As magma (a mixture of molten rock, minerals, chemicals, and gases) rises from deep within the earth, it escapes through surface fissures, creating dazzling displays of natural fireworks known as volcanic eruptions.

Leaving the visitor center, follow Crater Rim Drive for 11 miles as it encircles Kilauea Caldera. Stops along the way include the Jaggar Museum, panoramic overlooks of multiple craters, and short walks to steam vents. The half-mile-long Devastation Trail winds through what had been an ohia forest before a 1959 eruption devastated the area. At Thurston (Nahuku) Lava Tube, thick tree ferns and ohia trees nearly engulf lava tunnels, leftovers from an ancient flow.

Barren landscapes quickly give way to forested slopes as the loop draws to a close. Descending 4,000 feet from volcanic marvels to a black lava shoreline, the drive reveals more of the scenic diversity of Hawaii's Big Island paradise.

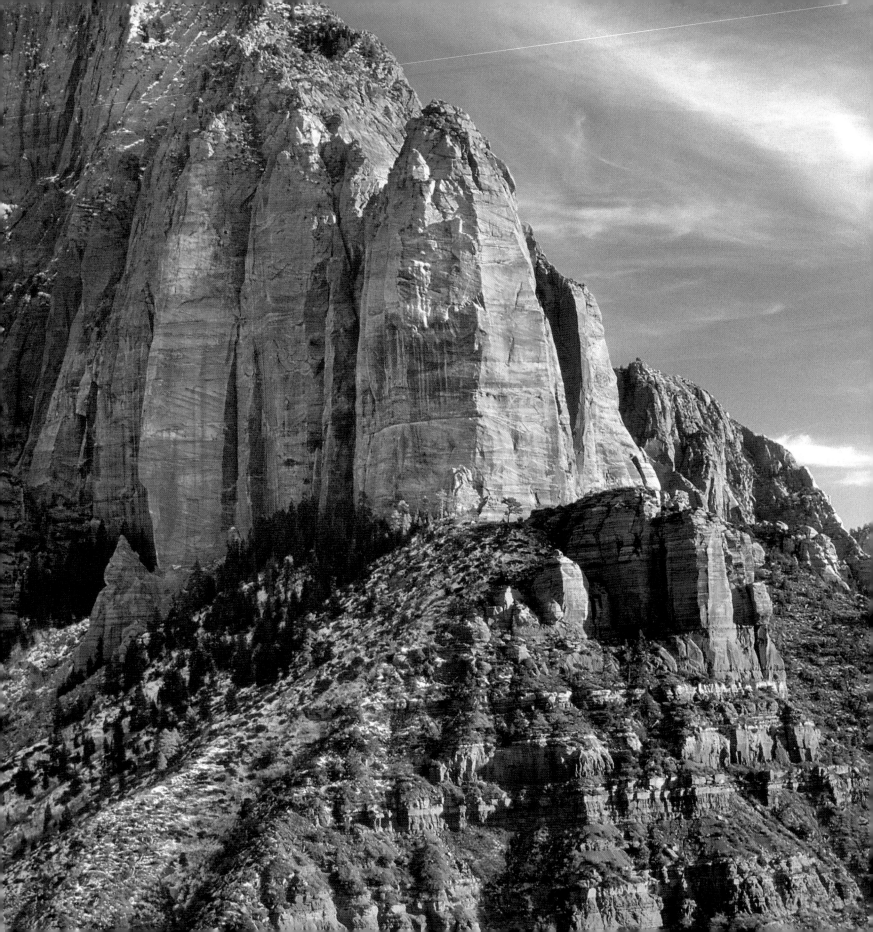

PART 2

The Rocky Mountain States

Idaho Heartland

Departing from Boise, the state's charming capitol, this long-distance drive traverses
a vast backcountry of white-water rivers, hard-edged mountain peaks,
and miles of rolling prairie that turn golden in the summer sun.

Dworshak State Park, located on the western bank of Dworshak Reservoir, is a popular fishing, boating, and archery spot.

Idaho, located at the crossroads of the Rocky Mountains and the Pacific Northwest, enjoys an incredible wealth of scenic diversity. Here, where the members of the Nez Perce tribe have made their home for centuries, a few hours' drive in almost any direction can take you from desert to mountain or from valley to prairie, and then back again. Best of all, some 4 million acres of the state are federally protected wilderness areas; they remain much as they have always been since the Lewis and Clark expedition first ventured into the area, crossed the Bitterroot Range in 1805, and beheld an unspoiled land they decided might best be called, simply, paradise.

1 Boise

French Canadian fur trappers, roaming the West in search of pelts, first explored this area in the early 1800s. Impressed by the abundance of cottonwoods along the riverbanks, they decided to name the place *Boisé*, which means "wooded." American settlers eventually followed, traveling west on the Oregon Trail, and today, with more than 140,000 residents, Boise is Idaho's largest city as well as the state capital.

In a wide valley backed by the silvery ridges of the faraway Owyhee Range, Boise boasts an appealing mix of the old and the new, the natural and the man-made. The capitol, with its neo-classical dome, is the stately centerpiece, while the historic district, Old Boise, lies at the east end of downtown. Also worth a visit are the sprawling grounds of Julia Davis Park, which contains Zoo Boise and offers charming narrated excursions aboard an antique steam-engine train. The Boise Greenbelt, perhaps the city's proudest achievement, features nearly 30 miles of trails along the banks of the Boise River—the very area that inspired the early fur trappers.

2 Payette River Scenic Byway

For a refreshing contrast to city life, head north on Rte. 55, the Payette River Scenic Byway. Leading into wooded wildlands, it soon becomes one of the loveliest roadways in the state. The scenery really picks up at mile 23, where an overlook affords a view of Horseshoe Bend, a lengthy curve in the Payette River.

At Banks, some 14 miles farther along, the river splits into two branches. Winding upward between steep, forested slopes, the byway follows the northern fork, which makes a tumultuous 1,700-foot descent in a mere 15 miles.

3 Cascade Reservoir

A dam on the North Fork Payette River, completed in 1948, created this large reservoir, which comes into view about three miles north of Cascade, a popular resort town. Pine forests cloak the mountain

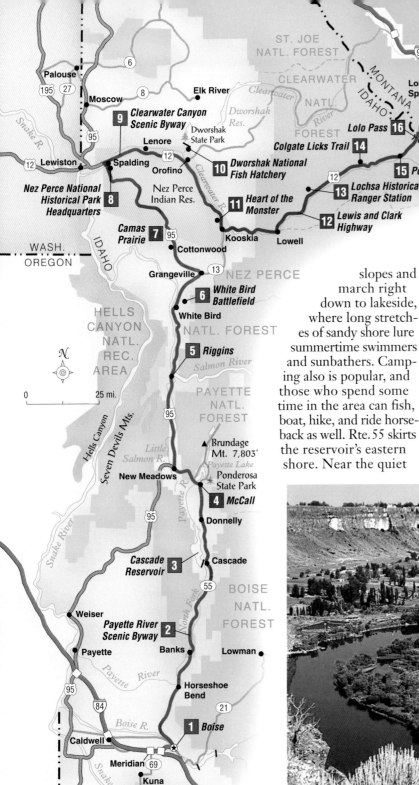

slopes and march right down to lakeside, where long stretches of sandy shore lure summertime swimmers and sunbathers. Camping also is popular, and those who spend some time in the area can fish, boat, hike, and ride horseback as well. Rte. 55 skirts the reservoir's eastern shore. Near the quiet little town of Donnelly, the route crosses a broad plateau, where herds of cattle graze contentedly in lush green pastures of tall grass.

4 McCall

The town of McCall, nestled beside Payette Lake, traces its beginnings to 1891, when Tom McCall and his family—part of a wagon train heading to the west—stopped and decided to stay. It's easy to see why: Payette Lake, with its azure water and forested shores, is indeed an enchanting place.

Word of the lovely setting has long since spread, and the town is now a popular vacation spot, with each season offering something special. In spring you can troll the lake's depths for rainbow trout and kokanee salmon. Summers are an ideal time to take a dip and then dry off in the bright mountain sunshine. Hiking, of course, remains excellent most of the year, but the trails at Ponderosa State Park are especially pleasing when autumn colors contrast vividly with the lake. Come winter, nearby Brundage Mountain attracts skiers with its fine powder snow. From the slopes visitors can enjoy a heart-stopping panorama that stretches from the gentle scoop of Long Valley to Seven Devils Mountains and neighboring Oregon.

5 Riggins

Like a world-class museum that offers one masterpiece after another, the drive reveals new delights with nearly every turn. Veering away from the North Fork Payette River, it hooks up with Rte. 95 at the town of New Meadows and heads north along the

Opportunities abound in the Snake River Canyon for white-water rafting, off-road recreation, and hiking.

Little Salmon River. Both the road and the river pass through meadows ablaze with wildflowers in summer, descending toward the tiny town of Riggins and the confluence of the Little Salmon and the Salmon rivers.

With a population of just 450, Riggins is a pleasantly typical Idaho town—friendly, unpretentious, and encompassed on all sides by soothing forested slopes. Once, logging drove the area's economy, but when the local mill burned down in 1980, recreation took center stage. A variety of trips down the Salmon River are now available, with outfitters in Riggins offering guides, rafts, and kayaks. The town also serves as a jumping-off point for expeditions into the wilderness. The Payette National Forest lies to the southeast; to the west are the Seven Devils Mountains and awesome Hells Canyon—at an astounding 8,000 feet, the deepest gorge in North America.

6 White Bird Battlefield

The rolling hills here, covered with grasses that sway gently in the breeze, were not always so peaceful and serene. Back in 1877 a group of Nez Perce Indians and their chief, White Bird, clashed with a party of soldiers and civilian volunteers from Fort Lapwai. What was supposed to be a time for making peace turned violent when, without warning, one of the civilians fired on the Indians. In the ensuing battle, the Nez Perces killed 34 of the government's troops, a third of the fort's force; the Indians had suffered no casualties. Brief and brutal, the battle was the opening salvo of what came to be known as the Nez Perce War.

The White Bird Battlefield, one of 38 widely scattered sites that make up the Nez Perce National Historical Park, occupies about 1,100 acres. A shelter on Rte. 95 offers one of the best places to view the area, with a sweeping panorama of the grassy hills. After taking in the vista, head down the hill to the town of White Bird, where road signs give directions to the battlefield and recall the events of that fateful day.

7 Camas Prairie

Heading north from White Bird, Rte. 95 traverses the lush Camas Prairie, a tapestry of green and gold beneath bright blue skies. For centuries the Nez Perces came here each spring to harvest the nutritious bulbs of the camas lily. No less generous today, the land now produces bumper crops of alfalfa, peas, and wheat.

Grangeville, in the heart of the golden fields, is an agricultural center situated at an elevation of 3,300 feet, the highest—and wettest—point on the Camas. But farming hasn't always been the area's main enterprise; during a gold boom in the late 1800s, the town served as supply depot for the nearby Gospel Mountain and Buffalo Hump mining districts.

The mines have long since closed down, and as in so many places in Idaho, the prospectors of old have been replaced not only by farmers but also by back-packers, anglers, and white-water enthusiasts. The adventurers come to sample the vast pristine tracts of surrounding countryside, including the Selway-Bitterroot, Gospel Hump, Frank Church–River of No Return, and Hells Canyon wilderness areas. Together these tracts form an expanse larger than the combined total areas of Connecticut and Rhode Island.

8 Nez Perce National Historical Park Headquarters

Turning to the west, the drive gradually descends toward Lewiston. As the miles roll by, the temperature as a general rule rises, and golden wheatfields yield to dry hills of tall grass. Notable sights on the way include the trestle bridge at Lawyers Canyon and the wayside at Cottonwood, site of several skirmishes between the Nez Perces and army troops.

Just past Cottonwood, the road enters the Nez Perce reservation and, some 40 miles later, brings you to the headquarters of the Nez Perce National Historical Park. The visitor center, located in the town of Spalding, looks out from its grassy hilltop to lazy Lapwai Creek; it also provides an excellent introduction to the history and culture of the tribe.

9 Clearwater Canyon Scenic Byway

A short way past Spalding, turn east on Rte. 12 for the start of a winding ascent beside the Clearwater River. Lewis and Clark came this way in 1805, and relatively little has changed since then. The towns along this stretch are small and far apart, resulting in a wild, unspoiled landscape—forged in large part by ancient volcanic activity—that teems with a seemingly endless supply of rugged beauty.

Pause at the overlook just a mile past the intersection of Rtes. 95 and 12 to look for the unusual basalt formations known as the Ant and the Yellowjacket. You might also want to visit the Lenore Archaeological Site, about 15 miles to the east, where Indian artifacts, some of them 10,000 years old, have been unearthed. Then, 12 miles farther upriver, the road leads to Canoe Camp, once a bivouac of Lewis and Clark. Preparing for their trip west, the explorers spent their time there making canoes, using the traditional Nez Perce method of burning out tree trunks.

10 Dworshak National Fish Hatchery

After crossing the Clearwater at Orofino (a Spanish word meaning "fine gold"), a short side trip on Rte. 7 wends to the Dworshak National Fish Hatchery. Every year this high-tech facility—the largest of its kind—releases about 4 million young steelhead and salmon into the Clearwater River. The fish then swim 500 miles to the Pacific, only to return years later to spawn. Behind the hatchery Dworshak Reservoir stretches its blue finger 54 miles into the timbered wilds.

The Salmon River near Riggins is a favorite spot for days of white-water rafting and kayaking.

11 Heart of the Monster

What the Garden of Eden is to Jews and Christians, Heart of the Monster is to the Nez Perces—the place where life began. According to ancient belief, the god Coyote slew a great monster from whose blood and flesh arose most Indian peoples. From the beast's heart, Coyote fashioned a race known as the Nee Mee Poo, today's Nez Perces. The Heart of the Monster, a 30-foot basalt outcrop near East Kamiah, sits on the banks of the Clearwater River, exactly where Coyote left it.

12 Lewis and Clark Highway

Just east of Lowell, a sign warns travelers that there are no service stations for the next 84 miles. Here begins one of Idaho's emptiest stretches of highway—empty, that is, of all but the most dramatic and unspoiled scenery. To the southeast lie the Lochsa River and the Selway-Bitterroot Wilderness; to the north, a woodland of Douglas firs and western red cedars covers a precipitous 6,000-foot ridge. Years ago, the only way through these mountains—as Lewis and Clark found out—was a tortuous Indian path called the Lolo Trail.

13 Lochsa Historical Ranger Station

Built in the 1920s, this station could not be reached by road until 1952, and all the buildings and furnishings on display were either made from local timber or were packed in. (One piece, a good-size desk, is said to have been slung to the side of a mule with a large ham and two bales of hay hung on the other side as counterbalances.) When forest fires raged through this area in 1934, residents of the ranger station jumped into the Lochsa River to escape the flames; miraculously, the ranger station itself survived. A walking tour through the site visits the eight original buildings and a museum of U.S. Forest Service memorabilia, one of the finest collections of its kind and tribute to those whom dedicate their lives to trees.

14 Colgate Licks Trail

Lochsa means "rough water," and the Lochsa River really delivers, especially for the next few miles. Ever-narrowing canyon walls squeeze the river into a series of exhilarating roller-coaster rapids so rough that even the most experienced white-water boatmen are tested to their limits. About 27 miles upriver, you can stretch your legs and walk the Colgate Licks Trail, which leads to two natural hot springs. Bring along a camera, for the mineral deposits at the springs attract a variety of wildlife, particularly at dawn and dusk. Be patient and you might spot elk, deer, and possibly even a bear.

15 Powell

Thirteen miles short of the Montana border lies Powell, a rest stop where food, fuel, and lodging are all available. (Fill the tank: the next service station is more than 50 miles away.) Traveling westward in the fall of 1805, the explorers Lewis and Clark paused here—also for a rest. Starving, exhausted, and soaked by persistent rains, they reluctantly were forced to butcher one of their own colts for food. Clark commemorated the event by naming a nearby stream Colt Killed Creek.

Another corner of this wilderness recalls the name of an award-winning author, conservationist, and historian—Bernard De Voto—who camped beside a branch of the Lochsa while he edited the journals hew as writing of Lewis and Clark. Just upstream on the riverbank, a grove of majestic red cedars is known as the De Voto Memorial Grove.

16 Lolo Pass

This high mountain pass, perched at an elevation of 5,233 feet, was once traversed by local Indians, who migrated in a seasonal pattern back and forth between their bison hunting grounds in present-day Montana and the fertile fields that spread across the wide prairies of Idaho.

A visitor center at the pass offers historical accounts of Lewis and Clark, whose expedition made an arduous trek over these wind-swept peaks, part of the craggy Bitterroots. (Once over their ridges, you will want to adjust your watches to the mountain time zone, an hour later.) Beyond, the roadway makes a twisting descent toward Lolo Hot Springs, a gateway town for the equally spectacular wilds of Montana, known far and wide to visitors and locals alike as Big Sky Country.

The Seven Devils Mountains parallel the Idaho–Oregon border in the Hell's Canyon area.

Salmon–Bitterroot Country

High in the Rocky Mountains of Idaho and Montana, this winding drive, following in places in the footsteps of Lewis and Clark, tours sharp-edged peaks and swift rivers.

Stanley Lake at the base of Mt. McGown in the Sawtooth National Recreation Area.

The ancestral home of two Indian tribes, the Shoshones and Flatheads, the Salmon and Bitterroot valleys witnessed an influx of adventurers in the 1800s—from trappers, mountain men, and gold and silver prospectors dreaming of riches to cowboys hoping only to survive the winter. No matter who has come and gone, the remote backcountry remains an inspiring realm, with roiling rivers, craggy peaks, and far-off vistas that lure you ever onward.

1 Stanley

Looking just as jagged as their name implies, the Sawtooth Mountains form a striking backdrop for Stanley, a throwback to the Old West, where the citizens take pride in a relaxed boots-and-jeans lifestyle. The Salmon River, the longest free-flowing waterway located in the lower-48 states, orginates high in the hills, fed year-round by melting snows—and passes right through town.

Rte. 75 follows the river, which snakes out of the Stanley Basin between high cliffs. Douglas firs and other conifers predominate in the forests, but aspens appear here and there as well, brightening the mountains' evergreen slopes with autumnal splashes of gold.

2 Sunbeam

Once in the town of Sunbeam, you'll notice the ruins of an old dam. The only such structure ever built on the Salmon River, it was erected in 1910 to supply power for a nearby mill and mines. Since it prevented salmon from swimming upstream to spawn, however, residents agreed to circumvent it, and in 1934 a well-placed charge of dynamite once again unleashed the river's flow.

Partially unpaved forest roads lead north out of Sunbeam to two early gold-mining camps, Custer and Bonanza. Both communities boomed when rich veins of ore were discovered around 1875, and both were all but abandoned by 1911. Sightseers can explore the ghost towns, where dance halls once resounded with rollicking piano tunes. A museum in Custer's old schoolhouse tells the story of those earlier days.

3 Challis

The drive to Challis, a small town with lodging and services, offers many opporunities to observe the region's wildlife. At Indian Riffles, for example, an overlook on Rte. 75 offers views of spawning salmon in the fall. The road then heads east and north, never straying far from the river.

Along the way, you might spot dippers, aquatic birds that resemble chubby brown wrens. Overhead, golden eagles sail across the sky, their graceful flight a nearly perfect symbol of the freedom one finds among the Rockies. The area is also inhabited by bighorn sheep,

::::: **Trip Tips** :::::

Length: About 250 miles.

When to go: Driving conditions are best in summer; winters are cold and snowy, especially at higher elevations.

Nearby attractions: Painted Rocks State Park, with camping and watersports, southwest of Hamilton, MT, on Rte. 473. Lake Como, nestled in a valley to the west of Darby, MT, on Como Rd.

Further information: Idaho Travel Council, 700 West State St., Boise, ID 83720; tel. 800-635-7820, www.visitidaho.org.

which winter on the alpine slopes, and mountain goats, sure-footed creatures that roam the uppermost cliffs at will.

4 Cronks Canyon

By the time the drive reaches the town of Ellis, low bare hills give way to the steep walls of Cronks Canyon. Farther along, the landscape opens once again, and farms and ranches abound. Keep an eye out here in springtime for Idaho's state bird, the mountain bluebird.

5 Salmon

Hemmed in by sheer cliffs, the dangerous, churning rapids of the Salmon River—a powerful torrent that the Shoshone tribe believed no human could survive —have earned the waterway the nickname River of No Return. Eventually, however, boatmen learned to master its white water, and today thrilling raft trips and jet-boat tours are available.

Surrounded by tall mountain ranges, the town of Salmon is also the home of the Sacajawea Interpretive and Education Center, celebrating the Lemhi-Shoshone woman who served as interpreter for Lewis and Clark as they crossed the Bitterroot Mountains. A one-mile-long walk brings her historic culture to life.

White-water outfitters offer a variety of trips, which range in length from a few hours to several days. Despite the remoteness of the setting, a day spent shooting rapids ends not with a can of beans but with a sizzling steak at a comfortable camp under the stars.

6 Lost Trail Pass

After being told by Shoshone Indians that the Salmon River could not be navigated, the explorers Lewis and Clark decided to scale this pass on September 3, 1805. What they encountered was by no means a leisurely hike. In fact, one member of the party described their route as "the worst...that was ever travelled." Today, following in the footsteps of Lewis and Clark, Rte. 93 zigzags up through dense forests and then, cresting at about 7,000 feet, descends into Montana. Farther along, the East Fork of the Bitterroot River comes into view, its chilly waters rushing to the valleys below.

7 Bitterroot Range

The byway continues through a fairly narrow valley, which eventually widens to permit glimpses of the Bitterroot Range to the west. Bitterroot, the plant that gave these mountains their name, once was a staple food of Indians, who boiled or baked the roots to lessen the bitter taste. Today it is Montana's state flower, and locals cherish the lily's pinkish bloom as a sure sign that spring has come. Other plant life includes towering ponderosa pines, cedars, firs, and larches, all of which blanket the lower slopes of the Bitterroots. The mountain crests, however, remain bare, their granite crowns battered by the elements into knife-edged horns and arêtes. South of the town of Darby, Trapper Peak rises some 10,157 feet.

Big Hole National Battlefield is a short detour from Lost Trail Pass.

8 East Side Highway

Near Hamilton, towering cottonwoods arch over the Bitterroot River, which meanders gently now after its tumultuous fall from the highlands. Exit onto the East Side Highway (Rtes. 269 and 203), which ventures to two noteworthy sites. The first is the Daly Mansion, a 42-room showplace begun in 1897 by a mining magnate. Then, at Stevensville, the highway nears the Lee Metcalf National Wildlife Refuge, where ospreys are making a welcome comeback.

9 Travelers Rest Historic Site

Before heading west for the Bitterroot Mountains and Lolo Pass, Lewis and Clark camped at this site just off Rte. 93. Nine months later—their trail-blazing journey nearing completion—they bivouacked here again, then returned to St. Louis and the heroes' welcome they so richly deserved.

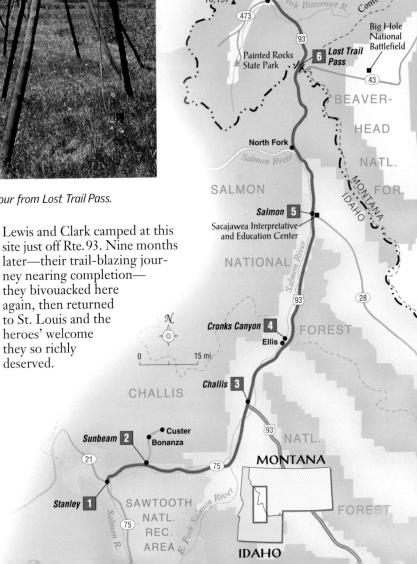

Sawtooth Sampler

Crowned with jagged crests that seem to slice the sky,
the Sawtooth Range extends like a sturdy spine
through the forests of south-central Idaho.

Redfish Lake, near Stanley, is one of the most picturesque lakes in the Sawtooth National Recreation Area.

Travelers in the largely untrodden domain of Sawtooth country are all but guaranteed a surfeit of scenic splendors. As this drive climbs into the rugged mountains of the backcountry—a realm of forests and alpine meadows, rivers and jewel-like lakes—it soon becomes evident why Ernest Hemingway, for one, praised these wilds as being among the most beautiful anywhere.

1 Shoshone Falls

In the city of Twin Falls, an eastward detour on Falls Avenue is rewarded with a look at Shoshone Falls. Plunging an impressive total of some 210 feet, the cascade roars loudest in spring, when snowmelt floods down from the uplands. By summer, though, moderation takes the place of tumult as the Snake River slows down and the once-rampaging falls are tamed.

2 Shoshone

Heading north from Twin Falls, Rte. 93 leaps across the Snake River Canyon on a lengthy bridge that arches 486 feet above the abyss. Beyond the bridge the drive enters a stark, striking landscape, with sagebrush and rumpled lava beds flanking the road. At Shoshone, an old mining center, continue north on Rte. 75 (the Sawtooth Scenic Byway), which leads to Shoshone Ice Caves, chilly lava tubes that are open for tours.

The pink granite peaks of the Sawtooth Range, rising in the northwest, soon make their appearance. If you'd like to venture off the main road, a short side trip to the west leads to Magic Reservoir, a favorite with local anglers. A bit farther along, near the village of Bellevue, visitors in spring and fall sometimes encounter a quaint pastoral scene: shepherds busily tending their flocks.

3 Ketchum and Sun Valley

Encircled by long, steep slopes, these two towns—amply supplied with restaurants, shops, and lodging—spread across part of the Wood River valley, a popular resort center. When the snows come, visitors head for Sun Valley's Bald Mountain, a world-famous ski area. In the warmer months the nearby wilds come alive, inviting nature lovers to linger and explore.

Ernest Hemingway, a onetime resident of this area, often stayed in the opulent Sun Valley Lodge, where he penned portions of *For Whom the Bell Tolls*. Admirers of the novelist can pay their respects at his grave in northern Ketchum's small cemetery.

4 Sawtooth National Recreation Area

Wildflower enthusiasts will want to time their visits for early summer, when the slopes of the Sawtooths are abloom with the brilliant colors of such beauties as lupines, scarlet gilias, fireweeds, bluebells, and columbines. Miles of trails thread through the forests of firs, pines, and aspens, and crystal-clear streams and rivers lace the large recreation area. If you decide to stay awhile, the visitor center is a valuable resource; located eight miles north of Ketchum, it offers trail maps and guidebooks. When exploring, be on the lookout for mountain goats, pronghorns, bighorn sheep, and elk.

5 Galena Summit Overlook

A half-mile past Galena Summit, which stands at an elevation of 8,701 feet, this overlook, perched near a terraced hillside with aspen groves and willows, commands a not-to-be-missed view. In the distance to the north lies the Sawtooth Range. Nearer at hand the Salmon River dominates the scene: some 2,000 feet below, the Salmon Valley spreads out like a vast rumpled cape, its rounded contours molded by the same slow passage of glaciers that honed the jagged peaks thousands of years ago.

A five-mile descent leads to the valley floor and the Salmon River, where chinook salmon hatch in the spring, then begin their long journey—about 400 miles—to the Pacific Ocean. To learn about the remarkable fish, visit the Sawtooth Hatchery on the river's western bank. Another springtime sight, the sandhill crane, can often be found high-stepping through the wetlands that line portions of the highway. If you'd like to take advantage of local camping, consider Alturas Lake, good also for picnics and swims.

6 Redfish Lake

Named for the sockeye salmon that spawn there, Redfish Lake, nestled as it is among tall peaks, resembles a polished mirror ringed with mountain gems. Redfish Lodge offers a relaxing escape from civilization, and if you feel like roughing it, several campgrounds are available. Little Redfish Lake, just up the access road,

The Snake River Canyon near Twin Falls, upstream from Shoshone Falls.

a super storm that sent flames 200 feet into the sky. It took nearly three weeks for more than 2,300 firefighters, working around the clock, to tame the inferno.

At final count some 46,000 acres were devastated by the Lowman burn. The damage to the forest, in spite of the fact that much clearing and replanting has been done, is quite evident as you drive through the area. As an aid to understanding the blaze, interpretive signs, placed at intervals along the highway, detail the fire's path and its aftermath.

10 Idaho City

Outfitted with powerful hydraulic pumps, large dredges were once a common sight in Idaho City, where one of our country's largest gold booms occurred in the 1860s. Remnants of those early times flank the byway: century-old gravel mounds and neatly piled cobblestones that were left behind at old excavations. For insights into the past, visit the Boise Basin Historical Museum, which traces the history of local mines. Rte. 21 then leads travelers back to city life in Boise, but not before unveiling a succession of scenic views that include rivers, lakes, forests, and boundless skies.

bans motorized craft, a rule that makes for a particularly peaceful day spent fishing, canoeing, kayaking, and exploring.

7 Elk Mountain Overlook

The drive continues north to the town of Stanley, then switches onto Rte. 21, the Ponderosa Pine Scenic Byway. For one of the finest vistas in the area, take Stanley Lake Road—about five miles farther along—to Elk Mountain Overlook. The view includes Stanley Lake, a shimmering alpine oasis in a forest of lodgepole pines.

Back on Rte. 21, the drive threads a pathway through the jagged peaks of the Sawtooths. Blocks of lightly colored granite are exposed at intervals along the road. A close look at these rocks reveals dark veins embedded in their faces—evidence, geologists say, of past upheavals.

8 Sawtooth Overlook

Past Cape Horn, as Rte. 21 nears the edge of Boise National Forest, it loops abruptly southwest toward Banner Summit, then descends through a narrow, steep-walled canyon. Before long, you'll come to Sawtooth Overlook, not only a favorite with photographers but also a spot that offers a last chance to glimpse the Sawtooth Range, now cresting in the east.

This part of the drive, battered by heavy snows, is sometimes closed in winter. Yet, even during the chillier months, Kirkham Hot Springs remain open. Held in tubs, their thermal waters can refresh the weary traveler, and the Forest Service provides a soothing dip free of charge.

If you prefer flowing water—and cooler temperatures—sample the South Fork Payette River. Popular for its trout fishing, it can be just as satisfying for those who are content to simply wet their toes and watch the rapids. About 800 elk live in the river's canyon, which also serves as a wintering area for hundreds of mule deer.

9 Lowman

In July 1989, lightning ignited three separate blazes in the forests near the town of Lowman. Feeding on the thick forest, the fires grew unabated, eventually merging into

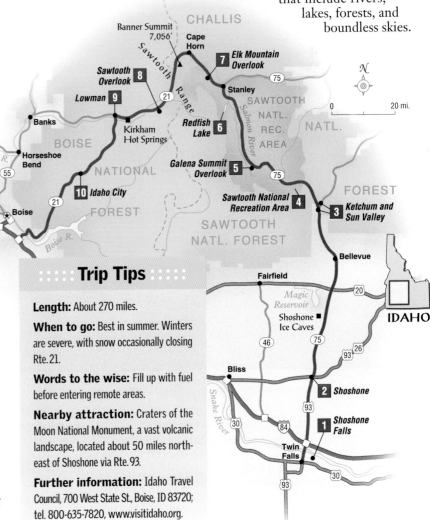

:::::: Trip Tips ::::::

Length: About 270 miles.

When to go: Best in summer. Winters are severe, with snow occasionally closing Rte. 21.

Words to the wise: Fill up with fuel before entering remote areas.

Nearby attraction: Craters of the Moon National Monument, a vast volcanic landscape, located about 50 miles northeast of Shoshone via Rte. 93.

Further information: Idaho Travel Council, 700 West State St, Boise, ID 83720; tel. 800-635-7820, www.visitidaho.org.

In Flathead Indian Country

Cradled between the sky-high peaks of the Rocky Mountains, the broad valleys of Flathead Country unfold as a patchwork of golden hayfields, rolling rangeland, and fragrant cherry orchards.

The sky colors with dusk as twilight settles over Flathead Lake.

Montana may be known as Big Sky Country, but in the state's rugged northwestern corner, the landscape looms just as large. Like the cowboys, prospectors, and pioneers who staked their claim to its riches, nature exists on an epic scale in Flathead Country—where the mountains seem the highest, the valleys the broadest, the rivers the wildest, and the lakes the bluest of blue.

1 Missoula

A brawny western town, Missoula sits in a fertile basin where the Clark Fork, Bitterroot, and Black-foot rivers converge. Through the years the site has served as a natural thoroughfare—first for Salish Indians crossing the mountains to buffalo-hunting grounds on the eastern plains, and much later for travelers on the Northern Pacific Railway, which chose the burgeon-ing town of Missoula as one of the main stops on the line.

Despite a devastating fire in 1884, much of historic Missoula remains. The old downtown district on the north side of the Clark Fork showcases many lovely old structures, including the Missoula Mercantile Building, the county courthouse, and Higgins Block, a group of turn-of-the-century commercial buildings decorated with intricate ironwork and ginger-bread cornices. Across the river the University of Montana, a major research institution, is surrounded by leafy blocks of lavish 19th-century homes. Each day at noon the caroling of bells resounds from the tower at University Hall.

Missoula's mile-long Greenough Park provides a refreshingly scenic hike through stands of conifers and cottonwoods lining the banks of Rattlesnake Creek. Bird-watchers gather here to glimpse warblers, pileated woodpeckers, American dippers, Bohemian and cedar wax-wings, and other avian rarities.

2 Flathead Indian Reservation

Traveling northwest from Missoula on I-90, the drive traces the Clark Fork for eight miles through grassy bottomland and then turns sharply north on Rte. 93, where it begins to climb. Seven miles later—and about a thousand feet higher, amid forests of Douglas fir and ponderosa pines —you arrive at Evaro and the southern boundary of the Flathead Indian Reservation. Home to more than 5,000 Indians, the reservation encompasses over 1.2 million acres, including much of the valleys to the north and the mountain ranges on either side.

From Evaro, the road descends into the Jocko Valley to Arlee, site of the largest powwow in the northwest, held every summer in July. From there a short, steep climb leads to a turnout with an eye-popping view of the Mission Mountains. Reaching 10,000 feet, these stunning peaks form a barricade of ice and stone that seems to launch skyward from the valley floor. So protected is Mission Valley that the Indians knew it as the "place of encirclement."

3 St. Ignatius Mission

As early as 1840, Jesuit missionaries—known to Indians as Black Robes—visited western Montana, choosing this hillside spot to build their mission in 1854. The structure's plain brick exterior gives little hint of the beauty to be found within; about 50 murals and frescoes with biblical themes adorn the walls and ceiling. Created by Brother Joseph Carignano, a cook at the mission who had no formal training and worked only in his spare time, the paintings—incredibly—were completed within just 13 months.

Encompassing some 18,500 acres, the National Bison Range is a refuge for bison, bighorn sheep, deer, elk, and other creatures.

4 National Bison Range

Backtracking five miles south on Rte. 93 to Ravalli, take Rte. 200 west to Rte. 212, then head north to Moiese, the starting point for a drive through the National Bison Range. Once darkening the plains by the millions, these splendid, shaggy beasts were the victims of wholesale slaughter by the white man in the 19th century. Today relatively few remain, but their numbers are growing, and the National Bison Range is a cornerstone of these restoration efforts. A 19-mile auto tour weaves through a rich pastiche of high-country landscapes—swirling grasslands, timbered hillsides, streamside groves—where bison and a variety of other wild animals

live much as they did before Europeans set foot in the New World.

5 Ninepipe National Wildlife Refuge

Continuing a few miles farther north on Rte. 212, you will reach the Ninepipe National Wildlife Refuge. It encompasses a wetland habitat of marshes, reservoirs, and glacial pothole ponds that each year attract more than 200 species of birds, including Canada geese, mallards, pintails, herons, gulls, cormorants, pheasants, and bald eagles. A viewing site on the east side of Ninepipe Reservoir offers some of the most fascinating viewing, especially in the spring and fall, when the refuge serves as a stopover for migrating flocks.

6 Polson

Famous for its cherry orchards, Polson sits atop the rough glacial moraine fronting Polson Bay, at the southern end of Flathead Lake. It's an energetic town, with a busy waterfront of shops, restaurants, and docks that is perfect for an afternoon stroll. At the bay's southwestern corner, the lake drains into the Lower Flathead River, which runs into a canyon plugged at one end by the Kerr Dam—a spectacular concrete edifice that measures 204 feet in height. To reach the dam, which is two miles downstream, head west on Seventh Avenue to Kerr Dam Road and follow the signs; a long flight of steps leads to a lookout point above the dam with bracing views of the Lower Flathead canyon, a landscape where roiling rapids contrast with arid hills that are virtually inaccessible by road.

7 Flathead Lake

First visible from the top of a gentle rise near Polson, Flathead Lake is the largest natural freshwater lake west of the Mississippi, and one of the loveliest. Embraced by rolling hills, deep green forests, and snowcapped granite peaks, the lake recedes 28 miles into the distance, where its shining surface mingles with the sky. Wooded islands and white sails dot the surface; tidy coves, rocky points, and picturesque camps line its shores. Like the glacier that created it some 12,000 years ago, Flathead Lake leaves an indelible impression on all who behold it for the first time.

Heading northwest from Polson, Rte. 93 cuts briefly inland across grassy hills and then rejoins the lakeshore at Big Arm. At the town marina you can rent a boat for a trip to Wildhorse Island, just off shore. The island—so named, according to legend, because the Flathead Indians once used it to safeguard their horses from enemies—now supports about 100 bighorn sheep.

After arcing around westward-pointing Big Arm Bay, the road heads due north, hugging the lake's ragged shoreline for about 15 miles. Evergreen forest marches straight to the water's edge, and toward sunset the Mission Mountains to the west drape long shadows across its surface.

mile trip on paved and gravel road to the lakeshore, hemmed in on all sides by a close, hilly forest of ponderosa pines. At dusk the only sound you are likely to hear is the splash of jumping trout and salmon, which reach record sizes in these protected mountain waters.

9 Lone Pine State Park

A pretty state park with trails that wind through wildflower meadows

es from Kalispell to the jagged peaks of Glacier National Park, serrating the horizon.

10 Kalispell

Situated on grassland within sight of Swan Peak and the Whitefish Range, the town of Kalispell—from an Indian word for "prairie above the lake"—stands as a living monument to the entrepreneurial spirit and good timing of one man,

the better of him; on a tip from the head of the Great Northern Railroad, Conrad took a chance and moved his enterprise to the Flathead Valley. When the railroad arrived in 1891, Conrad was waiting, and Kalispell was born.

Since those days Kalispell has served as the northern Flathead Valley's unofficial capital, a prosperous rail-and-river town with a busy commercial district and tree-lined residential neighborhoods with the proverbial white-picket fences. The Conrad family mansion, on Woodland Avenue, is the city's showpiece. An elegant Norman-style home with 23 rooms decorated in period furnishings, it abuts a picturesque city park with rose gardens and a duck pond, part of the original Conrad estate.

11 Whitefish

Fifteen miles north of Kalispell, Whitefish is home to Montana's largest ski resort, 7,000-foot Big Mountain. The peak lures visitors in the warm months too, when its slopes are dressed with wildflowers and the views from up top stretch all the way from Flathead Lake to southern Canada. A gondola will whisk you swiftly to the summit, or you can take a "Walk in the Tree-tops" at Big Mountain on platforms and paths 30–60 feet high, in a canopy of fir, cedar, and tamarack.

At the foot of the mountain, Whitefish Lake stretches seven miles into Flathead National Forest. The town of Whitefish, on the lake's southern tip, touts itself as the "recreation capital of Montana" and hosts one of the state's most exuberant winter carnivals, held each February.

12 Hungry Horse Dam

How they survived is a mystery, but when a feisty pair of freight horses named Tex and Jerry wandered away from their logging team during the winter of

St. Ignatius Mission continues a Jesuit tradition that dates to the 1840s.

8 Lake Mary Ronan

Lake Mary Ronan may seem positively petite—and pleasantly secluded—compared to immense Flathead Lake. To reach it, take the turnoff in Dayton; then follow the signs for a short, three-

and forest glens, Lone Pine would be worth a stop even if it didn't offer some of the most arresting views in Flathead Country. From the visitor center a loop trail leads to three cliffside lookouts whose commanding perspective stretch-

Charles Conrad. His Virginia plantation lost in the Civil War, Conrad headed west to Montana, establishing a successful freight operation in Ft. Benton. In the process he amassed a considerable fortune, but restlessness got

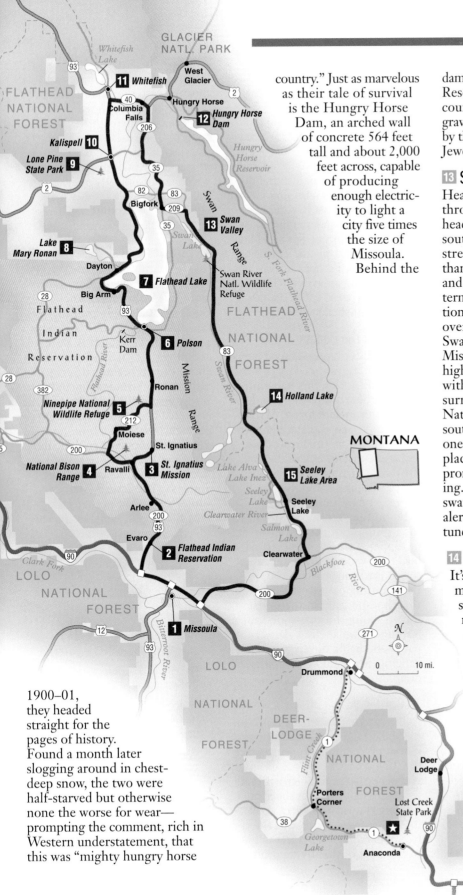

country." Just as marvelous as their tale of survival is the Hungry Horse Dam, an arched wall of concrete 564 feet tall and about 2,000 feet across, capable of producing enough electricity to light a city five times the size of Missoula. Behind the dam, 34-mile-long Hungry Horse Reservoir reaches deep into backcountry forest. Encircled by a gravel road, the reservoir is flanked by the Great Bear Wilderness and Jewel Basin Hiking Area.

13 Swan Valley

Heading south, the drive passes through the village of Bigfork, heads east on Rte. 209, and turns south onto Rte. 83—a beautiful stretch of road that, for more than 90 miles, parallels the Swan and the Clearwater rivers before terminating at Clearwater Junction nearly due south. Presided over by the stony peaks of the Swan Range to the east and the Mission Range to the west, the highway seems to meld gracefully with the idyllic wilderness that surrounds it. The Swan River National Wildlife Refuge, at the southern tip of Swan Lake, is but one of several pleasant stopping places along the route, and it promises superb wildlife watching. In this undeveloped tract of swampland and lakeshore, keep alert for signs of moose, bears, tundra swans, and bald eagles.

14 Holland Lake

It's hard to say precisely what makes this small body of water so special. Perhaps it's the lake's remoteness, its splendid sense of isolation; perhaps, too, it's the unassuming beauty of the place, the utter calm of the lake's blue surface in the mists of dawn or the blaze of an evening sunset. Located at the edge of the vast Bob Marshall Wilderness Area, Holland Lake also serves as a trailhead for one of the most popular hiking and horseback riding routes into this immense natural reserve.

Star Route

★ Pintler Scenic Route

Beginning at Anaconda, an old copper-smelting town, Rte. 1 traces an arc of about 60 scenic miles northwest to Drummond. Near Anaconda, mountain goats scale 1,000-foot limestone cliffs at Lost Creek State Park. As the drive heads west through Deerlodge National Forest, it skirts lovely Georgetown Lake and enters Flint Creek Valley, where the surrounding mountains harbor garnets, sapphires, and intriguing fossils. Paralleling Flint Creek, the drive stretches north past old mining towns (some are now ghost towns) and cattle ranches to its terminus on I-90 at Drummond.

Larger than the state of Rhode Island, "the Bob" (as it is known locally) straddles the Continental Divide and embraces almost 2 million acres of forest.

15 Seeley Lake Area

Flowing south to the Blackfoot, the Clearwater River forms a chain of picture-perfect lakes—Alva, Inez, Seeley, and Salmon—with wide-open views of the Mission and Swan mountains. A unique way to explore the area is by taking the Clearwater Canoe Trail, a three-mile downstream float with a one-mile hike back to the put-in point. Splendid by day, the ride is doubly so at dusk, when loons suffuse the air with their tremulous, haunting cries. Farther on, the drive turns west on Rte. 200 at Clearwater. It then returns to Missoula via the Blackfoot River corridor, the locale so movingly celebrated in *A River Runs Through It*, Norman Maclean's memoir of his boyhood and youth in Montana.

1900–01, they headed straight for the pages of history. Found a month later slogging around in chest-deep snow, the two were half-starved but otherwise none the worse for wear—prompting the comment, rich in Western understatement, that this was "mighty hungry horse

Going-to-the-Sun Road

Twisting and turning as it climbs through the mountains
of northwestern Montana, this drive reveals
the wild and wondrous essence of Glacier National Park.

St. Mary Lake, with tiny Wild Goose Island seemingly adrift in its center.

At the first signs of spring, workers begin to clear the snow—up to 80 feet deep in places—from Going-to-the-Sun Road, a job that takes two months to complete. The time and effort prove worthwhile, though, for when traffic finally begins to flow, visitors are treated to a nonstop show of stirring views. Most who make the trip will be inclined to agree with Glacier's founding father, who dubbed the park the Crown of the Continent.

1 Lake McDonald

Before heading into the heart of the park, you might want to acquaint yourself with some of its plants and animals, which are featured in exhibits at the Agpar visitor center. Thus informed, you can be on the lookout for the real thing as you set out on Going-to-the-Sun Road. For 10 miles or so, the highway hugs the once wooded shore of Lake McDonald, the site of forest fires in 2003 that charred many of the trees on its opposite shore.

Leaving the lake, the drive tunnels through a forest of mountain hemlocks and red cedars as it begins its climb beside McDonald Creek. Along the way, it passes McDonald Falls, where a thunderous roar heralds a stunning view of the cascade. Just beyond lies a marshy area frequented by moose. They come to probe the pond bottoms for aquatic plants, a favorite summer food. Perhaps surprisingly, the hulking animals—a bull can weigh more than 1,000 pounds—are accomplished swimmers.

2 Trail of the Cedars

Thick stands of moss-draped hemlocks and fragrant cedars cast a cool shade across this half-mile elevated boardwalk that winds through an ancient forest. Myriad ferns and mosses, glistening with dew, flourish on the forest floor, and at the eastern end of the trail, the faint murmur of Avalanche Creek, slipping through a small gorge, lends a musical note.

Be on the alert along streams for a glimpse of the water ouzel, or dipper, a small slate-colored bird that walks underwater in its search for food. Listen, too, for the haunting calls of the varied thrush, especially in the moist forests along the two-mile trail leading to Avalanche Lake. At the path's end half a dozen waterfalls, dancing down 2,000-foot cliffs, drain into the sparkling lake.

3 Garden Wall

As the road begins its steady ascent, the cedars and hemlocks give way to scattered stands of spruces and firs. Once past Red Rock Point, you may gasp as the Garden Wall first comes into view. A sheer ridge cresting thousands of feet above, its spine makes up part of the Continental Divide. Water falling to the west of the divide drains toward the Pacific; to the east it flows toward the Atlantic.

A fire in 1967, sparked by lightning, blazed through the woodlands in this area. Reduced to mere matchsticks, the charred skeletons of trees now punctuate the slopes, which are turning green again as shrubs and fledgling pines make a comeback, reclaiming this rugged, once-devastated landscape.

4 Birdwoman Falls

Just beneath the Garden Wall's great shadow, the drive meanders along a lengthy zigzag known as the Loop. Climbing ever higher into the thinning air, it arrives at a landscape of waterfalls, peaks, and plunging valleys. Perched above the timberline, this realm boasts many wonders, including Birdwoman Falls. At its best when bolstered by meltwaters, the cascade gushes down a mountainside. Two miles farther along lies Weeping Wall, where several streams descend a craggy cliff. Some say the cascades lament winter's end, but perhaps they shed tears of joy, celebrating the advent of spring.

::::: Trip Tips :::::

Length: About 50 miles.

When to go: Going-to-the-Sun Road is usually open from June through mid-October.

Nearby attraction: Waterton Lakes National Park, contiguous to Glacier, lies north of the U.S.–Canada border. The two together are known as Waterton-Glacier International Peace Park.

Words to the wise: Bring sunscreen and warm clothing, such as sweaters and rain gear.

Further information: Glacier National Park, West Glacier, MT 59936; tel. 406-888-5441, www.nps.gov/glac/.

Lake McDonald

MONTANA

5 Logan Pass

The drive's pinnacle at 6,646 feet, Logan Pass is a high point in terms of scenery as well, with massive domes and spinelike ridges looming boldly above the alpine wilds. A stunted forest of contorted firs marks the timberline, but the open slopes and meadows beyond are awash in summer in a sea of wildflowers. Yellow glacier lilies pushing through the last patches of snow are among the showstoppers, along with shooting stars, Indian paintbrushes, and stately wands of beargrass topped with bold clusters of white flowers—airy snowballs that sway in the breeze.

Trails begin and end at the visitor center at Logan Pass, including a boardwalk that wends through a lovely area called the Hanging Gardens. Here as elsewhere at Glacier, remember to scan the surrounding slopes for glimpses of one of the park's signature creatures, the shaggy mountain goat.

6 Jackson Glacier Overlook

This scenic viewpoint, one of many in the park, affords a splendid view of the frozen, gray-blue mass of Jackson Glacier. Jackson, like the 50 or so other glaciers in the park, is but a feeble reminder of the stupendous ice-age glaciers that shaped so much of this region's stunning scenery many years ago.

7 St. Mary Lake

Aspens, alders, and birches, their leaves green in summer but golden in the fall, line the road as the drive descends toward St. Mary Valley and its namesake lake. One glance at the mile-high peaks surrounding the blue expanse of water is enough to explain why Blackfeet Indians called it "the inside lake."

For one of the best roadside views of this mountain gem, pull over at the Wild Goose Island Overlook. Named for a pair of geese that once nested on its shores, the little island seems to float on the otherwise uninterrupted surface of St. Mary Lake.

Cresting in the distance is another unusual sight—Triple Divide Peak, which forms part of the Continental Divide. Imagine three rain drops falling on the mountain: one might flow west toward the Pacific, and the second toward the Atlantic. But the third might flow north across Canada and into the Arctic Ocean.

Up ahead the views open wide, and meadows of bunchgrass fan across the wilds. At Divide Creek the heart-stirring wonders of the park are left behind as you venture on to the vast plains lying to the east—unless, of course, you succumb to the urge to turn around and travel the drive through Glacier National Park again.

Alpine wildflowers fill meadows during Glacier National Park's brief warm spring.

Charlie Russell Country

Under the proverbial Big Sky, where the northern
Great Plains sweep up to the Rocky Mountains,
Montana's classic western landscapes are as bold and grand as ever.

In a scene that might be found anywhere in the region, autumn leaves and weathered wood mark the season's turn.

At the northwestern fringe of our fabled shortgrass prairie, Rte. 89 traverses the country immortalized by turn-of-the-century artist Charles M. Russell. Beginning at the stony peaks of Glacier National Park, near the Canadian border, the route stretches south across a vast patchwork of green and gold to Yellowstone at the northern edge of Wyoming.

1 Browning

Travelers descending the eastern ramparts of the Rocky Mountains in Glacier National Park are often startled by the sight of a yellow sea of grass that seems to go on forever. Few natural boundaries in North America are as abrupt as this, where the grasses of the Great Plains meet the willows and aspens that grow at the base of the Rockies' steep eastern face.

Early travelers ventured here with some trepidation, for this was the fiercely guarded domain of the buffalo-hunting Blackfeet. Today, however, the Indians' descendants welcome visitors to their 1½-million-acre reservation, headquartered in Browning and promoted as a year-round recreation mecca. Browning's Museum of the Plains Indian offers lively displays of the culture that once flourished here.

2 Blackleaf Wildlife Management Area

At the town of Bynum, turn west off Rte. 89 onto Blackleaf Road and drive 16 miles to the Blackleaf Wildlife Management Area in the foothills of the Rockies. Here a gravel road winds through forests of limber pine, ending at Blackleaf Canyon. Stippled in spring with trillium and ladyslipper and visited by a modest herd of mountain goats, the canyon is so beautiful you may want to continue on foot. Look for golden eagles and prairie falcons soaring overhead, and listen for the odd booming sound made by sharp-tailed grouse performing their spring mating dance.

3 Pine Butte Swamp Preserve

As the route continues south, treeless hill country stretches out like an ocean of enormous swells. A few of the wheat farms on the horizon are Hutterite colonies—self-sufficient religious communities begun by European immigrants in the 19th century. Hutterite women all dress alike (in dirndls, plaid aprons, and polka-dot scarfs), and each man has assigned duties (cow boss, pig boss, and the like).

About five miles north of Choteau, the highway reaches the shimmering Teton River, whose pebbly shallows gurgle softly, mimicking the quaking aspens along its banks. Heading west off Rte. 89, a side road follows the Teton for 17 miles. A turn south then leads across the Teton to the Pine Butte Swamp Preserve, an 18,000-acre wildlife sanctuary owned by the Nature Conservancy. The refuge encompasses a tangled swampy bottomland as well as hills, grasslands, and a 500-foot-high sandstone butte. The preserve's peace and quiet is often enlivened by the voices of more than 150 species of birds, which squawk, chitter, quack, trill, hoot, caw, and whistle in blissful abandon. The preserve is also a refuge for grizzlies, whose numbers have decreased markedly since pioneer days, when more than 100,000 roamed throughout western North America.

4 Choteau

Montanans have an expression for the kind of sunlight that breaks through the clouds, casting luminous beams on the prairie below: God Light, they call it. Inspired as much by Montana's broad horizons as by its often celestial light, novelist A. B. Guthrie, Jr., who lived in Choteau, titled his best-known work *The Big Sky*.

Alternating bands of yellow and black (grain and fallow soil) mark the rhythm of planting around Choteau, known for its abundant wheat and barley harvests. The rough quarry stones of the old courthouse reflect the town's pioneer pride, but Choteau also looks to even earlier times. The Old Trail Museum on Main Street displays the fossilized bones of the duck-billed Maisaura dinosaurs, which thrived here long ago. Nearby Egg Mountain, a Maisaura nesting area, yielded the first dinosaur egg found in the Western Hemisphere. Paleontologists from the Museum of the Rockies conduct digs at local "bone beds." Human history is ancient here too: winding across the prairie just west of the Sawtooth Range lies a trail said to have been blazed thousands of years ago by Mongol "proto-Indians" who crossed the land bridge from Asia

Charles M. Russell

Born in Missouri in 1864, Charlie Russell had a special fascination with the cowboys and Indians of the West, which he precociously depicted in his earliest drawings. His parents, concerned about his indifference to schoolwork, sent Charlie to Montana at age 15, hoping the visit would cure him of his obsession with the wild frontier. Instead, Charles Marion Russell became a rough-and-tumble cowboy himself, and over the decades he vividly chronicled—in thousands of inspired oils, watercolors, and bronzes—a way of life that has since faded from the American scene.

during the Pleistocene ice age.

5 Freezout Lake

About 10 miles south of Choteau, the marshes of Freezout Lake appear to the west. During waterfowl migrations in spring and fall, you'll find more birds here than anywhere else in Montana. Well over a million descend upon the 12,000-acre sanctuary, including some 300,000 snow geese and legions of other birds as lovely as their names: long-billed curlews, marbled godwits, black-crowned night herons, white-faced ibises, sandhill cranes, tundra swans, cinnamon teal—even shorebirds from California and gulls from Peru.

6 Great Falls

When Meriwether Lewis first viewed the Great Falls of the Missouri in 1805, he pronounced them the grandest sight he'd ever seen. They *were* grand, those lovely cascades—until the

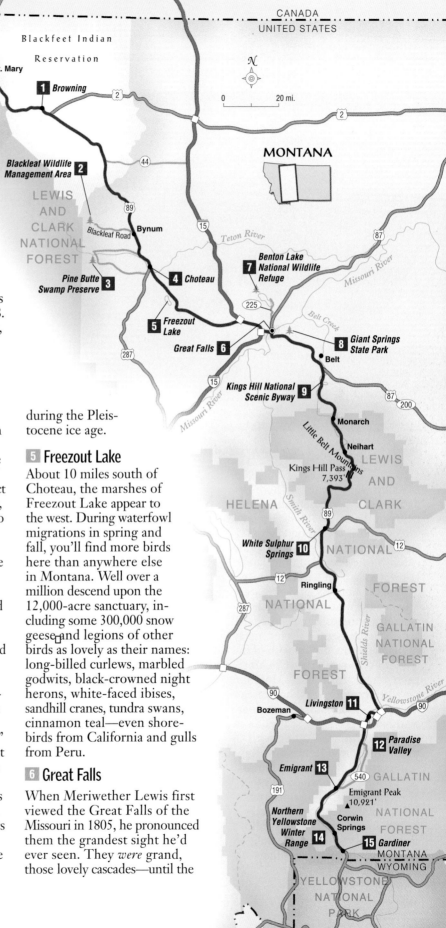

Tepees on the Blackfeet Indian Reservation are a timeless reminder of the past.

Missouri was fattened up here by hydroelectric dams, stopping up many of the original falls. Today Great Falls is the second-largest city in Montana, and its civic pride is based more on commerce and kilowatts than on natural beauty.

The city and its environs are, however, the heart of Charlie Russell country. The renowned artist lived in Great Falls for much of his life, drawing a wealth of inspiration from its cow-punching past. The C. M. Russell Museum on 13th Street North showcases his work—you'll find oil paintings, watercolors, sketches, sculptures in wood and bronze—along with many illustrated letters and Russell memorabilia. Included in its collection are the works of other Western artists. The museum complex also features Russell's house and the log cabin studio in which he produced the bulk of his remarkable work documenting his times.

7 Benton Lake National Wildlife Refuge

Located about 12 miles north of Great Falls, this refuge provides a 12,000-acre way station for ducks, geese, swans, and other migrating birds. Its ponds are prairie potholes, created by the melting of buried blocks of glacial ice. One way to see the refuge is via the Prairie Marsh Wildlife Drive.

The farmlands surrounding the refuge came under the plow after the Civil War, when paddle wheelers brought sodbusters 2,000 miles up the Missouri to nearby Ft. Benton, an old cavalry outpost said to be the world's most inland port. The fort's ruins—on a quiet riverbank below chalk-white bluffs—do seem a long way from St. Louis, to say nothing of New Orleans.

8 Giant Springs State Park

East of Great Falls on the Missouri's south bank, between the Black Eagle Dam and Rainbow Dam, 190 million gallons of chilly mineral-rich water still gush daily from rock fissures at Giant Springs State Park. One of the largest freshwater fonts in America, it is thought to be fed by rain and melting snow from the Little Belt Mountains southeast of town. Viewed from Great Falls, the range's glacier-worn contours bring to mind a huddle of sheep.

9 Kings Hill National Scenic Byway

Much of the country south of Great Falls has been plowed, logged, or mined, but its grandeur and serenity remain undiminished. There's God Light here: sunbeams and cloud shadows caress the rolling prairie and fields of grain.

Tracing some 70 miles, much of it along Belt Creek, the Kings Hill National Scenic Byway heads due south from the junction of Rtes. 87 and 89, near Belt, to White Sulphur Springs. Early on, the dusky brow of Tiger Butte looms to the west as the road climbs Monarch Canyon, whose corridor of pale limestone passes a chute of navigable Belt Creek white water known as the Sluice Boxes. Lodgepole and ponderosa pines mark the fringe of the Lewis and Clark National Forest, which cloaks the slopes of the Little Belt Range. When breezes stir, aspens seem to applaud your arrival in Monarch, an 1880s silver-mining town in the morning shadow of Sun Mountain. Like nearby Neihart, Monarch prospered briefly, but the boomtowners' hopes were dashed when silver prices plummeted in 1893. The sleepy hamlets now rely mainly on silver from skiers, but the towns' Victorian-style homes serve as monuments to a hopeful past.

Southbound from Neihart, the road climbs to 7,393-foot Kings Hill Pass and the Showdown Ski Area. From Porphyry Lookout atop the ski area (open to motorists in July and August), an exquisite panorama takes in the Little Belt peaks and—on a clear day—the Absaroka Range to the south. If you can see the steeples of the Absarokas, your gaze extends some 100 miles to the south, nearly to Yellowstone National Park. From Porphyry Lookout the road makes a rapid descent through evergreen forest to the arid fringe of the Smith River valley, a rumpled gray-green blanket of sagebrush patchworked with hay meadows and pastures.

10 White Sulphur Springs

The steaming mineral baths of this mountain-ringed hamlet are just hot enough to soothe aching muscles (they also supply the heat for the local bank). To the south the Shields River plain opens out onto farmland and ranchland so lovely it lured circus impresario John Ringling to the area—hence the name of the town 20 miles south of White Sulphur Springs.

11 Livingston

Established by the Northern Pacific Railroad near the confluence of the Shields and Yellowstone rivers, Livingston was once a brawling trainman's town, home

:::::: Trip Tips ::::::

Length: About 370 miles, plus side trips.

When to go: Popular year-round.

Nearby attractions: Lewis and Clark Caverns State Park, east of Whitehall. Museum of the Rockies, Bozeman. Ulm Pishkun State Park (prehistoric bison kill site), west of Great Falls.

Further information: Charlie Russell Country, Box 3166, Great Falls, MT 59403; tel. 800-527-5348, www.russell.visitmt.com.

to Martha Jane Cannary—better known as Calamity Jane—the celebrated hell-raiser. Its townsfolk and neighbors now include a cadre of writers, artists, and film stars. Gentrification has made inroads: feed and hardware stores rub shoulders with galleries and boutiques, and cowboy bars compete with chic cafés. Still, few of Montana's vintage red-brick communities work harder at preserving their past: more than 400 of Livingston's buildings, including a remarkably handsome turn-of-the-century railroad depot turned museum, are listed in the National Register of Historic Places. A trout-fishing mecca, Livingston's holiest shrine is Dan Bailey's Fly Shop—revered among fly casters—with a mail-order business spanning the globe.

12 Paradise Valley

Framed by the Absaroka and Gallatin ranges, this sparsely settled alluvial plain, which opens out south of Livingston, is traversed by the pristine Yellowstone River. At least one fly-fishing sage considers this stretch of river to be America's premier cold-water trout stream. Both Rte. 89 and East River Road (Rte. 540) parallel the river, on opposite banks, southbound through old ranchland. Rising to the east, the lush North Absaroka Mountains crown the Absaroka-Beartooth Wilderness. Some lingering volcanic activity is present here—a geologic heartburn that keeps the baths at nearby Chico Hot Springs Lodge on perpetual simmer.

13 Emigrant

As you roll south through the little town of Emigrant, 10,921-foot Emigrant Peak looms ahead, a reminder that the Absarokas (reaching 12,799 feet) are Montana's highest mountains. Mineralized hardwoods in the Gallatin

The Yellowstone River teems with fish and fishermen—the former seeking places to spawn and the latter hoping for epic battles. For casual visitors, it's also a great place to take photographs of the monumental landscape, mountains, and flowing water.

Petrified Forest, 12 miles west of Rte. 89, are identified as tropical, suggesting that in the age of dinosaurs, this region was vastly different. If you fancy taking a specimen with you, pick up a permit in Livingston or Gardiner before you take the gravel road west from Tom Miner bridge to the petrified forest.

14 Northern Yellowstone Winter Range

Farther south on Rte. 89, the granite walls of Yankee Jim Canyon close in, forming a gorge. The Yellowstone tumbles through it, slamming furiously against boulders and debris. During spring runoff these daunting rapids are a fearsome challenge reserved for white-water experts only.

Just beyond Corwin Springs a reddish slash known as Devils Slide appears on the flank of 7,176-foot Cinnabar Mountain to the southwest. Early prospectors mistook this eroded vein of iron-stained sandstone and shale for the ocher ore of mercury, giving Cinnabar Mountain its name.

Watch for wildlife from late fall to spring: this region is the winter range of the biggest, most diverse population of hoofed mammals in the lower 48 states—bighorn sheep, pronghorn antelope, mule deer, elk, bison, and other species that summer in Yellowstone.

15 Gardiner

This rustic little community, with a population of about 600, is the only year-round auto gateway to Yellowstone National Park. The brownstone Roosevelt Arch here was Yellowstone's original northern portal, opened in 1903 by the Rough Rider himself. Teddy's dedication, chiseled across its top, seems fitting not just for what lies beyond but also for the route that brought you here: "FOR THE BENEFIT AND ENJOYMENT OF THE PEOPLE."

Beartooth Country

A craggy granite pinnacle known as the Bear's Tooth lends its name to this upland, where glaciers fill mountaintop nooks, waterfalls tumble from cliffs, and wildflowers dot the alpine tundra.

Beartooth Lake mirrors the colorful, bedded sandstone of Beartooth Butte, a rich source of ancient marine fossils.

Sprawling across the borders of Montana and Wyoming, a vast expanse of scenic wildlands centers on the Beartooth Mountains, which dominate the horizon like a staircase to the sky. This drive, following Rtes. 78 and 212 (the Beartooth Highway), traverses the region and, as a bonus, ends at Yellowstone National Park. Once on the road—passing swift creeks and snowy uplands—you will see why the late television commentator Charles Kuralt hailed Rte. 212 as America's most beautiful highway.

■ Scenic Route 78

Heading south from Columbus, a quiet town on the banks of the Yellowstone River, Rte. 78 skirts the northern edge of the Beartooth Range. The road at first parallels the Stillwater River and its canyon to the little town of Absarokee, which was once the heart of Crow Indian territory. In Absarokee you might choose to take a side trip on Rte. 420, which leads farther up the Stillwater, or in summer, catch one of the rodeos that are held here.

Continuing south from Absarokee, Rte. 78 follows East Rosebud Creek to Roscoe, where the road and the creek part company. But here again a secondary road offers the opportunity for a pleasant side trip: Rte. 177 continues alongside the waterway, corkscrewing a route into the wilds. Usually passable, the gravel road skirts arid patches of sage and ancient, eroded cliffs, and finally dead-ends at East Rosebud Lake. Replete with a clutch of rustic cabins, piney woodlands, meadows, and steep mountain slopes, the area is a hiker's paradise. One trail snakes west into the Beartooths; a second remains with the creek, which spills though a dramatic canyon.

■ Red Lodge

Crossing myriad creeks that are fed in part by melting snow in the up-country, Rte. 78 climbs 1,000 feet more before arriving at Red Lodge, a town that was settled in the late 1800s to tap coal deposits. Although the mines are no longer active, a historic district conjures up the lifestyles of the settlers.

Now an important gateway to the wilderness, Red Lodge has earned special renown as the eastern terminus of the Beartooth Highway. Opened in 1936, this extraordinary 68-mile stretch of road begins with a series of switchbacks, then climbs through glacier-gouged Rock Creek Canyon. It continues to higher elevations, passing through an area that averages 200 inches of snow per year. The road's gradient, however, remains reasonable—about 4 percent—and turnouts invite drivers to pull over and enjoy the views.

■ Rock Creek Vista Point

A steady ascent, about a dozen miles in length, overlooks seemingly bottomless valleys and leads to Rock Creek Vista Point. Here, at an elevation of some 8,000 feet, the panorama takes in fields of sage, Rock Creek Canyon, and the road ahead, twisting and turning like a ribbon into the distance.

Although the area seems forbidding, wildlife is plentiful. Two hardy survivors—agile mountain goats and mountain sheep—can sometimes be seen leaping across the ledges. Spiraling overhead, hawks and eagles keep watch for potential prey.

■ Twin Lakes Headwall

Named for a pair of icy blue lakes, Twin Lakes Headwall, a long, sloping incline, is permanently covered with snow. A roadside turnoff looks out on the area, where young ski racers, some perhaps destined for the Olympics, gather each summer to schuss down the hill—its steep slopes pitched at a challenging 58° angle.

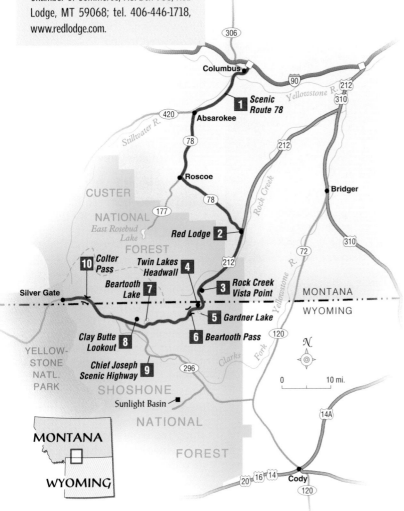

5 Gardner Lake

The 10-mile-long Beartooth Loop National Recreation Trail begins at Gardner Lake. Skirting creeks and lakes, the path traverses a stretch of austere alpine tundra, a landscape similar to that found near the Arctic Circle. Dainty but hardy wildflowers such as bluebells, gentians, and forget-me-nots flourish on the shores of the lake as well as on the trail; their 45-day growing season usually peaks in mid-July.

6 Beartooth Pass

Marking the crest of the byway, the pass, at 10,947 feet above sea level, makes this section of road one of the world's highest. Turnouts allow you to stop and breathe the pure, crisp—and very thin—air. And the view (visibility can reach 75 miles) takes in snowcapped peaks, glacier-etched valleys, flowery meadows, and coniferous forests. Look to the north for the Bear's Tooth, a rocky peak piercing the sky.

7 Beartooth Lake

The road descends 2,000 feet to this shimmering lake, which lies in the shadow of Beartooth Butte. The great rock—bulky and banded with colorful layers—was once part of an ancient seabed. Today archaeologists search its slopes for fossils, some more than 500 million years old.

But scientists aren't the only ones who enjoy this area; the lake and the surrounding plateau attract anglers, campers, and hikers. Even admirers of waterfalls can have their fill: Beartooth Falls, on the opposite side of the highway, makes a plunge of 100 feet.

8 Clay Butte Lookout

The fire tower at Clay Butte, another imposing monolith, permits a far-reaching vista. The dramatic, jagged skyline is defined by the Bighorn, Beartooth, and Absaroka ranges; standing guard on the distant northwest horizon is 12,799-foot Granite Peak, the highest point in Montana.

9 Chief Joseph Scenic Highway

After descending through a forest of pine, spruce, and aspen, Rte. 212 meets the Chief Joseph Scenic

A narrow isthmus of land—a terminal moraine—was left when a receding glacer melted, dividing Twin Lakes.

Highway (Rte. 296). Consider taking a side trip along the road: it rambles beside the Clarks Fork Yellowstone River, which has carved a stunning gorge 1,200 feet deep. Of particular note along the way is Sunlight Basin, where a secluded 50,000 acres of verdant hills are laced with willow-lined creeks and roamed by an array of wildlife, including coyotes, moose, deer, and elk.

10 Colter Pass

Back on Rte. 212, the drive proceeds along the Clarks Fork River toward Colter Pass. To the south lie Pilot and Index peaks, two ragged horns that have long been relied upon as landmarks.

Watch for black bears, moose, eagles, and other wildlife before rejoining civilization at Cooke City and Silver Gate. The two towns, both onetime mining settlements, lie nestled among towering mountains—and just miles from the northeastern entrance to Yellowstone National Park.

North to Jackson Hole

Winding through canyonland and primeval forest, Route 89 traverses three states on a journey north to Jackson Hole—a broad valley bordered by some of the craggiest peaks in the West.

The first rays of sunlight at dawn hit the rugged spires of the Tetons in Grand Teton National Park.

Bold and larger than life were the trappers, hunters, homesteaders, and prospectors who trod the ranges and ridges of Utah, Idaho, and Wyoming a century and more ago. On this drive you'll travel in their footsteps, following them through still-untamed country that seems both remote and accessible, forbidding and beautiful. The reward at the end of the road is a relatively small but priceless jewel—glorious Grand Teton National Park.

1 Logan Canyon Scenic Drive
From Logan, Utah, Rte. 89 follows the Logan River northeast toward Bear Lake. On either side of the river, whose moist banks nurture willows and birches, rise the steep slopes and dramatic limestone cliffs of Logan Canyon. Among the intriguing stops along the route is the Preston Valley Campground, where a sign calls attention to a slab of quartz tunneled by tiny seaworms some 400 million years ago. Another is the Wood Camp Campground, from which a trail leads to the Jardine Juniper, an evergreen believed to be more than 1,500 years old.

2 Bear Lake Summit
After a climb of some 3,000 feet between Logan and Bear Lake Summit, the drive rewards travelers with a breathtaking view of Bear Lake, which shimmers with a shade of blue-green so vivid it looks like a tropical lagoon—or a suburban swimming pool. A mile farther on, another commanding view overlooks not only Bear Lake, but a horizon rimmed by the Sawtooth Mountains to the northeast, the Trump Range to the east, and the Uintas to the southeast.

3 Bear Lake
Turning north at Garden City, Rte. 89 parallels the western shore of Bear Lake, whose aquamarine waters—colored by tiny suspended particles—straddle the border between Utah and Idaho. Because geologic upheaval long ago isolated it from surrounding bodies of water, Bear Lake has managed to nurture four species of fish found nowhere else in the world. The wide sandy beach at the lake's northern shore, part of Bear Lake State Park, is a local mecca for swimmers and picnickers. Just north of the beach is Bear Lake National Wildlife Refuge, 18,060 acres consisting mostly of wetlands that provide nesting places for snowy egrets, white-faced ibises, and Franklin's gulls.

4 Greys River Road
The fast way north to Jackson is via well-traveled Rte. 89 through the Star Valley, where the rugged mountains of Wyoming flatten and slide toward blandly bucolic Idaho farmland. A more adventurous route is the 80-mile, two-lane gravel detour by way of the Smith Fork and Greys River roads, beginning at a turnoff about six miles south of Smoot. Following a verdant valley tucked between the Wyoming and Salt River Mountains and cloaked with lodgepole pines (part of the Bridger-Teton National Forest), the road runs along the trout-rich Greys River. Frequent turnouts invite hungry travelers to pause for a picnic and tempt eager anglers to wet a line in the flowing waters.

:::::: Trip Tips ::::::

Length: About 240 miles.

When to go: May to October.

Nearby attractions: Fossil Butte National Monument (fossil displays), west of Kemmerer, Wyoming. Lava Hot Springs, Idaho (known for its hot mineral pools). Periodic Spring (the spring gushes every 18 minutes from an opening in a canyon wall), in Bridger-Teton National Forest, near Afton, Wyoming.

Visitor centers: At Colter Bay, Jenny Lake, and Moose in Grand Teton National Park.

Further information: Grand Teton National Park, P.O. Drawer 170, Moose, WY 83012; tel. 307-739-3300, www.nps. gov/grte/.

5 Jackson

As the road approaches Jackson, look down the highway and you'll see a strip of retail stores. Beyond Jackson, look toward the Tetons and you'll see a classic Ansel Adams image of natural grandeur. These are the two faces of Jackson Hole, a broad valley surrounded by mountains (what 19th-century trappers called a hole) that serves as the opening corridor to Grand Teton National Park. Though Jackson is a welter of boutiques, galleries, and restaurants, it is a great base camp for the loop drive through Grand Teton National Park. Be sure to make reservations for the busy summer season.

6 Jackson Hole Aerial Tram

An effortless alpine experience is provided by the aerial tram that in 10 minutes glides to the summit of 10,450-foot Rendezvous Peak, offering a view north into the sharp-edged tableau of the Tetons. The tram operates daily, late May through September,

from the Jackson Hole Ski Resort off Rte. 22, west of Jackson.

7 National Elk Refuge

Early in this century, Jackson Hole's majestic elk were dying by the thousands in bitter-cold winters. Consequently, in 1912 the federal government established a winter range for thousands of elk, which evolved into this 25,000-acre refuge. Elk dot the snowy meadows from October to April or May but head for the higher elevations in summer. Rte. 89 skirts the refuge's western boundary, often affording somewhat distant views of the antlered beasts. For a closer look, follow the signs from Jackson to the National Wildlife Art Museum and ride through the herd in a horse-drawn sleigh.

8 Gros Ventre Loop

For a lesson in the geologic history of Jackson Hole, take this 25-mile loop through a part of Grand Teton National Park overlooked by most visitors. Turn east at Gros Ventre Junction, paralleling the Gros Ventre River to Kelly. One mile north of Kelly, turn east on the narrow, winding road that leads through groves of white-barked aspen to the site of a relatively recent geologic cataclysm: the Gros Ventre Slide. In June 1925 a mile-long layer of sandstone suddenly tore loose from Sheep Mountain and slid downhill, damming the Gros Ventre River and forming Lower Slide Lake. Two years later a part of the lake burst through its natural dam and sent a wall of water rushing downstream toward the town of Kelly, which was virtually destroyed.

9 Teton Point Turnout

The route follows Antelope Flats Road west to rejoin Rte. 89 (now called the Jackson Hole Highway) and then heads three miles north to Teton Point Turnout.

The Wild West is just a ride away in Jackson, marked by its signature antler arch.

While you are here, look up to an imaginary point three-quarters of a mile directly above you: that is where the surface of the ice lay when glaciers filled Jackson Hole. To the west is a superb view of

the towering Tetons. Though the mountains are relatively young (less than 10 million years), some of them contain the gneiss and schist of far older rocks, nearly 3 billion years old.

10 Snake River Overlook

This turnout, atop a giant glacial moraine deposited thousands of years ago, affords a panoramic view across Jackson Hole to the Teton Range. The Snake River, as serpentine as its name suggests, is lined with willows, cottonwoods, and aspens—an ideal habitat for beavers, whose dams dot the myriad streams that feed into the great winding river.

11 Cunningham Cabin Historic Site

About a mile beyond the Snake River Overlook lies Hedricks Pond, a nesting site for rare trumpeter swans and other waterfowl. A bit farther along, an unpaved road turns west off Rte. 89, leading to the remains of a two-room, sod-roofed cabin that was once the home of Pierce and Margaret Cunningham. Exemplars of the pioneering spirit, the couple worked this harsh land tenaciously from 1890 until 1928, surviving in spite of the region's harsh winters, short summers (the growing season lasts only three months), and extreme isolation.

12 Oxbow Bend Turnout

Just south of Moran the drive crosses the tiny Buffalo Fork River, where Walter Delacy prospected for gold in the 1860s. He found no gold, so he journeyed north and discovered an even greater treasure, whose name at least *sounds* golden: Yellowstone. The artless map he made of the area inspired two major Yellowstone expeditions, the latter of which led in 1872 to the establishment of our first national park.

Far off to the west is 12,605-foot Mt. Moran, named for artist Thomas Moran, whose paintings of the West wowed the folks back east. Farther down the road, at the Oxbow Bend Turnout, moose and mule deer roam the thickets

along the Snake River, and its whispering waters are home to beavers, otters, and muskrats. For a closer look at the meander itself, take the short unpaved road south to Cattlemans Bridge. Because the water is slow-moving here, plants are anchored to the fertile riverbed and fish gather in schools, attracting pelicans, great blue herons, cormorants, and bald eagles.

13 Signal Mountain

At Jackson Lake Junction turn south on Teton Park Road (closed in winter). A few miles farther along, turn east onto Signal Mountain Road, a paved spur leading to the top of Signal Mountain, about 1,000 feet above the valley floor. The

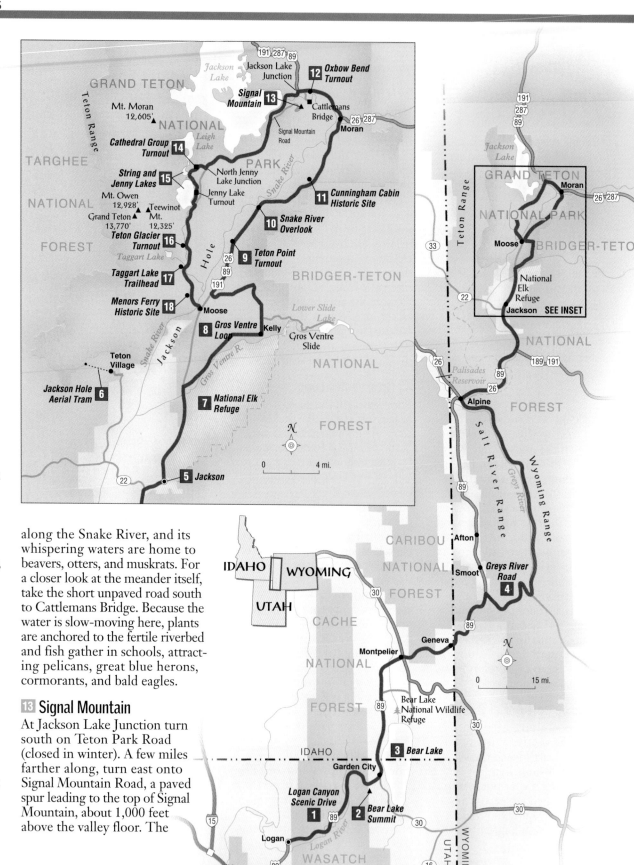

views from this road are perhaps the grandest in the Jackson Hole area. At the Jackson Point Overlook, half a mile short of the summit, a sweeping panorama faces west, toward the Tetons. The view was etched into the national consciousness when, from this exact spot in 1878, William Henry Jackson photographed Mt. Moran reflected in the surface of Jackson Lake. (Despite his contribution, the valley is not named for that particular Jackson. It was casually christened Jackson Hole in the early 1800s because an itinerant trapper, David Jackson, considered it his turf.) From Signal Mountain's summit you can see all the way north to Yellowstone. Two gleaming lakes—Emma Matilda and Two Ocean—lie to the northeast, the Snake River loops to the east and south, and the Gros Ventre Mountains rise beyond a flat expanse of sagebrush.

14 Cathedral Group Turnout

At North Jenny Lake Junction, bear right onto the one-way road leading to one of the park's most spectacular viewpoints. As though they had risen abruptly from the valley floor, the majestic trio of peaks known as Teewinot, Grand Teton, and Owen do indeed echo in granite the spires and symmetry of a great Gothic cathedral.

15 String and Jenny Lakes

An easy 3½-mile hiking trail encircles String Lake, the narrow connector between Leigh Lake to the north and Jenny Lake to the south. In early summer the path winds past clumps of calypso orchids, which look like pink, spoon-tailed birds in flight. They are one of the loveliest and most delicate of the park's 15 orchid species.

Farther south, a turnout looks across cerulean Jenny Lake—its shores clothed with stout spruce—into Cascade Canyon. Down the

At the Snake River Overlook, evening light sets the river aglow. To the west, across Jackson Hole, are the Tetons.

road near the ranger station, you can take a summer shuttle boat across the lake to the Cascade Canyon Trail. Its lower section wanders through a wonderland of evergreens and wildflowers to such inviting locations as Hidden Falls and Inspiration Point, overlooking Jackson Hole.

16 Teton Glacier Turnout

At the south end of Jenny Lake the drive rejoins Teton Park Road southbound. To the west lies Timbered Island—not a spot of land in a lake, but an oasis of evergreens amid a sea of sagebrush, growing on a patch of moist soil. Early on a summer morning or evening, you may see elk feeding amid the trees. From the turnout up ahead, you can view Teton Glacier, one of 12 still active rivers of slowly flowing ice in the range—a reminder that the natural forces that formed these mountains continue imperceptibly but steadily, uninterrupted by our brief passage.

17 Taggart Lake Trailhead

Another of those natural forces is fire, and to the west at Taggart Lake Trailhead, you can see the scar of a 1985 blaze that burned out of control with such intensity that sap-soaked lodgepole pines literally exploded with the fury of fireworks, and boulders cracked from the heat. Despite their seeming destructiveness, however, forest fires ignited by lightning cleansed and regenerated forests for eons before Smokey the Bear decided they were evil, and ecologists now question whether such blazes should automatically be quenched. An incidental legacy of the fire near Taggart Lake, at least for hikers, is unblocked mountain views and, in the summers that followed, a riot of wildflowers.

18 Menor's Ferry Historic Site

Exhibits at this site include an old homestead dating from 1894, a smokehouse, a well, Teton memorabilia, and a replica of the old cable ferry that operated here until 1927. Most important, at this site in 1923 a meeting was held among farsighted conservationists that led eventually to the creation of Grand Teton National Park.

Yellowstone's Grand Loop

On a map of the American mind, where wilderness is a place transcending time, all roads lead to primeval Yellowstone, a venerable but ever-volatile kingdom of fire, water, earth, and air.

Lower Yellowstone Falls in the Grand Canyon of the Yellowstone.

Occupying the northwestern corner of Wyoming and spilling over slightly into Montana and Idaho on the north and west, Yellowstone is the oldest of our national parks. It is a domain of dense forests and velvety meadows that give way to yawning gorges and steaming wetlands, all traversed by an intriguing assortment of wild creatures. The size of Rhode Island and Delaware combined, Yellowstone is also a treasury of geologic phenomena and a testament to the raw power of the elements.

1 Mammoth Hot Springs
The drive begins at the stately Roosevelt Arch, located at the northernmost entrance to Yellowstone National Park. Heading south, the road journeys through Gardiner River Canyon to the Albright visitor center and the limestone terraces of Mammoth Hot Springs, perhaps the eeriest and most hauntingly beautiful of Yellowstone's year-round thermal theatrics. Formed of calcium carbonate that has been leached from limestone beneath the earth's surface and deposited above as a glowing white travertine, the springs take their delicate colors from the algae and bacteria that thrive in the steamy water. Among the most active of the terraces—some of which grow by as much as eight inches a year— are Opal Terrace, which each year takes another bite out of the sloping lawn of the nearby housing area, and regal, multi-hued Minerva Terrace. For a panoramic view of a half-dozen other springs and their colored pools, follow the one-way loop called Upper Terrace Drive. After rejoining the main road, the route swings south, skirting sooty Bunsen Peak and the stark black basalt pillars of Sheepeater Cliffs.

2 Obsidian Cliff
The land along this stretch of road and many others throughout Yellowstone was badly scorched by the fires that raged here in 1988. One highlight of this otherwise forbidding landscape is the glittering black face of Obsidian Cliff, formed by the rare, high-speed cooling of a lava eruption thousands of years ago. Indians used the obsidian for arrowheads, which have been discovered as far away as Ohio.

3 Norris Geyser Basin
According to geologists who have been monitoring the area for years, Norris Geyser Basin is perhaps the hottest hot spot on earth, and certainly one of the most geologically active. Puffs of steam rise from the ground like involuntary sighs all day long, and the basin is richly endowed with active geysers: Dark Cavern, which erupts several times an hour; the fan-shaped, silica-spraying Whirligig; and Steamboat, the world's tallest geyser, with plumes of up to 380 feet— about three times higher than the eruptions of Old Faithful.

4 Virginia Cascade
A quick detour to the east leads to one-way Virginia Cascade Drive, which skirts the 60-foot waterfall that gives the road its name. A visit to the nearby willow meadows in the quiet of early morning or late afternoon may yield a glimpse of elk or moose, which regularly appear at the edge of the clearing.

5 Firehole Canyon Drive
Doubling back to Norris, the drive heads south to Madison, where the Grand Loop begins to cut across the edge of the great Yellowstone Caldera—the collapsed remains of a cataclysmic eruption that blew the center of the present-day park high into the sky some 600,000 years ago. Nearly 50 miles long and 28 miles wide, the basin lies above a still-churning core of molten rock. Its intense heat acts upon ground-

:::::: **Trip Tips** :::::

Length: About 150 miles, plus side trips.

When to go: Popular year-round.

Food, fuel, and lodging: Canyon Village, Grant Village, Mammoth Hot Springs, Old Faithful.

Words to the wise: Most park roads are closed from November through April, but park snowmobiles can be rented in winter.

Nearby attractions: Beartooth Highway (Rte. 212). Grand Teton National Park.

Visitor Centers: Canyon Village, Fishing Bridge, Grant Village, Mammoth Hot Springs, Old Faithful.

Further information: Yellowstone National Park, Box 168, Yellowstone National Park, WY 82190; tel. 307-344-7381, www.nps.gov/yell/.

water-filled fissures to create Yellowstone's chorus of bubbling springs and hissing geysers, its restless repertoire of fumaroles, spitting mud pots, and unearthly steaming craters.

Beginning just below Madison, Firehole Canyon Drive follows the twisting course of the Firehole River for a distance of two miles. The sheer canyon walls rise to a height of 800 feet above the river. The Firehole takes its name from naturally occurring Jacuzzi blasts below the water's surface, which keep the river from freezing during the long Wyoming winter and permit geese and ducks to find shelter here through the coldest months. At Firehole Falls the river plummets 40 feet, then races downstream over the black lava steps of the Firehole Cascade, eventually carving a foamy path through a forest of lodgepole pine.

6 Fountain Flats Drive

This three-mile spur passes meadows of purple gentian where elk and bison graze, and it ends at Goose Lake, a secluded spot for a picnic. Farther south on the main road lie the spewing and spitting mud springs of Fountain Paint Pot, a favorite with visitors. Along the boardwalk are a series of improbable displays—dense, bubbling clay

(Above) The steaming waters of the Grand Prismatic Spring are colored by algae, while the surrounding rock is stained by precipitated minerals. (Right) Old Faithful Geyser is the premier attraction among Yellowstone's more than 200 geysers.

Yellowstone's bison are reminders of America's wilderness past.

pools and geysers that toss pink, mineral-rich mudpies into the air.

7 Firehole Lake Drive

A one-way northbound loop off the main road, this three-mile drive takes in part of the Lower Geyser Basin, which boasts the park's second-highest concentration of geysers. Check the ranger postings to avoid missing the rival eruptions of Great Fountain Geyser (one of the world's grandest) and White Dome Geyser (with its massive, imposing cone).

8 Midway Geyser Basin

A wooden footbridge over the Firehole River overlooks sleeping Excelsior Crater, which last erupted in 1985 and now shoots its scalding broth into the river instead by way of a series of flumes. Continue along the boardwalk for a leisurely look at Grand Prismatic Spring, Yellowstone's largest and most colorful hot spring—a brilliant blue medallion more than 300 feet in diameter and ringed by throbbing, brilliant bands of yellow, green, red, and orange algae.

9 Old Faithful

With rapt attention crowds await the next scheduled performance of this world-famous geyser, whose timing is almost as predictable as its subterranean clockwork is complex. First comes the overture: splashing, gurgling, and throat-clearing as spurts of white are launched into the blue sky. Then, suddenly, a roaring column of spray erupts full force, causing jaws to drop and necks to jerk back in awe and amazement. Old Faithful has again lived up to its name.

Were it somehow to fail, visitors would still find spectacle enough within walking distance of the famed geyser. Morning Glory Pool, Castle Geyser, Chromatic Pool, Chinese Spring, Grotto Geyser, Punch Bowl Spring, and other

spots create an intriguing variety of pools and waterspouts great and small, each gurgling and blowing to its own peculiar rhythm. Of the 500 or so active geysers in the world, more than 200 are found in Yellowstone, and close to 125 of these thermal wonders are right here in Upper Geyser Basin.

10 Yellowstone Lake

Travelers experience an abrupt change of scene and scent as the Grand Loop swings east and climbs to the Continental Divide, passing through dense evergreen forests mercifully untouched by the fires of 1988. At 8,000 feet the road bridges tiny Isa Lake, which straddles the divide and drains both east and west. Just past the lake is a matchless view south toward the towering Tetons. Approaching the town of West Thumb, the forest finally parts like a curtain to reveal the diamond-bright surface of Yellowstone Lake, the highest mountain lake in North America—and one of the largest at 14 by 20 miles. Pelicans glide overhead, and flocks of honking geese alight along the tree-lined shore. The drive hugs the water's edge on its northward journey, and near Bridge Bay a mile-long spur leads west to the lovely Natural Bridge, a 30-foot span of pale stone arching high above the ground.

11 Fishing Bridge

It's been years since angling was last permitted here, but this still-popular stop offers a fine vantage point for communing with nature. In summer you can watch the cutthroat trout as they spawn, or hike nearby trails in hopes of catching a glimpse of a black bear. Moose sightings are frequent along the north shore of Yellowstone Lake and east of the bridge. Once you resume the journey north on the loop drive, follow the scent of

Excelsior Geyser contributes its boiling water to the Firehole River.

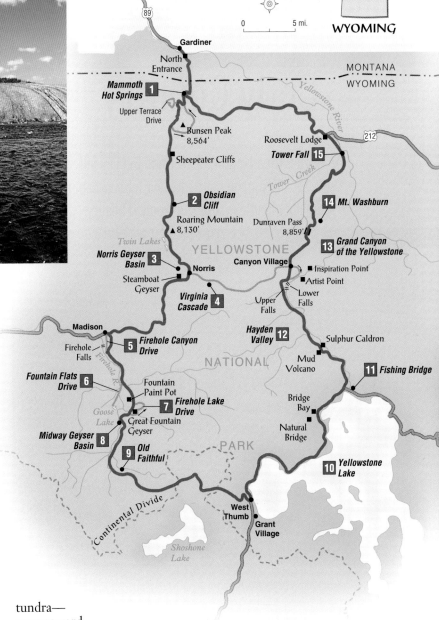

rotten eggs (hydrogen sulfide gas) to the Mud Volcano Trail, less than one mile long. Though somewhat infernal—replete with sulfurous fumes, churning mud springs, and yellow acid pools—the ground is warm enough in winter to melt falling snow, providing a welcome haven for bison.

12 Hayden Valley

Following the gentle curves of the Yellowstone River as it weaves through the verdant saucer of Hayden Valley, the road unfurls across fields of brilliantly colored wildflowers, past herds of grazing moose, elk, and the occasional solitary bison at the meadow's edge. Since the area's garbage dumps were closed down, most of the once-numerous grizzlies have retreated to the encircling pine forest, but the valley is celebrated for its rich bird life—including the magnificent trumpeter swan, only 1,500 of which are known to remain in the world.

13 Grand Canyon of the Yellowstone

You can hear it long before you see it: a swelling natural fanfare that prepares you for the drama to come. It's the sound of white water rushing ever faster through a narrowing passage before tumbling into the great golden gash known as the Grand Canyon of the Yellowstone. "It is grand, gloomy, and terrible," wrote one early visitor. Another spoke of the "mingled awe and terror" he felt in its presence. There is certainly something extraordinary about this gargantuan, 20-mile slice etched in the earth's crust, whether contemplated from a dizzying lookout at 1,200 feet or from a rainbow-framed perch at the water's edge. For the best view of the 109-foot Upper Falls, follow the trail that parallels South Rim Road; then descend Uncle Tom's Trail 700 steps toward the canyon floor and feel the spray of the thunderous 308-foot Lower Falls. For an unsurpassed view down the center of the glistening yellow canyon itself, hike the trail or drive along South Rim Road to Artist Point. On the opposite side of the river, a one-way road from Canyon Village leads to Inspiration Point for a final glimpse of the Lower Falls.

14 Mt. Washburn

If you park the car at the Dunraven Pass picnic area and hike three miles to the summit of Mt. Washburn—through woods of whitebark pine and blossoming tundra—your reward will be a grand view of the section one just traversed. In fact, this 10,243-foot remnant of a 50-million-year-old volcano—one of many that ring the caldera—offers a panoramic view of virtually the entire park. Wildflowers border the trail in summer, and pausing to catch your breath on the way up, you may well see a bighorn sheep waiting patiently for you to pass by before continuing slowly on its regal way.

15 Tower Fall

Meadows of sagebrush spotted with bright yellow monkeyflower border this last leg of the drive as it swings by the graceful 132-foot cataract of Tower Fall, the nearby Roosevelt Lodge, and the Petrified Tree, a fossilized redwood buried by volcanic ash some 50 million years ago when they were common throughout the area. The road then arcs west across Blacktail Deer Plateau, closing this captivating loop where it began, at Mammoth Hot Springs.

Cody Country

As filled with adventure as Buffalo Bill himself, northwestern Wyoming captivates with its sweeping, seemingly limitless supply of rugged beauty.

Layered rock formations cut by the Bighorn River at Bighorn Canyon.

By no means an isolated island of natural splendor, Yellowstone National Park is surrounded by remarkable wilds. This drive, following Rtes. 14 and 14A, offers an ideal encore, leaving the fabled preserve for points east, where an ever-changing realm runs the gamut from shadowy forests to wide-open grasslands. Between these extremes are lazy rivers, waterfalls, rolling fields, tall mountains, and deep canyons—a monumental mosaic of scenic grandeur that carries the visitor back in time and memory to the Wild West.

1 Pahaska

In the early 1900s many visitors to Yellowstone savored their last taste of civilization at Pahaska, where William F. Cody, alias Buffalo Bill, had built a hunting lodge known as the Pahaska Tepee. The lodge can still be toured in summer, and the resort still serves as a jumping-off point for excursions into the backcountry. Pahaska attracts outdoor enthusiasts, who come not only to enjoy the bounties of Yellowstone but also those of Shoshone National Forest, where more than 2 million acres encompass wilderness areas, rushing streams, granite peaks, and meadows abounding with wildflowers.

2 Wapiti Ranger Station

Rte. 14, which overlaps here with Rtes. 16 and 20, winds eastward along the north fork of the Shoshone River. Dotted with lodges and resorts, this stretch of highway passes through an amazing landscape forged by volcanic fires. Appearing one after another are hundreds of dramatic rock formations—multicolored spires, towering pinnacles, and layered columns, some of which are identified by roadside signs.

The national forest's Wapiti Ranger Station, erected in 1903, lies just off Rte. 14 and is a good place to relax and enjoy the sights. Open in the summer months, a visitor center at the station offers an informative video on grizzlies, the undisputed king of these woods. On the way out of the forest, the drive slips between Signal and Flag peaks, two mountains cresting at the preserve's eastern boundary.

3 Buffalo Bill State Park

As the road winds down from the mountains, the vegetation also changes, with dense forests yielding to open expanses of sagebrush and scrubby juniper. This arid landscape is not without its oases, however, for cottonwoods and willows flourish along the banks of the gradually widening Shoshone River. Then, a few miles farther along, the road skirts the shores of Buffalo Bill Reservoir, the centerpiece of Buffalo Bill State Park and an irresistible mecca for campers, windsurfers, and boaters.

The town of Cody, east of the reservoir, also recalls the popular scout and showman, who lent his magnetic name in the hope of attracting crowds. The plan was a success: today nearly 750,000 visitors come each year. One of the town's most popular attractions, the Buffalo Bill Historical Center, boasts a superb collection of western art and memorabilia. Come Independence Day, the Wild West also springs to life during the Cody Stampede, an entertaining show complete with parades and rodeos that marks the high point of Cody's summer festivities.

As it leaves town, the drive switches onto Rte. 14A, which heads toward Bighorn National Forest. Locals say the A stands for adventure, and once under way, you'll soon find out why. The route angles northeast through the Big Horn Basin, a broad, windswept valley. Far-reaching views of grassy rangelands are the norm in summer, but winter is another story: the snow, blowing unimpeded, accumulates in deep drifts that close the road from mid-November to mid-May.

4 Bighorn Canyon National Recreation Area

Passing through flat grazing lands and fields of sugar beets, the drive enters Lovell, a small town nicknamed the City of Roses. Beyond Lovell the earth begins to rumble, and rolling badlands dominate the scene. Take heart, though, for just ahead you'll come to Bighorn Canyon National Recreation Area, where a dam on the Bighorn River has formed a reservoir 70 miles long. Hemmed in by lofty peaks and multicolored cliffs, the lengthy man-made lake extends north well into Montana.

To enjoy the sights, follow Rte. 37, which curves atop Bighorn Canyon's western plateau and parallels the Bad Pass Trail, an ancient footpath worn by native Americans and, centuries later, by fur trappers. This neck of the woods is also the site of the Pryor Mountain Wild Horse Range, a large sanctuary where more than 100 mustangs roam the countryside. Though they tend to stay out of sight, the horses, whose Crow name means "wind drinkers," have bold markings in an array of colors.

Rte. 37 will also take you to the overlook at Devil Canyon, just across the Montana border, where the earth drops off below your feet, and the view looks down 1,000 feet into the water-filled canyon. Far below, the boats and sails on the lake's surface resemble toys floating in a faraway bathtub.

5 Medicine Wheel National Historic Landmark

Zigzagging up and down through Bighorn National Forest, the next leg of Rte. 14A—remember, the A is for adventure—was modeled after routes in the Alps. One of the most expensive stretches of highway ever built, the road slithers around cliffs, slices a few scant feet away from seemingly bottomless dropoffs, and forces cars to struggle up 10 percent grades.

But all is not perilous up here. A side trip to the north on Rte. 12, an unpaved forest road, wends three miles to Medicine

Wheel, one of North America's most mysterious landmarks. Reminiscent of England's Stonehenge, this native American version features limestone rocks that form a circle 80 feet in diameter. Located on a grassy mountaintop nearly 10,000 feet in elevation, the wheel was possibly used to mark the summer solstice and other celestial events. Tribe members, still holding the site sacred, continue to come for ceremonies, often tying prayer tokens to the fence that encloses the historic landmark.

6 Sheep Mountain Road

About three miles past the turnoff for Medicine Wheel, Sheep Mountain Road exits Rte. 14A for another brief backcountry tour. Most visitors make the trip to admire two local waterfalls, which are accessible via short trails. Porcupine Falls, the first along the way, lies half a mile off the road and plummets 200 feet. Another hike of three miles leads to Bucking Mule Falls: dropping about 600 feet into Devil Canyon, this hidden treasure is one of the West's tallest cascades.

Back on Rte. 14A, a viewing area just past Sheep Mountain Road takes in the long sweep of the multicolored Bighorns. The mountain chain, its jagged silhouette rising and falling for miles into the distance, arcs slightly toward the southeast. On a clear day you can also see north into Montana and west to the snowcapped Rocky Mountains.

7 Shell Falls

Moose and elk can sometimes be spotted in the willow bottomlands found just before you come to Burgess Junction. Once in town, the drive veers south and west onto Rte. 14, climbing back into the high mountains to the summit of Granite Pass—at 8,860 feet, the highway's loftiest point.

The road then slopes into Shell Canyon, curving between steep walls of pink granite and rosy sandstone. The sandstone is embedded with an abundance of fossils. The ancient creatures (some of the earliest hard-shelled animals on earth) were saltwater inhabitants that lived here when the area was covered by a sea.

Toward the southern end of the canyon, Shell Falls makes a 120-foot leap. It may not be the tallest cascade in the Bighorns, but it is one of the loudest, letting out a roar as some 3,600 gallons hurtle down the cliff every second. A visitor center features exhibits, and trails crisscross the area.

Leaving the mountains yet again, the drive descends to the plains and Greybull, a business

Shell Falls tumbles down a rift with a deafening roar.

and farming center founded in the 1890s by German settlers. Rte. 14 then rolls across vast plains on the way back to Cody, offering unbroken solitude and endless vistas.

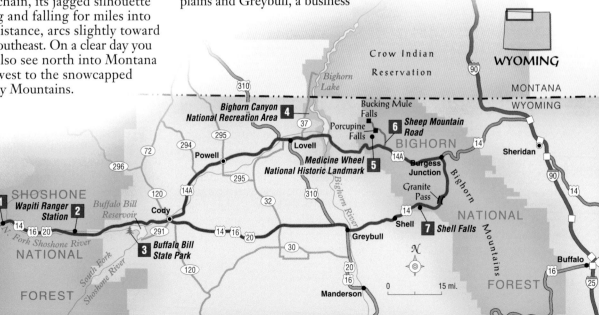

Devils Tower Loop

Devils Tower, rising high above the Wyoming hills, is revered by Plains Indians as a symbolic link to the heavens, despite its diabolical name.

The Belle Fourche River and Devils Tower, in Devils Tower National Monument.

Thanks to the Black Hills, the northeastern corner of Wyoming looks quite different from the rest of the state. In contrast to the tall peaks and vast plains found elsewhere, its gently rounded contours, snug valleys, small towns, and farmlands are reminiscent of the relative tameness of the Appalachians. This drive makes a full tour of the area, reaching a crescendo at Devils Tower, a geological marvel visible for miles and miles that in 1906 became America's first national monument.

1 Newcastle

The grassy plains of the open range meet forested foothills at Newcastle, an early railroad stop founded in 1889. Sample the town's historic sites, then follow Rte. 85 to the north, where it quickly climbs out of the broad flatlands into rolling hills cloaked with a dense, dark forest of ponderosa pines.

Red Butte, a sandstone formation that looms just off the road, provides a colorful counterpoint to the woodlands. Despite its steep sides, both Indians and frontiersmen scaled the butte and used it as a lookout point. Farther along, the road dips out of the hills and back onto grass-covered plains near Four Corners, a tiny community where the drive heads northwest on Rte. 585.

2 Sundance

The Sioux Indian Sun Dance, a grueling four-day ceremony that tested the fortitude of young braves, has lent its name to this town and to neighboring Sundance Mountain. Performed as thanksgiving, to cure disease, and to offer prayers, the intricate ritual was above all a way to symbolize the triumph of good over evil.

One white man who did not win that particular struggle was Harry Longabaugh, whose crimes as part of the Hole-in-the-Wall Gang earned him the nickname the Sundance Kid. The life and legend of the Kid, who was imprisoned for a short time in the local jail, are recalled by exhibits at the Crook County Museum and Art Gallery.

To enjoy the town's natural treasures, follow Rte. 14 to the north, where a paved spur road leads visitors to the Warren Peak Lookout. The fire tower offers a preview of Devils Tower off to the northwest and, nearer at hand, a look at the somber black hills of the Bear Lodge Mountains.

Departing Sundance via Rtes. 14 and I-90, the drive skirts the eastern edge of the Bear Lodge Mountains, then switches onto Rte. 111, which heads due north through a landscape of farms, ranches, and quiet creeks.

3 Aladdin

The modest settlement at Aladdin offers little more than a general store—a venerable old building, erected in 1890, that continues to serve as a gathering place where locals come to swap tales and pass the time of day. In August, however, the town's peaceful ways are pleasantly interrupted by the Bronc Match and Horseshow, complete with an old-time rodeo that always draws a crowd.

The next leg of the drive follows Rte. 24 into the westernmost sector of Black Hills National Forest. Meadows, tree-lined creeks, and 23-acre Cook Lake are among the notable sights in the area. Also memorable are the distant views of the vast plains to the north that are revealed by occasional gaps between trees and hills.

The forests are at their loveliest in the fall, when the leaves of aspens, oaks, and birches explode into a riot of reds and golds that contrast vividly with the dusky dark green of the predominant ponderosa pines. Any time of year, though, offers opportunities for spotting white-tailed deer, wild turkeys, and even elk.

4 Belle Fourche River

Beyond the tiny town of Alva, a slow, gentle climb leads to Hulett, perched next to the narrow, lazily meandering Belle Fourche River. Small bluffs close in here and there on its grassy banks, and cattle graze the many fields that fan away from the water's edge. Take advantage of the services and supplies that are available in Hulett, then continue south beside the Belle Fourche on

The Black Hills National Forest is dotted with numerous ranches.

Rte. 24, for Devils Tower is now just 10 miles away.

5 Devils Tower National Monument

After you've traveled for miles with only tantalizing glimpses of the tower now and then appearing above the treetops, the giant finally comes out of hiding. Rising 1,265 feet above river level, it dwarfs everything in sight, including even tall ponderosa pines that ring its base. Move closer and its neck-craning immensity becomes virtually overwhelming.

Scientists tell us that the tower was formed when a mass of molten rock welled up within the earth's crust, then cooled, and was later exposed by erosion. But the Kiowa Indians have their own way of explaining its creation. According to legend, several maidens were out picking the flowers from prickly pear cacti when they startled a large bear. Snarling with rage, the animal chased the girls to a huge tree stump where they cowered, praying for help. A kindly god, heeding their call, hurled a bolt of lightning at the stump, which caused it to rise toward the heavens, sparing the young maidens. The angry bear, left behind, clawed furiously at the stump, incising it with the grooves that visitors can still see today.

Fact or fiction, most everything about the area is on a grand scale. The national monument, encompassing more than 1,300 acres, contains a mix of grassy hills and scattered stands of pines. Two hikes —the Tower Trail and the longer Red Beds Trail—loop around the base of the monolith, enabling visitors to savor the ever-changing kaleidoscope of light and shadow as the sun's rays play across the accordion-pleated surface of the stump. Try, if possible, to visit in the morning or in the evening, when the effects of light are at their best—and the crowds are at a minimum. The weather, too, can add to the drama, as low clouds shroud the crest in veils of mist, or snow dusts the cracks between the columns, decorating the tower with streaks of white.

The looming bulk of Devils Tower also makes it a mecca for rock climbers, who regard it as a first-class challenge. Initially scaled in 1893, the tower now offers some 200 established climbing routes. A map in the visitor center shows the many paths that have been taken to the top. Bring binoculars and you can watch teams of climbers slowly making their way to the 1½-acre, flat-topped crest.

For more down-to-earth entertainment, pause near the national monument's entrance to view the resident prairie dog colony. Sociable creatures, their playful antics never fail to delight.

6 Keyhole State Park and Reservoir

Leaving Devils Tower, continue on Rte. 24 to Devils Tower Junction, where the drive veers southwest on Rte. 14 toward Keyhole Reservoir. Formed when a dam was built across the Belle Fourche, the lake is nestled among rolling slopes covered with sagebrush, pines, and shrubs.

Moorcroft, just to the southwest, was once a major livestock shipping center. There the gentle hills and pine forests finally disappear, and the land flattens into the sweeping plains of a vast basin spotted with sagebrush.

:::::: Trip Tips ::::::

Length: About 150 miles.

When to go: Popular year-round, but driving conditions are best during the warmer months.

Words to the wise: No fuel is available between Sundance and Hulett. Bring comfortable shoes or boots for hiking.

Nearby attraction: Thunder Basin National Grassland, offering views of wildlife. Largest sector is west of Newcastle.

Further information: Wyoming Division of Tourism, I-25 at College Dr., Cheyenne, WY 82002; tel. 800-225-5996, www.wyomingtourism.org

127

Flaming Gorge Getaway

Crossing the frontier that separates northeastern Utah and southern Wyoming,
this drive never veers far from its centerpiece—a massive reservoir more than 90 miles in length.

The white light of the midday sun washes out the colorful rocks of Flaming Gorge. It's best to visit at sunrise or sunset.

Mountains, forests, canyonlands, and high desert—a variety only the West can supply—are all parts of this tour. Yet there's a bonus too: an opportunity to glimpse relics of the distant past. Dinosaur fossils, footprints left by ancient reptiles, and billion-year-old rocks are among the reminders of a time long, long ago.

1 Vernal

Barely 8,800 people live in Vernal, but in this corner of Utah, that makes for a metropolis. At first the town was little more than a homestead or two, but today it has become a commercial center and the gateway to outlying countryside.

Travelers to Vernal can visit the age of dinosaurs, both at the Utah Field House of Natural History and at nearby Dinosaur National Monument. The Field House delights with its full-scale replicas of ancient animals in action poses in re-created environments. At the national monument, a vast tract of more than 200,000 acres spreading across the Utah-Colorado border, many fossils of prehistoric animals are embedded in sandstone cliffs. Painstakingly unearthed by scientists, the fossil bones are the remains of giants that roamed the earth about 145 million years ago.

2 Ashley National Forest

Designed to disrupt the landscape as little as possible, Rte. 191 rises and falls with the terrain on its climb into and through Ashley National Forest. Pines and aspens grow along the highway, but frequent breaks in the woodland afford views of far-off meadows. The grassy realms extend toward the Uinta Mountains, a series of rounded peaks that define the northern horizon.

What distinguishes this drive from other mountain routes, though, are the numerous roadside kiosks and interpretive signs that dot the byway all the way from Vernal to Manila. Visitors can learn about the area's past and present as they pass near petrified forests, primeval rocks, and ancient fossils. Habitats of some of the area's modern-day denizens—beavers, otters, elk, and songbirds—are also explained.

3 Flaming Gorge Dam

It took six years of hard work and nearly a million cubic yards of concrete to trap the combined flow of the Green River and the many smaller waterways that pour into Flaming Gorge. The dam, completed in 1964, rises to a height of 502 feet and contains the waters of Flaming Gorge Reservoir, an emerald expanse between colorful cliffs of quartzite (sandstone that

Length: About 130 miles, plus side trips.

When to go: Pleasant at any time of year, but winters often close roads at higher elevations.

Nearby attraction: Steinaker State Park, north of Vernal.

Lodgings: Reservations are necessary in summer.

Further information: Dinosaurland Travel Board, 55 East Main St., Vernal, UT 84078; tel. 800-477-5558, www. dino land.com.

has turned into solid quartz). To view the dam and the dramatic southern end of the gorge, continue on Rte. 191 for seven miles past its junction with Rte. 44.

4 Red Canyon

Backtrack to Rte. 44 and join the traffic heading northwest to Manila. Traveling through stands of ponderosa pines and aspens, you'll soon come to a well-marked forest road that leads north to Red Canyon Overlook. The area has a visitor center and several hiking trails and overlooks. One, perched on the edge of the canyon's rim, offers a bird's-eye view of the reservoir, shimmering far below, and the imposing cliffs that shoot up along the opposite shore.

5 Dowd Mountain Overlook

It was explorer-geologist John Wesley Powell, one of the first white men to set eyes on this area, who in the 1870s named this river-carved chasm Flaming Gorge. His thrill of discovery can be relived by sightseers today at the Dowd Mountain Overlook,

reached via an unpaved access road (closed in winter). The view takes in a lengthy stretch of the reservoir and the reddish walls of the gorge.

Paths wind through the nearby woods, where you may spot deer, elk, or sage grouse. One trail, though fairly difficult, threads its way to Hideout Canyon, a hill-hidden nook that was so named because Butch Cassidy and other outlaws sought refuge there from pursuing posses.

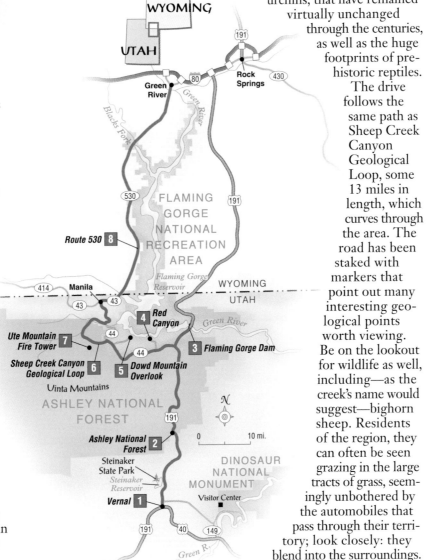

6 Sheep Creek Canyon Geological Loop

Millions of years ago the earth's crust shifted here along a giant fault, forming mountains 10,000 feet high and plunging ravines. Most of these highlands have been worn away since that time by the forces of erosion, the towering slopes today are teeming with fossils. Among the ancient creatures frozen in the stones are a variety of now-extinct marine animals. The fossil finds also include other creatures, such as sea urchins, that have remained virtually unchanged through the centuries, as well as the huge footprints of prehistoric reptiles.

The drive follows the same path as Sheep Creek Canyon Geological Loop, some 13 miles in length, which curves through the area. The road has been staked with markers that point out many interesting geological points worth viewing. Be on the lookout for wildlife as well, including—as the creek's name would suggest—bighorn sheep. Residents of the region, they can often be seen grazing in the large tracts of grass, seemingly unbothered by the automobiles that pass through their territory; look closely: they blend into the surroundings.

7 Ute Mountain Fire Tower

Early forest rangers, concerned about the devastation that fires leave in their wake, used high-platform lookouts to keep an eye out for smoke. Today most of the fire lookouts have gone the way of the dinosaurs, as helicopters and airplanes have been mobilized to keep a wary watch over the vast woodlands.

One of the earliest fire lookouts in Utah—designated a national historic landmark—still stands at Ute Mountain. It can be reached by a short, unpaved road off the Sheep Creek Canyon Geological Loop. The panorama from the tower's platform includes the Wyoming desert and the forest-clad ridgetops and valleys of the Uinta Mountains.

Once the loop road returns to Rte. 44, consider heading south five miles to Sheep Creek Overlook for a view of the dramatic meeting place of Sheep Creek and Flaming Gorge. Then the drive follows Rte. 44 north to Manila, a small town ringed by crests and peaks.

8 Route 530

After a short stretch along Rte. 43 east, a sign welcomes you to Wyoming. Rte. 530, the final leg of the drive, continues to the north, where the terrain quickly—almost magically—changes from mountains to high desert. Though the land through which you travel may for the most part seem barren, the 45 miles to Green River have an austere beauty all their own: lonely buttes cresting rumpled hills, piles of rocks shaped like giant beehives, and a weather-worn badland called the Devils Playground. Farther along, sand, sagebrush, and cactus accompany you to the town of Green River and its namesake waterway—the celestial knife that slowly carved Flaming Gorge.

Utah Byways

A journey through Utah's most secluded corner reminds us that this high, lonesome country is not just a landscape of legend and lore but a real place after all.

Vistas rival the Grand Canyon at Dead Horse Point, near Moab.

Sculpted by wind and water over countless millennia, the remote canyons and plateaus of southeastern Utah were among the last parts of the American West to be seen by travelers from the East—indeed, much of this country remained uncharted until well into the 20th century.

1 Fishlake Scenic Byway

Beginning at the little hamlet of Sigurd, the drive follows Rte. 24 southeast through miles of sage-brush country. After turning north onto Rte. 25, the road climbs to a lofty perch of nearly 9,000 feet. Here, cradled amidst the meadows and aspen groves of Fishlake National Forest, lies blue-green Fish Lake, its deep, cold waters teeming with four kinds of trout. A shoreline path and numerous mountain bike trails lead to views of snowcapped peaks as well as to glimpses of wildflowers, waterfowl, deer, elk, and moose. Boat rentals, campgrounds, and cabins enable travelers to enjoy the area and take their time exploring the gemlike lake. To continue the drive, double back to Rte. 24 and head east toward Torrey.

2 Torrey

The high Southwest is a landscape of surprising transitions, where cool wooded valleys can give way in a few short miles to otherworldly formations of sunset-colored sandstone. Rte. 24 makes just such a passage from one terrain to another as it follows the Fremont River, swinging south and east of a great plateau crested by the lofty ramparts of Thousand Lake Mountain. By the time you see the ruddy shaft of Chimney Rock rising high above the highway east of Torrey, the pine-scented woods surrounding Fish Lake will seem far away indeed. You are now at the gateway to Capitol Reef National Park, where nature has practiced the fine art of sculpture but has left the horticulture to humans.

3 Capitol Reef National Park

Named for a white sandstone dome that suggested the U.S. Capitol to approaching pioneers, Capitol Reef National Park is a 70-mile strip of stark and surreal terrain whose "reef" is its centerpiece. The nautical term in fact was grimly metaphorical: this age-old aggregation of sheer outcrops, a result of the gradual creasing and folding of the earth's crust, blocked the way for settlers' wagon trains just as ocean reefs stymie seafarers. Still, a handful of hardy souls did penetrate these polychrome ramparts.

Vivid petroglyphs, drawings etched into stone that depict desert bighorn sheep along with human figures holding shields and wearing headdresses, testify to the presence of the mysterious Fremont Indians 1,000 years ago. Later came the Paiutes and the Navajos, who gave the multicolored rock layers a name that means "sleeping rainbows."

As the last century closed, Mormon families sought solace in the shadow of Capitol Reef. In their tiny, optimistically named community of Fruita, these peaceable souls planted orchards, tended farms, and grazed livestock for more than 50 years, until the hamlet's utter isolation made living here intolerable. At the site of their abandoned community, a restored one-room schoolhouse—empty since 1941—and other wooden structures tell of a land brought to life by the Fremont River. Peaches, apricots, cherries, pears, and apples are still here for the picking, for a nominal Park Service fee, from trees in orchards that have long outlived the dreams of the men and women who once planted them.

4 Hickman Bridge

About midway along the main road through Capitol Reef National Park is a trail that follows the lush banks of the Fremont River, then climbs through stands of cottonwood and fragrant juniper to Hickman Bridge, a graceful 133-foot natural span. The sandstone arc leaps from a jumble of rock and makes a grand symmetrical sweep above a streambed, framing Capitol Dome (the signature formation of the national park).

5 Lake Powell Overlook

Along the lonely highway connecting Capitol Reef to Hanksville, the Henry Mountains rise in arid desolation to the south. Outlaws once hid rustled cattle in the shadows of these weathered peaks. Bison still wander in the foothills, where prospectors have sought gold for a hundred years and more.

Fifteen miles south of Hanksville, off Rte. 95, an unpaved side road leads to the russet-hued canyon of the Dirty Devil River, so named in the 1800s by explorer John Wesley Powell because of its mud and stench.

At the overlook some 35 miles to the south, the panorama of Lake Powell (named for the explorer) comes into view. Nearly 200 miles long, the lake took 17 years to fill Glen Canyon after the Colorado River was dammed; in the process, it wandered into so many side canyons that its shoreline extends for a staggering 2,000 miles—longer than the entire West Coast. The rich red walls of those inundated canyons rise abruptly from the waterline, contrasting sublimely with the lake's cerulean waters.

6 Hite Crossing

Named for Cass Hite, a prospector who in the 1880s ferried wayfarers across the Colorado River, Hite Crossing is now the northernmost passage across the portion of the river that has become Lake Powell—but instead of a ferry, a bridge now takes traffic across the transformed canyon. For travelers on Rte. 95, Hite Crossing is the threshold of the Glen Canyon National Recreation Area, more than a million acres of wilderness playground surrounding Lake Powell. The local marina rents houseboats and smaller craft, enabling visitors to explore the endless array of azure bays and ruddy canyons that branch out all along the lake.

7 Natural Bridges National Monument

Spanning the twisting streambeds of White Canyon and eons of geologic time with equal grace, three natural bridges attest to the patience and persistence of flowing water. Fashioned of tawny sandstone millions of years old, the bridges—called Sipapu, Kachina, and Owachomo—are the centerpieces of Natural Bridges National Monument, some 50 miles southeast of Hite Crossing. Atop a 6,500-foot-high plateau that commands a southerly overview of Arizona's Monument Valley, a road and hiking trail link the three bridges, which were formed by silted floodwaters that scraped out shortcuts between tight loops in the canyons. Sipapu, first along the drive, is the second-largest such bridge in the world; its height is equal to that of a 20-story building, and its span is nearly the length of a football field. Kachina, the youngest bridge, is the least worn down by wind and water. Owachomo, the oldest, is apt to be the first to fall: at 180 feet across, its span is a comparatively delicate strand barely nine feet thick.

Human engineering, too, shaped the scenery at Natural Bridges. Along Bridge View Drive the entrances to ancient Anasazi dwellings gape from a steep rock slope. Few places on earth can boast a climate and an architecture in such perfect harmony—if the vanished ancient peoples were to return tomorrow, their desert-preserved homes would be waiting just as they had left them some 800 years ago.

8 Mule Canyon Rest Area

Another long-abandoned Anasazi settlement survives in the South Fork of Mule Canyon, a 15-minute drive from Natural Bridges on Rte. 95. Among the stone and adobe structures—scarcely different in hue and texture from the rock that surrounds them—are a circular tower and a kiva, an underground chamber where members of the community met. Drought most likely drove the Anasazis from the area in the 13th century.

Mountain bikers enjoy the Needles District of Canyonlands National Park.

More of their sunbaked ruins are found in Arch Canyon, visible from a side road found off Rte. 95 a mile to the east.

9 Comb Ridge

Like a stockade wall flung up by giants, Comb Ridge rises with daunting abruptness from the floor of Comb Wash, east of Mule and Arch canyons. Rte. 95 ascends the 800-foot-high ridge, where the view encompasses this massive upthrust of the earth's crust as it extends toward the southern horizon.

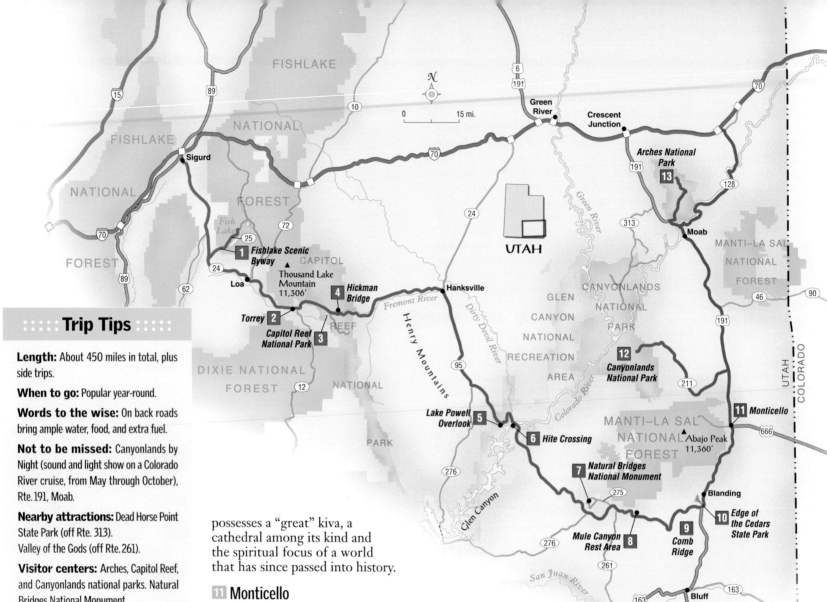

Length: About 450 miles in total, plus side trips.

When to go: Popular year-round.

Words to the wise: On back roads bring ample water, food, and extra fuel.

Not to be missed: Canyonlands by Night (sound and light show on a Colorado River cruise, from May through October), Rte. 191, Moab.

Nearby attractions: Dead Horse Point State Park (off Rte. 313). Valley of the Gods (off Rte. 261).

Visitor centers: Arches, Capitol Reef, and Canyonlands national parks. Natural Bridges National Monument.

Further information: Utah Travel Council, 300 No. State St., Salt Lake City, UT 84114; tel. 800-200-1160, www.utah.com.

10 Edge of the Cedars State Park

The sense of a dim, forgotten age permeates the Anasazi ruins at Edge of the Cedars State Park, in Blanding off Rte. 191. Here six complexes of residential and ceremonial structures have been noted by archaeologists, and a sizable Anasazi pottery collection is housed in a park museum. Each site has its kiva, and one even

possesses a "great" kiva, a cathedral among its kind and the spiritual focus of a world that has since passed into history.

11 Monticello

Head north 22 miles from Blanding to reach Monticello, the little San Juan County seat perched high in the foothills of the Abajo Mountains. The early Spanish explorers who saw these rounded summits as *abajo* ("low") must have been duped by a desert illusion; Abajo Peak itself, accessible on foot or by four-wheel-drive vehicle, rises to an elevation of more than 11,000 feet. Today these Blue Mountains, as they are also called, are part of the 1.2-million-acre Manti–La Sal National Forest, where cool pine woods offer respite from arid canyons and sun-seared plateaus. A haven for campers year-round

and a winter magnet for skiers, Manti–La Sal represents the green side of a land that, while beautiful, is typically limned in shades of ocher and vermilion.

12 Canyonlands National Park

About 60 miles from Monticello by way of Rtes. 191 and 211, Canyonlands is the largest yet least developed of the national parks in Utah. It encompasses a vast expanse of mesas and canyons surrounding the muddy confluence of the Green and Colorado rivers—a landscape

characterized by explorer and surveyor John Wesley Powell as "a wilderness of rocks…with ten thousand strangely carved forms in every direction."

The rivers divide the park into four unique districts: the Island in the Sky, the Needles, the Maze, and the rivers themselves.

Among the strangest of these districts is the Needles, a surreal jumble of stone turrets, towers, and minarets fashioned from Permian sandstone that is banded in shades of cream and rust. Here

Formed as soft, underlying layers of sandstone eroded, Mesa Arch is in the heart of the Island in the Sky section of Canyonland National Park.

awed visitors gaze at giant spires—some up to 30 stories high—that have been standing at attention for millennia—long before there were humans to see them.

Historic people of many cultures have visited Canyonlands over a span lasting more than 10,000 years—relying on and exploiting the rich resources that hide in the desert landscape. Many prehistoric campsites exist within the park's boundaries.

For several miles after entering the park, Rte. 211 snakes by sites with such names as Wooden Shoe Overlook, Squaw Flat, and Pothole Point and reaches a dead end at Big Spring Canyon. Four-wheel-drive roads and trails lead deep into the Needles backcountry—among them the harrowing Elephant Hill Road, where one particular turn can be made only after backing up to the edge of a sheer precipice that has no guardrail. Short trails lead to an ancient Anasazi granary and to an abandoned cowboy's camp that features century-old wooden and iron hand-made furnishings.

13 Arches National Park

Returning to Rte. 191, the drive heads north to Moab, then crosses the Colorado River and arrives at the entrance to Arches National Park. Given the singularity and variety of the rock formations here, it's not surprising that early explorers mistook them for the ruins of an ancient civilization. Within the park are more than 2,000 named arches, as well as other natural sculptures—domes, walls, spires, precariously balanced rocks, and figures resembling monumental chess pieces.

In the section of the park called The Windows stand several giant arches, and a few miles north is the often-photographed, freestanding Delicate Arch, regarded by many as the park's crown jewel. Farther to the north, at Devils Garden, is another collection of awesome arches with such names as Dark Angel, Pine Tree, Tunnel, Double O, and the long, graceful but alarmingly thin Landscape Arch.

Departing from Arches, the drive heads south for a few miles on Rte. 191 before turning northeast on Rte. 128, a 44-mile scenic byway that terminates at I-70. Paralleling the Colorado River most of the way (look for rafters in summer), the route skirts Castle Valley, a famous backdrop for Hollywood films; the high mudstone ramparts of Fisher Towers; and the old Dewey Bridge, a one-lane wood-and-steel suspension bridge built in 1916 and now closed to all but foot traffic. From the perspective of the route just traveled, this retired structure reminds us that man-made bridges are short-lived compared to arches of sandstone fashioned by nature.

Bryce Canyon Country

Giant chess pieces? Soaring sandcastles? Monks turned to stone? Not at all—just another of nature's masterpieces, the magical place called Bryce Canyon.

Dramatic sandstone chimneys, spires, and arches form the background for outdoor recreation in Kodachrome Canyon State Park.

To one explorer, it resembled "a mighty ruined colonnade." To an early settler, Ebenezer Bryce, it was "a hell of a place to lose a cow." But to the thousands of annual visitors to Bryce Canyon National Park and the surrounding area, it is quite simply unforgettable. State Route 12, an All American Road, and other nearby scenic byways take you deep into this city of stone and beyond, where time, water, and the elements have fashioned a soul-stirring landscape of fairy-tale castles and ramparts.

1 Red Canyon

Heading east across sagebrush flats, the drive quickly enters seven-mile-long Red Canyon, which offers all the dramatic splendors of Utah's canyonland in miniature. The canyon was carved by the same erosive forces that created Bryce and boasts stunning scenery of its own. But one big difference prevails: this little jewel of a canyon is far less visited than its big brother, so its trails remain virtually pristine. A U.S. Forest Service visitor center at the west end of the canyon directs visitors to a separate trail network that caters to human-powered and motorized forms of recreation. Many of Red Canyon's prettiest vistas can be seen along Rte. 12, which burrows through terra-cotta tunnels as it heads east. Slicing across Dixie National Forest, the drive passes glistening ponderosa pines and twisted stone formations tinted pink and scarlet by iron-rich minerals.

The canyon's myriad nooks and crannies once made it an ideal hideaway for outlaws, and you may stumble upon one of their lairs as you hike or ride horseback along the area's many serpentine trails.

Two of the easiest treks—both crossing dusty scrubland brightened by vermilion-colored rocks—leave from a visitor center located about two miles into the canyon. There you can get acquainted with the surrounding wilderness of Dixie National Forest. The Bird's Eye Trail, nearly one mile long, climbs high enough to offer an overview of the canyon below. The Pink Ledges Trail, even shorter, features some of the region's most intriguingly shaped rock formations. The most dramatic time of year to view these marvels is in winter, when the light is crystalline and snow clings to cracks, creases, and crevices like the vanilla icing on a gingerbread house.

2 Dixie National Forest

In a region dominated by desert, water is a precious resource. That makes Dixie National Forest—the largest in the state, encompassing nearly 2 million acres—a valued neighbor. Were it not for the mountains and plateau tops of this alpine forest, nearby cities and towns would never have been able to flourish. Throughout the winter, snow accumulates at high elevations, later melting into cold, clear mountain streams that feed sparkling lakes—much-needed moisture when the hot, dry summer arrives. Anglers prize these waters for their wealth of trout, including such varieties as brook, rainbow, brown, and cutthroat. Also varied are the forest's trees (spruce, fir, and a host of pines) and the birds that inhabit them (including numerous red-tailed hawks, Steller's jays, and, in summer, protected peregrine falcons).

State Rte. 22, one of several roads on which you can explore the forest, leads to the turnoff for Powell Point. Watch for Rte. 132 to Pine Lake Campground, but climb to the top of the plateau beyond the camp only if you have a high-clearance all-wheel-drive vehicle. Some 10,000 feet above sea level, this promontory looks out on the red-and-pink cliffs of the Claron Formation below and, beyond it, Arizona.

Animal lovers may opt to drive the East Fork of the Sevier River Scenic Byway, a must for wildlife viewing; look for Rte. 87, about 11 miles east of the Rte. 89 and State Rte. 12 junction. From its numerous pullouts, sightings of pronghorns, prairie dogs, and jackrabbits are more than likely, and in summer and autumn, perhaps an elk will saunter into view.

▣ Bryce Canyon National Park

The first thing to be said about Bryce Canyon is that it's not a canyon at all. Extending for 18 miles along the eastern edge of the Paunsaugunt Plateau, this enchanting fairyland of stone is a series of huge, horseshoe-shaped amphitheaters, carved over millions of years by countless rivulets.

Time, wind, and water—that masterful team of sculptors—also collaborated to create one of the park's most popular attractions: the fanciful rock formations known as hoodoos.

Over the ages, as water seeped into the cracks of alternately hard and soft layers, the rock underwent relentless freeze-and-thaw cycles called frost wedging. The result is a stone army of lifelike spires that populates the Claron Formation. Some of the rock formations here have names nearly as whimsical as their evocative shapes—Alligator, Queen Victoria, and The Hat Shop.

The intense palette to be savored here makes this 36,000-acre national park one of the most photogenic in America. The rocks' vivid hues have been created by the oxidization of various minerals. At dawn they wear gowns of reddish brown that slowly turn to light gold as the sun bathes them in its morning glow. Soon they don their afternoon play clothes, a careless hodgepodge of flaming orange, brick red, and deep tan. At day's end they slip into their long-awaited evening attire, festive ensembles of pink, red, and purple.

Making this kaleidoscope of color even more dramatic are the vast backdrops nature has provided for contrast: thick stands of evergreens and a seamless sky of cobalt blue. Perhaps some of this grandeur can be gleaned from photographs brought home by visitors. But only those who see Bryce Canyon for themselves can forgive the excess of exuberance displayed by one early surveyor of the park, who described it as "the wildest and most wonderful scene that the eye of man ever beheld."

Star Route

★ Brian Head–Panguitch Lake Scenic Byway

A year-round feast for the eyes, this 55-mile side trip serves up meadows confettied with wildflowers in summer, vivid aspens and maples in fall, and—in every season—the radiant reds of nearby Cedar Breaks National Monument, an exquisite limestone amphitheater. Heading southwest from Panguitch on Rte. 143, the drive arcs past lovely Panguitch Lake, passes Rte. 148—the access road to Cedar Breaks—then veers north to Brian Head, a prime ski resort. Then it hairpins along the white rocks of Braffit Ridge and the vermilion cliffs of Parowan Canyon before reaching the town of Parowan.

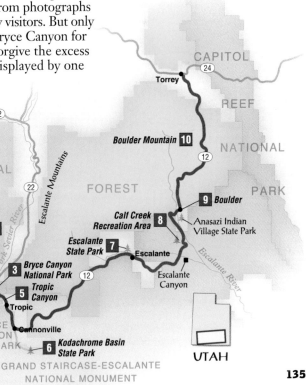

4 Bryce Canyon Scenic Drive

The beauty of Bryce Canyon can be sampled along an 18-mile drive that traces much of its rim. Scenic overlooks—many with views that on a clear day extend 100 miles or more—provide plenty of opportunities for picture taking or wandering along some of the park's 61 miles of trails.

Before venturing into the canyon, stop at Ruby's Inn, an all-purpose facility just north of the visitor center. There you can buy supplies, rent mountain bikes, cross-country skis, and horses or arrange to take a helicopter ride over the park's many and varied scenic wonders.

Once inside the park, head for the turnoff to Bryce Canyon's main amphitheater, which is ringed by

Coyote gulch is a stopping point for hikers in Grand Staircase–Escalante National Monument.

four eminently accessible and drop-dead gorgeous viewpoints plus the salmon-tinged hoodoos that stand within. By following signs to Sunrise Point, you'll be able to drive or walk to Sunrise, Sunset, Inspiration, and Bryce points. Keep in mind that elevations in the park range from 8,000 to 9,000 feet, oxygen is scarce, and that trails that lead down mean you must climb back up them. Wear proper hiking shoes; the trails' surfaces are covered with loose gravel, and you'll need traction to obtain a good footing. At Sunrise Point hike the Queen's Garden Trail, a short trek into the canyon below. The trail was named for the hoodoo at the bottom that bears a more than passing resemblance to Queen Victoria. At Bryce Point try the two-mile-long Hat Shop Trail, where you will see boulders and rock formations shaped like top hats and Easter bonnets.

The park's main road continues south six miles to Farview Point, whose high elevation offers sweeping views of the surrounding Dixie National Forest.

Higher still is Rainbow Point, several miles south, where the one-mile Bristle-cone Loop Trail leads to stands of the gnarled pines. More than millennium in age, these hardy trees are the oldest living things found in Bryce Canyon.

5 Tropic Canyon

The six-mile drive through this scenic canyon found just north of Bryce passes among more rock formations as it wends its way east to Tropic. The town is home to Ebenezer Bryce's old log cabin, which features a robust collection of Indian and pioneer artifacts.

6 Kodachrome Basin State Park

About seven miles south of Cannonville, a spur road leads to Kodachrome Basin State Park, where the scenery is as vivid as the park's name—conferred by the National Geographic Society—implies. Sixty-seven spires of rust-colored sandstone—some reaching heights as tall as 17 stories—soar skyward like frozen geysers.

The surrounding landscape is laced with numerous hiking trails. They range in difficulty from the quick-and-easy Nature Trail to the more daunting Eagle's View Trail, where intrepid hikers who climb a steep one-mile path up the mountainside are rewarded with heavenly vistas.

Southeast of the park the 37-mile-long Cottonwood Canyon four-wheel-drive dirt road takes you past Grosvenor Arch, an immense double span named for Gilbert H. Grosvenor, founder of the National Geographic Society. You have now entered the Grand Staircase–Escalante National Monument, one of the most remote regions of the American Southwest. This area is a favorite among locals, but bring plenty of water, provisions, and a current weather forecast if you venture into the district—untimely changes in the weather, including snow and flash floods, can be life-threatening and sometimes close the road—always come prepared for a long, cold stay.

7 Escalante State Park

Strewn about the landscape of this extraordinary 1,400-acre desert park are an abundance of ancient fallen logs that, through the magic of nature's alchemy, were slowly transformed into stone. Preserved beneath layers of sand and gravel, their wood was replaced by minerals painted in iridescent hues, then exposed by erosion. This fossilized wood—more than 5 million

tons of it—is a sight that never fails to dazzle visitors.

Located just west of the town of Escalante, the park displays its colorful collection of jewels along an interpretive trail. Geologic history is explained at a visitor center, along with Indian artifacts dating back to the 11th-century and dinosaur bones from the Jurassic. At nearby Wide Hollow Reservoir, rimmed with shady cottonwood trees, activities include swimming, fishing, and canoeing.

Continuing eastward on State Rte. 12, the drive connects with several scenic side roads. The Posey Lake Scenic Backway, just north of Escalante, passes Posey Lake, ringed by Ponderosa pines. Serenity gives way to excitement as you reach Hell's Backbone Road, a challenging ride leading to Hell's Backbone Bridge and stupendous views into the heart of Dixie National Forest and Grand Staircase–Escalante National Monument.

Another regional route, the Hole-in-the-Rock Scenic Backway, takes off from State Rte. 12 five miles east of Escalante. Again, a four-wheel-drive vehicle is recommended, as are ample provisions; the best sights lie far off the gravel-and-dirt road, close to the Escalante River—a territory suitable only for vigorous, well-equipped hikers.

The road leads to a gap in the 2,000-foot-high cliffs, through which 19th-century Mormons drove and dropped covered wagons on their journey westward. Be forewarned, though; just before you reach Hole in the Rock, the road becomes nearly impassable, and it's best to hike. Stop at Devils Rock Garden, where hoodoos provide an offbeat backdrop for a picnic, and Dance Hall Rock, where settlers once held rollicking shindigs.

8 Calf Creek Recreation Area

There's a surprising abundance of water in this high desert. East 15

miles from Escalante on State Rte. 12, you'll see Calf Creek. A stiff six-mile hike leads to its lower falls, passing prehistoric ruins and rock art before reaching the pot of gold: a 126-foot-tall cascade tucked away in a shady cul-de-sac. Dip your toes into the pure, icy waters of the pool at the bottom as your reward.

9 Boulder

Continuing north to Boulder, the drive crosses the Hogsback, a narrow ridge with steep cliffs on either side. Just south of town lies the 66-mile Burr Trail, which retraces the century-ago steps of pioneer rancher John A. Burr.

At Boulder, head for the Anasazi Indian Village State Park, a museum and partially excavated settlement that, over the years, has revealed pottery shards, axe heads, and other artifacts. While Boulder may feel as though it sits at the end of the earth, it's actually a quaint, accommodating ranch town with surprisingly good restaurants.

10 Boulder Mountain

Paying a return visit to Dixie National Forest, Rte. 12 climbs across a cool mountain landscape endowed with silvery aspens and sweetly scented evergreens. Atop the 9,670-foot-high summit of State Rte. 12, enjoy views of the 100-mile-long Waterpocket Fold monocline within Capitol Reef National Park to the east and south. From the elevated vantage points of this easternmost segment of the drive, the austere beauty of Utah's canyon country is laid bare for all to see—a sprawling monument to the power of water carving sandstone away by erosion, which continues to redefine this remarkable landscape, one grain at a time.

Lower Calf Creek Falls is a cool oasis in an area known for ancestral Puebloan ruins and rock art.

Zion Canyon Loop

Lofty in height as well as in name—Angels Landing, Great White Throne, Court of the Patriarchs—
the wonders of the Zion region lend southwest Utah a majesty that borders on the sublime.

Painted rock formations reach high into the indigo-blue sky in Zion National Park.

No one who visits Utah's spectacular array of sandstone columns,
canyons, and arches is likely ever to
forget them. The soaring monoliths
in Zion National Park—viewed from
a number of angles along this scenic
loop—combine with the stark, stadium-
like chasm at Cedar Breaks to make
this journey a sumptuous banquet for
the eyes.

1 St. George

The population of Utah is two-
thirds Mormon, and its history
is suffused with the hopes of the
Church of Latter-day Saints. In
1861 Mormon leader Brigham
Young, who dreamed of a western
"Dixie" that would provide the
cotton that was unavailable from
the South during the Civil War,
sent 309 families southwest from
Salt Lake City to St. George to
plant cotton. Though the climate
was fine for the crop, the experi-
ment failed after the Civil War
since cotton from the original
Dixie was so much less expensive.

The St. George of today is a
relatively small city, but not without its unique attractions. Among
them are Brigham Young's winter
home and two imposing Mormon
structures built in the 1870s. The
tabernacle, made of hand-hewn
sandstone blocks, is open to visitors. The white-walled temple,
which is the oldest Mormon temple in the world still in use, is
open only to Mormons.

2 Snow Canyon State Park

The route heads northwest on
Rte. 18 from St. George to Snow
Canyon, an eerie landscape comprising an assortment of lava flows,
extinct volcanoes, and canyons. A
half-mile off Rte. 18 at the park's
Panorama Point, jet-black chunks
of volcanic ash pepper a red sandstone moonscape. Petroglyphs by
ancient Indians appear in various
places throughout the park, and
carvings by 19th-century pioneers

Star Route

★ Smithsonian Butte Backway

Beginning at Rockville, just west of Zion Canyon, this nine-mile backway crosses the orchards and cattle pastures of the Virgin River valley before heading south on a gravel road that climbs to the summit of Wire Mesa. There a turnout offers stunning views of Zion's towering rock formations to the northeast and the massive, 6,632-foot Smithsonian Butte to the east. Swinging west and then due south, the road flattens out, ending at Rte. 59. To take in all the views, travelers are advised to drive this route back in the opposite direction.

decorate Johnson's Arch. After bidding farewell to Snow Canyon, the drive circles back to St. George via Santa Clara.

3 Hurricane

Once you head north on I-15 and then twist east on Rte. 9 through miles of arid landscape, a refreshing change awaits you at the town of Hurricane (named for the violent gusts that swirl off the surrounding hills). The fertile farms here, including orchards of apples, apricots, and peaches, owe their lushness to irrigation. A canal built long ago by intrepid Mormon settlers once linked this area with the Virgin River, and today a pressurized irrigation system keeps the land moist. As you leave town and cross the barricade-like Hurricane Cliffs, look northwest for views of the Pine Valley Mountains.

4 Kolob Terrace Road

Zion's salmon-colored monoliths, jagged towers, and huge cliffs—dubbed temples by the first trailblazers—lie dead ahead along the

Cross-bedded sandstones once were ancient dunes, according to geologists.

muddy Virgin River as you near the town of Virgin. Before you begin your final approach to the park's main entrance, however, consider taking a scenic detour 18 miles north from Virgin along the Kolob Terrace Road. The drive up Zion's western fringe onto the Kolob Plateau is usually uncrowded, and it offers dramatic views of such red-walled mesas and bluffs as Tabernacle Dome and the two Guardian Angels. Note that some parts of the road are unpaved, and they may be impassable after rains; much of the road is closed throughout the winter.

5 Grafton

South of Rte. 9 near Rockville lurk the haunting remains of Grafton, a famous ghost town dating from the 1850s. The settlers were bedeviled in turn by drought, flood, and hostile Paiute Indians. By the early 1900s, even the most stalwart had moved to one of the neighboring towns. The road to Grafton is unpaved, but the town's time-worn buildings and haunting ambience are well worth the trip. Frequently filmed and photographed, the town served as the backdrop for the bicycle scene in the movie *Butch Cassidy and the Sundance Kid*.

6 Zion Canyon

Returning to Rte. 9, the drive approaches the main entrance to Zion, where visitors' anticipation is stirred by the looming presence of the Watchman and the West Temple. These and the other ancient monuments of Zion were formed from sediment deposited in a succession of inland seas, rivers, and streams. The cliffs themselves, now thousands of feet high, are composed of Navajo sandstone—the remains of ancient dunes. In some places, dinosaur tracks send the imagination careering back to times when these giants walked the earth. Even Zion's human history dates from the Paiute Indians who hunted there to the Anasazi, more than a thousand years earlier.

In the 1860s one of Brigham Young's enthusiastic pioneers, Isaac Behunin, is said to have christened the area by proclaiming, "This is my Zion!" (The biblical reference names the hill in Jerusalem where the Temple was built.)

Today's visitors, regardless of their religion, are similarly awed by the wonders here. For the most direct access to the park's premier delights, follow the Zion Canyon Scenic Drive into the seven-mile trench that forms the centerpiece of the park. The canyon was carved over eons by the deceptively serene but relentless Virgin River. The canyon floor, an oasis of cottonwoods and box elders, is surrounded by awesome rock formations. The cluster of sky-high monoliths known as the Court of the Patriarchs seems to suggest a meeting of Titans. The Great White Throne, to the north, is a mass of Navajo sandstone with a flat, pale crown that sparkles in the sun. Topped by juniper and pine, Angels Landing forms a high ridge on the canyon's western side. At the scenic spur's terminus the popular Gateway to the Narrows Trail leads up the river to a deep, narrow chasm.

7 Zion–Mt. Carmel Tunnels

Returning to Rte. 9, the drive heads east on a steep stretch of road, completed in 1930, that zigzags around—and tunnels through—Zion's formidable bulk. The first and longer of the tunnels, more than a mile in length and some 800 feet above Pine Creek, is a marvel of engineering. Although blasted from solid rock, it affords scenic passing glimpses through occasional windowlike openings. Just east of the first tunnel, you can stop and stretch your legs along the well-marked Canyon Overlook Walking Trail—an easy one-hour stroll permitting views of Zion Canyon and Pine Creek that are normally reserved for Steller's jays and ravens. Just below the overlook, the singular Great Arch of Zion resembles a cathedral's flying buttress. Beyond the second tunnel, along Zion's high plateaus, lie petrified sand dunes and other surreal monuments. Among them is Checkerboard Mesa—a giant grayish formation cross-hatched over time with gridlike cracks.

8 Coral Pink Sand Dunes State Park

The road east from Zion coasts into Mt. Carmel Junction, then veers south on Rte. 89 to a 12-mile spur that leads to Coral Pink Sand Dunes State Park. The picturesque dunes there are formed by brisk winds that slice through the gap between the Moquith and Moccasin mountains, eroding sandstone and carrying off its crumbled remains. As rosy in color as their name would suggest, the dunes—up to several hundred feet high—extend to a horizon bedecked by the Vermilion Cliffs and rows of ponderosa and piñon pines.

9 Mt. Carmel

Returning to Rte. 89, the drive heads north through the orchards and verdant fields in and around Mt. Carmel, then passes through the tiny towns of Orderville and Glendale. In the distance are ranges of rough red-and-yellow plateaus that isolate these little villages and offer eloquent testimony to the independent spirit of the pioneers.

10 Strawberry Point

Veering west at Long Valley Junction onto Rte. 14 (the Markagunt Scenic Byway), the road climbs into Dixie National Forest, replete with juniper, Douglas fir, Engelmann spruce, aspen, and oak. (The forest's unlikely name is a further reminder of Brigham Young's unfulfilled hopes for a western land of cotton.) For a rare glimpse of Zion from the northeast, follow Forest Road 058 nine miles south to reach the panoramic perch known as Strawberry Point.

11 Duck Creek

Civilization briefly reasserts itself at Duck Creek, a village bordered by meadows that draw cross-country skiers in the winter and hikers and picnickers throughout the summer. If you're passing through on the weekend nearest Valentine's Day, expect the hills to be alive with the sound of snowmobiles. Each year in mid-February, Duck Creek hosts one of the nation's largest snowmobile races.

Another of the village's claims to fame is its use as a location for Hollywood movies: both *How the West Was Won* and *My Friend Flicka* were filmed here.

12 Navajo Lake

Navajo Lake is small—barely 3½ miles long—but its waters are astir with rainbow and brook trout. If you were to pace every inch of the lake's shoreline, you'd be hard-pressed to find a surface outlet. The lake, it seems, was formed by lava flows that sealed up its eastern edge; its water drains instead through underwater sinkholes, eventually feeding into Duck Creek and Cascade Falls (visible via Forest Road 054). Sometimes, if the weather has been dry, three of the sinkholes are visible from a turnout at the east end of Navajo Lake.

13 Cedar Breaks National Monument

Imagine a giant, natural amphitheater, three miles from rim to rim and 2,500 feet deep. Then fill that giant bowl with countless shapes and kaleidoscopic colors and you have Cedar Breaks. Like Zion, Cedar Breaks was named by Utah pioneers: "cedar" for the junipers found in Dixie National Forest, and "breaks" for the nearly insurmountable badlands that fill the mammoth hollow.

Snow closes the road through Cedar Breaks from mid-October to late May, making it less traveled (but no less beautiful) than neighboring Zion, Arches, and Bryce Canyon national parks. The drive through the park is a five-mile stretch along recently designated Rte. 148 (Rte. 143 on older maps), which heads north off Rte. 14.

Each of four separate overlooks, at elevations greater than 10,000 feet, offers a unique perspective on the myriad columns and canyons within the amphitheater. Toward sunset the shadows grow long, their drama deepened by a medley of oranges and reds that are as bright as glowing embers. In midsummer the purple and crimson colors of the rocks mingle with a floral palette of lupine, larkspur, and Indian paintbrush. These wildflowers contrast sharply—in both size and age—with the bristlecone pine, the granddaddy of trees. Contorted by age and weather, a few of these venerable Cedar Breaks veterans have inhabited the plateau since the last days of the Roman Empire some 16 centuries ago.

14 Zion Overlook

Returning to Rte. 14, the drive continues northwest to a turnout known as Zion Overlook, midway between Cedar Breaks and Cedar City. The vista takes in the majestic buttes of Kolob Terrace and, in the distance, the towers of Zion.

15 Kolob Canyons Road

At Cedar City, turn south on I-15 and follow this four-lane highway 20 miles to the exit for Kolob Canyons Road. Winding through the rugged landscape of Zion's backcountry, this paved 5½-mile spur begins at the Kolob Canyons visitor center, and it skirts the

Over 3,500 feet tall, the Watchman Peak presides over southern Zion National Park.

fascinating Finger Canyons—so named because they are divided by long, narrow sandstone ridges that are parallel to each other.

Although you can't see it from the road, the largest known freestanding arch in the world, Kolob Arch, is seven miles to the east. When the weather is warm and the air is clear, hikers often make overnight pilgrimages to visit the dizzying 310-foot span, among the most noted landmarks of the park.

Once you've left Kolob Canyons Road and rejoined I-15, it's only about a half hour to the drive's starting point at St. George. After traversing this remarkable loop—with its cliffs and summits rising heavenward—one can easily see why Mormon pioneers so revered this superb corner of Utah.

Rocky Mountain Ramble

Spanning America's rooftop, the drive traverses
a northern Colorado landscape once trod only by hooves, paws,
Indian moccasins, and trappers' boots.

Clouds billow up from the valley below, cloaking the ridges in mist.

For anyone who has ever dreamed of soaring like an eagle from one mountaintop to the next, Trail Ridge Road is a fantasy fulfilled. Travelers along this heavenly highway ascend, curve by sinuous curve, to elevations that are literally breathtaking. From ethereal overlooks in Rocky Mountain National Park, the drive winds south through forested valleys, along the shores of azure lakes, and across raging rivers, ending at a charmingly preserved Victorian-era mining town.

1 Park Headquarters

A quiet prelude to the stunning vistas to come, Rte. 36 winds lazily westward from the gateway town of Estes Park to the high ramparts of Rocky Mountain National Park. After pausing at park headquarters for a brief orientation, visitors enter a domain where more than 60 peaks soar higher than 12,000 feet into the alpine world above the tree line. Within the park are 147 lakes and over 350 miles of trails ranging from easy strolls along glacier-fed streams to strenuous hikes that crest the Continental Divide. Perhaps the best time to visit is in September, when the summer throngs have thinned, elk come down from the high country to feed in lush meadows, and the leaves of quaking aspen shimmer like gold coins.

2 Deer Ridge Junction

As Rte. 36 climbs the flank of Deer Mountain, the view to the rear embraces a line of lofty summits crowded shoulder to shoulder. The champion is Longs Peak, towering above its neighbors at 14,259 feet.

At Deer Ridge Junction the drive joins Rte. 34—the start of legendary Trail Ridge Road. Bisecting the national park, the 48-mile route rises to more than 12,000 feet, meandering for 11 miles across stark tundra that looks as though a part of Alaska had been transplanted to Colorado.

3 Many Parks Curve

In the language of Colorado pioneers, a "park" was a mountain-ringed meadow—an invitingly flat place to homestead in this otherwise rugged region. Upper Beaver Meadows and Moraine Park sprawls below the observation point at Many Parks Curve; visible in the distance is Estes Park, where the drive began.

As it winds through forests of Engelmann spruce and subalpine fir, the road passes a sign marking an elevation of two miles above sea level. A bit farther is Rainbow Curve, where another of the park's panoramas embraces a seemingly infinite expanse of mountains and valleys. An early mountaineer thought the configuration of peaks on the northern horizon resembled a swathed, supine figure and so named it the Mummy Range. The long scar on the hillside below is a reminder of the fearful flood that occurred on July 15, 1982, when the Lawn Lake Dam broke, sending a wall of water down Roaring River into Horseshoe Park and scattering giant boulders as though they were mere dice.

4 Forest Canyon Overlook

Beyond Rainbow Curve, the drive skirts stunted pines that have been contorted into odd shapes by the relentless wind. Scattered among them are "banner trees," whose limbs grow like flags on the leeward side of their trunks. As the road continues to ascend, even the trees disappear, yielding to tundra: a world of grasses and wildflowers only inches high. Although the growing season is brief (just 6 to 12 weeks in midsummer), it manages to produce a glittering display of blooms— sky pilot, clover, moss campion, phlox—in an otherwise bleak alpine landscape.

From the overlook high above Forest Canyon, the distinctive U shape of this glacial valley is quite evident, once filled hundreds of feet deep with moving ice. Echoing the glacial era are the Gorge Lakes; cupped in ice-sculpted bowls called cirques on the canyon's far wall, they remain frozen until well into summer.

Turnouts on the road allow numerous opportunities to see the wilderness close up. Above the tree line, alpine meadows stretch into the distance.

5 Tundra Nature Trail

For a close-up look at tundra vegetation, stop at Rock Cut Overlook and walk the half-mile Tundra Nature Trail. Here bucktoothed marmots sun themselves on rocks or scamper across the ground. Less at home are human visitors, who often gasp at the slightest exertion in the thin air at 12,000 feet. But inhospitable as this setting may seem in the warmer months, the scene in winter is truly forbidding: the wind can top 200 miles an hour, the temperature plunges to 60°F below zero, and snowdrifts can reach as much as 30 feet deep.

6 Lava Cliffs

The "lava" here is really volcanic ash deposited 26 million years ago and compacted under heat and pressure into the rock called tuff. Glaciers, the architects of the Rockies, later stripped away overlying material to expose this remnant of the area's volcanic past.

Within the next mile the road arrives at its highest point: 12,183 feet above sea level. Far to the west rise mountains that inspired one of the park's most poetic names; because snowfields on their upper slopes remain visible all year, the white-patched peaks are called the Never Summer Mountains.

7 Alpine Visitor Center

Barren though it may seem, tundra harbors a fascinating array of life, from seldom-seen pocket gophers that tunnel just below the ground to perky little rosy finches that pluck frozen insects off glacial ice. Exhibits at the Alpine visitor center highlight these and other forms of wildlife in this treeless world, comprising nearly a third of the park. (The latticework of massive logs on the visitor center's roof is there to hold it in place during hurricane-force winter storms.)

Trail Ridge Road now descends to Medicine Bow Curve, a hairpin turn overlooking the Medicine Bow Mountains. Far below lies the Cache la Poudre River, named by French trappers who once stored their gunpowder nearby.

8 Milner Pass

Back below the tree line, a one-mile trail leaves the road and heads uphill to the Crater, one of the park's best spots for sighting bighorn sheep. Males use their big curved horns to battle for dominance; when two rams butt heads, the crack echoes through the mountains like a rifle shot.

Just after passing Poudre Lake, whose waters eventually drain into the Mississippi River, the drive crosses the Continental Divide at Milner Pass. Beyond this point raindrops from a summer shower join the Colorado River and pass through the Grand Canyon before flowing into the Gulf of California.

9 Farview Curve

The overlook at Farview Curve perches above the Kawuneeche Valley, carved by a glacier that extended for 20 miles along what is now the west side of the park.

Just below, Trail Ridge Road begins a dizzying series of switchbacks as it descends to the flat, marshy valley floor, where the Colorado River meanders aimlessly in braided channels. *Kawuneeche* is Arapaho for "valley of the coyote"; the wild canines are common here, as elsewhere in the park, but their yipping night song is heard more often than the singers

are seen. Meanwhile, watch the meadows for the stately profiles of moose as they forage for plants.

10 Grand Lake

Rte. 34 leaves the national park—and Trail Ridge Road ends—just beyond the Kawuneeche visitor center. Grand Lake, less than a mile to the east, is Colorado's largest natural lake. (It is, however,

Star Route

★ Granby to Kremmling

Traversing Rte. 40 for some 29 miles between the towns of Granby and Kremmling, this charming stretch of road is part of the Colorado River Headwaters Scenic and Historic Byway. The route follows the Colorado River through a varied landscape of canyons, mountains, and pastures. One choice stop along the way is the Grand County Museum in Hot Sulphur Springs, which features intriguing exhibits on everyday life in the Old West.

Views are endless and traffic is sparse in Rocky Mountain National Park.

much smaller than its man-made neighbors, Shadow Mountain and Granby lakes.)

The town of Grand Lake was one of Colorado's first mountain resorts; founded for the well-to-do after the turn of the century, its yacht club is among the highest in the world. Each August, sailors compete for the Lipton Cup, originally awarded in 1912 by Thomas Lipton, the famed tea magnate, who had a vacation home here. Grand Lake's rustic architecture, featuring logs of lodgepole pine, is a reminder of that genteel era.

11 Tabernash

After skirting Shadow Mountain Lake, Rte. 34 passes between Lake Granby to the east and flat-topped Table Mountain to the west, where Indians mined jasper for tools and arrowheads. The drive then turns south on Rte. 40, passing through Granby and along the Fraser River valley into ranching country. Near the small community of Tabernash are some remarkable views of the

peaks of the Continental Divide, less than 10 miles to the east. The solitary rock column called Devils Thumb rises from the crest of the ridgeline, marking the route of a hiking trail over the mountains.

12 Winter Park

The region around Winter Park, where mountains squeeze in tight beside the Fraser River and Rte. 40, has seen major changes since pioneers arrived here in the late 1800s. Ranching and timber were the first lures. Later on, railroad workers moved in to build the famed Moffat Tunnel, which runs for more than six miles under the Continental Divide. (Completed in 1927, it is one of the longest railroad tunnels in the world. Rail fans and other curious travelers can see its western portal from an overlook in Winter Park.)

Now, as the interweaving trails on the mountainside to the west

A small group of young bull elk listen to older bulls fight.

attest, Winter Park is one of Colorado's more popular ski resorts. Today's luxurious lodges and high-tech lifts could hardly have been envisioned when Denver inaugurated the ski area. On that day in January 1940, lift tickets cost the grand sum of $1 each.

13 Berthoud Pass

Taking a serpentine course up the steep mountain slopes, Rte. 40 once again crosses the Continental Divide (back to the Atlantic side) at 11,307-foot Berthoud Pass. Renowned mountain man Jim Bridger was a member of the survey party that charted this route over the highlands in 1861. Pause a moment here to relax and savor the celestial view, for another series of white-knuckled roller-coaster curves awaits you on the way down to I-70.

14 Georgetown

No time capsule could have preserved the historic mining village of Georgetown as well as did a single turn of economic fate: silver, which built the town in the 1870s,

plunged in value when America adopted the gold standard in 1893. The boomtown went bust, and its fine Queen Anne, Gothic Revival, and Italianate buildings were saved from the wrecking ball of modernization. More than 200 of Georgetown's original structures remain intact today, many beautifully and authentically restored. The Hamill House, built by the town's richest silver miner and now a museum, dazzles the eye with ornate walnut woodwork, gleaming gaslights, original wall coverings, and Renaissance Revival furnishings.

A ride on the nearby Georgetown Loop Railroad affords breathtaking views down the narrow, rugged valley—especially from Devils Gate Bridge, perched on stilts 100 feet above Clear Creek. The chugging steam locomotive and open-air excursion cars recall the days when miners sought and made their fortunes here. Nestled against the wooded mountainside in the distance sits Georgetown, where the legacy of another era lives on in the city still known as the Silver Queen of the Rockies.

Peak-to-Peak Scenic Byway

The gold may be gone, but Colorado's Peak-to-Peak Scenic and Historic Byway continues to unfurl a wealth of natural treasures as it climbs through hushed forests to mirror lakes that reflect the cathedral peaks of the Continental Divide.

Longs Peak is the loftiest summit in Rocky Mountain National Park.

With almost 1,100 peaks soaring higher than 10,000 feet—55 of them rising above 14,000 feet—Colorado has justly been dubbed "the state nearest heaven." Originally conceived as part of a link between Longs Peak and Pikes Peak, this route skirts between two scenic alpine gems: Roosevelt National Forest and Rocky Mountain National Park. Designated a Scenic and Historic Byway in 1918, it is Colorado's oldest.

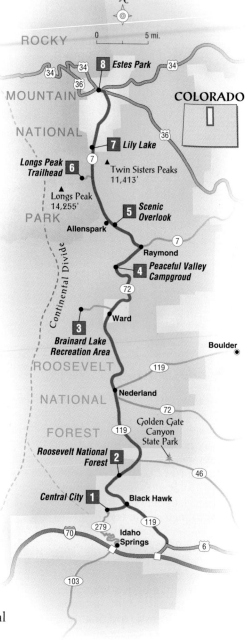

1 Central City

The rush for gold is still on in Central City, where shiny $5 slot machines have breathed new life into the former mining town. But the present revival is nothing compared to 1859, when some $2 million in gold was gouged from the nearby hills, earning Central City the sobriquet "richest square mile on earth."

The resulting boom financed many Victorian structures that still stand—the handsome Teller House, for example, where President Ulysses. S. Grant stayed, and an elegantly restored opera house once frequented by such luminaries as Oscar Wilde and Buffalo Bill Cody. A short, steep hike west from Central City leads to the ghost town of Nevadaville, where a few rickety houses still cling precariously to slopes scarred by mining.

2 Roosevelt National Forest

As Rte. 119 climbs a precipitous gorge into the expansive Roosevelt National Forest, it offers glimpses of magnificent Mt. Evans, whose snowy bulk to the south rises to 14,264 feet. Rolling over hills and ridges, the drive then passes the entrance to Golden Gate Canyon State Park, where downtown Denver can be seen twinkling in the purple twilight.

Just past the cozy town of Nederland, Rte. 72 twists and turns for nine miles as it approaches Ward, a once-rowdy mining camp that lost its luster along with its gold. Follow Rte. 112 west toward the Indian Peaks Wilderness Area, a two-mile-high wonderland of deep pine forests and alpine lakes where snowdrifts linger through July.

3 Brainard Lake Recreation Area

Soon the drive reaches Brainard Lake Recreation Area, where two looking-glass lakes (Red Rock and Brainard) offer fine trout fishing. Take the short, paved trail to Long Lake Trailhead for splendid views

Arrowleafs, grounsels, and mountain bluebells carpet the highlands of Rocky Mountain National Park.

of peaks haloed by clouds. But beware in winter, for the area's serenity is sometimes shattered by the roar of a distant avalanche.

4 Peaceful Valley Campground

Back on Rte. 72, the road drops into a valley along a dancing creek and hairpins at the aptly named Peaceful Valley Campground, where it's not unusual to see a bear lumber by. From here the drive descends into a tunnel-like canyon walled by granite cliffs and then turns west onto Rte. 7.

5 Scenic Overlook

With the new road comes a change in scenery, including verdant valleys, wooded ravines, willow thickets, and meandering creeks. Three miles past the junction, a scenic overlook faces north to Mt. Meeker and the Wild Basin in Rocky Mountain National Park. The largest national park in Colorado, this 265,000-acre preserve boasts an abundance of natural skyscrapers—114 named peaks that soar above 10,000 feet, 78 of them topping 12,000.

About four miles north of Allenspark, the 14,255-foot-tall profile of Longs Peak comes into view to the west. Its flat-topped summit, visible to half of Colorado's population, long served as a landmark to westward-bound pioneers.

6 Longs Peak Trailhead

To reach Longs Peak, continue another mile and follow a spur road west to the Longs Peak Trailhead. The 15-hour round-trip hike to the summit is strictly for the hardy but well worth the effort, offering a grand vista of the Central Rockies.

Back on Rte. 7, continue north another half-mile to the Enos Mills monument, built to honor the founding father of Rocky Mountain National Park. Mills's one-room cabin, filled with books, photographs, climbing equipment, and other memorabilia, is nestled among nearby pines. Behind the cabin loom the craggy silhouettes of Twin Sisters Peaks. In mid-September, when the aspens turn yellow, look for the so-called butterfly burn, a stand of trees that sprouted on a previously burned slope and resembles a giant butterfly.

7 Lily Lake

The lilies are long gone from Lily Lake—early homesteaders periodically drained its waters, causing the flowers to die—but they live on in its name. Full once again, the lake lures a steady stream of ring-necked ducks, mallards, and migrating Canada geese. Exhibits at the visitor center recall the days when the lake was a shimmering pool of yellow blooms.

8 Estes Park

Winter comes early to the Rockies, with snow dusting the hills, then deepens as the days grow shorter. In early fall elk wander down from the high country for their annual mating ritual, which you can see—and hear—from the highway. The road coils around Prospect Mountain before plunging to Estes Park, the eastern gateway to Rocky Mountain National Park and a popular year-round recreational center. (The town's name reflects the western custom of referring to any open, grassy valley as a park.)

During ski season a maze of Nordic trails shoelace up the snow-draped mountains that hover over this storybook town. (In summer an aerial tram whisks visitors to the summit of Prospect Mountain for panoramic views.) The historic Stanley Hotel, a sugar-white grand dame with a red roof, is a popular warming spot for visitors.

By late April, winter loosens its grip on the valleys and hillsides as distant thunder signals the return of spring. Rivers swell with snowmelt while luminescent wildflowers —alpine buttercups, shooting stars, and forget-me-nots—bloom through early May, transforming the low country into a land of Oz.

::::: Trip Tips :::::

Length: About 60 miles.

When to go: Year-round.

Not to be missed: The Oh My God Road, a narrow byway winding a tortuous course from Idaho Springs to Central City.

Nearby attractions: Mt. Evans Byway, one of the highest paved roads in North America, Idaho Springs. Eldora Mountain Resort, Eldora. Wild Bear Center, providing environmental education, Nederland.

Further information: Tourism and Recreation Program, P.O. Box 679, Nederland, CO 80466; 866-435-3672, www.colorado.com.

Colorado Springs Loop

A journey into the past as well as into the
mountains, this drive climbs to prehistoric fossil beds,
centuries-old Indian trails, and relics from the gold-boom era.

★ Shelf Road

For thrill seekers willing to leave
the ease of highway travel behind
in order to explore the untamed
Colorado countryside via an unpaved backcountry byway, Shelf
Road is the route of choice. The
challenging, white-knuckle drive
leads from Cripple Creek to Canon
City, passing numerous geological
marvels, Window Rock among
them, then comes to "the Shelf,"
where the road is just a ledge
sliced into the wall of Fourmile
Canyon. At Red Canon Park 100-
foot spires cast their lengthy
shadows, and the site of fossil
excavations awaits at the broad
mountain valley that encircles
Garden Park, a prime locale for
spotting wild turkeys.

1 Colorado Springs

Colorado Springs was established
on dreams of health, wealth, and
proper living. Founded in 1871 as
a model community for "upright"
people, the city counted among
its assets its clean, crisp air and an
average of more than 250 days of
sunshine a year. Within decades
the area was booming, complete
with polo and cricket fields, palatial hotels, and sumptuous homes.
Well-to-do travelers, often seeking
cures for tuberculosis and other
ailments, were flocking to the area.
Before long the town had become
so cosmopolitan that some began
to call it Little London.

Today about 361,000 people live
in Colorado Springs, where wide
boulevards, spacious sidewalks,
shady parks, and excellent museums complement the natural setting. The Rampart Range rises just
to the west, offering superb unobstructed views of the city below.
One of the best vistas can be seen

Sandstone formations at Garden of the Gods, some of time's finer creations, were carved by eons of erosion.

It was only a bit at a time that
early adventurers began to chart
this region, a landscape so rugged
that none but the bravest dared to
enter. Yet trappers, soldiers, geogra-
phers, and early settlers did in time
explore the area, opening the way for
others to follow. And come they did
when gold was found, spurring an influx of miners. The inevitable bust
brought an end to hopes for material
wealth, but for modern visitors, the
rivers, the peaks, and the lush valleys
are reward enough, the singular ingredients of truly priceless panoramas.

from the tower at the Will Rogers Shrine of the Sun. Inside, memorabilia recall the renowned cowboy-philosopher, and murals depict events from Colorado's history.

Heading out of town on Rte. 24, the drive, a lengthy loop, quickly ascends the first line of Rocky Mountain peaks. A not-to-be-missed stop along the way is Garden of the Gods, a 1,350-acre parkland filled with sandstone formations that have eroded into every imaginable shape and size—and quite a few unimaginable ones. To some eyes the sculpturelike spires and outlandish outcroppings resemble strange monsters, a roster that includes both giants and gargoyles.

2 Pikes Peak Highway

Cresting at 14,110 feet, Pikes Peak was named for Zebulon Pike, who led an expedition sent out in 1806 by Thomas Jefferson to survey the newly acquired lands of the Louisiana Purchase. Pike, a lieutenant at the time, glimpsed the mountain as he was crossing the prairie, perhaps 100 miles away. After a failed attempt to scale the peak, he concluded that the summit could never be reached.

Despite the lieutenant's dour prediction, present-day visitors can choose among three separate routes to the top: a hike along the Barr Trail, a chug aboard the Pikes Peak Cog Railway, or a drive on Pikes Peak Highway—one of the most spectacular mountain roads in the country.

The 19-mile highway, a toll road first opened in 1916, climbs through small canyons, traverses steep slopes, and winds around hairpin curves as it gains almost 7,000 feet in altitude. The uphill journey passes firs, pines, and aspens that are interspersed with flowery alpine meadows. Near the 12,000-foot mark, the trees begin to grow stunted, then farther on

disappear, as craggy rocks—for the most part Pikes Peak granite—dominate the landscape all the way to the broad, level summit.

High in the sky, the crest remains chilly most of the year. Yet its alpine tundra manages to sup-

This early homestead was settled on the grassy floor of the Florissant Valley.

port an array of vibrant wildflowers that bloom in the summer. Although the growing season is brief, the views seem to go on forever. On clear days you can see the suburbs outside Denver, the San Juan and Sangre de Cristo ranges rumpling toward New Mexico, and the immense sea of grass that comprises the Great Plains.

Such grandeur, it seems, is deserving of an equally sublime response, and Katharine Lee Bates, a college professor and poet, rose to the occasion. After visiting the summit in 1893, she recorded her impressions in a poem, including a lyrical passage that praised the "purple mountain majesties above the fruited plain." Her verses, set to music in 1913, became *America* *the Beautiful*, the cherished unofficial national anthem.

3 Mueller State Park and Wildlife Area

Long before man built highways, nature provided a path of its own through the mountains: Ute Pass, where ancient earthquakes cleared a route between the peaks. By the time white men arrived, Indians had worn a trail along the boulder-strewn fault, which Rte. 24 skirts up ahead.

At the town of Divide, Rte. 67 turns due south to Mueller State Park and Wildlife Area. Once a hunting ground of the Ute Indians, the park contains 12,100 acres of varied terrain—rounded outcrops, dense forests, and grassy meadows. Some 85 miles of hiking trails crisscross the preserve, where you might spot elk, mule deer, and bighorn sheep. One trail, short but steep near the top, climbs to Grouse Mountain, the loftiest point in the park and one of the

best places to glimpse hawks, golden eagles, and—looming as large as ever—Pikes Peak.

4 Cripple Creek

One of the best things about this mountain town is getting there—a drive on Rte. 67 running parallel to the mountains of Pike National Forest. The slopes support scattered stands of aspens and spruces, and above the timberline, rolling alpine tundra is dotted with forget-me-nots, dwarf columbines, lilies, and other summer wildflowers.

As precious to some as the views were the gold mines near Cripple Creek, where one of the richest claims in American history was filed in 1890. At the height of the boom, this was a small city—home to a population of about 16,000—and an important financial center, complete with three stock exchanges. Present-day visitors for a change of pace can ride an early narrow-gauge train, the Cripple Creek & Victor Railroad, which curls past dozens of old, abandoned mines.

Victor, a few miles to the southeast, can be reached via Rte. 67. Back in the area's heyday, the two towns were rivals, and at one time Victor, not to be outdone by Cripple Creek, had streets that were literally paved with gold—ore that was deemed too low-grade to ship out. After a period of decline, the twin towns thrive once again as centers for tourism.

5 Florissant Fossil Beds National Monument

The rumblings of ancient volcanoes—massive mountains that erupted repeatedly—are responsible for the fossils here. Mudflows dammed a stream, and the backed-up waters partially inundated the surrounding forest. Then thick rains of ash and pumice buried the region, thereby preserving the area's plants and animals as fossils.

The climate was much different then, a time when sequoia, cedar, hickory, beech, and even avocado trees thrived in a warm, humid realm. Conditions were perfect for insects, and they are among the most frequently found fossils—from butterflies to the tsetse fly, a species that today occurs naturally only in Africa. Mammals, too, were captured in stone and now form a prehistoric menagerie that includes a large rhinolike creature about 14 feet in length. Two short trails, A Walk Through Time and the Petrified Forest Loop, guide sightseers through the scattered forests and summer wildflower meadows that cover the numerous fossil-bearing shales.

6 Eleven Mile State Park

Large lakes are few and far between in this rugged, steep landscape, so humans have stepped in and, at Eleven Mile State Park, created a reservoir. Although visitors are not allowed to swim in the cold, cobalt water, they can cast a line and try for trophy-size trout. To enjoy the area's impressive

views—panoramas that take in several mountain ranges—explore the hiking trails that crisscross the surrounding wilds.

Back on Rte. 24, the drive leads to Wilkerson Pass, ascending to 9,507 feet. On the way back down, the view opens to reveal South Park, one of Colorado's largest upland basins. The valley, about 900 square miles in

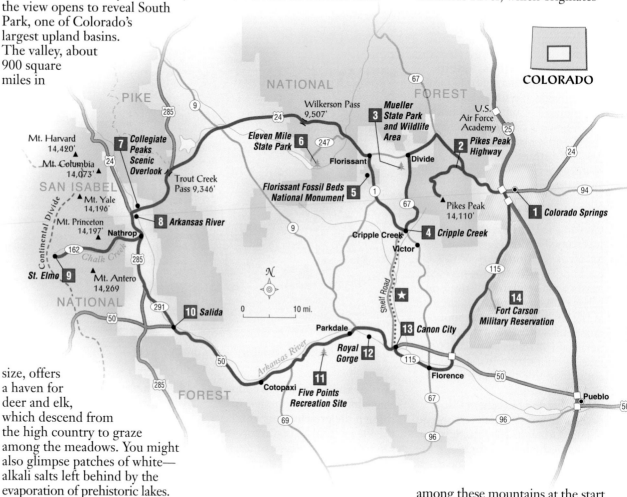

size, offers a haven for deer and elk, which descend from the high country to graze among the meadows. You might also glimpse patches of white—alkali salts left behind by the evaporation of prehistoric lakes.

7 Collegiate Peaks Scenic Overlook

The drive begins another demanding ascent as it climbs the western slope of South Park to Trout Creek Pass, which tops off at 9,346 feet. Tracing a 19th-century railroad's course, the highway slices up barren hillsides, snakes through shadowy canyons, and passes abandoned, weatherworn cabins that were built along the way by early pioneers

who settled the area in numbers in the 19th century.

One of the region's finest vistas awaits at the Collegiate Peaks Scenic Overlook, perched above the Arkansas River valley. The view looks west across a fertile basin—

spotted with willows and cottonwoods—to the snowcapped crowns of the Collegiate Peaks. Part of the Sawatch Range, the mountains were named in 1869 for the prestigious universities of the East—Harvard, Columbia, Yale, and Princeton. Rising more than 14,000 feet, each qualifies as a Fourteener, and together their sturdy backbone marks the Continental Divide's route through these precipitous parts.

8 Arkansas River

When the snow begins to melt, many of the local outdoor enthusiasts put their skis away and dust off their kayaks. They are bound for the roiling rapids of the Arkansas River, which originates

among these mountains at the start of what will be a 1,450-mile course to the Mississippi.

As the drive veers to the south, it crosses the river, then follows near its course via Rte. 285. Much of the river is encompassed by the Arkansas Headwaters Recreation Area, a protected corridor that was established in 1989. The river's rapids range from the fairly tame to frothy stretches that are rated among the state's most difficult. (A number of outfitters offer tours and supplies.) Ruby Mountain Recreation Site, a put-in point with camping and fishing, lies just up-river from Browns Canyon, where the Arkansas swirls between the towering pink walls of 6,600-acre Browns Canyon Wilderness Study Area. The river, however, does not have a monopoly on recreational activities here; inviting trails lace the region, and hikers can hope to catch glimpses of mule deer, elk, eagles, and peregrine falcons.

9 St. Elmo

A side trip, Rte. 162, turns away from the river and heads west for a nearly 2,000-foot climb. Mts. Princeton and Antero, both Four-teeners, stand sentinel on opposite sides of the road, which meanders next to Chalk Creek and its canyon, a prime foraging ground for big-horn sheep. Agnes Vaille Falls, one of the largest in these parts, can be reached along a short trail that begins just beyond Chalk Cliffs. The tumbling water creates a steady, soothing music, and the abundant spray keeps the ledges green with ferns and mosses.

Aspen groves, especially brilliant in the fall, dot the area's steep slopes for most of the ascent; then at higher elevations thick forests of Engelmann spruce and Douglas fir appear on the mountainsides. St. Elmo flourished during the region's gold rush but is now a ghost town, where visitors can view old buildings and follow a railroad line to Alpine Tunnel, which burrows beneath the Continental Divide.

10 Salida

As the drive continues, it never strays far from the Arkansas River, which has widened and become tamer after its escape from Browns Canyon. Farther along, switch onto Rte. 291 and follow the river to Salida, a small town backed by the Sangre de Cristo Mountains. Sightseers can tour its historic

The world at 14,000 feet: the sculpted summits of the Collegiate Peaks.

district, soak in hot springs, or stroll through Riverside Park.

Thanks to the surrounding mountains, which drain the passing clouds of most of their moisture, portions of this area are said to be high desert. The riverbanks remain lush with grasses, cottonwoods, and willows, but as you depart Salida on Rte. 50, the region becomes decidedly more arid. Rabbitbrush, piñons, and junipers are scattered across dry valleys. Two additional plant species also show up on the scene: oak brush and cholla cactus, whose pink flowers appear in spring.

11 Five Points Recreation Site

Just east of Cotopaxi the roadway dips into Bighorn Sheep Canyon, an aptly named locale where visitors can spot bighorn sheep. An interpretive facility at Five Points Recreation Site explains the habits of these creatures, which prove

their mountain-climbing skills as they roam the jagged canyon walls. Although the animals can be difficult to make out—their brownish coats blend into the surroundings—distinctive white patches on their rumps give them away.

12 Royal Gorge

This gorge, carved over eons by the Arkansas River, has walls—regally colored in an array of reds—that plummet more than 1,000 feet to the riverbank. An aerial tramway and the world's highest suspension bridge both span the abyss, offering vertigo-inducing views deep into the chasm. For yet another perspective, ride the incline railway to the gorge's faraway floor. In a thrilling descent the cars inch down a 45-degree slope to the swirling rapids of the Arkansas River. As you look up from the bottom, the towering walls obscure all but a sliver of sky.

13 Canon City

Farther east the drive snakes over the crest of the Dakota Hogback via the Skyline Drive, then descends to Canon City. One of its first mayors, a poet named Joaquin Miller, wanted to dub the rowdy mining camp Oreodelphia, a high-falutin' name that the miners insisted they could neither spell nor pronounce. "The place is a canyon," they said, "and it's goin' to be called Canon City."

The town is host to one of Colorado's major penitentiaries, besides other attractions better worth stopping for. A hint of its past still exists in the town's historic district, complete with museums, and visitors can also drive by the ornate mansions built by early mining magnates.

Take time to ride the scenic railroad through Royal Gorge. Its trestles span clefts, and its tracks cling to ledges with a view of the Arkansas River far below.

14 Fort Carson Military Reservation

Rte. 115 follows the river southeast to Florence, where the downtown district has become a mecca for antique lovers, then branches northeast through rolling hills studded with junipers, piñons, and sagebrush. At Fort Carson, an army installation off limits to the public, some 130,000 acres provide diverse habitat for wildlife. Elk, pronghorns, and mule deer roam the grasslands; songbirds fill the cottonwood groves; and grebes, mallards, and other waterbirds nest in the wetlands. Raptors—golden eagles, prairie falcons, and hawks—can also be spotted from the road.

The drive nears its completion with a dramatic flair as the roller-coaster loop twists on its self to make a winding descent from the foothills. The views take in Colorado Springs and the sun-soaked plains stretching east.

San Juan Skyway

Highlighting the ruggedly beautiful San Juan Mountains,
this stunning loop weaves through ranchland,
old mining towns, and ancient Indian digs.

Autumn aspens stand in multihued contrast to the conifers of Red Mountain Pass.

The locals call their homeland "Colorful Colorado," and a ride along the San Juan Skyway in the southwestern corner of the state proves the aptness of the nickname. As you climb from dusty lowlands to snowy peaks, you'll see nearly every shade in nature's kaleidoscopic palette, from creamy sands and rusty bluffs to multihued alpine meadows and the shimmering gold of aspens in autumn.

1 Durango
Though Will Rogers once described Durango as "out of the way and glad of it," by the late 1800s it was in fact a bustling railroad hub. Today visitors can recall that era by strolling through the restored downtown, with its gaslit street lamps and Victorian shops that sell everything from Mailpouch tobacco to mink earmuffs. Mexican cantinas, Irish pubs, and vintage Old West honky-tonks invoke the robust days when miners and cattlemen clomped in for a pint of brew.

Another way to relive the town's halcyon past is to board the Durango–Silverton Narrow Gauge Railroad, which runs between May and October, for a daylong round-trip journey through stunning mountain scenery. In one of the great engineering feats of its time, a part of this route was blasted into a sheer rock wall 400 feet above the Animas Canyon. Today, with guests settled into a variety of cars—open gondolas, coaches, or 1882 parlor cars—the train sounds a plaintive whistle as it chugs up the Animas River valley through the San Juan–Rio Grande National Forest, making occasional stops for backpackers. The end of the line is Silverton, a mining town seemingly frozen in time.

2 Animas River Valley
Departing from Durango, the Skyway itself (here Rte. 550) roughly parallels the rail route from Durango to Silverton, meandering along the Animas River. Passing green pastures grazed by cattle, and red-rock cliffs that rise abruptly from the valley, the Skyway climbs to the alpine heights enfolding Durango Mountain Resort, a down-home ski resort that used to be called Purgatory. Its unpretentious spirit is touted in an ad that proudly declares, "No Movie Stars Here!"

Looming above are the San Juan Mountains, a jumble of imposing peaks draped across southwestern Colorado. Two million years of periodic glaciation sculpted this awesome landscape, leaving behind precipitous gorges, broad valleys, craggy ridges, and skyscraping peaks—more than 100 of which exceed 13,000 feet in height. Volcanic eruptions played a part as well, spewing lava and ash over the region. Deposits of gold, silver, lead, copper, zinc, and other metals enriched the landscape, ultimately yielding billions of dollars to those with the fortitude to retrieve them.

Approaching Silverton, the Skyway zigzags to 10,910-foot Molas Pass, overlooking an array of lofty peaks, ridges staircasing up from the canyon floor, and the turquoise gem known as Molas Lake.

3 Silverton
From Molas Pass the Skyway drops sharply into the town of Silverton, strikingly set between high mountain walls. According to local lore, the town was named by a miner who once exclaimed, "We may not have gold here, but we have silver by the ton."

The quaint streets of Silverton are lined with historic relics—the gold-domed county courthouse, once-elegant hotels such as the Grand Imperial, and a former red-light district where locals stage mock gunfights on summer evenings. At nearby Hillside Cemetery, perched above town, grave markers tell of young men who lost their lives in mining disasters.

4 Million Dollar Highway
From Silverton the Skyway climbs to Red Mountain Pass, the highest point on the tour at 11,018 feet. The breathtaking view from here takes in Bear Mountain, so named because its contours resemble a giant bear licking a honeycomb.

A portion of the road between Silverton and Ouray is known as the Million Dollar Highway. Built between 1880 and 1920, the old toll road served as a mail, stage, and freight route. Depending on whom you ask, the highway was named for the amount of gold and silver mined in the area, the value of the low-grade ore tailings used to pave the road, the cost of the construction, or the rewarding views.

Despite the splendid scenery, motorists should definitely keep their eyes on the road along this stretch of the Skyway: it threads a tortuous, two-lane path around precipitous slopes—without the benefit of safety guardrails. From

November to May, blinding blizzards dump up to four feet of snow in one day, transforming the Skyway into a slick chute through treacherous avalanche country. During heavy snowstorms, crews close the road and fire cannons to trigger slides, which they then plow away. A rumbling sound, like distant thunder, announces that somewhere an avalanche is on the move, crushing everything in its path.

5 Ouray

As the highway curlicues down to Ouray, it noses through a tunnel blasted through solid rock, skirts the spectral remains of old mines, and breezes past waterfalls crashing down from invisible heights.

Nestled in a narrow, steeply walled valley, Ouray and its environs have been called the "Switzerland of America." Its steep streets are lined with Victorian hotels and shops—even a public pool fed by hot springs that sends billows of steam into the air as guests who

have come to "take the cure" gaze up at snowcapped peaks.

At Box Canyon Falls and Park, the turbulent waters of Clear Creek thunder 285 feet down a narrow gorge. A steel suspension bridge and well-marked trails offer glorious vistas.

6 Ridgway

From Ouray, the Skyway leaves the San Juan Mountains behind and coils into a broad valley where elk and deer graze in verdant meadows. Turning west on Rte. 62, the drive eases into Ridgway, which may look vaguely familiar, for this former Wild West town was used to film scenes in a number of Hollywood westerns, including *True Grit* and *How the West Was Won*.

If time permits, follow Rte. 550 north to Montrose and turn east on Rte. 50 to the road (Rte. 347) that leads to the Black Canyon of the Gunnison National Park. Here a menacingly deep gorge was carved over 2 million years by the erosive power of the Gunnison

River. Its charcoal-gray walls are shrouded in shadow for most of the day, hence the name Black Canyon. One of its prominent

COLORADO

The Durango–Silverton Narrow Gauge Railroad is a worldwide draw for steam enthusiasts.

features, the 2,200-foot behemoth called the Painted Wall, is the highest cliff face in Colorado.

7 Dallas Divide

From Ridgway, Rte. 62 rolls west past broad ranchlands dotted with cattle, climbs to scrub oaks and aspen, and finally enters the spruce-covered hills of the Dallas Divide. It overlooks the Mt. Sneffels Wilderness Area—an array of jagged, snowcapped peaks whose centerpiece is 14,150-foot Mt. Sneffels (named for a mountain in Jules Verne's *Journey to the Center of the Earth)*. From the Dallas Divide, the highway descends to cottonwood country and into the tiny town of Placerville, where it turns south on Rte. 145. After several miles the route veers east to Telluride.

8 Telluride

Its fanciful setting and gingerbread architecture give Telluride the kind of ambience you'd expect from a fairy tale come to life. The

quaint streets of this turn-of-the-century town are crowded with a mixture of colorful clapboard houses and brick buildings. Mountains rise a mile above the valley floor, their flanks adorned in spring with tumbling waterfalls.

Some locals claim Telluride is a contraction of "To hell you ride," a reference to the town's rowdy past. (Butch Cassidy robbed his first bank here in 1889.) Actually, the town was named after a mineral compound often found with gold and silver that, ironically, is extremely rare in Telluride.

Because of its remote location, Telluride was once "hell" to get to as well—especially in winter when snowdrifts blocked the winding roads. But thanks in part to a new airport that accommodates small jets, the town has become a popular destination. This may explain why the price of real estate around Telluride has soared higher than the peaks, and why part-time residents include a bevy of high-profile celebrities. The town is

shared as well by a new breed of buckaroos: kamikaze skiers and mountain bikers who hurtle themselves down the surrounding slopes. On some days it seems all roads lead to Telluride: the burgeoning ski town is also the Festival Capital of the Rockies, hosting throughout the year a number of world-famous film, arts, music, and even hang-gliding festivals.

A must for Telluride visitors with some time on their hands is the relatively easy two-hour round-trip hike to Bridal Veil Falls. Accented by rainbows as it plunges off a 425-foot-high cliff, Bridal Veil has the longest freefall of any waterfall in Colorado.

9 Lizard Head Pass

After retracing the spur from Telluride to continue south on Rte. 145, the drive heads across a high plateau of grasslands and dense aspen groves, with Wilson Peak and Sunshine Mountain towering to the southwest. In spring (mid-June in these parts), lilies bloom

from snowfields—vast canvases that also bear the tracks of passing animals in search of food. Put an ear to the snow and you may hear the soft tinkling of hidden streams.

Farther on, the road passes the defunct town of Ophir, glistening Trout Lake, and a campground with the ambitiously alpine name of Matterhorn. It then climbs to 10,222-foot Lizard Head Pass (named for a reptilelike monolith near the road). Indians used the pass for thousands of years, and highway markers note that the Rio Grande Southern Railway passed through here until 1952.

Several miles ahead, the road twists through a glaciated valley dotted with beaver dams before easing into the town of Rico.

10 Rico

Adopting the Spanish word for "rich," this once-booming mining town is lined with stone and brick Victorian structures from the 1880s. For the next 30 miles or so past Rico, the route follows the Dolores River, which takes a leisurely, meandering course through a valley of aspens and spreading cottonwoods.

11 Dolores

The pleasant town of Dolores is perched above McPhee Reservoir, popular for recreation and the site of ancient ancestral Puebloan settlements. Some of the remains that were excavated here before the gorge was flooded are on display in the Anasazi Heritage Center, located on a bluff overlooking the Montezuma Valley about four miles south of town on Rte. 145. The center also features a 25-room ruin and a full-scale replica of a pit house dwelling.

Colorful silt, washed from the mountains into the gorges, colors creek bottoms.

Descending past ranches and farms, the drive reaches the strip town of Cortez. Nearby are scenic desertscapes backed by the La Plata Mountains and unique Mesa Verde National Park.

12 Mesa Verde National Park

More than 700 years have passed since the ancient pueblo peoples occupied cliff dwellings along Mesa Verde's precipitous walls. Even so, when visiting crowds dissipate in late autumn and snow dusts the distant peaks, you can almost sense the presence of "the Ancient Ones," the name given to them by the Navajos. One imagines these cliff-dwelling people shaping pots, harvesting corn and storing it in preparation for winter, telling fireside stories passed down from their ancestors, or chanting prayers from the depths of ceremonial kivas.

The dwellings were first discovered in 1888 when two ranchers, Richard Wetherill and Charlie Mason, set off in a snowstorm in search of cattle that had strayed away and stumbled instead upon the perfectly preserved Cliff Palace —a large dwelling that was once the home of more than 200 ancient

A tongue-twisting name belies the haunting beauty found at Uncompahgre Gorge near Ouray.

pueblo people. The next day they found Spruce Tree House, naming it for the tree that grew beside the ruin, and Square Tower House, the tallest structure in the park.

Today, visitors can experience a similar sense of discovery as they roam through these apartment-like cliff dwellings, most built in the middle of the 12th century. The majority were tucked into alcoves facing south-southwest to let in low winter sun but not the searing overhead rays of summer. They range in size from one-room "studios" to structures containing hundreds of rooms.

At the Chapin Mesa Museum, lifelike dioramas and various exhibits on basket weaving, pottery, masonry, and other skills trace the evolution of Puebloan culture from its beginnings in settlements along the Colorado River to its demise nearly eight centuries later.

Many have speculated about the reasons this ancient people abandoned their homes, but no one knows for sure. Some suggest the soil became exhausted from overfarming. Others claim a period of relentless cold drove them away. One of the more plausible explanations suggests that, beginning one summer in the 13th century, the rain stopped and did not return for more than 20 years. By then, the cliff dwellings had become ghostly ruins where nothing moved but the wind.

With no written language to tell their story, we can only guess at the fate of these people, but it is likely that they dispersed throughout the Southwest and that some of the Indians who now live in northern Arizona and New Mexico are among their descendants.

13 Mancos

From Mesa Verde National Park, the drive continues east on Rte. 160 to a lush valley occupied by the ranching town of Mancos, which exudes Old West ambience. Nearby Mancos Lake State Park has a lovely campground in the midst of a ponderosa pine forest, and the lake itself is a paradise for boaters and anglers.

Heading east again, the road passes through ranchland and aromatic sagebrush flats to Cherry Creek, the locale where novelist Louis L'Amour penned the westerns that immortalized southwestern Colorado. The wide-open spaces continue all the way to Durango, the drive's point of origin. Thrilled by the captivating views throughout the San Juan Mountains area, many a motorist has simply turned around and driven the entire route back in the opposite direction.

Highway of Legends

Early Spanish settlements, bustling villages turned to ghost towns, and a cast of characters as colorful as the countryside set the mood for this Colorado idyll.

A volcanic dike, one of many in southern Colorado, points to West Spanish Peak.

Southern Colorado, a captivating blend of mountains and valleys, witnessed the meeting of three separate cultures: Indian, Spanish, and pioneer American. Tales of paradise, of hidden gold, and of miracles spread like wildfire through the region, but the most dramatic story of all continues to be told by the land itself.

1 Walsenburg

Since prehistoric times, few could resist the fertile Cucharas Valley, long the home of hunting-and-gathering Indians. Spanish farmers were the first Europeans to settle the region, bestowing their language on landmarks and their heritage on local culture. The town of Walsenburg, though, did not spring up until the arrival of American pioneers in the 1870s. The most important stimulus for development, boosted by the arrival of the railroad, was coal, for some very large and accessible deposits were available in this area.

Today the mines are all silent, and farming and tourism have taken center stage. Remnants of the old excavations—huge slag heaps—still line Rte. 160, the first leg of the drive. But as the road swings west, it soon arrives at Lathrop State Park, where Martin and Horseshoe lakes sparkle amid a patchwork of grasses, yuccas, junipers, and rabbitbrush on rock-strewn slopes.

For an inspiring panorama, hike the two-mile trail from Martin Lake to the crest of a volcanic hogback (a steep, sharp-edged ridge). Looking north, you'll see the Wet Mountains and Pikes Peak; in the west are the bold summits of the Sangre de Cristo Range, which stretches south into New Mexico.

2 La Veta

As Rte. 160 continues westward, it parallels the Cucharas River, which snakes across the broad Cucharas Valley. The waterway runs tame, its banks giving way to miles of rangeland and rolling hills lightly forested with piñons and junipers. Off to the south the paired Spanish Peaks form an imposing presence on the horizon. Slowly curving toward the two mountains, the drive leads to La Veta, a former trading post. Once in town, stop at the must-see Fort Francisco Museum for an informative look at life on the fabled frontier.

A much older chapter of history awaits to the south, where Rte. 12 passes numerous textbook examples of the geological features known as dikes. The formations—long, narrow, steep-sided outcropings—were created when masses of molten lava long ago forced their way into faults beneath the earth's surface. The heated magma cooled, then centuries of erosion wore away the softer sediments above, exposing the fault-filling, more resistant rock. Devil's Stairsteps, one of the most dramatic of the dikes, stands high above the road about six miles south of La Veta. Farther along, many more volcanic dikes come into view, baring their sharp-edged contours in a variety of sizes and jagged configurations.

Most of the dikes radiate from the Spanish Peaks. The prominent profiles of these giant ribbons of rock, formed about 35 million years ago, tower above the Cucharas Valley and have long served locals as landmarks.

3 Cucharas Pass

Cuchara means "spoon" in Spanish, and the elevated valley does in fact bear a vague resemblance to a spoon. The drive, following an old Indian trail, heads up the spoon's handle to Cucharas Pass, which tops off at 9,941 feet. Alpine meadows, despite their fairly steep slopes, support uncounted thousands of blue-flowered columbines in early summer. Autumn visits are well rewarded too, as groves

::::: **Trip Tips** :::::

Length: About 80 miles.

When to go: Year-round, but winters are snowy and fairly cold.

Nearby attraction: Great Sand Dunes National Park and Preserve. The tallest dune in North America is located in this 55-square-mile preserve. (Rte. 160 west to Rte. 150 north, about 45 miles from La Veta.)

Further information: La Veta/Cuchara Chamber of Commerce, P.O. Box 32, La Veta, CO 81055; tel. 866-615-3676, www.laveta cuchara_chamber.com.

of aspens turn to gold, creating a vibrant contrast to the encroaching stands of dusky green Douglas firs and Engelmann spruces.

Just before the pass, an unpaved forest road, now part of the official National Scenic Byway route, will take those willing to climb even higher to the aptly named Blue Lake, perched at about 10,500 feet. A trail from the lake ascends farther yet, winding to the alpine tundra below the 13,517-foot summit of Trinchera Peak.

4 Monument Lake

The tears of two Indian chiefs, saddened by long days of drought, are said to have formed Monument Lake. Unfortunately, they did not have a chance to enjoy the rewards of their sobbing, for a nearby volcano erupted and entombed them in a pillar of stone— a 15-foot-high rock that still breaks the lake's surface. Today, though, the area is a cause not for sorrow but for rejoicing. Visitors can fish for trout and take hikes or leisurely horseback rides along the tree-lined shores. Campsites also are available, or you can stay at the adobe-style Monument Lake Resort, built in the 1930s by the Depression-era Works Progress Administration.

5 Stonewall

Several creeks come into view as Rte. 12 continues to the village of Stonewall, which—not surprisingly —was named for a lengthy, looming wall of sandstone. Passing through a gap in the escarpment, the drive leaves Stonewall, then elbows eastward beside the Purgatoire River. Its banks lined with cottonwoods, the river twists through fairly dry pastureland ringed by rounded foothills.

Farther along, several hamlets— Vigil, Weston, Segundo—recall the area's Spanish heritage. Complete with plazas, or town squares,

the communities contain an abundance of log-and-adobe buildings. Look closely at the window frames and doorways; these were painted with bright blue paint to keep out restless devils.

6 Cokedale National Historic District

Several of the Spanish settlements were overrun by coal companies at the turn of the century. Some have since become ghost towns, but one—Cokedale, a model mining center built in 1907—has survived. Its main business was to produce coke, coal refined in special ovens to burn at higher temperatures. Although the legions of coking ovens that once flamed day and night are now black and weather-worn, most of the town—homes, a doctor's office, and a variety of company buildings—still stands as a nearly intact page in the annals of Colorado history.

7 Trinidad Lake State Park

With each passing mile toward the east, the landscape along the

Man and best friend amid flat-topped hills and high plains.

route tends to grow drier, but at this park a dam across the Purgatoire River has created an oasis of sorts: three-mile-long Trinidad Lake. Although the water level in the lake fluctuates according to irrigation and flood-control needs, in the warmer months you can usually count on ample opportunities for such activities as boating, windsurfing, and angling for trout, bass, and an assortment of other fish. Of historical note on the surrounding ridges are ancient teepee rings, circles of stones that once were used to anchor the tent-like homes of nomadic Indians.

8 Trinidad

After crossing the plains, stagecoach drivers paused to rest in Trinidad, where they prepared for the dangerous mountain route yet to be traveled on the Santa Fe Trail. Among the oldest communities in Colorado, the onetime stage stop was later a hub to the homesteaders and the farmers

who settled along the Purgatoire River. By the 1900s cattle and sheep ranchers also came, but as in Walsenburg, it was coal-mining activity that really put the town on the map.

Over the years a rootin'-tootin' cast of characters appeared on the scene. The historic downtown, El Corazón de Trinidad ("The Heart of Trinity"), testifies to those bygone glory days. Take a leisurely stroll through the downtown streets for a look at an architectural mélange that reflects the varied backgrounds of Trinidad's inhabitants—an odd lot that at one time or another included Doc Holliday and temperance activist Carrie Nation, who denounced Trinidad as "the devil's carnival ground." Life in El Corazón de Trinidad is more civilized nowadays, but the legends and lore of the old Wild West still live on, as they do in most of the stops on this intriguing and historical route.

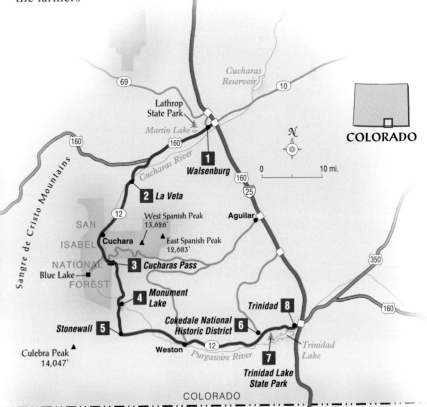

Monument Valley Meander

On this quiet journey through the heart of the Southwest, the Hopis meet the Navajos, four neighboring states meet each other, and visitors meet a landscape immortalized by countless Hollywood westerns.

Listening to mission bells while dozing beneath a shady cottonwood tree…watching the last glimmer of daylight as it turns a distant mesa from fiery red to faded umber…hearing the call of a coyote beneath a full desert moon. The pleasures of the Southwest are simple and subtle yet deeply satisfying. And they are found in abundance along this drive through the Arizona–Utah border country.

1 Dinosaur Tracks
The land of the Navajos is one of timeless splendor and quiet grandeur. Both of these virtues are embodied in the dinosaur tracks that can be seen just a few miles west of Tuba City as the drive heads northeastward on Rte. 160. The fossilized footprints bear silent testimony to the reptiles who once lumbered across Jurassic sediments that have long since turned to sandstone. Farther along, the drive passes two more ancient landmarks: massive twin buttes called the Elephant Feet. Also composed of sandstone, these monuments were worn by time and the elements into the wrinkled, leathery finish that inspired their name.

2 Navajo National Monument
With the bulk of Black Mesa brooding to the south, Rte. 160 forges northeast into Navajo country. No less than today's travelers, the Navajo people, too, have played the role of stranger in these parts. Long before they arrived, some four centuries ago, this was the home of the mysterious Anasazi people, possibly ancestors of the modern Hopis. A remnant of this lost tribe can be seen at Navajo National Monument, which sprawls across broken high country at the end of Rte. 564, a nine-mile drive through pygmy junipers and piñon pines.

Here, in the clear, dry air nearly a mile and a half above sea level,

Monument Valley Navajo Tribal Park on the Utah-Arizona border has been featured in countless commercials and films.

the remains of Anasazi pueblo villages slumber beneath beetling ocher cliffs, accessible to hikers by trails through steep terrain and sand. Note that backcountry travel requires ranger guides or permits.

Clustered within a great cavern in a canyon wall, the 700-year-old ruin called Betatakin contains inner walls still sooty from cooking fires long since extinguished.

Another site, Keet Seel, is one of the best-preserved cliff dwellings in the Southwest. It welcomes only those visitors hardy enough to venture eight miles on foot or horseback from the Navajo National Monument visitor center.

3 Agathla Peak

At the wind-scoured little town of Kayenta, veer north on Rte. 163 and traverse a mile-high valley where ravens often can be seen wheeling overhead. Before long, as if to announce the approach to Monument Valley, a sentinel pierces the desert sky: to the east stands Agathla Peak (Spanish explorers called it El Capitán), a great black thunderhead of a mountain believed to be the core of a prehistoric volcano. Across the road, on the west side of the highway, another monolith commands attention—the sandstone needle of Owl Rock, which soars from the edge of Tyende Mesa.

4 Monument Valley Navajo Tribal Park

Even if this is your first trip to the Arizona-Utah border country, you probably aren't seeing Monument Valley for the first time. Chances are good that a man named John Ford has already shown it to you. Beginning in 1938 with his landmark film *Stagecoach* and continuing a decade later with his cavalry trilogy (*Fort Apache*, *She Wore a Yellow Ribbon*, and *Rio Grande*), the celebrated director used this setting so often that it came to epitomize the rugged terrain of the Old West.

Within this vast tableland—punctuated by spires, buttes, and pillars—lies the 30,000-acre Monument Valley Navajo Tribal Park. Visitors can explore the area on a well-marked, scenic 17-mile route. (But be forewarned that a guided tour will save your car a good deal of wear and tear, since the road is unpaved and rutted.)

However you experience it, the valley is a wonder to behold, a harsh yet hauntingly beautiful landscape. View it in early morning, when shadows lift from rocky marvels with names such as Rain God, Thunderbird, Gray Whiskers, and Spearhead. Admire it in springtime, when tiny pink and blue wildflowers sprinkle the land with jewel-like specks of color. Try to see it through the eyes of the Navajos, who still herd their sheep and weave their rugs here.

Spaced grandly apart on a wide-open range, these stark buttes and sculpted pinnacles form one of the most dramatic assemblages of rock formations to be found anywhere on earth. The ingredients of stone, water, and time combine here to form a whole that's infinitely greater than the sum of its parts.

5 Goosenecks State Park

This stretch of Rte. 163—called the Trail of the Ancients in honor of the vanished Anasazis—cuts across Monument Valley at the

Betatakin—one of three Anasazi pueblos at Navajo National Monument—clearly reflects its name, which means "ledge house."

Like a sidewinding rattlesnake, the Moki Dugway slithers to the top of Cedar Mesa.

Utah border on its way to the little town of Mexican Hat. Named for a rock formation there that resembles an upside-down sombrero—a whimsical footnote to the magnificence of Monument Valley—Mexican Hat is the nearest settlement to Goosenecks State Park, just ahead and to the west via Rtes. 261 and 316.

The Great Goosenecks of the San Juan River are what geologists call entrenched meanders: by anyone's definition they are a prime illustration of the unhurried power of natural forces. Look down a thousand feet or more at the waters of the San Juan River. The lazily looping pattern of the river's gooseneck turns took shape over 300 million years, with the result that in six meandering miles, the San Juan makes a westing of barely a mile and a half on its way to Lake Powell.

Snaking between its eroded walls of sandstone, limestone, and shale, the gorge looks like something akin to the Grand Canyon tied into knots, a reminder that although we might consider a straight line to be the shortest distance between two points, nature couldn't care less.

6 Muley Point

In this famously vertical landscape, there are six primary directions: north, south, east, west—and up and down. For proof, head north on Rte. 261 beyond the Goosenecks State Park overlook, climbing another 1,000-plus feet, and enjoy what is undeniably one of the most arresting panoramas in all of the Southwest—the lofty view from Muley Point. From the coiling Goosenecks far below to distant vistas of Monument Valley's ruddy stone cathedrals, the magnificence of the Four Corners region unfolds before you.

Taking the road up to Muley Point means traveling the notorious Moki Dugway, three miles of harrowing, unpaved switchbacks that accomplish an ascent of 1,100 feet via grades of up to 10 percent. All the while, your creeping progress is mocked by the aerial ease of whistling canyon wrens and plunging swallows—no more concerned with notions of up and down than they are with the four points of the compass.

7 Valley of the Gods

Having made it all the way up the Moki Dugway, the next challenge is to make it back down—"Easy does it" is the best advice. At the bottom, instead of following Rte. 261 back to Rtes. 316 and 163, turn east onto a 17-mile rough dirt road that wanders through the heart of the Valley of the Gods.

If nature had needed a model for Monument Valley, the Valley of the Gods could easily have filled the bill. As in so much of this water- and wind-sculpted high country, the valley's medium is red sandstone, a rock that seems almost to seize sunrises. Towers stabbing skyward, rocks balanced precariously on slender pedestals, buttes bearing homespun names such as Rooster and Sitting Hen—all invest the Valley of the Gods with an eerie ambience that lingers in the bones long after you've departed.

8 Bluff

At the end of the Valley of the Gods road, turn east onto Rte. 163. Though it's only 15 miles or so from here to the little settlement of Bluff, traversing this brief stretch must have seemed an eternity to the party of Mormon pioneers who first ventured into southeastern Utah in 1880.

The Mormons came here by wagon train from Escalante, more than 100 miles to the northwest. In the final miles before the pioneers reached the San Juan Valley, they had to surmount the nearly vertical upwarp of the earth's crust called Comb Ridge. Today, modern travelers on Rte. 163 scale and descend the same barrier with far greater safety and comfort. Still, one can imagine how daunting that 800-foot climb must have seemed to pioneers when it first came into view.

Once across the ridge, the exhausted Mormons found rest on the banks of the San Juan River, at a place they named Bluff. The town never prospered (there are only a few hundred residents today, not counting those buried in the little hilltop cemetery), but it is a pretty enough spot, with sandstone towers—the Navajo Twins—standing guard over the river.

Three miles south, beneath the cottonwoods that line the riverbanks at Sand Island, rafters set out for float trips on the San Juan. Just downstream you'll find a cliff adorned with Indian pictographs that portray a band of mythological flute players—images that were already centuries old when the first covered wagons rattled into Bluff.

The pioneer spirit that brought the Mormons into this southeastern corner of Utah was still very much alive in 1943 when Fr. Harold Lieber founded St. Christopher's Episcopal Mission two miles northeast of Bluff. A serene spot, the mission is a shady haven built of locally quarried sandstone. About a mile past the mission, you can sample pioneer engineering with a nerve-jangling walk across a swaying, planked suspension bridge five feet above the San Juan River. The adventure is worthwhile: once across the river, a one-mile walk leads to the ruins of a 14-room Anasazi

Faithful to years of tradition, a Navajo woman spins yarn.

dwelling, built against a cliffside decorated with the ocher-tinted handprints of the Ancient Ones.

9 Hovenweep National Monument

To the Ute Indians, the mesas and canyonlands along the Utah-Colorado border territory north of the San Juan River were *hovenweep*, a word meaning "deserted valley." The Utes must surely have wondered who had populated and abandoned this desolate land, where strange stone towers (oval, square, D-shaped, and round) stand in ruined splendor along the canyon rims. We now know that these sturdy structures—clearly the work of master builders—were created by the Anasazis. But their purpose remains a mystery. Some believe they were used for defense; others think they might have been granaries or platforms for observing the heavens.

To reach Hovenweep, among the most remote of the great western monuments, take Rte. 191 north out of Bluff, then swing east on Rte. 262 toward the Colorado border. Another turnoff continues seven miles to the Hatch Trading Post, the last outpost before the 16-mile journey (by dirt road) to the site's headquarters at the Square Tower ruin. The best preserved and most accessible of these six ancient villages, Square Tower includes the imposing Hovenweep Castle and a ranger station that provides information on tours of the other ruins.

10 Four Corners Monument

From Hovenweep, follow Rtes. 262, 41, and 160 to the Four Corners Monument, the place where Arizona, Utah, Colorado, and New Mexico meet, and the only such four-point border in the United States. Go ahead—climb onto the concrete marker and stand in four states at once.

Then look out across the unbroken desert and up at the borderless blue sky. You'll come away with the sense that nature disdains our attempts to draw lines all over its creations and to parcel tidy territories out of such sprawling majesty.

161

Arizona Indian Country

Ancient traditions still survive among the towering mesas and deep canyons of northeastern Arizona, where the Hopi and Navajo peoples have lived for centuries.

Canyon de Chelly National Monument is a moonscape of bedded sandstone cliffs.

Nowhere in America is Indian territory so extensive as in northeastern Arizona, where the Hopi and Navajo Indian reservations comprise some 30,000 square miles. Part of the Colorado Plateau, the region, though sere and barren, abounds with a serene, uncrowded beauty. Measure the riches here not in material wealth but in such things as the vast vistas to be seen from atop tall mesas, and in the magical colors that paint the desert sky at sunup and sunset.

1 Coal Canyon

As the drive heads southeastward away from Tuba City on Rte. 264, it soon sweeps into Moenkopi. Though the village is surrounded by the Navajo Indian Reservation, it is a Hopi community, the first of several to be seen along the way. The settlement's name means "place of running water," and year-round springs do indeed keep the surrounding fields green and the fruit trees productive.

The road climbs gradually away from Moenkopi and crosses the northeastern limits of the Painted Desert—a dry and daunting realm that supports little more than tufts of grass, resilient sagebrushes, and scrubby junipers. The desert rolls far into the distance, where mesas loom along the horizon. What makes the unbroken vistas truly special, though, are the vivid colors of exposed sandstones and shales, which are banded with an array of reds and pinks.

For a complete change of scene, pause at Coal Canyon, which can be reached by a short side trip. The access road exits at a windmill (there are no signs) and leads northward to an overlook. Peering down into the chasm, you'll see black veins of coal—a resource that has been tapped for centuries by native Americans.

2 Third Mesa

Soon the desert and the highway meet the southern fringes of Black Mesa, an enormous tableland that spreads across northeastern Arizona. Along its southern edge the giant formation, composed mostly of sandstone, tapers into three fingerlike extensions: First, Second, and Third mesas. These lofty, flat-topped areas have long been inhabitated by the Hopis, who survive by irrigating the land below, planting fields of corn, beans, and squash.

Passing through a steep, narrow canyon, Rte. 264 climbs from the desert floor to the crest of Third Mesa. Of special note at the top is Old Oraibi: dating all the way back to 1150, it is said to be America's oldest continuously inhabited village. A patchwork of stone dwellings, the settlement sits 650 feet above the desert floor.

3 Second Mesa

Proceeding on Rte. 264, the drive crosses cottonwood-lined Oraibi Wash (a dry streambed) and small plots of Indian farmland, then ascends to the top of Second Mesa. The Hopi Cultural Center, located at the eastern edge of the promontory, displays tribal artifacts, and its restaurant serves traditional Hopi fare. Several small villages are clustered atop the mesa, where the views extend far across the desert to distant buttes and peaks. This lonely place, according to Hopi legend, is the Sacred Circle—the center of the universe.

4 First Mesa

First Mesa, which has the steepest sides and is the narrowest of the three, rises to a height of 600 feet. The route makes no attempt to scale its boulder-strewn west wall but skirts the rocky rubble at the base to the town of Polacca, where a paved side road hugs the eastern cliff as it makes a daring ascent.

Once on top, the road wends through two villages—both of them hundreds of years old—then suddenly ends. The mesa, though, continues, narrowing to just 15 feet in places. Near the tip is

:::::: Trip Tips ::::::

Length: About 215 miles.

When to go: Conditions are best from May through October.

Nearby attraction: Petrified Forest National Park, where a scenic drive leads through the petrified remains of an ancient forest, off I-40 east of Holbrook.

Words to the wise: Respect the privacy and traditions of the Indians, who usually prohibit photographs and unguided tours. Always ask rather than assume.

Further information: Arizona Office of Tourism, 1100 West Washington St., Phoenix, AZ 85007; tel. 800-842-8257, www.azot.com.

Walpi, perhaps the most dramatic of all the Hopi villages. Fashioned from the pale sandstone of the mesa, the 300-year-old dwellings look so at one with their surroundings that they seem to have sprouted from the earth itself. (Hour-long guided tours begin 9:30–4:00 at Ponsi Hall Visitor's Center.)

5 Keams Canyon

Visible at intervals along the way, dry creek beds are about the only breaks in the sameness of the desert until the drive reaches the town of Keams Canyon. Although it has a center for native crafts, this is a government outpost, not a Hopi village. A short side trip to the northeast leads into the town's namesake canyon.

6 Hubbell Trading Post

As Rte. 264 continues eastward, it climbs yet another mesa and reenters the Navajo Indian Reservation. The land is dotted with octagonal hogans, traditional homes constructed of logs held together with dried mud. More mesas, miles away, rise to the south, a pleasing contrast to the stark desert plateau. Farther along, the drive makes a steady descent into Steamboat Canyon, named for a giant rock that seems to sail on a sea of sand and boulders.

Continue past the junction with Rte. 191 to visit Hubbell Trading Post, a national historic site. Still active, the post was established by John Lorenzo Hubbell in 1878, and its ambience definitely belongs to that era: dim lighting, extrawide counters designed to prevent theft, and floorboards creaky from the passage of countless boots. Among the wares on sale are brightly colored Navajo rugs adorned with sacred symbols and geometric patterns. Learn how they are made at the visitor center next door, where Navajo women demonstrate the traditional craft.

7 Canyon de Chelly

The next leg of the drive turns to the north, following Rte. 191 past red rock mesas to Rte. 64 and Canyon de Chelly (pronounced duh-shay) National Monument. As you approach, the desert sands give way and bare sandstone dominates the landscape. Beyond the visitor center, where you'll find interpretive exhibits and helpful information, the highway branches into two: South Rim Drive and North Rim Drive, both with several well-marked scenic overlooks.

Follow South Rim Drive (Rte. 7) for four miles to Junction Overlook, where Canyon de Chelly's sheer cliffs stand about 400 feet high. As colorful as they are awesome, the walls seem almost to glow, especially at sunset when the hues range from peach to fiery orange. In niches in the walls are two Anasazi cliff dwellings, or pueblos. Some of these ancient homes were built more than 800 years ago by the now-vanished tribe. Far below, the usually shallow and tame Rio de Chelly meanders along the canyon floor.

South Rim Drive eventually leads to the overlook viewing the White House ruins. A trail (the only one where visitors are allowed to travel without a Navajo

guide) descends 550 feet to the canyon floor and to the ancient ruins. Fifteen miles farther on, the road ends, but the scenery has one last surprise in store: an overlook offers views of Spider Rock, an impressive free-standing stone spire that rises 800 feet in height above the canyon floor.

8 Canyon del Muerto

In 1805 Spanish soldiers massacred more than 110 Navajos here. The Canyon of the Dead, however, takes its name not from the terribly bloody battle, but as a result of a peaceful expedition led by archaeologists who found a burial ground among the cliffs in the 1880s. To view the chasm, a branch of the larger Canyon de Chelly, backtrack to the visitor center, then follow North Rim Drive.

Canyon del Muerto has even more Anasazi ruins than are to be found in its southern neighbor. One pueblo, which can be seen

Ruins of Anasazi cliff dwellings in Canyon de Chelly.

from Antelope House Overlook, was a bustling village, with 91 rooms occupying four stories. Farther along, the overlooks provide views of 1,000-foot cliffs, talus slopes (piles of fallen boulders), and sheer buttes that rise dramatically from the canyon and are painted with colorful minerals.

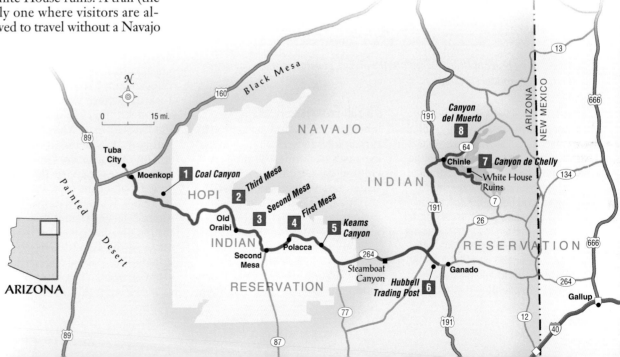

Grand Canyon Loop

From the slopes of Arizona's highest peak, the road spins through pine forests and flatlands to America's deepest, most gorgeous gorge: the incomparable Grand Canyon.

At the eastern border of Grand Canyon National Park stand the titanic, limestone-laden ramparts of Marble Canyon.

From trappers and explorers, the stories drifted east—stories of a canyon so huge, so awesome, that it seemed the stuff of tall tales. In the era before landscape photography, eyewitness accounts were, quite simply, beyond belief. In time, though, as more travelers saw the canyon for themselves, the legendary rift became undeniably real: this "canyon of canyons"—one of the certifiable wonders of the world—leaves visitors to ponder its haunting depths.

1 San Francisco Peaks

The drive begins in Flagstaff, a city surrounded by seemingly endless expanses of ponderosa pine. A cultural oasis complete with museums and a university, Flagstaff also manages to retain a turn-of-the-century frontier flavor in its well-preserved downtown district.

Heading northwest on Rte. 180, the drive winds by the San Francisco Peaks, which are really several mountains in one. The mountain,

an inactive volcano, is part of the San Francisco Volcanic Field. It erupted repeatedly for more than a million years and now embraces a number of peaks with such names as Agassiz, Doyle, and Humphreys.

The mountains have inspired admiration and awe since ancient times. Hopi Indians believe the crests to be the home of kachina spirits and a source of rain; the Navajos, too, consider the peaks to be so sacred that they are the objects of their prayers.

For a view from on high, take Snow Bowl Road off Rte. 180 to a ski resort chairlift that whisks visitors to an elevation of 11,500 feet on Agassiz Peak. Those so inclined can hike the nine-mile round-trip trail through twisted bristlecone pines to the alpine tundra atop 12,633-foot Humphreys Peak, the loftiest point in Arizona.

2 Kaibab National Forest

Traveling northwest, Rte. 180 descends to a drier landscape; piñon pine and juniper give way to the sagebrush flats around Valle. Due north, near Red Butte, a prominent mountain just east of the highway, the route enters Kaibab National Forest and rises again into an open woodland of ponderosa pine and Gambel oak. For a closer look at the forest habitat, take a few minutes to walk the graveled half-mile nature trail at Ten-X Campground, south of Tusayan, where you may spot a mule deer, Abert squirrel, mountain chickadee, or white-breasted nuthatch. For detailed information on the forest flora and fauna found in the area, visit the district ranger's office in Tusayan. And be aware that Kaibab National Forest is much larger than it may seem at first: another giant section lies north of the Grand Canyon, and still another part of the national forest occupies a huge tract of land west of Flagstaff.

3 Grand Canyon Village

The crowd gathered on the edge as you approach most likely includes first-time visitors—as hushed as pilgrims in a great cathedral. Tread gently as you near them, for they've just experienced a telling and powerful moment: the Grand Canyon, its image already seen in hundreds of photographs, has become a glorious, three-dimensional reality. Buttes stack up beyond gorges, and cliffs rise above plateaus in a blazing rainbow of red, orange, yellow, and buff—a symphony for the eyes that comes not one measure at a time, but as suddenly as a thunderclap. The sheer scale of the chasm staggers the imagination. One formation serves as the backdrop for another all the way to the North Rim, physically just 10 miles away, but more than 200 miles by highway. Three Empire State Buildings stacked one atop another would still not span the height—more than a mile—from the canyon floor to the rim. It is, as one visitor wrote a century ago, truly dizzying to "gaze down, and still farther down, into its depths, and realize for the first time your own utter insignificance."

Such is the panorama at Mather Point as the drive nears Grand Canyon Village and national park headquarters. The overlook takes in many of the canyon's most famous features, including Bright Angel Canyon, sharp-tipped Isis Temple, and flat-topped Wotan's Throne. As you view the expanse spread before you here, remember that for all its breadth, it encompasses only a third of the canyon's total length of 277 miles.

Bright Angel Trail, which begins at Grand Canyon Village, is the park's most popular hike; the nine-mile round-trip to Indian Gardens makes a fine day trip. The famed Grand Canyon mule rides are an alternative to hiking, but reserva-

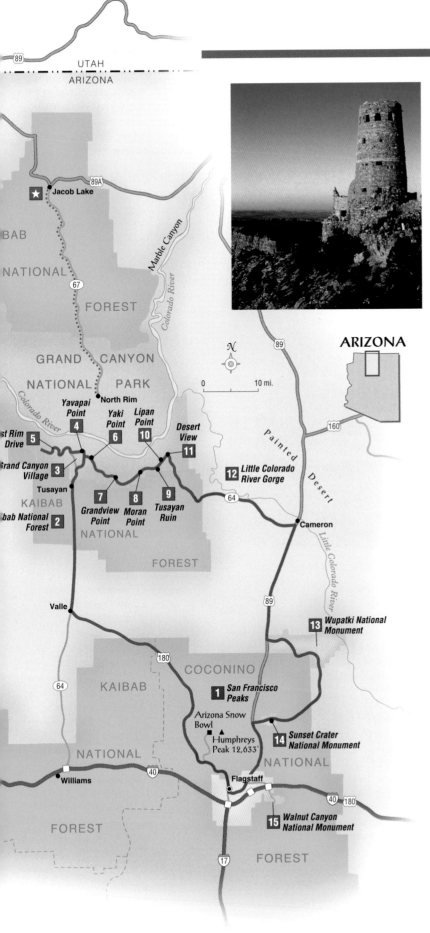

Desert Watchtower stands as a lonely sentinel over the Grand Canyon.

tions must be made far in advance for this popular adventure—and bear in mind that for the soreness your feet are spared, other parts of your body must pay.

4 Yavapai Point

As you view the panorama here, imagine silt drifting to the bottom of a shallow sea, building up bit by infinitesimal bit over eons of time and eventually being compressed into solid rock. Now envision the Colorado River cutting its way down through it all, creating mile-deep chasms, and you'll have some idea of the long and complex formation of the Grand Canyon—a layer cake of the earth's history preserved in rock. Its deepest point, in the black-walled Inner Gorge, reveals rocks nearly 2 billion years old.

The museum at Yavapai Point is the best place to learn about the deposition and erosion processes that created the canyon; as a bonus, the museum's windows make it a fine viewpoint during summer storms and on cold winter days. On nice days visitors can take an easy hike on the South Rim Nature Trail west from the museum to Hermits Rest.

5 West Rim Drive

West Rim Drive, an eight-mile road west of Grand Canyon Village, also ends at Hermits Rest. The road is closed to private vehicles during the busy summer months, but regular shuttle buses make it easy to visit the drive's many overlooks. A memorial here honors Major John Wesley Powell, the courageous one-armed Civil War veteran who led expeditions down the Colorado River in 1869 and 1871 to survey the river and take photographs.

As you near the end of the drive, Pima Point offers views into what Powell called the "grand, gloomy depths" of the canyon bottom. From the rim the Colorado seems only a narrow creek; in reality, the river is between 200 and 300 feet wide, and what appear to be gentle ripples are in fact wildly roaring rapids that toss river-runners' 20-foot rafts about like so many corks in a whirlpool.

6 Yaki Point

The drive doubles back to Grand Canyon Village and heads east on East Rim Drive to Yaki Point. Prominent in the view here are the switchbacks of the South Kaibab Trail, which in 6.3 miles drops steeply to the Colorado River. Hiking into the canyon can be an exhilarating experience, but be sure to carry plenty of water and allow adequate time (twice as long to come back up as you spend going down). Descending below the rim is like entering a desert—and the lower you go in the canyon, the hotter it gets. In summer, temperatures on the canyon floor often exceed 105°F.

Star Route

★ North Rim Parkway

Just 1 out of 10 Grand Canyon visitors makes it to the North Rim (10 miles from the South Rim as the crow flies but 215 miles by car), and the lack of crowds is part of its appeal. From Jacob Lake, Rte. 67 (open May to October) travels south across the Kaibab Plateau through pine forests and grassy meadows. After it enters the park, the road winds through rockier terrain, culminating at historic Grand Canyon Lodge, where a short trail leads to the dazzling views at Bright Angel Point.

Pueblo ruins at Wupatki National Monument date from the 1400s, when prehistoric farmers settled in small groups beneath the shadows of the San Francisco Peaks.

kivas, survives as the haunting, silent testament to a departed people—ancestors of the Hopi Indians of today—who farmed and hunted here some 800 years ago.

10 Lipan Point

In the canyon depths below Lipan Point, the Colorado River makes a sinuous S curve as it bends toward the west. Cottonwoods and willows grow in spots along its banks and, like oases in the desert, create an important habitat for wildlife.

There is much to see above the rim as well. Mule deer, with their enormous ears, are often spotted by the road, while elk, their massive, stately cousins, are more elusive. In the nearby ponderosa pines, look for a large, bushy-tailed squirrel with long tufted ears; this charming and playful creature embodies a fascinating lesson in ecology. Over the centuries squirrels on the North Rim evolved into a white-tailed form known as the Kaibab squirrel; the closely related, dark-tailed Abert squirrel is found on the South Rim. Though the two populations live only a few miles apart, the impassable gulf of the Grand Canyon separates them so completely that they might as well be on separate continents.

11 Desert View

East Rim Drive saves one of its finest sights for last: just before Rte. 64 turns south to leave the national park, Desert View offers a vista northward into Marble Canyon as well as a panorama of the vast plain known as the Marble Platform, stretching eastward toward the Painted Desert. (The "marble" for which these features were named is actually limestone.)

The 70-foot-tall Watchtower, perched precariously on the very edge of the canyon rim here, was built in the 1930s. Its rustic rock design was based on similar round

7 Grandview Point

Trying to choose a favorite view of the Grand Canyon can prove as frustrating as counting the stars in the sky. Every vista, every visit, reveals something new and extraordinary. Nonetheless, Grandview is a favorite of many who know the park well, with Horseshoe Mesa, Angels Gate, and Vishnu Temple among the majestic formations arrayed below.

Like a kaleidoscope in constant motion, the canyon's colors change with each nuance of light and season, from winter's gray mists to summer's blazing light. Shades of black, gray, green, red, rust, yellow, brown, and white all paint the canyon walls; the depth and hue of these horizontal bands offer clues to the age and composition of the rocks that form them.

8 Moran Point

While you're admiring the wild beauty of the Grand Canyon, save a bit of gratitude for the landscape painter Thomas Moran, who stopped here on his travels across the West in the late 19th century. Moran's dramatic paintings played an important role in persuading the federal government to preserve the canyon for all Americans, at a time when private commercial development was spreading insidiously across the South Rim. This view, named in his honor, looks west toward the slanted rock layers and jagged outline of the formation known as the Sinking Ship.

9 Tusayan Ruin

Nineteenth-century explorers, artists, and prospectors were not the first to behold the Grand Canyon's marvels. Before them came Spanish conquistadors, and before them the Anasazis, who built pueblo settlements in many places across the Southwest. The restored Tusayan ruin, with its rock-walled living quarters and round ceremonial

⋮⋮⋮⋮ Trip Tips ⋮⋮⋮⋮

Length: About 250 miles.

When to go: March to November.

Lodging: Make reservations in advance for overnight stays at Grand Canyon Village.

Nearby attractions: Meteor Crater, east of Flagstaff. Museum of Northern Arizona, Flagstaff.

Visitor centers: Grand Canyon Village. Sunset Crater, Walnut Canyon, and Wupatki national monuments.

Further information: Arizona Office of Tourism, 1100 West Washington, Phoenix, AZ 85007; tel. 866-298-3312, www. azot. com.

towers constructed by the Anasazis hundreds of years ago.

12 Little Colorado River Gorge

Continuing south and east, Rte. 64 descends from the Coconino Plateau to a broad plain where vegetation is sparse—mostly desert plants such as sagebrush, creosote bush, and Mormon tea. Two overlooks just north of the highway provide dizzying views into the Little Colorado River gorge. Like an old photograph taken of someone that is now full grown, the narrow, 1,200-foot chasm may show how the Grand Canyon looked as the Colorado River first began to erode its bedrock in its youth—millions of years ago.

13 Wupatki National Monument

The drive joins Rte. 89 at the village of Cameron, and 20 miles south a side road leads to Wupatki National Monument. Indians now called the Sinaguas (*sin agua* is Spanish for "without water") lived here some 800 years ago. The multistoried sandstone and limestone pueblos they built (one contains more than 100 rooms) were home to about 2,000 people.

14 Sunset Crater National Monument

The scenic loop continues south from Wupatki across the desert, rising as it approaches the dramatic, almost otherworldly vision of Sunset Crater. A little over 900 years ago—only a heartbeat in geologic time—a series of volcanic eruptions built this stunning, symmetrical, black cone of rock, ash, and cinders in an eruption that lasted only a few years; its peak rises 1,000 feet from the ponderosa pines and lava fields around its base. The crater took its colorful name from particles of oxidized iron and sulfur, which tint its rim in the fiery "sunset" shades of red and yellow. While it's inviting to climb, prepare for slow progress; loose cinders slide from underfoot.

15 Walnut Canyon National Monument

At the junction of Rte. 89 and I-40 near Flagstaff, the drive turns east to Walnut Canyon. In this deep horseshoe-shaped gorge, the Sinagua Indians built pueblos under the ledges of limestone cliffs, sheltered from sun, rain, and snow. Living in family groups, they grew corn, beans, and squash on the canyon rim, gathered wild berries and walnuts, hunted deer and rabbits, and traded with surrounding tribes. The sturdy pueblos attest to their builders' skill and ingenuity. Yet after 150 years in this idyllic home, the Sinaguas abandoned the canyon about A.D. 1250. Bones tell us what they ate, and macaw feathers prove that their trade routes went as far as ancient Mexico, yet the cause of their final journey is a mystery that may never be solved.

Sunset Crater is a relatively recent volcanic cinder cone. To climb it means scrambling steps up and sliding back down.

Red Rock Country

Switching like the tail of a miner's mule, this old wagon trail scales steep desert hills and plunges into cloistered canyons as it journeys through the heart of Arizona.

::::: **Trip Tips** :::::

Length: About 79 miles, plus side trips.

When to go: Popular year-round.

Nearby attractions: Lowell Observatory, Flagstaff. Tlaquepaque district, Sedona (a four-acre architectural tribute to Old Mexico featuring gardens, fountains, courtyards, and galleries). Fort Verde Historic Park, Camp Verde. Sharlot Hall Museum, Prescott. Phippen Museum of Western Art, Prescott. Smoki Museum, Prescott (a collection of Indian artifacts).

Visitor centers: Tuzigoot and Montezuma national monuments.

Further information: Sedona-Oak Creek Canyon Chamber of Commerce, Box 478, Sedona, AZ 86339; tel. 800-288-7336, www.visitsedona.com.

The Red Rock Country near Sedona includes this signature formation, which is called Coffee Pot Rock, banded in ochre and crimson.

When the great American architect Frank Lloyd Wright first laid eyes on the town of Sedona, he declared that "nothing should ever be built here." And Wright wasn't the first traveler to be so transfixed by Red Rock Country; for centuries Indians and whites alike have gazed in wonder at these sandstone monoliths, shaped by the same patient forces that carved the Grand Canyon. Strung along the length of Arizona's famed Rte. 89A, they form the vivid backdrop for this sinuous spin through some of the state's most bewitching desert wilderness.

1 Oak Creek Vista Point
Road maps say the distance from Flagstaff to Sedona is only about 30 miles, less than an hour's drive. But in fact, Sedona, tucked in a parched basin 2,600 feet below the cool alpine forests of the Coconino Plateau, seems a world away. To get there, Rte. 89A makes a dramatic descent down mile-wide Oak Creek Canyon, truly one of the most spectacular stretches of road in the entire state.

Pause a few miles south of Flagstaff at the Oak Creek Vista Point to get a sense of what lies ahead. A short trail leads from the parking area to a breathtaking overlook, where sheer rock faces of orange, red, pink, and chalky white plunge more than 1,000 feet to the canyon floor. (At Sedona, a half-hour drive to the south, the brilliantly dappled canyon walls stand nearly twice as high.) Though words strain to capture the scene, Western novelist Zane Grey came close in *Call of the Canyons.* "The very forest-fringed earth," he wrote, "seemed to have opened into a deep abyss."

2 West Fork Trail
Like a great winding staircase, the road descends from Oak Creek Vista Point in a series of dizzying hairpin turns to the canyon floor. Though each switchback brings a

fresh perspective on this fabled gorge, the neck-craning view from below is just as dramatic. Near the bottom lies the Sterling Springs Fish Hatchery, which supplies Oak Creek with trout.

Along the canyon floor the road traces the west bank of Oak Creek for 14 miles downstream to the lovely town of Sedona. While the upper canyon is densely forested with aspen, maple, ash, and oak (making for a dazzling display in early November), subtle changes in vegetation take place mile by mile, as the higher-altitude flora gradually yield to the piñon pine, juniper, shrub oak, and prickly pear cactus of the upper Sonoran desert.

The eastern wall of the canyon is nearly as impenetrable as it looks, but to the west the Red Rocks Secret Mountain Wilderness—a maze of canyons, cliffs, and crystalline streams—is threaded with trails. One of the best, tracing the West Fork of Oak Creek, begins a mile south of Cave Springs Campground at the Call of the Canyons Day Use Area. Just three miles long, West Fork Trail leads through lush vegetation into an ever-narrowing canyon whose red walls tower hundreds of feet overhead. Pack your waterproof boots: in places the canyon becomes so tight you'll have to wade through the ankle-deep stream.

3 Slide Rock State Park

Of the various stops along Oak Creek, there's no such thing as a bad choice. Pause to fish the clear waters (trout flourish in the cool depths), picnic in the shade of cottonwoods and willows, or simply contemplate the red rocks, whose striking contours never grow tiresome. On a hot summer day, however, one particular spot shouldn't be missed: Slide Rock. Snaking along a sandstone chute made slippery by algae, the creek drops suddenly to a frigid pool, creating

an exhilarating ride for swimmers. Farther down the canyon, at the Grasshopper Swim Area, the creek curves through a narrow canyon pass and gathers in a series of still basins, where visitors can swim.

4 Sedona

Myriad stories tell of the magical effect Sedona has on visitors, none more persuasive than the tale of a New York stockbroker who visited in 1973, took one look, and bought a house the very next day. When asked if he thought this was a bit impulsive, he shook his head. "No," he explained, "impulsive would be the same day."

Indeed, since Theodore and Sedona Schnebly settled there in 1902, Sedona (named for Mrs. Schnebly) has inspired more than one newcomer to linger. The town itself is pleasant enough, with a busy arts community, nearly flawless weather, and a handsome downtown of restaurants, hotels and shops. But what truly puts Sedona on the map is its stunningly beautiful landscape. In this grand geological garden, brightly banded mesas, buttes, and spires flank the town on all sides, thrusting to heights of more than 2,000 feet from the valley floor. If you stand and watch for a while, you'll see a fresh array of colors almost hourly, as one mountain recedes into violet shadow and the next takes on a vivid orange glow. Some take the spell of Sedona quite literally, believing that "vortices" of natural psychic energy occur here. Bell Rock, for example, is said to attract UFOs, while Cathedral Rock, in West Sedona, purportedly radiates a sense of well-being to all who approach within 500 yards. Whether you believe all this or not, it hardly matters; the vortices double as excellent picnic spots, as do Capital Butte, Chimney Rock, and Shrine of the Red Rocks, which looks out from the summit of Table Top

Mountain. South of town, Sedona's best-known man-made structure, the Chapel of the Holy Cross, is hard to miss. Both sculpture and house of worship, the chapel—a wedge of concrete with a 90-foot cross bisecting its face—seems to emerge from the red rocks and point straight to heaven.

5 Schnebly Hill Road

A popular scenic route, Schnebly Hill Road winds for six miles up a series of steep switchbacks through Bear Wallow Canyon to the summit at Schnebly Hill Vista, where spectacular views take in the Verde Valley, Sedona, and the mouth of Oak Creek Canyon. To begin the climb, drive a half-mile south from Sedona on Rte. 179 and turn east onto Schnebly Hill Road. Though the road is less steep than the descent into Oak Creek Canyon, only the first mile is paved; where the road turns to graded dirt, it's five more miles to the turnaround at Schnebly Hill Vista. Perched on the edge of a high precipice, the overlook takes in a sweeping view of Red Rock Country from Steamboat Rock to Mingus Mountain, which rim the Verde Valley to the west.

6 Red Rock State Park

Returning to Rte. 89A, head south for another three miles to Lower Red Rock Loop Road. Turn east again, and follow the signs to Red Rock State Park.

Straddling a 1½-mile section of Oak Creek, this 286-acre park—the region's newest—keeps a "hands-off" philosophy toward its

natural surroundings. The wild creekside habitat, where sycamores and cottonwoods grow in tangled profusion and shrubs of poison ivy rise eight feet tall, is left in its natural state without man's help or management. More than 150 species of birds have been catalogued (check at the visitor center for the latest sightings), and the many trails that wander through the property offer fine bird-watching. Try Smoke Trail, a half-mile loop beginning at the visitor center, or Eagle's Nest Trail, a scrambling mile-long hike to an overlook above the creek.

7 Dead Horse Ranch State Park

When Calvin Ireys went shopping for a ranch in the Verde Valley in the early 1950s, he visited this spot, only to find that the owner's horse had just died and the carcass

Cathedral Rock, like twin skyscrapers over Oak Creek, near Red Rock Crossing.

In the Verde River valley, 800-year-old ruins spill down the sides of a hilltop at Tuzigoot National Monument.

the theory that the Sinaguas were menaced by warring neighbors.

On the other side of the valley (about a 45-minute drive from Tuzigoot via Rtes. 279, 260, and 17) lies another Sinagua wonder: Montezuma Castle, a five-story structure tucked high on a sandstone cliff. It owes its romantic but misleading name to early explorers who mistakenly concluded that the dwelling was built by Aztecs of Montezuma's army who fled north.

9 Sycamore Canyon

Paralleling Oak Creek Canyon roughly 15 miles to the west, Sycamore Canyon offers the same splendor as its neighbor, without the crowds. Only hikers and those on horseback are allowed within the area, and even so, a trek should not be attempted in summer, when temperatures on the canyon floor flirt with the 100°F mark. To reach the canyon from Tuzigoot, take the national monument road and turn left after crossing the Verde River. The road dead-ends at the head of Parsons Trail, which runs the 21-mile length of Sycamore Creek. Yawning five miles wide in some spots, the gorge has been likened to a miniature Grand Canyon.

10 Verde River Canyon Excursion Train

No roads penetrate the upper Verde River Canyon, so it's not surprising that this excursion train —the holdover of a once-busy railroad serving the area's copper mines—is so popular with visitors. Hugging the south side of the river, the diesel-powered locomotive chugs along at a lazy 12 miles an hour through the craggy canyon, past Indian ruins, across spectacular trestle bridges, and down one long mountain tunnel, making the 40-mile round-trip between Clarkdale and the ghost town of Perkinsville in 4½ hours.

was awaiting pickup. Later that night, when his family sat down to dinner, Ireys asked his children which ranch he should buy. Their reply: "the one with the dead horse." Ireys did as they suggested, and the name stuck.

Today Dead Horse Ranch State Park occupies more than 300 acres along the Verde River, with excellent camping facilities and leisurely hiking trails that meander along the riverbanks and into the surrounding desert. The park's lagoon is regularly stocked with panfish, bass, and trout, which are easy pickings for anglers.

8 Tuzigoot National Monument

Strewn across the Verde Valley are remnants of an ancient people, called the Sinaguas, who first appeared in this region about 2,000 years ago. No one knows for certain who they were. Probably they moved down off the Mogollon Rim around A.D. 1125 onto lands vacated by the Hohokams, another group of people who had moved north. Adopting the irrigation practices of neighboring tribes, the Sinaguas farmed the fertile bottomlands of the Verde Valley and began to build apartment-style pueblos, a practice they may have learned from the Anasazis. For some 300 years the Sinaguas thrived; then they simply vanished. Some archaeologists think a devastating drought was responsible; others cite tribal warfare as the cause. The mystery is deepened by the seeming permanence of the structures they left behind.

The hilltop village known as Tuzigoot housed as many as 250 Sinaguas at its peak, around 1300. Built almost entirely without exterior doors, the two-story pueblo was entered by ladders through rooftop hatches, giving credence to

The valley is home to a variety of birds and mammals, and the train's dawdling presence does not disturb them. Look for bobcats, black bears, bald eagles (the canyon is the winter home to a flock of these quintessentially American birds), and great blue herons, throngs of which nest in the cottonwoods near the end of the line.

11 Jerome

Clinging to the sides of Cleopatra Hill, Jerome looks like a city poised to jump. In fact, that's exactly what has happened more than once, when dynamite blasts from nearby copper and silver mines shook buildings—including the town jail—right off the hillside.

Jerome's history is no less interesting than its precarious placement. Named for mining financier Eugene Jerome (who never actually set foot on Cleopatra Hill), the town was born in 1882, when the United Verde Copper Company began operation. It quickly grew to become the territory's fifth-largest city—and a veritable mecca of sin. At the turn of the century, so many saloons, gambling dens, and brothels crowded Jerome's crooked streets that a New York newspaper tagged it "the wickedest town in America." As if to purge it of its unseemly reputation, fires raged through Jerome so many times that people lost count. Somehow, the town always bounced back.

The mines are long gone, of course—shut down for good in 1953. What remains is a picture-perfect, turn-of-the-century Victorian town located in one of the steepest places you've ever seen. So precipitous are the town's switchbacking streets that, as a Phoenix newspaper once observed, "Your neighbor in Jerome can't look into your back windows, although he can look down your kitchen chimney from his front porch."

Three museums invite visitors to relive the city's past: the Jerome State Historic Park's opulent Douglas Mansion, with fine views from its upstairs balconies; the Jerome Historical Society Mine Museum, featuring displays of old mining paraphernalia and ore samples; and the Gold King Mine Museum, sporting a replica of a mine shaft that visitors can enter.

12 Prescott

Cresting Mingus Mountain at a soaring 7,023 feet, the highway makes its final switchback descent

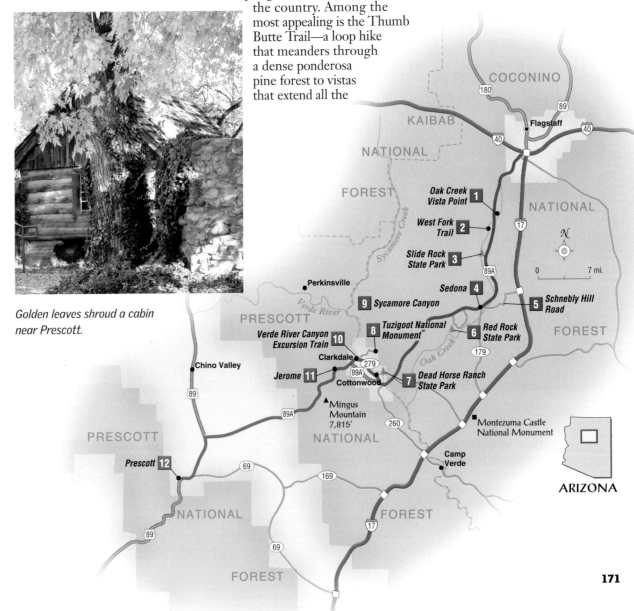

Golden leaves shroud a cabin near Prescott.

into Prescott Valley, a wide basin of grass and ranchland. End to end, this soothing expanse stretches more than 25 miles, from the base of Mingus Mountain to the former territorial capital, Prescott. Nestled in the cool pine forests of the Bradshaw Mountains, the city exudes a mellow Western charm, especially around its central plaza, which was once home to the infamous Whiskey Row.

Prescott is wedded to the beauty of its surroundings, and a variety of wilderness excursions offer tempting choices for exploring the country. Among the most appealing is the Thumb Butte Trail—a loop hike that meanders through a dense ponderosa pine forest to vistas that extend all the way to the San Francisco Peaks, near Flagstaff. A few miles north of town via Rte. 89 lies another popular spot for hiking and picnicking: the Granite Dells. Sometimes called Arizona's Garden of the Gods, this labyrinthine jumble of giant boulders attracts avid hikers and rock climbers. Nearby Watson Lake Park, just south of the Dells, is a fine place to swim, and campers drift off to sleep under the moonlight, fueling their dreams with memories of this dazzling journey through Red Rock Country.

Apache Trail

In the shadow of Arizona's Superstition Mountains arcs an old Indian path
so studded with desert delights that it is a treat for any traveler.

::::: **Trip Tips** :::::

Length: About 145 miles.

When to go: Best in winter, spring, and autumn.

Supplies: Start with a full tank of gas and plenty of water.

Words to the wise: Despite its short length, the drive can take a full day due to low speed limits.

Nearby attraction: Superstition Mountains Museum, Apache Junction.

Further information: Tonto National Forest, 2324 E. McDowell Rd., Phoenix, AZ 85006; tel. 602-225-5200, www.fs.fed.us/r3/tonto/.

Tonto National Monument borders the shores of Theodore Roosevelt Dam and Lake.

Many people have tried to capture the mystique of this historic highway, but few have been more exuberant than President Theodore Roosevelt. "The Apache Trail," he declared, "combines the grandeur of the Alps, the glory of the Rockies, and the magnificence of the Grand Canyon."

starkly beautiful Sonoran Desert and the strikingly handsome Superstition Mountains. The desert, a vast landscape of prickly cacti, hardy mesquite, and thorny paloverdes, is named for the Mexican state of Sonora, which lies to the south. The mountains, born of ancient volcanoes, tower above the desert floor, their jagged peaks spanning some 40 miles. Looking more like a mighty fortress than a mountain range, these silent reminders of nature's majesty are visible along much of the trail.

1 Apache Junction

Located some 30 miles to the east of Phoenix, this gateway to Arizona's desert lake region is the spot where Rte. 60 meets Rte. 88, also known as the Apache Trail. But another meeting also takes place here: an encounter between the

2 Lost Dutchman State Park

The next stop, at Lost Dutchman State Park, offers numerous campsites and nature trails. The 300-acre park derives its name from one Jacob Waltz, a shadowy figure who—according to legend—discovered a rich gold mine during the late 1800s but never revealed its exact whereabouts. Over the years, at least 36 treasure seekers have died or disappeared as they sought the elusive lode.

3 Tonto National Forest

As the trail winds around the base of the Superstition Mountains, a number of other stony wonders come into view: chunks of volcanic debris, bronze cliffs, and weird-looking whirlpool rocks (they resemble frozen masses of swirling water). Soon the drive enters Tonto National Forest, 3 million acres of rugged terrain featuring colorful canyons, pine-covered peaks, sparkling streams, and more than 400 kinds of animals. A turn onto Rte. 78 leads to the Superstition Wilderness Area, laced with over 180 miles of hiking trails.

4 Needle Vista

Back on Rte. 88 the drive heads north to Needle Vista, where, far off to the south, you can catch a glimpse of Weavers Needle, an imposing lava plug. The soaring spire has long served as a landmark for gold diggers in search of the Lost Dutchman's mine.

5 Canyon Lake

Rambling through steep, rocky hills, the trail passes varied vegetation that ranges from desert scrub to mountain chaparral. At Canyon Lake Vista Point, visitors look out on the azure waters of Canyon Lake, guarded by tall reddish cliffs. The 950-acre lake is one of four reservoirs that nourish nearby Phoenix and the Salt River valley. In addition to fishing and water sports, the lake offers cruises on a double-deck stern-wheeler.

6 Tortilla Flat

Another view of Canyon Lake can be glimpsed from a small vista point that also overlooks the town of Tortilla Flat, a mile and a half away. Once a stagecoach stop, this resurrected ghost town has a café, country store, and a permanent population of six. But its weekend visitors—lured by souvenir shops, prickly-pear ice cream, and the cool waters of Tortilla Creek—are far greater in number.

7 Fish Creek Hill

Soon after leaving Tortilla Flat, the pavement gives way to a dirt road, making for a rather dusty drive over the next 22 miles. The scenery, however, more than makes up for the rough road conditions. The route—dotted with willows, cottonwoods, and sycamores— passes countless craggy peaks before arriving at one of the trail's most photographed sites, Geronimo Head Cliff. The adjoining wilderness teems with wildlife, including deer, bobcats, coyotes, javelinas, mountain lions, and bighorn sheep.

At Fish Creek Hill the drive reaches its most thrilling—and treacherous—course. Hugging the canyon wall, the one-lane road (with numerous pullouts for passing) twists and turns as it plunges a dizzying 1,000 feet in just a mile and a half. In late afternoon, the setting sun adds a golden glow to the Wall of Bronze, multihued rocks near the canyon floor. A short trail at the edge of Fish Creek Hill leads north to Fish Creek Vista, where buff-colored cliffs skirt the canyon below.

8 Apache Lake

A few miles farther along, Apache Lake Vista Point looks out across the water to flat-topped Goat Mountain and the colorful Painted Cliffs. At the overlook a turnoff leads to the Apache Lake Recreation Area, which offers a marina, campground, and rock and mountain climbing. This is also a good place for spotting eagles, ospreys, and red-tailed hawks.

9 Theodore Roosevelt Dam and Lake

Back again on Rte. 88, the next leg of the journey heads through cactus-covered hills before arriving at Theodore Roosevelt Dam. Dedicated in 1911, this mammoth structure is the world's largest masonry dam. Without it, the Apache Trail would never have existed, for the road was built to transport materials and equipment, hauled by 20-mule teams, from the nearest railroad to the construction site. The labor force for the dam consisted of both white men and Indians—groups that had been fierce foes only a generation earlier. Roosevelt Lake today offers fishing, boating, and camping.

10 Tonto National Monument

Just east of the dam lies Tonto National Monument, which preserves two apartment-style cliff dwellings occupied more than 600 years ago by the Salados Indians. The lower part of these ancient ruins, nestled in caves, can be visited on a short self-guiding tour.

11 Queen Creek Canyon

Near the town of Globe, the drive leaves the Apache Trail and heads back west on Rte. 60. Along the way, it passes through Queen Creek Canyon, a dramatic stretch where the highway is lined with ridges, buttes, and pinnacles. Just beyond Queen Creek Tunnel, you arrive at Superior, an old mining town. Nearby Apache Leap was allegedly named for a large party of warriors who, after being cornered by the U.S. Cavalry, chose to plunge off the cliff in a suicide pact rather than surrender.

12 Boyce Thompson Arboretum

Desert marigold, Mexican gold poppy, and crimson sage are but a few of the more than 2,000 desert plants you'll see along the trails of this renowned research

Wildflowers bloom after spring rains in the Superstition Mountains.

facility, founded by mining mogul William Boyce Thompson. Colors are at their peak in spring, of course, but with so many species from around the world on display here, every season brings its share of blooms.

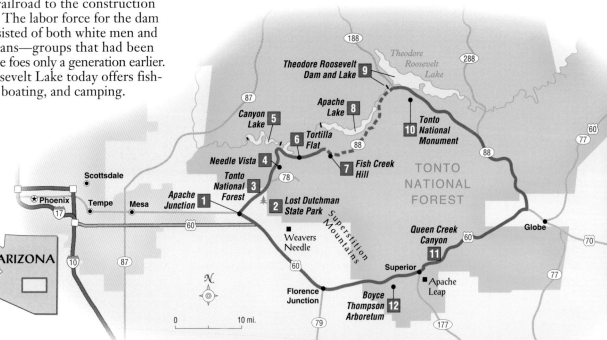

Coronado Trail

Named for the Spanish explorer but known to locals as the "white-knuckle road,"
this wildly curving wilderness byway roller-coasters across the wooded ridges of eastern Arizona.

A side road, primitive but passable, wanders through the aspens and evergreens near Blue Vista Point.

Seeking to enrich the already plentiful coffers of the Spanish crown, Francisco Vásquez de Coronado led an expedition through this area in 1540. His goal was to find the Seven Cities of Cíbola, mythical places said to have streets paved with gold. The journey, needless to say, was a wild-goose chase, and Coronado returned empty-handed.

But gold or no gold, one fact remains: these out-of-the-way wilds along the Coronado Trail overflow with history, natural wonders, and truly superlative scenery.

1 Springerville

Rustic little Springerville sits in a wide grassy valley dotted with cinder cones—small, shapely hills composed of volcanic debris. The town began as a trading post, a hub for the Mormon ranchers who settled the region in the 1870s. Most signs of the town's early days have long since disappeared, but on Main Street an 18-foot-tall statue recalls the era. The monument, known as the "Madonna of the Trail," depicts a pioneer mother cradling a child in her arms, a tribute to the brave women who helped settle the West.

2 Apache-Sitgreaves National Forest

Heading south out of Springerville, Rte. 191—the Coronado Trail—quickly bids farewell to town life as it climbs into hills and canyons of Apache-Sitgreaves National Forest. The vastness of Apache-Sitgreaves virtually guarantees a wealth of scenic diversity: myriad mountains, canyons, secluded lakes and creeks, and woodlands that change in character depending on elevation. The untamed terrain, however, makes for another cer-

---

::::: **Trip Tips** :::::

Length: About 130 miles.

When to go: Year-round, but snow sometimes closes the road, especially from Alpine to Morenci.

Nearby attractions: Casa Malpaís (House of the Badlands), an ancient pueblo of the Mogollon Indians, north of Springerville. Luna Lake, with water sports and campsites, Rte. 180 east of Alpine.

Further information: Apache–Sitgreaves National Forest, P.O. Box 640, Springerville, AZ 85938; tel. 928-333-4301, www.fs.fed.us/r3/asnf/.

A lone windmill near Escudilla Mountain draws precious water from the depths.

tainty: travelers must be cautious. Signs all along Rte. 191 warn motorists: "Go Slow." With its many curves and hills, the Coronado Trail, though fairly short, takes at least four hours to drive. Allow plenty of extra time, too, since opportunities abound for pulling over and taking in the views of pristine countryside—the perfect remedy for the rigors of the road.

3 Escudilla Mountain

Cresting at 10,877 feet, Escudilla's rounded crown dominates the eastern horizon. Its name is Spanish for "soup bowl," most likely an allusion to the bowl-shaped crater at the summit of the extinct volcano. A large grove of aspens covers the northern slopes, where a fire in 1951 ravaged the firs and pines that once grew there. In the rangeland and clearings that fan away from the peak's base, tangles of raspberries, snowberries, and gooseberries flourish among the other shrubs and grasses.

A forest road exits Rte. 191 three miles south of Nutrioso and leads visitors closer to the peak's steep slopes. For the best view from the top, take the well-kept trail that begins at Terry Flat and guides hikers to the summit and to the

Escudilla Lookout, the loftiest fire tower in Arizona.

Continuing southward, Rte. 191 ascends through a forest-filled valley to Alpine Divide, about 8,550 feet in elevation, then winds downhill through a slender canyon to Alpine. A picturesque town in the heart of the high country, Alpine serves as a center for outdoor activities, including some of the state's best cross-country skiing. (Before heading south, fill your fuel tank here; the next service station is 89 miles away.)

4 Hannagan Meadow

Scattered stands of aspens, pines, spruces, and firs surround the aptly named village of Hannagan Meadow, with its historic lodge dating to 1926. Several trails branch away from the lodge and thread through the wooded backcountry, home to coyote, deer, elk, and black bears. In various seasons, the area becomes a magnet for those who hike, fish, horseback ride, snowmobile, or cross-country ski.

In this region, known for its wealth of wildflowers—black-eyed Susans, four o'clocks, lupines, asters, and primroses, for example —August usually offers the most brilliant spectacle. Among the avian inhabitants are such rarities as peregrine falcons, bald eagles, and spotted owls. Of special note, too, is one of the Southwest's largest virgin stands of ponderosa pines. The trees shade segments of the Bear Wallow Trail No. 63, which follows a creek for a distance of about seven miles.

5 Blue Vista Point

The showstopper here is the Mogollon Rim, a massive, almost continuous cliff that towers up to 1,000 feet in height as it runs northwestward nearly all the way to the Grand Canyon. Atop the rim Blue Vista Point looks out on a good-size portion of southeast-

ern Arizona, a sprawling jumble of ridges, wooded slopes, and maze-like canyons. In the south stands 10,717-foot-high Mt. Graham and the Pinaleno Mountains; to the east the thin ribbon of the Blue River shimmers in the distance. The Forest Service has also cut a nature trail near the viewpoint. Marked with interpretive signs, the pathway switches back and forth across the clifftop.

6 Rose Peak Lookout

Twisting and turning along a convoluted course, Rte. 191 makes its way down the steep face of the Mogollon Rim. Along the way, spruces and firs yield first to oaks, then to a grassland spotted with piñon pines and junipers.

Farther south an uphill stretch leads to yet another fine vantage point: Rose Peak Lookout. An unpaved road—bumpy and steep in places—climbs to the isolated forest tower, where the view takes in the rugged Blue Range Wilderness Area, a backpackers' mecca far off to the east.

7 Clifton

The 10 miles of the Coronado Trail descending into Morenci are the steepest. Down and down the drive plummets, passing through a series of switchbacks toward far-off desert valleys simmering beneath a blanket of haze. Just before the town of Morenci, you'll skirt a site that explorer and gold-seeker Coronado could not even have imagined: one of the world's largest open-pit copper mines. A roadside overlook reveals the western edge of the chasm, overwhelming for its sheer size—two miles in diameter.

The final leg of the Coronado Trail coasts to Clifton, a quaint, historic town wedged between canyon walls. The community has seen its share of ups and downs since its founding in 1872.

Most of the early buildings— some restored, others in need of repair—have survived.

Be sure to see the old jail blasted into a cliffside by one Margarito Verala. On payday, Verala shot up a local dance hall and became the jail's very first occupant.

New Mexico North

Vivid tableaux of bold colors and eye-catching forms, the panoramas of northern New Mexico take in purple peaks, ruddy buttes, bloom-bedecked meadows, and flaming skies at dusk.

::::: **Trip Tips** :::::

Length: About 410 miles, plus side trips.

When to go: Popular year-round.

Words to the wise: Roads can be icy and snowpacked in winter and early spring.

Not to be missed: Northern Navajo Nation Fair (October), Shiprock.

Nearby attractions: Aztec Ruins National Monument, Aztec. Bisti Wilderness and Chaco Culture National Historical Park, south of Farmington. Heron Lake State Park, near Rutheron. Kit Carson Home and Museum, Taos.

Further information: New Mexico Tourism Department, 491 Old Santa Fe Trail, Santa Fe, NM 87503; tel. 800-545-2040, www.newmexico.org.

At Taos Pueblo, stucco-covered adobe blocks—straw mixed with clay—form thick walls, providing excellent insulation.

Traversed long ago by ancient Indians, Spanish conquistadors, and traders from the East, the richly varied journey along Rte. 64 showcases rainbow-hued deserts, pine-cloaked mountains, and windblown plains that ripple toward the horizon. But the trip is especially remarkable because, thanks to its splendid isolation, the landscape looks much as it did when the first Spaniards arrived here more than four centuries ago.

1 Shiprock

A thriving center of Navajo trade, and the site of the tribe's annual fall festival, the town of Shiprock occupies a land where nearly every monument has been sacred to this people for centuries. Southwest of the town lies Shiprock Peak, for example, a volcanic core that soars some 20 stories higher than the Empire State Building. The Navajos dubbed it Winged Rock, and down through the generations they have told how the hallowed monolith once sprouted enormous wings to rescue their ancestors from enemies. (Early explorers gave the peak its present name because of its resemblance to a high-masted sailing ship.)

For scenes of a different sort, head east out of town on Rte. 64, which slices through verdant fields nourished by the San Juan River—a gift of life to civilizations present and past that tried to make their homes in this high desert. One not-so-lucky group was the Anasazis, who lived at Salmon Ruins (just west of Bloomfield) nearly eight centuries ago, until drought forced them to move away. Still standing as testimony to their fate are the remains of a C-shaped pueblo, with over 200 apartment-like dwellings overlooking a central plaza, and the Great Kiva, a religious chamber where urgent prayers for water evidently went unheeded.

2 Angel Peak

Angel Peak is easy to spot even from afar: hulking above a pastel-painted canyon, this monolith resembles an angel with outstretched wings. You can drive to the peak, and the national recreation area that surrounds it, by turning south at Bloomfield onto State Rte. 44. Bear in mind, however, that despite the area's austere beauty, visitor facilities are limited.

Views of Angel Peak and other natural features throughout the region are enhanced by the crystal-clear air of northern New Mexico. At more than 5,000 feet above sea level, the air is free of smog and humidity, making mountains seem closer, the sky bluer, and the hues of the landscape more radiant. For centuries this luminous terrain has cast a spell on unsuspecting visitors, enchanting everyone from Spanish explorers, whose name for the area means "Land of Clear Light," to modern artists such as the celebrated Georgia O'Keeffe.

As the drive continues east on State Rte. 550, it passes a number of fanciful buttes, mesas, and hoodoos (mushroom-shaped spires) that lord above the flat terrain. These geological marvels—tinted orange, pink, and ocher—are the sandstone remains of an ancient seabed that was sculpted over eons by wind, rain, and frost.

The moon peeks from behind the 1,700-foot eroded volcanic spire of Shiprock. It is a spiritual center for the Navajo people.

3 Navajo Lake State Park

Swinging north on State Rte. 511, the drive cruises into Navajo Lake State Park, a 21,000-acre Eden. Beckoning boaters to its cool waters, the lake—one of New Mexico's largest—contrasts intriguingly with the piñon-pine dotted tableland seared brown by the relentless sun. On this arid terrain surrounding the park, an eerie stillness seems to reign. But occasionally, even while the sky is clear and blue, a distant rumble heralds the arrival of a thunderstorm. Billowing black clouds sweep in, eclipsing the sun and throwing dark shadows across the plain. Cued by brilliant flashes of multipronged lightning bolts that stab the peaks beyond, thunder crashes like a chorus of angry titans. Cascades of water swell the arroyos, and then, just as suddenly as it began, the spectacle is over. Within minutes shafts of light make the soggy earth shine, gossamers of steam float skyward, and the sky turns blue again.

4 Jicarilla Apache Indian Reservation

Continuing east, Rte. 64 twists through a rolling countryside of pine-clad mountains and alpine lakes, of sandstone bluffs and sagebrush prairie. These mixed lands belong to the Jicarilla Apaches, whose ages-old nomadic way of life ended abruptly when they were forced onto this reservation in 1887. Known for their intricately woven baskets, the Jicarillas (meaning "little basketmakers") reside for the most part in and around Dulce, the hub of the tribal community. The reservation land, rich with a variety of game, is a mecca for fishermen angling for trout and for hunters seeking deer, elk, mountain lions, ducks, geese, and wild turkeys.

For a closer look at the lovely Jicarilla landscape, follow State Rtes. J-8, J-15, and 537 on a scenic loop south from Dulce that takes in five lakes sparkling among piñon-flecked hills. The route is alluring in fall, when Gambel oaks blaze with scarlet and migrating geese honk from the sky.

5 Cumbres Pass

Soon after crossing the Continental Divide, Rte. 64 enters the little town of Chama. From here, the Cumbres and Toltec Scenic Railroad has huffed and puffed its way up and over Cumbres Pass and along precarious Toltec Gorge since the 1880s. The narrow-gauge railway was built to transport miners to Colorado's bountiful lodes, but today it carries tourists who come to ogle such sights as the aspens that shimmer on mountain slopes in autumn.

If you prefer to drive, State Rte. 17 more or less parallels the part of the train's route that stretches between Chama and Cumbres Pass.

6 Brazos Cliffs

From the little town of Tierra Amarilla, tucked in a valley beside the slopes of the San Juan Mountains, Rte. 64 curls upward past aspen-fringed lakes, fields of buttercups, and grazing cattle. The road crests at an elevation of over 10,500 feet, where turnouts and picnic spots along the ridge afford splendid views of the Brazos Cliffs. A part-time waterfall, the product of melting snow in spring and thunderstorms in summer, spills

gracefully down the face of the cliffs. From here the drive breezes east through Carson National Forest. Its 1.5 million acres of aspen, fir, and spruce—punctuated by sunny fields and murmuring streams—are a paradise for backpackers and anglers. Among the superb recreational areas that entice motorists to the forest is Hopewell Lake, set in a lovely mountain meadow.

7 Rio Grande Gorge

The high sagebrush plain east of Tres Piedras is broad and flat, offering no hint of the invasive gash in the earth that lies ahead. Then suddenly, on one of the highest suspension bridges in America, the road soars across the chasm of the Rio Grande Gorge. From this 650-foot perch, which quakes under the weight of passing trucks, you can see the raging Rio Grande far below, its green waters encased by walls so steep and narrow that the sun's rays manage to illuminate them only in summer—and even then only at midday. Golden eagles, which nest on the cliffs, glide gracefully over the gorge.

8 Taos

This picture-perfect town, with its tan adobe architecture, sits in a charmed landscape of snowy peaks and turquoise-blue skies. No wonder it has lured artists for well over a century—and continues to do so today. Saturated with painters and writers, the town sports such cultural trappings as galleries, craft shops, bookstores, and museums.

At the heart of town, Taos Plaza is lined with an eclectic mix of eateries and boutiques. The plaza itself is a legacy of the Spaniards, who came in the 1600s searching

Leaping Lizards

While pausing along the drive to stroll through rocky, arid terrain, you may spot one of these colorful creatures. Named for the striking bands around their necks, collared lizards are a foot long on average and are often seen basking on boulders to soak up the sun. When hunting—for insects, mice, and even smaller lizards—they run on their hind legs, with forelimbs and tail in the air, and leap nimbly from rock to rock to seize their prey.

for gold and stayed to colonize the valley and convert the Pueblo Indians to Christianity. Their strategy did not altogether succeed; though they left behind such imposing structures as the Church of St. Francis of Assisi, located in a nearby village, they did not thoroughly convert the Indians, whose descendants still reside north of town at Taos Pueblo. Today, you can wander among the pueblo's twin multitiered adobe dwellings, nestled at the base of Pueblo Peak, and watch shawl-covered women prepare bread in large hornos (outdoor beehive ovens), just as they have for generations.

9 Enchanted Circle

A stunning patchwork of pine-covered peaks, picturesque valleys, and deep-blue lakes accounts for the poetic name of this scenic 80-mile detour north of Taos on State Rtes. 522 and 38. The centerpiece is lofty Wheeler Peak, a popular ski center that, at 13,161 feet, is New Mexico's highest mountain. Near San Cristobal lies the D. H. Lawrence Ranch where, in the 1920s, the British author wrote some of his most celebrated works. As the route swings around the mountain, you can pause at Red River, a ski resort with Texan flair;

Elizabethtown, a gold-mining ghost town; and Eagle Nest Lake, where windsurfers fueled by fierce gusts from the mountains skitter across the whitecapped expanse of blue.

10 Cimarron Canyon State Park

Zigzagging down from the Sangre de Cristo ("Blood of Christ") Mountains—at sunset they have a scarlet glow—Rte. 64 winds between the red granite palisades of narrow Cimarron Canyon. Blue spruce and the rushing Cimarron River complete the idyllic scene, considered by many to be the route's prettiest stretch. Under a dark awning of trees, husky mule deer forage at dawn and twilight, nibbling twigs and leaves and twitching their huge ears at the slightest sound. In winter the mule deer have good reason to be vigilant, for hunters comb the wilderness surrounding Cimarron Canyon State Park in search of a take-home prize.

11 Cimarron

The 25,000 Boy Scouts who visit Philmont Scout Ranch near Cimarron each year, enjoying its many acres of mountains, valleys, and forests, know quite well to "Be Prepared"—to build a fire, raise a tent, or employ some other wilderness skill. But in the days when the West was still wild and

Cimarron was overflowing with the likes of Doc Holliday and Wyatt Earp, that motto would have had a different meaning: be prepared for a quick draw. Boasting 15 saloons, the town was so raucous that on one occasion a journalist noted, "Everything is quiet in Cimarron. Nobody has been killed for three days." The St. James Hotel, where Buffalo Bill organized his Wild West extravaganza, was a nefarious hangout and didn't escape injury. No fewer than 400 bullet holes were found in the ceilings of the hotel's saloon, hallways, and rooms during a 1901 renovation, and you can still see some today. Redolent with history—and not just the rowdy kind—the St. James was built in 1872 by a chef who had once served Abraham Lincoln. Years later Lew Wallace penned part of *Ben Hur* while staying at the hotel, and Zane Grey composed a novel here.

12 Sugarite Canyon State Park

In the 1800s thousands of eager traders and their loaded freight wagons rumbled across the land between Raton and Cimarron—part of the 850-mile Santa Fe Trail. After negotiating Raton Pass, an axle-breaking route over the mountains, they may well have stopped for a breather at Sugarite Canyon, a quiet niche (now a state park) that seems to epitomize New Mexico: flower-strewn meadows meet high palisades, and a serene mountain lake reflects aspen-clad slopes and the wide blue sky.

13 Capulin Volcano National Monument

Armed with flint spearheads, primitive humans known as Folsom Man (for the little town where their bones and spear points were discovered) hunted such prehistoric animals as giant ground sloths and woolly mammoths. And it is

San Francisco de Asis church, built of adobe in 1813–1815, is one of the oldest churches in New Mexico and the West. It is one of the outstanding remaining examples of authentic mission architecture from the Spanish colonial period.

possible that Folsom Man may have witnessed, and been terrified by, a dazzling display of pyrotechnics: Capulin Mountain—a nearly symmetrical, extinct volcano—exploded many thousands of years ago, spewing ash and steam high into the atmosphere.

For a present-day view of the volcano, the surrounding plains, and—on a clear day—Colorado and Oklahoma, take the narrow road that ends just below the summit, then walk the rim trail. Another trail descends a quarter mile into the crater.

14 Clayton Lake State Park

A century ago, a vast sea of tall, saddle-high grass rippled across the Great Plains in an unbroken prairie that extended for thousands of square miles. It's gone now, done in and turned under by the farmer's plow and eaten by grazing cattle. But a few remnants survive here and elsewhere. At Kiowa National Grasslands, a 136,505-acre preserve east of Clayton, it is still possible to imagine straight-horned bison and prehistoric hunters watching an endless sea of grass as it swayed to the distant horizon.

Aeons before the first Indians arrived in North American and the prairie took root, dinosaurs roamed the muddy banks of an ancient sea, one whose shores stretched from the Gulf of Mexico to Canada. The enormous beasts left their mark at Clayton Lake State Park, northwest of Clayton, where 500 elephantine footprints (discovered after a scouring rainstorm in 1982) are embedded in a two-acre swath of sandstone: a fitting finale for visitors taking a journey imbued with images from the recent and distant past.

Jemez Mountain Trail

Natural forces and ancient peoples have left their marks on this area of New Mexico, a color-streaked landscape where shimmering desert gives way to forested mountains.

The landscape that inspired famed painter Georgia O'Keeffe, who lived at Ghost Ranch, is found here in northern New Mexico.

To venture into the Jemez Mountains is to leave the modern world behind—to travel a route that is measured not only in miles but also in time. For this region—a realm of canyons, mesas, and mountains—has remained virtually undisturbed for centuries, recalling an era when ancient Indians first colonized there, then yielded to the Anasazis, a long-extinct culture that built their villages into the cliffsides and led seemingly peaceful, simple lives.

1 Jemez River Canyon

Looming like distant thunderheads, the Jemez Mountains darken the desert horizon as Rte. 44 curves northwestward past sunbaked hills. The ridges, rising as an unbroken barrier, prove impassable until the road reaches San Ysidro, where the thin ribbon of the Jemez River guides State Rte. 4 into the tree-covered mountains. In fewer than 10 miles, the landscape here undergoes a drastic change—from arid, rocky lowlands to the lush pine woodlands of Santa Fe National Forest. The transition is particularly evident at the Jemez River Canyon, where the river and the road are hemmed in on both sides by high-climbing sandstone slopes. Shrubs and ponderosa pines claim the lower elevations, then yield their dominance to thick stands of spruces, firs, and aspens that take over the landscape, providing welcome relief for the eyes.

2 Jemez Springs

The volcanic forces that forged the Jemez Mountains a million years ago remain active today—though on a far less violent scale. Hot springs, proof of the underground unrest, bubble to the surface at Jemez Springs, a peaceful town where in winter puffs of steam rise like smoke signals into the chilly air, inviting visitors to take a dip.

Two structures of historical note stand on the northern outskirts of town: a long-abandoned Indian pueblo and a church erected by Spanish missionaries in 1622. Preserved as Jemez State Monument, their walls are slowly crumbling as the ravages of time take their toll.

One of nature's monuments, Soda Dam, in contrast, is being painstakingly enlarged. The steady accumulation, layer upon layer, of calcium carbonate formed the bizarre barrier—a process that continues to this day. Standing about 40 feet high, the marblelike monument partially blocks the flow of the Jemez River. In addition to the slow crafting of the

:::::: **Trip Tips** ::::::

Length: About 170 miles, plus side trips.

When to go: Year-round. Higher elevations provide relief from the heat during the scorching days of summer.

Nearby attraction: Heron Lake State Park, 11 miles west of Tierra Amarilla via Rte. 95.

Not to be missed: Feast Day, held August 2 and November 12 at Jemez Pueblo. Visitors can observe traditional dances.

Further information: New Mexico Tourism Department, 491 Old Santa Fe Trail, Santa Fe, NM 87503; tel. 800-545-2040, www.newmexico.org.

Multistory cliff dwellings dot Bandelier National Monument.

dam, hidden volcanic forces make themselves evident in another way: sulfurous fumes escape from underground chambers, tinging the air with a pungent smell.

3 Valle Grande

You'll soon catch your first glimpse of Battleship Rock, a massive monolith of basalt that seems to navigate the confluence of the Jemez River's forks. Farther on, State Rte. 4 leads to the Jemez Falls Campground, where a short trail twists to graceful Jemez Falls. An overlook amid the wooded countryside offers a clear view of the cascade, which fans out as it splashes down a jagged cliff.

The foliage thickens along the next leg of the drive, a climb that approaches the 9,000-foot mark, where groves of towering firs and spruces cover the mountainsides.

Then, stunningly, the forest floor falls away, with views of a vast meadowland. This is the heart of the Jemez Mountains: a great valley spreading across an area that was once a massive volcanic peak is called Valle Grande. Its energy spent, the fiery giant collapsed into itself, forming a caldera that covers about 175 square miles.

4 Bandelier National Monument

As an ancient home of Anasazi Indians, Bandelier abounds in mystery. The tribe, vanishing from history with few hints as to why, arrived in this area in the 12th century, carving dwellings into the cliffs of tuff (composed of ash and other fine volcanic particles). They were farmers who raised corn, beans, and squash among the ponderosa pines and box elders that line Frijoles Creek. The community flourished, and as the centuries rolled by, the population snowballed into the thousands. About A.D. 1550, however, the Anasazis abandoned the site, never to return. Yet their onetime presence remains indelible, and trails—some of them steep and equipped with ladders—lead through the ruins of their bygone civilization.

5 White Rock Overlook

Up ahead lies the Pajarito Plateau, an arid realm spotted with piñon pines and junipers—hardy survivors that often grow side by side. The drive slowly descends as it follows State Rte. 4, passing several small canyons, each cut into the plateau's eastern slope by the steams that tumble down to the Rio Grande. Inviting as the area may seem, parts of it are off-limits for good cause. Much of the land here is controlled by the Los Alamos National Laboratory, where scientists working in utmost haste and secrecy developed the atomic bomb during World War II.

The White Rock Overlook, perched on the crest of a mesa, offers a panorama from above the steep-sided Rio Grande Valley. A dizzying 700 feet below, the river runs through a gauntlet of rocky rapids, its furious white water contrasting dramatically with the dark slopes of the valley.

6 Puye Cliff Dwellings

After traveling through open country above the Rio Grande, the drive switches onto State Rte. 502 east, then follows State Rte. 30 north to the turnoff for the Puye Cliff Dwellings, another ancient home of the Anasazis. The narrow road to the ruins leads through red hills cloaked with patches of shrubs and forest. Farther on, the drive encounters a mesa with two rows of caves carved into the cliffs. On the mesa's flat summit, the Indians built a pueblo—a large structure that contained about 740 rooms.

Although Bandelier was even more extensive, Puye's site is more accessible, with roads rambling through the area. The caves can be explored by those willing to climb ladders and inch along narrow ledges. Peering into the openings, visitors glimpse ceilings blackened by long-vanished fires and walls with faded petroglyphs.

7 Scenic Route 84

The drive continues to Española, a hub for the region, then heads northwest on Rte. 84. As your odometer slowly counts the miles, you'll notice the land becoming more and more colorful, especially near the town of Abiquiu. This region was made famous by Georgia O'Keeffe, an artist who used bold hues and forms to capture the essence of the local landscape, an area she penned as "a beautiful, untouched lonely-feeling place—part of what I call the Far Away." One does not need to be an painter, though, to appreciate hills and cliffs decorated with a kaleidoscope of maroons, oranges, golds, and bands of white.

Farther along, pause at Ghost Ranch, once a dude ranch with a name derived from an Indian legend that a canyon hereabouts was home to spirits. Sample the ranch's museums and zoo, then head for Echo Amphitheater. Shaped like a band shell, this natural chamber was carved by wind and water into the sandstone. The drive's final leg, a gradual climb, leads to Rte. 64 and Tierra Amarilla, where green fields meet rolling foothills.

New Mexico's Scenic South

In this land of stunning contrasts, piñon-spotted plains meet alpine peaks, and vast ridges of black lava share azure skies with a sea of dazzling dunes.

Three Rivers Petroglyph National Recreation Site, north of Alamogordo.

When Spanish explorers ventured into this region, they dubbed the twisted lava fields *mal país*, "bad land" and concluded that this territory might best be left alone. And so it was to a large extent, except for the occasional outlaw who took refuge from a pursuing posse of the law in the harsh terrain. Today, in contrast, the very extremes that kept people away in the past have become an invitation to sightseeing adventures.

1 Organ Mountains

As Rte. 70 sweeps eastward out of Las Cruces, the irrigated green fields that ring the city give way to the Organ Mountains, steep, rugged peaks that have been beautifully sculpted by erosion. Near the little town of Organ, the 6½-mile Baylor Canyon Road, unpaved but well-maintained, offers access to Organ Mountains Recreation Area, where several trails crisscross the countryside. Springtime hikers along the Baylor Pass Trail are rewarded with the cheerful white saucers of prickly poppies. But for many the highlight here is the Dripping Springs Natural Area, so named for the cliffside seeps that, during the rainy season, are transformed magically into a gushing waterfall.

Once back on Rte. 70, you will climb to the overlook at San Augustin Pass, cresting at 5,719 feet. The bird's-eye view takes in the Organ and San Andres mountains, their ridges rumpling on for miles; the stark Tularosa Basin, a desert lowland punctuated by mesquite and creosote bushes; and on clear days, billowing white dunes of sand shimmering in the northeast.

As strange as it might seem, herds of African antelopes can be spotted farther ahead on Rte. 70. The oryx, with long, straight horns and a black-and-white face, was introduced to the Tularosa Basin.

2 White Sands National Monument

Like colossal waves, the dunes of White Sands National Monument roll across the northern horizon. The preserve, covering an astounding 230 square miles, contains in essence one of the world's largest, most beautiful sandboxes. Composed mostly of gypsum—a mineral deposited in an ancient sea —the area, as its name implies, is also remarkable for its color, a brilliant, sparkling shade of white.

Many dunes are not only shaped like waves but also move like them. Pushed by the prevailing winds, sand grains slowly climb one side of the dune, crest, and then slide down the opposite face. Sunrise and sunset, the most colorful hours for viewing this sandy sea, paint the dunes in pastel pinks, oranges, and yellows. Meanwhile, the desert silence is broken only by the low whistle of the wind.

Locked in a struggle to eke out a living, the animals that inhabit this region must constantly cope with extreme conditions—blistering heat, chilly nights, scant moisture, and strong winds that sometimes stir up sandstorms. Yet they manage to survive. For most, including mammals such as coyotes and kit foxes, the trick is to stay out of the noontime sun, so they remain in burrows during the day, then go on the prowl by night.

Humans, fortunately, can simply admire the terrain, then head back to air-conditioned comfort. The Dunes Drive, an eight-mile road into the national monument, makes the trip convenient as well as scenic. It begins at the visitor center, and at any one of the several pullouts along the route, visitors can park and explore the dunes—some up to six stories in height. You might even spot sand surfers slashing down the steeper slopes.

3 Cloudcroft

The next leg of the drive makes a steep, serpentine ascent on Rte. 82. The gain in elevation from the desert floor to the Sacramento Mountains brings cooler temperatures and an increase in vegetation. The roadsides, green now, are edged with pine trees and apple orchards. Stop along the way at Tunnel Vista, an overlook that provides simultaneous viewing of both the forested mountains and the desert basin.

Cloudcroft, perched at 8,700 feet, began as a logging town and retains much of its turn-of-the-century flavor. Today it's also known as the home of the southernmost ski resort in the country. To sample the cool stands of Douglas-fir and spruce trees in the surrounding Lincoln National Forest, choose from among many roads and trails.

If you have the time, you'll certainly enjoy the 15-mile Sunspot Scenic Byway. The two-lane road

White Sands National Monument is part of the world's largest gypsum dune fields.

real claim to fame, however, began when a bear cub was discovered clinging to a tree in the wake of a devastating forest fire in 1950. Rescued and cared for, the little foundling went on to achieve lasting fame as the country's symbol for fire prevention: Smokey Bear. At the historical state park, visitors can learn all about the popular bear and follow a short path through land-

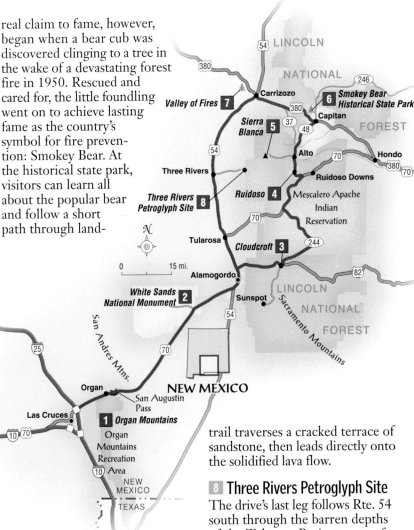

passes evergreens and meadows bedecked with raspberries and wildflowers on its way to Sunspot. At drive's end is a solar observatory, where visitors can stop by for a firsthand look at sunspots and solar flares.

4 Ruidoso

Thick, cool woodlands crowd in around State Rte. 244 as it snakes through the mountains to join Rte. 70. Still farther, the drive veers west on State Rte. 48 to Ruidoso—a Spanish word meaning "noisy." It's

a mountain resort town, a bit larger and brassier than Cloudcroft, named not for its hubbub but for its gurgling stream.

5 Sierra Blanca

The White Mountain—Sierra Blanca—has been in sight over much of the drive, its bold 12,003-foot summit visible wherever the view is unobstructed. In summer its slopes are speckled with asters, sunflowers, and other wildlings. Come winter, downhill skiers flock to Ski Apache, a resort run by the Mescalero Apache Indians. To reach the ski area, follow State Rte. 532, a narrow, twisting road. Stop off en route at the Windy Point Vista Lookout, where on clear days the views take in mountains up to 100 miles away.

6 Smokey Bear Historical State Park

Back on State Rte. 48 the drive maneuvers down mountain slopes lush with a nearly continuous forest of pines and firs. At lower elevations piñon and juniper trees decorate the foothills, which in turn give way to the basin floor and Capitan, a hub for the area's ranchers since 1900. Capitan's

scaped grounds that lead to the site of Smokey's grave.

7 Valley of Fires

Underscoring yet again the region's dramatic diversity, the drive dips out of the cool forest via Rte. 380 and leads to the Valley of Fires. Scorched by red-hot rivers of lava some 1,500 years ago, the land today lies buried beneath black volcanic rock, a jagged realm of ridges and caves. Though mostly barren, this recreation area has been colonized here and there by tenacious, drought-resistant desert plants. A three-quarter-mile loop

trail traverses a cracked terrace of sandstone, then leads directly onto the solidified lava flow.

8 Three Rivers Petroglyph Site

The drive's last leg follows Rte. 54 south through the barren depths of the Tularosa Basin to one of the country's largest collections of ancient rock etchings, or petroglyphs. Carved centuries ago by the Jornada Mogollon Indians, this remarkable desert display includes depictions of symbolic figures, sunbursts, masks, rattlesnakes, and much more. Standing amid this gallery of primitive art, you are also treated to a grand panorama. Sierra Blanca crests in the east; the San Andres Mountains run along the western horizon; and in the south, hills of white sand shine brightly, beckoning you back toward the beginning of your journey leading through the Land of Enchantment.

Trip Tips

Length: About 210 miles, plus side trips.

When to go: Year-round.

Nearby attractions: Mescalero Cultural Center, Mescalero. International Space Hall of Fame, Alamogordo.

Words to the wise: Government tests at White Sands Missile Range can cause brief closures on Rte. 70 between Las Cruces and Alamogordo.

Further information: New Mexico Tourism Department, 491 Old Santa Fe Trail, Santa Fe, NM 87503; tel. 800-545-2040, www.newmexico.org.

PART 3

The Central States

North Dakota Sampler

A natural highway linking East with West, the Missouri River guided explorers and pioneers across the American frontier. Today pastoral roads parallel its historic path from rolling prairie to rugged badlands.

Banded buttes of the Badlands in western North Dakota glisten in the late summer sun.

Theodore Roosevelt often said that if it hadn't been for his experiences in North Dakota, he would never have become president. He was not exaggerating. Overwhelmed by the loss of his wife and mother (both of whom died on the same day—Valentine's Day), the feisty young man returned here in 1884 to renew his strength. His spirit was fired by the Badlands, where he triumphed over his grief by living the arduous life of a ranchman. The untamed grandeur he so admired— the "vast silent spaces" that later inspired him as president to expand our national parks system—still endures. From meandering rivers to craggy canyons, from the meadowlark's song to the distant rumble of bison on the move as they graze endless grasslands, North Dakota's riches remain gloriously unspoiled.

1 Fort Abraham Lincoln State Park

Military and American Indian history are culturally entwined at Fort Abraham Lincoln State park, located seven miles south of Mandan on State Rte. 1806. Once home to Lt. Col. George Armstrong Custer and the 7th Cavalry, it earlier was home to the Mandan Indian people living at On-A-Slant Village. Today, American Indian and military history can be seen in the reconstructed home of Libbie and George Custer, the military barracks, the commissary, the stables, the medicine lodge, several earthlodges, and a museum. Take a trolley ride from Mandan through the cottonwood trees along the Heart River to the fort and back. In July, the park features living-history demonstrations at the American Legacy Exposition; the 7th Cavalry encampment features displays of military skills and drills, and you'll follow delicious smells to the Nu'eta Corn and Buffalo Festival at On-A-Slant Village. In August, the Fur Traders' Rendezvous provides reenactments, music, and demonstrations throughout the state park.

2 Missouri River Valley

The "Skyscraper on the Prairie" is the name given to North Dakota's 19-story state capital building. Walking paths on the capital grounds lead past figurative and abstract metal sculptures, statues, flowering plants, and native trees. While traveling on State Rte. 1804 along the Missouri River, enjoy the serene beauty of cottonwood forests and the rolling high plains.

The Big Muddy, as the river is sometimes called, has been tamed by dams. But this free-flowing segment has changed little since explorers Meriwether Lewis and William Clark passed this way in 1804 on their way to the Pacific. Visit Double Ditch State Historic Site and view the landscape seen by expedition members, virtually unchanged today, as you camp, kayak, canoe, fish, and ski along the Missouri River and view soaring bald eagles and white-tailed deer. State Rte. 1804 joins Rte. 83 just a few miles outside the city of Washburn.

3 Cross Ranch State Park

The undeveloped stretches of the Missouri River and North Dakota's Cross Ranch State Park has an extensive trail system to explore on foot in summer or on cross-country skis during the winter. The ranch offers 5,000 acres dedicated to the nature preserve with river-bottom and cottonwood forests, mixed-prairie grasslands, and woody draws. Visitors often see the buffalo herd roaming the park's neighboring nature preserve. The park preserves the natural beauty of the land and creates a wildlife habitat for birding. Annual events include the High Plains Rendezvous and the Missouri River Bluegrass and Old-Time Music Festival.

4 Knife River Indian Villages

Continue on Rte. 83 to Washburn, site of the Lewis and Clark Interpretive Center. Focused on the

Children reenact Fort Mandan's past.

complete expedition, it is filled with rare artifacts and interactive displays. It also houses the rare, complete collection of Karl Bodmer's historic artwork, which dates from the 1830s. Authentically reconstructed Fort Mandan, just west of the interpretive center, brings history to life with

demonstrations and reenactments during Lewis and Clark Days in June and the Heritage Outbound Summer Adventure in August.

From Washburn, follow Rte. 200 to the Knife River Indian Villages, a National Park Historical Site located just north of Stanton. This historically important settlement was established by the ancestors of the modern Hidatsa people. The women of this tribe once gardened in the rich soil, growing squash, pumpkins, beans, sunflowers, and a variety of corn. They traded abundant crops to nomadic tribes and fur traders, gaining staples, foodstuffs, and buffalo hides.

By the early 1800s, the village was a burgeoning marketplace. Here Lewis and Clark met and hired a French fur trader and his wife, Toussaint Charbonneau and Sakakawea, as interpreters for their Corps of Discovery. They wintered together at Fort Mandan in 1804–1805.

Today the village site offers a free tour of the museum, exhibits, and artifacts, including circular depressions in the ground that once were homes of the Hidatsa Indians. Visit in July to watch the Northern Plains Indian Culture Fest.

5 Sakakawea State Park

When Lewis and Clark added Charbonneau to their expedition, they could never have dreamed that Sakakawea would become a heroine of the American West. During the winter of 1805, while wintering at Fort Mandan, she gave birth to a son, Jean Baptiste Charbonneau. Carrying her baby, she provided translation and guided the party on its arduous journey across the Rockies.

Sakakawea's legacy lives on in the name of an expansive reservoir on the Missouri River, as well as a beautiful state park along the shoreline near Garrison Dam. The park's main entrance offers visitors a new welcome center with information for the area and entire state. Enjoy its swimming beaches, campsites, and boat ramps; throughout summer the park hosts numerous regattas, with sailboats, catamarans, and sailboards skimming the blue waters of Lake Sakakawea like birds in slow, stately flight.

6 Garrison Dam

It would take 2 million freight cars to carry the material used to build the immense Garrison Dam, which holds back the waters of the mighty Missouri for nearly 200 miles upstream. At 382,000 acres, Lake Sakakawea is one of the largest man-made reservoirs in America. After crossing the two-mile-long dam, the drive rejoins Rte. 83 near the town of Coleharbor.

7 Audubon National Wildlife Refuge

Few sounds in the natural world are as evocative as the mellow, throaty honking of a flock of Canada geese—a true call of the wild that floats down from the skies as the big

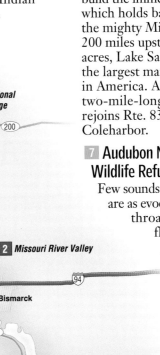

birds pass overhead. Geese gather at this lakeside refuge in the fall, along with thousands of other waterfowl, feeding in preparation for their flight south. Other winged wildlife that may be spotted along the refuge's eight-mile auto-tour route include peregrine falcons, whooping cranes, piping plovers, and bald eagles—all rarities eagerly sought by birders.

Not so rare, but perhaps more fun to watch, is the sharp-tailed grouse, a chickenlike bird that spends most of the year hidden amid tall grasses. In early spring males assemble at traditional mating grounds called leks, where they spread their tail feathers, inflate purple air sacs at the sides of their necks, and rapidly stamp their feet. Females watch this spectacle from

nearby, choosing the best entertainers as mates. The birds' movements inspired traditional Indian dances still performed at powwows across the West. Although the natural grassland has disappeared from much of the country, the Audubon refuge is one place where sharp-tails still gather for a ritual as old as the prairie.

8 Fort Stevenson State Park

If you have any doubts that fishing is the major draw at Lake Sakakawea, drop by the city park in Garrison, off Rte. 37. There, Wally Walleye, a 26-foot fish statue, underscores the town's claim as the walleye capital of North Dakota. Fort Stevenson State Park, on Garrison Bay just south of town, is a popular launch

point for anglers heading out for salmon, smallmouth bass, northern pike, and of course, walleye.

9 New Town

West of Garrison, State Rte. 1804 traverses farm and ranch country. Soon you are entering the million-acre Fort Berthold Indian Reservation, home to Three Affiliated Tribes (the Mandans, Hidatsas, and Arikaras). New Town, the major city on the reservation, was a planned community built in the 1950s to replace villages flooded by Lake Sakakawea. Today it boasts a joint-tribal museum, a casino, and the intricately girdered Four Bears Bridge, just west of town on Rte. 23. Spanning Lake Sakakawea, this mile-long structure is best appreciated from the Crow Flies

High Butte observation point on the western edge of town. Heading north and then west on State Rte. 1804, the drive crosses the Little Knife River.

10 Lewis and Clark State Park

As the drive heads toward the park, rocky buttes in the distance foreshadow the shift from rolling plains to rugged Badlands. Located on an upper bay of Lake Sakakawea, this site contains one of the largest tracts of native prairie in the state park system. In late spring, when the quiet landscape suddenly explodes with festive wildflowers, this is a fine place to enjoy prairie clovers, purple coneflowers, and other blooms that form part of nature's multihued palette. After a stroll along one of the park's nature trails, you'll no doubt agree with Meriwether Lewis (a better explorer than speller) that these plains, so often thought barren, are "verry handsom" indeed. The expedition camped nearby on April 17, 1805.

11 Fort Union Trading Post

The world of fashion may seem to have little in common with the Great Plains, but this settlement was founded in 1828 by John Jacob Astor's American Fur Company. Beaver pelts—bought from trappers or taken in trade from Indians —found their way into hats worn by smart dressers around the globe.

Visiting Indians camped on the grassy plain 25 miles southwest of Williston, near Fort Union Trading Post. The partially reconstructed post, a national historic site, features a replica of the 1851 residence of the "bourgeois," or postmaster. It has a two-story front porch, a broad facade, and a lookout tower on the roof—all designed to convey the power behind what one 19th-century missionary called the "vastest and finest" fort

Broadway-style musicals are held nightly in the modern Burning Hills Amphitheater, cut into the Badlands near Medora.

::::: Trip Tips :::::

Length: About 400 miles plus side trips.

When to go: Mid-May through mid-September.

Words to the wise: Keep a safe distance from bison, which can run as fast as 35 m.p.h.

Not to be missed: Medora Musical, a Western-style revue (early June to early September), Medora. Jaycee Rodeo Days (early July), Mandan. Dam Regatta (late August), Garrison. United Tribes Powwow (early September), Bismarck.

Nearby attraction: North Dakota State Fair (late July), Minot.

Further information: North Dakota Dept. of Commerce, P.O. Box 2057, Bismarck, ND 58502; tel. 800-435-5663, www. ndtourism. com.

on the Missouri. Fort Buford was one of several military posts that protected overland and river routes used by immigrants settling the West, but it is probably best remembered as the place where the famous Hunkpapa Sioux leader, Sitting Bull, surrendered in 1881.

Located a half-mile east of the fort, the Missouri-Yellowstone Confluence Interpretive Center tells the story of these two mighty rivers and provides the same magnificent view that Lewis and Clark's team enjoyed in 1805–1806.

Backtracking on Rte. 1804, head south on Rte. 85 until you reach the entrance to Theodore Roosevelt National Park's North Unit.

12 Theodore Roosevelt National Park (North Unit)

Mention the word badlands and the image that springs to mind is one of a desolate, dangerous place. One can easily understand why General Alfred Sully, who caught his first glimpse of this region of North Dakota in 1864, said that it looked like "hell with the fires out."

Over centuries, the Little Missouri River, its tributaries, and the relentless forces of wind and rain have carved deep, rugged canyons through western North Dakota's plains. Dramatic pyramid-shaped buttes and steep bluffs with bands of red, orange, pink, yellow, gray, and black can be seen along a 14-mile scenic drive that winds from the North Unit's visitor center to Oxbow Overlook.

Like its counterpart Unit to the south, the area is rich with all sorts of wildlife. Longhorn cattle can be seen drinking water at the bison corral. Golden eagles soar overhead, hunting unwary prairie dogs. Here and there, mule deer (named for their large ears) pause as they graze to watch cars pass by. But for most visitors the tour's highlight comes when bison, the park's proudest residents, are seen. Up to 60 million of these massive mammals, standing six feet tall and weighing more than a ton, once roamed the Great Plains. Today these icons of the Old West are scarce; only 100 are found in the park's North Unit, with about 300 in the South Unit.

13 Little Missouri National Grassland

As Rte. 85 makes its way south, it skirts the eastern border of the Little Missouri National Grassland, one of the largest and most varied of the 20 grasslands found in the West. The region—embracing more than a million acres of open prairie, buttes, and badlands—was overgrazed and abandoned in the drought-stricken Dust Bowl 1930s, but it was later reclaimed for cattle ranching and recreation.

A number of scoria—red—knobs may be seen throughout the area. They are composed of sediment that was baked red by burning lignite coal. You'll also note a

The Lewis and Clark riverboat plies the Missouri between Bismarck and Mandan.

number of petrified wood stumps. These are millions of years old, all that remains of North Dakota's once-extensive forests of sequoias.

For the best views of the grasslands, follow the Maah Daah Hey Trail, a 96-mile-long horseback riding, hiking, and mountain biking route through the Badlands that joins the North and South Units of Theodore Roosevelt National Park.

14 Theodore Roosevelt National Park (South Unit)

The savage artistry of the Badlands is well displayed at the Painted Canyon Overlook, just north of I-94, where wind and water have shaped rolling hills, undulating plains, and colorful cliffs. When Theodore Roosevelt came here in 1883 on a hunting trip, he was so captivated with the region that he became a principal partner in the Maltese Cross Ranch. Visitors can tour his restored cabin near the Medora visitor center at the park's entrance.

Motorists on the South Unit's 36-mile-loop drive will see many romantic reminders of a bygone era, including wild horses racing across the plains. Here, one can choose between the splendid isolation of a land little changed since cowboys rode herd or the Old West festivals and other attractions in nearby Medora. For all its scenic wonders, the park's greatest gift to visitors may be its sense of endless free space.

Badlands and Black Hills

The unique and varied landscapes that make up this corner of South Dakota—
resonant with history and lore—were fashioned both by the elements and by human hands.

Peter Norbeck Scenic Byway

Named for the South Dakota politician and conservationist who championed it, this carefully engineered double-loop drive through the Black Hills was designed in the 1920s to enhance—not disrupt—the rugged natural scenery. The byway includes Needles Highway, threading its way through tunnels and between towering spires, and Iron Mountain Road, where "pigtail" bridges (supported by rustic timber trestles) spiral upward and the exits to tunnels perfectly frame the four faces on Mt. Rushmore.

Scenic overlooks on Badlands Loop Road provide striking views of eroded pinnacles and buttes in Badlands National Park.

They've been called "the vest pocket Rockies" and "the West's most intimate mountain range." But it was the Lakota who deemed them sacred and named them *Paha Sapa,* or "Hills of Black," because of the dense,

dusky pine forests that cloak their stony crags and canyons. Indeed, despite their modest size, the Black Hills have always loomed large in the American mind. Rising from the austere beauty of the Badlands and

the South Dakota plains, this land embraces a remarkably diverse wonderland of domes, needlelike spires, rolling prairie, endless caverns, old-fashioned mining towns, and monumental works of art.

1 Prairie Homestead

The settlers who laid claim to the Dakota Territory were a hardy and resourceful bunch. With few trees to supply lumber, they built houses from the only material at hand—the earth itself. Most of these structures have long since washed away, returned to the very ground from which they came. A rare exception is the sod-and-log home of Edgar and Alice Brown, who homesteaded 160 acres near the Badlands in 1909. Built of rough-hewn logs and bricks of buffalo-grass sod, the house is partly dug into an embankment to shield it from the biting prairie winds. Crude pioneer furnishings, many of which belonged to the Browns, decorate the dim interior, lending it a hardscrabble homeyness. To reach the site, exit I-90 at Cactus Flat and head south two miles on Rte. 240, which also leads to the northeast entrance to Badlands National Park.

2 Badlands National Park

French fur traders who explored the West in the early 1800s called them *mauvaises terres*—that is, "bad lands"—and the name stuck. First glimpsed near the park's northeast entrance, the Badlands are truly awe-inspiring—a moonscape of tormented ridges, crumbly spires, and precipitous canyons stretching as far as the eye can see. Touring the West in 1935, the renowned American architect Frank Lloyd Wright exclaimed, "I've been about the world a lot and pretty much over our own country, but I was totally unprepared for the Dakota Bad Lands … an endless supernatural world more spiritual than earth but created out of it."

The tortured appearance of the Badlands suggests some great natural calamity. But in fact, the bizarre terrain was formed inch by inch over millions of years as wind and rain sliced into volcanic ash and the soft sediments left behind by an ancient marshland. During the Oligocene epoch (between 37 and 23 million years ago), early mammals roamed these plains in vast numbers, and today their fossilized remains peep from the walls and sandy ridges with the starkness of cave paintings. It is largely due to finds in the Badlands' rich fossil beds that scientists have deemed the Oligocene the golden age of mammals.

All of Badlands National Park's 244,000 acres are open to hiking, but the topography is treacherous and, lacking easy reference points, can be disorienting. Novice hikers

and anyone without a topographic map should stick to marked trails. Many are clustered in and around the Ben Reifel visitor center, a wise first stop to orient yourself to the terrain and discover its geology, history, and wildlife. Door Trail, a quarter-mile, open-access round-trip, shows off the Badlands. Beginning at the northern end of the Doors and Windows parking area, the trail passes through a hole in the rim wall and ascends to a startling panorama of intricately eroded canyons and castlelike buttes. The quarter-mile, wheelchair-accessible Fossil Exhibit Trail, five miles west of the visitor center on Rte. 240, the Scenic Loop Road, showcases fossils under transparent domes—a

reminder of the mighty and minor beasts that lived here eons ago.

Despite scorching summer temperatures and icy winter winds, life goes on in the Badlands. Nearly 50 different grasses and 200 types of wildflowers thrive here, the latter adding brilliant dashes of color to the gullies that drain the surrounding plains. Bison, mule deer, and pronghorns make occasional appearances, and sure-footed bighorn sheep clamber up and down the crumbly buttes and sawtooth ridges. Higher still, cliff swallows and white-throated swifts flit to and from their nests among the park's loftiest, least accessible perches, while every so often a golden eagle plunges earthward to seize its prey.

3 Sage Creek Rim Road

A number of overlooks—13 in all—along Rte. 240 provide rich opportunities to view the Badlands wildlife and landscape. About 22 miles beyond the visitor center, the highway veers sharply north, but the drive, trading blacktop for gravel, continues west on Sage Creek Rim Road. Immediately you enter the Sage Creek Wilderness Area, a 64,250-acre subsection of Badlands National Park. Hikers who venture off the highway into the grassy lowlands will find no trails to guide them, save those worn by the tread of bison. Some five miles west of the turn onto Sage Creek Rim Road, look for Roberts Prairie Dog Town, an underground community for the

The tallgrass prairie is a place where the earth meets the sky and the eye beholds the ever-changing spectacle.

endearing rodents housing hundreds of the Badlands' most sociable and industrious inhabitants.

4 Buffalo Gap National Grassland

Where the gravel ends at the town of Scenic, the drive turns onto Rte. 44 and heads northwestward across a sprawling sea of mixed prairie grasses trembling in the ever-present breeze. Early in the 20th century, settlers by the thousands flocked to this part of the plains to become ranchers, only to see their hopes dashed either by drought or by the Great Depression, when homestead after homestead was abandoned.

Today, Buffalo Gap—one of three national grasslands in South Dakota—embraces more than a half-million acres of grassland restored to its original lushness. Though it may be tempting to rush through this wide, wind-blown expanse, slow down to savor one of North America's most striking landscapes. In some places table-flat, in others gently rolling, the prairie—occasionally punctuated by patchy incursions from the Badlands—seems boundless, as vast as the sky above.

5 Rapid City

Today it's the state's second-largest population center, but Rapid City nearly disappeared before it had even begun. The city planners who founded the town in 1876 as a supply depot for the Hills' prosperous goldfields were dismayed to discover that the lure of mineral riches a few miles farther on was so great that no one wanted to stop here. Luckily, residents soon persuaded the railroad to build a line through town, and nearly overnight Rapid City's future was assured.

For a bird's-eye view of the town and a glimpse of the Black Hills beyond, take a quick jaunt up Skyline Drive, cresting the hill that bisects the town. (Be prepared to share the view with Rapid City's strangest residents: seven concrete dinosaurs, remnants of the Depression-era Works Progress Administration, stand atop the ridge, as if surveying their lost domain.)

Buildings in the old commercial district have been restored, and many street corners feature life-sized bronze statues of U.S. presidents. West Boulevard Historic District includes stately Queen Anne– and Colonial-style homes. North of Historic Downtown, on New York Street between Fifth Street and E. North Street, visit the Journey Museum—filled with exhibits that tell the story of the western Great Plains.

6 Black Hills National Forest

On Rte. 79, jog south to the town of Hermosa and then west on Rte. 40. The drive rises gently through foothills, then begins a sharper climb into the pines that make up Black Hills National Forest. If you sense the presence

Mt. Rushmore National Memorial immortalizes four U.S. presidents.

of something timeless, it's no wonder. Though not the most imposing mountains in America, the Black Hills are ancient, thrust upward from the plains some 60 million years ago, just as the dinosaurs exited the stage.

7 Mt. Rushmore National Memorial

Like a magnificent mirage, the four presidential faces that gaze out from Mt. Rushmore—Washington, Jefferson, Teddy Roosevelt, and Lincoln—first peek through the trees just south of Keystone. It isn't until you reach the site itself and stand on the viewing terrace 1,400 feet away that the full dimensions of this man-made marvel hit home. Each face, carved with consummate craftsmanship, measures a full 60 feet from brow to chin. The eyes alone are masterpieces: granite columns inside each pupil catch the light in such a way that they seem to twinkle. Whether bathed in the amber glow of the morning sun or lit by spotlights at night, the faces of Mt. Rushmore seem almost alive.

Credit for this triumph of artistry and engineering belongs to Gutzon Borglum, an Idaho-born sculptor. Two South Dakotans, Doane Robinson and Peter Norbeck, shared his vision and gained permission from the federal government, authorization from the state legislature, and the donations of citizens to match federal funds for the million-dollar project. Beginning in 1927, Borglum and his crew of unemployed miners—who became accomplished during the succeeding years—blasted, drilled, and hammered away, removing 800 million tons of rock from the granite mountainside.

Tragically, Borglum himself did not live to see his vision fully realized. His plan was to carve each of the four presidents to the waist, but in March 1941, after 14 years of labor, the sculptor died suddenly. Borglum's son, who had worked beside his father, took over and declared the project completed later that year. Even so, Mt. Rushmore remains one of America's most durable icons and one of the greatest pieces of public artwork the world has ever known. Borglum chose his medium well; the granite of the sculpture erodes, on average, less than an inch every 10,000 years, and his creation will stand for ages to come.

8 Custer State Park

From Rushmore, the drive pushes south toward Custer State Park on Iron Mountain Road, part of the Peter Norbeck Scenic Byway. Challenged to make this section of road one of the most visually pleasing in the state, engineers pulled out all the stops: the highway vaults from ridge to ridge on spiraling bridges, and the openings to three strategically placed tunnels frame views of Mt. Rushmore. As you ascend to Norbeck Overlook, the highest point along the route, look to the west at

::::: Trip Tips :::::

Length: About 360 miles.

When to go: Popular year-round.

Words to the wise: Some sections of the Peter Norbeck Scenic Byway are closed in winter.

Nearby attractions: Bear Butte State Park, northeast of Sturgis. Devils Tower National Monument, Wyoming. Wounded Knee, south of Badlands National Park.

Visitor centers: Badlands National Park. Mt. Rushmore National Memorial. Wind Cave National Park. Jewel Cave National Monument.

Further information: South Dakota Office of Tourism, 711 E. Wells Ave., Pierre, SD 57501; tel. 800-732-5682, www.travelsd.com.

Wind Cave National Park near Hot Springs is one of the world's longest limestone caves.

7,242-foot Harney Peak—the greatest of the Black Hills' many domes and, in fact, the loftiest mountain between the Rockies and the Swiss Alps.

From the overlook, the road descends to Lakota Lake and Iron Creek (lined with 300-year-old pines and a lush understory of ferns and berry bushes) and then continues on to Custer State Park's 71,000 acres in the heart of the Black Hills' gold rush country. When Lt. Col. George Armstrong Custer and his men discovered gold nearby in 1874, a party of would-be prospectors pitched camp here, violating a treaty that had kept the Hills in Indian hands. They were escorted out of the Hills by federal officers less than a year later. A replica of their encampment (named the Gordon Stockade, for the party's leader) offers an intriguing glimpse into the lives of the first white settlers in the area.

The park is best known for its wildlife, including bison—at 1,500 head, one of the largest public herds in the nation. To view these imposing creatures (watch them from the safety of your car), drive the 18-mile-long Wildlife Loop Road through the sumptuous grasslands where they graze.

9 Needles Highway

No less intriguing than Iron Mountain Road is Needles Highway (Rte. 87), named for the finger-like spires that line the road. Twisting and turning like a restless rattler, the route threads a course through eerie formations of billion-year-old granite, said to resemble everything from praying hands to pipe organs. To the north, Harney Peak punches the skyline with its robust dome. From idyllic Sylvan Lake, where Rtes. 87 and 89 meet, a challenging three-mile trail leads to the summit and sweeping views of the Black Elk Wilderness Area.

10 Wind Cave National Park

After looping south on Rte. 89 and east on Rte. 16A, the drive breezes down Rte. 87 to Wind Cave National Park. Here a rich assortment of wildlife large and small—prairie dogs, coyotes, elk, bison, pronghorns, mule deer—share more than 28,000 acres of sunlit mixedgrass prairie and shady pine forest.

The main attraction, however, is underground. Wind Cave may have been known to local Indians for centuries, but it wasn't until 1881 that white settlers learned of its existence. Lured by a strange whistling sound, brothers Jesse and Tom Bingham stumbled upon a small hole, the cave's only natural entrance. So forceful was the wind that blew through the opening—caused by the difference in barometric pressures above and below ground—that Jesse's hat blew clean off his head.

Word of the men's discovery spread quickly. In time it became evident that the Bingham brothers had stumbled upon not just one cave but an entire network ringing the hard granite core of the Black Hills—a vast subterranean labyrinth that, scientists believe, remains 95 percent unexplored.

The spirit of the Dakota, Lakota, and Nakota Sioux come alive at a powwow.

A variety of guided tours—one is lighted by the flickering glow of handheld candle lanterns—offer enticing glimpses of the delicate calcite formations (given fanciful names as flowstone, frostwork, boxwork, and popcorn) that adorn the cave's multitude of narrow halls and enormous chambers.

11 Jewel Cave National Monument

After swinging north almost to the town of Custer, the drive spurs west on Rte. 16 across a high mountain valley to the next stop, Jewel Cave. As intriguing as its geological cousin to the south, Jewel Cave is so named for its resplendent calcite crystals, some of which sparkle like precious gems when they are illuminated. Once you return to the light of day, the pine-cloaked hillsides and wildflower meadows of the park's Hell Canyon offer a warm, welcome contrast to the cave's chilly depths—just right for a post-spelunking picnic.

12 Crazy Horse Memorial

A massive sculpture-in-progress, the Crazy Horse Memorial honors the highly esteemed Lakota war-

rior who helped defeat Custer and the U.S. 7th Cavalry at the Battle of the Little Bighorn. The idea for this Herculean undertaking originated in 1939, when Lakota Chief Henry Standing Bear wrote a letter to sculptor Korczak Ziolkowski (then assisting Borglum at Mt. Rushmore) and asked him to design a similar monument to Indian culture. "My fellow chiefs and I," he explained, "would like the white man to know the red man has great heroes, too." Duly persuaded, Ziolkowski set to work —often alone—and continued until his death in 1982. Today his work honoring the great chief is overseen by his wife and seven of his children, using the detailed guidelines he left behind.

Ziolkowski's plans were grand, to say the least. Unlike Mt. Rushmore, which represents the presidents' faces in relief, the Crazy Horse Memorial is slated to be a three-dimensional sculpture-in-the-round that depicts the bare-chested warrior charging out of the mountainside atop his galloping horse. When completed, it will dominate the landscape on an unprecedented scale, standing 56 stories tall and more than two football fields in length. So far, the warrior's face and outstretched arm have emerged, with the upper half of the 22-story horse's head roughly blocked out. A scale model at the visitor's complex shows how the monument will appear when it is finished. In June, an annual volksmarch is held to ascend to the top of the outstretched arm.

13 Hill City

So authentically Western is this old gold-rush town that the cars parked along its Historic Main Street seem truly out of place. More in keeping with the town's character is the Black Hills Central Railroad, offering two-hour excursions to Keystone and back aboard a vintage 1880s steam train. Just a few miles north on Rte. 385, Sheridan Lake Recreation Area makes an ideal camping spot, with good swimming from its sandy shores. There's superb hiking to be found on the Flume Trail, following an old flume bed strewn with artifacts from mining days. Hill City is a trailhead for the 109-mile George S. Mickleson biking and hiking trail with four hardrock tunnels and over 100 converted railroad bridges.

14 Pactola Reservoir Recreation Area

Embraced by a heavy growth of oaks, birches, and ponderosa pines, Pactola Reservoir is a local favorite for water sports, camping, and hiking. The reservoir is a haven for fishing; it is stocked with 200,000 rainbow-trout fingerlings each year. A state-of-the-art visitor center located on Rte. 385 is open daily from Memorial Day until Labor Day.

15 Deadwood

The history of white settlement in the Black Hills offers no shortage of colorful characters, and many can be found right here—six feet under. Laid to rest in the Boot Hill section of Mt. Moriah Cemetery are the mortal remains of any number of hard-living real-life legends, including Calamity Jane and James Butler Hickok, better known as Wild Bill Hickok.

Calamity, who lived by the creed "never go to bed sober, alone, and with one red cent in your pocket," survived to see the 20th century; Hickok was not so lucky. Arriving in Deadwood in the summer of 1876, the one-time lawman and full-time gambler was killed less than one month later, shot in the back of the head while playing poker at a local saloon. As he slumped forward, the mortally wounded Hickok is said to have been clutching black pairs of aces and eights—known to this day as the "dead man's hand."

Visitors to the Deadwood of today will find that the spirit of the town has changed little since gold-rush days. When gambling was legalized in South Dakota in 1989, investors were quick to capitalize on Deadwood's notoriety, and more than 80 gaming establishments now call Deadwood home. The town is no Las Vegas,

though; Deadwood is listed as a National Historic Landmark, and the casinos are housed in lavishly restored period buildings that double as museums. (At the Old Style Saloon No. 10, for example, look for the chair that Bill Hickok was sitting in when he got shot.)

The gold that enriched Deadwood actually came from nearby Lead, where there's no lead at all; the town's name, pronounced "leed," is a miner's term for gold-bearing gravel deposits. You might not know it to look at them, but

below these tilted hills lie the 8,000-foot-deep shafts of the Homestake Gold Mine, which at one time was believed to be the longest continuously operating gold dig in the world. The Black Hills Mining Museum, the Homestake visitor center, and the Adams Museum and House combine to offer visitors a complete course in the

history of gold mining, from the hit-and-miss drudgery of river panning to the use of massive ore-crushers.

16 Spearfish Canyon Scenic Byway

Soaring limestone palisades enclose this cozy canyon byway on Rte. 14A as it runs for some 20 miles along serpentine Spearfish Creek (named for the angling technique used long ago by the Lakota and Cheyenne Indians). Scenic in all

seasons, the canyon is especially so in autumn, when the display of color in its forest rivals any in New England. Two crystal-clear cascades, Roughlock and Bridal Veil falls, punctuate the serene gorge, used as the setting for the final scenes of the film *Dances With Wolves*. At the end of the road is the town of Spearfish, founded in the 1876 gold rush. Tinged as Spearfish is by both history and scenic beauty, it seems an apt spot to bid farewell to the Black Hills.

Mountain goats are agile climbers that often can be seen at Mt. Rushmore.

Northern Minnesota Circle

The tug of a walleye on the line, the spicy scent of countless pines, a crackling campfire on the shore of a secluded lake—life's little pleasures abound in the watery, wooded reaches of northern Minnesota.

Autumn brings flamelike color to the hardwoods of Chippewa National Forest.

Fur traders and lumberjacks were the first to join the Indians who long inhabited this remote realm of sparkling lakes and dense green forests—an enchanted land that has inspired more than its share of legends, folklore, and of course, stories about the fish that got away. As you drive through the region, where wild orchids brighten hidden bogs and the Mississippi is but a gentle woodland stream, it's easy to see why so many tall tales have been born here.

1 Grand Rapids

Situated on the banks of the Mississippi River, the city of Grand Rapids has long served as a gateway to the surrounding forests and lakes. Scandinavian and German immigrants came here in waves during the logging boom of the late 1800s, then headed north to nearby lumber camps. Today, visitors passing through are more likely to be heading for resort cabins and campgrounds. But many also pause to enjoy the attractions of Judy Garland's hometown. Outstanding among them is the Forest History Center, where costumed interpreters re-create the life of a turn-of-the-century lumber camp.

2 Avenue of Pines Scenic Byway

Heading out of Grand Rapids on Rte. 2, the drive soon links up with Rte. 46, the aptly named Avenue of Pines Scenic Byway. Nearly 40 miles in length, the byway slices through the Leech Lake Indian Reservation and Chippewa National Forest, a vast tract of cultivated fields and stands of red pines, aspens, birches, firs, and spruces. Wetlands abound in this outdoor Eden, and hundreds of lakes are scattered among the wooded hills.

3 Lake Winnibigoshish

Local storytellers claim that the northern lakes were formed by the heavy hooves of Paul Bunyan's companion, the hulking blue ox named Babe. Even Babe, though, was not large enough to create Lake Winnibigoshish, or Big Winnie. That called for another kind of giant—one that was white, not blue—a glacier. The ice sheet buried the area 10,000 years ago, gouging out lakebeds and depositing natural dams as it advanced and retreated. Today a man-made dam makes Big Winnie even larger, about 14 miles in length.

Fishing is the pastime of choice here, with a catch that includes walleye, northern pike, bass, and sunfish. Not even the short, frigid days of winter can deter fishermen, who drill holes through the ice to get at their prey and build closet-like shacks to protect themselves from the elements.

Requiring neither rod nor reel, another talented fisher, the bald eagle, can be seen from viewpoints along the shores of Big Winnie. Once nearing extinction, the majestic birds can be found in substantial numbers in this part of Minnesota. Scan the tallest trees to spot their nests—huge structures that can weigh up to two tons.

4 Cut Foot Sioux Visitor Center

As Rte. 46 continues north, it slips through a corridor of red pines, many of them planted in the 1930s by the Civilian Conservation Corps. Here and there, towering above the younger trees, are scattered old-growth monarchs, venerable survivors that are well over 100 years in age and 12 stories in height.

Another longtime survivor, a 1908 log cabin that was used as a ranger station, stands near the Cut Foot Sioux Visitor Center. (The center was named for a brave who lost his life in a skirmish between the Sioux and Chippewas.) The Cut Foot Sioux Scenic Drive, a leisurely 20-mile loop, begins at the visitor center and travels to backcountry lakes, secluded campgrounds, and numerous points for observing wildlife. Hiking trails also lace the area. Segments of the 22-mile Cut Foot Sioux Recreation Trail retrace a route that once was traveled by Indians and fur traders.

5 Laurentian Divide

As the drive delves deeper and deeper into the forest, Rte. 46 crosses the Laurentian Divide, a rise in the land that determines which way running water flows. Rivers and streams north of the divide run into chilly Hudson Bay; those to the south eventually drain into the faraway Gulf of Mexico.

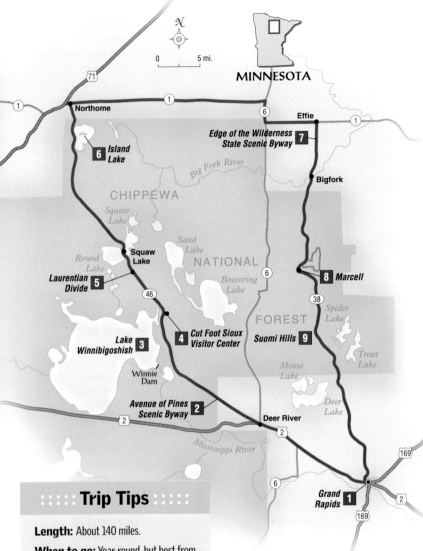

N

0   5 mi.

71

MINNESOTA

Northome

1

6

Effie

1

Edge of the Wilderness State Scenic Byway 7

Island Lake 6

Big Fork River

Bigfork

CHIPPEWA

Squaw Lake

Sand Lake

Round Lake

Squaw Lake

NATIONAL

6

Marcell 8

Laurentian Divide 5

46

Bowstring Lake

38

Spider Lake

FOREST

Lake Winnibigoshish 3

Cut Foot Sioux Visitor Center 4

Suomi Hills 9

Trout Lake

Winnie Dam

Moose Lake

Avenue of Pines Scenic Byway 2

Deer Lake

2

Deer River

Mississippi River

2

169

6

Grand Rapids 1

2

169

:::::: **Trip Tips** ::::::

Length: About 140 miles.

When to go: Year-round, but best from late spring through fall. Winter brings frigid temperatures.

Words to the wise: Bring insect repellent; mosquitoes and other pests thrive in these woods.

Nearby attraction: Itasca State Park, featuring Lake Itasca, the source of the Mississippi River. About 20 miles north of Park Rapids on Rte. 71.

Further information: Grand Rapids Convention & Visitors Bureau, 1 NW 3rd St., Grand Rapids, MN 55744; tel. 800-472-6366, www.grandmn.org.

In past centuries Indians and fur traders paddled across these myriad waterways in handcrafted birchbark canoes. The Ojibwa Indians, a local tribe, still use the streamlined craft when harvesting wild rice, an aquatic grass that grows abundantly in the Squaw Lake area. Slowly paddling and poling among the tall stalks, they gently tap the ripe grains into their canoes—an ancient practice demonstrating that patience and harmony with nature can bring their own rewards.

6 Island Lake

The forest grows thinner and the views open up as you continue to the north, where stands of aspens, birches, and balsam firs ring meadows and wetlands. Rte. 46 then passes along the shore of Island Lake, so named for the large island found rising from its waters. At Northome the drive switches onto Rte. 1, heading eastward through a mostly uninhabited realm of still more woodlands interspersed with low-lying wetlands.

7 Edge of the Wilderness State Scenic Byway

At Effie the drive veers south onto Rte. 38, the Edge of the Wilderness State Scenic Byway, a 47-mile stretch that wends through a hilly, lake-splashed landscape. Reminders of the ice age—in the form of the low gravelly ridges that are known as eskers—are prevalent in this area, especially near Turtle Lake. You'll also revisit the Laurentian Divide, where a roadside kiosk supplies information.

8 Marcell

Circling the wilds east of Marcell, a 17½-mile self-guiding auto tour, known as the Chippewa Adventure, showcases the rich and varied habitats of the Chippewa National Forest. Although quite primitive in places, the route abounds with opportunities for spotting wildlife:

Edge of the Wilderness State Scenic Byway.

an osprey diving for fish, a white-tailed deer bounding through the forest, or even a black bear feasting on wild blueberries.

Back on Rte. 38, the drive enters a stretch that is particularly rewarding in the autumn. Throwing aside all modesty, the hardwoods south of Marcell bedeck themselves with a glorious red-gold display that can make sightseers gasp.

9 Suomi Hills

Continuing south, the drive passes near the Suomi Hills and Trout Lake recreation areas. Miles of hiking and cross-country ski trails lead to out-of-the-way lakes and splendid wildlife-watching locales in these semiprimitive tracts. Off-limits to motorized vehicles, the regions also offer a golden silence broken only by the whispers and calls of birds echoing in the wild northern woods.

North Shore Drive

Lake Superior's chilly waters form a bold blue backdrop
for Minnesota's ever-alluring coastline—a 150-mile ribbon
of tangled woodlands, towering cliffs, and tumbling waterfalls.

Split Rock Lighthouse State Park has a beacon that lives up to its lofty name.

The "shining Big-Sea-Water" of Henry Wadsworth Longfellow's *Song of Hiawatha,* Lake Superior is as magnificent as it is mesmerizing. Its moody blues are forever shifting in color—one moment a sun-shot sapphire, the next a stormy gray as dim as the wilderness that shades its shore. As the coastline curves toward Canada, civilization gives way to nature, and breaking the evening hush is heard the clarion call of the Great North Woods: the piercing cry of the loon.

1 Duluth
Each year hundreds of ships enter this inland port, the final destination of a long journey from the Atlantic Ocean through the St. Lawrence Seaway and beyond. En route the ships pass beneath Duluth's aerial-lift bridge, an extraordinary structure that rises vertically to allow ships to pass by. For visitors, however, the city is not an end but a beginning: the starting point for an equally scenic trip along lovely North Shore Drive.

As Rte. 61 sprints northeast through Duluth, turn west on 60th Avenue East to reach one of the town's prime natural attractions, Hawk Ridge. As many as 33,000 raptors have been sighted on a single October day along these 600-foot bluffs, making this one of the premier hawk-watching spots in North America.

2 Two Harbors
As Duluth's grain towers fade away in the distance, Lake Superior sprawls to the east, its immensity glimpsed from the breakwater in Two Harbors. The world's largest freshwater lake, Superior is so extensive—nearly 32,000 square miles in surface area—that it breeds its own weather. The lake's moderating waters also serve as a

Canoe Country
At Illgen City Rte. 1 winds northwest through Superior National Forest on its way to the Boundary Waters Canoe Area. The 1-million-acre wilderness is laced with rivers, streams, and more than a thousand lakes linked by a unique network of canoe trails. Placid and pristine, these waters are accessible (with a forest service permit) from numerous points around Ely, a small resort and outfitting community that serves as a gateway to the canoe area.

season-stretcher, causing spring to arrive sooner, and fall later, along the shore than inland. Locals boast of their "second spring" and "second fall," which keep lilacs blooming well into June and cause roses to flower against the golden aspens of autumn.

Two Harbors' turn-of-the-century boom days—it was Minnesota's first iron-ore port—are vividly recalled at the Lake County Historical Museum. Also visit the ornate *Edna G,* an 1890s tugboat that retired in 1981. The town's other harbor, Burlington Bay, shelters a pleasure boat landing and a campground.

3 Gooseberry Falls State Park
Countless streams drain into Lake Superior, but none so dramatically as the Gooseberry River, whose Upper and Lower Falls plunge 30 and 60 feet, respectively. The mouth of the river washes over the aptly named Agate Beach, a good place to find samples of Minnesota's state gemstone.

Embracing some 1,700 acres, Gooseberry Falls State Park lures visitors not only with its five splendid cataracts but with 18 miles of trails, all of them threading through a green-and-silver tapestry of birch, aspen, and spruce. In winter some trails are groomed for cross-country skiing.

The park's superbly crafted buildings, steps, and retaining walls were constructed of native granite, quarried and cut by the Depression-era Civilian Conservation Corps. Gooseberry Falls is linked to six other state parks along the North Shore by the Superior Hiking Trail—a narrow 300-mile path that, when completed, will parallel the entire length of Lake Superior's rocky rim, from Duluth to the Canadian border, and will provide hikers with unique perspectives of the beauty to be found in the area.

4 Split Rock Lighthouse State Park

Seven miles farther along, a turnoff leads to one of the North Shore's most famous attractions: Split Rock Lighthouse. After six ships were wrecked within 12 miles of the Split Rock River during a fierce storm in November 1905, the federal government commissioned a lighthouse to be built atop the forbidding 100-foot cliff that overlooked the disaster. Completed in 1910, the octagonal structure is now surrounded by 1,900-acre Split Rock Lighthouse State Park. Its powerful beam, visible from up to 20 miles away, shone steadily until 1969, when electronic navigational equipment rendered it obsolete.

Swooping along the shore like the gulls that bank overhead, the road passes through the towns of Beaver Bay and Silver Bay—where cranes and gantries feed the maws of giant iron-ore freighters—before regaining the rocky heights.

5 Palisade Head

The rusty, weathered cliffs of Palisade Head form a promontory prized by the daring climbers who spider across its sheer faces, and by the kayakers who paddle among the wind- and water-scoured caves below. Some 350 feet high, this scarp marks the beginning of the Lake Superior palisades, a ragged wall that extends some 40 miles eastward. A short road leads to a scenic overlook where the most dramatic views are available early in the morning, when the rays of the rising sun fire the rock and gild the dwarf spruces that cling to its crevices.

6 Tettegouche State Park

From Palisade Head you can look north and spot Shovel Point, the 170-foot-high monolithic remnants of ancient lava flows. Atop the reddish-black rock that forms the eastern boundary of Tettegouche State Park, winter gales and icy spray have razored down the stubborn dwarf spruce to a fuzzy crown. Although the park covers barely a mile of shoreline, its 9,000 acres encompass four lakes, undisturbed groves of northern hardwoods, and the Baptism River, whose 70-foot falls are among the highest in the state.

7 George Crosby–Manitou State Park

The George Crosby–Manitou State Park is located a short distance inland on Rte. 7. This road, built on the grade of an old logging railroad, is a reminder that timber was once the chief industry in the great northern woods. Severe deforestation left the North Shore a battered landscape, but the only remaining evidence today is an occasional three-foot white pine stump, moss-covered and moldering beneath the new growth. The revived ecosystem supports moose, black bears, and timber wolves, which prey on white-tailed deer.

Threading through the heart of the 3,400-acre park is the Man-itou River, a rough braid of turbulent waterfalls and peaceful peat-dark pools full of trout. Its gorge, scraped through the granite bedrock by drainage from an immense glacial lake, is one of the deepest along the North Shore, with sides so sheer that the river can't be seen from the brink. Twenty-three miles of trails explore cedar-scented glades atwitter with waxwings and warblers and offer hilltop panoramas reaching all the way to the Wisconsin shore.

8 Temperance River State Park

Back on the main highway, the drive soon reaches Temperance River State Park. The river, which romps over a rocky basalt bed, owes its name not to prim and proper behavior, but to a pun. Streams foaming down the slopes into Lake Superior carry gravel and sand, which is deposited at their mouths when the water enters the lake and loses velocity. While a small bar can be seen today, it didn't exist in 1864 when the river was named Temperance.

9 Sawbill Trail

Three miles farther up the coast, the town of Tofte is the jumping-off point for both the Sawbill Trail (yet another access route for the Boundary Waters Canoe Area) and a scenic 60-mile round-trip sojourn through 3-million-acre Superior National Forest. Paved in some parts and gravel-surfaced elsewhere, the road bores through walls of northern hardwoods (including oaks, maples, and basswoods), whose fall fireworks brighten the otherwise solid backdrop of evergreens. Moose gravitate to the spruce swamps, where they emerge—dappled with duckweed—from conveniently located beaver ponds. Notoriously shy, they are best spotted at dawn or dusk, which are also good times to watch for beavers, deer, and loons.

The forest primeval is punctuated by Carlton Peak, which rises

Palisade Head warms in the first rays of dawn.

to 1,526 feet and is accessible by the Superior Hiking Trail. A steep scramble to its rocky summit yields 360-degree views of two wildernesses—a watery one that shimmers to the south and east and, to the north and west, a wooded one that marches toward the Sawtooth Mountains.

199

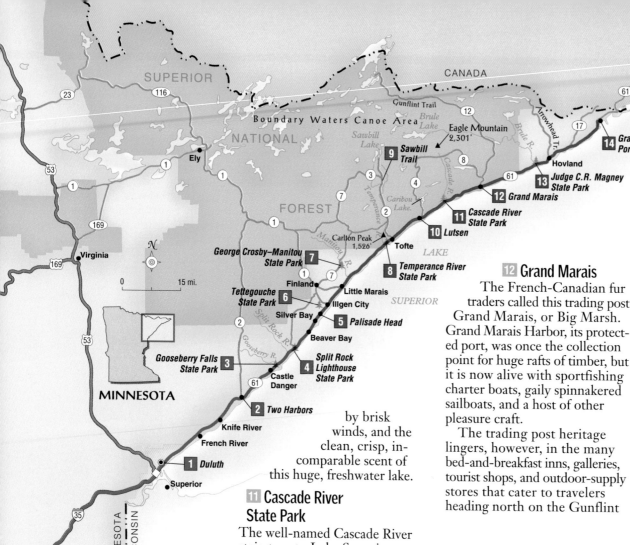

Map Labels:

SUPERIOR

CANADA

23

116

Gunflint Trail

12

Boundary Waters Canoe Area

Brule Lake

NATIONAL

Sawbill Lake

Eagle Mountain 2,301'

17

61

14 Grand Portage

Ely

1

53

1

9 Sawbill Trail

8

Hovland

61

13 Judge C.R. Magney State Park

FOREST

3

4

Temperance R.

Cascade R.

12 Grand Marais

169

7

Caribou Lake

2

11 Cascade River State Park

Virginia

1

10 Lutsen

Carlton Peak 1,526'

Tofte

LAKE

George Crosby–Manitou State Park

7

53

169

Manitou R.

8 Temperance River State Park

N

Tettegouche State Park

6

1

7

Finland

Little Marais

Illgen City

SUPERIOR

0   15 mi.

Silver Bay

5 Palisade Head

2

Split Rock R.

Beaver Bay

Gooseberry R.

Gooseberry Falls State Park

3

4 Split Rock Lighthouse State Park

Castle Danger

61

MINNESOTA

2 Two Harbors

Knife River

French River

1 Duluth

Superior

35

MINNESOTA WISCONSIN

200

---

by brisk winds, and the clean, crisp, incomparable scent of this huge, freshwater lake.

11 Cascade River State Park

The well-named Cascade River stairsteps to Lake Superior through five separate waterfalls, whose constant spray splits sunbeams into rainbows. This moist environment also sustains an abundance of delicate mosses, lichens, and white cedars that shade the slippery rocks. Orange jewelweeds, pale orchids, buttery clintonias, and dainty Canada mayflowers thrive in this dim, dewy realm. Between the crashing currents lie peaceful pools—filled with rootbeer-colored water due to leached tannins—where trout and fishermen both idle patiently. In contrast to the shadow-dappled world found in the depths of Cascade River Gorge, the 500-foot summit of nearby Lookout Mountain is full of sunlight, cheerful flowers, and dazzling vistas.

10 Lutsen

If you're in the mood for still more panoramic views, check out the lakeside resort of Lutsen, where a two-mile gondola Sky Ride takes in scenery that stretches for hundreds of miles—from the Apostle Islands in distant Wisconsin to the rumpled ridges of Minnesota's North Shore. As the drive barrels northeast, stop at one or more of the many overlooks to sample Lake Superior's many moods: the glimmering haze that mists its surface on calm summer days, the shoreless horizon, snapping whitecaps fanned

12 Grand Marais

The French-Canadian fur traders called this trading post Grand Marais, or Big Marsh. Grand Marais Harbor, its protected port, was once the collection point for huge rafts of timber, but it is now alive with sportfishing charter boats, gaily spinnakered sailboats, and a host of other pleasure craft.

The trading post heritage lingers, however, in the many bed-and-breakfast inns, galleries, tourist shops, and outdoor-supply stores that cater to travelers heading north on the Gunflint

Trail (Rte. 12), a two-lane paved road through the Sawtooth Mountains. The 58-mile trail provides yet another portal to the land of lakes—the Boundary Waters Canoe Area—and its Canadian counterpart, Quetico Provincial Park.

13 Judge C. R. Magney State Park

The coast road hopscotches countless streams, including the Brule River, backbone of the 4,514-acre Judge C. R. Magney State Park. Boreal forests of fragrant balsam firs, dotted with ghostly birch and aspen groves, frame blueberry-choked meadows. Long before the Brule's upper and lower falls come into view, the dull thunder of water crashing against stone can be heard. But the best is yet to come. At Devils Kettle the river divides into two channels that flirt with a lip of rock. The eastern fork plunges 70 feet into the gorge below; the western one mysteriously disappears into a pothole just before the brink.

The road continues its curve into the northeastern corner of the state, sometimes referred to as Arrowhead Country for its distinctive triangular shape. North of Hovland the Arrowhead Trail (a two-lane gravel road) branches off to the north, an invitation to explore the Grand Portage State Forest and the many lakes of the Boundary Waters.

14 Grand Portage

The Chippewa Indians had long bypassed the risky rapids of the Pigeon River by an overland route, to which they gave a name meaning "great carrying place." With the expansion of the far-flung fur-trading empire of the North West Company in the

18th century, the nine-mile haul (dubbed Grand Portage by French-speaking voyageurs) became the gateway to the rich fur-trapping grounds of the Canadian wilderness. After the ice broke up each spring, the voyageurs took their valuable pelts to a trading post on the shore of Lake Superior, where they would exchange them for goods and money. Their historic headquarters have been re-created on the spot as a national monument. The Grand Portage itself still exists as a hiking trail, although present-day travelers rarely tote birchbark canoes—it's far more likely that you'll see the ultimate in high-technology fiberglass and carbon-fiber composites used to build today's streamlined kayaks.

For a dramatic view of Lake Superior, board a ferry to Isle Royale National Park, a roadless wilderness 22 miles offshore. At dusk the island's remaining timber wolves sometimes greet visitors with haunting howls.

Gooseberry Falls, in the state park of the same name, has five magnificent cascades of tumbling water tinged root-beer brown by leached minerals from the soil and foliage.

Wisconsin North Woods

Balsam, wild rice, and walleye pike—the forests and lakes of upper Wisconsin offer a natural abundance and wild beauty that travelers find irresistible.

Potato River Falls, a moment of beauty near Hurley.

Trees grow tall in this authentic northern wilderness. But it's the lakes—thousands of them, some big enough for squadrons of water-skiers, some small enough for a pair of loons to nest in solitude—that make the Wisconsin North Woods so appealing. Sports enthusiasts are lured by world-class fishing, canoeing, cross-country skiing, and snowmobiling, while others are drawn by the promise of serene days spent in a simple cabin by a lake.

1 Rhinelander

Whereas 100 years ago the streets of Rhinelander bustled with loggers clad in flannel shirts, nowadays they are filled with legions of visitors who (at least in summer) wear T-shirts and tote fishing poles. Even so, tourism has not wholly supplanted the loggers: the Rhinelander Paper Company, on the Wisconsin River, is a substantial producer of paper. The loggers' legacy also lives on at the Logging Museum in Pioneer Park, where a reproduction of a 19th-century camp features massive old-growth white pines felled by crosscut saws.

2 Northern Highland–American Legion State Forest

Pushing northeast on Rte. 17, the drive approaches the town of Eagle River. Once you enter the city limits, stop off at Carl's Wood Art Museum, which features life-size figures of people and animals (including an enormous grizzly bear) carved with a chain saw. Natural wood oddities, such as tree burls, are also on view at the museum.

Here the drive turns west on Rte. 70, easing through the second-growth pines, red maples, and balsam firs of Northern Highland–American Legion State Forest. The gentle terrain gives no clue that mountains taller than the Rockies stood here countless ages ago—granite peaks that were gradually worn away by the ele-

ments, especially by ice. In fact, every bit of this landscape was crafted by the great glaciers that long ago entombed all of northern Wisconsin. When the ice finally retreated, it left the land dotted with hundreds of depressions large and small that we now know as everything from tiny ponds to the Great Lakes.

At Woodruff the drive turns south on Rte. 51 to Minocqua, the gateway to the region's extraordinary concentration of freshwater lakes. These pristine pools draw family vacationers and fishermen in search of muskellunge (muskie), northern pike, walleye, and panfish. In winter, when the lakes are locked in ice, recreation shifts to cross-country skis and snowmobiles; fishing moves into snug ice shacks, some outfitted with heaters and (yes) even television sets.

3 Lac du Flambeau Indian Reservation

Some 200 years ago, a visitor to Lac du Flambeau might have seen birchbark canoes gliding through the shallows as the Chippewas harvested wild rice, the silence broken only by the occasional honks of geese flying overhead.

The name Lac du Flambeau was used by 16th-century French fur traders and refers to the local Indians' practice of fishing the lake by torchlight. Today the descendants of these Indians display a variety of artifacts at the George W. Brown Jr. Ojibwe Museum and Cultural Center. The exhibits and demonstrations there highlight beadwork, decoy carving, basketry, and moccasin making.

4 Hurley

"Hayward, Hurley, and Hell," midwesterners commented at the turn of the century, shaking their heads at the hamlets where loggers and miners came to drown the memory of months in the deep

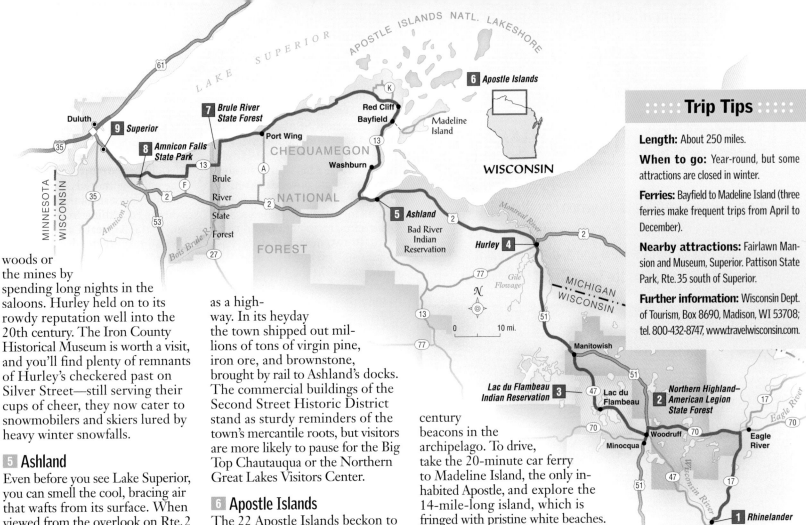

Trip Tips

Length: About 250 miles.

When to go: Year-round, but some attractions are closed in winter.

Ferries: Bayfield to Madeline Island (three ferries make frequent trips from April to December).

Nearby attractions: Fairlawn Mansion and Museum, Superior. Pattison State Park, Rte. 35 south of Superior.

Further information: Wisconsin Dept. of Tourism, Box 8690, Madison, WI 53708; tel. 800-432-8747, www.travelwisconsin.com.

woods or the mines by spending long nights in the saloons. Hurley held on to its rowdy reputation well into the 20th century. The Iron County Historical Museum is worth a visit, and you'll find plenty of remnants of Hurley's checkered past on Silver Street—still serving their cups of cheer, they now cater to snowmobilers and skiers lured by heavy winter snowfalls.

5 Ashland

Even before you see Lake Superior, you can smell the cool, bracing air that wafts from its surface. When viewed from the overlook on Rte. 2 on the way to Ashland, the gigantic lake is blue to the point of blackness: a virtual ocean of the North.

Asaph Whittlesey, who founded Ashland in 1854, saw the lake not so much as a thing of beauty but

as a highway. In its heyday the town shipped out millions of tons of virgin pine, iron ore, and brownstone, brought by rail to Ashland's docks. The commercial buildings of the Second Street Historic District stand as sturdy reminders of the town's mercantile roots, but visitors are more likely to pause for the Big Top Chautauqua or the Northern Great Lakes Visitors Center.

6 Apostle Islands

The 22 Apostle Islands beckon to the northeast. To get closer, turn north on Rte. 13, following the shoreline of the Bayfield peninsula. Here you'll find Bayfield, another once-bustling, now quirky port town. The burghers' white clapboard mansions serve as bed-and-breakfast inns, while the old county courthouse, built of locally quarried brownstone, houses the visitor center for the Apostle Islands National Lakeshore.

On the islands, it's an intoxicating blend of water and wilderness: 50-foot sandstone cliffs line secluded coves, and wildflowers brighten the forests above. The islands appeal to sailboaters and kayakers, serviced by half-day excursion boats departing from Bayfield. From the ferry, you'll see Raspberry Island and its lighthouse, one of six 19th-

The lighthouse at Sand Island.

century beacons in the archipelago. To drive, take the 20-minute car ferry to Madeline Island, the only inhabited Apostle, and explore the 14-mile-long island, which is fringed with pristine white beaches.

7 Brule River State Forest

West of the drowsy lakeside town of Port Wing lies one of the most renowned trout streams east of the Mississippi: the Bois Brule. Five presidents have tested their mettle against its wily brook trout. Whitewater canoers also love the stream; from its headwaters it meanders gently, but north of the highway it plunges down a series of brisk rapids. In autumn the Bois Brule's banks explode with color.

8 Amnicon Falls State Park

Continue west on Rte. 13 and dip south on Rte. U to Amnicon Falls. Faults in the 600-million-year-old sandstone bedrock divide the Amnicon River into three 30-foot cascades. A half-mile trail winds to a long covered bridge that vaults the cataract, leading to an enchanting

island between the falls—a nearly perfect place for a picnic.

9 Superior

Superior (and its sister, Duluth) is a major seaport, thanks to the series of locks and channels that connect it to the Atlantic Ocean more than 2,000 miles away. Watch massive grain and ore freighters entering and leaving the harbor by driving Wisconsin Point Road along a sandspit to the lighthouse at its end —a popular spot for driftwood campfires on summer evenings. From nearby Barkers Island, site of the *S.S. Meteor* Maritime Museum, visitors can cruise the harbor, a finale to this drive beside the greatest of the Great Lakes.

Door County Byways

Quaint waterside villages, towering limestone bluffs, and 250 miles of convoluted coastline give this peninsula such a look of vintage New England charm that it has come to be known as the Cape Cod of the Midwest.

Cave Point's plunging cliffs and pounding surf near Whitefish Dunes.

The Door Peninsula is often likened to a thumb jutting from the mitten we call Wisconsin. But a better description would be a double-edged sword, for the watery margins of this narrow spur of land represent two different faces of nature. The Green Bay coast offers cozy harbors and calm waters, while the Lake Michigan side lures visitors with its wild surf, sandy beaches, and superb fishing. Whichever one of these two worlds you fancy, it is never far away. With 250 miles of shoreline, the most of any county in the country, Door County can guarantee that you'll never be more than 10 minutes from a scenic view.

■ Potawatomi State Park

Traveling north from Green Bay on Rte. 57, a short side trip leads to Potawatomi State Park. Located at the mouth of Sturgeon Bay, this 1,200-acre preserve is named for the Indian tribe that once occupied the land. The park is dominated by dense forests of sugar maples, pines, and birches but also contains a beach sprinkled with granite boulders brought from Canada by glacial ice. On clear days the park's 75-foot-high observation tower affords a majestic view all the way to Michigan's Upper Peninsula, some 16 miles away.

2 Sturgeon Bay

The gateway to Door County and its largest city, Sturgeon Bay is named for the huge numbers of these fish that were once caught in its waters. This former lumbering community now boasts one of the biggest shipyards in the nation, producing vessels as varied as luxury yachts, racing craft, and naval ships. Its two historic districts have more than 100 distinguished old buildings. Visit the Door County Maritime Museum to discover its watery past.

3 Whitefish Dunes State Park

About 12,000 years ago the movement of a glacier left an indentation in the shoreline of what is now Door County, creating the basin of Clark Lake and Whitefish Bay. Over time, lake currents deposited sand in the bay and then moved it shoreward, forming the large sandbar that cut off Clark Lake. The dunes here are among the most imposing in Wisconsin, with the tallest, Old Baldy, rising 93 feet above lake level. At nearby Cave Point County Park, the waters of Lake Michigan create a not-to-be-missed spectacle: whipped by winds, waves pound against cliffs up to 50 feet tall.

4 Baileys Harbor

The oldest village in Door County, Baileys Harbor (founded in 1851) is home to the Ridges Sanctuary, one of the largest wildflower preserves in America. Named for its corduroy-like ridges of sand—the product of centuries of wind and wave action—this sun-dappled sanctuary holds some 1,200 acres of wooded ridges, boglike wetlands, and sandy beaches. Among the highlights of these rare ecological communities are carnivorous pitcher plants, 27 species of native orchids, and a century-old white

Rock Island State Park

Newport State Park **8**

7 Washington Island

Ellison Bay

Ephraim **9**

6 Gills Rock

Peninsula State Park **10**

5 Sister Bay

Fish Creek

Egg Harbor

4 Baileys Harbor

Potawatomi State Park **1**

3 Whitefish Dunes State Park

2 Sturgeon Bay

LAKE MICHIGAN

11 Algoma

Kewaunee

Green Bay

12 Point Beach State Forest

Two Rivers
Manitowoc

0   10 mi.

WISCONSIN

spruce. For a treat, visit nearby Cana Island Lighthouse, a favorite with photographers.

5 Sister Bay

The road from this waterside village north to Ellison Bay passes some of Door County's celebrated cherry and apple orchards, where you can pick your own fruit and buy jelly, jam, and juice at roadside stands. The area is especially beautiful in late May, when the trees are in full bloom. Another memorable sight—Al Johnson's restaurant in Sister Bay—is noted for both its traditional Swedish cuisine and its strikingly unconventional roof, which is sodded in the style of an old European farmhouse. For an unforgettable vista, visit Ellison Bluff Park near Ellison Bay.

6 Gills Rock

Nearly everyone calls this part of Door County the Top-o'-the-Thumb because of its position on the tip of the Wisconsin "mitten." In the waters offshore of the tiny village of Gills Rock, you'll find some of the best fishing in the entire Great Lakes area.

7 Washington Island

So many Indians had fallen victim to the turbulent currents between the tip of the peninsula and Washington Island that the Indians called it "place of death." On hearing this some 300 years ago, French explorers dubbed the strait Porte des Morts (loosely translated as Death's Door), from which Door County derives its name. Visitors can safely traverse these same waters on a brisk ferry ride to Washington Island. Once there, you'll find the oldest Icelandic settlement in America. With more than 100 miles of roadways, the island is ideal for biking. At Jackson Harbor you can take another ferry (no cars allowed) to Rock Island State Park, the site of Potowatomi Lighthouse—the first one built on Lake Michigan.

8 Newport State Park

Back on the mainland, this 2,400-acre park was once the site of a logging village and is now a semi-wilderness containing several forest, wetland, and meadow communities and 11 miles of shoreline. Though nature has certainly reclaimed the land, traces of Newport's early days can still be seen amid the ruins of old loggers' cabins. Adjoining the park is Europe Lake, a spot so serene that it's hard to believe it lies only a few miles from the spirited surf of Lake Michigan.

9 Ephraim

As you approach Ephraim's white steeples and white picket fences, you quickly discern that this is a place of elegant simplicity, a town that reflects the purity and plainness of its Moravian founders. When they arrived at this lovely site in 1853, they called it Ephraim, a Hebrew word meaning "the fruitful land." Their spirit lives on in the Moravian church, which

uing south on Rte. 42, visit Fish Creek, a lively vacation village. From Egg Harbor, take Road G into Road B to enjoy a relaxing tour of Green Bay's coast along quiet country byways.

Cana Island Lighthouse's spire near Baileys Harbor has inspired thousands of photos.

contains a pulpit handcrafted by the first pastor. Nestled along the shore of Eagle Harbor, Ephraim hosts a festive regatta every July.

10 Peninsula State Park

Stop at Peninsula State Park for a glimpse of what the north woods looked like before Door County was settled. Grayish-white cliffs, deep green forests, beige beaches, and the bright blue waters of Green Bay combine to form an ageless portrait of nature's splendor. With three-quarters of its 3,800 acres unspoiled by man, the park is the largest in Wisconsin. Stupendous views can be seen along Shore Road and Skyline Road, and from Eagle Tower and Eagle Bluff Lighthouse. Contin-

11 Algoma

Looping back through Sturgeon Bay and continuing south, the drive passes through Algoma. The town has a scenic walkway along the Ahnapee River that affords views of boats, old fishing shanties, and the Algoma lighthouse.

12 Point Beach State Forest

As its name implies, the 2,800 acres at Point Beach State Forest encompass the best of both worlds: in addition to a sunny lakefront beach, the preserve includes a shady northern pine forest. Bulging out into Lake Michigan, Point Beach features some six miles of sandy shore, as well as nature trails, picnic areas, and outdoor beauty at its best.

Great River Road

Like Tom Sawyer and Huck Finn, the Mississippi and the Great River Road are bosom buddies, ever inseparable as they wander about in Wisconsin, Minnesota, and Iowa.

Beyond the birches and maples, all along the Great River Road, the Mississippi rolls by, as lazy and lovely as ever.

To Mark Twain, who as a young man knew the Mississippi River as well as anyone, its upper reaches were "as reposeful as dreamland." And anyone who travels this portion of the Great River Road (a mere 470 miles of its entire 6,000-mile length) would surely agree with him. For unlike the bustling commerce of the Lower Mississippi, the Upper Mississippi is a place of quiet splendor. Running up one side of the river and down the other, this magnificent roadway—marked by green-on-white signs featuring the image of a steamboat pilot's wheel—is truly a worthy companion to America's greatest waterway.

1 Cassville

Nelson Dewey, Wisconsin's first governor, lobbied to make Cassville the state capital, but it lost to Madison and instead became a major steamboat center during the mid-1800s. At Nelson Dewey State Park, which contains five original buildings from the governor's homestead, visitors can enjoy picnicking, camping, hiking, and lovely views of the Mississippi. Adjacent to the park is Stonefield Historic Site, where life of an earlier era is evoked in a reconstructed town from the 1890s. In midwinter Cassville is a good place to spot bald eagles, which roost there.

2 Wyalusing State Park

Perched atop bluffs 600 feet high, this riverside park affords sensational views of the Mississippi River valley. Sprawling over some 2,700 acres, the park has 20 plus miles of trails, including some that wind among curious rock formations, canyons, and prehis-

Trip Tips

Length: About 470 miles.

When to go: Popular year-round, but best in summer because of river activities, and in fall for spectacular foliage.

Not to be missed: Riverboat excursions from several cities, including LaCrosse, Prairie du Chien, and Dubuque.

Nearby attractions: River Museum, a group of six museums focusing on Mississippi River history and lore, Dubuque, IA. *Field of Dreams* baseball diamond, setting for the popular motion picture, Dyersville, IA. The Mall of America, the country's largest shopping mall, Bloomington, MN.

Further information: Mississippi Valley Partners, P.O. Box 610, Stockholm, WI 54769; tel. 715-442-2900, www.mississippi-river.org.

toric Indian mounds. A few miles south of the park's entrance, the village of Wyalusing adjoins a riverfront beach.

3 Prairie du Chien

One of the oldest European settlements in Wisconsin, this town was a fur-trading post during the late 1700s and early 1800s. Among those who profited from the local trade was Hercules Dousman, whose 1870s mansion, Villa Louis, sits atop a 1,000-year-old Indian burial mound.

Leading north from Prairie du Chien to La Crosse is an especially scenic route—a 60-mile ribbon of roadway shadowed by towering bluffs. Stop at the Old Settlers Overlook (two miles north of Genoa) for a panoramic view of Old Man River.

4 La Crosse

Unlike the northern and eastern parts of Wisconsin, where plateaus and rolling hills were planed down by glaciers that scraped across the terrain, the state's southwestern corner was untouched by those colossal sheets of ice. The result is a region of remarkable beauty— a land of deep valleys and high ridges. In the heart of this territory sits the lively city of La Crosse, often called the Gateway City largely because of its location at the confluence of the Mississippi, Black, and La Crosse rivers. The view from Grandad Bluff, a 500-foot-high summit, takes in parts of three states—Wisconsin, Minnesota, and Iowa.

In summer, La Crosse is sometimes a port-of-call for two floating palaces, the *Delta Queen* and the *Mississippi Queen*. Both paddle wheelers offer overnight trips, but shorter excursions are available on boats departing from numerous towns along the river. An ideal way to spend a lazy afternoon is to take a rambling cruise down the river

and savor the sights: tiny tugboats pushing and towing block-long barges, princely paddle wheelers splashing up memories of a bygone era, and houseboats of every description hugging the shore.

5 Trempealeau

To walk down the streets of this drowsy town is to step back in time—back to the days when riverboats rolled by all afternoon and the best bargain in town was a 25-cent dinner at the Trempealeau Hotel. Just west of town is 1,400-acre Perrot State Park, where bluffs 500 feet tall afford majestic views of both the Mississippi and Mt. Trempealeau. The peak, which is shaped like a squat volcano, was considered sacred ground by local

Indians. Nature lovers will want to visit Trempealeau National Wildlife Refuge, a 6,000-acre preserve, home to white-tailed deer, bald eagles, and many waterfowl.

6 Fountain City

Nestled beneath the green brows of two cliffs, this river town is named for the area's many springs. Terraced gardens, hillside homes, and handsome 19th-century brick buildings combine to give Fountain City its quaint appearance. Nearby Merrick State Park, which covers 325 acres, offers camping, hiking, and swimming and is especially popular with anglers who enjoy fishing for a variety of panfish, including bluegill, crappie, northern pike, and walleye.

7 Alma

As technology brought bigger and bigger barges to the Mississippi, deeper water was needed to accommodate them. So in 1930 the U.S. Army Corps of Engineers began to build an elaborate system of 29 locks and dams to make the waters of the upper river navigable. One of the best places to appreciate this engineering triumph is in the town of Alma. From a downtown observation deck (or from nearby Buena Vista Park), you can view Lock and Dam No. 4 and marvel at one of man's most ingenious attempts to tame the mighty Mississippi River.

8 Pepin

Pepin has two claims to fame— one natural, the other literary. Lake

Viewpoints from vast heights, as seen here in Great River Bluffs State Park, abound on this drive overlooking the river valley.

Pepin, a large natural lake on the Mississippi, is an aquatic-lover's paradise. Nearly 3 miles wide and 20 miles long, it is guarded by tall bluffs and surrounded by rich, rolling farmland. The town is also near the birthplace of Laura Ingalls Wilder, author of the ever-popular series of books that includes *Little House on the Prairie*. Seven miles north of Pepin, you can visit the Little House Wayside, a replica of the log cabin Wilder immortalized in her frontier tales. On the way to Stockholm, the drive reaches one of its highlights: a 20-mile stretch that is considered one of the most scenic spots to be found in the entire Midwest.

9 Stockholm

As its name suggests, this quiet village was founded by Swedish settlers. In the early 1970s a new wave of immigrants arrived—artists from Midwestern cities. Their work is displayed at local shops and galleries and at an annual art fair. But the most memorable sight here is the sweeping view of Lake Pepin from Maiden Rock, two miles north of Stockholm. In legend, it was named for a lovelorn Indian princess who leaped off the cliff to avoid marrying the man her father had chosen for her.

10 Prescott

Just outside of this old river town, turn off of Rte. 35 onto Freedom Park for an overview of the river's "color line"—the spot where the clear, bluish waters of the St. Croix River merge with those of the brown and muddy Mississippi. Mercord Mill Park, downtown, offers a close-up of the junction where the rivers meet. Traveling west on Rte. 10, cross the bridge into Minnesota.

11 Hastings

From early summer through early fall, history takes center stage in Hastings. In May the town hosts Front Porch Days, a festival featuring traditional front-porch pastimes, including a rocking-chair marathon. The third weekend in July brings Rivertown Days, highlighted by a flotilla of brightly illuminated boats. And September heralds Main Street Festival, held in the historic downtown district.

12 Red Wing

Heading south on Rte. 316 and connecting with Rte. 61 South, the drive ventures deep into the heart of Hiawatha Valley, where lush hills and hardwood forests make autumn an eye-popping time of year. The picturesque town of Red Wing, named for a great Dakota Indian chief, was once a major wheat center, but today it is known for its pottery and shoemaking industries. For stunning views of the Mississippi—which makes its sharpest bend just to the north—visit nearby Memorial Park, Barn Bluff, and Sorins Bluff.

13 Frontenac State Park

Campers, hikers, sightseers, and bird-watchers all give raves to this 1,754-acre park. Situated beside the widest expanse of the Mississippi, the park has unparalleled views of the surrounding river valley. Flanked by Minnesota and Wisconsin, the river here is buttressed by so many bluffs that some say it resembles the Rhine. During the late 1800s, Old Frontenac—surrounded by the park—evolved from trading post to trendy resort. Handsome homes became so ubiquitous that the area was dubbed the Newport of the Northwest.

14 Winona

Leaving Frontenac State Park, you will pass Lake City, then Wabasha, then arrive in Winona. Built on a huge sandbar formed by the Mississippi thousands of years ago, the town sits in the shadow of lofty limestone bluffs that afford magnificent views of the river and Lake Winona. In this vicinity Rte. 61 parallels the Upper Mississippi National Wildlife and Fish Refuge, a vast network of wetlands, islands, forest, and prairie that border the Mississippi. Extending for some 260 miles through four states, this 200,000-acre preserve shelters some of the finest and rarest wildlife communities in the Mississippi Valley, including 292 species of birds —huge flocks of tundra swans congregate here in early November— 118 kinds of fish, and many types of aquatic plants. For more information, write or call the refuge: 51 East Fourth St., Winona, MN 55987, or tel. 507-452-4232.

Lake Pepin, a narrow 12-mile-long section of the Mississippi River, is bounded by forests and craggy bluffs.

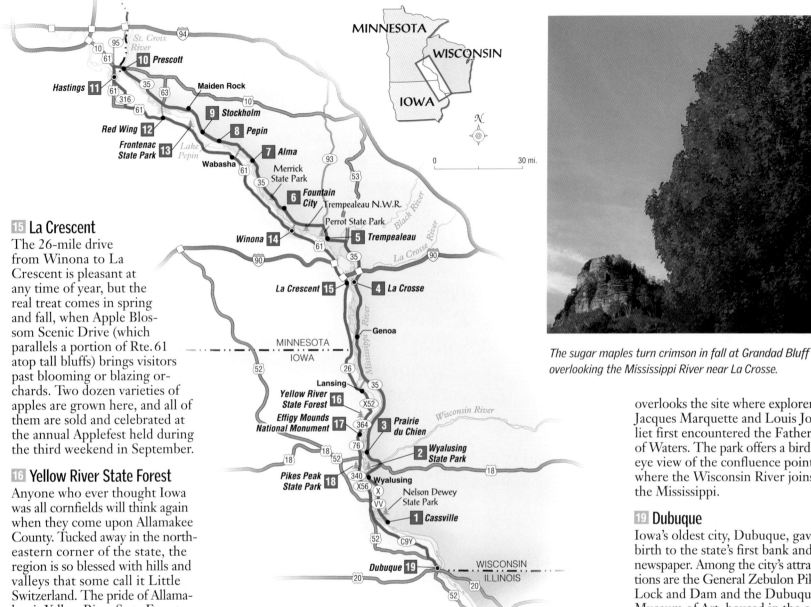

The sugar maples turn crimson in fall at Grandad Bluff overlooking the Mississippi River near La Crosse.

15 La Crescent

The 26-mile drive from Winona to La Crescent is pleasant at any time of year, but the real treat comes in spring and fall, when Apple Blossom Scenic Drive (which parallels a portion of Rte. 61 atop tall bluffs) brings visitors past blooming or blazing orchards. Two dozen varieties of apples are grown here, and all of them are sold and celebrated at the annual Applefest held during the third weekend in September.

16 Yellow River State Forest

Anyone who ever thought Iowa was all cornfields will think again when they come upon Allamakee County. Tucked away in the northeastern corner of the state, the region is so blessed with hills and valleys that some call it Little Switzerland. The pride of Allamakee is Yellow River State Forest—8,500 acres of lush landscape traversed by an enticing series of sparkling trout streams.

17 Effigy Mounds National Monument

To honor their dead, the early Indians in this area marked burial pits by topping them with low, rounded earthen mounds. Nearly 200 such monuments—some shaped like birds and bears—can be seen at this 2,500-acre preserve.

Most of the mounds are reached by a steep path that leads to 11 miles of trails. Take Fire Point Trail to the observation terrace for a memorable view of the Mississippi.

18 Pikes Peak State Park

Most explorers would be proud to have even one place named in their honor, but General Zebulon Pike could claim two: one peak in Colorado that became famous, and a bluff in Iowa that few people have ever heard of—despite the fact that Pike sighted it a year before its legendary counterpart.

During his 1805 expedition to map the Upper Mississippi, Pike chose two locations for forts, one of them atop a summit on the west side of the river. The area is now occupied by a 1,000-acre park that overlooks the site where explorers Jacques Marquette and Louis Jolliet first encountered the Father of Waters. The park offers a bird's-eye view of the confluence point where the Wisconsin River joins the Mississippi.

19 Dubuque

Iowa's oldest city, Dubuque, gave birth to the state's first bank and newspaper. Among the city's attractions are the General Zebulon Pike Lock and Dam and the Dubuque Museum of Art, housed in the old county jail. (The building is one of the few remaining examples of Egyptian Revival architecture in America.) The best views are from the top of the Fenelon Place Elevator—built in 1882 to connect blufftop homes with downtown businesses, it is one of the world's steepest and shortest railways—and from Eagle Point Park, with sweeping vistas that overlook broad areas of Iowa, Wisconsin, and Minnesota.

Upper Peninsula Drive

Ore, timber, and trade all played a part in the long history of Michigan's wild north woods, and today recreation lures travelers to this handsome hinterland, hemmed in by three of the largest lakes in the world.

Miner's Castle is a picturesque stopping point on the Lakeshore–North Country Trail in Pictured Rocks National Lakeshore.

The Chippewa Indians told haunting tales of spirits of the wilderness that roamed this vast northern swath of land and water. As this multifaceted journey unfolds, you may find yourself, if not in the company of spirits, at least entranced by the natural beauty of the Upper Peninsula—as were such notables as Longfellow and Ernest Hemingway, who once traversed the woods of this unspoiled Eden, a setting the former chose for Hiawatha.

1 Menominee

An Algonquian word meaning "wild-rice men" gave this town its name, but it was timber, harvested from virgin forests, that spelled out the destiny not only of Menominee but of the entire Upper Peninsula. Nestled on the west coast of Green Bay, the city mushroomed into one of the largest pine-shipping ports in the world in the last decade of the 19th century.

White pines towering to 150 feet were the glory of these forests. A single tree in those days could furnish enough wood to build a five-room house. Although timber barons savaged the pine woods in just a few decades, they left behind an unforeseen legacy: among the remaining evergreens grew oaks, aspens, and other hardwood trees that blaze with color in autumn.

Pushing north on Rte. 35, which traces the Green Bay shoreline, the drive breezes past J. W. Wells State Park, about halfway between Menominee and Escanaba. Here are many cedars and some of the last virgin hemlocks in the area. You can enjoy their aroma overnight, if you like, from one of the rustic cabins fronting Green Bay. Across the water lies Wisconsin's Door Peninsula, pointing northeast like a great green finger. Its tip, the ominously named Porte des Morts ("Death's Door"), is a treacherous channel whose unusual wave action and turbulent currents have sunk hundreds of ships. The bay is much kinder to anglers; the 300-pound sturgeon that Indians used to catch are long gone, but smallmouth bass, walleye, and brown trout still can fill the average creel.

2 Hiawatha National Forest

Once past the bayside towns of Escanaba and Gladstone, the drive eases into the western unit of Hiawatha National Forest. (The eastern unit lies north of the Mackinac Bridge.) The forest, extending across the peninsula from Lake Superior to Lake Michigan, was named for the Indian leader in Henry Wadsworth Longfellow's poem *The Song of Hiawatha*.

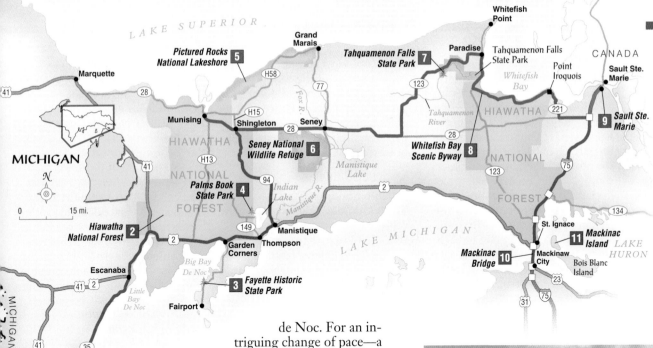

MICHIGAN

Lake Superior

Marquette

Pictured Rocks National Lakeshore **5**

Grand Marais

Tahquamenon Falls State Park **7**

Whitefish Point

Paradise

Tahquamenon Falls State Park

Point Iroquois

Sault Ste. Marie

CANADA

Whitefish Bay

Whitefish Bay Scenic Byway **8**

HIAWATHA

Sault Ste. Marie **9**

Munising

Shingleton

Seney

Fox R.

Tahquamenon River

NATIONAL

Seney National Wildlife Refuge **6**

HIAWATHA

Palms Book State Park **4**

Manistique Lake

FOREST

Indian Lake

Manistique R.

Manistique

Thompson

Garden Corners

NATIONAL

LAKE MICHIGAN

St. Ignace

FOREST

Mackinac Island **11**

LAKE HURON

Mackinac Bridge **10**

Mackinaw City

Bois Blanc Island

Escanaba

Little Bay De Noc

Big Bay De Noc

Fayette Historic State Park **3**

Fairport

J. W. Wells State Park

1 Menominee

Marinette

Green Bay

MICHIGAN

0   15 mi.

Hiawatha National Forest **2**

---

as Kitch-iti-kipi (meaning "Mirror of Heaven"), you can board a wooden raft and, using a guide cord, pull yourself across the 200-foot-wide pond. The raft has observation windows that allow you to look deep into the crystal-clear depths, where oversize trout glide among the limestone-coated trunks and branches of fallen trees. The underground aquifer below maintains the water

Wind-whipped waves come ashore at Lake Superior.

In its verses Lake Superior, the largest of the Great Lakes, is called "Gitche Gumee, the shining Big-Sea-Water." And water—not just the biggest kind—is a recurring theme in this national forest. It is dotted with tiny lakes, gorgeous waterfalls, and canoe trails such as the Au-Train, where paddlers can spy on snapping turtles, muskrats, mink, and an assortment of waterfowl and songbirds. From the trails that weave through Hiawatha's woodlands, hikers may catch a glimpse of such creatures as black bears, white-tailed deer, ruffed grouse, the occasional moose, and wild turkeys.

3 Fayette Historic State Park

Veering east on Rte. 2 at Rapid River, the drive pushes through the southern reaches of Hiawatha National Forest, skirting the tips of Little Bay de Noc and Big Bay

de Noc. For an intriguing change of pace—a look at Michigan's industrial past—head south on Rte. 183 along the shore of the Garden Peninsula to historic Fayette townsite. Here, being restored to its 19th-century ambience, you'll find a fascinating iron-industry community. About a hundred years ago Fayette was a bustling company town where barges delivered ore and ships took away tons of pig iron—the product of Fayette's gigantic smelting furnaces. The furnaces and many of the town's original buildings are still here, including a hotel, several houses, the town hall, and the remains of a company store. Tours of the village begin at the town site's visitor center.

Fayette Historic State Park is a fine spot for a picnic, and some seven miles of hiking trails wind through beech and maple forest, along sandy beaches, and atop 90-foot-high limestone cliffs that overlook Green Bay.

4 Palms Book State Park

Doubling back to Rte. 2, the drive jogs east to the village of Thompson and then turns north to Palms Book State Park. Here, at a 45-foot-deep natural spring known temperature at a constant 45°F, even in the subzero winter.

At nearby Indian Lake State Park, an 8,000-acre body of water was named for the Indians who lived there more than a century ago. Today its pristine beaches attract swimmers and sunbathers, and its whitecapped waters are a lure for anglers.

After rejoining Rte. 2, head east into Manistique and cross the unique Siphon Bridge. Designed to float like the hull of a boat, this remarkable road lies four feet below the surface level of the Manistique River.

5 Pictured Rocks National Lakeshore

From the Manistique area the drive pushes north on Rte. 94, crossing the peninsula and arriving at the little town of Munising, the gateway to Pictured Rocks National Lakeshore. Extending for some 40 miles along the shore of Lake Superior from Munising to Grand

Marais, this arresting wilderness area contains a wealth of multi-hued sandstone cliffs, fortresslike rock formations, windblown forest, bright, sandy beaches, and impressive dunes. Hiking trails abound in this stretch of lakeshore paradise, the most traveled being the Lakeshore–North Country Trail, which hugs the coast for the entire length of the park. Two spots along the trail are as rewarding as they are accessible (you can drive to each via back roads if you prefer to spare your feet). One is Miners Castle, where a lovely stream, forming a waterfall and an idyllic little lake, empties into Lake Superior; the mouth of the stream is flanked by the nine-story-high "castle" to the west and a very inviting sandy beach to the east. Stand on the cliffs to have the best view. The other choice spot is Chapel Basin, a day-hiker's dream that invites leisurely exploration of its streams, ponds, waterfalls, beaches, and high cliffs.

For the most dramatic and revealing views of the red, green, blue, and white Pictured Rocks, get out into the lake. Between June and October, excursion boats depart daily from Munising on three-hour tours of the colorful cliffs.

6 Seney National Wildlife Refuge

From Munising the drive sidles east on Rte. 28 across a flat expanse of forestland before turning south on Rte. 77 to Seney National Wildlife Refuge. No avid angler or bird-watcher should miss this wealth of wilderness—nearly 100,000 acres of wetlands dotted with drainage ditches, dikes, and small bridges. Visitors to these wild marshes can hear the cries of more than 200 kinds of birds: the whistled notes of the wood duck, the honk of the Canada goose, the high-pitched screech of the bald eagle, or the rare bray of the trumpeter swan. Motorists can cruise the seven-mile Marshland Wildlife Drive

(between mid-May and mid-October), while hikers and bikers have 70 miles of gravel roads from which to choose.

At nearby Seney the drive crosses the Fox River, believed by some to be the setting for Ernest Hemingway's classic fishing story, *Big Two-Hearted River* (the real Two-Hearted River is actually many miles away). The celebrated author, a native of Michigan, wrote fondly of the trout stream, "pebbly-bottomed with shallows and big boulders" and the trout "keeping themselves steady in the current with wavering fins" and changing their positions "by quick angles, only to hold steady in the fast water again."

7 Tahquamenon Falls State Park

Reached by a turn north on Rte. 123, the caramel-colored Tahquamenon River is none other than "the rushing Tahquamenaw" of Longfellow's *The Song of Hiawatha*. Beside its waters the poem's Indian hero builds a birch-bark canoe that "shall float upon the river like a yellow leaf in Autumn." Even Hiawatha's skill, though, couldn't have carried him safely over Upper Tahquamenon Falls, where the river pushes up to 50,000 gallons a second over a sandstone precipice in a wide copper-hued arc. Called the little Niagara, the Upper Falls (as distinguished from the more modest-size, multitiered Lower Falls farther downstream) is second in the volume of water flow only to Niagara itself in the eastern United States. Stairs and observation platforms allow close-up views of the wide, raging cataract, whose waters eventually flow into Lake Superior.

The root-beer color of the water at Tahquamenon Falls stems from tannins leached from plants.

Trip Tips

Length: About 395 miles, plus side trips.

When to go: Best in spring, summer, and fall.

Ferry: Service to Mackinac Island from St. Ignace and Mackinaw City begins in spring and continues to December or January, weather permitting.

Not to be missed: If you are anywhere near the Mackinac Bridge on Labor Day, join the crowd of 50,000 who hike the span between St. Ignace and Mackinaw City.

Nearby attractions: City of Marquette. Great Lakes Shipwreck Museum, Whitefish Point. Museum of Ojibwa Culture, St. Ignace.

Further information: Michigan's Upper Peninsula Travel and Recreation Association, P.O. Box 400, Iron Mountain, MI 49801; tel. 800-562-7134, www.uptravel.com.

8 Whitefish Bay Scenic Byway

After heading south from the village of Paradise, on Whitefish Bay, the drive turns east onto the well-marked Whitefish Bay Scenic Byway. Here the pines of Hiawatha National Forest (the eastern unit) slope to glistening white beaches along the bay. A number of scenic turnouts dot the byway, which culminates at Point Iroquois Lighthouse, built in 1870. Visitors can climb its spiral staircase for a lofty view of the Canadian shore.

9 Sault Ste. Marie

Canada looms even closer as the drive nears Sault Ste. Marie at the narrow end of Whitefish Bay. Here 1,000-foot-long freighters laden with ore from Minnesota mines or grain from the Canadian prairies point their bows east into the St. Marys River, which flows from Lake Superior into Lake Huron, connecting the two lakes. Some of the longest, busiest canal locks in the world await these giant cargo

Pictured Rocks National Lakeshore is a locale of bright-colored sandstone and dunes.

vessels at "the Soo," as locals refer to Michigan's oldest city. Visitors can gawk up at the locks' concrete walls from a sightseeing boat, or they can peer down from above at the mammoth ships squeezing through. But the best views of all await tourists atop the nearby 21-story Tower of History.

10 Mackinac Bridge

Tooling south on I-75, the drive arrives at St. Ignace, which juts into the Straits of Mackinac. Each summer about a million tourists surge through this historic crossroads of the Great Lakes, where massive chunks of Michigan geography—the Upper Peninsula, the Lower Peninsula, Mackinac Island, Lake Michigan, and Lake Huron—converge like pieces of a colossal jigsaw puzzle. It's not hard to see why this stunning confluence of land and water played a strategic role for the New World empires of France and England during the French and Indian Wars. A

generation before the American Revolution, the blasting guns of hostile forts threatened travelers on this treacherous strait, but times have obviously changed. Today you can vault the straits by car in 10 carefree minutes on the Mackinac Bridge. The "bridge that couldn't be built" opened in 1957, casting its ribbon of steel across five watery miles. Known locally as Mighty Mac, it is one of the longest suspension bridges ever erected.

11 Mackinac Island

One of the most popular destinations in northern Michigan, lovely Mackinac Island holds an unusual distinction. Its state highway is the only one in the country where there has never been an automobile accident. For good reason: Mackinac Island has outlawed motor vehicles since the 1930s. After you leave your car at one of several parking facilities in St. Ignace (or in Mackinaw City across the bridge), prepare to enter a bygone era. A short ferry ride takes you to the island's 19th-century harbor village, nestled next to wooded bluffs. Victorian-era storefronts with bright canvas awnings greet visitors, as do horse-and-buggy "taxis" waiting at the docks. At the waterfront you can rent bicycles and hire porters with old-fashioned drays to follow behind, toting your baggage to its destination.

One such destination might be the elegant Grand Hotel or some other island hostelry. Day-trippers, however, can head straight to Fort Mackinac, a restored citadel offering reenactments of local history. Visitors can also explore the island on foot, by bicycle, or in a horse-drawn carriage, stopping off at such rock formations as Skull Cave and Arch Rock. A captivating potpourri of land, water, and history, Mackinac Island seems to embody the essence of the Upper Peninsula.

Lake Michigan Tour

Caressed by waves and bathed in sunshine, the eastern shores of
Lake Michigan have been dubbed the Riviera of the Midwest.

Point Betsie Lighthouse warns lake mariners clear of the coast.

Once the province of Chippewa, Huron, and Ottawa Indians, the crystalline waters and densely wooded shores of Lake Michigan (Michigan is an Algonquian word meaning "great lake") have served as a mecca for explorers, traders, and settlers. Today, however, this is a year-round haven for nature lovers, retirees, and visitors who come from all over to enjoy the only one of the Great Lakes that lies entirely within U.S. borders.

1 Ludington

Anchored on the eastern shore of Lake Michigan, the town of Ludington is just a four-hour ferry ride from Manitowoc, Wisconsin. As a result, this quaint fishing port is popular not only with local tourists but also with nearby Wisconsinites, who frequently drop in on their lakeside neighbors for visits. Here you'll find a trim, neat harbor, open beaches, blue lake water, white sand dunes, and abundant stands of emerald-green forest that encompasses the port. For a foreign note, a towering cross overlooks the harbor; it memorializes Père Marquette, the French explorer and missionary who trekked through the area and is thought to have died nearby in 1675.

From Ludington, head north on Lakeshore Drive to Rte. 116 and follow it to Ludington State Park. Bookended by Lake Michigan and Hamlin Lake, this 5,300-acre park abounds with waterside campsites. Fishing, boating, and waterskiing can be enjoyed at both lakes, and canoeing is possible not far away on the Big Sable River.

Returning to Ludington, the drive takes Rte. 10/31 east, then continues north on Rte. 31 through a mix of farmland and forest. When you reach Forest Trail Road, follow signs to the Lake Michigan Recreation Area.

2 Lake Michigan Recreation Area

Swimming, picnicking, camping, and trails aplenty make this recreation area one of the most popular in the state. But if you're seeking a little more peace and quiet, you won't have to go very far. The adjacent 3,500-acre Nordhouse Dunes Wilderness—a glorious untouched mile of rolling sand dunes, interdunal wetlands, and mixed stands of juniper, jack pine, and hemlock—is an oasis of solitude. No motorized vehicles are permitted in this federally designated wilderness area, so the only noise you are likely to hear as you stroll along the wide, sandy beach are the sweet sounds of nature— the shriek of gulls, rustling leaves, or the crash of the waves.

3 Manistee

Back on Rte. 31 the drive continues north through a glacier-sculpted landscape where tiny sapphire lakes are surrounded by an emerald forest. The region's natural wonders are explained at the U.S. Forest Service ranger station just south of Manistee, an old lumber town named for the Chippewa spirit of the woods.

Like many busted boomtowns, Manistee has undergone a com-

mercial renaissance in the age of tourism. Manistee's prosperous past is still visible in the grand Victorian-era buildings that make up its downtown (the entire area is listed on the National Register of Historic Places). An 1883 commercial building houses historical exhibits, while several churches reflect the Irish, German, and Scandinavian heritage of the town's early settlers. Just north of Manistee lies Orchard Beach State Park, which, from its perch high atop a bluff overlooking Lake Michigan, offers splendid views. Several miles east of the park, switch over to Rte. 22 and follow it north as it hugs the shore.

4 Point Betsie Lighthouse

With uninterrupted views up and down the coast, the tiny community of Arcadia is every bit as bucolic as its ancient Greek counterpart. Savor this tranquil spot, then move on to the bustling town of Frankfort (which, incidentally, also has a historic marker in honor of Père Marquette). Before curving around Crystal Lake, turn left onto Point Betsie Road and go to the venerable Point Betsie Lighthouse—one of the oldest and most photogenic beacons on the Lower Peninsula. From here, the dunes, lakes, and rivers of Sleeping Bear Dunes National Lakeshore dominate the coastline for the next 35 miles.

5 Sleeping Bear Dunes National Lakeshore

By the time you crest the 150-foot Dune Climb, you may be as exhausted as the legendary bear for whom this 71,000-acre preserve is named. The Chippewas tell the tale of a mother bear who swam across Lake Michigan with her two cubs to escape a Wisconsin forest fire, only to watch her weary youngsters drown before reaching shore. In pity, Manitou, the great spirit, turned the cubs into the

Manitou Islands and the mother bear into Sleeping Bear Dunes.

In reality, however, this is not a place of sadness but one of great beauty. Six thousand acres of cream-colored dunes tower high above the waters of Lake Michigan; inland lakes and birch-lined streams teem with pike, trout, and bass; and maple-beech forests echo with the tuneful trills of the wood thrush. Just beyond the visitor center in Empire, lookout points along the 7.4-mile Pierce Stocking Scenic Drive offer a preview of the park's many treasures: Glen Lake (a sand-dammed inlet of Lake Michigan), the sandy slopes of Sleeping Bear Dunes, crescent-shaped Sleeping Bear Bay, and the misty Manitou Islands.

Called "perched dunes" because of their position atop high bluffs, the Sleeping Bear Dunes—some of which reach up to 480 feet in height—are among the tallest in the world, their shifting sands barely stabilized by beach grass, sand cherry, and other pioneer plants. Along the four-mile looping Dunes Trail, look for the skeletal remains of so-called "ghost forests." Once buried by shifting sands, these dead trees are now partially exposed and can be seen poking up from their sandy graves. Equally spooky are the tales of 50 shipwrecks in the dangerous Manitou Passage; they are vividly illustrated with exhibits at the maritime museum, located near the village of Glen Haven. Rest overnight at the Homestead in nearby Glen Arbor; it claims to have the best ski runs in the Midwest, though cross-country skiing enthusiasts can follow trails nearly anywhere.

6 Pyramid Point

Whether you rough it in the lakeshore's D. H. Day Campground or lounge in comfort at the nearby lodge, head past the Glen Arbor sandbar to adjacent Pyramid Point.

A leafy three-mile trail there leads to a lookout point that offers what is perhaps the best view available of the Manitou Islands (reachable by ferry from nearby Leland).

7 Leland

Lured by an annual snowfall exceeding 100 inches, "snowbirds" flock to the rolling hills of the lakeshore every winter.

In summer postcard-pretty Leland, a fishing port sandwiched between Lake Michigan and Lake Leelanau, is a perfect place to idle while waiting for the Manitou ferry or a fishing charter. Turn-of-the-century shanties, now scrubbed and spruced up, have reemerged as Fishtown, a collection of charming quayside restaurants, galleries, and shops.

A visit to the nearby islands of North and South Manitou is a must for nature lovers. The North Manitou wilderness beckons backpackers and fishermen, while its smaller sibling, South Manitou, is celebrated for the Valley of the Giants—a 500-year-old virgin white cedar forest where one of the trees is believed to be the largest of its kind in the world. Off South Manitou's southern coast rests the wreckage of the *Francisco Morazan*, its rusty remains as clear a warning of danger as any beacon.

Back on the mainland, orchards in this area overflow with fruit from summer through autumn, starting with cherries and berries in July and ending with apples and grapes in September. During that same month energetic coho salmon can be seen leaping the Leland dam on their way to their upstream spawning grounds.

8 Leelanau State Park

The little finger of Leelanau Peninsula crooks protectively around the mouth of Grand Traverse Bay as the highway ambles to Northport, a picturesque hamlet chock-full of boutiques, antique shops, restaurants, and bed-and-breakfast inns. With its abundant orchards, award-winning wineries, and fine swimming beaches, Leelanau lives up to its

Manistee Lighthouse extends far into Lake Michigan near Orchard Beach State Park.

Day's end in autumn colors the water with shimmering reflections of golden and scarlet.

::::: **Trip Tips** :::::

Length: About 320 miles plus side trips.

When to go: Popular year-round.

Not to be missed: The National Cherry Festival, Traverse City.

Nearby attractions: Colonial Michilimackinac, a reconstructed fur-trading village and exhibits, Mackinaw City. Mackinac Island, "the Bermuda of the North," accessible by ferry from St. Ignace and Mackinaw City.

Further information: West Michigan Tourist Association, 950 28th St., Suite E-200, Grand Rapids, MI 49508; tel. 800-442-2084, www.wmta.org.

hogback, passing orchards that explode in a filigree of creamy pink blossoms in May and, in autumn, past blazing hardwood thickets.

Though Old Mission Lighthouse is the focal point of the state park at the tip of the peninsula, only the campground and neighboring swimming beach are open to the public. Brush up on local history at a reconstructed 1839 Indian mission, then drive west across the peninsula and go south on Peninsula Drive to the hook of historic Bowers Harbor, which delights visitors with its gourmet restaurants, rumors of ghosts, and views of Power Island.

name, a Chippewa word meaning "land of delight."

At Leelanau's fingertip you'll find the Grand Traverse Lighthouse, part of 1,300-acre Leelanau State Park. The historic beacon still guards rocky shoals once so intimidating to French fur trappers that they christened the bay Le Grand Traverse—"the big crossing." Pine- and cedar-scented trails lead away from a tiny campground, down to deserted beaches at Cathead Bay and Christmas Cove.

9 Traverse City

A temperate climate such as one finds in Traverse City is just right for growing premium grapes. So it is small wonder that the area boasts fifteen wineries, all of them open for tours and tastings.

Nevertheless, it wasn't grapes but cherries that put this former timber town on the map. Traverse City is the self-proclaimed Cherry Capital of the World, producing 100 million pounds per year (one-third of the world's crop). The National Cherry Festival is held

here in July, and February brings another annual event, a North American cross-country ski championship. Sixteen miles southwest of town, the Interlochen Center for the Arts offers year-round entertainment in the form of classical and popular music, art, and dance.

10 Old Mission Peninsula

A narrow spur bisecting Grand Traverse Bay, Old Mission Peninsula is as timeless as Traverse City is trendy. The 18-mile drive along Rte. 37 lazes northward via a high

11 Charlevoix

Rte. 31 winds its way around the east bay toward the prosaically named town of Acme. There you can buy a slice of cherry pie or pluck a basketful of orchard-ripe fruit for a picnic at Elk Lake or Torch Lake. The beach at Fisherman's Island State Park, several miles past Norwood, is a perfect place to view one of Lake Michigan's million-dollar sunsets.

Farther along, the drive reaches the resort town of Charlevoix, whose main street is flanked by

Sunset comes to South Manitow Island, accessible by ferry from Leland.

Shore Drive—you may see some of the rarities found on the Lower Peninsula, including Lake Huron tansy, Pitcher's thistle, showy lady's slipper, wide-eyed saw-whet owls, and pileated woodpeckers.

From here the highway twists and turns for the next 14 miles through a landscape that provides stunning views of Lake Michigan. Occasional corridors of hardwoods and hemlocks give this stretch of the drive its name—the Tunnel of Trees. At the end of Rte. 119 sprawls Cross Village, an old Indian community settled by the Chippewa and Ottawa tribes. From Cross Village, head north along Sturgeon Bay to Lakeview Road, then east about five miles to Cecil Bay Road (Rte. 81). When the road ends at Cecil Bay, follow the signs west to Wilderness State Park.

two pretty shores—one is found on Lake Charlevoix and the other at nearby Lake Michigan. Charlevoix is the departure point for ferries to Beaver Island, some 32 miles offshore. Dubbed the Emerald Isle by homesick 19th-century Irish settlers, this charming island once sheltered a breakaway sect of Mormons who were driven from Illinois in 1847. Their leader, James Strang, reigned as "king" until he was brutally murdered in 1856. The island's Mormon and Irish heritage survives in the old Mormon Print Shop and in the brogue of natives.

12 Petoskey

The road to Petoskey winds through a pastoral setting reminiscent of England's lovely Lake District, which may be why Ernest Hemingway's family chose "Windemere" (after the largest of those lakes) as the name for their summer cottage on nearby Walloon Lake. Still, the jewels of Petoskey are not lakes but stones—350-million-year-old polished pebbles adorned with fossilized coral that the lake dredges up from its bottom every spring and which beachcombers quickly pocket. The stones are among the wares on sale in the Gaslight District, a local shopping mecca. But this historic community on Little Traverse Bay has its spiritual side as well. In summer a Methodist camp called Bay View sponsors concerts, lectures, and other activities.

13 Tunnel of Trees

Across tranquil Little Traverse Bay glitters the fashionable enclave of Harbor Springs, where Detroit's well-to-do banish cars from their gated compound and party-hop between mansion-size "cottages" and elegant yachts. But north of town, just off Rte. 119, it's nature that puts on the show.

At Thorne Swift Nature Preserve—a 30-acre sanctuary of dunes, wetlands, and mixed forests located just off Lower

14 Wilderness State Park

Although golf, hunting, bass fishing, hiking, picnicking, and water sports all have their place here, it's wildlife that is the real star at this 8,200-acre preserve on the northwest tip of the Lower Peninsula. Rustic cabins provide temporary homes for naturalists hoping to spot seldom-seen birds and plants: rare orchids grace the park in spring; nesting piping plovers sequester among the dunes and marshes in summer; dabbling wood ducks, pintails, and other waterfowl glide through the wetlands; and craggy tree snags hide the young of great horned owls from predators while their parents seek prey.

Beyond Wilderness State Park, on the northeast horizon, looms a man-made wonder that magnificently complements those found in nature. Spanning the Straits of Mackinac—the place where Lake Michigan and Lake Huron meet—the Mackinac Bridge (one of the world's longest suspension bridges) links Mackinaw City with Michigan's Upper Peninsula. It's a fitting place to end your drive to Michigan's north.

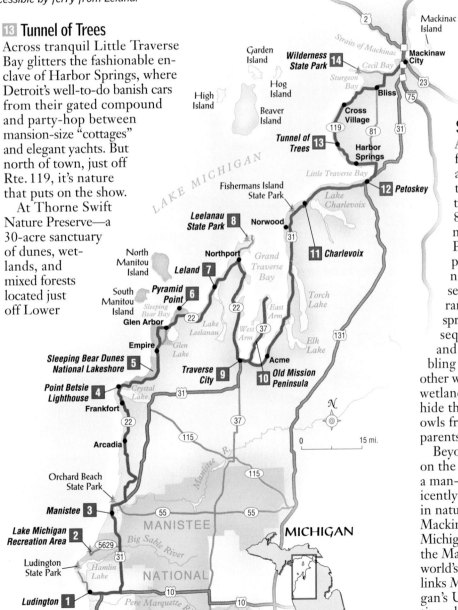

217

The Scenic Sunrise Shore

With Lake Huron lapping endlessly at the shores of Michigan's east coast, a delicate give-and-take forever unfurls in the land where the countryside meets the lakeside.

Historic Fort Michilimackinac frames the Mighty Mac bridge at Mackinaw City.

Michigan's state motto says it all: "If you seek a pleasant peninsula, look about you." That's no empty boast, as the spectacular scenery along the state's shorelines illustrates. This drive, with the vast expanse of Lake Huron never far from view, hugs Michigan's northeastern coast—an ever-changing lakefront complete with pleasant Victorian villages, century-old lighthouses, mixed forests, sugary sand beaches, and windswept limestone ledges.

1 Bay City State Park

In the late 1800s the fortunes of Bay City, like those of many other towns in Michigan, were closely tied to the timber industry. The Victorian mansions of the lumber barons who settled here remain as a testimonial to their once-opulent prosperity. Other architectural gems from that era can been seen in the Midland Street Business District, including a château-style Sage Library.

Climb the stairs at the City Hall Bell Tower for views of the area. Then hurry off for a swim at Bay City State Park, which lies but five miles up the coast. Nestled on the curving shore of Saginaw Bay, the park not only has lovely beaches but also contains Tobico Marsh, a 1,700-acre wetland where two observation towers provide opportunities for spying on mink, deer, waterfowl, and other wildlife.

2 Tawas Point State Park

Heading north on Rte. 13 and then eastward on Rte. 23, the drive seldom veers far from the coast, passing stands of cedars, pines, and scrub oaks that grow along the golden beaches. Just past the town of East Tawas, a side road down the small peninsula that shelters Tawas Bay leads to Tawas Point State Park. Soft beaches invite leisurely exploration, as does the Sandy Hook Nature Trail, a pleasant stroll that begins at the Tawas Point Lighthouse, an 1876 structure that is still in use.

3 River Road National Forest Scenic Byway

Once so dense with white pines that only the slimmest of sunbeams penetrated to the forest floor, the woodlands of eastern Michigan were severely depleted by the late 1800s—the trees felled to supply the lumber that built the West. Part of an effort to replant and protect the woods, Huron National Forest was created in 1909. Today its landscape is once again lush, with majestic pines, maples, cedars, and birches fanning away from the banks of the Au Sable River. To sample the legacy of this early conservation effort, take a drive on the River Road National Forest Scenic Byway, a 22-mile sylvan odyssey that accompanies the river westward from Oscoda. Supplying fine views at nearly every turn, the road leads to camp-grounds, historic sites, and trails atop riverside bluffs.

Back on Rte. 23 the drive meanders for miles along Lake Huron's shore. The water—pale green in fair weather, steely gray on stormy days—laps gently against the coast, and small tufted dunes rumple the tawny beach. For a relaxing escape along the way, stop at Three-Mile Beach, an undeveloped expanse that is ideal for swimming, wading, or simply for beachcombing for pieces of driftwood.

Farther along, four miles north of Harrisville, the Sturgeon Point Lighthouse rises above Lake Huron. The lone beacon, a white brick structure built in 1869, has been converted into a museum furnished with antiques and exhibiting remnants of ships that were wrecked in the area.

For yet another opportunity to walk the water's edge, pause at Negwegon State Park. A short path leads to seven miles of remote, unspoiled beach, where birds soar overhead and small, smooth stones cover parts of the shore.

4 Alpena

According to Indian lore, two rival braves, each courting the same maiden, were out on Thunder Bay in canoes when they fought a duel. One fired an arrow that accidentally struck the girl, who fell from her boat and drowned. Outraged, the gods churned up turbulent currents and frothy waves that roil unpredictably to this day.

No matter how one explains the treacherous conditions on Thunder Bay, its waters have long been a hazard for sailors. About 80 shipwrecks lie on its murky floor, all of them protected in the Thunder Bay Underwater Preserve. One ill-fated steamer, the wooden *Shamrock*, went down in a storm in 1905. Its skeletal remains rest in 12 feet of water offshore from the Alpena City

Au Sable River drains the watersheds of Hurnon National Forest.

Marina; divers often visit the site in the summer to peer into the submerged hull.

Alpena itself, known as The Town That Wouldn't Die, has had its share of ups and downs. Fires destroyed its downtown twice, and the city's economy has followed the seesaw fortunes of the lumber industry. True to its nickname, though, Alpena has endured each setback and is once again on the upswing as an industrial and recreational center.

For a look at the region's logging past, visit the Jesse Besser Museum and take note of the early timber tycoons' stately homes, which line the waterfront. North of town a one-mile trail at the Besser Natural Area winds past an abandoned village, an azure lagoon, and a virgin forest of white pines.

5 Presque Isle

Continuing northward, the drive skirts Grand Lake, whose limestone floor causes the water to sparkle like a translucent green jewel. Presque Isle—its harbor long a haven for ships plying Huron's trade routes—is located on the neck of land separating Grand Lake and Lake Huron.

The Old Presque Isle Light, now a museum, began guiding mariners into the harbor in 1840. In 1870 a larger structure, the Presque Isle Light, was erected about a mile to the north, putting

the older lighthouse out of commission. Bordered by a 100-acre park, the newer beacon, one of the loftiest on the Great Lakes, stands more than 110 feet tall.

6 Rogers City

Though the drive passes through forest as it leads north, the economy in these parts is fueled not by lumber but by rocks: one of the world's largest limestone quarries has been carved into the earth at Rogers City. At Quarry View visitors can take a look at the action in the immense pit—three miles long and two miles wide.

A side trip to the west on Rte. 68 leads to Ocqueoc Falls, the largest in lower Michigan. Songbirds flit through the cedars that line the trails to the terraced falls,

Trip Tips

Length: About 220 miles, plus side trips.

When to go: Spring through autumn, but the peak summer season can be crowded.

Nearby attraction: Bois Blanc Island, a rustic getaway accessible by ferry from Cheboygan.

Further information: Travel Michigan, 300 N. Washington Square, 2nd Fl., Lansing, MI 48913; tel. 888-784-7328, www.michigan.org.

and hikers can top off their treks with a refreshing dip in a pool at the base of the tumbling cascade.

Continuing north again on Rte. 23, you'll come to P. H. Hoeft State Park, a 300-acre refuge with a mile-long beach. Although winds and currents can combine to make the water chilly and the shore bottom pebbly, fine views of Lake Huron remain a constant. You can while away the hours by watching huge freighters pass on their way to and from the quarries at Rogers City—a sight that is equally impressive at night when the ships' lights flicker and dance across the darkened water.

7 Cheboygan

Several roadside overlooks, complete with picnic areas, make the sightseeing easy as you travel northward. The curving wooded shoreline and the expanse of Lake Huron form panoramic patchworks of green and blue all the way to Cheboygan. The town sits on the banks of the Cheboygan River, which is part of Michigan's Inland Waterway. Meandering between willow-shaded banks, the passageway has two locks and passes through three rivers and three lakes on its way across northeastern Michigan. In addition to boating and fishing opportunities, Cheboygan boasts trail-laced parks and historic sites, including lighthouses and an old-time opera house—an elegantly restored music hall dating from 1877.

8 Mackinaw City

Located at the northernmost tip of Michigan's Lower Peninsula, Mackinaw City affords visitors the rare opportunity of watching the sun rise over one Great Lake,

Lake Huron, and set over another, Lake Michigan. Sightseers can also tour Colonial Michilimackinac, a reconstruction at the site of a once-thriving fur-trading post and palisaded fort. Here, too, is Mighty Mac—the Mackinac Bridge, one of the world's longest suspension bridges. Spanning the swirling Straits of Mackinac, it provides an impressive gateway to the wooded wilds that spread across Michigan's Upper Peninsula, a fitting end to your drive.

Nebraska Heartland

Rippling like waves into the distance, grassy dunes extend for miles across central Nebraska, where vast, unbroken expanses of land and sky offer the promise of escape to solitude and serenity.

The High Plains Homestead near Crawford offers rustic accommodations combined with authentic cattle-drive grub.

Making up one of the world's largest dune systems, which covers about one-fourth of the state, the Sand Hills of Nebraska are a major feature of this drive. The gently undulating grasslands, which stretch from the Platte River valley in the south to the plains and hills in the north, prove a welcome counterpoint to our often overcrowded world.

1 Grand Island

Today a bustling railroad and manufacturing city, Grand Island was founded in 1857, when German families settled near the banks of the Platte River. Westward-bound pioneers and the short-lived Pony Express would soon pass through. And then the transcontinental railroad came, its builders laying the framework of the present town some five miles north of the immigrant community.

To experience the region's distinctive heritage, visit the Stuhr Museum of the Prairie Pioneer. It's easy to spend hours exploring Stuhr's many attractions, complete with an abundance of antiques and a re-created early railroad town.

Heading out of town toward the northwest on Rte. 2, the drive passes through a pastoral midwestern landscape in which fields of corn and beans eventually give way to grasslands where sheep and cattle graze. This shift from crops to livestock reflects the fact that soil in the area tends to be low on nutrients and vulnerable to the effects of strong winds.

Indeed, blowing soil, sand, and snow are a major concern on these open plains, where gusting winds meet few obstructions. That's why windbreaks occasionally parallel the highway. One of the longer ones, between the towns of Cairo and Ravenna, is made up of a mixed planting of ponderosa pines and eastern red cedars.

2 Broken Bow

Broken Bow is so named because, quite simply, settlers found an Indian's broken bow here. The comparatively new shops around the town square are quite a contrast to the sod houses and dugouts of the pioneers, whose struggles to build new lives on the prairie were often

Star Route

⭐ Rte. 2 to Ellsworth

The great expanse of the Sand Hills could never be seen on just one drive. To explore more of this remote and distinctively beautiful region, continue west on Rte. 2 out of Thedford. The road rises and falls with the terrain and, as a reminder that civilization does indeed exist, windmills and quiet towns—Seneca, Mullen, Hyannis—dot the area. Ranches here are measured not in acres but in square miles, and toward the drive's western end, the wide-open skies are reflected in numerous lakes and ponds.

fraught with hardships. Although modern-day travelers have most difficulties solved for them, it is always a good idea to fill the fuel tank and pack some food before heading out to sparsely populated stretches of countryside.

Once again following Rte. 2, you will notice that the plains become drier. Many animals nonetheless manage to survive in these surroundings, including pheasants, grouse, quail, and wild turkeys. And remember to look skyward from time to time: you might spot soaring hawks and eagles, as well as huge flocks of ducks and groups of geese flying in their characteristic V-shaped formation.

Sandhill Cranes

One of the great spectacles of the bird world can be witnessed in the Grand Island area. From the beginning of March until mid-April, large flocks of sandhill cranes pause to rest and feed along the Platte River. An estimated 80 percent of the cranes' total population visits the area, with the heaviest concentrations found along the 40-mile stretch between Grand Island and Kearney to the west. For further information on the best viewing locations and guided outings, contact the Grand Island Visitors Bureau (309 West Second St., P.O. Box 1486, Grand Island, NE 68802).

3 Victoria Springs State Recreation Area

Rte. 2 soon leads to the small town of Anselmo, where a large brick church—complete with a Gothic-style tower—provides a welcome vertical relief to the far-stretching horizon of the plains. A side trip of about six miles along Rte. 21A passes through more cattle country and takes you to Victoria Springs State Recreation Area. Its sprin water, like that of many others in America, was once considered a tonic and a cure. Today there is no promise of good health, but this oasis certainly is restful. As at all state-run parks in Nebraska, permits are required for entry.

4 Sand Hills

Back on Rte. 2 outside of Anselmo, you'll soon pass a sign indicating that you are entering the Sand Hills. The immense system of dunes, sometimes compared to the Sahara, was created when the sands of an ancient sea were carried here by the wind.

The hills can reach heights of more than 350 feet, but what most distinguishes this region from other sandy areas are the flourishing grasses, which include Indian, bluestem, prairie sand reed, and sand love grasses. Their presence is vital, for their roots are the fabric holding the dunes in place. Without the grasses, the sands would be swept away by the wind.

5 Nebraska National Forest

Stands of trees on the prairie? As strange as it might seem, some do exist, and the Bessey Division of the Nebraska National Forest soon appears on the horizon. Many of its trees—ponderosa pines, eastern red cedars, and jack pines—were planted and tended by humans, beginning in 1903 at the suggestion of Dr. Charles E. Bessey, a University of Nebraska botanist.

Although trees do occur natural-

Trail riders pass beneath chiseled bluffs in Fort Robinson State Historical Park.

ly along rivers and lakes, they often require a helping hand to survive in this sometimes harsh landscape. To observe the practices of the forest's caretakers, stop by the Bessey Arboretum, where several million trees began their lives before being transplanted to the forest and other parts of the country.

The national forest offers a variety of activities: swimming, canoeing, fishing, and camping,

for example. You can also drive or hike to the Scott Lookout Tower for a panoramic view of the surrounding forest and hills. If you keep an eye out for the preserve's many animals, you might spot an endangered black-footed ferret, a peregrine falcon, a golden eagle, or several of the many songbirds. A word of caution, though: like many parts of Nebraska, this is rattlesnake country.

6 Valentine National Wildlife Refuge

Just east of Thedford, the drive heads north on Rte. 83 toward Valentine National Wildlife Refuge. Nebraska lies directly on the migration routes of many birds, and the refuge offers great opportunities for observing them. Ducks, upland sandpipers, long-billed curlews, and white pelicans are among those likely to be seen.

White-tailed deer live in the patches of woodland, while mule deer, preferring open areas, bound across the plains. But that's not all, for coyotes, minks, skunks, weasels, and raccoons also roam through the refuge.

The many lakes and ponds here are fed in part by the Ogallala Aquifer. Holding enough water to fill Lake Huron, this huge underground reservoir stretches from South Dakota to Texas. It was formed because the sand acts like a sieve, allowing surface water to seep in with very little runoff. The water saturates the sand and gravel below, while an even lower impermeable layer of rock holds the liquid in place. Many thousands of years old, the aquifer is an extremely valuable resource.

7 Fort Niobrara National Wildlife Refuge

Continue north on Rte. 83 to Valentine, a quiet town set amid some of our country's most productive grazing grounds, then drive four miles east on Rte. 12 to Fort Niobrara National Wildlife Refuge. Prairie dogs have built a town near the visitor center; in addition to the antics of the little rodents themselves, be on the lookout for burrowing owls and various snakes that have moved into their abandoned burrows. Herds of bison, elk, and deer roam across the sanctuary's grasslands and among the patches of pines

Northeast of Valentine in the Sand Hills region, Smith Falls drops 70 feet.

that grow there. Watch, too, for Texas longhorns, which can weigh up to a ton and have hornspans of as much as nine feet.

You can also see wildlife from the comfort of your car. The refuge features several unpaved roads, usually negotiable except in times of rain and snow. An even more appealing alternative might be to head for the Niobrara River, where you can put in a raft or a canoe (outfitters have set up shop in the area) and drift downstream with the lazy currents.

The visitor center displays a model of an 1879 fort, and additional exhibits give a good introduction to the refuge's wildlife. To increase your chances of observing the animals in their natural settings, it's best to search for them in the early morning hours or just before sunset. Walk with a light step, making as few noises as possible, and take along a pair of binoculars—an essential tool for the nature watcher.

8 Samuel R. McKelvie National Forest

Backtrack to Valentine, then follow Rte. 20 west and Rte. 16F south into the Samuel R. McKelvie National Forest. (It's time to turn your watches back an hour, for you've now crossed into the Mountain Time zone.) Really more prairie than woodland, the "forest" —bordered by the Snake and Niobrara rivers—is blanketed with an assortment of native grasses.

Toward the eastern boundary of this peaceful preserve lies Merritt Reservoir State Recreation Area, where the damming of the Snake River has created a large lake. You can camp along its shores, put in a boat, or drop a line to sample some of the state's best fishing.

9 Arthur Bowring Sandhills Ranch State Historical Park

Return to Rte. 20 west, then follow Rte. 61 north to this state historical park, where time stands still as ranchers tend to herds of Hereford cattle. The area was donated to the state by a well-known Nebraskan couple, and their former home—brimming with fine antiques and Sand Hills memorabilia—is open for tours. You can also learn about local geology, homesteading, and wildlife at the park's visitor center.

10 Chadron State Park

Continuing to the west, the drive leaves the Sand Hills and, at the Chadron State Park, enters an area with a rich mix of terrain,

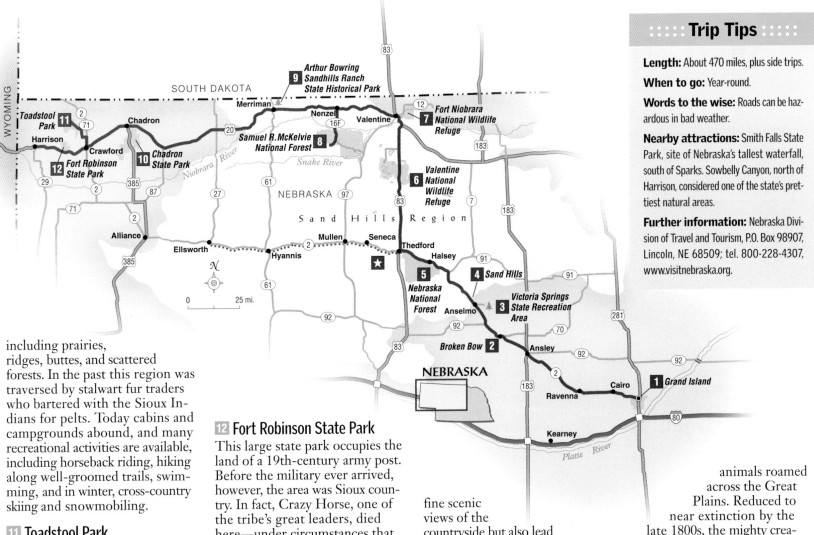

including prairies, ridges, buttes, and scattered forests. In the past this region was traversed by stalwart fur traders who bartered with the Sioux Indians for pelts. Today cabins and campgrounds abound, and many recreational activities are available, including horseback riding, hiking along well-groomed trails, swimming, and in winter, cross-country skiing and snowmobiling.

11 Toadstool Park

The forces of nature have sculpted a peculiar landscape at Toadstool Park, where hills composed mostly of sand and clay—bare and severely eroded—protrude from the grassland like some great mountain range in miniature. Just as fanciful are the landmarks that give the park its name. These "toadstools" were created when harder rocks were left perched atop softer materials that have been eroded away and now form pillars. Delightfully different from the rolling Sand Hills and sweeping plains found elsewhere in Nebraska's heartland, they are a whimsy to see and a pleasure to explore.

12 Fort Robinson State Park

This large state park occupies the land of a 19th-century army post. Before the military ever arrived, however, the area was Sioux country. In fact, Crazy Horse, one of the tribe's great leaders, died here—under circumstances that are still clouded in mystery.

Take some time to explore the park's roads, which offer not only fine scenic views of the countryside but also lead to the grazing grounds of bison herds. It is estimated that in the past some 60 million of these animals roamed across the Great Plains. Reduced to near extinction by the late 1800s, the mighty creatures have been making a slow but steady comeback.

Any time is a good time to observe the herd, but during the later summer months, the bulls add a special note of drama; stirring up dust with their huge, powerful hooves, they threaten and charge other males in battles over mating rights. The winners of these encounters are guaranteed the largest harems, which can consist of up to 50 cows, and the calves are usually born in late May and early June.

You'll find eroded bluffs as well as toadstools at Toadstool Park.

Platte River Road

In the heart of Nebraska's panhandle, where rolling prairies give way to remote, rocky plains, the Platte River Road unfurls as a highway back through history.

Try your hand at riding a prairie schooner wagon near knifelike Chimney Rock.

When French explorers tried, and failed, to navigate the shallow Platte River, they understood why the Oto Indians had given it a name that means "flat water," and they followed suit, calling it the Platte. But while this stream did not actually take travelers to the longed-for land of the West, it certainly led them there. In the mid-1800s the river paralleled the Pony Express route and the Oregon, Mormon, and California trails, helping some 350,000 pioneers across Nebraska in the greatest westward migration in American history. Today you can follow them in spirit on the Platte River Road.

1 Ogallala

They called it the Gomorrah of the Plains—and with good reason. Located at the end of the long, lonely Texas Trail, Ogallala was the place where rowdy cowboys were finally able to let off some steam. The town, one visitor noted, was so godless that "amongst its half hundred buildings, no church spire pointed upward." Though the Ogallala of the Old West was certainly no place for women and children, the town of today offers delightful family fare. On Front Street the past comes to life as gunslingers reenact showdowns, and the Crystal Palace Revue—named for a 1875 dance hall—kicks up a storm. There's even a golf course nearby.

2 Lake McConaughy

Just a short drive north from Ogallala, Lake McConaughy—with more than 100 miles of sandy shore and 35,000 acres of clear, deep water—certainly lives up to the nickname Nebraska's Ocean. A 5,500-acre park borders the lake, which is a popular spot for fishing, camping, boating, and water sports. During late winter and early spring, keep an eye peeled for bald eagles and sandhill cranes.

3 Ash Hollow State Historical Park

For some 6,000 years, spring water has drawn visitors to this oasis on the plains. Traces of their presence remain throughout the 1,000-acre park, which is named for its shady ash groves. Near the visitor center is a rock shelter that served as an Indian campsite for 3,000 years. And nearby Windlass Hill, one of the first steep slopes faced by westering pioneers, is still scarred by tracks made by wagon wheels as they slid downhill. Along the highway beyond Ash Hollow, travelers might encounter somewhat stranger relics, for Nebraskans follow the curious custom of leaving old cowboy boots turned upside down on their roadside fence posts.

4 North Platte River

Continuing north, cross over the North Platte River, which parallels Rte. 26 as the road heads westward across the prairie. (Nourished by snowmelt from the Colorado Rockies, the 665-mile-long river merges with its smaller sibling, the South Platte, to form the main-stem Platte River in central Ne-braska.) Wetlands, rocky buttes, and sandbars are frequently in view along the way, as are the countless unkempt cottonwoods that fringe the river. Planted by settlers, many of these trees are now dying off, but their remains provide shelter for such creatures as raccoons and wood ducks.

5 Crescent Lake National Wildlife Refuge

Golden eagles soaring overhead in search of prey, a lone coyote stalking a white-tailed deer, pot-hole lakes that shimmer in the setting sun, a sea of sunflowers in full bloom—such are the sights that await visitors at Crescent Lake Wildlife Refuge, located 28 miles to the north of Oshkosh. Here the hills and valleys fringing the North Platte River give way to open prairies dotted with grazing cattle.

Encompassing some 46,000 acres of marshes and meadows, the refuge lies within the Nebraska sandhills—the largest dune formation in the Western Hemisphere. (Because of sandy roads, four-wheel-drive vehicles are recommended.) Among the rarities that can be seen here are the prong-horn antelope, the bald eagle, and the endangered peregrine falcon, together with many more common species of wildlife.

6 Courthouse Rock and Jail Rock

After 500 weary miles on the co-joined Oregon, Morman, and California trails, westward-bound pioneers must have welcomed the sight of this picturesque pair of natural sedimentary promontories. Courthouse Rock and Jail Rock—so named because they reminded travelers of man-made structures remembered from back home—were the first of several natural "road signs" encountered on their grueling 2,000-mile journey across the plains.

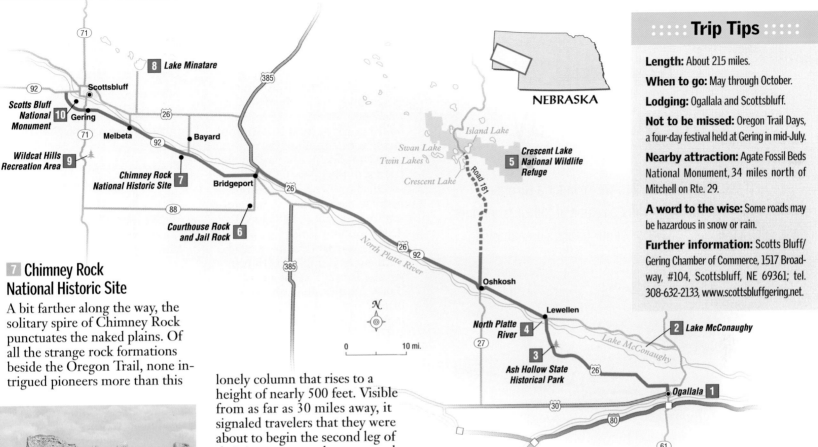

7 Chimney Rock National Historic Site

A bit farther along the way, the solitary spire of Chimney Rock punctuates the naked plains. Of all the strange rock formations beside the Oregon Trail, none intrigued pioneers more than this lonely column that rises to a height of nearly 500 feet. Visible from as far as 30 miles away, it signaled travelers that they were about to begin the second leg of their journey—a trek across much rougher terrain. Chimney Rock looks especially dramatic after dusk, when it is illuminated for several hours. Just west of Bridgeport on Rte. 26, modern-day travelers can sample the pioneer spirit at the Oregon Trail Wagon Train, which offers Connestoga wagon treks ranging from three-hour jaunts to six-day adventures.

8 Lake Minatare

A short side trip leads to Lake Minatare, one of Nebraska's most popular outdoor spots. The 2,000-acre lake boasts superb fishing for walleye, crappie, and bass; good camping; and one of Nebraska's two "lighthouses"—the other is at Ashland—a 55-foot-tall observation tower on a spit of land that juts out into the lake. Park at Lighthouse Point for a good view of the shores of Lake Minatare.

Visitors to Monument Shadows in Gering play golf at the foot of soaring bluffs.

9 Wildcat Hills Recreation Area

Whether they come for hiking, camping, or scenery, visitors at this recreation area won't be disappointed. Encompassing 935 acres of rocky buttes and forested canyons, Wildcat Hills offers three miles of rugged hiking trails, stone shelters with fireplaces, and magnificent views of the North Platte River valley. At the adjoining Big Game Reserve, elk, deer, and bison sometimes venture close enough to the fence to be photographed.

10 Scotts Bluff National Monument

It first appears as a dot on the horizon. But the fact that it loomed in the distance for days told approaching pioneers that—whatever it was—it had to be big. When they finally reached this gigantic mound of clay, sandstone, and volcanic ash, they were awed by its dimensions: over 500 feet high and half a mile wide.

Some years earlier, fur traders had named the site Scotts Bluff, after a fellow trapper who had died there mysteriously during an 1828 expedition. But travelers soon discovered that its Indian name, meaning "the hill that is hard to go around," was far more apt. Forced to detour around the badlands that lay between the bluff and the North Platte, wagons moved in a single file through a narrow shortcut called Mitchell Pass, which still displays ruts etched there more than a century ago. For a breathtaking view, take Summit Road to the top of the bluff.

Loess Hills Scenic Byway

If you think Iowa is flat, you're in for a surprise when you visit the Loess Hills, a region of tall, grassy ridges along the western fringe of our nation's breadbasket.

The Loess Hills are punctuated with wetlands that teem with waterfowl.

Ranging north to south near the Missouri River, the Loess Hills (pronounced "luss") are imposing reminders of the ice sheets that once covered much of present-day Iowa. Silty debris left behind after the ice melted here was piled high by the wind into dunelike drifts—some as tall as 200 feet. Thanks to a group of Iowans who banded together to establish the Loess Hills Scenic Byway, this distinctive landscape can now be toured in the comfort of your car.

1 Waubonsie State Park

Begin your survey of the Loess Hills at this 1,200-acre preserve, where three towering bluffs afford views into four states: Iowa and neighboring Nebraska, Kansas, and Missouri. Here, too, you'll catch your first glimpse of the Missouri River as it lazes across the plains.

Located 9 miles north of Hamburg off Rte. 2, the park is laced with more than 15 miles of hiking trails and bridle paths, offering up-close views of the loess formations. Due to its extremely fine texture, the soil erodes and drains quickly, leaving behind knife-edged ridges that are as sharply crested as meringue. As is evident at many road cuts, however, loess can also hold a nearly vertical face without giving way (a result of the way its grains interlock). Another notable feature of the Loess Hills is the so-called cat steps. Visible on the park's western slopes, these miniterraces are caused by loess's tendency to slump.

From the park the drive heads north on Rtes. L44 and J18 before joining Rte. 275 at the town of Tabor. Farther along, the highway briefly merges with Rte. 34, heading west before continuing north at Glenwood to Council Bluffs. Named for an 1804 meeting between explorers Lewis and Clark and members of the Otoe Indian tribe, Council Bluffs today is a busy river town and the northernmost point on one of Iowa's best hiking or biking routes—the Wabash Trace Nature Trail. Following an old railroad right-of-way, this 63-mile pathway wanders through forests, farmlands, and meadows spangled with wildflowers, ending just a few miles short of the Missouri border.

2 I-680 Scenic Overlook

Gliding through some of the most fertile farmland in the state, the drive heads northeast from Council Bluffs on Rtes. 191 and L34, then veers west on I-680. A few miles ahead a gravel access ramp (closed in winter) leads to a scenic overlook, with lovely views of billowing hills and the Missouri River valley.

3 Hitchcock Nature Area

A sharp turn south on Rte. 183 brings you to one of Iowa's loveliest parks, the 580-acre Hitchcock Nature Area. As elsewhere in the western part of the Loess Hills, the terrain here is rugged yet lush, making it hard to imagine that, only a few miles away, the vast flatlands of the western prairie stretch toward the horizon.

Hitchcock also displays the same odd mix of vegetation that is characteristic of this region. While the shaded inner hollows of the Loess Hills support dense forests of oak, hickory, and red cedar, their western slopes are almost desertlike in appearance, with faces raked by sun and wind. Look for hardy survivors such as yucca and purple beardtongue—plants found again only hundreds of miles to the west. Looping back to I-680, the drive continues north to Logan, where it heads southwest to the DeSoto National Wildlife Refuge.

4 DeSoto National Wildlife Refuge

On any given day at the height of the tourist season, some 4,000 visitors flock to this wetland refuge on the Missouri River, but they're outnumbered 100 to 1 by the geese—snow geese, to be precise. Each fall nearly half a million of these high-flying birds alight on the shores of DeSoto Lake—the midpoint of a 3,000-mile migration between Arctic nesting grounds

Trip Tips

Length: About 220 miles.

When to go: April to November.

Words to the wise: Check local road conditions and beware of slow-moving farm equipment.

Nearby attractions: Henry Doorly Zoo, Omaha, NE. Elk Horn Danish Villages, Elk Horn, IA.

Further information: Harrison County Welcome Center, 2931 Monroe Ave, Missouri Valley, IA 51555; tel. 712-642-2114, www.goldenhillsrcd.org.

Bluff tops provide views of Sioux City and the Big Sioux and Missouri rivers.

and their winter home along the Gulf of Mexico. So vast are the flocks that at takeoff they blot out the sky like a blizzard, and the din of their honking can make it difficult to converse with someone just a few feet away. The preserve's other seasonal and full-time inhabitants include, among others, wood ducks, mallards, warblers, piping plovers, and bald eagles.

The visitor center is a starting point for several trails and roads that lead through the refuge. It also houses a fascinating display of Civil War–era artifacts recovered from the Bertrand, a stern-wheeler that foundered nearby in 1865.

Birders are frequent visitors to DeSoto National Wildlife Refuge.

5 Murray Hill Scenic Overlook

After returning to Logan, the drive continues northwest on Rtes. 127 and 183, passing through a rustic mosaic of handsome farmsteads, rustling ridge-top grasslands, and drowsy apple orchards. In friendly towns such as Logan, Magnolia, and Pisgah, a cup of coffee at the village café may lead to an afternoon of unhurried conversation with locals—a hallmark of midwestern hospitality.

Just a few miles to the west of Pisgah, the Murray Hill Scenic Overlook reminds visitors how richly varied this landscape can be, as the snug valley of the Little Sioux River gives way to the wide greenish-brown belt of the Missouri River floodplain.

6 Preparation Canyon State Park

During the 1850s a band of idealistic Mormons settled here and established the School of Preparation for the Life Beyond. Before long, however, their leader—a con man named Charles Thompson—robbed them of their property. Although Thompson was eventually

run out of town, many of his followers became so disillusioned that they decided to move on as well. By the turn of the century, the community existed only in memory.

Happily, Preparation Canyon State Park, just off Rte. 183, does a far better job of fulfilling its promises. Here you can explore over 300 acres of steep loess terrain—accompanied, some say, by the ghosts of a few of the cheated settlers. Keep an eye peeled for such creatures as wild turkeys, white-tailed deer, and red foxes.

7 Sioux City

The drive eases toward its finish with a long climb to Sioux City. Though it boasts only about 80,000 residents, Sioux City ranks as one of the country's largest grain and livestock centers, with diversions aplenty along its busy waterfront. Drop by the Sergeant Floyd Museum of riverboat history, take in a bluff-top view of the Big Sioux and Missouri rivers from Floyd Monument, and finish with a hike to Dakota Point Overlook in Stone State Park, an 1,100-acre recreation area at the north edge of town.

8 Dorothy Pecaut Nature Center

Within the boundaries of Stone State Park, you'll find the extensive Dorothy Pecaut nature center

with exhibits that include a "walk-under" prairie, an aquarium of native fish, natural history dioramas, and a hands-on discovery area that appeals to children and adults alike. Continuing northwest on Rte. 12 to Akron, the drive bids farewell to the Loess Hills as the slopes themselves recede from view, their proud tops melting into the gently folded plains.

IOWA

Illinois Northwest

With the Father of Waters as its frequent companion, this graceful stretch of road through the northwest corner of Illinois takes a riverside journey back through time.

The sense of spring is noticeably in the air at this panoramic viewpoint on the bluffs in Mississippi Palisades State Park.

Geologists call this part of Illinois the Driftless Area or the Land the Glaciers Forgot. Stopping short of the eastern bank of the Mississippi, the great sheets of ice that elsewhere flattened the Prairie State left untouched the high, commanding bluffs that overlook the river and mile after mile of rolling hills and farmland.

1 Galena

Setting out from East Dubuque, the drive breezes southeast via Rtes. 20 and 84 to Galena, a 19th-century boomtown beautifully preserved as a living museum. Perched above the Galena River, a Mississippi tributary that once carried lead ore to market, Galena (Latin for "lead") was a bustling port in the middle of the 19th century. Ultimately, however, the mines played out, the river silted up, and railroads undercut the price of river shipping.

Since then time has stood still for Galena, and today's visitors are nothing less than grateful. Charmingly restored brick and limestone mansions are now bed-and-breakfast inns, and Main Street is lined with antique stores and galleries. When touring the town, be sure to visit the Galena History Museum, and don't miss the Belvedere Mansion, the limestone Dowling House, Old Market House, or the handsome brick mansion that Galena presented to adopted son Gen. Ulysses S. Grant on his triumphant return from war in 1865. Six miles north of town, visitors don hard hats for a tour of the Vinegar Hill Lead Mine, hosted by a descendant of the Irishman who staked his claim there in 1822.

2 Scales Mound

From Galena the drive follows the well-marked Stagecoach Trail, climbing rugged hills to Scales Mound. A fascinating collection of preserved frame houses and period commercial structures including the Warren Community Building, Scales Mound is on the National Register of Historic Places. Two miles northeast of town, at the Wisconsin border, is Charles Mound—a modest 1,235 feet, it's the highest spot in Illinois.

3 Apple River Canyon State Park

Continuing east on Stagecoach Trail past the town of Apple River, the route turns south on Canyon Park Road to 300-acre Apple River Canyon State Park. Here the air is filled with the charming sounds of a babbling stream, and the sky echoes with the trills of many different kinds of songbirds. Rare bird's-eye primrose grows from crevices on sheer limestone cliffs that soar high above the river as it winds through a lush landscape laced with hiking trails. Mosses and lichens carpet the pitted canyon walls, as do rare ferns, relics of the preglacial era, which survived in this untouched zone.

4 Long Hollow Scenic Overlook

After driving south to Rte. 20 and then two miles west just past Elizabeth, pause at the Long Hollow Scenic Overlook. The pagoda-like tower there affords a fine view of the surrounding countryside: to the northeast lies the just visible crest of Charles Mound, while below, the green hills roll away in soft velvet folds that generations of farmers have embellished with shade trees, tall grain and silage silos, trim white farmhouses, and red-sided, steep-roofed barns.

Turning south on Rte. 84, the drive soon arrives at Hanover, home to Whistling Wings' duck hatchery, where visitors can view ducklings through glass windows. This self-proclaimed Mallard Capital of the World husbands more than 200,000 ducks a year.

::::: **Trip Tips** :::::

Length: About 110 miles.

When to go: Popular year-round, but most beautiful in autumn.

Not to be missed: Annual eagle watches: Albany, Fulton, Galena, and Rock Island. Nouveau Wine Festival, November, Galena.

Nearby attraction: Mt. Carroll (historic 19th-century town), nine miles east of Savanna on Rte. 52/64.

Further information: Illinois Bureau of Tourism, 100 W. Randolf St., Chicago, IL 60601; tel. 800-226-6328, www.enjoy illinois.com.

5 Mississippi Palisades State Park

There's no toe-dipping to be had in the water along this stretch of the Mississippi, where the banks rise steeply from the river to form a magnificent row of tree-lined bluffs looking out to the west. Experienced climbers can sometimes be seen scaling the sheer cliffs from below, and hikers can travel some 13 miles of trails at the top, many of which trace old Indian paths through the dense growth. In spring visitors can pluck fresh watercress from spring-fed streams or hunt morel mushrooms amid the riot of wildflowers topping the palisades. Though the Great River Road (which runs on either side of the river along most of this drive) hums with traffic nearby, the park is home to such wild creatures as muskrats, white-tailed deer, wild turkeys, and pileated woodpeckers.

6 Savanna

From the Savanna–Sabula Bridge at Savanna, an impressive vista sweeps out over the wide Mississippi, punctuated here and there by a waterbird skimming the surface or an eagle circling overhead. Constructed of 1930s metalwork resembling that of an old toy Erector Set, the bridge joins the town of Savanna and the midriver island community of Sabula, Iowa. Farther downstream a diked-off portion of the river known as Spring Lake offers fishing and bird-watching. Continuing on Rte. 84, the drive heads south through flattening plains. Just outside of Thomson you can buy a slice of fresh watermelon grown in moist, sandy soil near the Mississippi.

7 Thomson Causeway Recreation Area

Situated adjacent to the Upper Mississippi River National Wildlife and Fish Refuge, this little island (managed by the U.S. Army Corps of Engineers) is a peaceful spot for picnicking, camping, and wildlife viewing. Bring your binoculars and be on the lookout; you might see great blue and lesser herons, egrets, beavers, painted turtles, and other water-loving creatures that reside on this appealing sandbar.

The elegant Belvedere Mansion in Galena was built in 1857.

8 Lock and Dam No. 13

One spectacle that rivals the river itself is the sight of a great Mississippi barge "locking through" at one of the 29 locks built by the U.S. Army Corps of Engineers between Minneapolis and Granite City, Illinois. At No. 13 you can view the process from a visitors' observation platform.

9 Fulton

At the north end of Fulton, a riverside town named for the inventor of the steamboat, lies the model pioneer village of Heritage Canyon, complete with smithy and one-room schoolhouse. Before ending at Rapids City, the route stops off at Port Byron, an 1828 steamer town where the Mississippi River Tug Fest is held every August, with teams at either end of a rope stretched across the river—a unique annual celebration of the mighty Mississippi.

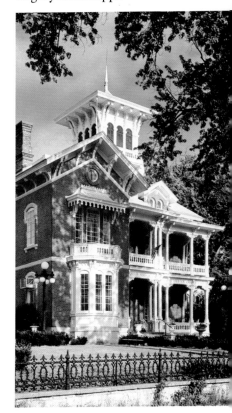

Shawnee Hills Scenic Byway

A zigzagging seam in the rich fabric of southern Illinois, the Shawnee Hills Scenic Byway threads through mellow farmlands, picturesque river towns, and rugged wilderness.

Deep in the heart of Shawnee National Forest, a lengthy ledge forms the perfect launchpad for Burden Falls.

Mention Illinois and most people think of Chicago. The state's attractions, however, go far beyond the urban glamour of its northern reaches, as the beauty of its southern tip clearly proves. The towers here are made of sandstone, not steel, and the thickly wooded slopes of the Shawnee Hills—known to some as the Illinois Ozarks—overlook the beauty of the mighty Ohio and Mississippi rivers.

1 Shawnee National Forest
From its beginning in the flat farmlands around Harrisburg, the drive heads south on Rte. 34 and soon begins to snake through the first line of the Shawnee Hills. This rumpled stretch of countryside, spared by the glaciers that leveled most areas to the north, is part of Shawnee National Forest. In the forest's 270,000 acres, the works of humankind are for the most part left behind, and nature steals the scene with an array of lonely lakes and streams, shady gorges and rocky bluffs, and a host of flowering shrubs and leafy hardwoods. The diversity of landforms, in turn, supports a range of wildlife: from ubiquitous white-tailed deer to waterfowl, wild turkeys, and even bobcats.

Miles of roads and trails create a web of opportunity for visitors to follow, allowing access to all but the remotest corners of the forest. Driving and hiking are not the only ways to get about. Some enjoy the area on horseback, while others bring canoes and float silently downstream on the forest's creeks and rivers beneath a cooling green canopy of trees.

2 Garden of the Gods
A few miles past Herod, turn east on Karbers Ridge Road, where tulip poplars, elms, and maples deck the hillsides. The drive then follows a marked turnoff to Garden of the Gods, whose oddly shaped sandstone formations—rounded, grooved, and streaked with crimson and orange—lie strewn and scattered about like toys left behind by some playful giant.

Names such as Mushroom Rock, Anvil Rock, and Devils Smokestack help conjure up a picture of these fanciful towers, overhangs, and balanced boulders. To understand their origin, though, one must go back millions of years to a time when this region formed the bed of an inland sea. The water eventually receded, leaving behind sandy sediments that compacted into stone. Faults in the earth's crust then exposed the rocks to the elements, and ever since, wind, water, and other erosive forces have been sculpting the sandstone into these outlandish forms.

3 Pounds Hollow Recreation Area
As Karbers Ridge Road meanders eastward, it passes the Rim Rock National Recreation Trail, which

:::::: Trip Tips ::::::

Length: About 100 miles, plus side trips.

When to go: Pleasant year-round, but best from spring through fall.

Nearby attractions: Burden Falls Wilderness Area, southwest of Mitchellsville. Old Shawneetown, historic town with a few restored buildings, Rte. 13 at Ohio River.

Further information: Shawnee National Forest, 50 Hwy. 145 South, Harrisburg, IL 62946; tel. 800-699-6637, www.fs.fed.us/r9/forests/shawnee.

curves beside an ancient Indian wall and continues along the top of an escarpment. The view overlooks the region's crown jewel: Pounds Hollow Lake, reached by an access road farther ahead on Karbers Ridge Road. The tree-lined drive follows a ridge top on its way down to the lake and the Pounds Hollow Recreation Area, where swimming, camping, and fishing are some of the diversions available to visitors.

4 Cave-in-Rock State Park

The drive veers to the south as it follows Rte. 1 to the Ohio River and Cave-in-Rock State Park, which offers campgrounds, overlooks of the waterway, and trails that wend through groves of oak and hickory trees. Though peaceful today, this spot was once a hideout for river pirates, who used the park's namesake—a 160-foot-deep cave in a limestone bluff—as a den in the decades following the Revolutionary War. The bandits lured into the cave early pioneers rafting down the Ohio River, then took their possessions—and sometimes their lives. By the mid-1800s the villains had been apprehended and brought to justice, and the cave enjoyed a more respectable role as a refuge from inclement weather for latter-day travelers.

For a different perspective on the state park, take a cruise aboard a ferry that departs from the nearby town of Cave-in-Rock. Like old-time travelers, passengers can view the chalky limestone cliff and the opening of the cave as they cross the Ohio River.

5 Tower Rock

The drive briefly backtracks, then heads west on Rte. 146, a gently meandering highway that proves anew that travel at its best is much more than just a journey between two points. Miles of rolling farmland border the two-lane road, which also passes stately stands of maples and oaks. For camping and for unobstructed views of the Ohio River, take the turnoff to Tower Rock. The giant cliff—it rises 160 feet above water level—is the tallest bluff on the Illinois bank of the Ohio River.

6 Elizabethtown

Looking at the river today, one is likely to see many sleek pleasure boats—a marked contrast to times past when the only craft would have been steam-powered vessels and makeshift rafts. In those days travelers and pilotmen often stopped at Elizabethtown to provision their barges and escape the rigors of river life, perhaps spending the night at the Rose Hotel.

Opened in 1812, the Rose was first a boarding house, then a hotel that was once the pride of southern Illinois; today the completely refurbished hotel—a national historic landmark operated by the Illinois Historic Preservation Agency—continues to provide lodging as a bed-and-breakfast. Relaxing on its veranda, visitors can dream of the past as they watch the river glide by just yards away.

Rosiclare, yet another rustic river town, lies a few miles to the southwest. A century ago, if you wanted to cross its Main Street, chances are you would have had to wait for a passing wagon laden with either coal or fluorspar. Today fluorspar, a mineral chiefly used in glassmaking, is still mined in Rosiclare, though many of the region's mines have been closed down.

7 Illinois Iron Furnace

In a wooded valley northwest of Elizabethtown stands the Illinois Iron Furnace, a massive smelter originally built about 1838 and restored in 1967. It produced pig iron, which was shipped out for further refinement and, according to local legend, was used in cannons and ironclads during the Civil War. Today the grounds around the historic furnace attract picnickers, who can walk beside the scenic Big Creek.

8 Golconda

Handsome 19th-century architecture throughout Golconda testifies to the town's glory days when its commerce on the Ohio River brought vast riches. Although trade has long since peaked, fishermen still find plenty of rewards here as they cast off the docks at the local marina for bass, bluegills, sunfish, and catfish.

Recalling a sad chapter from the past, a historical marker just outside town indicates the route of the so-called Trail of Tears. Thousands of Cherokees, escorted by the army, crossed the river here in the fall and winter of 1838–39 on their way to reservation lands in Oklahoma. The hardships encountered on the 1,200-mile journey—lack of food and brutal cold—proved unbearable for many, and some 4,000 Cherokee people perished.

9 Smithland Locks and Dam

Pioneers and the Ohio River had at least one thing in common: both were traveling west. But even then it was obvious that the waterway needed to be tamed, and today the Smithland Locks are just one link in a system of 20 locks and dams that slow the river into a series of steplike pools. A visitor center tells about the locks, which you can observe as huge barges pass through, and it traces the history of the Ohio River and the impact it has had on the surrounding states of Illinois and Kentucky.

Kansas East and West

Familiar icons of the Old West—from covered wagons and cattle drives to Indians and bison—come to mind on this drive paralleling the Santa Fe Trail across Kansas.

It may once have been "Queen of the Cowtowns," but Dodge City is fun to visit today.

Untold thousands of iron-rimmed wagon wheels rolled along the Santa Fe Trail in the 19th century, traversing a seemingly endless prairie. Today travelers on Rte. 56, which skirts a segment of the trail, can explore this historic route while savoring the silence of the open range.

1 Santa Fe Trail

In the mid-19th century, the Santa Fe Trail linked Independence, Missouri, with New Mexican trading partners far to the southwest. For about six decades, wagons laden with wares lumbered the 900 miles between Independence and Santa Fe, slowed only now and then by outbreaks of war. In 1866, the peak year for traffic on the trail, some 5,000 wagons rumbled along the popular and well-worn route, now a National Historic Trail.

This scenic drive traces a portion of the Trail—from the outskirts of Kansas City west across most of Kansas to Dodge City. The drive begins in the Kansas City suburb of Olathe, where tree-shaded streets are lined with stately Victorian homes. Here visitors can stroll through the restored Mahaffie Stagecoach Stop and Farm, once a frontier transportation stop. Nearby, at the Prairie Center, acres of wildflowers shimmer in summer amid a billowing blanket of tall green grasses. In Edgerton, southwest of Olathe, the meticulously restored one-room Lanesfield School recalls a now-bygone era, and a half-mile-long nature trail weaves through the prairie.

From Rte. 56 between Edgerton and Baldwin City, turn south at the Black Jack historical marker to reach the Ivan Boyd Prairie Preserve. Here you'll find indelible reminders of the droves of freight wagons that once rolled westward: deep ruts etched into the ground, still evident a century after the last wagons passed over these plains.

2 Council Grove

The 75 miles separating Baldwin City and Council Grove belie the Kansas reputation for flatness. In this part of the state, Rte. 56 sails across rolling farmland and into the more rugged, open grassland of the Flint Hills.

Council Grove played a major role in the growth of the Santa Fe Trail. In 1825 Osage chiefs and negotiators for the U.S. government signed a treaty here that granted whites safe passage through Indian lands. The oak tree beneath which the two groups met survived until a violent windstorm toppled it in 1958, but the city has preserved its stump as a historic shrine.

3 Marion Lake

West of Council Grove you'll enter the Grand River valley, the southern margin of Kansas's Lake Country. As you motor toward Marion on Rte. 56/77, crossing streams bordered by sycamores, redbuds, cottonwoods, and cedars, try to imagine making this trip 150 years ago. In those days travel

Pelicans migrate to Kansas wetlands.

on the Santa Fe Trail was tough even when the weather was good, but it became downright dangerous when the skies opened up and the rivers rose. A cloudburst a century ago could easily slow a caravan to a crawl as wagon wheels sank axle-deep into the mud. Worse, fording rivers such as the Cottonwood or the Arkansas could be fraught with peril as the lazy waters became swollen torrents.

To help control flooding in the 20th century, the strategically placed dam for Marion Lake was constructed north of Marion in the 1960s. Nestled in the lovely Cottonwood River valley, it is surrounded by a network of hiking trails that wander among hardwoods, flowering shrubs, and wildflowers, and its waters offer tempting opportunities for swimmers, boaters, and anglers.

West of Marion the drive eases into the little Mennonite community of Hillsboro. Be sure to visit the Pioneer Adobe House, built by Mennonite settlers in 1876. The home, constructed of adobe bricks, is a fine example of the resourceful use of prairie materials. Attached to the house is a barn filled with displays relating to pioneer life.

4 Maxwell Wildlife Refuge

It might have begun with a low murmur, like the rumble of far-off thunder. Then the ground would tremble, suggesting an earthquake. But soon it became clear that the sound belonged to neither storm nor quake, but to the pounding hooves of an approaching herd of

bison—the occasional companion of the wagons rolling along the Santa Fe Trail. Some 60 to 75 million bison once roamed the prairies, each bull weighing up to 2,000 pounds. Now only a tiny fraction of that number remains, and about 200 bison wander the 2,200 acres at Maxwell Wildlife Refuge six miles north of Canton on Rte. 86. After touring the preserve, return to Rte. 56 and continue west to McPherson. At Maple Street, a block past Main Street, you can glimpse the town's venerable limestone courthouse, built in 1894.

5 Quivira National Wildlife Refuge

Pulling out of McPherson, Rte. 56 unspools due west, surrounded by farmland and prairie—a flat expanse stretching to the horizon.

When you reach Lyons, turn south on Rte. 14 to Sterling. The two-lane highway winds through quiet, open countryside dotted with occasional clusters of cottonwoods. At Rte. 484, turn west into Quivira National Wildlife Refuge—the first of two Wetlands of International Importance and a 22,000-acre home to white-tailed deer, black-tailed prairie dogs, beavers, badgers, and more than 250 species of birds, including the exceedingly rare whooping crane.

6 Cheyenne Bottoms

About 13 miles beyond the salt marshes at Quivira's western border, follow Rte. 281 north through Great Bend to Cheyenne Bottoms, sometimes called the Jewel of the Prairie. Here some 41,000 acres of cattails and marshland serve as a major waystation for migrating shorebirds and waterfowl. During the spring and fall migrations, the honks and cries of hundreds of thousands of Canada geese, gulls, mallards, pintails, wigeons, cranes, and other birds make for lively crescendos. Because these waters are set in an enormous basin bordered by surprisingly high bluffs of sandstone, limestone, and clay, visitors entering Cheyenne Bottoms can sometimes hear the cacophonous chorus before laying eyes on the birds themselves.

Bison in Maxwell Wildlife Refuge north of Canton.

7 Fort Larned National Historic Site

Continuing on Rte. 56 to Larned, the drive sidles west on Rte. 156 to the Santa Fe Trail Center, where exhibits depict the Kansas of a century ago. Farther along, amidst the elms and box elders that dot the grassland, are nine buildings that once comprised the U.S. Army's Fort Larned, established in 1859 to garrison troops policing the Santa Fe Trail. The stone quarters here served as shelter for, among others, the then up-and-coming Indian fighter, Lt. Col. George Armstrong Custer.

8 Dodge City

Dodge City's checkered reputation has inspired a cluster of highly colorful nicknames, including the Wickedest Little City in America, Buffalo Capital of the World, and Queen of the Cowtowns. The place still evokes minds-eye images of old-time dance halls and saloons where lawmen Bat Masterson and Wyatt Earp tried to keep order. Commerce played a key role as well: in the 1870s, buffalo hides and cattle by the millions passed through the town as drovers pushed herds to Dodge City from as far away as Texas and Montana.

Nine miles west of Dodge City, on the north side of Rte. 50, a vast swath of deep wagon ruts remains as yet another enduring vestige of the great path that once linked east and west, among the few places where such tracks survive. Though the trail survived the Mexican War, the Civil War, and the Plains Indians Wars, its ox-drawn wagons were no match for the iron horse: when the first locomotive steamed into Santa Fe in 1880, the earthen highway became little more than a dusty memory.

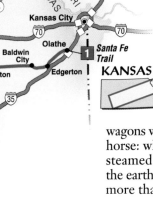

Flint Hills Highlights

A lonely, rolling landscape spotted with lakes, the Flint Hills crinkle the land north to south across the prairies of eastern Kansas—a heartland delight where the pioneer spirit proudly endures.

Covered wagons—like ships plying a sea of prairie rippling in the wind—re-create the pioneer lifestyle in El Dorado.

A Kansas newspaperman, Rolla Clymer, captured the essence of the Flint Hills when he wrote that their "gay colors and the magic softness of their outline...send forth a constant message of repose and quiet and abiding peace." Travelers will find those qualities and much more in this region, where wildflowers spangle prairies lush within a virtual sea of grasses that grow taller than a person can reach.

1 Hollenberg Pony Express Station

As regularly as clockwork in the early 1860s, the silence near the present-day town of Hanover in northeastern Kansas was broken by the thumping of hoofbeats as a dusty Pony Express rider galloped in on his horse. He'd jump to the ground at the Hollenberg Pony Express Station, transfer his saddlebags filled with mail to another mount, then be off again, pausing barely long enough for a drink of water. The scene would be repeated by riders all the way to Sacramento, California—a journey that was completed in just 10 days.

The Hollenberg station, a state historic site on Rte. 243, had other roles as well: the weathered wooden structure also served as a store, tavern, and inn along the Oregon-California Trail. The travails and triumphs of both the riders and the pioneers who passed this way are remembered at the station, which perches on a sweeping grassy knoll surrounded by scattered trees.

2 Tuttle Creek Lake

At Marysville the drive turns south on Rte. 77, then, at Randolph, takes Rte. 16 east to Carnation Road, which links up with Rte. 13 south as it passes Tuttle Creek Lake, a lengthy expanse wedged between grassy hills. Parks dot the scalloped shores, enticing travelers with such pastimes as swimming and camping. The lake is also well stocked, and fishermen try their luck in the many coves for catfish, walleye, sunfish, and bass.

Bald eagles, which winter here roosting in tall cottonwoods, are among the avian anglers that are likewise drawn to Tuttle Creek Lake. Just as thrilling for wildlife watchers are the flocks of white pelicans that pause at the lake to feed and rest during their spring and fall migrations. Soaring majestically, the birds circle silently down from the sky and land on the water with a gentle splash.

3 Konza Prairie

"Eternal prairie and grass, with occasional groups of trees" is the way one visitor described the Flint Hills in 1842. Although most of America's original tallgrass prairie has been lost to cropland, these rolling hills, stretching on for some 200 miles, remain much as they were when the first settlers arrived. Their name hints at the reason:

Trip Tips

Length: About 190 miles.

When to go: Year-round.

Nearby attractions: Fort Riley, military installation with historic buildings and museums, west of Manhattan; Kansas State University, Manhattan.

Further information: Kansas Travel and Tourism Division, 1000 S.W. Jackson St., Suite 100, Topeka, KS 66612; tel. 800-252-6727, www.travelks.com.

the hills are formed of limestone and chert, a hard, fine-grained rock also known as flint. Rough and difficult to plow, the prairielands here thus survived largely intact.

Rte. 901, a side trip off Rte. 177, leads to the headquarters of Konza Prairie, a good place to sample the grassland. Complete with bison, this 8,600-acre preserve was set aside for research use. As a result, much of it is off-limits to visitors except during special events. Visitors, though, are always welcome to walk the preserve's three well-marked trails, which begin at the park headquarters.

The predominant grasses on the prairie are big and little bluestem, along with switchgrass and Indian grass. Growing up to eight feet tall, the grasses are accented in summer with the golden heads of sunflowers, spikes of liatris, coneflowers, compass plants, and countless other wildflowers. Here and there, bur oak, hackberry, green ash, and honey locust trees add a pleasing vertical note.

4 Council Grove Lake

As the drive rolls gently southward along Rte. 177, it crests low ridges blanketed with native grasses—grazing grounds for the region's large, prosperous cattle ranches. Traveling beneath the vast azure

dome of sky, visitors here discover extraordinary solitude. But for the thin gray ribbon of the road, a lone sign of human presence is the long lines of barbed-wire fences extending to the horizon.

The serenity of the scene, however, can vanish quickly when dark thunderheads mushroom overhead. As locals are acutely aware, such clouds mean keeping a wary watch for the whirling funnels of nature's most fearsome windstorms, the tornadoes—most likely to occur in April through June.

Farther along, Rte. 177 parallels the eastern shore of Council Grove Lake, a local favorite for swimming, sailing, and waterskiing. Turnouts let you stretch your legs and enjoy the views. Just to the south, on the banks of the Neosho River, lies the historic town of Council Grove, once a supply point for the Santa Fe Trail.

5 Tallgrass Prairie National Preserve

Local lore has it that S. F. Jones came to Chase County in 1878 "with money sticking out of every pocket." Intending to establish one of the grandest cattle ranches in the country, he soon built an elaborate limestone mansion that left no doubt as to his determination. Even the outbuildings, which include a three-story barn, were made of native limestone (a common building material in this relatively treeless region). Today his ranch is the site of an 11,000-acre national tallgrass prairie preserve, where buffalo and antelope might once again roam, as free as the wind that whips the waves on a boundless inland sea of grass.

Just a few miles south is the town of Strong City. In June, they hold an authentic western rodeo.

6 Cottonwood Falls

If the Chase County Courthouse, with its steep red roof, intricate

ironwork, and clock-tower cupola seems impressive today, imagine the excitement it caused back in 1873. In those days the three-story edifice in Cottonwood Falls must have seemed a picture-book palace come to life. Farmers and ranchers came from miles around to celebrate its completion with a festive ball. Be sure to go inside for a look at the handsome woodwork, especially the spiral staircase with its black-walnut balustrade. Another historic structure worth a look is the Grand Central Hotel.

7 Cassoday

Like contestants before a panel of judges, male prairie chickens gather each spring to "dance" for an audience of potential mates. The grasslands around the little town of Cassoday—the self-styled Prairie Chicken Capital of the World—support a healthy population of these grouses, which have disappeared from much of their former range. Hunters converge on Cassoday in the fall to stalk the elusive fowl, while birders flock here in early spring to catch a glimpse of the birds' ritual.

8 El Dorado Lake

Continuing southward, the drive skims the shores of El Dorado Lake, cupped in the prairie like a glistening blue gem. Another large reservoir, it is adjoined by a park offering many different recreational opportunities.

For recreation of a different sort—a taste of 19th-century pioneer life—contact Flint Hills Overland Wagon Trips in El Dorado or Country Boy

Carriages & Prairie Adventures in Newton. On selected weekends in the summertime, passengers caravan in covered wagons, stopping for a campfire dinner and a night under the stars. After a hearty breakfast comes a return to the trail, where wagon wheels play a creaky counterpoint to the meadowlark's whistled melody.

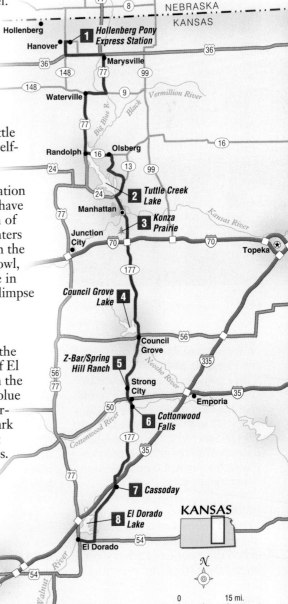

Missouri Rhineland

Reminiscent of an Old World pastoral, this splendidly secluded river valley is embellished with gentle scenes of German villages, sun-dappled vineyards, and meadows dotted with docile cattle.

Historic downtown St. Charles retains its Germanic-inspired architecture.

Tracing the seductive curves of the Missouri River past cornfields and limestone bluffs, Rte. 94 crosses a once-wild landscape surveyed by Lewis and Clark. If the explorers could visit the region today, they would notice a few changes—among them steel bridges and sleepy towns—but they would still be able to pronounce this fertile patch of central Missouri "most romantic."

1 St. Charles

When French-Canadian settlers arrived here in the 1700s, they called this spot Les Petites Cotes, after "the little hills" on which they built their homes. Although the name has changed—the settlement blossomed into the town known today as St. Charles—the old spirit lives on in the Festival of the Little Hills, a crafts celebration held every year in late August.

At one time, St. Charles was the last outpost for westward-bound pioneers. (It was here that Lewis and Clark launched their historic expedition to the Pacific.) The city also served briefly as Missouri's first state capital. Both key roles undoubtedly stemmed from St. Charles's strategic location on the banks of the Missouri River. Plied by low-slung barges transporting goods from America's interior, this muddy-green waterway parallels Rte. 94 as it exits town, and remains a constant companion for the rest of the drive.

2 August A. Busch Memorial Conservation Area

Among the best ways to discover the varied habitats you will traverse along the drive is to visit this 7,000-acre preserve, located about 10 miles to the west of St. Charles. Numerous trails weave through rolling prairie, white pine forest, and river bottomland—all of them home to thousands of birds. Fleet-footed sandpipers race across the mudflats. Plovers scurry madly to no place in particular, only to halt abruptly and then start up again. And chunky woodcocks, wanderers of the night sky, plummet toward the earth in zigzags, landing gracefully in marshy thickets, where they poke their lengthy bills into the ground in search of earthworms.

At the nearby Weldon Springs Conservation Area, a portion of the 225-mile-long Katy Trail twists along an old rail bed, showcasing a very different assortment of natural attractions—tiger lilies, black-eyed Susans, trumpet vines, and a host of other seasonal wildflowers. On summer weekends the scenery is further brightened by swarms of bicyclists and hikers sporting kaleidoscope tights.

3 Defiance

As it meanders southwest, Rte. 94 enters a hardwood forest thick with maples, elms, hickories, and oaks and rich in frontier lore. Traveling this way in 1804, explorers Meriwether Lewis and William Clark are thought to have visited a then-aged Daniel Boone in his wilderness home, adjacent to Boonesfield Village, a reconstructed 19th-century village. The legendary frontiersman had moved to this isolated spot in the pretty Femme Osage Valley, just north of present-day Defiance. His distinguished four-story, Georgian-style house with a breezy veranda and walnut mantels—a far cry from the rustic cabin one might expect for such a pioneer—stands with many of its original furnishings, providing a worthwhile reason for a detour.

Leaving Defiance, the drive hugs the banks of the Missouri River, following its lazy course through countryside confettied with tidy farmhouses, red barns, white country inns, and fields of corn and soybeans. Along the way, the road ventures now and then across the wooded hills and valleys that form the northernmost reaches of the Ozarks, which are not mountains—despite what many believe—but are the remains of an ancient plateau that, over eons, was dissected by the relentless forces of wind and water.

4 Augusta

Golden vines cascade down the gentle rounded slopes surrounding Augusta, the heart of Missouri River wine country—or Rhineland, as it is sometimes affectionately called. Nostalgic German immigrants, reminded of their beloved Rhine River valley, flocked to the Missouri River in the 1800s, bringing with them their Teutonic architecture, fondness for flowers, and traditional winemaking skills. Back then, when Missouri's vineyards were second only to California's, 11 wineries flourished here—that is, until Prohibition turned off the taps. Several dozen have since reemerged along Missouri's wine region, opening their cellar doors both to judges (who have awarded gold medals to a number of fine vintages) and to visitors. A perfect place to sample some of this prize-winning nectar is the Mt. Pleasant Winery, where a shady veranda overlooks countryside and rivers.

5 Dutzow

As Rte. 94 continues west, it passes through the little German town of Dutzow, founded in 1832 by members of the Berlin Emigration Society. One point of interest that's easy to miss is the cemetery, just down the road, where the earthly remains of Daniel Boone may—or may not—be laid to rest.

Boone's body lay here beside that of his wife for 25 years after his death in 1820. Then the state of Kentucky insisted that its founding father be moved back home. Missouri acquiesced, but some skeptics maintain that Kentucky got the bones of a young slave—a story supported by a forensic expert—while the great backwoodsman remains exactly where he wished, on this hill overlooking his beloved Missouri bottomland.

Boone wasn't the only one lured by the river bottom; farmers love its rich soil as much as

builders appreciate its level terrain. But for those who live close to the river's banks—as pretty as they may be—flooding is a perennial threat. Serving as a poignant reminder is the St. Johns of Pinckney United Church of Christ. Sitting picture-perfect on a river bend three miles past the village of Treloar, it is the only structure in the area that survived the high, raging floodwaters of 1993.

6 Washington

From Dutzow the drive detours south on Rte. 47, crossing the Missouri River to reach Washington. With a population of 14,000, this town is, by local standards, considered something of a metropolis. A bit of history was made here in the 1860s when a woodworker mechanized the manufacturing of corncob pipes. The factory that supplied such aficionados as Mark Twain and Gen. Douglas MacArthur still stands on Front Street, turning out some 4,000 pipes a day.

7 Hermann

Back on Rte. 94, the drive proceeds west until it intersects with Rte. 19, where it once again leaps across the river on its way to Hermann. This flower-decked town with its salmon-colored brick buildings—many of them brightened by lacy white curtains—echoes the tastes of its prim and proper German founders. At the Deutschheim

Daniel Boone Home in Defiance was his final residence.

State Historic Site, two houses filled with original furnishings recall domestic life in the 19th century. History still in the making can be found nearby at Stone Hill, one of Missouri's biggest and oldest vineyards. Wine flows freely and oompah music fills the air during Oktoberfest, the traditional fall harvest celebration.

8 Jefferson City

Passing through one drowsy town after another, the road continues across green velvet countryside dotted with old farms. Some 40 miles beyond Hermann, Rte. 94 approaches Jefferson City, Missouri's genteel capital. Proudly announcing the city's main business and the reason it was first erected in 1826—government—the gray dome of the state capitol building dominates the city's skyline, presiding over modern buildings as well as the 1871 Governor's Mansion and other official buildings.

Missouri Ozarks

Much more than mountains, the Missouri
Ozarks offer a multitude of eye-soothing scenes, from
rushing rivers and bubbling springs to
lush forests, high cliffs, and mysterious caves.

Morning mists rise from Council Bluffs Lake in the Mark Twain National Forest.

Spewing from limestone crevices deep in the subterranean aquifer and gurgling into tranquil pools, the turquoise springs of the Ozark Mountains are among the largest and most plentiful on earth. Remarkably clear, curiously constant, and each with its own personality, they tell a tale as old as the hills that surround them and as lively as the rivers they feed. As you drive through the quiet Ozarks, you'll discover historical settings that seem unchanged from the days of the settlers.

1 Onondaga Cave State Park

On the drive south from I-44 on Rte. H, the rocky slopes and folded hollows on all sides conceal a vast honeycomb of caves and underground streams. Missouri, in fact, boasts a total of some 5,000 grand and small limestone caverns. In the minds of many, Onondaga Cave, the focal point of a state park near Leasburg, is the most spectacular of them all.

It's an excellent place to learn about the secrets of these hidden worlds. The Onondaga Cave's story began about 550 million years ago, when a shallow marine sea covered this entire region. Sediments beneath the sea hardened into limestone and dolomite, and for eons after, either the sea receded or the land was uplifted, percolating groundwater dissolved away the stone, opening flooded underground channels and, as the water levels dropped, the open cavities we call caves.

Water filtering through the semiporous stone then leached out calcium carbonate and deposited it on the walls, floors, and ceilings of Onondaga Cave as the water carrying it evaporated, creating the intricate calcite deposits that decorate it today. As you tour this silent wonderland, lights cast an eerie glow on walls encrusted with cave coral or draped with silky-smooth flowstone. Ceilings are festooned with dripping "soda straws," and lily pad–shaped stones seem to float on the waters' pools.

2 Meramec Spring Park

Once back in the light of day, you can swim, hike, or picnic along the shores of the Meramec River, which flows through Onondaga Cave State Park. Or you can drive to another park, located just a few miles away, that shelters the Meramec's pristine source.

To get there, follow the gravel road out of Onondaga Cave State Park for three miles through the Huzzah Wildlife Area, heading south on Rte. E to the junction with Rte. 8. Then veer west and continue through Steelville to the rugged hills of Maramec Spring Park, named for the largest of the springs that nourish the river. Once the site of a 19th-century mining community, the 1,800-acre park is crisscrossed with nature trails.

Scotch-Irish farmers from the Appalachians began trickling into the Ozarks in the late 1700s, but it was Shawnee Indians who led keen-eyed Ohio businessmen to this area. The Indians had pointed out the "red earth" they used as body paint, and the white men correctly suspected the presence of iron ore. In 1826 the first successful ironworks west of the Mississippi was established here, and it continued to operate for 50 years. One lonely furnace is all that remains today, but the ironworks are recalled at the park's museum.

3 Mark Twain National Forest

The rough-hewn yet city-polished Mark Twain probably never set foot in the 1.5-million-acre forest that bears his name, but you can: turn south on Rte. 19, which dominates much of this drive and serves as the scenic backbone of the Missouri Ozarks. Once you reach Cherryville, continue south on Rte. 49, which snakes into Mark Twain National Forest.

Its rocky slopes and deep, shady hollows—where white-tailed deer

:::::: Trip Tips ::::::

Length: About 310 miles, plus side trips.

When to go: Popular year-round.

Words to the wise: Heavy rains can make rivers rise suddenly, so choose campsites that allow a route for escape. Swim only in clear, calm water and look below the surface for submerged objects.

Nearby attractions: Elephant Rocks State Park, Rte. 21 near Belleview. Clearwater Lake, Rte. 34, east of Garwood. Meramec State Park, Rte. 185 near Sullivan.

Further information: Ozark National Scenic Riverways, Box 490, Van Buren, MO 63965; tel. 573-323-4236. Mark Twain National Forest, 401 Fairgrounds Rd., Rolla, MO 65401; tel. 573-364-4621, www.fs.fed.us /r9/marktwain/.

forage and rabbits dart about—are at their most captivating in spring, when redbuds and dogwoods blossom into pink-and-white clouds beside babbling springs and frothing rivers. In the autumn, hardwoods cast a mantle of reds and golds across the hills.

The national forest is managed for multiple use, which means that interspersed with its trail-laced wilderness areas are bustling resort lakes, grazing lands, active mines, and logging operations. If you had visited these wooded slopes seven decades ago, you would have seen something quite different: a denuded wasteland—the result of clear-cutting—with gravel washing down eroded hillsides into the rivers and streams.

Renewal began in the 1930s when the Civilian Conservation Corps planted millions of pine, hickory, and oak trees. Populations of deer and wild turkey soon grew as they regained their habitats. The waters now teem with bass, bluegills, sunfish, crappies, and catfish, and squirrels, raccoons, and opossums share the trees with 175 species of birds—all in all, a notable environmental success story.

Dillard Mill State Historical Site, one mile south off Rte. 49, is a picturesque spot for a picnic in the recovered forest. Nestled among grassy, pine-topped bluffs overlooking Huzzah Creek, it was built in 1900 and was one of many gristmills that depended on the Ozarks' most plentiful natural resource—free-flowing water—for its power.

4 Indian Trail Conservation Area

Following Rte. 19 southwest from Cherryville to Rte. 117, the drive dips into 13,000-acre Indian Trail State Conservation Area, where the paths once were traveled by two different tribes. Generations of Osage Indians trod stealthily through the woodland, leaving an ancient trail known as the White River Trace. The second forest footpath, tramped out by Indians on their forced march to Oklahoma in 1838, is part of the infamous Trail of Tears, during which thousands of Cherokees died.

5 Montauk State Park

Continuing on Rte. 19 to the town of Salem, the drive turns west onto Rte. 32 and then south again on Rte. 119. This 22-mile side trip along forested ridges atop the Ozark Highlands leads to Montauk State Park, supposedly named by homesick pioneers from Montauk, Long Island, who in the early 1800s settled in this secluded river valley about 35 miles southwest of Indian Trail State Forest.

Here the cold, driving headwaters of the Current River, which emerge steadily from Montauk Springs, provided the water power that ran mills, and several were built in the 19th century. One, a gristmill constructed in 1896, still stands and is open to visitors. The clear, fast-flowing waters also make a perfect home for rainbow trout, attracting anglers to the river from miles around. Just south of the park the river lures paddlers, who consider the Current one of the best canoeing rivers in the Midwest.

6 Ozark National Scenic Riverways

The Current River and its southern tributary, the Jacks Fork, form 130 miles of free-flowing, spring-fed, federally protected waters known as the Ozark National Scenic Riverways. Meandering down narrow valleys, diverted by frequent gravel bars, often no wider than a country road, and varying in depth, the two rivers

Otherworldly formations proliferate in the eerie recesses at Onondaga Cave State Park.

are generally safe and easy to navigate. To ply the waters, canoes, inner tubes, and johnboats (traditional flat-bottomed fishing boats that navigate shallow waters) can be rented along both rivers.

About 30 miles south of Salem on Rte. 19, you can park your car and walk across a bridge for a lovely view of the Current River. Early in the morning it is often draped with low-lying veils of

mist. Later in the day, especially on hot summer weekends, it is crowded with flotillas of fun seekers paddling canoes.

7 Alley Spring

About a half-mile from the bridge that spans the Current River, you'll come to Round Spring. Its waters rise from a circular basin formed by a collapsed cave and then pass under a low natural bridge.

Some 13 miles farther south, beside the Jacks Fork on Rte. 19, the drive reaches Eminence, a hamlet that embodies the home-spun flavor of the Ozarks. Old-timers congregate outside the bank for "spit and whittle" sessions, kids spin on stools as they wait for their ice cream sodas in Winfield's drug store, and Saturday nights resound with bluegrass music at the local Veterans of Foreign Wars hall in this hillside town.

A six-mile jaunt west on Rte. 106 leads to Alley Spring and its historic red rollermill, one of the most photographed sites in the Ozarks. Equally photogenic are the limestone bluffs of the Jacks Fork valley, seen from a foot-bridge that spans the Jacks Fork.

Beyond the bridge a path winds down to the turquoise pool formed by a dam on Alley Spring.

8 Blue Spring

About 12 miles east of Eminence on Rte. 106, along the stretch of the Current River appropriately known as Owls Bend, barred owls and screech owls do indeed perch on high ledges. Here, at the end of a gravel road, in a rocky basin beneath a black-and-buff dolomite cliff, you'll find the deep, dazzling waters of Blue Spring, shimmering like a liquid sapphire.

Of the 1,100 or so springs scattered across Missouri, the largest are in the Ozarks, and many bear simple names that humbly describe their most obvious characteristics. In a state that prides itself on plain speaking, a spring in a round basin is called Round Spring and one whose waters are blue is dubbed Blue Spring. But what a blue it is: pure, serene, and so clear that it invites inspection. Gazing down into its transparent depths, you take a moment to realize that this is not a still pool: millions of gallons of rushing water are surging up toward you from a hidden source some 250 feet below and spilling into the creek. Nurtured by the crystalline waters, a luxuriant carpet of watercress rings the spring's gravelly shore.

9 Big Spring

Big Spring, located farther south on the Current River, is one of the largest single-outlet springs in the world. You can float to it from Blue Spring, but if you're driving, you'll have to loop through the forest on Rtes. 106, 21, and 60. The final four-mile stretch, on Rte. 103 (called Skyline Drive), is dramatic. From the busy fishing and tubing resort of Van Buren, it wriggles south along the top of a ridge with commanding views of the valley.

A massive limestone bluff forms the backdrop for the turbulent spectacle of Big Spring. Its outflow—277 million gallons a day on average, but reaching up to a billion in times of flood—emerges as a gushing white-water river that momentarily calms itself in a huge

Dillard Mill State Historic Site on Huzzah Creek near Dillard.

mile-long canyon before joining the Eleven Point River and more than doubling the river's volume.

11 Grand Gulf State Park

Just north of the Arkansas border, near Thayer, the drive veers west onto Rte. W, a six-mile spur leading to Grand Gulf State Park. As parks go, it's a place of modest size —about 160 acres—but it harbors a fascinating treasure: a narrow, mile-long gulf, or chasm of stone, with vertical walls some 13 stories high. This Little Grand Canyon, as Grand Gulf is sometimes called, provides a visible outline of what was once a system of underground limestone caves whose roofs have long since collapsed. A portion of the ceiling that is still intact forms a natural bridge from which visitors can peer down into the cleft—an unusual glimpse into a hidden recess of the Ozarks, whose subterranean splendors are most often concealed beneath hundreds of feet of limestone. To view this gulf is symbolically to take part of the Ozarks home as a memory of the drive just finished.

Alley Spring, near Eminence, has inviting turquoise-blue waters found in a setting surrounded by limestone bluffs.

basin before racing ahead to its confluence with the even larger Current River.

10 Eleven Point National Scenic River

From Big Spring Rte. 60 winds west through pine and hardwood forests to Winona, where Rte. 19 leads south toward the Eleven Point National Scenic River, one of the lushest areas in Mark Twain National Forest. Rushing rapids alternate with deep, slow-moving sections of river as this 44-mile-long stretch of moving water carves its way past soaring bluffs, wooded valleys, and low-lying pastures.

Wildlife thrives in this protected riverside habitat. Kingfishers scan the water for prey; huge pileated woodpeckers and their smaller downey cousins drum on tree trunks; great blue herons wade beneath aged sycamores that lean out from the shoreline; and portly wild turkeys strut across the forest floor. In springtime blossoming azaleas contribute dashes of bold, spectacular color to a scene that seems painted by a watercolorist's brush.

For a more intimate look at this sylvan paradise, follow the one-mile footpath that leads from a parking area on Rte. 19 to nearby Greer Spring. While some Ozark springs roil, others gush. But versatile Greer Spring does both at the same time. Some of its water bubbles up from the streambed, while the rest surges from the mouth of a dark cave. The spring water then spills through a rocky,

Fall color sweeps the limestone cliffs of Jefferson City.

241

Cherokee Country

*A hilly, wooded realm replete with rivers
and lakes, northeastern Oklahoma offers travelers
a hospitable mix of both history and scenery.*

Day's end at the Grand Lake O' the Cherokees, a good spot for fishing.

An interest in America's Native American heritage certainly enriches a visit to this corner of Oklahoma. The Cherokees, who had farmed and hunted in the southern Appalachians for centuries, were forced by the government to relocate here in the 1830s. On their way thousands succumbed to sickness and cold along a trek that has come to be called the Trail of Tears. Yet those members of the Cherokee nation who survived gallantly began their new lives, at home once again in a spirit-soothing, forested terrain where hope could be reborn.

1 Gore

Several years before the march along the Trail of Tears, some members of the Cherokee tribe, known as the Western Cherokees, were already living in present-day Oklahoma. Their government —a democracy that took the U.S. Constitution as its model—was centered about three miles east of Gore, where a re-creation of the 1829 Cherokee Courthouse can be seen. Also on view at the site are a log cabin from the early 1800s, drawings, early photos, and a collection of tools and other artifacts.

The little town of Gore itself, flourishing as people discover the delights of eastern Oklahoma, serves as gateway to this drive, which leads north on Rte. 100. Rambling through the Cookson Hills, a lush, gently rolling landscape, you'll soon come to Tenkiller Lake and its dam. An overlook, affording far-reaching vistas, lets you preview the scenery before continuing northward.

2 Tenkiller State Park

Big, blue, and beautiful, Tenkiller Lake extends for 34 miles or so, but its shoreline, full of twists and turns, totals about 130 miles—a diverse mix of bluffs, woodlands, manicured lawns, and bathing beaches. Rte. 100 follows along the water's edge, rolls right across the top of the dam, then skirts Tenkiller State Park, one of more than a dozen spots that can serve as convenient bases for camping, fishing, boating, and even scuba diving.

3 Cherokee Heritage Center

Rte. 100, which overlaps here with Rte. 82, roughly parallels the eastern shore of Tenkiller Lake. A few miles before Tahlequah, stop in nearby Park Hill to see the stately Murrell Home, an elaborate mansion built in 1843. Its original owner, a businessman from Virginia, married a Cherokee chief's niece, a union that helped forge a link between Cherokees and the settlers. In addition to touring the sumptuously furnished home, visitors can follow a nature trail through the grounds, green with flowery gardens, shrubs, and trees.

Follow Rte. 82 through the oak and hickory forest to the Cherokee Heritage Center in Tahlequah. One could easily spend a whole day at the complex: the Cherokee National Museum offers exhibits on tribal life, both past and present, a re-created village depicts life in the 1500s, and actors at an outdoor theater dramatize the tragedy of the Trail of Tears.

4 Tahlequah

More Cherokee history awaits in nearby Tahlequah, where marchers on the Trail of Tears ended their journey. Here the tribe's eastern and western branches joined hands and crafted a constitution for the Cherokee nation. The area's first newspaper, the *Cherokee Advocate*, was published in town, offering its readers articles in both the newly created Cherokee written language and English. Self-guiding tours of Tahlequah are available; stops along the way include the Old Cherokee National Capitol, the Cherokee Supreme Court Building, and the campus of Northeastern State University, with its restored 1889 Cherokee National Female Seminary Hall.

5 Illinois River

The meandering channel of the Illinois River—born in the nearby Ozarks of Arkansas—accompanies scenic Rte. 10 northeast. In the spring, redbud and dogwood trees, bursting with blooms, make the stretch particularly pleasing. Come summertime, the big attraction is the river itself: fairly tame, the

Rafts, canoes, kayaks, and free swimmers dot the Illinois River, a popular spot for leisurely float trips.

> ### :::::: Trip Tips ::::::
>
> **Length:** About 130 miles, plus side trips.
>
> **When to go:** Year-round, but best conditions occur from April to October.
>
> **Nearby attraction:** Sequoyah's Home Site, log cabin built by the genius inventor of the Cherokee alphabet and namesake to the world's largest trees as well as many geographic locations, northeast of Sallisaw via Rte. 101. Spavinaw State Park, on the shores of Spavinaw Lake, off Rte. 10.
>
> **Further information:** Oklahoma Tourism and Recreation Department, P.O. Box 52002, Oklahoma City, OK 73152; tel. 800-652-6552, www.travelok.com.

Illinois is the perfect avenue for lazy float trips beneath a lofty canopy of sycamore trees.

6 Grand Lake O' the Cherokees

A maze of bays, creeks, and wooded hollows welcomes motorists to yet another watery wonderland: Grand Lake O' the Cherokees. Autumn here, in addition to the seasonal treat of blazing foliage, offers a special thrill: the sight of hundreds of white pelicans cruising in to fish and to make landings on the lake.

To get out on the water yourself, take a narrated cruise aboard the *Cherokee Queen I* or the *Cherokee Queen II*, paddle wheelers just like the ones that used to rule America's inland waterways. The boats depart from Grove, the hub of the region. Har-Ber Village, one of this area's pleasant stopovers, is nestled on the lakeshore a little more than three miles to the west. Its carefully re-created 1800s pioneer town and huge collection of antiques truly help to bring the past era to life for today's visitors.

7 Honey Creek State Park

On the shores of Grand Lake O' the Cherokees and south of grove off Rte. 59 is another Oklahoma jewel, Honey Creek State Park. With camping, fishing, boating, swimming, and waterskiing, it is a popular destination for many locals and out-of-state visitors, both to sample its many attractions and to spend time on the banks of Grand Lake.

8 Twin Bridges State Park

After passing through rolling hills, swing west on Rte. 60. Where the Neosho and Spring rivers feed into Grand Lake O' the Cherokees is Twin Bridges State Park.

Just northwest lies the friendly, homey town of Miami ("my-am-ah" to Oklahomans) and old Rte. 66, the highway of many legends. Another early treasure here is the Coleman Theatre Beautiful, a 1929 vaudeville showplace for many performers, among them Oklahoma's own native son, Will Rogers. The master of homespun humor was himself part Cherokee, and his life, though cut short by tragedy, was a colorful example of how Cherokee heritage in eastern Oklahoma is woven into the broader fabric of American life.

Talimena Scenic Byway

In this woodland world of dwarf trees
and gigantic vistas, civilization seems far removed,
and the clouds seem close enough to touch.

The Talimena Scenic Byway spans mountain peaks from Talihina to Arkansas.

One of the first highways to be designated a scenic byway by the U.S. Forest Service, the Talimena Scenic Byway crosses the Ouachita Mountains (pronounced *WASH-i-taw*), whose ridges extend across the Oklahoma-Arkansas border. Skimming the crests of these elongated hills, the drive dips and loops like a roller coaster, often rising to overlooks with views of steep slopes, narrow valleys, and a nearly seamless carpet of trees. The Ouachitas—the name is taken from a Caddoan word that means "good hunting grounds"—are relatively modest in height, topping off under 2,700 feet. Yet they seem to tower over the surrounding ter-

rain, making visitors feel that they are indeed on top of the world.

1 Talihina
The ping of hammers on metal spikes rang through the woods like an alarm call in 1888, when the Frisco Railroad pushed its tracks through these rugged hills. The Choctaw Indians knew that the coming of the "little houses all hooked together" signaled yet another change in their traditional way of life; some 50 years earlier, they had been forced to leave their ancestral homeland east of the Mississippi and resettle in what was then designated Indian Terri-

tory. The Choctaws called the rail line *talihina*, meaning "iron road," and the name stuck to this track-side community. When Indian Territory officially became a state in 1907, two Choctaw phrases meaning "red people" were put together to form its name: Oklahoma. Similarly, the word *Talimena* grew out of the names of the towns at opposite ends of the rail line—Talihina and Mena.

2 Ouachita National Forest
Traveling east on Rte. 271, you'll soon reach Talimena State Park, just inside the boundary of Ouachita National Forest. Just ahead, where Rte. 271 intersects with Rte. 1, lies the West End Visitor Center, where you can get a map and information on overlooks and recreation areas along the drive. The Talimena Scenic Byway officially begins here, then continues all the way into Arkansas.

Some 480 miles of superb hiking trails crisscross the forest, including the well-known Ouachita National Recreation Trail, which begins at Talimena State Park and runs 225 miles to the outskirts of Little Rock, Arkansas. Paralleling parts of the drive's route, the trail leads backpackers through some of the roughest, wildest, loneliest terrain to be found in the region. Ouachita National Forest can also be ex-

plored by canoe. Float trips along the Ouachita River begin at two sites: Pencil Bluff and Mt. Ida.

3 Winding Stair Mountain
As Rte. 1 climbs the thick, forest-covered flank of Winding Stair Mountain to the ridge top, it encounters not only a landscape of steep-sided mountains and compact valleys but also evidence of one of the greatest cataclysms ever to occur in North America. More than 200 million years ago, a continental plate "crashed" into the southern edge of this region, sliding beneath it with such force that the earth's surface was folded into

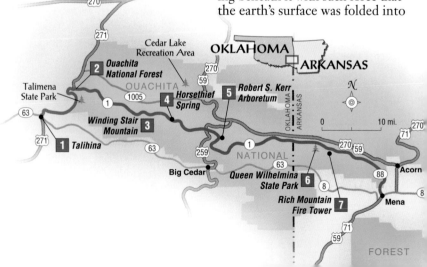

long, narrow ridges. As a result, the Ouachita Mountains (one of the oldest landmasses in America) stretch east to west—unusual for this continent, where nearly all other ranges run north to south.

Despite its abundance of lovely scenery and varied attractions, Ouachita National Forest remains a relatively well-kept secret. The oldest (established in 1907) and largest (1.6 million acres) national forest in the South, Ouachita is home to white-tailed deer, bobcats, foxes, and a host of birds, including hooded warblers, great horned owls, and—in winter—golden eagles. In the 1930s the forest was a candidate for national park status, but political issues overruled the region's unquestionable beauty.

4 Horsethief Spring

In the late 1800s bold entrepreneurs operated a thriving—if illegal—business in these parts. They smuggled stolen horses across the Ouachitas to Texas. So blatant were their activities that the route became known as Horsethief Trail; a watering hole where the bandits often camped—now a grassy picnic site—was even dubbed Horsethief Spring. The Anti-Horse-Thief Association, organized at nearby Heavener, put an end to these shenanigans shortly after the turn of the century. Nowadays, the ones drawn to this spot are horse lovers. At Cedar Lake Recreation Area, just north of Horsethief Spring, an equestrian camp adjoins a trail system that extends more than 200 miles through the countryside.

5 Robert S. Kerr Arboretum

Sandy soil underlying the Ouachitas favors the growth of pine forests, making this area one of the country's leading sources of timber. While shortleaf pine is common, hardwoods—including oak, maple, and elm—are also present in these parts in large

From the air, the Ouachita Mountains resemble wrinkles on a rumpled bedspread.

numbers, providing splashes of red-orange that, in autumn, blaze in bright contrast to the subdued, emerald evergreens. In early spring pink blossoms of redbud, white dogwood blooms, and pale yellow buckeye flowers create lacy swirls of color in the woods, delighting the eye.

For an informative introduction to the many types of trees, shrubs, and flowers that are found in the Ouachita Mountain region, visit the Robert S. Kerr Arboretum

and Nature Center, where three well-marked trails focus on soil formation, vegetation, and ecology. Farther along the highway watch the ridge tops for "dwarf" forests of mature oaks, stunted to miniature size by winter's wicked winds and ice storms and twisted by nature into bonsailike sculptures.

6 Queen Wilhelmina State Park

As the drive crosses from Oklahoma into Arkansas, the route number changes along with the state (Rte. 1 becomes Rte. 88), but the views remain as boundless as ever. A few miles beyond the Arkansas state line, 460-acre Queen Wilhelmina State Park and its mountaintop lodge come into view. Investors from the Netherlands built the original structure here in 1898 and named it in honor of their young queen, hoping she would be flattered enough to visit. Wilhelmina never came, however, and the hotel closed after only a few years.

Today's modern facility retains the royal title and enjoys the same panoramic vistas that gave its predecessor the nickname Castle in the Sky. Along the highway near the lodge, lucky travelers might catch a glimpse of a white-tailed deer, a black bear, or one of the scores of different types of birds.

7 Rich Mountain Fire Tower

At 2,681 feet Rich Mountain is the highest peak in Ouachita National Forest. Taking advantage of this lofty location, the Forest Service erected a tall steel tower here to spot fires. Now that helicopters and other aircraft have taken over that task, the site has become a popular picnic spot. As the drive nears its endpoint at Mena, several overlooks offer vistas of the surrounding summits, which stretch toward the horizon like a billowing ocean of green.

Scenic Highway 7

Rolling with the rhythmic rise and fall of the hills and valleys in western Arkansas, this scenic drive is often rated as one of America's top 10.

The overlook at Petit Jean State Park provides grand vistas of the Arkansas River.

Forested slopes appear around almost every new bend along Scenic Highway 7—a route that traverses one national park and two national forests, the Ouachita *(WASH-i-taw)* and the Ozark. Side trips meander farther into the countryside, leading to nature preserves, tall mountain peaks, sparkling lakes, towering waterfalls, and outlandish yet appealing rock formations.

1 Hot Springs

A lively atmosphere pervades the city of Hot Springs, an engaging mix of tree-lined streets, coffee houses, antique shops, art galleries, hotels, and Victorian homes. What especially earns the place its far-flung renown, however, is Hot Springs National Park, where heated, mineral-laden waters flow to the earth's surface at numerous springs. Although the park may be smaller and far less pristine than our grand nature preserves, its unique character and colorful history are pleasing compensations.

A row of ornate bathhouses on Central Avenue (Rte. 7) recalls the early 1900s, when health-seekers traveled to the springs in pursuit of cures. Today only one of the facilities—the Buckstaff—remains open but visitors still come to bathe in its soothing waters and stroll through the landscaped grounds, lush with magnolia trees and fountains. The Fordyce, another of the old bathhouses, operates as a museum and visitor center. In addition to its exhibits on the workings of the springs, the Fordyce details the region's past, especially the city's heyday, when gangsters and movie stars gambled in local casinos.

Secondary roads wind up and down the ZigZag Mountains, the idyllic background for the city and park. One unforgettable drive— with hairpin curves and steep ascents—leads to the observation tower at the crest of Hot Springs Mountain. The view looks out on the dense forests that cover both the nearby and faraway mountains, an especially dazzling sight when autumn colors the leaves.

New to the spa city is breathtaking Garvan Woodland Gardens, located on a wooded peninsula jutting into Lake Hamilton. Its floral landscapes, streams, and waterfalls —as well as hundreds of native and exotic plant species—make a visit well worthwhile.

2 Lake Ouachita State Park

Before continuing on Rte. 7, consider a side trip on Rtes. 270 and 227 to Lake Ouachita. Set amid a forest of pines, the park offers nature talks and tours, cabins, and camping, as well as springs and trails. The lake—large, scalloped with coves, and notable for its cleanliness—is ideal for all sorts of water sports. For those who try fishing, the catch might include bass, bream, trout, and catfish.

3 Ouachita National Forest

Heading north from Hot Springs, Scenic Highway 7 passes souvenir shops, stores offering quartz and other rocks, fruit stands, sparkling creeks, and tree-covered hills. Farther along, the highway carves a course for more than 23 miles through Ouachita National Forest.

Soon after entering these wooded wilds, the drive runs downhill beside Trace Creek, which rushes beneath a canopy of shortleaf pines and hardwood trees. Thousands of wildflowers—orchids, lilies, and irises, among them—also thrive along the road.

Campsites are plentiful, and to while away the day, visitors can be on the watch for such creatures as white-tailed deer, beavers, great blue herons, and wild turkeys. In the morning a chorus of songbirds greets the dawn, and come nighttime, owls and frogs sing their own peculiar brands of music.

4 Holla Bend National Wildlife Refuge

After descending from the rounded hills of the Ouachita Mountains, Rte. 7 wends on to the Arkansas River and the large fertile valley floodplain it has helped to create over millions of years.

At Centerville, head east on Rte. 154 to the turnoff for Holla Bend National Wildlife Refuge, where bobcats, coyotes, beavers, and deer are among year-round denizens.

A waterfall at Garvan Woodland Gardens.

An eight-mile driving tour starts near the Arkansas River and leads past levees, lakes, marshes, farmlands, and forests.

5 Petit Jean State Park

Farther east on Rte. 154, pause for a visit at Petit Jean State Park, a mountaintop preserve that can be explored on a self-guiding auto tour. Among the sights to be seen are a pioneer cabin, panoramic overlooks, and Cedar Falls, where a stream makes a 94-foot plunge into Cedar Creek Canyon.

6 Dardanelle

Back on Rte. 7, beside the Arkansas River, lies the town of Dardanelle. Historic homes, parks, and stately oaks (one of which had set down its roots years before Columbus and his expedition chanced upon the New World) add to the charm of this community.

7 Mt. Nebo State Park

On the way to popular Mt. Nebo State Park, wayside overlooks make for easy viewing along steep and sharply curving Rte. 155. Once at the 1,800-foot summit, hikers have their pick of fine trails and, after a day's exploration, can enjoy swimming or camping.

For a chance to see humans fly like birds, stop at Sunrise Point. Hang gliders, harnessed in kitelike devices, run down the slopes and take off to sail on thermals (wind currents created by rising hot air).

8 Mt. Magazine

The southern border of the broad Arkansas River valley reaches its apex at Mt. Magazine. Its steep slopes, composed mostly of sandstone and shale, rise to an altitude of 2,753 feet, the highest point in the state.

To explore this lofty wilderness, where temperatures during the often hot summer months average about 10°F cooler than in the surrounding lowlands, take scenic Rte. 22 west along Lake Dardanelle, which was created by a dam on the Arkansas River. From the town of Paris, head south on Rte. 309 across the river valley and its fertile farmlands.

The drive then climbs the northern face of Mt. Magazine, where oaks, hickories, and maples grow among the more-numerous shortleaf pines. Adding to the beauty of the scene are the ferns and wildflowers that carpet the forest floor.

At the summit, you'll find the new Mt. Magazine State Park visitor's center that welcomes you to the park, provides information, and offers exhibits. A lodge will be completed on the site in 2006.

In stark contrast to its north face, the southern slopes of the mountain, having a drier climate, support patches of prickly-pear cactus, stunted and twisted oak trees, prairie grass, and occasionally in spring, the purple-petaled Ozark spiderwort.

These rich and varied wildlands harbor many animals—black bears and foxes, opossums and skunks, mockingbirds and whippoorwills, to name just a sampling. Of special note are the middle-toothed land snail—look closely for them in the leaf litter under trees—and the maple-leaved oak tree—two very rare species that survive on the slopes of Mt. Magazine.

9 Ozark National Forest

Once back on Rte. 7, the drive proceeds across the Arkansas River into Russellville, then continues up the northern flank of the Arkansas River valley. Pasturelands, horse farms, and craft and antique shops line the byway. Near the town of Dover, the Ozark Mountains begin to rise, and the drive soon enters Ozark National Forest.

This diverse treasure (it encompasses more than a million acres) contains mountain springs and streams, caves and waterfalls, odd rock formations, and trail-laced forests full of pines, shrubs, and colorful wildflowers.

10 Long Pool Recreation Area

One of the first places to park and enjoy Ozark National Forest, Long Pool is reached via Rtes. 1801 and 1804. Lapping at the

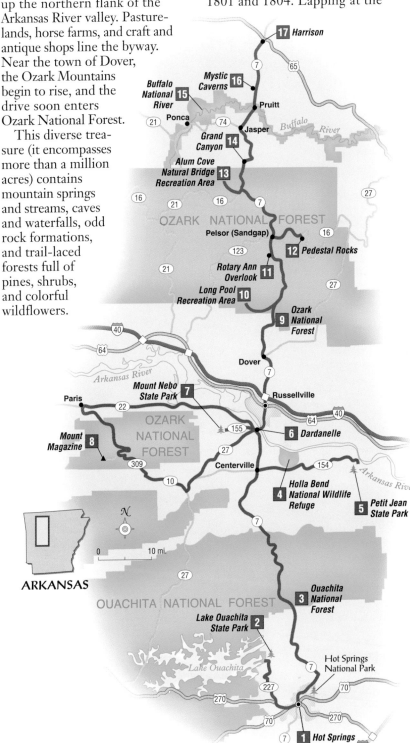

Spring tulips and azaleas paint Garvan Woodland Gardens near Hot Springs.

base of the high bluffs that tower above the banks of Big Piney Creek, the pool is a refreshing swimming hole. After a dip, sample one of the many hiking trails that crisscross the hilly terrain.

11 Rotary Ann Overlook

Scenic Highway 7 slips through Moccasin Gap, climbs even higher into the Ozarks, and then twists and turns to the Rotary Ann Overlook. Back in the 1930s, the wives of Rotary Club members were instrumental in the development of this popular roadside viewing point. It comes complete with picnic facilities, interpretive signs, and far-reaching vistas of the jagged mountains—all things considered, it's a delightful place to admire the forest and stretch the legs.

12 Pedestal Rocks

At the little community of Pelsor, Rte. 16 leads east for about four miles to Pedestal Rocks. A mile-long trail passes by wooded hollows and hillsides to these sandstone formations. Natural forces—millions of years' worth—have carved the rocks so that large boulders rest on pillarlike ones.

13 Alum Cove Natural Bridge Recreation Area

Another side trip, to the west along Rtes. 16 and 1206, traverses the slopes of Henderson Mountain to this recreation area. Here, among craggy hillsides, the combined actions of wind, water, and gravity have transformed a huge mass of sandstone into an imposing natural bridge. With a total span of about 130 feet, the bridge averages 20 feet in width.

A nature trail crosses the bridge, overlooking the magnolias and beech trees that flourish below. In spring, blossoming dogwoods—found throughout the region—lend a contrasting brightness to the scene, with their clouds of white flowers resembling snowflakes that refuse to land.

Habitats such as Alum Cove, where overhanging rocks form numerous nooks and crannies, sometimes provide ideal conditions for uncommon species. Botanists for that very reason find this area an exciting place, especially when they come upon French's shooting star, an extremely rare wildflower that flourishes beneath just a few sandstone ledges.

14 Grand Canyon of the Ozarks

Although Rte. 7 soon departs from Ozark National Forest, the splendid scenery is far from ended, for Arkansas's own "Grand Canyon" soon appears. The deep, wide valley, etched by the Buffalo River, teems with wildflowers. Overlooks, especially the one at the Cliff House, provide superb vantage points. The panorama includes red bluffs and the sharply defined Boston Mountains, which give way to smoother and smaller plateaus in the north.

15 Buffalo National River

In a steep descent some six miles in length, the highway slopes down to the town of Jasper and then leads on to the Buffalo National River. Congress declared the waterway the country's first national river in 1972, ensuring that neither dams nor other obstacles would impede its flow or taint its purity.

The river courses for nearly 150 miles through the Ozarks, starting high in the forest and with an outlet where it flows into the White River. Swollen with water after rainstorms, the river occasionally overflows its banks. At other times the dry spells of late summer take their toll and it slows to a trickle.

Towering limestone bluffs jut up in many places from the river's blue-green water. Where no cliffs rise, oak and hickory trees are the predominant cover. Their leaves

Known far and wide as the crossroads of the Ozarks, Harrison's town square is also the center of a bustling district with many craft stores.

and branches cast a patchwork of sun and shadow across the forest floor, where the fertile soil supports a colorful array of wildflowers.

Ponca, one of the best gateways to the national river and the encircling wilds, can be reached via Rte. 74 west. The town is a popular put-in point for canoers and kayakers, and several outfitters offer boats and tours. Just to the north, a

trail leads to Hemmed-in-Hollow, where a veil of water falls 209 feet from the crest of a limestone bluff. To the south lies Lost Valley, a scenic woodland worth visiting.

16 Mystic Caverns

The subterranean wonders of the two caves at Mystic Caverns prove Arkansas's beauty is even found underground. Stalactites hang from

the ceiling, and stalagmites grow upwards from the cave floor. Formations resembling a giant pipe organ and a huge crystal dome are among the other sights that you'll savor on guided tours here.

17 Harrison

A lovely old town square greets visitors to Harrison, known as the crossroads of the Ozarks. Along

its streets, you'll find museums, craft shops, and inviting lodgings.

For a change of scenery, head for Baker Prairie, west of town. A remnant of a once-huge grassland, the prairie offers serenity and wide-open spaces in which to picnic and wander trails—brightened from March until October by a riot of wildflowers that colors the meadows in a rainbow of inviting colors.

Big Bend and Beyond

In southwest Texas, where the Rio Grande cradles a region of mountains and desert, travelers will find a land as grand as a ten-gallon hat—Big Bend Country.

Named for the great curve in the Rio Grande where it rounds the southern elbow of Texas, Big Bend Country lies at the heart of an untamed sector of the American Southwest. A land little changed since the days of Spanish conquistadors and Apache warriors, this remote region on the edge of the Chihuahuan Desert is home to sprawling ranches, eerie ghost towns, and one of our largest and least-visited national parks.

1 Balmorhea State Park

Big Bend Country is a land of surprises, and the first one comes not long after the drive begins at the intersection of I-10 and Rte. 17, about 190 miles east of El Paso. As you head south through the desert on Rte. 17, you'll soon reach Balmorhea State Park, which features a welcome oasis—a two-acre concrete swimming pool that was formed by containing the waters of San Solomon Springs. But the pool's size isn't the only thing that makes it unusual. Its bottom features sand, rocks, and native aquatic plants, and its waters teem with freshwater fish that are native to the area. Ten different kinds inhabit these waters, including green sunfish, silvery Mexican tetras, and two endangered species, the Pecos mosquito fish and the Comanche Springs pupfish. Thanks to the pool's crystaline water, swimmers, snorkelers, and divers can observe these creatures at any depth.

2 Fort Davis National Historic Site

Water is a very precious resource in western Texas, so it's not surprising at all that, when the U.S. Army wanted to build a fort to protect westward-bound pioneers from Indian raids, it chose this site on the bank of Limpia Creek. What

Rafters enjoy a quiet moment as they ride the Rio Grande at Santa Elena Canyon.

★ Davis Mountains Scenic Loop

Star Route

Fort Davis is not only the highest town in Texas but also the starting point for a 74-mile scenic side trip through the Davis Mountains. After heading northwest on Rte. 118, turn south on Rte. 166 to loop back to Fort Davis. Along the way you can stop at 2,100-acre Davis Mountains State Park and at the W. J. McDonald Observatory, where visitors can peer through the only world-class telescope in America that's available for public viewing. Call 915-426-3640 at least four months in advance for reservations to use the facility.

does come as a surprise to most visitors is the majesty of its setting. Bordering a parade ground that is about 900 feet long, the fort's restored buildings are silhouetted against the red-rock walls of Hospital Canyon, the remains of an ancient lava flow.

Most of the original wooden structures, dating back to 1854, were burned to the ground by Apache raiders when the fort was abandoned during the Civil War. When it was reactivated in 1867, the new outpost was built with thick walls of stone and adobe that insulated against both the summer's heat and the winter's cold. The fort was closed in 1891, but its buildings proved so durable that they survive to this day. Like troops in full dress uniform, 13 of the former officers' quarters—each adorned simply with a prim white-columned porch—stand beside the parade ground in perfect symmetry. They are a poignant reminder of the soldiers who once marched in formation there during their parade drills.

Enhancing this view from the south rim of the Chisos Mountains are agaves, also called century plants because some varieties take several decades to bloom, then die.

3 Alpine

As befits its high-sounding name, Alpine sits among lofty mountains, several of which top 6,000 feet.

Rising from the rocky land along Rtes. 118 and 90 are two of the range's most prominent pinnacles —Paisano Peak and Mt. Ord— both remnants of ancient volcanic activity. At Marathon the drive turns south on Rte. 385 and winds past the Santiago Mountains into the vast northern Chihuahuan Desert, an expanse of harsh terrain that extends southward from Texas into Mexico.

251

THE CENTRAL STATES

4 Big Bend National Park

All but two percent of Big Bend National Park is covered by desert and desert grassland. But what makes this place so extraordinary is the contrast between this vast, sere territory (Big Bend is about the size of Rhode Island) and the tiny remainder of the park. Within Big Bend the desert exists side by side with two dramatically different environments—those of the Chisos Mountains, which lie at the heart of the park, and the Rio Grande, which rolls along its southern boundary. The result is a world of astonishing variety, an entrancing realm of sandy slopes and grassy fields, deep canyons and towering peaks, tiny springs and one of the longest rivers in North America.

No less varied than the park's terrain is its wildlife. About 1,200 species of plants (including more than 60 kinds of cactus) thrive within its 800,000 acres, as well as 75-odd species of mammals, 66 species of reptiles, and more than 400 kinds of birds—a greater number than are found at any other national park.

As you enter the park at Persimmon Gap (44 miles south of Marathon), it is not uncommon to see mule deer and jackrabbits roaming the roadside and hawks soaring overhead. To the south looms Big Bend's magnificent centerpiece, the Chisos Mountains, crowned by 7,835-foot Emory Peak. Like a green island in a desert sea, the Chisos Range is forested with such high-country trees as Douglas firs, ponderosa pines, and even quaking aspens, isolated here far from their primary ranges. If you arrive in early spring, it's a good idea to take the side road to Dagger Flat. Depending on the timing of recent rainfalls, hundreds of giant dagger yuccas may be in bloom there, each one adorned with massive clusters of gleaming white flowers.

5 Rio Grande Village

At Panther Junction, drive southeast on Hot Springs Road until you reach Dugout Wells, once a ranch and schoolhouse and now a pleasant picnic spot. As the road rambles on toward Rio Grande Village, two of the park's most prominent peaks come into view. Look for aptly named Elephant Tusk off in the distance to the south and, closer to the road, Chilicotal Mountain.

At Rio Grande Village (an excellent spot for bird-watching), a short nature trail loops across the lush floodplain before climbing to a ridge that overlooks the Sierra del Carmen in Mexico and, of course, the endlessly flowing ribbon of the Rio Grande.

Here and elsewhere throughout the park, enjoy the dazzling array of vegetation to be found in this living desert—ubiquitous bluebonnets, fragrant creosote bushes, prickly pear cacti, and the striking sword-shaped leaves of lechuguillas, to name just a few. Returning to Panther Junction, head west on Rte. 118 until you arrive at the turnoff for Basin Drive.

6 Basin Drive

Shaped like a gigantic bowl, the Chisos Basin offers such amenities as a lodge, a campground, and a restaurant. But it's the green surrounding peaks of the Chisos Mountains that make this spot a highlight of the drive. Among the pinnacles towering over the basin is Casa Grande, a monumental stone castle that is truly breathtaking in scale. Like its fellow spires, Casa Grande was formed when molten rock forced its way up through limestone bedrock; much of the limestone was later eroded away, leaving these dramatic summits standing free.

Trails here range from Window View, an easy stroll affording vistas through a break in the basin wall, to strenuous hikes into the highlands. White-tailed deer, mountain lions, and many black bears range through these mountains, but the park's most famous critter is the tiny gray-and-yellow Colima warbler. Naturalists from all over the world trek to Boot Canyon to see this bird, which nests nowhere else in the United States.

7 Ross Maxwell Scenic Drive

Back on Rte. 118, the drive heads west toward Santa Elena Junction, where a turnoff leads south onto the Ross Maxwell Scenic Drive—a 31-mile tour (requiring at least half a day) of some of the park's most striking scenery. Burro Mesa lies to the west, while the mighty Chisos Mountains loom in the east. After a few miles, a view opens up back down and into the basin, with Casa Grande beautifully framed by the so-called Window, a V-shaped cleft in the peaks that is particularly photogenic at sunset.

A few miles beyond Sotol Vista (the last stop for those with trailers and recreational vehicles, both of which are too large to negotiate the sharp curves and steep grades that lie ahead), a spur road leads to a view of Mule Ears Peaks, a pair of pointed hills. As you near the next landmark, 1,000-foot-tall Cerro Castellan, stop at Tuff Canyon, carved millions of years ago by Blue Creek. After visiting Cas-

252

tolon, an old army post that once protected residents from Mexican bandits, follow the paved road to Santa Elena Canyon, about eight miles farther to the west.

8 Santa Elena Canyon

Of all the sublime scenery at Big Bend, the sight that awaits you here may well be the most awesome. Over untold millennia, the gritty, silt-laden Rio Grande has—like a never-ending strip of sandpaper—worn its way through the limestone Mesa de Anguila, carving a narrow chasm with sheer sides

of astonishing height. As you make your way along the trail into Santa Elena Canyon, the walls of the abyss rise hundreds of feet above you like skyscrapers on a city street, until the sky seems like just a thin ribbon high overhead.

As you explore Santa Elena, your companions are likely to include not only ravens, but river rafters. White-water float and canoe trips through this and the park's other canyons, Mariscal and Boquillas, can be arranged through outfitters in nearby towns. Check current water conditions by calling park service staff before departing for the river. Some trips take a few hours; others, several days. But all provide memories that will endure for a lifetime.

9 Terlingua

To exit the park near Maverick, either backtrack along the Ross Maxwell Scenic Drive to Santa Elena Junction and then head west, or follow the Old Maverick Road (a well-graded dirt road that's more direct but sometimes closed after heavy rains). Once outside the park, follow Rte. 170 west until you reach Terlingua. Formerly a thriving mining center, Terlingua is a popular tourist destination.

The town's two biggest claims to fame are its World Championship Chili Cookoff, a boisterous celebration held in early November, and the Cookie Chilloff, a spoof of the event, held in early February.

10 Big Bend Ranch State Park

The fast-growing town of Lajitas is the gateway to the Barton Warnock Environmental Education Center, which showcases the flora and fauna of the Chihuahuan Desert. The facility also serves as a visitor center for the Big Bend Ranch State Park, a 270,000-acre desert garden, which is traversed by the drive. With scenery that rivals that of Big Bend National Park, the park contains—among other types of animals—the smallest and largest bats in America.

11 El Camino del Rio

The ruggedness of the terrain traversed by El Camino del Rio ("The River Road") is underscored by one of the route's early nicknames, Muerte del Burro, meaning "Donkey's Death." At times dropping to within yards of the Rio Grande, then winding into the cliffs above, this highway—once a Spanish trail, later a smuggler's route—is unquestionably one of the state's finest scenic drives. Passing beside steep, heavily eroded bluffs and fancifully shaped rock formations, you begin to understand why ancient Native American legend holds that Big Bend Country is the place where the Great Spirit

dumped all the rocks that were left over after he created the world.

12 Fort Leaton State Historic Site

Built in the late 1840s, this adobe-and-wood structure was the private fortress of Ben Leaton, a trader who ran his empire with such ruthlessness that he earned a host of less-than-flattering nicknames, including scalp-hunter, desperado, and *un mal hombre*—"a bad man." Overlooking the Rio Grande valley, the restored fort recalls frontier days with exhibits, historic artifacts, and tours.

13 Shafter

At Presidio, the drive veers north on Rte. 67 toward Shafter. Just before you reach town, look west for the uncanny likeness of Abraham Lincoln's profile on a nearby mountain. Watch out as well for deerlike pronghorns, which sport tan fur and a distinctive white patch on the rump.

Shafter was once dubbed "the richest acre in Texas" because of the millions of dollars' worth of silver that were extracted from local mines. Today, little remains of the town except crumbling ruins, but veins of the precious metal still run through the surrounding hills.

14 Marfa

Movie buffs may recall that the 1955 classic *Giant* was filmed on a ranch 15 miles outside of Marfa. But West Texans know the town as the home of the mysterious "Marfa ghost lights," strange glowing spots that have baffled watchers and investigators since the 1880s. Explanations have ranged from UFO's to atmospheric disturbances to reflections of automobile headlights, but you can judge for yourself: an official Marfa light-viewing station is located about nine miles east of town on Rte. 90.

Trip Tips

Length: About 450 miles.

When to go: Best from late February through May, October through December.

Nearby airports: Midland (225 miles); El Paso (325 miles); San Antonio (400 miles).

Lodging: Gage Hotel, Marathon; Chisos Mountains Lodge, Big Bend National Park (three-month advance reservations required).

Supplies: Available at Chisos Basin.

Words to the wise: When hiking, wear cool, rugged clothing for protection from prickly plants and take along at least one gallon of water per person per day.

Vehicles: On dirt roads, high-clearance vehicles are necessary to avoid large rocks.

Fuel: Panther Junction, Rio Grande Village.

Nearby attraction: Museum of the Big Bend, Sul Ross State University, Alpine.

Visitor centers: Persimmon Gap, Panther Junction, Rio Grande Village, Chisos Basin.

Further information: Big Bend National Park, P.O. Box 129, TX 79834; tel. 432-477-2251, www.nps.gov/bibe/. Brewster County Tourism Council, P.O. Box 335, Terlingua, TX 79852; tel. 877-244-2363, www.visitbigbend.com.

The Rio Grande west of Big Bend National Park.

Texas Hill Country

Here in the heart of the Lone Star State,
serene backroad byways wander among the sculpted hills
of a land once set atremble by the hooves of longhorns.

The cabin that belonged to rancher Sam Ealy Johnson, President LBJ's grandfather.

Geologists call the uplands west of Austin an eroded plateau. To Texans they're known simply as the Hill Country, and they've been a favorite retreat since pioneer days. Here tree-shaded rivers wind beneath limestone bluffs, their waters pooling at picture-perfect swimming holes. Woodland wildlife ranges from white-tailed deer and wild turkeys to armadillos and endangered songbirds. German and Mexican influences blend with the Texas ranching tradition to form an invigorating potpourri that typi-fies the Southwest region. And all this rich variety is neatly bookended by two of the state's most beautiful and historic cities.

1 San Antonio

If this is your first visit to San Antonio, begin your stay at Hemis Fair Park's 750-foot-high Tower of the Americas—a soaring spire set in a landscaped oasis on the edge of the downtown area. A glass-walled elevator zooms to an observation deck where you can make out the rolling green Hill Country to the northwest. Nearer at hand, as you look down, you will see that the city straddles a fault zone: a long slope dividing the Hill Country from the Gulf Coastal Plain to the southeast.

Back on the ground, you'll soon discover that San Antonio bridges history as well as geography. The Alamo—the little Spanish mission where Texas, in a symbolic sense, was born—is just steps away from the elegant hotels and restaurants that line the River Walk (or Paseo del Río), an immensely popular series of flagstone and cobblestone paths beside the San Antonio River.

In the midst of this thoroughly modern metropolis, reminders of a proud and diverse heritage endure: the Victorian mansions of the King William District; the arts community at La Villita, where adobe and limestone buildings recall one of the city's original settlements; and the venerable churches of San Antonio Missions National Historical Park, including Mission Concepción, Mission San José, and several others.

2 Bandera

Pushing northwest on Rte. 16, the drive glides through San Antonio's suburbs and enters the Hill Country, where the terrain ranges from gently rolling to rugged but is always a delight for the eye. This distinctive landscape was formed in stages: first, a thick layer of limestone (originally sediment deposited on an ancient seabed) was lifted high above the Coastal Plain, creating what geologists call the Edwards Plateau. Rivers and streams then etched deep valleys into the rocky upland, leaving the erosion-resistant hills we see today.

The little town of Bandera, once a center for cattle drives, now celebrates its past by claiming to be the Cowboy Capital of the World. Each year the numerous dude ranches

in Bandera and its environs are visited by thousands of city slickers, who, after a few days on horse-back, leave saddle-sore but mellow, having sampled fresh air, hearty campfire cooking, and the robust flavor of the cowboy life.

3 Utopia

The drive continues west on Rte. FM470, winding among grassy hillsides dotted with junipers and live oaks. White-tailed deer graze near the highway, and in spring and summer, wildflowers decorate the hills and meadows along the way.

Set in the picturesque Sabinal River valley, Utopia is a historic ranching and farming community dating from 1852. In a grove of pecan trees behind the Methodist Church, the town has held outdoor dinners, church revivals, games, and camp meetings since the 1890s —all with a style that can fairly be called utopian.

4 Garner State Park

Imagine yourself in a swimsuit on a hot, lazy afternoon, easing into an oversize inner tube and drifting down a cool, crystal-clear river. Tubing, in fact, is one of the Hill Country's most popular summertime pursuits, and an invigorating place to try it is the Frio ("Cold") River at Garner State Park.

Stately bald cypresses (a species of tree usually more associated with swamps) tower over the Frio, creating shade for the floaters and illustrating a lesson in natural history. The river valleys of the Edwards Plateau are like fingers of America's humid East reaching into territory where the uplands are most definitely part of the drier West. Species from both regions coexist here: pecan and mesquite trees, for example, are neighbors in the Hill Country; and the Carolina wren, an eastern species, sings its tremulous song within earshot of the canyon wren, a western bird. Few places in the country boast such an intriguing diversity of flora and fauna.

5 Lost Maples State Natural Area

The scenery along Rte. FM337 east of Leakey is among the Hill Country's finest. The drive twists through valleys below oak-covered ridges and climbs to panoramic-view-offering heights of the eroded plateau and its many hills.

Where the highway descends toward the Sabinal River, turn north on Rte. FM187 to Lost Maples State Natural Area, by any standard one of the loveliest places in Texas. The "lost" bigtooth maples here are actually relics of a prehistoric age when the climate was wetter and cooler. Surviving in a deep canyon carved by the Sabinal, the maples (along with oaks, walnuts, and other trees) are protected from the hot summer temperatures and drying winds

found throughout the entire Hill country region.

Guadalupe bass, found only in central Texas streams, glide along the rocky Sabinal, while tiny green kingfishers not much bigger than sparrows patrol the river for prey. Rare golden-cheeked warblers and black-capped vireos nest on hillsides above the river. Endangered, these birds symbolize the area's unique natural heritage.

Bluebonnet Fields Forever

One of Texas's most enjoyable spectacles is the kaleidoscope of wildflowers that carpet its roadsides—the result of decades of planning. Beginning in the 1930's, the state harvested tons of seeds from donors and planted them along the highways (thus eliminating mowing expenses). In 1982 one of the program's most ardent champions, Lady Bird Johnson, founded the National Wildflower Research Center in Austin, where visitors can enjoy the sight of such native wildflower species as the Texas bluebonnet, the official state flower (shown here in the scattered company of red Indian paintbrushes).

6 Kerrville

Before turning northeast on State Rte. 16 at Kerrville, stop at the Cowboy Artists of America Museum for a look at historic and recent artwork that captures the romance and vitality of the largely bygone era of open range ranching. Nearby Kerrville-Schreiner State Park, along the Guadalupe River, is a fine spot for a short hike, a picnic, or a refreshing swim.

7 Fredericksburg

Shortly after German immigrants settled here in 1846, the town's leaders offered a peace treaty to their fierce and feared Comanche neighbors. While talks were under way, one family's children became frightened by Indian signal fires on nearby hills. Their mother calmed them by saying that the Easter Rabbit had started the fires to boil eggs for the holiday. To this day,

Fredericksburg celebrates a yearly Easter Fires Pageant in memory of that story—and of the fact that the treaty became the only one in Texas history never to be broken by either side.

Fredericksburg still echoes its strong German influences, from the cuisine in local restaurants to the town's Old World *fachwerk* (timber and stone) architecture. Distinctive "Sunday houses" were

built around the turn of the century by farm families who came to town on weekends to shop and to attend church; many of these simple dwellings have been renovated for modern use, including service as bed-and-breakfast inns.

8 Enchanted Rock State Natural Area

Indians, who heard strange noises and saw eerie lights emanating at

night from this colossal mound of pink granite, believed it was possessed by supernatural powers. Today we know that the sounds are caused by expansion and contraction of the rock, and the illumination results from reflected moonlight—yet Enchanted Rock retains its magical appeal. Geologists call it a batholith and claim it is more than a billion years old. Visitors, with or without scientific interest, are awestruck by its sheer enormity. Encompassing 70 acres and rising to 400 feet in the air, Enchanted Rock is included among the largest monolithic masses of exposed granite in the United States, nearly comparable to Stone Mountain in Georgia. The view from the summit rewards those who hike the trail to its top.

9 Ranch Road 1

President Lyndon B. Johnson, like his fellow Texans, pronounced the Pedernales River as *PURd-'n-allis*. As you drive along Ranch Road 1, which branches north off Rte. 290 and parallels the river into the heart of LBJ country, you'll quickly understand why this land was so beloved by the late presi-

dent. The meandering Pedernales, flanked by rolling pastures and scattered groves of live oaks, seems to be the very embodiment of true pastoral serenity.

10 Lyndon B. Johnson State Historical Park

Cattle that escaped from Spanish ranchers in 18th-century Texas

had to be tough to survive. And so they were—a hardy breed with extralong horns to combat predators, and an ability to thrive on the sparse vegetation. Texas longhorns were popular in pioneer times, but as modern breeds were introduced, their count declined. Mindful of its heritage, Texas now maintains a herd of longhorns

★ Highland Lakes Tour

This lake-hopping excursion follows the chain of man-made gems that stairstep along the Colorado River northwest of Austin. Setting out from Cedar Park on Rte. FM1431, you'll first see serpentine Lake Travis to the south, followed by Lake Marble Falls and Lake Lyndon B. Johnson, the latter ringed by steep hills and domes. Farther along, the drive skirts the south end of giant Lake Buchanan and loops around tiny Inks Lake on Park Road 4 before terminating at Rte. 281.

that thrive at Lyndon B. Johnson State Historical Park.

Another of the park's attractions is the Sauer-Beckmann Farm. Here folks in period costumes demonstrate the daily chores—canning, milking, churning, plowing—of a Texas-German farm family at the turn of the century.

Buses leave from the state park for tours of the LBJ Ranch—the Texas White House—where Johnson conducted official business on his visits home. The route passes the reconstructed house where he was born, a one-room school he attended, and the cemetery where he is buried under a large oak tree.

11 Johnson City

For five years after the Civil War, Sam Ealy Johnson (LBJ's grandfather) drove Texas longhorns up the Chisholm Trail to markets in Kansas, running the business from his ranch near the Pedernales River. When the price of beef

Indians both feared and revered the huge granite dome known as Enchanted Rock.

dropped so low that cattle drives could no longer turn a profit, he returned for good to his home turf.

Here, at a unit of the Lyndon B. Johnson National Historical Park, visitors can browse every part of Sam Johnson's original farmstead. In town, at the visitor center, they can view a film and displays relating to the life and times of LBJ and tour the white Victorian house where the longtime politician spent his formative years. Authentic family furnishings—even toys—create the illusion that the Johnsons have just stepped out, perhaps for a walk down one of the town's quiet, tree-shaded streets.

12 Pedernales Falls State Park

Hill Country geology is plainly written in the landscape at this attractive park on the north side of Rte. FM2766. At the falls the Pedernales cascades down broad slabs of limestone tilted like tables with broken legs—evidence of the Llano Uplift, which long ago raised the Edwards Plateau. Deer and wild turkeys roam the hillsides, and farther downstream there is a fine spot for a refreshing swim.

The short, easy Hill Country Nature Trail, which begins in the park campground and winds down to Twin Falls Overlook, provides a close look at native plants. Mesquite, shin oak, Ashe juniper, Texas persimmon, and sycamore are among the trees you'll see along the way. In spring and summer also

take time to listen for the short, buzzing notes that flow from the golden-cheeked warbler's throat.

13 Austin

Almost fifteen feet higher than the U.S. Capitol in Washington, D.C., the Texas-size state capitol in Austin is the largest in the entire country. Its construction in the 1880s called for some 15,000 railroad carloads of pink Hill Country granite. The immense building is just as imposing indoors, with details in its oak, walnut, cherry, cedar, ash, pine, and mahogany woodwork.

The capitol is open for tours daily; a gallery and balcony on the fourth floor offers visitors impressive views of the finely worked terrazzo tile floor below and the sweeping arch of the rotunda above.

The city of Austin is studded with parks, among them the famed swimming hole at Hamilton Pool; Zilker Park with its formal gardens; Wild Basin Preserve; and nearby McKinney Falls State Park.

The Bob Bullock Texas State History Museum in downtown Austin engages visitors with the compelling story of Texas, using interactive exhibits and an IMAX motion picture as large as the state itself. From its signature Lone Star sculpture out front to a campfire scene with enduring appeal to the westerner in all of us found inside its lobby, the museum brings Texas to life.

For nature lovers an especially intriguing spot is the Congress Avenue Bridge across the Colorado River, south of the city center. Over a million Mexican free-tailed bats live here during the summer months—the largest urban bat colony in the country. Emerging each evening to feed on nocturnal insects, the swirling swarms of tiny mammals create one of the Lone Star State's most wondrous wildlife spectacles.

East Texas Ramble

Sun and surf at the Texas shore mark the start of this drive,
which then heads northward to wooded wilds, sprawling lakes, and historic towns.

Woods and water commingle at Caddo Lake, where bald cypresses stand like sentinels with knobby knees.

Linger awhile in East Texas and you will discover why Stephen Austin, known as the Father of Texas, was so determined to settle the region. But fertile farmlands and forests are only a part of this drive, which also offers sandy beaches along the Gulf of Mexico, saltwater marshes that teem with birds, an Indian reservation, and 19th-century towns.

1 Galveston

A drive down Seawall Boulevard on a summer day quickly reveals the casual, carefree character of Galveston. Hundreds of pedestrians, skaters, and cyclists share the broad sidewalk atop the lengthy seawall that protects the city from stormy seas; anglers cast from rock jetties; and swimmers and sun-bathers enjoy the beach. On the inland side of the street, the windows of inviting boutiques display their wares, and restaurants serve tempting fare.

Yet the resort also happens to be one of the state's most historic places. Just before the turn of the century, Galveston was considered the second-richest city in America, but a disastrous hurricane changed all that in 1900, claiming thousands of lives and destroying most of the buildings. Luckily, some of them survived: the restored 1894 Grand Opera House and 1893 Bishop's Palace both recall the city's early days of glory.

2 Anahuac National Wildlife Refuge

Free of charge, a ferry transports travelers on State Rte. 87 across Galveston Bay to Bolivar Flats Shorebird Sanctuary. Thousands of birds pause to feed and rest along the Bolivar Peninsula during their migrations. From the tiny least sandpiper to pelicans, herons, and roseate spoonbills, they throng the salt marshes and mudflats and fill the air with their constant calls.

For equally rewarding bird-watching, turn north on Rte. 124, then west on Rte. 1985 to the access road for Anahuac National Wildlife Refuge, where more than 30,000 acres of wetlands attract huge flocks of ducks and geese in winter. American alligators share these wetlands with the birds, and the reptiles can often be seen sunning themselves near the refuge's unpaved roads. Be sure to give them plenty of room: they might seem sluggish and lazy as they float on the water as still as logs, but they can run with a surprising speed that they surpass when swimming.

3 Big Thicket National Preserve

Thanks to its richly varied plant life, Big Thicket has earned a special renown among botanists and other observers of nature. Nearly all of East Texas was once covered by this semitropical wilderness—a tangle of woodlands, swamps, bayous, and bogs that few dared to enter. Over time, however, Big Thicket was tamed as farmers and lumbermen moved in. Today only scattered fragments of the original wilds are protected in Big Thicket National Preserve, yet each separate unit is pleasantly evocative of the region's original appearance.

Of particular note are the nearly 1,000 species of flowering plants in the preserve, including 20 kinds of wild orchids and four out of America's five types of insect-eating plants. To learn about the best places for spotting the carnivorous pitcher plants and sundews, stop at the main visitor center, which sits just east of Rte. 69 on Rte. FM420.

4 Alabama-Coushatta Indian Reservation

A side trip to the west on Rte. 190 brings motorists to the home of the Alabama-Coushatta Indians, who have protected 4,600 acres of forest since the mid-1800s. Also preserved here are the tribes' time-honored traditions: visitors can observe traditional dances and the making of authentic handicrafts. If you have time, be sure to take a tour of the area's virgin woodlands.

5 Sam Rayburn Reservoir

After returning to Rte. 69, the drive winds through the rolling countryside to Rte. FM147 and the Sam Rayburn Reservoir. For about two miles the highway skims right across the man-made lake, which is hemmed in by Angelina National Forest, part of what local Texans call the Piney Woods. Several recreational areas dot the lake's shores, and the forest's designated pathway, the Sawmill Hiking Trail, parallels the Neches River as it passes the remains of an early mill and wends beneath towering long-leaf pines, oaks, sweet gums, and beeches—a reminder of East Texas as it was before the advent of large-scale logging.

6 San Augustine

Rte. FM147 soon sweeps into San Augustine, a town that took root as a Spanish mission in 1716. More than a century later, Sam Houston, the man of boundless bravery who led Texas in its fight for independence from Mexico, could be seen striding down the streets here. For a sampling of residential life in that spirited, glamorous era, visitors can tour the Ezekiel Cullen Home, an 1839 mansion.

7 Marshall

Heading north from Tenaha, Rte. 59 passes through Carthage, home of the Texas Country Music Hall of Fame and Tex Ritter Museum. The drive next crosses the Sabine River on the way to Marshall. This community's legacy as one of the first cities in Texas lives on in buildings such as the 1896 Ginocchio Hotel, with Victorian architecture, and Maplecroft, a well-preserved Italianate home built in 1870. The town is also the home of Marshall Pottery and Museum, found 2½ miles south on Rte. FM31. The star attraction in Marshall, though, is its Christmastime Wonderland of Lights: about 6 million bulbs adorn the city in one of the nation's largest and brightest holiday displays.

8 Caddo Lake State Park

Festooned with wispy strands of Spanish moss, bald cypresses tower above the waters of Caddo Lake. Miles of "boat roads" lead down channels in this watery wilderness, where anglers in search of bass and catfish might hear the drumming

:::::: **Trip Tips** ::::::

Length: About 275 miles, plus side trips.

When to go: Spring and fall.

Nearby attractions: Nacogdoches, one of the state's oldest towns, with historic sites and museums. Sabine National Forest, offering wildlife and water sports.

Not to be missed: Dickens Festival (first weekend in December), re-created scenes from Charles Dickens' *A Christmas Carol*, Galveston.

Further information: East Texas Tourism Association, P.O. Box 1592, Longview, TX 75606; tel. 903-757-4444, www.east texasguide.com.

of the pileated woodpecker or the curious "Who-cooks-for-you?" call of the barred owl. The lake itself, geologists say, was created as a result of an earthquake, which formed a natural dam on a bayou. The Caddo Indians, according to legend, were forewarned of the earthquake by the Great Spirit.

9 Jefferson

Few spots in Texas can match Jefferson's nostalgic charm. Among its many restored structures is the Excelsior House Hotel, where the guests have included such notables as Ulysses S. Grant, Rutherford B. Hayes, John Jacob Astor, and Oscar Wilde. Another patron was railroad baron Jay Gould, whose private railcar rests just a few steps from the hotel. Local lore says that Gould prophesied the town's doom when its citizens refused to let his railroad pass through. And Jefferson did in fact undergo a decline—but that very lack of progress places today's visitors on the threshold of Texas as it looked more than 100 years ago.

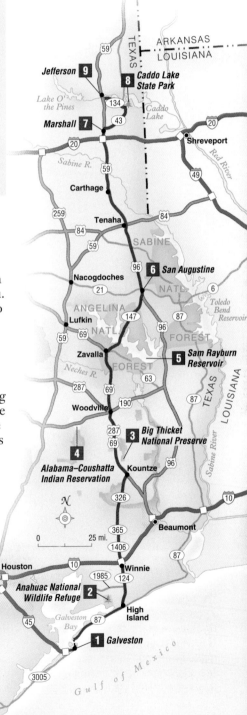

Bayou Byways

Like a hearty gumbo, this southern sojourn brims with zesty delights—coffee-colored bayous, stately sugar plantations, ancient cypress swamps, and more.

The bird sanctuary at Avery Island is home to cattle egrets, here in mating colors.

At 600,000 acres the Atchafalaya Basin is America's largest river swamp—a place so big that when I-10 was built in the early 1970s to make the region more accessible, the challenges of extending a road across soggy land made this stretch of interstate one of the most costly ever. Lazing from New Orleans to Lafayette, this nearby drive leads visitors into that lush, liquid world of slightly exotic surprises: French accents, abundant wildlife, and flavorful food and music found nowhere else in America.

1 Jean Lafitte National Historical Park and Preserve

Crossing the Mississippi River at New Orleans, the Greater New Orleans Bridge soars over grassy embankments that, from above, look not much larger than speed bumps. In fact, these man-made levees, built to protect against flooding, are about 23 feet high—a hint of the water-logged land that lies ahead. Once across the bridge, follow Rte. 90 (the West Bank Expressway) west to Rte. 45, which leads south to the Barataria unit of Jean Lafitte National Historical Park and Preserve.

Set on 8,600 acres of coastal wetlands (a medley of swamps, freshwater marshes, and hardwood forests), the preserve is a fragile yet fertile breeding wildlife ground. On guided tours and float trips, rangers point out snoozing alligators, posed like bumpy logs, and some of the 200-odd species of migratory birds that breed, pass through, or winter here. Five hiking trails weave among bottomland hardwoods, natural levees, a swamp of tupelo gum and bald cypress trees, and a bayou once frequented by Jean Lafitte, the pirate turned patriot.

Leader of a large band of smugglers who prowled the waters of Barataria Bay in the early 1800s, Lafitte was branded a pirate by Louisiana's American governor, who issued a $500 bounty for his arrest. A self-proclaimed privateer —he considered himself licensed to raid ships on the high seas— Lafitte is said to have doubled his offer to anyone who kidnapped the governor. During the War of 1812, the British approached Lafitte for help in capturing New Orleans, but he tipped off the authorities and cast his lot—men, ammunition, rifles, and military advice— with General Andrew Jackson to help him win the Battle of New Orleans. Lafitte later moved his

Star Route

★ Creole Nature Trail

Louisiana boasts some 2.6 million acres of marshland, and you can tour a largely unspoiled portion of it along the Creole Nature Trail, an 85-mile loop that travels past salt domes and rice fields. Starting at Sulphur (about 80 miles west of Lafayette), take Rte. 27 south through the 125,000-acre Sabine National Wildlife Refuge, one of several to be found along the trail. At Holly Beach the drive continues east along the Gulf Coast on Rte. 27/82, accompanied by stands of ancient live oaks on its way to Creole, where it veers sharply northward on Rte. 27, then follows Rte. 14 north and west to Lake Charles.

operation to Texas, leaving behind a rich legacy of treasure tales that still fire the imagination.

2 Kraemer

The drive returns to Rte. 90 and heads southwest. Just beyond Des Allemands, veer off onto Rte. 3199 for a short distance, then turn north on Rte. 307, where sugarcane fields give way to wetlands as you follow the road to Kraemer, a base for alligator processing and swamp tours. As you approach Kraemer, you'll glimpse some of the region's most typical vegetation: floating carpets of duckweed (one of the world's smallest flowering plants), ubiquitous lavender-flowered water hyacinths, and bald cypress trees draped with wispy gray shawls of Spanish moss.

Be on the lookout as well for great blue herons, which can be seen high-stepping through roadside ditches as they stalk minnows or crawfish. When hunting, this beautiful bird stands as motionless as a lawn ornament, with its eyes focused below the water's surface. Suddenly its coiled neck springs forward, and with the aid of its sharp beak, the bird snatches its unsuspecting prey.

3 Houma

Rte. 90 bypasses Houma; take the turn into the town on Rte. 182, crossing one of the 55 bridges that give this seafood center its nickname: the Venice of America. Lots of fishing boats line the waterways, so don't be surprised if one of them sneaks up alongside as you stroll on one of Houma's bayou-hugging streets, which in bygone days were used as towpaths for vessels.

Houma's location at the confluence of seven bayous makes it a major base for swamp tours. If you are willing to tolerate the high humidity, the best time to explore the area's countless waterside wonders is from April through September, when alligators—the premier natural attraction in these parts—are most likely to be spotted. Measuring up to 14 feet in length, these fearsome reptiles patrol the waters like submarines. When winter arrives, the cold weather sends the alligators into hibernation, but it replaces one

eerie presence with another: fog steals across the bayou, rising from the warm water like steam from an oversize kettle.

4 Franklin

At Patterson the drive detours from Rte. 90 onto Rte. 182, where it mimicks the bends of its watery companion, Bayou Teche. As brown and sinuous as the snake from which its name is derived, this 125-mile-long waterway— perhaps the longest of Louisiana's thousands of bayous—was thought so strategic to commerce during the steamboat era that sugar barons built their palatial homes conveniently right alongside it.

As Rte. 182 nears Franklin, you can't help but notice that you are indeed in sugarcane country. In spring rows of newly planted crops fan out from the highway, each stalk yielding about one tablespoon of sugar. In fall, cane trucks heading for the mills slow down traffic, and stalks burned off before they are harvested fill the air with plumes of sweet-smelling smoke.

In town roam beneath tunnels of live oaks, which shade some 400 historic buildings, or follow Irish

Lake Martin is near Breaux Bridge, the self-proclaimed crawfish capital of the world.

Bend Road to Oaklawn Manor. Once the hub of a 12,036-acre sugar plantation, this restored 1837 Greek Revival structure is named for its surrounding groves of live oaks—among the largest in America. As

you amble beneath them in their shade, examine their branches for signs of resurrection ferns. In dry weather these plants shrivel into nondescript brown curls, but rain transforms them into lush, lacy green fronds.

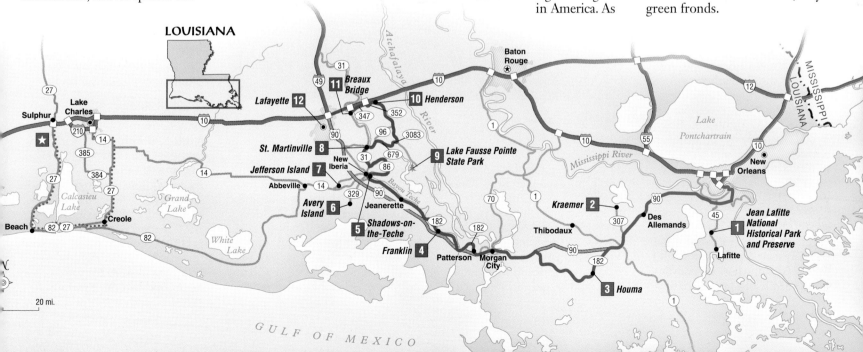

5 Shadows-on-the-Teche

Near Jeanerette several antebellum homes hide like shy southern belles behind fans of magnolias and live oaks. But the real treat lies farther ahead in New Iberia, site of an exquisite 1834 plantation house called Shadows-on-the-Teche. Breaking with tradition, this coral-brick, white-columned mansion stands with its back to the bayou. Beginning in the 1920s the builder's great-grandson, William Weeks Hall, used the estate to entertain celebrities, including the film director Elia Kazan, who described it as "the most beautiful house I've seen in the South."

6 Avery Island

Saucy scenery lies south of New Iberia on Rte. 329 at Avery Island, a lush island of greenery in this region of swamplands. A toll road bisects plots of the peppers used to make Tabasco sauce—a mixture of vinegar, red pepper, and salt that was first bottled in 1868. The company offers tours through glass-walled corridors, which eliminate all but the faintest whiff of this sinus-clearing concoction, a staple of Cajun cuisine.

Secluded paths and gravel roads loop among the compound's more-than-200-acre Jungle Gardens, which feature an egret rookery built on bamboo piers. Once prized for their showy feathers, egrets were hunted nearly to extinction. In 1892 the Tabasco company's founder, E. A. McIlhenny, helped in their recovery by capturing and nurturing seven young birds, which in less than 25 years increased to 20,000—the largest egret colony ever established in America.

7 Jefferson Island

After returning to Rte. 90, head southwest on Rte. 14 toward Jefferson Island, where an oak-lined boulevard leads, appropriately

The Bittersweet Home is a fixture in the historical district of Franklin.

enough, to Live Oak Gardens—25 acres of semitropical gardens bordering Lake Peigneur. More than 1,000 species of flowering plants can be seen here, and in nearby Rip Van Winkle Gardens. Surveying the scene is a graceful Victorian mansion that was once the winter home of Joseph Jefferson, a celebrated American actor.

8 St. Martinville

After leaving Jefferson Island, the drive swings east on Rte. 675, then continues north on Rtes. 86 and 31 until it reaches St. Martinville. The town was established as a military post in 1714 and settled by French expatriates and Spanish soldiers. The Acadians—or Cajuns, as they came to be called when the word was contracted—eventually settled here after being driven out of Nova Scotia by the British in 1755, and have indelibly branded the area with their customs. During the French Revolution so many Royalist refugees came to St. Martinville that it was dubbed Le Petit Paris.

But it is literature, not history, that draws most visitors to St. Martinville, for this charming hamlet is the setting for *Evangeline*, Henry Wadsworth Longfellow's epic poem about star-crossed lovers. The Longfellow-Evangeline State Historic Site, a 157-acre park just north of town, has a museum and visitor center that explain the history of the region's French-speaking peoples, including the colorful Cajuns. Also on the grounds are a reconstruction of a 19th-century plantation and a house that, according to legend, once belonged to Louis Arceneaux, the real-life counterpart of *Evangeline's* hero, Gabriel.

Of all the town's *Evangeline*-related sites, perhaps none is more popular than the Evangeline Oak. Found at the end of Port Street, this ancient moss-draped tree is said to be the place where Emmeline Labiche (whose story inspired Longfellow) met her long-lost fiancé. Nowadays the hoary oak is a shady spot for musicians who sometimes gather to play Cajun tunes beside the bayou.

9 Lake Fausse Pointe State Park

While you hum along with Zydeco and Cajun songs on the radio, continue to Lake Fausse Pointe State Park, site of one of the region's oldest bald cypress groves. To reach the park, take Rtes. 96 and 679 east, Rte. 3083 south, and turn off onto the Atchafalaya Levee Road.

This 6,000-acre recreation area sits on land that once periodically disappeared beneath Atchafalayan floodwaters; levees on the park's eastern border now protect it from such flooding. Acting like a giant sponge, the 15-mile-wide by 70-mile-long Atchafalaya Basin absorbs much of the soil and water runoff of the Mississippi's drainage system. Consequently, this root-snarled habitat nurtures a bonanza of creatures—bass, crappies, frogs, snakes, alligators, black bears, eagles, herons, and ibises, to name just a few.

10 Henderson

Swamp tours of the Atchafalaya Basin shove off from McGee's Landing and Whiskey River Landing in Henderson. At first they journey into a bald cypress graveyard, where severed stumps are all that remain from a stand of 100-foot-tall trees that were logged in the 1930s. The tombstone stumps give this part of the swamp a lake-like appearance, but deeper in the basin, the waters are punctuated by willow, sweetgum, and bald cypress trees. Most tours float beneath the twin spans of I-10,

Jefferson Island's Rip Van Winkle Gardens mimics the tranquil Zen gardens of Japan. The area is noted for its botanical treasures.

:::::: Trip Tips ::::::

Length: About 210 miles, plus side trips.

When to go: Spring and fall.

Words to the wise: If you rent a pirogue (a canoelike boat) for a private swamp tour, be careful; they tip over easily.

Nearby attraction: The French Quarter in New Orleans, a colorful and historic residential district.

Not to be missed: Guided tours of the swamps are available in Kraemer, Houma, and Henderson.

Further information: Lafayette Convention and Visitors Commission, P.O. Box 52066, Lafayette, LA 70505; tel. 800-346-1958, www.lafayettetravel.com.

which was built to link this watery realm with the rest of civilization.

11 Breaux Bridge

According to Cajun legend, when the Acadians left Nova Scotia, the local lobsters grew lonesome and swam after them, becoming so exhausted by the long journey that they shrank to the size of shrimp. But there's nothing modest about the size of the crawfish in Breaux Bridge, located west of Henderson at the end of Rte. 347.

The town calls itself the Crawfish Capital of the World, and a festival held every May underscores the point, causing traffic to swell to a level higher than the Atchafalaya at flood stage. Cajun music, carnival rides, and a parade of floats play second fiddle to crawfish races and, of course, crawfish-eating contests. (The record stands at 33 pounds consumed in one hour.) As the drive nears its end, it heads north out of town on Rte. 31, then leads west on I-10 and south on Rte. 90 to Lafayette.

12 Lafayette

Located in the heart of Cajun country, Lafayette offers a dance card full of activities, ranging from the foot-shuffling that closes various downtown streets to traffic on Friday evenings during spring and fall to the Cajun-style two-stepping that is featured at dance halls every night.

In spring blossoming azaleas lure drivers along the 20-mile Azalea Trail, a well-marked tour that skirts lush private gardens and such landmarks as the Lafayette Museum (once the home of the city's founder). Among the most notable attractions here are murals near Lafayette Centre portraying scenes from Cajun history, and a man-made swamp—complete with alligators—found on the campus of the University of Southwestern Louisiana. At Vermilionville and the Acadian Village—two historical theme parks that are located at different ends of town—the daily life experiences of early Acadian settlers is brought vividly to life by costumed interpreters.

PART

4

The Eastern States

Maine Coast

Although Rte. 1 offers its share of eye-catching delights, the twists and turns
that characterize the coast in this corner of America are best seen from secondary roads
that meander down long peninsulas and across out-of-the-way islands.

Saltbox houses cascade down to the water's edge at the harbor at Blue Hill Peninsula.

Rocky, rugged, and interrupted by few sandy beaches, Maine's craggy midcoast is the legacy of long-gone glaciers. During the ice age, the earth's crust here buckled under the unimaginable weight of the ice cap that once covered the region. When the ice melted, the sea rushed in, transforming valleys into coves and inlets, leaving its mountain ridges exposed as headlands and islands.

Fragrant mixed forests still march right down to seaside in some places, just as they did when Algonquian Indians were the sole inhabitants of this convoluted coast. But elsewhere the scenic grandeur is accented by quaint fishing villages, lonely lighthouses, and vacationers' waterside retreats.

1 Brunswick

The story of Brunswick began in the 1600s, when explorers from Europe recognized its potential as a center for the fur trade and for lumbering. Mills were eventually built to harness the power of the Androscoggin River, and by the late 1700s the town had grown so prosperous that Bowdoin College, the first in Maine, was founded there. Summer music festivals are held on the idyllic, tree-lined campus, and the college's art museum displays works by Winslow Homer, Andrew Wyeth, and other famous painters.

Brunswick also functions as the commercial hub of this region, whose population mushrooms in summer. Explore the town and you will find a traditional village green, Federal-style mansions, seafood restaurants, and an array of antique shops and artists' studios.

2 Bailey Island

Just east of Brunswick, Rte. 24 exits the sometimes traffic-choked Rte. 1 for small towns and natural splendors along a 16-mile run to Bailey Island. Among the cottages it passes is Pearl House, once the summer retreat of famous author Harriet Beecher Stowe.

Slow down at the Cribstone Bridge, a 1,200-foot span linking Orrs and Bailey islands, to notice its unusual construction. Massive granite blocks are arranged in a honeycomb pattern, with gaps that allow the tides and the runoff from spring thaws to rush through without causing damage.

From the docks at Bailey Island, sportfishing excursions depart in search of bluefin tuna, some of which weigh 500 pounds or more. At the island's far tip, a small beach nestles among granite boulders.

3 Bath

Located near the mouth of the Kennebec River, Bath has long

The northern fringe of Maine's coast is a magnet in autumn for lovers of fall color.

been a boat-building center. Visit the Maine Maritime Museum to learn about the industry. More evidence of the city's prosperous maritime past can be seen along Washington Street, where wealthy merchants and captains built their fine mansions.

Lying just before the Carleton Bridge is the sprawling Bath Iron Works, where ships continue to be built. (Traffic can be heavy here, particularly when the shipbuilders get off work in the afternoon.) While in Bath, stop by the revitalized business district, taking special note of the 19th-century storefronts, brick sidewalks, and lampposts along Front Street.

4 Popham Beach State Park

The Kennebec River empties into the sea here, some 150 miles from the source of its headwaters at Moosehead Lake. Sandbars, salt marshes, and a sandy beach are intermingled in this meeting place of fresh- and saltwater. Among the salt-tolerant vegetation that flourishes here is cordgrass, one of the plants characteristic of such salt marshes. Other hardy survivalists able to endure the alkaline conditions include seaside goldenrod, sea lavender, and beach pea, all of which can be seen along the paths that lead to the beach. At the end of a strip of land jutting into the sea, you can also visit never-completed Fort Popham.

5 Reid State Park

Passing through a landscape in which evergreen forest rims the ocean shore, Rte. 127 leads to Reid State Park, an attractive mix of rocky headland, marsh, and dunes. Piping plovers and least terns nest on the park's long beaches, which are salted with grains of feldspar and schist. Among the other minerals found here—don't be surprised if you come across a rock hound peering through a magnifying glass—are quartz, calcite, mica, garnet, and hornblende. Stroll along one of the many paths for an introduction to a rich blend of seaside vegetation, including blackberries, raspberries, meadowsweet, and—be on the lookout for and beware—poison ivy.

6 Wiscasset

In the early 1800s, Wiscasset was the home port for dozens of clipper ships that carried fish and lumber to distant lands. Today, though, with its picture-perfect setting of pretty homes on wooded slopes along the Sheepscot River, it seems hardly surprising that Wiscasset has become a haven for writers and artists.

Although traffic through the center of town can be heavy on summer weekends, the side streets are usually quiet. Among the delights to be sampled there are the old-time courthouse, clapboard mansions, bed-and-breakfast inns, and shops offering antiques, pottery, and artwork.

7 Boothbay Harbor

Once a little fishing village, Boothbay Harbor has evolved through the generations into a bustling summer resort. Windjammers and other craft set out from the quaint waterfront for sightseeing tours of lighthouses, seabirds, whales, seals, and offshore islands. Charter boats offer deep-sea fishing trips, searching the waters for bluefish and tuna. Rte. 96, which heads down to Ocean Point, is a particularly scenic byway, with glimpses of foamy, seething surf and thick pine forests along the way.

8 Damariscotta

The Indians who once farmed and fished here called the area Damariscotta ("meeting place of the alewives"). Every spring these small fish of the herring family swim up the Damariscotta River to spawn. To witness this yearly ritual, stop at the Damariscotta Reversing Falls—so named because the rush of incoming tides is sometimes strong enough to overcome the natural flow of the river.

Many species of birds also make annual migrations to this historic town, with the osprey being perhaps the most impressive. Usually arriving in mid-April and staying through September, these fish-eating hawks have wingspans of up to six feet. Thanks to excellent vision, they can spot prey from far above. The mighty predators then swoop down and plunge right into the water to snatch prey with their razor-sharp talons.

9 Pemaquid Point

Most visitors travel down Rte. 130 to Pemaquid Point for a glimpse of its famous lighthouse, a beacon to sailors since 1827. Also of interest here are the Fishermen's Museum, the Pemaquid Art Gallery, and the surf-pounded rock formations washed by the Atlantic Ocean. Living in tide-swept crevices amidst the stones are green sea urchins and limpets, snail-like mollusks known for their ability to cling steadfastly to the rock even in the most punishing surf.

Christmas Cove, off to the west and reached via Rte. 129, was reportedly visited by Capt. John Smith on Christmas Day in 1614. With its well-protected harbor, this summer hamlet is a favored destination for the many sailboaters who cruise up and down the rugged coast.

10 Waldoboro

Follow coast-hugging Rte. 32 up to charming Waldoboro, which was named for a wealthy Bostonian who tried to start a settlement here in 1748. Many hardships met the German immigrants who arrived with Samuel Waldo, and the community was soon dissolved.

Other adventurers eventually came ashore, however, and Waldoboro has been active in the shipbuilding business ever since. (It launched the world's first five-masted schooner in 1884.) Some 10 miles to the south, the village

A three-masted cutter carves a wake through the swell at Rockland's breakwater.

of Friendship is renowned for the gaff-rigged sloops that bear the town's name.

11 Port Clyde

The drive down the peninsula to Port Clyde passes tiny villages and peaceful, pristine wilds and seashore. Andrew Wyeth, the Amer-

ican painter, spent many boyhood summers here. To this day artists come from all over to find inspiration in the far-reaching vistas of islands, sea, and sky.

Some 12 miles offshore, appearing as little more than a speck in a lovely seascape, is Monhegan Island, which can be reached by ferry from Port Clyde. Although no cars are allowed on the remote and tranquil island, nature trails abound, winding through stands of red spruce and balsam fir to veritable gardens of wildflowers and the crests of wave-battered cliffs towering over the sea.

12 Rockport

In addition to its picturesque harbor and interesting shops, Rockport offers a variety of cultural entertainments. Chamber music concerts are presented weekly in the opera house, and works by well-known local painters hang

Popham Beach's crystalline, chilly waters entice children of all ages.

on the walls at the Maine Coast Artists Gallery. Pictures of a different sort can be viewed at the Maine Photographic Workshops, which also offers evening lectures.

13 Camden Hills State Park

Gray squirrels leaping through the treetops, woodpeckers hacking at the branches in search of insects, a harmless garter snake slithering for cover behind a rock —these are but a few of the animals found at Camden Hills State Park. Nature trails thread through the 5,000-acre refuge, and a toll road ascends Mt. Battie, where, at about 800 feet above the sea, an unobstructed view unfolds before your eye in every direction.

Below is the village of Camden, hugging the deepest part of a cove. Forests dotted with evergreens cloak the slopes that rise from the harbor's edge. These evergreens make a special contribution to the setting, for here as elsewhere along the Maine coast, the fragrance of pine needles mixes with the salty air of the sea to create a memorable sensation.

Camden is also a good place to learn about the region's settlers. The restored 18th-century Conway House, an early homestead complete with barn and blacksmith shop, is well worth a visit.

14 Castine

Farther up the coast—past the pleasant communities of Belfast, Searsport, and Bucksport on the shores of Penobscot Bay—follow Rtes. 175 and 166A to the historic village of Castine. This part of Maine, beginning with the eastern shore of Penobscot Bay and continuing to the Canadian border, is referred to by residents as the Downeast Coast. Here the signs of commercialism begin to thin out. The cottages, barns, meadows, and woodlands along Rte. 166A, for example, look much as they might have some 100 years or more ago.

Centuries-old homes, quiet inns, and grand elm trees line the streets of Castine. Spend some time sitting on the benches that overlook the town's peaceful dock, or take a walking tour of the town to gain insights into the history of the homes and other points of architectural and historical interest.

15 Holbrook Island Sanctuary

Nearby, Rte. 176 passes through rugged, unspoiled countryside and leads to the turnoff for Holbrook Island Sanctuary. An ideal spot for picnics and nature walks, the seaside refuge has some 1,250 acres of varied terrain—from pebble beaches to seaside crests.

Hikers enjoy the salt air and frost, which colors the low-growing foliage as red as the trees on Mt. Battie, near Camden.

16 Stonington

Farther south, Rte. 15 leaps across a narrow suspension bridge to Little Deer Isle, then continues on to land's end in Stonington. In the late 1800s the area was a booming mining center. The distinctive pink granite quarried here can be found in famous structures up and down the East Coast. Today the quarries are active again, though on a much reduced scale.

Town life is now geared mostly toward the sea, as witnessed by a harbor full of trawlers and other fishing vessels. Lobster traps are stacked high on the docks, and canneries are ever ready to process the day's catch. The shops along Main Street offer a variety of well-crafted wares, from pottery to clothing. For a glimpse of inland nature, head east on Indian Point Road to Ames Pond, where the water lilies bloom in pink and white from June to September.

17 Ellsworth

Passing by charming villages, saltwater ponds, meadows, and forest, the coastal highways lead along the eastern shores of the Blue Hill Peninsula to Ellsworth, which is the commercial center for this portion of the Maine coast. The First Congregational Church, with its sky-piercing steeple, is among the town's noteworthy buildings. Another example of outstanding architecture is the 1828 Colonel Black Mansion, which features antique furnishings appropriate to its age, and outstanding views of the Union River that flows alongside it.

Situated on the eastern side of the river is the Stanwood Wildlife Sanctuary, an animal refuge encompassing about 130 acres. The park is a peaceful place, lush with wildflowers, shrubbery, and a varied woodland. Viewing areas in key locations enable visitors to watch the many different species of birds that come to nest near and bathe in the sanctuary's three ponds. The grounds also contain a wildlife recovery center where injured birds find solice and care, and the onetime home of Cordelia Stanwood, a pioneering ornithologist whose efforts at observation and conservation made her quiet refuge a sanctuary for avian visitors and those who love them.

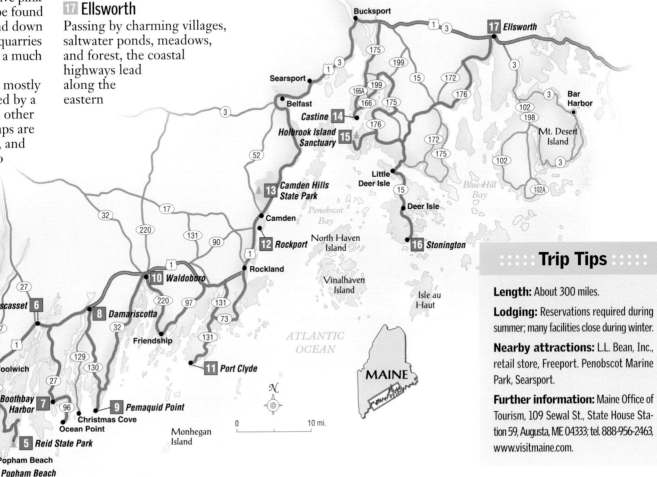

Trip Tips

Length: About 300 miles.

Lodging: Reservations required during summer; many facilities close during winter.

Nearby attractions: L.L. Bean, Inc., retail store, Freeport. Penobscot Marine Park, Searsport.

Further information: Maine Office of Tourism, 109 Sewal St., State House Station 59, Augusta, ME 04333; tel. 888-956-2463, www.visitmaine.com.

Mt. Desert Island

The mosaic of Mt. Desert Island is crafted from the choicest of ingredients—sea-sprayed cliffs, fragrant woodlands, the tallest peak on the eastern coast, and rustic villages that were settled long ago.

Northeast Harbor is a popular waypoint for coastwise sailers and fishermen.

Mt. Desert Island, at some 13 miles wide, ranks as the largest of Maine's myriad islands. A patchwork of picturesque villages dots its jagged coast; founded to reap the harvests of land and sea, today they serve as centers for tourism as well. Mt. Desert's distinguishing centerpiece, though, must surely be Acadia National Park, which occupies roughly half of the island, plus parts of nearby Isle au Haut and a mainland peninsula. Laced with inviting roadways, the park is a soul-satisfying place for savoring an especially dramatic meeting place of land and sea.

1 Hulls Cove Visitor Center

One of the best ways to learn about the mountains, seacoast, and the many animals and plants that can be found in Acadia National Park is to stop at the Hulls Cove visitor center. The wealth of helpful information available there includes maps of the more than 120 miles of trails that thread through the wilds, a film on the park's history, and a scale model of the area.

The beauties of the park, however, come at a price: traffic and crowds. Though one of the smallest of the national parks—some

40,000 acres—Acadia is also among the most visited. Thus it's a good idea to start your day early or to visit during the off-season. Autumn brings dazzling foliage, and winter offers its own very special rewards: cross-country skiing, snowshoeing, snowmobiling, ice fishing, and the stirring sights of seeing the snow-whitened wonderland.

2 Cadillac Mountain

Honed to its present form by long-gone glaciers, the rounded dome of Cadillac Mountain towers some 1,530 feet above the Gulf of Maine, making it the highest point along the whole eastern coast. The view from the peak overlooks not only the majority of Mt. Desert Island but also a vast expanse of sea dotted with countless islands.

Maples, birches, and a variety of evergreens maintain a toehold among the mountain's pink granite rocks, and trails traverse the slopes, occasionally passing huge boulders that seemingly have been

dropped in the middle of nowhere. Called erratics, these stones were transported here from distant peaks by the moving ice of Eocene and Pleistocene glaciers.

3 Park Loop Road

The one-way sector of the 20-mile Park Loop Road hugs the eastern side of the island, with turnouts and parking areas along the way that provide access to viewpoints, trails, and shoreline landmarks.

To gain a quick introduction to many of the park's plants, visit the Wild Gardens of Acadia. Although only about an acre in extent, the gardens are rich in variety, with samplings of native grasses, ferns, mosses, wildflowers, and trees.

Sand Beach, snugly set between headlands and forests, is a favored spot with sunbathers and swimmers (who must be game enough to brave the chilly ocean temperatures). A trail from the parking lot explores a small peninsula and leads to Great Head,

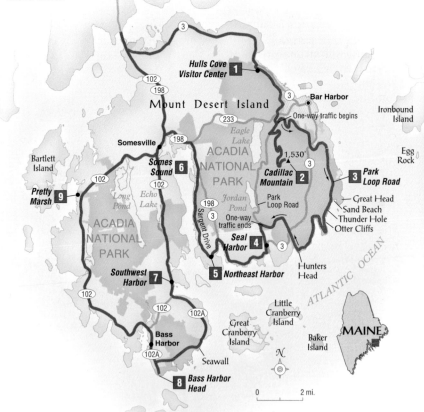

a volcanic rock that looms nearly 150 feet above the ocean.

Farther south, a trail leads to Thunder Hole, a chasm carved into the cliffs by the sometimes raging sea. When strong surf teams with an incoming tide, a booming blast resounds from the hole.

Another trail parallels Otter Cliffs, precipitous granite rocks that rise 110 feet. The view looks out on Egg Rock Island and its lighthouse, as well as Nova Scotia, which appears as a speck on the horizon. Wild roses grow here, and arctic plants thrive in the cool seaside climate. The ocean below also teems with life—harbor seals, starfish, rock crabs, barnacles, squid, herring, and many other marine denizens. Although many of the land animals stay out of sight for safety's sake, attentive observers might be rewarded with glimpses of foxes, coyotes, snowshoe hares, great horned owls, and hawks.

4 Seal Harbor

Continuing past Hunters Head and densely forested hillsides, the one-way section of the loop road soon joins two-way traffic. At that juncture the drive turns to the south and, after a short stretch, enters Seal Harbor, a pretty town with elegant homes and a sandy beach. At the intersection with Rte. 3, turn to the west for a seaside drive to Northeast Harbor, stopping on the way at the informal gardens surrounding Thuya Lodge in Asticou.

5 Northeast Harbor

With its large marina, beautiful homes, and upscale art galleries, the village of Northeast Harbor has long been a mecca for sailboaters and well-to-do vacationers. Throughout the warmer months, craft by the hundreds anchor in the harbor, periodically heading out to the ocean for regattas. Ferries also ply the choppy seas, shuttling to the historic Cranberry Isles.

6 Somes Sound

A fjord that nearly splits the island in two, Somes Sound is the star attraction along Sargent Drive, a spectacular route (open to passenger cars only) that traverses the clifftops on the waterway's eastern shore. Here, thousands of years ago, a glacier deepened a river valley, and then, as the ice melted, seawater flooded the deep gorge. A turnoff near the narrowest part of the fjord affords fine views of this sliver-shaped stretch of sea as well as Acadia Mountain, which rises beyond the opposite shore.

Near the head of the sound on Rte. 102 lies quaint Somesville. Founded in 1761, the island's oldest settlement has many examples of early New England architecture. Set along tree-lined brooks and beside quiet ponds, the buildings have a timeless charm.

As Rte. 102 leads down the western flank of Somes Sound, a side road exits to Echo Lake Beach, a popular spot for swimming. A short and fairly easy trail through

The wave-sculpted shoreline near Thunder Hole, south of Great Head and Sand Beach.

stands of firs and spruces climbs to the crest of Beech Mountain, where hikers can enjoy uninterrupted views of the lake and hills.

7 Southwest Harbor

A quiet fishing village with shops, galleries, and restaurants along its main street, Southwest Harbor is known for its maritime history and its museums. One of them, the Oceanarium, has exhibits on marine life and offers up-close glimpses of the animals that live in the local seas and tidepools.

Farther along, the town of Seawall looks out on the Cranberry Isles. The only creatures that flock here in large numbers are seabirds, and this corner of the park is an enjoyable spot to pass a quiet day.

8 Bass Harbor Head

Bass Harbor Head, at the southernmost point of Mt. Desert Island, is one of the finer spots for watching the sunset. A white-painted lighthouse crowns the rocky, sea-washed ledge here. Its flashing red light, visible as far as 13 miles away, has been guiding sailors safely into port through the nearby rocky reefs since 1858.

9 Pretty Marsh

After passing through the little fishing community of Bass Harbor, the drive follows the western branch of Rte. 102 to Pretty Marsh. A trail there switches back and forth through thick forests to the bayshore, an idyllic spot for picnics and bird-watching.

Seaway Trail

Tracing the northern border of New York State, this journey hugs the shores of two mighty rivers and one of the Great Lakes, which, in tandem, help link the Midwest to the sea.

The power of falling water is nowhere more evident than at Niagara Falls.

Wending southwestward along the island-dotted St. Lawrence River, the breezy coast of Lake Ontario, and the steep banks of the Niagara River, this waterside ramble terminates at the world-famous falls. Along the way, immense dams, power plants, and oceangoing ships contrast with sleepy rural hamlets, bountiful orchards, and historic lighthouses skirted by sprightly pleasure boats.

1 Dwight D. Eisenhower Lock

From Rooseveltown the scenic drive heads toward Massena on Rte. 37, veering north on Rte. 131 to this oft-visited exemplar of naval engineering. In 1959 Queen Elizabeth II and President Dwight D. Eisenhower stood on the viewing platform here to dedicate the St. Lawrence Seaway—a vast system of interconnecting channels, locks, and lakes—which opened the foundries and farmlands of the Midwest to seagoing cargo ships. The huge vessels, up to 740 feet long and 82 feet wide, use the locks to stair climb their way up toward Lake Ontario or downward to the Atlantic Ocean.

The visitors' approach road passes through a tunnel that burrows under the Eisenhower Lock —and provides motorists with an unnerving experience when a 100-ton tanker (visible above the tunnel entrance) is passing overhead.

Farther along you can see the vast arc of the Moses Saunders Power Dam, whose huge turbines are operated by the flow of 150 million gallons of water passing through every minute. Nearby you will find Robert Moses State Park, a forested retreat with a beach, a picnic area, campsites, and wetlands that harbor many kinds of migratory birds. Pause for a short stroll before heading back to the main road.

2 Ogdensburg

On days when the wind is high, the waves churn around the freighters that parade past Ogdensburg, the St. Lawrence River's midpoint and narrowest stretch. First a French fort, in 1749, the town is home to the historic 1809 Customs House, a Georgian structure that is the oldest federal government building still in use in the United States.

Another notable site, the Frederic Remington Art Museum, is located on Washington Street in a grand old mansion that was the home of the famed Western artist's widow. It houses a huge collection of his paintings, watercolors, and sculptures. One painting with an appropriately local theme shows fearless Chippewa Indians crossing the storm-tossed St. Lawrence River in a birchbark canoe.

For a shady picnic by the water, head for Greenbelt Riverfront Park,

complete with its own marina. It's also the starting point for a walking tour that describes the Battle of Ogdensburg, in which 400 British regulars routed a larger American force during the War of 1812.

3 Thousand Islands

As it exits from Lake Ontario, the upper St. Lawrence River is itself a broad lakelike expanse, dotted with the Thousand Islands. According to Iroquois legend, this idyllic collection of islets spilled like flowers from the Creator's basket as he was carrying the earthly paradise back to heaven. The islands, whose number is closer to 1,800 than 1,000, come in all sizes. Some are just large enough to accommodate a few trees; others are home to stately Victorian mansions accessible only by boat. It was the owners of these island estates who, on their return to the big cities, made Thousand Islands dressing a staple on so many menus.

Alexandria Bay, the commercial hub of the district, is a comely village with old shops such as the Cornwall Brothers Store, a bastion of quaint Americana. From the waterfront take the boat tour to Boldt Castle on Heart Island. This imposing 121-room structure, a replica of a castle on the Rhine, was built by George C. Boldt, the proprietor of the Waldorf-Astoria Hotel in New York, as a gift for his beloved wife. (He even had the island reshaped into the form of a heart.) When his wife suddenly passed away in 1904, Boldt sent his 300 workmen home and never set foot on the island again.

For dramatic aerial views of this idyllic archipelago, motor across 100-foot-high Thousand Islands International Bridge (off Rte. 12 a few miles southwest of Alexandria Bay), whose several spans connect the United States to Canada. From Hill Island, Ontario, you can take an elevator to reach the top of the Thousand Islands Skydeck—a 400-foot perch overlooking the river from Ogdensburg to Lake Ontario.

4 Wellesley Island State Park

Back on the American side, just west of the bridge, is the entrance to forest-covered Wellesley Island. Campsites at Wellesley Island State

Park are much in demand for views of Eel Bay. At the Narrows, visible from the park, seagoing vessels large and small pass by in a continual parade. Nearby Thousand Islands Park, a private community of broad streets and vintage Victorian homes, is a reminder of the way some of the well-to-do spend their summers.

As the drive continues southwest on Rte. 12, it whisks into the village of Clayton. Here the Antique Boat Museum offers a nostalgic tribute to the art of the wooden boat, including sleek and elegant runabouts that ferried summer revelers at exhilarating speeds.

5 Cape Vincent

Cape Vincent sits on a point of land that juts into Lake Ontario at the point where it meets the St. Lawrence. During the 1820s the town became the home of a French expatriate community—supporters of Napoleon Bonaparte. Though their plan to have the emperor join them never worked out, they left a legacy of French customs still celebrated in an annual festival. At the Cape's western tip, the 1827 Tibbetts Point Lighthouse still guides ships

between the lake and the seaway. From this simple stucco tower, sunset-tinted vistas extend across the length of the lake.

6 Sackets Harbor

South from Cape Vincent, the road winds by sinuous bays and inlets across rolling pastureland where dairy cattle graze. As you pass into the little town of Chaumont, notice its many intriguing structures built of locally quarried blue limestone. The route then swings into the quiet village of Sackets Harbor, used as a naval base from 1808 until the 1940s. During the War of 1812, the British tried to capture it, launching two furious but unsuccessful assaults upon the thousands of Americans occupying the town. Walking tours take

you to the battle zones, including the solid brick-and-limestone Madison Barracks, where Ulysses S Grant was stationed in the 1830s. Today the structure has been converted into a residential community.

7 Southwick Beach State Park

Known for its outstanding bathing beach, Southwick Beach State Park serves as the entry to the 3,400-acre Lakeview Wildlife Management Area, home to muskrats, otters, beavers, and herons. The area also contains Lake Ontario's most extraordinary network of dunes, some of them up to 60 feet high.

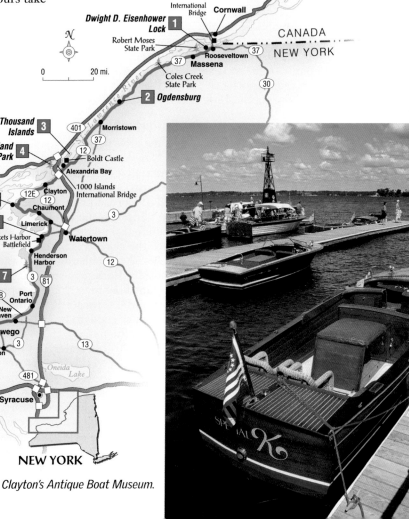

Clayton's Antique Boat Museum.

The sweeping light appears with sunset at Oswego Lighthouse, entrance to the Oswego River's harbor.

Farther to the southwest lies the shipping city of Oswego, located at the mouth of the Oswego River. Here Fort Ontario, begun in 1755, reflects the strategic importance of this waterway during the 18th and 19th centuries.

8 Fair Haven

This elegant town, which occupies both sides of narrow Little Sodus Bay, was at one time a busy shipping port. Nowadays, however, it is a delightful resort with charming lakeside inns and expansive green lawns that slope toward the bay.

9 Sodus Bay Lighthouse

After swinging inland for several miles through orchard country, the drive once again nears the lakeshore, where the gray limestone structure known as the Sodus Bay Lighthouse comes into view. It is said that slaves escaping via the Underground Railroad longed to see the Sodus Light, the last way station on their 1,000-mile trek. From here they sailed across the lake to freedom in Canada.

The lantern room atop the lighthouse overlooks the spectacular Chimney Bluffs. Shimmering in the distance, their twisted spires and serrated ridges trace intricate silhouettes against the sky.

10 Rochester

As the drive heads west, the skyline of New York's third-largest city materializes above acres of apple orchards. Standing at the northern end of a broad plain, Rochester was chosen as the terminus of a branch of the Erie Canal—and once the canal was built in the 1820s, the population grew dramatically. Entrepreneurs founded so many flour mills along the upper falls of the Genesee River that Rochester came to be called the Flour City.

The 100-foot waterfall in the Brown's Race Historic District is spectacular in itself, but all the more so for being right in the middle of town. Nearby are restored factories and mills from Rochester's early days, along with an interpretive center and an overlook affording a sweeping view of the river's deep gorge.

During the 1840s the Rochester mills went into decline, yielding to a booming horticultural trade. Accordingly, the city changed its nickname from the Flour City to the Flower City. Lovely Highland Park still lives up to that sobriquet: it features one of the world's most astonishing displays of lilacs, more than 1,200 plants in all, which perfume the air in May and paint the park with purples and blues.

For a look at a virtual anthology of American domestic architecture, drive through the East Avenue Historic District. There, set among tall trees, are the homes—past and present—of Rochester's many successful entrepreneurs. None was arguably more prominent than George Eastman, founder of the Eastman Kodak Company, whose 50-room Colonial Revival mansion now houses the magnificent International Museum of Photography and Film.

Another local institution, the Strong Museum, is a testament to one woman's faithfully indulged obsessions. Margaret Woodbury Strong, whose parents made a small fortune in buggy whips and were among the earliest investors in young Mr. Eastman's company, parlayed her inherited wealth into collections of everything from decorative buttons to more than 20,000 antique dolls.

11 Thirty Mile Point Lighthouse

Beyond the urban sprawl of Rochester—at a point just 30 miles east of the mouth of the Niagara River—sits the square limestone tower known as Thirty Mile Point Lighthouse. Now serving as the visitor center for Golden Hill State Park, the 61-foot-tall lighthouse was built in 1875 to mark a dangerous offshore sandbar. It commands a sweeping view across the widest stretch of Lake Ontario.

12 Old Fort Niagara

The drive elbows abruptly southward at the mouth of the Niagara River. Here at its outlet the river is so broad and placid that it's hard to believe it carries most of the water flowing out of Lake Superior and lakes Michigan, Huron, and Erie.

For more than three centuries Old Fort Niagara has stood guard at the river's mouth. Its most conspicuous feature, the 1726 French Castle, is among the oldest structures in the Northeast. In an effort to calm the fears of hostile Iroquois Indians, the architect disguised the fort's guardrooms, powder magazines, and soldiers' quarters in a building that resembles a large, unthreatening manor house.

13 Lewiston

Heading south on the Robert Moses Parkway, the drive eases into Lewiston, which was the site of Niagara Falls some 12,000 years ago. With continuous erosion, it has since receded seven miles to the south, leaving a spectacular gorge in its wake. Passing its brief course, the Niagara River descends more than 300 feet in elevation, making it one of the best sources of hydroelectric power in North America. Much of New York State's power needs are met by the dynamos that hum eight miles upriver at the Niagara Power Project. Its visitor center, complete with an observation deck and displays, also features a mural painted by Thomas Hart Benton that depicts one of the falls' European discoverers, Father Hennepin, and his first sighting of the Niagara Gorge in 1678. Awed by the falls, "it is without parallel in the Universe!" he reportedly exclaimed.

Nearby is the terraced woodland of Artpark, a 200-acre state park where visiting artists of all kinds polish their skills, compare notes, arrange exhibits, and stage musical and theatrical events.

14 Niagara Falls

Farther south on the Robert Moses Parkway, past a welter of industrial plants and tourist shops, is the celebrated trio of cataracts known as Niagara Falls. The American Falls are the highest at 184 feet, while the broad sweep of Horseshoe Falls (176 feet high) creates an amphitheater of white water, mist, and thunder that is simply breathtaking. Between them, in the gap between Goat and Luna islands, the slender Bridal Veil Falls adds its own blend of grace notes to the deafening din. Together the three waterfalls spill some three-quarters of a million gallons of water each second into the gorge below.

The main entry point for views of the falls on the American side is Niagara Reservation Park. They have been drawing visitors—often honeymooners—since 1803, when Napoleon's brother brought his American bride here. To get near the edge of the falls, walk over the pedestrian bridge to Goat Island, where you can look straight down into the cacophonous gorge as tons of white water plunge in shrouds onto huge dark boulders that appear and disappear in the mist. For a closer encounter, take the elevator to the rock-hewn tunnels that lead to the Cave of the Winds at the falls' base. Here, outfitted in a yellow slicker to protect you from the airborne downpour, you can look straight out at the thundering wall of water.

For an aerial perspective on the scene, ride the elevator to the top of the Prospect Point observation tower. Then descend to streamside, where a fleet of sightseeing boats that all bear the same name, *Maid of the Mist*, has been taking visitors into the maw of the falls for more than a century. Be prepared to get wet, with or without the protection of a hooded slicker.

Across Rainbow Bridge on the Canadian side, generations of visitors have gathered atop Table Rock, which affords a close-up view of Horseshoe Falls. From there, you can descend to the river on the Falls Inclined Railway—a harrowing ride for those subject to vertigo— or venture into the Table Rock Scenic Tunnels, which take you down behind the roaring cataracts. Nearby, the Skylon Tower, about twice as high as its counterpart on the American side of the falls, offers views from on high of the falls and its surroundings.

For a change of pace, take the short drive downriver on the Niagara Parkway to visit the swirling, churning waters of Whirlpool Basin. If you have the nerve to take a ride on the Niagara Spanish Aero Car, you can view the enormous whirlpool from directly overhead.

Return to the falls after sunset to watch the display of colored

Boldt Castle on Heart Island in Alexandria Bay was inspired by castles on the Rhine River.

lights that are projected across the cascade to create an unforgettable *son et lumière*—sound and light— that pulsates in rhythm as the water falls in a never-ending pattern of changing colors. Fittingly, the cascading water is both star and workhorse: the former provided by the roaring falls and the latter by the electric power the river generates along its stair-stepping journey to the sea.

Adirondack Adventure

The Adirondack Park, the largest wilderness east of the Mississippi, sprawls far and wide across upstate New York—a rugged, pristine realm where forests and mountains reign supreme.

The 16,000-acre Wilmington Flume Preserve on Rte. 86 is part of Adirondack Park.

Encompassing both public and private land, the Adirondack Park is shaped a bit like a giant oval, and it bounds an astounding 6 million acres— a tapestry of woodlands, meadows, high-shouldered peaks, and thousands of streams and lakes. Tiny villages are nestled across the countryside, and campgrounds and trails abound. It is no wonder, then, that visitors who come here tend to stay a while in order to savor the stunning scenery, protected since 1892 by a state law decreeing that the park shall remain "forever wild."

1 Prospect Mountain

For a good overview of the region, begin your Adirondack adventure with a drive to the lofty summit of Prospect Mountain, which crests at 2,030 feet. The highway, a toll road that is open in the warmer months, switches back and forth as it maneuvers up the slopes. It has many overlooks along the way to allow visitors to pause and enjoy the vistas.

Below lies Lake George, a glistening 32-mile-long expanse of blue wedged amid steep, forested ridges. Sparkling clean, the lake is a swimmer's delight, and its shores and myriad islands are virtually unbeatable when it comes to exploring and relaxing. Anglers too will find a piece of paradise here as they try their luck for bass, trout, perch, and other fish.

The Lake George area was not always so idyllic. In the 1700s the British and French waged battles for control of the territory, but of course neither country was destined to possess it in the end. The English erected Fort William Henry, which has been reconstructed just east of the village of Lake George, the touristy hub for the region. Visitors come to the reconstructed fort not only to learn about its history but also to take in the stunning views to be seen from the nearby water's edge.

2 Bolton Landing

Hugging Lake George's western shore, Rte. 9N passes waterfront homes, resorts, and rocky slopes softened by thick, fragrant stands of evergreens intermixed with broadleaf trees. Before long it arrives at Bolton Landing, a village complete with souvenir shopping, summer homes, a boat launch, and sweeping views of the lake. A narrow bridge connects the town to an island where the spacious Sagamore Hotel has been catering to guests for more than a century. A white clapboard structure with striking green trim, the resort first opened for business in 1883. The original structure burned down, was rebuilt, then caught fire again. The hotel standing today was erected in 1922.

3 Fort Ticonderoga

Nearly every sign of commercialism quickly fades from view as the drive continues northward, offering excellent views of Lake George and its mountainous surroundings. Pulloffs here and there provide motorists with opportunities to pause and enjoy the scenery. Deer's Leap, at the base of steep-sided Tongue Mountain, commands a vista back toward the lake's southern end. Farther along, the community of Hague, snugly situated on the water's edge, has a park that is just right for picnics.

At its northern end Lake George flows through the narrow channel of the La Chute River into Lake Champlain—a location so valuable in the past that it became known as the Key to the Continent. The French staked their claim on the area by building a fort on Champlain's shores in 1755, but a few years later the British captured the citadel, which they named Fort Ticonderoga. Years later, in one of the Revolutionaries' first victories, a force of independence-minded Americans—led by Ethan Allen and Benedict Arnold—took the fort in a surprise attack in 1775.

Their victory was destined to be famous, but it was short-lived:

Trip Tips

Length: About 270 miles, plus side trips.

When to go: Fine scenery year-round, with drastic and dramatic seasonal changes.

Nearby attractions: Lake George Beach State Park, with swimming and picnicking, east of Fort William Henry. Six Nations Indian Museum, with displays of native crafts, Rte. 30, north of Saranac Lake.

Words to the wise: Blackflies and other insect pests can be numerous, especially in early summer.

Visitor centers: Paul Smiths Visitor Information Center, Rte. 30, north of Saranac Lake. Newcomb Visitor Information Center, Rte. 28N, 14 miles east of Long Lake.

Further information: Adirondack Regional Tourism Council, P.O. Box 51, West Chazy, NY 12992; tel. 518-846-8016, www.adk.com.

the British regained the fort in 1777. Exhibits at Ticonderoga's museum tell the story of its past. (Come summer, a part of that past is reenacted with demonstrations of early soldiering that include cannon firings and fife-and-drum marching bands in period costumes.) As an added bonus, the views from the fort are splendid, looking out across the water to the Vermont shore and the distant peaks and ridges of the Green Mountains.

4 Paradox Lake

Changing direction, the drive next swings toward the west as it follows Rte. 74 to Paradox Lake. (The "paradox" lies in the fact that, in times of high water caused by floods, the lake's outlet, overwhelmed by the Schroon River, becomes an inlet.) Many other lakes, though smaller, are spotted throughout the surrounding countryside, a woodland crisscrossed by hiking trails.

5 High Peaks

Rte. 9 guides motorists northward beside the Schroon River to Rte. 73, a serpentine drive that leads into the heart of the high-climbing Adirondack Mountains. Elevations often exceed 4,000 feet in this area, where the rounded dome of Mt. Marcy—nicknamed the Cloud-Splitter—reigns as the tallest of all the state's peaks. Its peak tops off at 5,344 feet.

Embellishing the undulating beauty of the High Peaks region are its many waterways. The narrowest of brooks and the swiftest of streams splash down the slopes in all directions. They collect in lakes and ponds, many of which are situated in glacier-carved basins and U-shaped valleys that have become gathering places for wildlife.

Pine trees hem in Rte. 73 as it continues to twist and turn to idyllic Chapel Pond, where you'll drive through the mighty jaws of a deep gorge. Rock climbers come to scale the high cliffs, which also happen to be an important nesting ground for the endangered peregrine falcon. (To ensure that the birds are not disturbed, climbers are not permitted on certain cliffs during the birds' nesting season.)

Farther on, after dipping into a broad valley, the drive heads into the town of Keene. A side detour from there diverts to the west to the High Peaks Wilderness, where travelers can park and then head out on foot to sample some of the scenery afforded by the 238 miles of hiking trails that lace the area.

The trail to the summit of nearby Mt. Jo, a round-trip of less than two miles, is a fairly easy hike that culminates with a panoramic view of the sculpted summits. Lofty Mt. Marcy can also be climbed by trail, a trek—very difficult in places—that ascends amid maples, birches, alders, and spruces on its way to the treeless summit. Looking down, hikers can see tiny Lake Tear-of-the-Clouds, the extreme headwater of the Hudson River.

6 Lake Placid

Alpine skiing was introduced near the sleepy village of Lake Placid nearly 100 years ago. As the sport has grown, so too has the community, which hosted the Winter Olympics in both 1932 and 1980. The cheers and thrills that characterized the athletic events have long since subsided, but today Lake Placid—no matter what its name may suggest—remains the vibrant hub for the High Peaks region. Visitors to its downtown area can browse in art galleries, take a ride in a horse-drawn carriage, or simply enjoy the views of the lake.

Sightseers can also spend their time taking in the many signs of

Whiteface Mountain stands sentinel over the west branch of the Ausable River.

the past Olympics. Luge and bobsled runs slash down the hillsides at the Mt. Van Hoevenburg Recreation Area; two massive ski jumps, set atop a prominent knoll, tower high into the sky; and the Olympic Center houses ice-skating rinks. These areas are not just showpieces, either; many American athletes aspiring to one day win a gold medal come to train here and perfect their skills year-round.

A dreamer of a different sort, abolitionist John Brown, lived and farmed in the Lake Placid area more than 100 years ago—his 244-acre homestead lies to the southeast of town. Visitors

are welcome to explore its woods and fields and to learn about the man who was tried and executed for leading an attempted raid on the federal arsenal at Harpers Ferry, West Virginia.

7 Whiteface Mountain

For many visitors to the Adirondack Park, the drive up the slopes of Whiteface Mountain, whose bold summit stands at 4,867 feet, is the superlative experience. The winding eight-mile Veterans Memorial Highway, opened to traffic by President Franklin Delano Roosevelt, ends just 500 feet below the summit, which visitors can reach by means of a stone walkway or by an elevator that ascends through a shaft carved deep within the mountain's granite core.

An observation deck crowns the mountaintop, where the assault of winter weather is quite apparent. Only a few hardy lichens are able to survive—quite a contrast to the views of the forests that stretch all the way to the horizon in every direction. On clear days you also see Lake Champlain and the Saint Lawrence River.

Backtracking to Lake Placid, take the time to stop at High Falls Gorge, situated near the base of the Whiteface Mountain Ski Area. The deep cleft was sliced into a mass of layered rock by the West Branch of the Ausable River. A thundering waterfall shoots between the walls, dropping 100 feet, then another 600 feet over three downriver ledges. Bridges and pathways—wooden boardwalks that cling to the cliffsides—make for unforgettable views of the river, which rushes and roars below.

You should also keep an eye out for unusual vegetation. One plant, the rare Lapland rosebay, resembles a rhododendron and manages a toehold in the merest of crevices.

8 Saranac Lake

The thermometer's "mercury... curls up into the bulb like a hibernating bear," lamented the noted author Robert Louis Stevenson, who spent six months at Saranac Lake in 1887–88. He had come hoping that the crisp air would check his tuberculosis, which was being treated at a sanatorium established by Dr. Edward Livingston Trudeau. Stevenson's onetime cottage, preserved as a museum, displays memorabilia recalling his life.

The village of Saranac Lake, settled in 1819, provides travelers with yet another entryway to the wilds. Camping, hiking, canoeing, and fishing await among the interconnected lakes and streams, parts of which are designated as the St. Regis Canoe Area. Popular too is the town's Winter Carnival, an annual festival highlighted by the creation of an elaborate castle built of ice.

9 Tupper Lake

Rte. 3 passes beside the Saranac Lakes and then continues through forest-clad foothills and more lakes on its way to Tupper Lake, founded as a lumber camp in the late 1800s. Canoeists and anglers give high marks to this area's 40 miles of navigable waterways, while hikers enjoy the lakeside trails. A secluded site nearby, Follensby Pond, was the setting for the 1858 Philoso-

phers Camp, where writer Ralph Waldo Emerson and several other scholars he numbered among his friends came to enjoy the woods and exchange ideas.

10 Long Lake

After traversing through a mixed forest consisting of pine, maple, beech, and birch trees, the drive toward the town of Long Lake skims across miles of wetlands—vast stretches that close in on both sides of the road. In Long Lake itself, nature lovers can glimpse—and hear—an amazing array of bird life. The cantankerous chatter of ducks plays a counterpoint among the varied tunes of many species of songbirds. In the tamarack-fringed marshes, long-legged great blue herons stand out amid the carpeting of sedges, reeds, and wildflowers.

11 Blue Mountain Lake

Nestled at the base of Blue Mountain, Blue Mountain Lake is regarded by some as one of the most beautiful of the 2,800 lakes in the Adirondack Park. Indeed, the setting has long been an inspiration to writers, artists, and musicians, who make summertime pilgrimages to come to the Adirondack Lakes Center for the Arts.

Some highly regarded artwork can be seen at the acclaimed Adirondack Museum, which overlooks the lake and boasts an exhaustive collection of exhibits. Not surprisingly, the emphasis here is on Adirondack life, and more than 20 buildings—each dedicated to a particular subject—are spread across 30 acres. Visitors can spend days

Winslow Homer

Campers at the water's edge, trappers tramping through the woods on snowshoes, a lone angler canoeing across a pond in autumn—scenes from the Adirondacks stirred the imagination of American painter Winslow Homer, a frequent visitor to the region. The watercolor shown here, *Bear Hunting,* was completed in 1892. It is one of many vivid outdoor images that were inspired by his fishing and camping trips to these mountainous wilds.

delighting in everything from boats, furniture, handicrafts, and railroad cars to paintings by such American masters as Frederic Remington, Winslow Homer, and Thomas Cole.

12 Raquette Lake

Raquette Lake—a name that applies to both the lake and to this quaint and quiet village that stands beside it—consists of little more than a couple of dwellings, churches, and a general store. Golden Beach, situated four miles east of the hamlet, was named for the color of its soft sand. Families with small children favor swimming here since the water remains shallow for dozens of yards offshore.

In the late 1800s the glory of the Adirondacks began to lure some of America's wealthiest families. Buying large parcels of land, they built spacious summer homes—getaways that, perhaps a bit tongue in cheek, they referred to as "camps." Sagamore Road, an unpaved drive, leads to one of the grandest of these lodges, known today as Great Camp Sagamore.

Built by architect William West Durant in 1897, then sold to Alfred Vanderbilt, Sagamore contains numerous buildings set among the pine woods. But it is the main house, a chalet-style mansion constructed of logs, that commands center stage. Every detail of the place was supervised by Durant, who even ordered the huge fireplace to be rebuilt: one or two stones, it seems, were not set exactly as they were supposed to be. Traditional Adirondack chairs and lamps, a bowling alley, and wall coverings made of bark are among the many touches that make the mansion so endearing.

Recently the camp has gained a new lease on life as the Sagamore Institute, a center that conducts craft workshops and outdoor programs. Summer visitors can watch a slide show on the great camp era and take a two-hour tour.

13 Fulton Chain Lakes

Hoping to map a water route all the way to Canada, Robert Fulton, best known as the inventor of the steamboat, surveyed these lakes in about 1811. No such waterway could be found, but the lakes are part of a 125-mile canoe route—some short portages are required at impassible spots—between Saranac Lake and Old Forge.

The eight Fulton Chain Lakes are known simply by number—perhaps explorers just ran out of other names. On the eastern end of Fourth Lake sits the village of Inlet, a rustic place where the cooling shade of sky-high pine trees is never far away. You can rent a boat to explore the lake or continue on Rte. 28 to Old Forge, a forest-girt town that was first settled by one Charles Herreshoff.

Herreshoff dreamed of making a fortune by mining iron ore. Those who came with him, however, found the work as brutal as the winter weather; many packed up and departed. Adding to his disappointment, the mines frequently flooded, and Herreshoff ended as a broken man. Despite its bleak beginnings, Old Forge today is a haven where visitors can ski, hike, and perhaps glimpse a black bear wandering its way down Main Street.

Oseetah Lake offers boating and canoeing access between Lake Placid and Wilmington.

Lake Champlain Loop

First-time visitors to Lake Champlain share a sense of wonder: nestled between two mountain ranges, this glimmering giant rewards the eye from most any angle.

The layered walls of Ausable Chasm seem etched with ancient secrets.

Though it lies not far from some of the East Coast's largest cities, Lake Champlain remains truly unspoiled—one of America's lovelier repositories of natural beauty. Doubly blessed, this long, island-dotted jewel is set in the expansive valley between New York's Adirondacks to the west and the Green Mountains of Vermont to the east. Drivers on this loop tour may feel as though transported to faraway places: the peaks that loom above Champlain bring Switzerland to mind, and the juniper-topped bluffs along its shores recall the rugged seascapes of coastal Maine. For those who live beside it, however, this always enchanting, ever-changing blend of water, wind, and light is reason to stay right at home.

① Westport

Lake Champlain is 120 miles long and flows from Whitehall, New York, to its outlet at the Richelieu River in the Province of Quebec, Canada. The lake's unusual shape is drastically tapered at its southern tip, where it shrinks to the width of a weedy stream, and at Ticonderoga, the site of one of the lake's three ferry crossings, it seems as if anyone with a strong arm and a tailwind could hurl a baseball right across its quarter-mile-wide span. Just a few miles north, though, the lake broadens to truly impressive dimensions, reaching a maximum width of 12 miles near the Vermont town of Burlington.

From Ticonderoga, follow Rte. 9N/22 north along the western shore through Crown Point, Port Henry (not far from the Champlain Bridge, which will be crossed later in the drive when you return to New York from Vermont), and the lakeside town of Westport. The main street, perched above Westport's busy marina, offers sweeping

⁞⁞⁞⁞⁞ Trip Tips ⁞⁞⁞⁞⁞

Length: About 190 miles, plus side trips.

When to go: Popular year-round.

Ferries: Call 802-864-9804 for information on Lake Champlain ferries.

Nearby attractions: City of Montreal, Quebec. University of Vermont Dairy Farm, South Burlington, VT. Vermont Wildflower Farm, Charlotte, VT. Kingsland Bay State Park, Ferrisburg, VT.

Not to be missed: Ferry ride across Lake Champlain to New York, departing from Charlotte, Burlington, or Grand Isle.

Further information: Lake Champlain Regional Chamber of Commerce, 60 Main St., Suite 100, Burlington, VT 05401; tel. 802-863-3489, www.vermont.org.

panoramic views of the lake in all of its moods.

If you're especially patient—who knows?—you might manage to catch a glimpse of Champ, Lake Champlain's own version of the Loch Ness Monster. Samuel de Champlain, exploring these waters in 1609, was the first to note something of the sort, writing of a 20-foot-long serpentlike creature with a horse's head. Since then, Champ sightings have become a regular feature of life along Champlain, though somewhat ironically, this elusive creature has a knack for appearing only at those moments when no camera is available.

② Essex

Among the prettier villages on the New York side, tiny Essex is a slice of rural Americana that can becalm the most jangled city nerves. The town's tidy main street, which parallels the lakeshore, is lined with stately shade trees and Federal-style houses. Two small marinas occupy the snug natural harbor, which also serves as the landing for the Essex–Charlotte ferry. For a relaxing hour-long break from driving, take the round-trip cruise across the lake (you can take your car to explore the other side, or leave it in the Essex ferry lot). Spend a restful evening at one of the harbor's charming cafés, where you can watch the gilded glow of the Green Mountains as they catch the last rays of the setting sun. In the hour before darkness, the lake grows still as granite, and if the nearby commotion permits, the tiniest of sounds—the soft ping of a halyard, the cry of a gull—travels for miles across the surface.

3 Willsboro Point

For much of the journey north to Plattsburgh, the drive skirts the eastern slopes of the Adirondack Mountains, a region that embraces one of the East Coast's grandest tracts of wilderness. Taller and more rugged than their cousins across the lake, the Adirondacks amass in a great, brooding jumble near the lake's western shore. The mountains are so immense and densely forested that it's not always easy to get a clear view of them when one is in their midst. Be assured that they are all around you, and hold your breath for a better look at these stony giants when you reach the Vermont side of the lake.

Beyond Essex the highway follows the lakeshore for a stretch before veering inland to Willsboro, where New York State's first fish ladder affords migrating salmon the chance to overleap Willsboro Dam en route to their fall spawning grounds upstream—and enables visitors to witness this ageless, often repeated struggle.

Farther on, take the turnoff to Willsboro Point, a fingerlike peninsula that shelters one of Champlain's largest and perhaps most scenic inlets. Reminiscent of a Nordic fjord, four-mile-long

At sunset under an auburn sky, Lake Champlain appears to be filled with molten gold.

Willsboro Bay is walled on the west by sheer cliffs that tumble to the water's edge. To sample accommodations as they existed here some 200 years ago, visit the Adsit Cabin, a modest log structure built in the 1790s.

4 Ausable Chasm

This deep, tortuous gorge was one of America's first tourist attractions, and its grandeur has hardly paled over the years. Come early in the day to avoid the crowds, and take a leisurely stroll along the path below the chasm's beautifully textured, sheer sandstone walls—sculpted over millennia through Cambrian rock formed over 500 million years ago by the Ausable River on its way into Lake Champlain. In places these magnificent walls—between 100 and 200 feet high—stand as close together as 20 feet. On bright autumn days flaming foliage ignites the chasm's clifftops as well as patches along its walls, making for an especially breathtaking spectacle.

5 Plattsburgh

The largest town on the New York side, Plattsburgh was the site of the lake's last major naval battle during the War of 1812—not only a victory for the American fleet, but a tribute to the imagination of its commander, Commodore Thomas Macdonough. Using a cat's cradle of anchors and winches, Macdon-ough was able to swing his ships around and deliver double broadsides to the British fleet, which soon withered under his hammering assault. A limestone obelisk across from city hall commemorates the scene and the battle.

From Plattsburgh the drive continues north on Rte. 9 through Ingraham and Chazy (home to what locals say is the largest McIntosh apple orchard in the world), and follows Rte. 9B to Rouses Point (near the Canadian border) before veering east to Vermont on Rte. 2. From the Korean Veterans Memorial Bridge (still known by many as the Rouses Point Bridge), look northward to catch a glimpse of the stone ruins of Fort Montgomery. Aptly nicknamed Fort Blunder, it was inadvertently constructed north of the 45th parallel, on unquestionably Canadian soil.

Here Vermont's Alburg Peninsula and Champlain's islands segment the lake into a patchwork of bays. Remote and lovely, this area contains some of the Champlain Valley's richest farmland. On lingering summer days no lakeside tour would be complete without stopping to sample the fresh produce that is abundant in the many roadside stands.

6 Missisquoi National Wildlife Refuge

A short detour on Rte. 78 brings you to this pristine wetland preserve on the broad Missisquoi River delta. The refuge's 6,642 acres are evenly divided between brush, timber, and marsh, making this a perfect spot to observe wildlife of every stripe, from the migratory waterfowl and raptors that stop here each spring and fall to the white-tailed deer and other animals that inhabit the refuge's wooded uplands and wildflower meadows. Two well-marked nature trails—about 1½ miles in total length—guide visitors into this fragile mix of habitats. In the summer bring along a bucket and waterproof boots—and insect repellent—for blueberry picking in the bog off Tabor Road.

7 Isle La Motte

Northernmost of Champlain's islands, tiny Isle La Motte is sparsely touristed, as sequestered in spirit as it is in fact. Fittingly, the one spot that attracts visitors year after year is a place of quiet contemplation: it is St. Anne's Shrine, site of the first white settlement and the first Roman Catholic Mass to be held in Vermont, in 1666. Despite prayers to St. Anne (mother of the Virgin Mary), the settlers were driven off the island by inclement weather and hostile natives; the area was later reclaimed as a holy place by the Bishop of Burlington in 1892.

Take the serene water's-edge drive to Isle La Motte's southern tip, where lake breezes stir the trees and an occasional snowy egret haunts the rocky shores of an old, water-filled marble quarry.

8 North Hero Island

Island-hopping to the east, the drive crosses another bridge and alights on narrow North Hero. Here, just off Rte. 2, sits woodsy North Hero State Park, a mecca for campers on a handsome stretch of land overlooking Maquam Bay. Motoring south across the slender isthmus that connects the north

The elegant barn at Shelburne Farms, once a private family compound built by heirs to the Vanderbilt railroad fortune, has a grandeur that befits its setting.

blanket on the ground for a breezy picnic beside the whitecaps, or prowl the edge of the adjacent wildlife refuge, which offers some of the best bird-watching south of the Missisquoi delta.

11 Burlington

As the drive pushes south along Champlain's eastern shore, it offers distant views of Malletts Bay—a sheltered harbor bustling with pleasure boats and lined with family cottages. Then, after breezing through the beautifully restored river town of Winooski, the drive coasts into Burlington, the largest city in the state. A blend of rustic innocence and urban sophistication, this city of 40,000 or so is set on a steep, terraced slope beside the lake. The downtown is clean, upscale, and ideal for walking, with an open-air pedestrian mall of restaurants, pushcarts, and specialty shops. Spectacular views of Champlain and the Adirondacks appear around every corner. The slope above the city is crisscrossed with tree-shaded streets that are lined with regal Victorian homes, and crowning the hill are a white cupola and the cluster of stately brick buildings that grace the spacious campus of the University of Vermont, founded by Ira Allen in 1791.

Vermont was one of the last areas of New England to be settled, and in the years following the Revolutionary War, Ira and his brother Ethan (he of Green Mountain Boys fame) did much to promote Burlington's development from a frontier farming community to the cultural capital

and south sections of the island, and continuing beyond the town of North Hero, the drive arrives at Knight Point State Park. Poised on the island's very tip, this charming oasis is blessed with a sheltered, warm bay just right for swimming, and a view of the drawbridge connecting North Hero and Grand Isle. More spectacular still are the park's views of the Green Mountains to the southeast and the Adirondacks to the southwest. Beginning at the sandy beach, a grassy nature trail loops around the oftentimes breezy point to pass through groves of birches, oaks, and maples.

9 Grand Isle

Golden hayfields, fragrant orchards, and lush green pastures bordered by a choppy, wind-tossed lake is the largest of Champlain's islands. Like its neighbors to the north, Grand Isle has managed to avoid unchecked development— it's too cold in the winter, too far in the summer—but visitors who manage to pass through these parts are left with fond memories. To best sample this island's unique charms, take the East Shore Road south along the coastline to Grand Isle State Park, then follow Town Line Road to rejoin Rte. 2 near

Keeler Bay, a sheltered cove ideal for boating and fishing. A number of primitive camps—and the occasional upscale summer home—are huddled along the water's edge.

10 Sand Bar State Park

A narrow mile-long causeway crosses the waterway separating the southern tip of Grand Isle from the mainland. Deservedly, the protected beach at Sand Bar State Park draws hefty crowds on summer weekends, but autumn's first gasp of chilly air restores this stretch of sand and trees to an uncrowded tranquillity. Spread a of the state. Today the brothers are remembered as something akin to Burlington's patron saints. To pay your respects and pay a call on history, stop in at the Ethan Allen Homestead, the modest farmhouse at the north end of town where the patriot lived the last two years of his life. Adjacent Ethan Allen Park preserves a portion of the farm once owned by Allen, and nature trails snake through the nearby woods.

12 Shelburne

The greater Burlington area has grown rapidly in recent years, and the commercial strip along Rte. 7 south of town is proof that even in Vermont, scenery sometimes takes a backseat to worldly necessities. Happily, the malls, car dealerships, discount stores, and cineplexes disappear within a few miles, replaced by berry farms, apple orchards, dairy fields, and roadside antique barns crammed to the rafters with eclectic country treasures.

In Shelburne two special treats await—both associated with the Webb family, whose wealth stems from the Vanderbilt railroad fortune. For nearly a hundred years, the Webbs' walled compound on Shelburne Point—known as Shelburne Farms—was closed to the public, but a younger generation of Webbs has lately opened this magnificent 1,400-acre lakeside tract for a variety of public programs, including the Vermont Mozart Festival and tours of their award-winning farmstead cheese-making operation.

Just a few miles farther south on Rte. 7 lies the world-famous Shelburne Museum, which makes a spectacular virtue of the common-place. This "village" of 39 buildings (including a lighthouse, a round barn, a country store, a jail, and other buildings carted from elsewhere in the state) houses one of the world's great collections of 18th-

century folk art, furnishings, tools, toys, carriages, and other Americana assembled by Electra Havemeyer Webb beginning in the 1940s. The museum's largest oddity, a 1906 lake side-wheeler named the *Ticonderoga*, sits hard aground in the middle of town. Allow yourself at least one full day to tour the museum—a unique tribute to America's past.

13 Charlotte

A worthy detour west off Rte. 7 brings you to this pretty country town, whose name is pronounced the French-Canadian way: *SHAR-lot*. If you've yet to set out on the lake, Charlotte provides a fine opportunity; the ferry, which runs back and forth to Essex, New York, departs from the dock at the end of Lake Road. The road to nearby Charlotte beach, a mecca for wind-surfers, takes you across an old covered bridge with a broad, un-obstructed view or two of the Adirondack Mountains.

On the other side of Rte. 7, Mt. Philo State Park beckons visitors to make the corkscrewing drive—it's not recommended for trailers, though—or to hike to the summit of Mt. Philo for dazzling sunset views across the shimmering Champlain Valley.

14 Vergennes

South of Charlotte, the highway crosses the unofficial boundary separating the greater Burlington area from the rest of the state. This rolling portion of the Champlain Valley, replete with barns, silos, and black-and-white cows, resembles the Midwest with mountains.

At one square mile, Vergennes (pronounced *VER-jenz*) ranks as the smallest chartered city in Vermont, and it has an unstudied authenticity that recalls an earlier America. Park your car in the center of town for a pleasant warm-weather stroll, and then head west to But-

ton Bay State Park, named for the peculiar, button-shaped pebbles (some with holes) that wash up along this protected cove. Six miles west of Vergennes on Basin Harbor Road, the Lake Champlain Maritime Museum dishes up the region's most comprehensive display of navigational artifacts, many recovered from sunken Champlain steamboats.

15 Champlain Bridge

Before returning to New York, you'll pass through Chimney Point. Some allege that Ethan Allen downed an ale in the tavern here before storming Fort Ticonderoga. The story is probably apocryphal, since the attack on Fort Ticonderoga took place at dawn and Chimney Point is more than 12 miles distant from it. Linking two historic sites—Chimney and Crown points—the high, arching Champlain Bridge affords a fine farewell view of the watery expanse to the north.

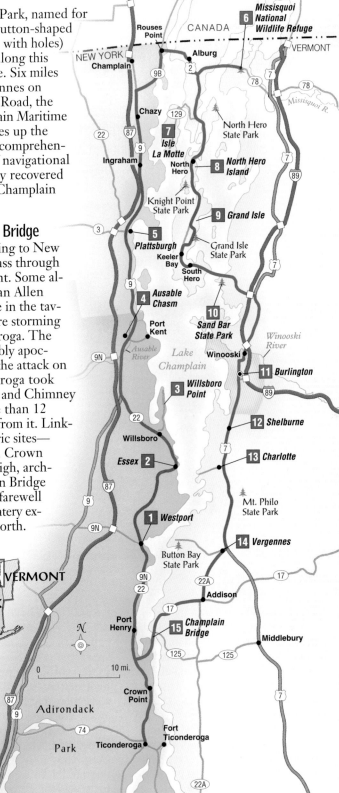

Hudson River Valley

Like Rip van Winkle, modern-day travelers
will find themselves spellbound by the ageless grace
of this lovely, legendary waterway.

Trophy Point and the U.S. Military Academy at West Point overlook the Hudson.

"He saw at a distance the lordly Hudson... moving on its silent but majestic course... and at last losing itself in the blue highlands." So wrote Washington Irving of Rip van Winkle, the napper of literary note, on the eve of his long snooze. Nearly 200 years later the description still holds, and the Hudson River valley remains a scenic treasure where the boundaries between fact and fancy blur as easily as the morning mists that drift across the water.

1 George Washington Bridge
The Swiss architect Le Corbusier called this awesome 3,500-foot span "the most beautiful bridge in the world." Its two towers are, he declared, "so pure, so resolute, so regular that here, finally, steel architecture seems to laugh." Cross over from New York to the New Jersey side, where the drive turns sharply north on the Palisades Interstate Parkway, and you're likely to agree—the graceful sweep of the bridge is a perfect counterpoint to Manhattan's serrated skyline.

The parkway, the first leg of the drive, runs north from the bridge to Bear Mountain State Park. At first it travels atop the Palisades, a wall of cliffs that here form the Hudson's west bank. Giovanni da Verrazano, who probably sailed up the river in 1524, was most likely the first European to glimpse the Palisades. For your own riverside views of the cliffs, take Exit 1 to the Englewood Boat Basin, or Exit 2 to the Alpine Boat Basin. Both have picnic tables, just right for a pleasant break. Beyond Exit 2, an off-ramp leads to State Line Lookout, with a dazzling vista of the Hudson, Manhattan Island, and the George Washington Bridge.

2 Bear Mountain State Park
Verrazano may have beat him by a century, but it was Henry Hudson and the crew of the *Half Moon* who gave this region its first detailed inspection in 1609. Believing that the great waterway might be the elusive Northwest Passage to China, Hudson sailed upriver as far as present-day Albany. The explorer never gave up hope completely, but it's easy to imagine his frustration as he saw the river plunge ever deeper into mountain wilderness and his dreams of a shortcut to Asia wither away.

Explorers of the Hudson River valley nowadays suffer no such disappointments. Especially during the October foliage season, the Palisades Interstate Parkway grows ever more wild and lovely as it approaches Bear Mountain State Park. With 5,067 acres on the Hudson's western shore, the park is a popular destination for downriver urbanites and can be crowded. But a drive to the mountain's rocky summit is not to be missed. Take Exit 19, where Seven Lakes Drive leads to the Perkins Memorial Drive, a picturesque route leading to the top of Bear Mountain. From this perch at 1,305 feet, the views are nothing short of sensational.

3 West Point
The Hudson Highlands, named for the steep mountain slopes that hem in the river like the walls of

Trip Tips

Length: About 100 miles, plus side trips.

When to go: Popular year-round.

Nearby attractions: Kykuit, the John D. Rockefeller mansion, North Tarrytown. Harriman State Park, accessible via the Palisades Interstate Parkway. Storm King Art Center, off Rte. 32 at Mountainville. Washington's Headquarters State Historic Site, Newburgh.

Further information: Hudson Valley Tourism, P.O. Box 284, Salt Point, NY 12578; tel. 800-232-4782, www.travelhudsonvalley.org.

a Norwegian fjord, are at their best from Dunderberg Mountain, opposite Peekskill, to Storm King Mountain, some 10 miles north. Long a challenge to painters who would capture its brooding beauty on canvas, the river here is indeed, as novelist Henry James described it, "mountain guarded and dim."

To sample the serenity of the Highlands, drive north from Bear Mountain on Rtes. 9W and 218. You'll soon arrive at the United States Military Academy, which stands guard above West Point, a strategic river overlook. Guided tours of the Military Acadamy's grounds begin at the visitor center found just outside its Thayer Gate. As you explore the historic campus, you can walk in the footsteps of military giants from Robert E. Lee to Dwight D. Eisenhower, as well as lesser comrades such as George Armstrong Custer; take in the stirring spectacle of a cadet parade; and examine the West Point Museum's collection of wartime memorabilia, one of the nation's richest. Perhaps most rewarding of all, you can revel in the sweeping views from Trophy Point; both upriver and down, they are among the finest along the Hudson.

4 Newburgh–Beacon Bridge

Leaving West Point, drivers with a taste for drama should shun Rte. 9W in favor of a higher challenge on Storm King Highway (Rte.218). Carved into the side of Storm King Mountain, this serpentine cliff-clinger seems to hang by its fingernails, twisting and turning its way north to Cornwall-on-Hudson, where it rejoins Rte. 9W. The views—for passengers, at least—are truly breathtaking.

At I-84 the Newburgh–Beacon Bridge returns the drive to the Hudson's eastern flank. The city of Beacon, hugging the river's edge, is named for Mt. Beacon, where Revolutionary War patriots lit warning fires to signal George Washington's army of British troop movements in the Highlands. To the west the massive hulk of Storm King Mountain punches the skyline, a magisterial presence looking over your shoulder as you continue driving south.

5 Cold Spring

Smack by the river, this pretty village seems to have one foot firmly planted in the 19th century.

Along its historic Main Street, one can practically hear the clip-clop of horsedrawn carriages, and the town's waterfront gazebo is a graceful spot for taking in a sunset over West Point.

South of town, history is played on an even grander stage at Boscobel, the first of several riverfront mansions along the drive. Built in 1804 by States Morris Dyckman and his wife, Elizabeth, descendants of Dutch settlers, Boscobel was originally located 15 miles downriver. Slated for demolition in the 1950s, it received a last-minute reprieve when it was dismantled and moved to its present site. Surrounded by green lawns and gardens, it sits high on a bluff with a grand view south toward Bear Mountain.

As special as it is on the outside, it is Boscobel's interior that draws visitors year after year. Room by sumptuous room, elegant Federal-period furnishings make it one of the finest museums of its kind.

6 Manitoga

Forest or garden? Work of nature, or of man? Manitoga is all of these,

A cooper plies his trade with a drawknife at Philipsburg Manor in Sleepy Hollow.

and more. When industrial designer Russel Wright purchased this 80-acre parcel on the east bank of the Hudson River in 1942, it was a tangled junk heap, scarred by decades of lumbering, quarrying, and human carelessness.

Wright, whose designs were celebrated the world over for their use of organic forms, chose Manitoga for his greatest work of all and, over the next 30 years, shepherded it back to health. Although the landscape seems guided by no force but nature, Wright's handiwork in fact is everywhere. Each detail is carefully scripted, like the furnishings of a grand outdoor room. A network of paths, made of stone reclaimed from the quarries, escorts you through the property, from view to view.

7 Tarrytown

Clustered along the river in Tarrytown and its bordering hamlets, a trio of estates showcase several different eras of life in the Hudson Valley. Philipsburg Manor, in Sleepy Hollow (formerly North Tarrytown), was once the home of Adolph Philipse, an 18th-century Dutch Colonial trader; his stone house, a reconstructed gristmill, and a working farm all are on public display, with exhibits and authentic architecture dating to Colonial times. Lyndhurst, a baronial Gothic Revival home, has an impressive list of former residents, from a New York City mayor to a railroad tycoon—and the Hudson River to serve as its backyard. Last but not least, in Irvington, is the noted and carefully preserved mid-19th-century home of author Washington Irving, Sunnyside. The creator of such imaginative works as *Rip Van Winkle* and *The Legend of Sleepy Hollow*, Irving portrayed both the beauty and the enchantment of the Hudson Valley in the many books that he penned within Sunnyside's walls.

Green Mountain Highway

This classic tour through the heart of Vermont passes green pastures grazed by contented cattle, tidy villages with quaint general stores, and mountains that seem as old as time.

In Plymouth Notch a cool autumn rain stirs the scent of damp fallen leaves.

Virtually bisecting the state from top to bottom, Rte. 100 has occasionally been called Vermont's Main Street. Beginning near the Massachusetts border and weaving northward past farms, villages, and mountain woodlands almost to the Canadian border, this charming drive comprises the scenic quintessence of Vermont.

1 Wilmington

Chartered a quarter century before America won its independence, tiny Wilmington once hewed its living from the surrounding forests. Today, this white-steepled village on the banks of the Deerfield River plies instead the Yankee innkeeper's trade, serving a cluster of nearby ski resorts.

Gen. John Stark passed this way during the Revolutionary War as he led his troops in 1777 to the Battle of Bennington, where he swore that the British would be defeated "or tonight Molly Stark sleeps a widow." Stark not only survived, he triumphed, and in tribute to him and his wife, Rte. 9 is now called the Molly Stark Trail.

Follow the trail east out of Wilmington for about three miles, and you'll arrive at Molly Stark State Park, where a path leads to the summit of 2,415-foot Mt. Olga. The most appealing views are off to the east, toward the rolling hills of New Hampshire, but in early autumn the mountain's own cloak of crimson maples and canary-yellow birches easily surpasses the lure of the distant horizon.

2 Green Mountain National Forest

Ever since it was settled by southern New England colonists hankering for elbow room, Vermont has meant many things to many people—survival on hardscrabble farms, the lonely grandeur of the Green Mountains, the sun's sparkle on freshly powdered mountain slopes. Rte. 100, wending its way north from Wilmington, visits all of these various Vermonts.

Within its first 10 miles north of the Molly Stark Trail, the drive links two of the state's many skiing meccas, Haystack and Mt. Snow—the latter named not for its stock-in-trade, but for the Reuben Snow farm that occupied this site until 1954. Farming was once far more widespread in the unforgiving uplands of Vermont. Much of the territory that makes up the nearly 400,000-acre Green Mountain National Forest, which Rte. 100 enters just beyond West Dover, was cleared of trees a century and a half ago. Today two great swaths of the state's rugged heartland comprises the national forest, established in 1932. A vast resource of timber, it also shelters species as diverse as the peregrine falcon and the eastern coyote (a resourceful predator that has expanded its range in recent years).

3 Townshend State Park

Tucked next to an oxbow bend of the West River, West Townshend lies one mile east of Rte. 100's convergence with Rte. 30 at East Jamaica. Two miles to the south at Townshend, you'll find the entrance to Townshend State Park. Nearby, the river is spanned by two very different structures—the Townshend Dam, built in 1961, and the Scott Covered Bridge. Dating to 1870, this bridge is one of the longest and handsomest of the state's 100-plus surviving wooden spans. Contrary to legend, these shedlike structures were enclosed to protect timbers and roadbeds from the elements, not to prevent horses from balking at river crossings. Today, these quaint bridges are as much a symbol of Vermont as dairy cows and cheese.

Townshend State Park serves as the trailhead for a path that leads to the summit of Bald Mountain. The trail meanders past an alder swamp, across a murmuring brook, and through a hemlock wood; it then ascends nearly 1,100 feet in less than two miles. The reward at the top is a splendid panorama of farms and forests along the West River valley.

4 Jamaica State Park

Returning to East Jamaica and Rte. 100, head north three miles to Jamaica State Park. Here, where the West River loops eastward around the great granite bulk of Ball Mountain, you can cool off at an old-fashioned swimming hole, watch as white-water canoeists and kayakers negotiate the river rapids, or hike to Cobb Brook's 125-foot plunge over the smooth chutes and jagged precipices of Hamilton Falls.

Though no sign of its untamed past lingers, this idyllic woodland was once at New England's western frontier. One day in 1748, as a party of Colonial scouts was returning to a fort on the Connecticut River from Lake Champlain, they were ambushed by

::::: Trip Tips :::::

Length: About 220 miles, plus side trips.

When to go: Popular year-round; fall foliage is especially beautiful in early to mid-October—newspapers have color reports.

Words to the wise: Book reservations early for fall foliage tours and accommodations. Mountain roads may be closed in winter. Some attractions are seasonal.

Nearby attractions: The Bennington Museum, Bennington. Village of Newfane. Vermont Historical Society Museum, Montpelier. Maple Grove Maple Museum (featuring exhibits on maple sugaring), St. Johnsbury.

Further information: Vermont Dep't. of Tourism & Marketing, 6 Baldwin St., Drawer 33, Montpelier, VT 05633-1301; tel. 800-837-6668, www.vermontvacation.com.

Abnaki Indians at the foot of Ball Mountain, and six of their number were killed.

5 Scenic Mountain Loop

Once you reach the hamlet of Rawsonville, you can proceed in one of two ways: north on Rte. 100 or west on Rte. 30. Rte. 100 passes through meadows and valleys punctuated by the streamside village of South Londonderry.

Rte. 30 opens a scenic highland circuit that passes through Green Mountain National Forest and the heart of southern Vermont's ski country. Just to the west of Rawsonville is the access road to Stratton Mountain, a giant alpine resort that features a gondola ride to the windy summit, where visitors are treated to views of four states. Past Stratton, turn right onto Rte. 11 and continue past the ski trails of Bromley Mountain, which presides over a 10-mile valley vista.

Before you get back to Rte. 100, you'll pass a turnoff leading to the toylike village of Peru—a handful of houses, a white church, and the venerable, squeaky-floored J. J. Hapgood Store, established in 1827 and still offering everything from penny candy to fishing line.

6 Weston

Lying in the shadows of Markham and Terrible mountains, Weston was one of the first of the classic Vermont hill villages to turn its face to the outside world. Here, beside the village green with its handsome little bandstand, tourists take photos and townsfolk pick up their mail at the tiny post office. On summer evenings local theater thrives at the Weston Playhouse.

Just up the street the Vermont Country Store—selling souvenirs, calico by the yard, and mail-order goods to the far corners of the globe—keeps a fire in its potbellied stove during the cold months. At a riverside bowl mill, craftspeople transform trees into woodenware, while innkeepers pamper travelers with candlelit dinners and canopy beds. North of town, near the fork of Rtes. 100 and 155, Benedictine monks at the Weston Priory hold to a tradition far older than the hill towns of Vermont, soothing daily visitors with inspirational songs of their own composition.

7 Ludlow

Rte. 100 leaves Weston the way so many roads depart Vermont towns —by climbing over a mountain. Terrible Mountain isn't really terrible, at least not by modern standards. But some 200 years ago, when Weston was a new settlement set against the mountain wilderness, the descriptive name probably made sense.

On the other side of the mountain, the road dips into Ludlow, an old factory town whose principal mill has been renovated and now contains eateries that cater to skiers taking a break from the slopes at nearby Okemo Mountain. In summer or fall follow a paved road to Okemo's 3,343-foot summit, where views extend across the Connecticut Valley.

8 Plymouth

When the warm, sunny days of March alternate with subfreezing nights, the sap begins to rise in sugar maple trees.

Soon clouds of steam rise from hundreds of sugarhouses, where sugarers boil tapped-off liquid sap until it has thickened into the incomparably delectable companion to pancakes, waffles, baked beans, and vanilla ice cream we all know and love.

Sugaring time is as old as the region's Native Americans and a link to all the generations of Vermonters. Surely, for example, it would have been a fact of life for the country's 30th president, Calvin Coolidge, when he was a boy in Plymouth. The entire village, 14 miles north of Ludlow via Rtes. 100 and 100A, has been designated the Plymouth Notch Historic District, and it encapsulates Coolidge's life and character. Here are the buildings where he was raised, the store his family kept, and the kerosene-lit room where his father, a notary

Moss Glen Falls, north of Granville, is a restful roadside oasis worthy of a pause to refresh one's spirit.

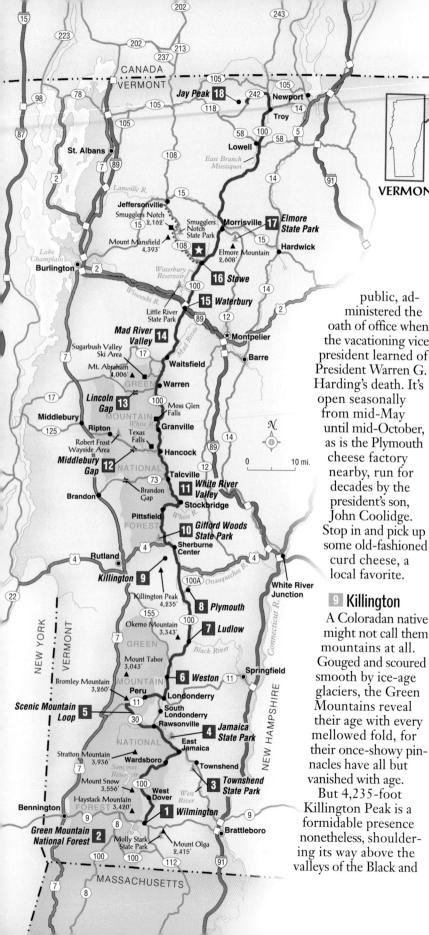

Ottauquechee rivers near the intersection of Rtes. 100 and 4. A century ago, central Vermonters liked to boast that Killington was the state's highest peak—until more accurate surveys gave the title to Mt. Mansfield, farther to the north. Nowadays, Killington still has its own claims to fame: it is one of the most popular ski areas in the Northeast, and the 5,998-foot double chairlift ride from Rte. 4 to the summit—a fine way to enjoy the fall foliage along with a rest from driving—reaches the highest lift-served elevation in New England.

10 Gifford Woods State Park

Beyond Killington Rte. 100 strikes north from Rte. 4, arrowing directly into deep forests of hardwoods and evergreens. In this rolling, mountain-shadowed terrain, signs of civilization trail off so rapidly that the big ski resort might well have been a mirage. Just beyond the intersection, the lordly maples and hemlocks of Gifford Woods State Park stand as a living link with the Vermont of ages past, for this is climax forest, a woodland never touched by axe or plow.

11 White River Valley

North of Stockbridge, Rte. 100 parallels the White River, which traces the eastern boundary of Green Mountain National Forest. To the west lie Mt. Carmel, Bloodroot Mountain, Round Mountain, and other peaks—hulking barricades that separate the lush Champlain Valley from Rte. 100. But there are clefts in this wall of mountains. Just north of tiny Talcville, Rte. 73 lurches west and ascends to 2,183-foot Brandon Gap, one of the major Green Mountain passes. At the gap the road crosses the Long Trail, Vermont's 270-mile "footpath in the wilderness" that follows the crest of the mountains from Massachusetts to

Canada. For a vigorous break from driving, set out on the trail for a while. To the south a wayside shelter awaits hikers less than a mile away; to the north a steep hike leads to the cliff-girded summit of Mt. Horrid.

12 Middlebury Gap

Farther north along Rte. 100, a turn west on Rte. 125 at Hancock leads to Middlebury Gap, named for the cozy college town that lies across the mountains. After climbing for three miles, the road's path reaches a short side route to the picnic area at Texas Falls, where the Hancock Branch of the White River roars over a granite escarpment to create one of Vermont's loveliest wilderness cascades.

Farther west, beyond the gap's highest point, a wayside honors

Star Route

★ Mountain Road (Rte. 108)

Setting out from the charming resort town of Stowe, Mountain Road leads northwest through a string of stunning attractions, beginning with Mt. Mansfield. The toll road or a gondola will take you most of the way up, but you'll have to hike the final distance to the spectacular summit. From there you can see Lake Champlain and the Adirondacks to the west, Canada to the north, and the White Mountains of New Hampshire to the east. Farther along, at Smugglers Notch, a dramatic pass flanked by high walls of silver rock, you can hike the Long Trail to lovely Sterling Pond or cool off in the dank recesses of Smugglers Cave. Descending from these high, rocky places, the drive breezes past a series of enticing picnic spots before arriving at Jeffersonville.

---

public, administered the oath of office when the vacationing vice president learned of President Warren G. Harding's death. It's open seasonally from mid-May until mid-October, as is the Plymouth cheese factory nearby, run for decades by the president's son, John Coolidge. Stop in and pick up some old-fashioned curd cheese, a local favorite.

9 Killington

A Coloradan native might not call them mountains at all. Gouged and scoured smooth by ice-age glaciers, the Green Mountains reveal their age with every mellowed fold, for their once-showy pinnacles have all but vanished with age.

But 4,235-foot Killington Peak is a formidable presence nonetheless, shouldering its way above the valleys of the Black and

Vermont Cheese

Introduced by English colonists in the 1700s, cheddar cheese has been a staple in Vermont ever since. Today the cheesemaking tradition continues at factories scattered throughout the state, including several not far from Rte. 100. For a look at the process, stop at the following: the Grafton Village Cheese Company in Grafton, Crowley Cheese in Healdville, Sugarbush Farm near Woodstock, or the Cabot Farmers Cooperative Creamery in Cabot. Others are listed at the Vermont Cheese Council website, www.vtcheese.com.

An 18th-century grist mill on the West River in the village of Weston evokes the Vermont of yesteryear.

poet Robert Frost, who lived for more than 20 years in the nearby village of Ripton. Frost once declared that along with New Hampshire, Vermont was "one of the two best states in the Union." Plaques along a footpath are inscribed with quotes taken from the poet's works.

13 Lincoln Gap

North of Hancock, the forests of the Green Mountain foothills take on a somber, almost melancholy cast. The heart of this cool, shadowy realm is the six-mile stretch called Granville Gulf, north of the little town of Granville. Wooded slopes close ever more tightly about the roadway, until the trees give way to sheer rock walls, dripping with the cold waters of cascading mountain streams.

The road up to the wildest and loftiest of the Green Mountain gaps begins at Warren, 10 miles north of Granville. As the Lincoln Gap road climbs westward away from Rte. 100, it is sheltered by tall ancient maples that in summer shroud the highway and, in winter, lies underneath an impassable blanket of snow.

When drivers reach the road's 2,424-foot crest, they discover that the venerable Long Trail has gotten there first and offers the challenge of a 2½-mile trek to the top of Mt. Abraham, a 4,006-foot perch commanding views of the Champlain Valley, Lake Champlain, and New York's towering Adirondacks.

14 Mad River Valley

Loosed from the tight grip of Granville Gulf, Rte. 100 makes the six-mile northward run from Warren to Waitsfield along the fertile fields of the Mad River valley. The stream runs to madness only when it's gorged with snowmelt in spring; during the rest of the year, it flows gently through a bucolic region of ski resorts and well-maintained family farms.

The ski areas—sprawling Sugarbush and smaller, tradition-minded Mad River Glen—both lie west of Rte. 100 between Warren and Waitsfield. The farms, like most in Vermont, are dairies, and their daily chores have hardly changed over the decades. The milking machines may be electric, but the farmer must still be in the barn before first light; capricious summer weather still spells out the fate of the vital corn crop used for the cattle's feed; and "Make hay while the sun shines" is more than a mere figure of speech.

15 Waterbury

Vermont milk and Vermont apples undergo a transformation into two kinds of ambrosia here in Waterbury. In 1977 a pair of free spirits named Ben Cohen and Jerry Greenfield took a correspondence course in ice-cream making and set up shop in 1978 in a converted Burlington gas station—and the dessert world hasn't been the same since. In 1985, when the un-

Though autumn hues cast their own particular spell on this well-known village, Stowe retains its classic New England charm throughout every season of the year.

likely moguls needed a new factory, they came to Waterbury, a quiet old red-brick town located where Rte. 100 crosses the Winooski River. The factory, now Ben & Jerry's headquarters, welcomes visitors to its assembly lines with free samples, a cheerful soda fountain, and more than a dollop of the zaniness that put the old gas station on the map. Just up the road, a more traditional Vermont treat is produced at the

Cold Hollow Cider Mill. You can watch the big press squeeze the rich bronze juice from tart locally grown apples, and you can shop for treats that range from apple pies to apple butter.

Head a mile and a half west from Rte. 100 on Rte. 2 to discover Waterbury's main outdoor attraction, Little River State Park. Its densely wooded grounds border the blue waters of meandering Waterbury Reservoir. Calm-water

canoeing, swimming from sandy beaches, and fishing for trout, perch, and bass all help work up an appetite for, well, fresh-squeezed cider and refreshing ice cream.

16 Stowe

Like a snow-white lance aimed skyward, the lofty and narrow spire of Stowe's Community Church identifies this most famous of Rte. 100's long skein of country villages. Stowe—the town, the

resort, and the mystique—seems to gather strength throughout the 10-mile drive north from Waterbury. Inns and ski shops tell the story, but none more strikingly than the great looming profile of Mt. Mansfield. At 4,393 feet, it is Vermont's highest peak.

For generations of skiers, the sport has been synonymous with the 241-year-old town. Vermont skiing didn't get its start here, but once Mansfield's first trails were cut in the early 1930s, the legend was irrevocably launched. Stowe's alpine cachet was helped immensely by the arrival, more than half a century ago, of an Austrian family named Von Trapp—the real-life inspiration behind the popular musical and stage play, *The Sound of Music.* Just outside the village, off Rte. 108, the Trapp Family Lodge commands a view of meadows and mountains that might have been imported from the Tyrol, along with the familiar strains of the Trapp family's music.

17 Elmore State Park

Beginning with a flicker of yellow in the high country, the blaze fully ignites in the cold valley pockets before raging through the temperate lowlands. The trees explode with color during fall foliage season, but strangely their beauty results from nature's closing up shop. Chlorophyll makes summer leaves green, and its supply diminishes as the days grow shorter, unmasking a kaleidoscope of pigments in the few precious weeks before the first gusts of late October winds strip the branches bare.

For a front-row seat at this annual spectacle, hike the trail that leads up Mt. Elmore, in Elmore State Park just east of Morrisville. From the abandoned fire tower at the summit, the colors of autumn —saffron, gold, scarlet, apricot, rust—radiate to the horizon and reflect in the clear waters of Lake Elmore far below.

18 Jay Peak

As the drive draws to a close, it skims the edges of Vermont's least-populated corner, whose nickname, the Northeast Kingdom, evokes a fairyland of fabled treasures. Rich it is, too—in solitude, timberlands, and wildlife. Travelers rarely meet another car on the scenic gravel roads that snake through the backcountry hills, but they might see a moose trudging within or alongside a beaver-dammed pond as it seeks water sedges to feed on.

Standing alone and apart near the end of Rte. 100, Jay Peak is the northern bastion of the long chain of Green Mountains. But for all the nearby wilderness, Jay is still part of the skier's Vermont. The beaklike shape you see at the top of the mountain is the summit station of an aerial tramway, its roomy cabs suspended by steel cables above a yawning forest gulf. You don't have to ski down— the tramway runs in summer and fall—and Jay's grand isolation will ensure views that reach as far distant as glittering Lake Champlain, Mt. Washington in far-off New Hampshire, and Canada to the north. Quebec Province is so close, in fact, that you are likely to hear French spoken on the mountain, though peculiarly accented with the Vermont twang.

Rte. 100 ends just south of the Canadian border at a junction with Rte. 105, next to a farmer's field. Travelers heading north from Massachusetts may lament that Vermont's Main Street, having led them to so many exciting places, ends here so anonymously. But for motorists driving in the opposite direction, that farmer's field marks the gateway to adventure.

As wavy and windblown as a Vermont lake, a thick blanket of snow envelops a farmer's field south of Newport Center.

Vermont's Quiet Corner

A glimpse of New England life awaits along
this drive, which wends through the White River Valley
to farms and villages farther north.

The dairylands and gentle hills near Tunbridge as seen from the air.

Even by Vermont standards, much of the northeastern corner of the state is an out-of-the-way place, wild and unpopulated. The narrow roads are weatherworn, dairy farmers live much as their 19th-century ancestors did, and the forests form a mantle of green brocade across the hills. For a rural rhapsody sampling such country charms, follow this drive through the Green Mountain State.

1 White River Valley

Two rivers and two interstate highways converge in the village of White River Junction, long a rest stop for weary travelers. Shady blocks of stately brick buildings comprise the downtown area, where the Hotel Coolidge, with its fine murals and antiques, has been offering accommodations ever since the railroad came through town in the late 1800s.

Before you head northward from White River Junction, consider a six-mile sidetrip westward on Rte. 4 to Quechee Gorge, Vermont's Little Grand Canyon. A bridge, perched 165 feet above the gorge's floor, offers dizzying views of the stone-strewn chasm, carved into the foothills by the Ottauquechee River. Several additional overlooks are positioned on both sides of the gorge's rim. Or to sample the area on foot, you can follow one of several hiking trails—some lead all the way down to the river.

2 Sharon

The bends and straightaways of the White River guide Rte. 14 north to Sharon. While lovely hilltop churches are signature sights in New England, a religious landmark of a different sort lies just a few miles north of town: the boyhood home of Joseph Smith, who was born in 1805 and, later founded the Church of Jesus Christ of Latter-day Saints. A steep, tree-lined turnoff leads to his family's farm, which today has been designated a Mormon shrine complete with a museum and a granite memorial dedicated to Smith. The site's fields and forests, about 360 acres in all, are a walker's delight.

3 Strafford

The drive switches onto Rte. 132, veering northeastward through a pocket of Vermont that has largely escaped the modern world. A patchwork of rustic villages, dairy farms, clapboard dwellings, and meadows grazed by Morgan horses fills the valleys between the hills. The West Branch of the Ompompanoosuc River, a gentle waterway, runs beside the road. Scan the horizon where the views open up at higher elevations: the White Mountains crest in the east; the more rounded Green Mountains rumble to the west.

Well-kept white houses grace the peaceful small town of Strafford. One standout here is the impressive pink mansion that was the residence of Justin Smith Morrill, a three-term U.S. congressman and longtime senator. Though fond of his estate, he represented Vermont in national politics for so long—more than 40 years—that much of his time was spent in Washington, D.C. One of his proudest achievements was the 1862 Morrill Act, which granted the states federal lands in order to finance the establishment of colleges.

4 Tunbridge

Winters are cold here, as the high-stacked piles of firewood testify. Many farmers, seeking ways to milk their cows without having to brave the brisk outdoors, have connected their homes to their barns with rambling additions or enclosed walkways, simple but sure examples of Yankee ingenuity.

Craftsbury Common has a spacious village green.

Covered bridges are another common sight in Vermont, and five of them can be found in Tunbridge alone. (The town, though, was named for an 18th-century nobleman, not a bridge.) The most prominent wooden span is the Howe Bridge, south of town. Dating from 1879, it is almost as old as Tunbridge's self-proclaimed World's Fair—a festival that has been held each autumn since the 1860s. The celebration features such pastoral pleasures as floral displays and fiddling contests.

5 Brookfield

At South Royalton, across the river from the white buildings of the Vermont Law School, take Rte. 14 north to Royalton, a town that was burned to the ground in 1780 by raiding British soldiers and Indians. Next you'll pass through three separate Randolphs: South, East, and North. (There's also a Randolph Center and Randolph Village—a small indication of how Vermonters can make the most out of anything, even a name.)

In Brookfield stop at Sunset Lake, site of the annual Ice Harvest Festival. If you're here the last weekend in January, you'll witness some of the area's hardiest residents using ice saws and tongs as they demonstrate the old-time skill of carving out block ice.

Still waters run deep at Sunset Lake—so deep that it has been impractical to connect the two sides of the lake with a conventional anchored bridge. The solution: a "floating bridge" buoyed by almost 400 barrels. Its simplicity is a perfect match for the understated beauty of Brookfield itself.

6 Barre

Forested mountains hem in Rte. 14 as it snakes northward through a chasm called the Williamstown Gulf. Farther on, after emerging from the deep valley, the drive enters the town of Barre, where the New England work ethic is clearly in evidence.

More than 1,500 residents are employed by local granite quarries and stonecutters, which produce one-third of the nation's memorial stones. The biggest pit of them all—the largest, deepest granite quarry in the world—lies to the southeast of Barre in aptly named Graniteville, where the Rock of Ages company has been mining stones from the earth since 1885. Guided tours are available in summer, and visitors can watch as skilled stonecutters reshape blocks weighing as much as 200 tons.

Spreading across the hillsides north of Barre, Hope Cemetery, like an outdoor sculpture garden, is replete with the finished products of the granite-carving artisans. The stones have been fashioned with consummate skill to resemble everything from racing cars, airplanes, and soccer balls to the detailed likenesses of people.

7 Craftsbury Common

Christened the Northeast Kingdom, this backcountry corner of

Vermont has a subdued rural grace that combines lakes, woodlands, and meadows. As Rte. 14 rolls through the region, it passes towns with names reflecting the area's French-Canadian and Yankee

heritages: East Montpelier and Calais, Woodbury and Hardwick.

Farther along, just past the serene expanse of Eligo Pond, detour onto Craftsbury Road for a visit to a string of hamlets that—probably not a surprise by now—also share a common name: East Craftsbury, Craftsbury, and Craftsbury Common. Elegant farmhouses and rolling ridges bedecked with apple orchards and evergreens are bountiful here. On the approach to Craftsbury Common, though, the trees part to reveal a splendid hilltop village green—a large and well-tended lawn surrounded by immaculate clapboard homes, steepled churches, and a grand country inn.

If you have the time and are inclined to continue still farther north on Rte. 14—perhaps all the way to Canada—you'll travel beside the Black River through a land much like the boreal forest that lies in the far north, just south of the Arctic Circle. Lakes and bogs speckle the countryside, and woodlands of spruce trees and other evergreens extend for miles. In the towns that populate this northern province, it is said, you are more likely to meet a moose than another person.

New Hampshire Highlights

From riverside lowlands this drive climbs
to higher ground, where waterfalls rush and tumble
and where the wind whips across mountaintops.

*The faint glow of autumn
light dances on the still
surface of Saco Lake.*

Granite, some say, is New Hampshire's most abundant crop, with the hard rock visible nearly everywhere. The farmer's curse, however, is the sightseer's blessing, giving form to the state's imposing cliffs and peaks—a ruggedness that is offset by the gentle grace of mixed forests and rushing streams.

1 Hanover

"It is … a small college, and yet there are those who love it," proclaimed Daniel Webster, one of Dartmouth College's most famous graduates. The same could be said of the school's home, Hanover, where town and gown seem intimately bound. Coffeehouses, bookstores, and other shops are signs of the school's influence. The College Green, the grassy heart of the campus, is flanked on one side by Dartmouth Row, a quartet of white Georgian-style buildings. Other notable sites include the Hood Museum of Art and the Baker Library, whose belfry rises even higher than the institution's towering elms and maples.

2 Orford

Leaving college life behind, Rte. 10 leads northward to Lyme—one of those pretty towns that everyone associates with New England. Here the drive mirrors the meandering curves of the Connecticut River, the natural causeway that brought commerce and culture to the area. Settlers blazed trails beside its banks, drawn by the fertile land of its floodplain and the virgin forests on the surrounding hills.

Even the rushing water was a resource to early settlers, a force able to set massive machinery in motion. Mills were erected at intervals all along the river. Today many of these brick structures have been renovated into inviting shops and restaurants, and the houses that the factory owners built still grace the towns.

One such community is Orford, where early mansions—some date back to the late 1700s—crown a ridge above the Connecticut River. Impressive too are the views, which take in 600-foot cliffs—the Palisades—that protrude along the Vermont side of the river in Fairlee, just a bridge crossing away.

3 Bath

The drive continues to parallel the Connecticut River as far north as Woodsville, where it veers northeastward on Rte. 302. A much smaller waterway, the Ammonoosuc River, now tumbles merrily beside the road, which soon enters Bath, also the site of an early mill. In town you can rattle across a covered bridge that is more than 370 feet long and was built in 1832. (In the days before iron and steel were used in bridge construction, wooden spans such as this one were roofed and sided with wood in order to protect their planked

::::: **Trip Tips** :::::

Length: About 120 miles.

When to go: Fine scenery year-round, Allow for extreme seasonal differences in weather that can occur in any season.

Nearby attraction: Saint-Gaudens National Historic Site, the home and gardens of the famed sculptor, south of Lebanon via Rte. 12A.

Not to be missed: Dartmouth Winter Carnival, featuring snow sculptures, ski races, and musical performances. Held in early February in Hanover.

Further information: New Hampshire Div. of Travel & Tourism Development, P.O. Box 1856, Concord, NH 03302; tel. 603-271-2665, www.visitnh.gov.

roadbeds and supporting timbers from the elements.)

Farther on, Rte. 302 ripples past hayfields and rolling pasturelands. Here you'll find that the Ammonoosuc River deepens into swimming and fishing holes. One of the largest of these pools, Salmon Hole, lies a few miles to the north in the town of Lisbon, where Rtes. 302 and 117 intersect.

4 Littleton

Though you won't see any skyscrapers, Littleton has been this region's "big city" since the early 1800s. Back then the factories kept people warm by producing buckskin mittens and gloves and woolen cloth—absolute necessities during a New Hampshire winter. An early settler could also purchase an axe, then get on with the never-ending chore of chopping firewood. Today the mills are gone, but Littleton's historical society (located at 2 Cottage Street) and several examples of early architecture help recall the bygone era.

5 Bethlehem

The drive soon begins to climb in earnest as Rte. 302 heads into the foothills of the White Mountains. On the way, be sure to tour Bethlehem, a longtime resort area that lies halfway up the granite shoulder of Mt. Agassiz. It was to this town at the turn of the century that many people suffering from hay fever—presidents and poets among them—came by the hundreds to escape the ill effects of summertime pollen. A walk through the thick stands of evergreens here—which drop their pollen in springtime and are free of it by summer—will quickly confirm the opinion of those earlier visitors: the fresh air truly is invigorating.

The terrain turns wonderfully wild and rugged as the drive rolls onward and upward to the Presidential Range, the tallest peaks of the White Mountains. Rocky and bruised by the often brutal climate, the summits slice the sky all along the eastern horizon. The seemingly endless woodlands in this region are protected as

part of the White Mountain National Forest, a vast tract that stretches into Maine. The Trestle Trail, one of the first places to sample the forest on foot, begins near the town of Twin Mountains. Though fairly short, the pathway wends past a surprisingly varied array of

plant life: patches of wild sarsaparillas, ferns, Canada mayflowers, and stands of red maple, birch, and balsam trees.

6 Bretton Woods

"The second-greatest show on earth" was P. T. Barnum's assessment of the view from atop Mt. Washington. To decide for yourself, take a ride on the historic Cog Railway. It departs from Bretton Woods and huffs and puffs as it inches all the way up to Mt. Washington's lofty 6,288-foot peak. Mixed forests yield to stunted evergreens along the way, until above the timberline only tundra plants can survive. Hardy well-equipped hikers can descend via the Jewell Trail, which skirts the 1,600-foot cliffs of the Great Gulf on the way back to Bretton Woods, where the tired can unwind at the Mt. Washington Hotel, a white palace of a place that sits in the shadows of the great peak.

7 Crawford Notch State Park

Hot on the trail of an elusive moose in 1771, a hunter by the name of Timothy Nash stumbled upon a gap in the mountains that no white man had ever seen. Today that steep-sided cleft is known as Crawford Notch, a rugged pass where the Saco River scoots between rocky ramparts washed by water racing down from the uplands. Silver Cascade can be seen from the road, while Arethusa Falls, the highest waterfall in the

Even granite gives way to the grind of Silver Cascade.

state, can be reached by a hike that passes Frankenstein Cliff, whose monstrous wall—covered with a glistening sheath of ice in winter—rises to an elevation of 2,451 feet.

8 Mt. Attitash

The familiar sight of rushing water accompanies the road as it snakes beside the Saco River. Just a little east of Bartlett, the trails of the ski area on Mt. Attitash trace thin lines among the trees—streamers of white in winter and ribbons of green in summer. Visitors can ride a chairlift to the 2,300-foot summit. In service year-round, it whisks passengers to an observation tower for a last glimpse of the Presidential Range, its peaks perhaps gilded by the setting sun.

White Mountain Wonderland

"The woods are lovely, dark, and deep," wrote Robert Frost, moved by the icy beauty of the White Mountains. But while these sugarcone peaks live up to their name only in winter, they are worth a visit at any time of year.

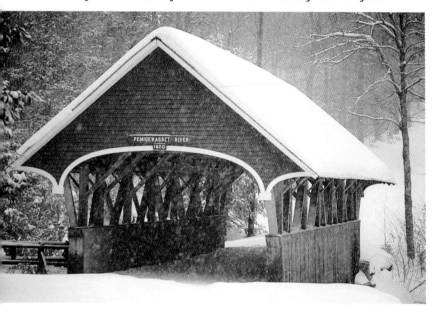

The covered bridge at Franconia Notch is just one of dozens in New Hampshire.

Though the northern tier of New Hampshire is home to fewer than one-tenth of the state's million or so residents, it boasts a majority of its tall peaks. The region is renowned for its 48 summits that rise above 4,000 feet—including Mt. Washington, the loftiest in the Northeast. All of them are embraced by the White Mountain National Forest, where 23 campgrounds, 50 lakes and ponds, 1,200 miles of trails, and 750 miles of fishing streams make this 770,000-acre tract of wildlands a paradise for lovers of the outdoors.

1 Franconia Notch State Park
Heading southeast from Franconia, Rte. 18 leads travelers to the Franconia Notch Parkway, a dramatic eight-mile stretch of Rte. 93 that climbs past craggy peaks, mountain lakes, mile-long slides, and gutted ravines on the way to Lincoln. Just west of the highway sprawls 6,500-acre Fran-

conia Notch State Park, built around a spectacular mountain pass. Take Exit 34B to the Cannon Mountain Aerial Tramway, the first of its kind in North America. A five-minute ride whisks visitors 2,000 vertical feet to the mountain's 4,180-foot summit, where an observation tower commands views that extend into four states and Canada.

From the tramway you can spot Echo Lake, sparkling far below like a turquoise jewel. A haven for fishing and boating, the looking-glass lake is fed by springs and surging streams that crash through a hushed forest of birch, beech, and spruce trees. Gangling moose stare from the woods, and graceful deer step lightly through the underbrush like four-legged ballerinas, pausing to nibble on buds.

Also along Exit 34B a pullout offers a view of the former site of the Old Man of the Mountain—a series of stacked granite ledges that resembled a human profile and was the state's emblem, but which fell in May 2003. As taciturn-looking as a New England farmer, the 40-foot-high rock formation was the inspiration for one of Nathaniel Hawthorne's tales and dubbed the Great Stone Face. What really made the image famous, though, was its appearance on New Hampshire license plates. It stood for years beyond its natural life with the surgical assistance of locals, who each spring rewired its stony countenance and patched its unsightly cracks. Back on the parkway, Basin Exit leads to a shimmering pool, located at the foot of a waterfall that swirls and foams with bubbles like a giant Jacuzzi.

2 Flume Gorge
Return once again to the parkway and take Exit 34A to the visitor center at Flume Gorge, where a shuttle bus takes visitors to within 500 feet of the entrance to the

A screech owl resting in its woody home.

gorge. There a cascading brook burbles through an 800-foot-long chasm hemmed in by towering granite walls. The gorge is especially lovely in springtime, when painted trilliums, trout lilies, wild cherry blossoms, and many other blooms upholster its banks.

Beyond the flume, hiking trails wander through the woods and across two covered bridges. On bright spring days sunlight filters through the dense canopy of trees, creating puddles of light on the forest floor. Farther ahead on Rte. 93, the drive briefly overlaps Rte. 3 and hugs the Pemigewasset River on the way to Lincoln. There the drive veers eastward on Rte. 112— the Kancamagus Highway (pronounced *Kan-ka-MAW-gus*).

3 Kancamagus Highway
Named for a Penacook chief, "the Kanc," as locals call it, rises to an elevation of 2,900 feet, making it one of the highest roadways in the Northeast. In autumn it's also one of the prettiest, corkscrewing as it does past birches, beeches, and maples that blaze against an emerald backdrop of spruces and hemlocks. This 34-mile byway passes near dozens of waterfalls but not a single restaurant or fuel station, so you may wish to stop at Lincoln before getting on Rte. 112. The White Mountain Visitors Center, just off Exit 32 on Rte. 93, is a good place to get acquainted with the scenery and sites that lie ahead.

From Lincoln the drive climbs 1,000 feet in just 10 miles, spiraling past jagged peaks and glacier-carved cirques. Strewn about the rugged landscape are countless boulders, many of which—poised on tiny toes of rock and leaning at unlikely angles—seem ready to roll with the next gust of wind.

4 Kancamagus Pass

At an elevation of almost 2,900 feet, Kancamagus Pass is the highest point on Rte. 112, making this stretch of road especially scenic. On the way up you'll see the trailheads of the Pemigewasset Wilderness Area, 45,000 acres of untamed territory bordered by the Appalachian Trail (one of many to be enjoyed here). Once you reach the pass, the dazzling scenery may tempt you to keep turning your head—but keep your eyes focused on the road. Before long you will encounter two hairpin curves, made all the more hazardous by

A branch from a silver maple floats in a pond at Franconia Notch State Park.

their lack of guardrails to stop vehicles from plunging down the hillside and into the valley.

Atop the pass, views open up to the Presidential Range, a jumble of 11 lofty peaks, six of them named for American presidents. Several of these summits top off at more than a mile above sea level, and the tallest of them—at 6,288 feet—is Mt. Washington, whose rocky crest is sometimes visible from as far as 70 miles away. Some of the best views of the Presidentials are available at the nearby C. L. Graham Wangan Ground, a former Indian meeting place that is now a lovely picnic spot.

5 Sabbaday Falls

With the Pemigewasset and Swift rivers as its companions, the road dips for several miles on its way to Sabbaday Falls, another nice place for a picnic, and Lily Pond. Spring transforms the pond into a floating garden. Just a short distance from the picnic grounds are the falls themselves, a three-level cascade that plunges to a pool where swimming, unfortunately, is not permitted. Named for the Sabbath, the falls remain a popular destination on any day of the week.

Several miles ahead lies the historic Russell-Colbath House, where a half-mile trail parallels an old railway grade that skirts neighboring woods and swamps. You can gain access to another nature walk at Bear Notch Road (just past the Jigger Johnson campground), which winds into ethereal evergreens and rock grottoes that on cloudy days are sometimes shrouded in mist.

6 Rocky Gorge Scenic Area

Sculpted by the erosive forces of the Swift River, this rocky medley of clefts, caves, and ledges can be explored by means of a footbridge that crosses the gorge. Nearby, another bridge—this one covered—

leads back to Rte. 112, which continues east along the Swift River until it reaches Conway.

7 Conway

At Conway, where the mountains give way to rolling uplands, the drive makes a sharp turn north. Several miles ahead lies its sister town of North Conway. Both villages have a quintessential New England charm, complete with 19th-century covered bridges, swimming holes, waterfalls, and a host of inviting inns. The stretch of Rte. 16 between them, however, is another story. Dominated by fast-food chains and factory outlets, the road can be a motorist's nightmare—especially on rainy days and weekends, when bargain hunters abound. North Conway offers two consolation prizes to those who brave the traffic: a grand view of Mt. Washington and a scenic railroad that tours through the surrounding valley.

8 Echo Lake State Park

From the north end of North Conway, River Road winds west to Echo Lake State Park, a 400-acre recreation area huddled beneath White Horse Ledge. A scenic road leads to another dramatic rock formation, 700-foot-high Cathedral Ledge. The drive returns to North Conway and heads north on Rte. 16/302, then branches northeast on Rte. 16A toward Intervale. The two-mile Intervale Resort Loop circles up and around

the towns of Intervale and Lower Bartlett, affording more fine views of Mt. Washington. The drive continues north on Rte. 16A to Jackson.

9 Jackson

With its skating pond, country inns, and covered bridge, Jackson is a Currier and Ives print come to life. Although its population is barely 650, each winter thousands of Nordic skiers come here to enjoy a 95-mile network of trails. In fact, some Jacksonites park their cars for the winter and ski to work.

10 Pinkham Notch

From Jackson the highway climbs to Pinkham Notch, a scenic pass offering a breathtaking view of Mt. Washington. Meandering through the woods, the Glen Ellis Falls Trail leads to a scenic overlook of the Ellis River as it crashes 80 feet to a churning pool.

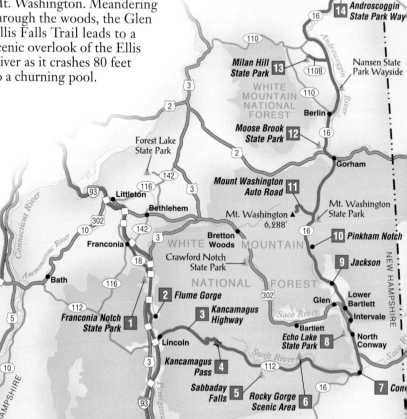

High atop Cannon Mountain, a hiker surveys the scene.

11 Mt. Washington Auto Road

They call Mt. Washington "the most dangerous small mountain in the world," and with good reason. Despite its relatively modest height, this central peak of the White Mountains has such fierce weather conditions—the highest gust of wind ever recorded on land was clocked here at 231 miles per hour—that Himalayan climbers use it for survival training.

Yet for all its hazards, Mt. Washington remains one of the most accessible summits of its size in the United States. Some of the thousands who visit it each year arrive by way of a well-maintained hiking trail, while others opt for a thrilling ride on the Cog Railway, which departs regularly from Bretton Woods on the western side of the mountain. But most come by way of the Mt. Washington Auto Road (open from May to October, weather permitting), which spirals eight miles up the eastern slope.

Hailed as a masterful feat of engineering when it was completed in 1861, the road was originally designed for stagecoaches from the Glen House Hotel, a stop once located at its base. Nowadays an assortment of vehicles—including unicycles, wheelchairs, and, of course, automobiles and trucks—tackle the same 12-degree grade during occasional scheduled races. If your car is not in tip-top shape, however, you would be well-advised to take one of the regularly scheduled chauffeured vans to the summit.

However you tour Mt. Washington, the trip will be worthwhile. "No other mountain," claims one admirer, "can boast of having a carriage road, railway, four hotels, two weather observatories, a radio station, and a television station." In addition to all that, there are the splendid views that can be enjoyed at the summit. From the peak of the mountain, you can see parts of Maine, Vermont, New York, Massachusetts, Canada, and the Atlantic Ocean.

12 Moose Brook State Park

After exiting the White Mountain National Forest, Rte. 16 passes through Gorham. A short side trip west on Rte. 2 leads to Moose Brook State Park, which is located in the heart of the Presidential Range. Despite its name (which comes from a brook), the 87-acre park is not inhabited by moose, but these massive antlered relatives of deer can be seen nearby on tours hosted by the Gorham Chamber of Commerce during the summer.

13 Milan Hill State Park

Continuing north, the drive passes through Berlin, where the scent of sulfur dioxide—rotten eggs—announces the presence of an enormous paper mill. But a breath of fresh air is just minutes away at Nansen State Park Wayside and, farther ahead, Milan Hill State Park, both ideal spots for hiking and picnicking.

Continuing north beside the Androscoggin River, Rte. 16 eventually enters the Thirteen-Mile Woods Scenic Area, where forested hills inhabited by moose, deer, and bear stretch for miles. Alternately lazy and wild, the river along this stretch of the byway lures fishermen as well as white-water canoeists.

14 Androscoggin State Park Wayside

Perched on a bluff overlooking a bend in the river, this pretty park—once the site of logging drives that floated logs downstream—abounds with picnic spots that offer bird's-eye views of canoeists braving the rapids far below. Just ahead is Errol, a tiny town that is surrounded on all sides by wilderness.

Plunging into an abyss, the Ellis River unleashes its full fury.

Mohawk Trail

Forested mountains, rich river-bottom farmlands, and riotous explosions of autumn color—the splendors of this Massachusetts drive have inspired the raves of travelers for generations.

A floral cascade blankets the streamside trail at Bridge of Flowers in Shelburne Falls.

Mohawk Indians once trod this route across the rugged Berkshire Hills to raid the Pocumtucks of the Deerfield River valley, and armies from Colonial Boston in turn traveled this way to defend the Western Frontier. But the real flood of traffic began in 1914 when the trail opened to automobile traffic—just six years after the first Model T rolled off Henry Ford's production line—for its panoramic vistas helped whet the nation's appetite for leisure-time touring.

1 Northfield Mountain

From the summit of Northfield Mountain, found north of Rte. 2 in western Massachusetts, the view arcs out across a crazy quilt of corn and tobacco fields, ponds and reservoirs, stands of oaks and maples, and 19th-century factory towns, all linked by the majestic sweep of the Connecticut River. On the mountain itself, Northeast Utilities maintains a 2,000-acre complex of woodland hiking paths and ski trails—the Northfield Mountain Recreation and Environmental Center. It's a fine spot to sample this corner of the state, whose character has long been defined by three key ingredients—farmland, mill town, and forest primeval.

2 Turners Falls

The life of the Atlantic salmon—a trout rather than a true salmon—is as fragile as it is astonishing. Each spring, tiny alevins by the millions hatch from eggs in freshwater streams throughout the Northeast. Most of them perish, but some survive and head downriver to spend the next year or two at sea. As adults they return, fighting their way upcurrent to spawn in the same streams where they were born—unless something stops them. And stopped these fish were, until recently, by power dams built across the Connecticut and other rivers. But at Turners Falls, Northeast Utilities has built state-of-the-art fish ladders that enable the salmon—and many shad as well as undesirable lamprey eels—to bypass their dam. At a special viewing area, open in May, you can experience the miracle of the fish's spring migration.

3 Shelburne Falls

Just beyond I-91, Rte. 2 begins its climb into the hills. Scaling the steep wooded slopes of Greenfield Mountain, the Mohawk Trail spins on past apple orchards, pastures, hay fields, maple-sugar houses, and old barns brimming with antiques. Shelburne Falls, the first of the hill towns, is a huddle of rambling Federal-style houses and a historic shopping district nestled beside the Deerfield River.

The first visitors here were Indians, who came to net salmon at the base of the falls, where a swirl of boulders in the closing years of the ice age scooped some 50 circular pools into the bedrock. One pothole, measuring 39 feet across, is said to be the world's largest. Nearby, the 400-foot-long Bridge of Flowers spans the Deerfield River. Originally built for trolley cars, it now displays bright seasonal borders that erupt in a nine-month display of color, from springtime's daffodils and summer's gladiolii to autumn's asters.

4 Charlemont

"There is no lovelier place on earth," once opined Archibald MacLeish, America's late poet laureate and sometime resident of Franklin County, "nothing more human in scale and prospect than our hills." He was opening the summer chamber music season at Charlemont's prim white clapboard Federated Church, perched above the Deerfield River. In summer the concerts and—more ruggedly active—white-water canoeing are the attractions here; in winter skiing is the draw. The Berkshire East Ski Area offers short, steep runs and a Grandma Moses view of town from atop the slopes.

Charlemont also is the center of a renewed Mohawk presence along the trail. Tribal groups from all over the Northeast gather at

:::::: Trip Tips ::::::

Length: About 60 miles, plus side trips.

When to go: Popular year-round, but best in fall for the foliage.

Nearby attractions: Historic Deerfield, featuring well-preserved 18th- and 19th-century homes. Natural Bridge, a 550-million-year-old marble formation, North Adams. The Sterling and Francine Clark Art Institute, Williamstown.

Further information: Mohawk Trail Association, P.O. Box 1044, North Adams, MA 01247; tel. 413-743-8127, www.mohawktrail.com.

Hail to the Sunrise *statue at Charlemont.*

Indian Plaza, east of town, to swap stories, perform native dances, and sell handicrafts. In a small park to the west, a statue of a Mohawk brave, *Hail to the Sunrise,* celebrates the trail's Indian heritage.

5 Mohawk Trail State Forest

Beyond Charlemont the trail rises steeply, reaching an abruptly wild terrain of gorges, tumbling brooks, sudden ridges, and rocky outcrops, all enveloped in a densely mixed forest made up of hardwoods and evergreens. The air, perfumed by pines and hemlocks, grows cooler here in Mohawk Trail State Forest. Hikers can sample trails that range from gentle to moderately ambitious. Anglers can try their luck for trout. And wildlife watchers will find that the woods are alive with wonders: even from the campground parking area, you might glimpse a deer, a porcupine, or a black bear.

6 Whitcomb Summit

Experienced leaf peepers, as they're known in these parts, pray for three things in early autumn: cool nights, warm days—and not too much

wind. But in almost any year, the transformation is breathtaking. At the town of Florida, the trail reaches its loftiest point, and from the 2,200-foot-high overlook at Whitcomb Summit, the hills and valleys below unfurl in all their autumn glory: the orange and scarlet of maples, the bright gold of birch, the purple of ash, and the deep green punctuation marks of hemlock and spruce.

The prospect calls out for a closer look, and you should take it. Just east of Whitcomb Summit, turn onto Whitcomb Hill Road and head down to the Deerfield River. As the road descends into the gorge, each switchback reveals new views. Hills shift and disappear; a stream gurgles past; the river glistens.

Once at the bottom you'll find an imposing historical landmark. A left onto River Road takes you to the Hoosac Tunnel, a five-mile-long railroad route through the granite spine of the Berkshires that was hailed as the engineering marvel of its day. It took 25 years to build and cost 196 lives—but it opened the rail link between Boston and Albany and led to the development of the lands between.

7 Hairpin Turn

At the Western Summit, a popular launching point for hang gliders, the view reaches on toward sunset. The trail then zigzags down,

turning a full 180 degrees at a dramatic Hairpin Turn. Back when the road first opened, cars ascending eastward from North Adams tended to overheat, and near this point the radiators of many would boil over. The owners would get water from the restaurant here—it's still in business—and gaze out over the valley and the mountains beyond.

8 Mt. Greylock

Rising to 3,491 feet above sea level, Mt. Greylock ranks as the highest peak in Massachusetts. And what a splendid vantage point it forms. From the observation tower at its summit, you can see the Catskills and Adirondacks in New York, the Green Mountains of Vermont, the high peaks of New Hampshire, and the entire sweep of the Berkshires. The road to the top, a 10-mile switchback detour along Notch Road, takes you through a state forest reservation encompassing some 12,000 heavily forested acres, including a 200-year-old stand of stately red spruces. Wildlife is plentiful, with beavers, porcupines, coyotes, foxes, snowshoe hares, black bears, and bobcats all lurking in the shadows. Spend time also looking at the plentiful wildflowers in spring and the shaded glens and moss-banked creeks in summer.

9 Williamstown

Somewhere in everyone's mental file cabinet there exists the image of a picture-perfect New England village. Williamstown comes close to that prototypical ideal. Classic white clapboard mansions line its tree-shaded streets, along with Gothic stone churches and the handsome buildings of Williams College, which has been thriving here since 1793. Its town parks are fine spots for impromptu picnics or sunbathing, with a chance to wind down—all in all, an idyllic climax to the varied scenery to be savored along the Mohawk Trail.

Hewn stone spires at Williams College.

Cape Cod's Sandy Shores

Sand dunes and seashores, sunsets and windmills, colorful lighthouses and gray-shingled cottages—such are the delights to be savored on a tour of Cape Cod.

Digging for clams is one of many popular activities at Cape Cod National Seashore.

To New Englanders, "the Cape" can mean only one place: "the bared and bended arm of Massachusetts," as Henry David Thoreau once called it. Less than two hours from Boston and reaching 70 miles out into the Atlantic, it abounds with idyllic beaches and quaint villages that draw huge crowds on summer weekends. But come mid-September, when mild sea breezes and crisp blue skies prevail, you'll have most of these beaches, marshes, and cranberry bogs almost all to yourself.

1 Sagamore Bridge

Though you have to cross a bridge to get to it, the celebrated spit of land known as Cape Cod is actually a peninsula, separated from the mainland by the seven-mile-long, man-made Cape Cod Canal. Three spans leap across this busy shipping corridor: the Bourne Bridge, connecting the mainland with the Cape's crowded southern coast; a railroad trestle (designed to lift its center span—one of the world's longest—for passing ships); and the Sagamore Bridge, gateway to Cape Cod's northern, or bay, side. Encircled by the Cape's crooked arm, the waters of Cape Cod Bay are calmer and colder than those to the south, and the land is less developed. The north coast, as a result, remains relatively unmarred by commercialism.

Once you cross the Sagamore Bridge, follow signs for Rte. 6A, also referred to as the Old King's Highway (a hint of the Cape's Colonial heritage). Slaloming past cranberry bogs, briny marshland, and the countless weathered cottages that have become hallmarks of Cape Cod, Rte. 6A has the feel of a quiet country lane, and locals much prefer it to the faceless efficiency of Rte. 6 (the Mid-Cape Highway), which parallels the route to the south.

2 Sandwich

The New England of yesteryear is alive and well in Sandwich. Incorporated in 1639, this historic town is the oldest settlement on Cape Cod and one of the oldest in North America. It later became the site of one of the largest glass factories in the nation, and the Sandwich Glass Museum, on Main Street, is a must-see, with a glittering assemblage of 19th-century glass—cut, beveled, enameled, and blown.

The best way to sample Sandwich is on foot—it is, after all, in essence a 17th-century English village. A goodly portion of the downtown district remains remarkably intact, and many original buildings are open for tours.

Among the town's more notable residents was Thornton Burgess, author of *Peter Cottontail* and other charming children's tales. A museum on Water Street—actually a restored house that was built in 1756—showcases many of his original manuscripts and illustrations. Another nearby site, the Green Briar Nature Center and Jam Kitchen, honors both Peter Cottontail's "briar patch" home and his creator's affection for the sweeter things in life. "It's a wonderful thing to sweeten the world, which is in a jam and needs preserving," Burgess quipped. If you have any doubts, stop to sample the kitchen's beach plum jelly and cranberry preserve.

Across the highway the Sandwich boardwalk rambles through marshland and dunes to Town Neck Beach. Destroyed in 1991 by Hurricane Bob, the boardwalk was later rebuilt by a corps of volunteers, many of whom carved messages into the planks—everything from literary quotations to eulogies for boats lost in the storm.

3 Sandy Neck Beach

One of the Cape's best-preserved shores, Sandy Neck occupies the eight-mile-long barrier beach that protects Barnstable Harbor. The south side of this peninsula is marshland—some 4,000 acres, teeming with shorebirds and other wildlife—while to the north, a long strip of sand (perfect for strolling) meets the bay's chilly waters. Allow some time for an exploration of this marvelous stretch of dunes, beach plums, and lapping waves. Along the waterline, sand gives way to water-smoothed stones that, when jostled by the waves, sound rather like marbles being shaken inside a paper bag.

4 Yarmouth Port

Back on Rte. 6A, the drive heads east into Yarmouth Port, a quaint village with many old sea captains' homes that have since been converted to bed-and-breakfast inns. Among the properties relating to the town's seafaring history is the Captain Bangs Hallet House, a Greek Revival structure crammed with treasures acquired by the good captain on his many voyages to the Far East.

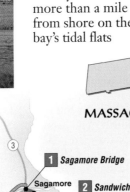

Glacial kettle ponds dot Dennis's charming landscape.

Behind the post office (located just off the town green), a nature trail of the Historical Society of Old Yarmouth leads through 50 acres of lush, lovely woodlands, where brilliant foliage bedecks the canopy in

autumn, and blossoming rhododendrons enliven the scene during the springtime.

5 Dennis

Though it rises only 160 feet above sea level, Dennis's Scargo Hill is a mountain by Cape Cod standards. On a clear day the view from its observation tower can extend all the way to Provincetown, some 40 miles away. Scan the landscape, too, for freshwater kettle ponds. These deep depressions were created many centuries ago when the glaciers that formed the Cape left behind, buried in debris, huge chunks of ice that later melted. Warmer and more secluded than nearby beaches, these shimmering pockets of fresh water make first-class swimming holes. Some 360 dot the Cape, and while a number of them are on private property, many others are open to the public. Check town maps to find their locations.

6 Brewster

The best time to visit Brewster is at low tide, when you can walk more than a mile out from shore on the bay's tidal flats

and wade amid tidepools filled with sea life. A good many ship captains once resided here; Thoreau noted in 1849 that Brewster had more mates and masters of vessels than any other town in the country. At the eastern edge of town, look for the entrance to Nickerson State Park, once the private fish and game preserve of a railroad tycoon. Laced with trails and dotted with ponds (several of them filled with jumping and biting trout), Nickerson boasts nearly 2,000 acres—a remarkable spread, given the Cape's small size. A bike shop provides rentals for excursions along the Cape Cod Rail Trail, a 20-mile-long paved path that runs through the park, en route from South Dennis beyond the National Seashore at Eastham to Wellfleet.

The Cape's beaches are ideal nesting sites for least terns.

7 Orleans

At Orleans the Cape's three main east–west arteries converge in a busy crossroads, making for such bustle that you might think you were entering the most populous quarter. But in fact the Lower Cape (as in lower arm, from the elbow to the fingertips) is, if anything, less visited, less developed, and more remote than its upper half. Here, where the Cape meets the turbulent Atlantic, the boundaries between sea and land blur, and one comes face to face with the fragility of this unique peninsula.

Orleans may be the commercial hub of the Lower Cape, but once off the highway, visitors will find that it possesses all the weathered charm of its neighboring towns. Go for a stroll in nearby bustling Rock Harbor, the home port for a small commercial fishing fleet. Then drive south on Rte. 28 until you reach Main Street, which leads east into Beach Road on its way to Nauset Beach, where for 15 miles sand dunes soar above the pounding surf.

The scene hasn't always been so serene; Orleans enjoys the dubious distinction of being the only place in the continental United States to be targeted by enemy gunfire during World War I. In 1918 a German U-boat off the coast fired on a group of

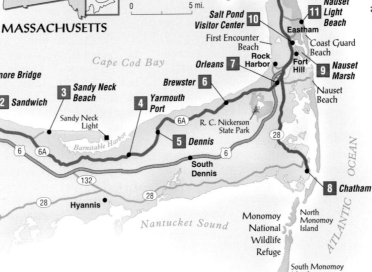

MASSACHUSETTS

Cape Cod Bay

Cape Cod Canal

Nantucket Sound

17 Race Point Beach

Province Lands Visitor Center

16 Provincetown

Truro 14

Wellfleet 13

Head of the Meadow Beach

15 Highland Light

SEASHORE

12 Wellfleet Bay Wildlife Sanctuary

Marconi Station

Great Island

Salt Pond Visitor Center 10

First Encounter Beach

11 Nauset Light Beach

Eastham

Coast Guard Beach

Rock Harbor

Orleans 7

Fort Hill

9 Nauset Marsh

Nauset Beach

Brewster 6

R. C. Nickerson State Park

5 Dennis

South Dennis

8 Chatham

1 Sagamore Bridge

Sagamore

2 Sandwich

3 Sandy Neck Beach

Sandy Neck Light

4 Yarmouth Port

Barnstable Harbor

Hyannis

Monomoy National Wildlife Refuge

North Monomoy Island

South Monomoy Island

Nauset Light in Eastham guides mariners with its trusty presence.

save their favorite spots around the bandstand.

The talk of the town remains the "Chatham breakthrough" of 1987, when a powerful nor'easter broke through the protective barrier beach outside Chatham harbor. Another storm in 1992 widened the gap and exposed miles of coastline to the ocean's rages. Across the drawbridge, Chatham Light tells another compelling tale: look 200 feet offshore to the wavetorn spot where the original Chatham Light stood until a tempest felled it in 1841.

9 Nauset Marsh

Backtracking north on Rte. 28, the drive leads into Rte. 6 as it heads toward Eastham. At Fort Hill, just east of the highway, a spur road dead-ends, looking out on a green pasture that reclines to Nauset Marsh. Follow the two-mile trail to the wetlands, where red maples fire the scene with blazing color in fall. A few miles west, at the end of Samoset Road, lies First Encounter Beach, whose name stems from the fact that it marks the site where Miles Standish and his band of fellow Pilgrims first clashed with the tribesmen of the Wampanoag in 1620.

10 Salt Pond Visitor Center

Farther north on Rte. 6, the Salt Pond visitor center welcomes travelers to one of Cape Cod's greatest natural treasures—the Cape Cod National Seashore. Signed into existence in 1961 by President John F. Kennedy (whose family home in Hyannis Port made him the first and only permanent Cape Cod resident elected to the White House), this park land occupies much of the shoreline from the Cape's elbow to its fist. The seashore preserves over 27,000 acres of dunes, scrub oak and pine forest, bountiful wetlands, and mile after shimmering mile of wild, windswept coastline.

11 Nauset Light Beach

From Nauset Light Beach and adjoining Coast Guard Beach—both linked to the seashore's visitor center by trail and road—you can walk 30 miles north without once leaving the sand. Though the landscape seems little changed since the days when Thoreau hiked on this stretch, an average of three feet of beach continues to recede each and every year, dragged northward by the ocean's currents and deposited near Provincetown.

A few miles to the south, Nauset Spit marks the site of Cape Cod's most famous literary landmark, The Outermost House. Naturalist Henry Beston spent a solitary year here writing a book about life on the great beach. The cottage where he lived was swept into the sea during the great storm of 1978, but the literary classic that bears its name, as well as the transcendent beauty of the place, lives on.

12 Wellfleet Bay Wildlife Sanctuary

No spot on Cape Cod is more than 10 miles from a waterside view, but as the drive heads north toward Wellfleet, the point is pretty much moot. Shrinking to a mere half-mile in width, the Cape's forearm tapers to little more than a slender sandbar. Here, overlooking Wellfleet Harbor, sprawls the Wellfleet Bay Wildlife Sanctuary. Managed by the Massachusetts Audubon Society, the preserve embraces 1,000 acres of pitch pine and oak forest, marshland, and moors spangled with huckleberries. Just off Rte. 6 are two spur roads— one leading to Marconi Beach, a strip of sand backed by bluffs, and the other to the site of Marconi Station, from which Nobel prize-winner Guglielmo Marconi transmitted the first transatlantic message from the United States to Europe in 1903.

13 Wellfleet

Fronting one of the Lower Cape's two great natural harbors, Wellfleet was once a lively whaling port, and the bells of the town's First Congregational Church still keep ship's time, ringing two, four, six, or eight bells according to the shipboard shedule used to change the crew's watches. From Commercial Street follow Chequessett Neck Road west along the water to Sunset Hill and Great Island. Sunset Hill is indeed a terrific spot to enjoy one, but Great Island is long overdue for a name change; though still great by any measure, it hasn't been an island since a sandbar connected it to the mainland more than a century ago. Seven miles of trails crisscross the dunes and salt marshes of this pork chop–shaped peninsula, where oysters and quahogs—the champions of Cape Cod clams—clot the mudflats like living stones. Digging for shellfish is allowed, but a town permit is required.

14 Truro

After returning to Rte. 6, the drive continues north to Truro. Knowing when you've reached the town, however, may not be easy. Truro

barges, sinking four of them. A lone shell, perhaps missing its target, is said to have fallen harmlessly on land. Once back on Rte. 28, continue south to Chatham.

8 Chatham

Although locals like to say that Chatham is the most "capey" of all the Cape's towns, it's also one of its most "tony." Chatham is known for its special main street, filled with boutiques, gourmet candy shops, and restaurants. If you find yourself there on a Friday, the evening band concerts, held from Memorial Day to Labor Day, draw more than a thousand visitors each week. Concert-goers put down their blankets as early as 6 a.m. in order to doesn't make much of a fuss over itself; the town center is a veritable pinpoint, with little more than a few stores, a library, a firehouse, and a police station. The beauty of Truro is its spaciousness. With about 1,400 year-round residents, Truro is one of the smallest towns on the Cape in population, but it's one of the largest in area, spreading over some 20 square miles of dunes and moors. Numbered among the many artists who have sought out Truro's inspiring blend of beauty and solitude was Edward Hopper, the American realist painter who summered and created his canvases here for 37 years.

15 Highland Light

Also known as Cape Cod Light, this bright beacon has been warning ships away from the treacherous sandbars found undersea off Truro's coast since 1857. The original lighthouse, erected in 1797, was torn down when the bluff started to erode. Today its replacement is also on shaky ground, as the bluffs below it crumble slowly into the sea and the ocean's waves undermine the shore. Just to the north is one of the Cape's loveliest beaches, Head of the Meadow. A strong pair of legs can carry you there from the Highland Light, or you can return to Rte. 6 and drive east on Head of the Meadow Road.

16 Provincetown

Although Provincetown is the northernmost town on Cape Cod, it certainly is no lonely outpost. P-town, as the locals affectionately call it, combines the jazziness of a small city with the lazy charm of a coastal village. In summer the town's population multiplies ten-fold, bringing together such diverse groups as sightseeing families, a large gay community, Portuguese-American fishermen, and bohemian painters hawking their wares.

Stroll the busy environs of Commercial Street, then watch the day's catch come in along MacMillan Wharf, one of only three surviving piers out of the 59 that once lined the harbor. (Throughout the mid-1880s Provincetown was known for a catch of a grander scale: it was the nation's third-largest whaling center, after the towns of New Bedford and Nantucket.)

No tour would be complete, of course, without a visit to Pilgrim Memorial Monument, built to commemorate the first landing of the Pilgrims here in 1620. From atop the 255-foot-high tower, a 360-degree view takes in the entire Upper Cape, a boundless blue apron of ocean, and the whole of Cape Cod Bay from Provincetown to Plymouth.

17 Race Point Beach

Curving west on Rte. 6, the drive grazes the south shore of Pilgrim Lake, then jogs north on Race Point Road at the Province Lands visitor center. Because Race Point Beach faces northwest into the Atlantic, you can watch the sun here set into open ocean—perhaps the only spot on the East Coast where such a feat is possible—a fitting end for one's first visit to Cape Cod.

Once the center of a thriving oyster industry, Wellfleet Harbor is a much quieter place nowadays, but plenty of fishing boats can still be seen along its sleepy shore.

Litchfield Hills

Tucked away in the northwestern corner of the
Nutmeg State, the Litchfield Hills exude
an 18th-century ambience that is pure New England.

A bird's-eye view of the Hill–Stead Museum in Farmington reveals highlights that include the sunken garden, the crown jewel to be found among the estate's 150 carefully manicured acres.

Graced by quaint country villages, inviting woodlands, and rolling fields in the green hills of northwestern Connecticut (or, if you prefer, the foothills of the Berkshires in Massachusetts), this backroad ramble tours a serene landscape that is colored by both innocence and elegance.

1 Farmington

An affluent outpost on the banks of the Farmington River, this old gem of a town has long lured admirers of art and architecture. A number of classic white clapboard buildings form part of the exclusive Miss Porter's School, a Farmington institution for well over a century. Even older is the carefully restored 18th-century Stanley–Whitman House (with an overhanging second story) and its adjacent gardens on High Street. The nearby Hill-Stead Museum, designed in 1898 by one of the country's first female architects (Theodate Pope Riddle, an early graduate of Miss Porter's School), houses a fine collection of French and American Impressionist paintings.

2 Topsmead State Forest

Motoring west on Rtes. 4 and 118, a right turn onto East Litchfield Rd. and a right onto Buell Rd. lead to Topsmead State Forest. A belief in the enjoyment to be found in woods, meadows, flowers, and wildlife led Edith M. Chase, another local grande dame, to bequeath her 500-acre estate to the people of Connecticut so that they might enjoy the land as she herself once did. Her antique-filled Tudor-style mansion is open to visitors on alternate weekends, but the real adventure here is having a chance to play lord of the manor in an idyllic outdoor setting. You can hike over open fields, lose yourself amid a 40-acre wildflower preserve, or trace an ancient stone wall as it winds through refreshingly cool, canopied woodlands.

3 Litchfield

"The only street in America more beautiful than North Street in Litchfield is South Street in Litchfield," quipped author Sinclair Lewis, who was more than passingly familiar with America's main streets. He might have added that between North and South streets lies one of the prettiest greens to be found in all of New England. Laid out half a century after the town's founding in 1720, this deeply shaded sward remains unchanged today but for the ever-increasing height of its oaks and maples.

Litchfield grew rich on mills, tanneries, and foundries, and it grew famous on the strength of its many prominent citizens, including Harriet Beecher Stowe (author of *Uncle Tom's Cabin*) and her brother Henry Ward Beecher, the famed preacher, both of whom were born on North Street. On South Street be sure to visit the venerable Tapping Reeve House and Law School, and pause at the green to admire the Congregational Church, with its soaring white steeple.

Travel a few miles to the south of Litchfield on Rte. 63 to a spot where the fine art of cultivation is on display in season at the prize-winning gardens and meticulously landscaped grounds of the White Flower Farm, a mail-order nursery.

⋮⋮⋮⋮ Trip Tips ⋮⋮⋮⋮

Length: About 70 miles, plus side trips.

When to go: Popular year-round.

Nearby attractions: Wadsworth Atheneum (containing fine collections of painting and porcelain), Hartford. Lock Museum of America (keys, locks, and hardware), Terryville. The American Clock and Watch Museum and the New England Carousel Museum, Bristol.

Further information: Litchfield Hills Travel Council, P.O. Box 968, Litchfield, CT 06759; tel. 860-567-4506, www.litchfield hills.com/.

4 White Memorial Foundation

From the architectural splendors of Litchfield, the drive swings southwest on Rte. 202 toward the woodlands and wetlands of the White Memorial Foundation, a 4,000-acre nature sanctuary crisscrossed with paths that were first traced by Indians. Deep within Catlin Woods, giant hemlocks intermingle with red maples and white pines, and beavers inhabit the shallow waters of Miry Brook. Both outdoor recreation (hiking, horseback riding, and cross-country skiing) and education (a nature center and museum) are well served in this extraordinary environment.

5 Mt. Tom State Park

From the rustic bluestone lookout tower atop Mt. Tom, the view across the treetops takes in the Catskill Mountains to the northwest and one of Connecticut's highest peaks, Bear Mountain, to the north. In the park's lower reaches, you can swim in a bracing spring-fed pond or picnic at the tree-shaded water's edge. At nearby Lake Waramaug State Park (reached via Rtes. 202, 45, and 341), you can camp, swim, fish, or rent a canoe and explore the hidden coves nestled along the lake's unusually scenic shoreline.

6 Kent

Veering west at Warren, the drive coasts along Rte. 341 toward the picture-postcard village of Kent on the banks of the Housatonic River. The Appalachian Trail, which cuts through town, remains largely unnoticed by the art and antique lovers who crowd Main Street. For a change of pace, head down to the river, where the serenity is broken only by the subdued oar strokes of the Kent School crew team.

7 Kent Falls State Park

In spring the dogwoods gleam like pale moon drops along Rte. 7 as it gently rises and falls on its journey north from Kent. History lovers should stop at the Sloane-Stanley Museum just outside of town to view its collection of early American tools. A few miles farther on, at popular Kent Falls

An autumn-hued maple shades an old stone fence on the grounds at Hill–Stead Museum in Farmington.

State Park, you can stroll across a grassy meadow to view the foaming cascades of a gorgeous multi-tiered waterfall.

8 West Cornwall

As Rte. 7 continues north, it passes through Housatonic Meadows State Park, where the rushing river is often dotted with canoes, kayaks, and fly fishermen. A few miles to the north, a turn onto Rte. 128 leads—by means of passing over a weathered red covered bridge—to the picturesque and diminutive hamlet of West Cornwall.

9 Canaan

The last leg of the drive, along Rte. 7 from West Cornwall to Canaan, offers pleasant diversions in the warm months. Fans of sports-car racing flock to nearby Lime Rock (via Rte. 112), and music lovers are lured to Music Mountain (at Falls Village) for the summer chamber-music festival. At the little village of Canaan, you may want to pause at an outdoor café before heading north to the Berkshires or looping back toward lovely Litchfield.

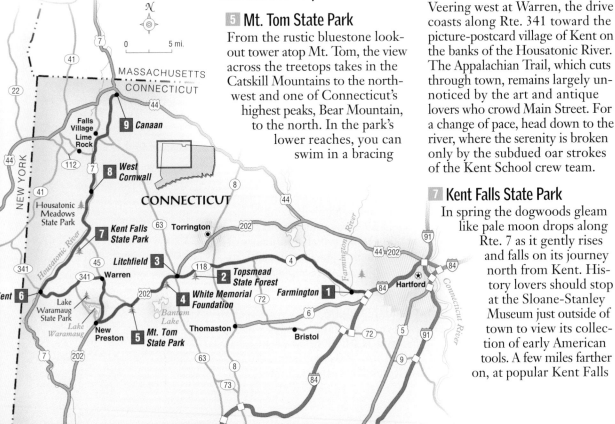

South County Coast

A drive along the restful, romantic shores
of America's smallest state proves once again
that good things can, indeed, come in small packages.

Castle Hill Light in Newport helps guide wayfarers of the sea to safe harbor.

Take one look at a map of Rhode Island and you will quickly see why this pint-size package is nicknamed the Ocean State. Despite its modest size—only 48 miles long and 37 miles wide—this New England nugget has 400 miles of coastline. Though officially named Washington County, the southern fringe of the state is known to locals as South County. No matter what you call it, though, the area is replete with scenic Rhode Island riches.

1 Watch Hill

Traveling south from Westerly, take Rte. 1A toward Watch Hill, one of the prettiest seaside resorts in South County. Built on a series of bluffs, the town has hills galore, many of them with handsome Victorian-style summer homes nestled into their slopes.

For one of the best beach walks in Rhode Island, follow the path at the end of Fort Road to Napatree Point. Situated at the westernmost tip of the state, this long peninsula is a good spot to watch migrating hawks and waterfowl. The Watch Hill Coast Guard Station (on Light House Road) offers a sensational panoramic vista.

2 Misquamicut State Beach

At Winnapaug Road head south to Misquamicut State Beach, the state's largest. Misquamicut, which is flanked by Winnapaug Pond and the ocean, is one of more than a dozen public beaches that dot the coast of Rhode Island. Continuing east on Atlantic Avenue, the road passes through the quaint ocean-side community of Weekapaug, where gingerbread-style homes punctuate the rocky shoreline.

3 Burlingame State Park

Back on Rte. 1A, the drive leads to one of Rhode Island's most popular camping sites, Burlingame State Park. This 2,100-acre park, located in a wooded area beside Watchaug Pond, offers freshwater swimming, boating, and fishing. On the pond's south side is Kimball Wildlife Refuge, a 29-acre preserve with several hiking trails and an abundance of oaks, maples, starflowers, and, in season, pink lady's slippers.

4 Ninigret National Wildlife Refuge

Set on a coastal plain that once served as a U.S. naval-air installation, this 400-acre sanctuary is bordered by a large saltwater pond. Yet the water is so shallow (only four feet deep in most spots) that sunlight can easily reach the bottom, promoting the growth of vegetation that in turn nourishes a wide variety of life—from shrimp and flounder to black ducks and snowy egrets.

In late September visitors may glimpse hordes of orange-and-black monarch butterflies as well as flocks of migrating hawks. A walk along one of the old airplane runways is a good way to spot a deer, fox, or even a coyote.

5 Trustom Pond National Wildlife Refuge

Piping plovers that fill the air with their whistling calls; mute swans gliding across the water with un-erring grace; American woodcocks that perform elaborate courtship rituals; ospreys that plummet down from nowhere, then suddenly soar skyward with a fish in their clutches…These are but a few of the 300-odd species that frequent this bird-lover's paradise. Once a farm, the 640-acre refuge—among the best wildlife preserves in Rhode Island—is now covered with abandoned orchards, a scrub forest, and

---

::::: Trip Tips :::::

Length: About 40 miles.

When to go: Popular year-round, but best in summer because of water activities.

Not to be missed: The Flying Horse Carousel, Watch Hill.

Nearby attraction: Block Island (take ferries from Galilee, RI, and New London, CT).

Further information: Rhode Island Tourism Division, 1 W. Exchange St., Providence, RI 02903; tel. 800-566-2484, www.visitrhodeisland.com. South County Tourism Council, 4808 Tower Hill Rd., Wakefield, RI, 02879; tel. 800-548-4662.

fields of alfalfa, which the refuge still cultivates to help make the area more inviting to wildlife.

6 Galilee

Legend has it that this bustling fishing village was named for its biblical counterpart by a Nova Scotia fisherman who settled here at the turn of the century. The best time to arrive is at sundown, when trawlers are returning with their catch of the day. Nearby Roger Wheeler State Beach (also known as Sand Hill Cove Beach) has calm, shallow waters, making it a good swimming spot for children. One mile east of Galilee is Point Judith, where visitors can enjoy spectacular ocean vistas and photograph an octagonal lighthouse.

7 Narragansett Pier

In its heyday—the period between 1878 and 1920—the Narragansett area (named for the tribe that once occupied the region) was a mecca

The waters of Rhode Island Sound off of the celebrated city of Newport are frequented by racing sailboats.

for affluent vacationers, who were lured to the region by its luscious landscapes and beautiful beaches. Reminiscent of those bygone days is the Romanesque arch that greets visitors as they enter Narragansett Pier. Once part of a lavish casino, The Towers, as the massive stone structure is called, now houses the chamber of commerce. The town beach offers fine white sand and long smooth waves that are ideal for surfing.

8 Saunderstown

Thoughts of New England don't normally conjure mental images of plantation life, but from the early 1700s until 1774 (Rhode Island was the first colony to prohibit the slave trade), South County had many large farms tended by slaves. Typical of these estates is the Silas Casey Farm in Saunderstown. Modest by southern standards, it is stately nonetheless; the homestead is named for the wealthy trader who owned it. With 300

acres of fertile land, this working farm has various animals (including horses, cattle, and sheep) and a two-story clapboard house with period furniture.

Several miles northwest of the farm is the birthplace of Gilbert Stuart, the most renowned American portrait artist of the Colonial era. The son of a Scottish immigrant, Stuart is perhaps best known for the likeness of George Washington that appears on the one-dollar bill. Stuart's home beside the Mattatuxet River is a simple barn-red structure that housed New England's first snuff mill. Inside are reproductions of a few of the hundreds of portraits the artist painted during his lifetime.

9 Wickford

With its snug, well-protected harbor and proximity to fertile farmland, this quaint village was once a chief port for shipping produce to the markets of nearby Newport. Hints of Wickford's prosperous past can still be seen in the dignified white clapboard houses and red-brick buildings that line its tiny, tidy streets.

Star Route

★ Ocean Drive

A drive over the Jamestown Bridge leads to the celebrated city of Newport, playground for the rich and famous. Many of their turn-of-the-century mansions and modern multimillion-dollar yachts can be seen along Ocean Drive, a 10-mile seaside loop. Though not marked, the route consists of Harrison Avenue, Ridge Road, Ocean Avenue, and Bellevue Avenue. The best views are from Cliff Walk, a 3½-mile trail that begins at Easton's Beach near Bellevue Avenue and runs along the bluffs.

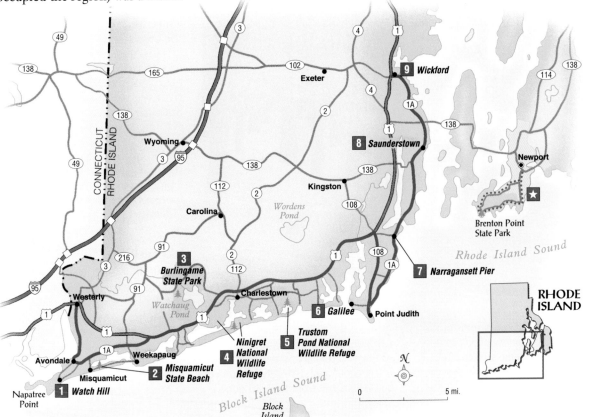

Across the Alleghenies

Pennsylvanians long ago dubbed this part of their state The Endless Mountain, and from countless points along this richly rewarding drive, the Alleghenies really do seem to roll on forever.

At Heart's Content Scenic Area, freshly fallen snow clings to red pines, turning the forest into a winter wonderland.

The longest continuous highway in the country until it was eclipsed by Rte. 20 in 1965, Rte. 6 extends from Bishop, California, to Province-town, Massachusetts, on Cape Cod.

Along the way, it tours some of the most diverse scenery of any road in America. This scenic stretch of Rte. 6, which spans the northern tier of Pennsylvania along old Indian trails,

is among its loveliest. Called the Grand Army of the Republic Highway in honor of Union veterans of the Civil War, it offers cool forests, friendly towns, and vistas that run from ridge to ridge.

1 Warren

Trim and tidy beneath the four clocks of its 1877 courthouse, the town of Warren (named for General Joseph Warren, a hero of the Battle of Bunker Hill) stands at an important junction in the history of American transportation. Early in the 19th century, when timber barons felled the forests of north-western Pennsylvania and western New York, they assembled their log drives here, at the confluence of the Conewango and Allegheny rivers. The logs splashed and thundered downstream and south to meet the Ohio River at Pittsburgh, and fortunes flowed into Warren's serene, mansion-lined streets.

2 Tidioute Overlook

Heading west on Rte. 6 out of Warren, take Rte. 62 south along the Allegheny River until you pass a narrow iron bridge that crosses into the hamlet of Tidioute. A spur road just beyond the bridge leads to the Tidioute Overlook, which affords sweeping views of the broad, smooth waterway.

The Allegheny has come a long way to reach this point. Rising near Denton Hill State Park, the river veers north into New York State, then winds back into Pennsylvania at the Allegheny Reservoir, northeast of Warren. Also visible from the overlook are the red-and-white houses of Tidioute, a patchwork of small farms, and Courson Island (part of the only federally designated wilderness to be found in Pennsylvania).

3 Hearts Content National Scenic Area

After leaving Tidioute Overlook, the drive begins its journey east through Allegheny National Forest. Situated atop a rugged plateau, this 512,000-acre national forest boasts 170 miles of hiking trails and 91 miles of shoreline, but it is most renowned for its timber.

Yellow poplar, white oak, and red maple are just a few of the hardwoods that contribute to the more than 65 million board feet of timber harvested here each year. The region's black cherry is prized by furniture craftsmen, but locals, perhaps, place an even higher premium on white ash, which is used to make a masterpiece of an entirely different sort—Louisville Slugger baseball bats.

One place in the forest, however, has been touched by neither saw nor axe. At the aptly named Hearts Content National Scenic Area, hemlocks, beeches, and white pines still stand straight and tall, as they have for more than 300 years. Absent are American elms that fell prey to Dutch elm disease late in the 1800s all across the continent. To reach Hearts Content, follow signs from the Tidioute Overlook. Once there, you'll find a mile-long trail that winds through the old-

growth timber stand and loops back to the picnic area.

The national scenic area lies at the threshold of another pocket of serenity, the 8,570-acre Hickory Creek Wilderness. Since no motorized vehicles are allowed there, you may prefer the conveniences of Chapman State Park, where campsites cluster around a trout-filled lake. The best way to get to Chapman is to take Rte. 3005 north to Warren, follow Rte. 6 south, and then head west at Clarendon.

4 Kane

Traveling southeast on Rte. 6, the drive reaches the town of Kane. General Ulysses S. Grant was once arrested here for fishing without a license, but the only Civil War hero you're likely to hear folks talk about is General Thomas L. Kane, who settled the community that now bears his name. A champion of persecuted Mormon pioneers and a mediator in the so-called Mormon War of 1857, Kane was one of the first Pennsylvanians to volunteer for service in the Union Army. He is buried in front of the chapel he built, which has been restored by grateful Mormons and is now maintained as a historic site.

5 Kinzua Bridge State Park

Spanning the Kinzua Creek valley north of Rte. 6, the Kinzua Bridge, at 301 feet in height, was the tallest railroad bridge in the world when it was erected in 1882. Rebuilt with steel in 1900 and abandoned by regular railway traffic in 1959, this towering monument to the golden age of railroads now serves the excursion trains of the Knox, Kane, and Kinzua Railroad, which can be seen chugging along the 2,053-foot-long viaduct from several vantage points in Kinzua Bridge State Park. From June to October you can get on board at Kane or, for an all-day trip, farther south at Marienville and let a vintage steam

locomotive carry you through the park's forests, across the historic bridge, and all the way back.

6 Ole Bull State Park

One of the great violin virtuosos of the 19th century, Ole Bull was renowned on both sides of the Atlantic. His greatest love after music was his native Norway, and since the rugged, deeply wooded hill country of northwestern Pennsylvania reminded Bull of his homeland, it was here that in 1852 he attempted to found a colony called New Norway. Problems with property titles and the hardships of

At a farm off Rte. 6, simplicity makes for memorable scenery.

wresting farmland from forest defeated Bull and his followers, but the landscape of his dream is preserved for posterity at 125-acre Ole Bull State Park, located along the banks of Kettle Creek. As you head south to the park on Rte. 44 at Sweden Valley, you'll be following the path of an old stagecoach route that was called the Jersey Shore–Coudersport Turnpike. Named for the towns at either end of the line, this roller coaster of a road must have challenged weary stagecoach drivers as much as its vistas now delight travelers.

7 Pennsylvania Lumber Museum

Several miles beyond Sweden Valley, Rte. 6 reaches its highest point in Pennsylvania. From the top of Denton Hill, in Denton Hill State Park, you can look down on the headwaters of the Genesee River, flowing northward toward Lake Ontario and the Gulf of St. Lawrence; Pine Creek, which feeds the Susquehanna River and, ultimately, Chesapeake Bay; and the headwaters of the Allegheny River, a tributary of the Ohio and Mississippi rivers. At the Pennsylvania Lumber Museum, just off the highway near Denton Hill, the river of time flows back 100 years to an era when burly men with big saws cut hemlock and white pine for as long as 70 hours a week. All the tools of their trade are on view here, set among the mills, mess halls, and bunkhouses where they lived and worked. The colorful history of the period comes to life in early July at the Bark Peeler's Convention, which features, among other activities, single- and double-bladed axe-throwing competitions and sawing demonstrations.

8 Grand Canyon of Pennsylvania

For nearly 50 miles Pine Creek winds southward along a route cut by glacial meltwater during the great ice ages. Nearly one mile across from rim to rim, the wooded gorge—locals proudly dubbed it the Grand Canyon of Pennsylvania —plunges to depths of 800 feet along much of its length, although it is nearly twice as deep near its southern end. Nowhere is this natural wonder grander (or more accessible) than at Colton Point

Pine Creek Gorge, better known as the Grand Canyon of Pennsylvania.

State Park and Leonard Harrison State Park, both located several miles south of Ansonia on opposite sides of the gorge. A visit to Colton or Harrison is immediately rewarded with glorious views from scenic overlooks.

At Harrison State Park those with enough stamina—and not to mention, the right kind of shoes— can venture along Turkey Path, a steep switchback trail that travels a little more than one mile from the main overlook to the bottom of the gorge. Somewhere between the rim and the shallow creek, deep

amid the rhododendrons and syc-amores, you may just happen to cross paths with that quintessentially American bird, the wild turkey. Once plentiful in these parts, these colorful critters came close to extinction as a result of hunting and habitat destruction. But in recent years they have made a surprising comeback.

Among the wariest of fowl, the wild turkey—despite its three-foot length, bright red wattles, and boastful fan of tailfeathers—is easily concealed by the forest and its own quick wits. One may appear

out of nowhere, a strutting flash of iridescent bronze, then suddenly dart—as quickly as you can say "gobble"—into a nearby thicket under a cloak of invisibility. But if you're lucky enough to see this bird, you'll long remember it.

9 Wellsboro

With its stately stone courthouse, Victorian homes, and gas street lamps, Wellsboro—which serves as gateway to the Grand Canyon of Pennsylvania—looks like a New England town that has been transplanted to Pennsylvania. And

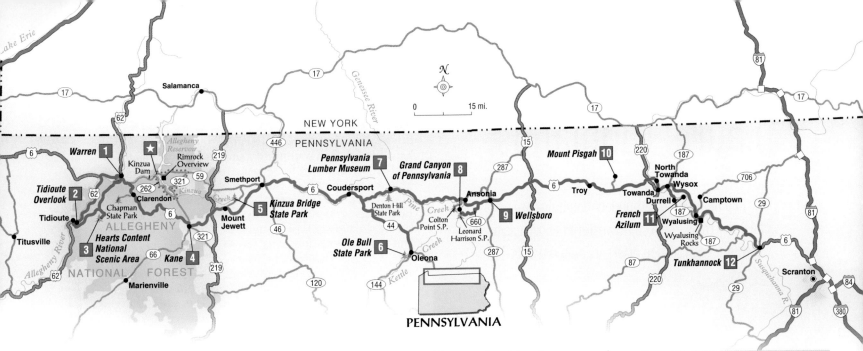

no wonder, for it was largely New Englanders who settled the community in 1806. Stroll along its shady streets, graced with maples and elms, to the town green, where a bronze statue depicts a scene from the beloved children's poem "The Dutch Lullaby." It shows Wynken, Blynken, and Nod adrift in their improbable craft—a seaworthy wooden shoe.

10 Mt. Pisgah

With the highest of the Alleghenies fading behind to the west, Rte. 6 descends toward the Susquehanna River valley. Between the town of Troy and the river lie two of the region's most delightful recreation areas: Mt. Pisgah state and county parks. Mt. Pisgah itself has a road all the way to its gently contoured summit. From here pastured valleys tumble away in every direction, their grassy folds cradling white farmhouses, big red barns, and herds of dairy cattle.

The two most venerable manmade and natural highways in Pennsylvania—famous Rte. 6 and the Susquehanna River—finally meet at North Towanda. The Susquehanna rises in Otsego Lake, north of New York State's Catskill Mountains. Snaking through eastern Pennsylvania in the shape of a long, backward S-curve, the swift, shallow river slices through five gaps in the Appalachian Mountains to drain the state's coal-mining and industrial valleys as it flows to the tidewaters found at the head of Chesapeake Bay.

From Wysox, head southward on Rte. 187 to Durrell, then follow the signs to French Azilum.

11 French Azilum

One of Pennsylvania's oddest footnotes to history can be found at a horseshoe bend in the Susquehanna River, some eight miles southeast of Towanda. In the autumn of 1793, several prominent Philadelphians sympathetic to royalists displaced by the French Revolution purchased land in the Susquehanna Valley and made it a refuge for exiled aristocrats.

The Azilum, or asylum, became a genteel community of comfortable log cabin homes, the largest of which, La Grande Maison, was reputedly intended for Marie Antoinette and her children. But any hopes the emigrés may have harbored for a new Versailles-on-the-Susquehanna were dashed when the queen was guillotined; not long after, the French community began to disperse. Some of its members headed south; others returned to France when Napoleon granted them amnesty; a few remained in northeast Pennsylvania, where their descendants live today.

Although none of the 50 or so original structures remain, the site of French Azilum is unquestionably one of the prettiest along the meandering Susquehanna River. A nature trail winds along the river where courtiers once sauntered, and the 1836 La Porte House, built by the son of one of the colony's founders, offers as close a look as we can get at the settlement's brief but historic heyday.

12 Tunkhannock

Return to Rte. 6 at Wysox and take a longer view up and down the Susquehanna River Valley from the Marie Antoinette Overlook, located about seven miles east of the village. Less than three miles farther down the road, another scenic vantage point commands a broad river view near the massive sandstone-and-shale outcroppings called the Wyalusing Rocks. A horse race once held from Wyalusing to nearby Camptown was immortalized by songwriter Stephen Foster, a resident of Towanda, in his familiar, catchy tune popular in the 19th century, *Camptown Races.*

:::::: **Trip Tips** ::::::

Length: About 300 miles, plus side trips.

When to go: Popular year-round, but especially scenic in autumn.

Not to be missed: Pennsylvania State Laurel Festival, a week-long series of activities held in mid-June, Wellsboro.

Nearby attractions: Peter J. McGovern Little League Baseball Museum, Williamsport; Buzzard Swamp Wildlife Area, Allegheny National Forest; Drake Well Museum, birthplace of the oil industry, Titusville; Seneca-Iroquois National Museum, Salamanca, NY.

Further information: Allegheny National Forest, 222 Liberty St., Warren, PA 16365; tel. 814-723-5150, www.fs.fed.us/r9/allegheny.

The drive through the Alleghenies began with sensational views of its one great signature river—the Allegheny—and at the picturesque town of Tunkhannock, it will end with those of another, the Susquehanna. Just ahead lies Scranton, a hardworking coal town and stop on the Lackawanna Valley railroad. In it, you'll find connections with I-81 to points north and south.

Laurel Highlands

Rolling fields and rounded mountains are
cause for rejoicing in southwestern Pennsylvania,
where each season offers its own rewards.

Daylilies add diversity to the sea of green near Ohiopyle State Park.

Mountain laurel, the state flower of Pennsylvania, lends its name to this rumpled region in the western foothills of the Allegheny Mountains. Covered with clusters of cuplike pink flowers in spring, the laurels often grow in thickets that brighten whole hillsides—one of many good reasons for a visit to this pleasing blend of forests and farmlands.

1 Bedford

Begun as a frontier outpost in 1766, Bedford boasts a wealth of historic sites. George Washington once established a headquarters at the Espy House, and the town's walking tour also visits the 1814 Anderson House, the residence of a physician who was instrumental in Bedford's development. To top off your journey into the past, drive northward to the re-created Colonial settlement of Old Bedford Village. Once across the Claycomb Covered Bridge, you'll find yourself in a spot that seems drawn from revolutionary times.

The drive then heads west on Rte. 30, tracing the course of what was once a wagon trail between two forts. Inns and taverns from the 1700s still stand along the way; some are spaced four miles apart—roughly the distance covered in a day's travel in that era.

2 Shawnee State Park

Farmhouses and weathered red barns dot the countryside as the drive approaches the tiny town of Schellsburg. Turn southward there on Rte. 96 for a visit to Shawnee State Park, which, like the area's other parks, showcases the Laurel Highlands' year-round beauty. In spring the blossoms of mountain laurels and rhododendrons decorate the hills. Patches of daisies spangle the fields in summer; then the lushness slowly fades and the trees take on autumn hues. With the onset of winter, heavy snowfalls wrap the entire region in a white embrace and a churchlike hush broken only by the occasional calls of ravens and owls.

Just west of Schellsburg, a lonely stretch of Rte. 30 leads to one of this area's earliest houses of worship. Built in 1806, the log-and-mortar church crowns a hill that overlooks a small, tidy cemetery.

3 Bald Knob Summit

Rte. 30 zips past more farmland, where cows graze in green pastures spotted with looking-glass ponds. Charming farm lanes branch off from the highway, only to disappear behind tangles of wild roses and honeysuckle. Many of the side roads ribbon down to secret worlds where small covered bridges span gurgling streams. The highway itself begins a slow curl to Bald Knob Summit. On the way, stop by the old Ship Hotel, where a viewpoint atop an isolated crest looks to the far-off forests and mountains of both Maryland and West Virginia.

4 Ligonier

From the summit the drive heaves and sighs across crests and valleys, then levels off as it rides across a plateau on the Seven-Mile Stretch. Farther on, the highway resumes its roller-coaster course as it descends through forests, fields, and small towns. Rte. 30 then parallels Ligonier's Main Street, where a picture-perfect village square, hemmed in by historic stone buildings, greets motorists. At regular intervals the chimes from three bell towers mark the time of the day, another note from a past that's ever present in this enjoyable town.

The next leg of the drive heads southward on Rte. 711, a backcountry byway passing amid hilly pastures that tumble and collide at unlikely angles, and small hollows that shelter farmhouses. After several miles the drive switches onto Rte. 31 and continues east for a short distance to Rte. 381 south. Here you'll dip into a valley laced by a stream and dotted with little towns. A bit farther along you can sample Bear Run Nature Reserve, a 5,000-acre parkland with impressive stands of towering oaks and hemlocks.

The Youghiogheny River speeds down several rapids at Ohiopyle State Park.

5 Fallingwater

Asked to draw up plans for a house that would look out on a waterfall, architect Frank Lloyd Wright went one step further and designed a structure he situated directly atop the ledge-leaping stream. Aptly named Fallingwater, the sandstone residence, surrounded by a dark woodland, blends so well with its setting that it seems to spring from the earth itself. Take the tour to hear the music of the splashing stream play in nearly every room.

6 Ohiopyle State Park

The name of this park, an Indian word, translates as "white frothy water"—and one look at the Youghiogheny River (pronounced *yoke-oh-GAY-nee*) will be enough to show you why. The river wraps around a large horseshoe bend, racing over a waterfall and across churning rapids that are much loved by white-water enthusiasts.

A gorge some 1,700 feet deep hems in the river with fern-choked cliffs. At the Ohiopyle Falls Day Use Area, platformed viewpoints overlook the Youghiogheny as it

spills over a series of massive sandstone ledges. The park also has numerous trails offering opportunities to explore its hushed forests and rhododendron thickets. Be on the lookout for wildflowers: Ohiopyle boasts such beauties as trailing arbutus, clintonia, false Solomon's seal, and the cloaked flowers of monkshood, among many others.

7 Laurel Hill State Park

The drive rolls past sleepy hamlets —quiet communities reminiscent of an earlier era—as it rambles on to Rte. 40, known as the National Road. Cut into the wilderness in the early 1800s, this was the first road to penetrate the 75-mile-wide wall of the Allegheny Mountains. As such, it opened a door to the frontier, enabling pioneers to flood westward and begin new lives.

The drive, in contrast, heads eastward on Rte. 40, then swings north via Rte. 281. Here you can camp, fish, and

hike at Youghiogheny Lake, a reservoir ringed by wooded hills.

Farther on, Rte. 281 enters New Lexington. In town turn westward onto Rte. 653, then follow the signs northward to Laurel Hill State Park. Mountain laurel erupts with a profusion of pink blossoms across the slopes of this preserve, and its hiking trails, sparkling lake, and quaint visitor center (an old farmhouse) help to make Laurel Hill an especially pleasant stopover.

8 Somerset

Gracious estates and historic government buildings line the streets of Somerset, a place also known for its towering maples. The trees are more than mere decoration: for over 100 years their sugary sap has been used to make maple syrup. To learn how pioneers went about that process, stop at the Somerset Historical Center, a large complex that re-creates many Early American crafts and activities. The center also supplies handy maps of the Covered Bridge Route. A whole day can easily be expended wandering along the back roads to these old-time spans.

Pennsylvania Dutch Country

The farmers who till these fertile fields may be called
the Plain People, but the views are far from ordinary in this land
where cars comfortably share the road with horse-drawn buggies.

Milk flows each morning from the tidy, understated Amish farms of the Pennsylvania Dutch near Lancaster.

The beauty of this gentle region lies not only in its rolling hills and tidy homestead farms but also in the well-preserved customs of the peaceful folk who live here. Clad unpretentiously in homespun shirts and dark trousers or long gingham dresses, they are proud to call themselves the Plain People and to keep their hands on the plow, their eyes on the soil, and their ears open to the voice of a stern but loving God.

1 Intercourse

Descendants of German Protestant sects, mainly Amish and Mennonite, the Pennsylvania Dutch (a corruption of *Deutsch*, for "German") believe in keeping life simple. In fact, any establishment that calls itself Amish probably isn't, for the Plain People never advertise or capitalize on either their religion or themselves.

A good spot to get an inside look at their enduring simplicity is the People's Place in the town of Intercourse, where a narrated slide presentation (motion pictures are too newfangled) provides a straightforward introduction to these fascinating sects. The handcrafted dioramas of folk artist Aaron Zook bring to life a barn-raising, an Amish funeral, and "buggy courting." Across the street are the Quilt Museum, filled with walls draped with dozens of antique classics, and a general store, where you can buy modern quilts and local handicrafts.

A couple of miles west on Rte. 340 is Bird-in-Hand, named for a tavern that served the Old King's Highway some 200 years ago. In nearby Witmer the 18th-century buildings of the Folk Craft Center and Museum contain displays of local home arts, from stoneware pots to Stiegel glass. Nearby, you can clip-clop lazily on a two-mile buggy tour of Amish country.

2 Ephrata Cloister

Head north on Rte. 772 through a prosperous checkerboard of fertile farms, and then turn right on Rte. 272 to arrive at the medieval-style compound of the Ephrata Cloister. "Spartan" might describe the life of the monastic Seventh-Day Baptists, followers of Conrad Beissel, who immigrated from Germany nearly 300 years ago. Here they built austerely beautiful clapboard buildings with tiny dormer windows—a style borrowed from the traditional houses of their native Rhineland. Known as the Society of the Solitary, they slept on hard benches with wooden blocks for pillows. Narrow hallways symbolized the straight and narrow path, and the low doorways (even short visitors have to duck) reminded sect members of humility. Beissel, who called their rigors "serenity," rests among the mossy stones of the old graveyard.

3 Landis Valley Museum

As you drive toward Lancaster on Rte. 272, stop three miles north of town at the Landis Valley Museum, where the numerous exhibits include a post–Civil War schoolhouse and the early-19th-century Landis Farmstead. Some 80,000 items—everything from potbelly stoves to cigar-store Indians to Conestoga wagons (built in Lancaster County)—make this one of the world's largest museums focusing on the Pennsylvania Dutch. Farm animals roam the grounds, and you can watch demonstrations of blacksmithing, weaving, and open-hearth cooking.

4 Lancaster

This was one of the largest inland cities in the 13 colonies during the American Revolution, and its Central Market goes back even further, to the early 1700s. Today it is a thriving outlet for much of what is produced in Pennsylvania Dutch

farm country. Arrive early to see families set up their stands under Pennsylvania-German nameboards that have been used for generations. Offerings range from such local specialties as shoofly pie, snitz (dried apples), and Bavarian pretzels to heaps of farm-fresh corn, tomatoes, celery, and other produce.

The market is just one of the stops on a 90-minute walking tour of the city. Led by a costume-clad guide, the tour takes in the gilded splendor of the 1852 Fulton Opera House, the heady aromas of the old Demuth Tobacco Shop, and the eclectic treasures of the Heritage Museum on Penn Square.

5 Marietta

Heading west out of Lancaster on Rte. 23, stop at Wheatland, the perfectly preserved Federalist home of James Buchanan, the only president from Pennsylvania. Farther along, as you approach the Susquehanna River, the expanses of plowed fields yield to sizable hills and then to the charming riverfront town of Marietta, nearly half of which is on the National Register of Historic Places. In its two centuries the town has been a boisterous port (well-known by rivermen for its taverns), a lumber depot, and an iron-smelting center. Each role is reflected in the lovingly restored buildings along the main street—including a well-preserved silk mill in the center of town.

6 Hans Herr House

Just south of Marietta on Rte. 441, rapids churn at the foot of Chickies Rock, which

Amish children in traditional garb take their wagons for a spin.

juts 200 feet above the Susquehanna. A short trail to the river overlook opens onto a watery vista studded with islands. The biggest—Three Mile Island—was made widely known after the accident at its nuclear facility in 1979. It lies a few miles to the north.

At Rte. 999 a turn to the east will lead you back into the heart of the Pennsylvania Dutch country, where Amish buggies are drawn by sleek, high-stepping horses. The road passes by large farmsteads, and cars sometimes have to wait for several minutes as a plodding herd of dairy cattle shambles from pasture to barn. The farms' names speak of many generations working the same soil: "Stone Cliff: 1892," for example, or "Eugenheiser's End: 1867." Other signs call attention to homemade crafts and quilts, and sterner ones show that these practical, productive folk always have one eye on the Lord: "Repent and Be Saved!" or "What Man Sows, That Shall He Reap."

When you reach the little town called Willow Street, stop at the Hans Herr House. Guides conduct tours of the oldest

home in Lancaster County (dating from 1719), and the visitor center has an exhibit on Mennonite farm life. The house was a frequent subject for paintings by Pennsylvania artist Andrew Wyeth, a descendant of Herr.

7 Strasburg

For railroad buffs Strasburg is a virtual heaven. At the enormous Railroad Museum of Pennsylvania, they can climb into old locomotives and railroad cars. Next door, the National Toy Train Museum offers miniature versions of the real thing in five huge tabletop displays. If you prefer to ride, you can take the nine-mile round-trip on the Strasburg Railroad. Accompanied by the cheerful wheezes and whistles of its steam engine, the old train chugs through fields of corn and tobacco as riders watch from plush Pullman seats and the conductor calls attention to local sights: an Amish farmer plowing with a six-mule team, or a telephone booth at a cornfield's edge for families that ban modern conveniences at their home.

The last leg of the drive traverses the gently rolling farmland along Rte. 741 toward the town of Gap. Dotted with roadside stands, the route offers a final chance to sample the bounty of the Plain People.

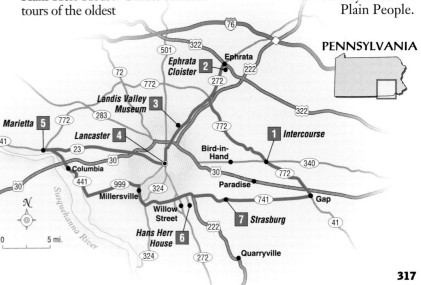

Delaware River Loop

Astride the border between Pennsylvania and New Jersey, a narrow notch in the Kittatinny Ridge provides a natural gateway to this pleasantly pastoral river valley.

Autumnal dazzler: the Delaware Water Gap viewed from atop Mt. Tammany.

To motorists on I-80, the Delaware Water Gap is little more than a magnificent minute at the border between New Jersey and Pennsylvania, where the highway briefly joins the Delaware River as it snakes through a deep cut in the Kittatinny Ridge. Unseen from the highway, however, is the quietly impressive countryside that lies upstream—a 40-mile corridor formed by millions of years of erosion and gradual uplift and now protected as the Delaware Water Gap National Recreation Area. In summers past, this forested valley—encompassing more than 70,000 acres—hummed with vacationers who flocked to fashionable resorts to savor cool mountain air and blissful views. Most of the resorts are gone, but this relatively unspoiled landscape can still be enjoyed by anyone with a craving for a preserve embodying scenery and serenity.

1 Kittatinny Point Visitor Center

Just off I-80 at the exit immediately to the east of the Delaware River Bridge, the drive sets out from the Kittatinny Point visitor center. In addition to its stunning views of the Kittatinny Ridge—a long, flat-topped range so straight that it would be the envy of any carpenter —the visitor center offers a good introduction to the Water Gap area. It also provides the only access to Old Mine Road, along the route of an 18th-century wagon trail. Although the historic path is now paved, the going is still slow on the narrow, winding roadway. (Nearby, a 3.7-mile trek along Dunnfield Creek meanders to secluded Sunfish Pond, one of many glacial lakes that dot the uplands.)

From the visitor center Old Mine Road heads north, paralleling the Delaware River through Worthington State Forest. The woods are dense with hardwoods and pines, but occasional openings afford wonderful glimpses of the wide, lazy river and the foothills beyond. The 5,800-acre forest, traversed by the famed Appalachian Trail, is popular with hikers and campers, not to mention black bears, which are fairly common in these parts. Three miles to the north, the Depew Recreation Site offers picnickers a chance to dine along the river's edge.

2 Millbrook Village

The first whites to settle the Delaware River valley in the early 1700s were Dutch farmers from New Amsterdam (now New York). The Van Campens, descendants of one of the families, sold their land so that a mill could be built beside a stream that came to be known as Van Campen's Mill Brook. This mill spawned Millbrook Village, a living museum and the first "town" inside the Delaware Water Gap Recreation Area. An adjoining glen makes a fine picnic spot, and while the brook isn't stocked, it boasts a healthy population of wild trout, which thrive in its cool waters and seem to exist solely to tempt anglers drawn to its waters.

Once a thriving crossroads, Millbrook, like so many remote hamlets, was practically deserted by 1900. Today its 23 restored buildings offer visitors a glimpse of an all-but-vanished world. Travelers who arrive on the first weekend in October may think they've wandered into a time warp, as local volunteers dress up in period attire to celebrate Millbrook Days, a recreation of daily life in a rural 19th-century town.

At the intersection of Old Mine Road and Flatbrook Creek, turn onto Rte. 615 and head north into Walpack Valley. One of the loveliest stretches of the drive, the exquisite scenery here is further enhanced by a gurgling stream, a valley lush with meadows and fertile farmland, and superb views of the nearby Kittatinny Ridge.

3 Walpack Center

As the most densely populated state in the country, New Jersey is perhaps the least likely location for a ghost town. But Walpack Center is just such a place. A few folks do live here, but not many; most left in the 1960s, when the federal government briefly planned to dam a section of the river here to form a reservoir. Though local opposition derailed the scheme,

Tortured layers of uplifted rock mark Kittatinny Ridge on the Delaware River.

Walpack Center never bounced back. It remains a mere shadow of its former self—a haunting place in hauntingly beautiful surroundings.

Walpack Center also provides access to Buttermilk Falls, the first of three cascades along the drive. To see them, follow Main Street past the old post office for about half a mile; at the cemetery take Mountain Road south for about two miles and listen for the sound of tumbling water. A short trail leads to the top of the falls, among the highest in New Jersey.

4 Peters Valley

In times gone by, the crafts practiced in this remote farming village were simple and basic. Folks made cloth because they needed something to wear; they worked with wood because they needed furniture; and when they painted, it was to decorate walls, not canvases.

Today, however, Peters Valley is synonymous with the Peters Valley Craft Center, where the handiworks on display range from basketry to photography. Classes are held throughout the summer, and tours of the artists' studios, all housed in restored 19th-century buildings, are available. The Peters Valley Craft Fair, held during the last full weekend in July, draws artists and exhibitors from all over the country.

5 Dingmans Ferry

Just how narrow is Dingmans Bridge? As you cross the Delaware River into Pennsylvania, you may hold your breath as you face oncoming traffic along this rattling wood-decked span. But not to worry: travelers have been squeaking by safely for nearly 100 years. Once across, reward yourself with a float trip on the river; canoe rentals are available just past the bridge, and you'll find the Dingmans Ferry boat ramp, the site of a Colonial-era ferry crossing, located across the road.

The Dingmans Ferry area is also blessed with a pair of magnificent waterfalls, both accessible along the same trail. From the Dingmans Falls visitor center, just south of the bridge on Rte. 209, a 10-minute hike through a hemlock forest passes Silver Thread Falls, then Dingmans Falls, where Dingmans Creek bounces down five rock steps before shooting to a pool 130 feet below. In the closed quarters of the ravine, the spray from the falls keeps the air cool even on the hottest of days.

6 High Point State Park

Back on the New Jersey side, the drive follows Old Mine Road north to Montague, then continues east on Rte. 521 and, briefly, south on Rte. 6, where it scrapes along the New York border before turning southwest on Rte. 23. From there the road begins its climb to High Point State Park and New Jersey's crowning summit, at 1,803 feet, atop the Kittatinny Ridge. A tall obelisk stands at ridgetop, where spectacular views unfold in all directions, including—on the clearest of nights— the distant, twinkling lights of the metropolis of New York City.

7 Stokes State Forest

Straddling some of the region's highest peaks, this 15,700-acre preserve is crisscrossed with 45 miles of trails. Sunrise Mountain, its name notwithstanding, offers stirring views at any time of day. Farther south on Rte. 521 lies another fine recreation area, 1,470-acre Swartswood State Park. Camping, fishing, and boating are all popular activities here, but some say the bird-watching to be had in these parts is second to none, both in number of species and the quality of the experience.

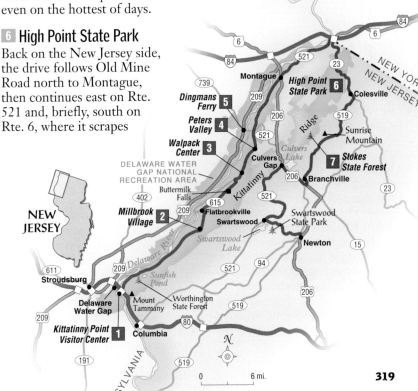

Maryland Panhandle

Hidden in the time-worn mountains of far western Maryland is a pristine province where rivers run deep, forests grow thick, and tiny mountain towns beckon with cozy inns and tales of frontier lore.

Though tranquil today, Antietam National Battlefield is littered with mementos of the bloody Civil War.

Creating a formidable barrier to settlers and colonists in centuries past, the peaks and valleys of the Allegheny Mountains still guard a corner of wilderness where locals—of which there are few—endure long blustery winters and extreme isolation from the rest of Maryland. But what outsiders don't know (and locals don't tell) is that this backcountry world offers a host of natural splendors—cascading streams, meadows strewn with wildflowers, and crystal-clear lakes—as well as hospitable towns with historic inns, tiny museums, and charming restaurants that serve up hearty, homestyle meals.

1 Swallow Falls State Park

Lured a century or so ago by blue-green mountains, cool forests, and swift, icy rivers, the well-to-do of Baltimore and Washington, D.C., built grand homes in and around Oakland, where the drive begins. Here they lolled away the summers with chilled lemonade and leisurely strolls. Many of their opulent homes still stand—mostly gingerbread Victorian in style—east of Oakland in the little town of Mountain Lake Park.

To get a sense of the unspoiled territory that first attracted these urban bluebloods, meander northwest from Oakland on Herrington Manor Road to Swallow Falls State Park. In the midst of this leafy paradise, serene Muddy Creek splashes over a rock ledge framed by mountain laurels, maples, hickories, and rhododendrons. Trails wander along sandstone cliffs beside the furious Youghiogheny River, whose rapids—with such knee-knocking nicknames as Triple Drop, Meat Cleaver, and Double Pencil Sharpener—are to many rafters a dream come true.

2 Deep Creek Lake State Park

Heading east on Swallow Falls Road, follow signs to Rte. 219 and then motor north to Deep Creek Lake, tucked among steep, forested slopes. This outdoor wonderland—and the 1,800-acre state park that lines its eastern shore—beckons sailors and water-skiers. Anglers come to entice walleye, and hikers tromp along trails that wind through groves of cherries, oaks, and sugar maples. In winter cross-country skiers glide beside the frozen lake past ice fishermen bundled up against the cold.

3 The Cove Overlook

Passing the high-steepled church in the town of Accident, Rte. 219 comes upon a picturesque pocket of farmland surrounded by the Alleghenies. Stop at The Cove Overlook to savor the tranquillity of this fertile valley fenced in by mountain peaks. Once reaching as high as the Alps, the Alleghenies—part of the Appalachian chain that stitches the eastern coast from Quebec to Alabama—are now relatively modest in size, softened and rounded by the elements over millions of years. The road winds north among these ancient mountains to the rugged summit of Keysers Ridge, where Rte. 40A veers east to Grantsville beneath the branches of oaks, hickories, and birches.

4 Grantsville

Chestnut-colored horses pull sleek black carriages through the streets of Grantsville, a mountain village populated mostly by Amish and Mennonites since the 1800s. A walk through the pleasant downtown brings you to the Casselman Hotel, a historic roadside inn with gleaming woodwork, a fireplace in every room, and the mouth-watering aroma of freshly baked bread wafting from the inn's on-site bakery.

Nearby at Penn Alps, a center that encourages local craft traditions, Amish people clad in black and white sell handwoven baskets, homemade apple butter, and colorful patchwork quilts. Next door at the Spruce Forest Artisan Village, a renowned whittler turns chunks of wood into graceful bird carvings that, from a distance, look like they just might fly away and join their real-life counterparts.

::::: **Trip Tips** :::::

Length: About 170 miles, plus side trips.

When to go: Best between May and October.

Not to be missed: The Western Maryland Scenic Railroad, from Cumberland to Frostburg and back.

Nearby attractions: Harpers Ferry National Historic Park, Harpers Ferry, WV. City of Washington, DC.

Further information: Allegheny County Visitor Bureau, Madison St. and Harrison St., Cumberland, MD 21502; tel. 800-508-4748, www.mdmountainside.com

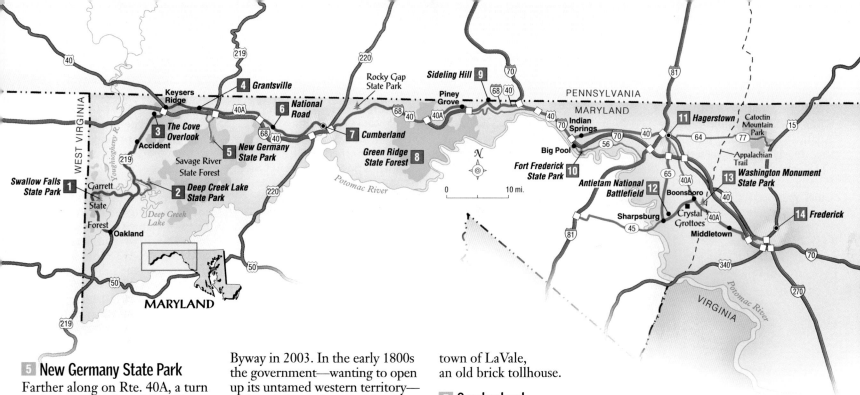

5 New Germany State Park

Farther along on Rte. 40A, a turn to the south leads to New Germany State Park, a comely patch of wilderness—with winding trails, hilly woods, and a trout-stocked lake—that showcases the seasons to perfection. In summer an emerald canopy of cherry, oak, and hickory trees shades these gentle slopes, until the days begin to shorten and gold and scarlet spread like wildfire across the hillsides. All too soon, an icy, arctic breeze blows the last leaves off the trees, a prelude to the blizzards that roar across the silent land, dumping so much snow—over 100 inches a year—that it lasts well past winter. Only in April or May do the rhododendrons and mountain laurels begin to show their pink and white blooms, acknowledging the arrival of spring.

6 National Road

All the way to Cumberland, Rte. 40A traces the well-trodden route of the old National Road, an ancient footpath first forged by Native Americans, then traipsed by explorers and militiamen into the unmapped lands beyond the Appalachians. This historic route was designated a National Scenic Byway in 2003. In the early 1800s the government—wanting to open up its untamed western territory—widened the path, paved it with broken stone, and dubbed it the nation's first federal road (it was generally known as the Pike). In no time long lines of covered wagons, their holds chock-full of pioneers yearning for a better life, churned westward toward Oregon and Santa Fe, joining herds of teamsters and stagecoach riders on the slow, bumpy trek. Mementos of that era include the crumbling stone mile markers scattered here and there along the roadside, the tiny village of Frostburg— which grew up around a cluster of taverns, smithies, and inns that served travelers plying the National Road—and in the

Built in 1813, the Casselman Bridge near Grantsville arcs gracefully beyond a carpet of maple leaves.

town of LaVale, an old brick tollhouse.

7 Cumberland

Beyond La Vale the road squeezes between the sheer 1,000-foot bluffs of Cumberland Narrows, then slides into Cumberland, an alluring town of historic red-brick buildings nestled in the mountains. Here in the early 1750s, George Washington, as a young lieutenant in the French and Indian War (his cabin stands in Riverside Park), dreamed of a magnificent canal that would carry goods between the frontier and the coast.

He never had the chance to build it, but the idea took form in 1828, when President John Quincy Adams broke ground (and, some say, the shovel) in Washington, D.C., and work was begun on the Chesapeake & Ohio Canal. The canal operated for nearly a century, its husky mules plodding beside the waterway with low-slung boats in tow. But the mules and canal boats were no match for the sleek engines of the Baltimore & Ohio Railroad (the nation's first), which came barreling up and over the mountains and eventually signaled the demise of the canal in 1924 after parts of it fell victim to flood damage. Today, the last lock to be built before all hopes for the canal were dashed stands down by the Potomac in Cumberland and has been transformed into Canal Place, commemorating the C & O Canal's terminus. It also has been designated Maryland's first certified heritage area. Throughout the summer season, here you'll be able to participate in a variety of activities including canal boat replica tours, scenic rail excursions, and festivals, culminating in the largest: CanalFest. It's also a welcome boon for the hikers, cyclists, and joggers who swarm to its scenic towpath—now part of a national historical park that meanders for more than 180 miles, all the way to Washington, D.C., along the old, leaf-shaded waterway. Plans in the future call for restoring a section of the canal itself and offering boat rides from the rewatered terminus of the C & O canal.

8 Green Ridge State Forest

Farther along, the road rambles across a succession of long ridges and gentle valleys with views of endless forest. At some point on this stretch of road, which heads into Green Ridge State Forest, stop the car and look to the sky for hawks, who like to swoop and glide on the thermals here.

At the southern tip of the state forest's lush carpet of oaks and hickories stands one of the C & O Canal's greatest engineering feats, the Paw Paw Tunnel—3,118 feet long and built of nearly 6 million bricks. A narrow gravel path disappears into the dark passage, a place where bats hang from ceiling crevices and ice-cold water oozes from the clammy walls. If you decide to embark on a trek through the pitch-black tunnel, bring a flashlight and wear a warm coat. When you emerge at the other end, you can spread a blanket at a charming grassy picnic spot.

9 Sideling Hill

From Green Ridge State Forest, the drive follows Rte. 40A to the town of Piney Grove, where it joins Rte. 40/68 and heads into Sideling Hill. When road workers blasted into the hilly landscape here in 1984 to make way for the highway, the resulting gash revealed eons of geological history. Among the lessons imparted here is how the mountain came to be—how, 230 million years ago, the continental plates of North America and Africa rammed into each other like a slow-motion car crash, their impact crumpling the land to create a mountain range. Also discovered here were the fossil remains of brachiopods left behind by an inland sea, and traces of swamp ferns dating from the days of the dinosaurs. These and other treasures are on display at the three-story exhibit center.

Ahead, the mountains melt into hills as the road enters the heart of Maryland's farm country. Old stone houses and classic red barns dot the velvet-green fields, and the hillsides are clad with fruit trees.

10 Fort Frederick State Park

Reached via a short side trip on Rte. 56, Fort Frederick is the sole survivor of a long line of sturdy forts that were sprinkled along the length of the Maryland Panhandle in the 1700s. Their purpose was to keep encroaching French colonists and their Indian allies away from the settlers trying to carve homesteads out of the wilderness. Fort Frederick, a great stone structure poised above the Potomac River, has massive walls 17 feet high and 4 feet thick. Inside the barracks uncomfortable iron

Blue Spring, one of the largest in the East, is nestled in a verdant woodland near Cumberland.

beds and plain stone walls evoke the nearly monastic austerity of a soldier's life in the old days. The fort—serving variously as a strategic supply base, a refuge for settlers, and a prisoner-of-war camp—figured in three major conflicts of U.S. history: the French and Indian War, the Revolutionary War, and the Civil War.

11 Hagerstown

To continue the drive, take Rte. 56 west and then turn north at Big Pool to Indian Springs. From there take Rte. 40 east through rolling green countryside and pastures to Hagerstown.

More than two centuries ago, a young, starry-eyed German named Jonathan Hager followed his true love (so it is said) across the Atlantic Ocean to America. They married and settled in the middle of the wilderness in a limestone house with a great stone fireplace. Young Hager named the village that grew up around them Elizabeth Town, though everyone else called it Hager's Town. Their old house—furnished with buffalo hides, split-oak baskets, and other frontier decor—still stands today as a reminder of the depth of the region's historic past.

Several miles east of town—via Rtes. 64 and 77—lies Catoctin Mountain Park, which harbors one of the nation's most carefully guarded enclaves—Camp David. Unless you're the president, you probably won't visit this secluded mountain retreat, which Franklin D. Roosevelt christened Shangri-la. But you can still enjoy the dense woods, intriguing nature trails, and trout-filled streams, and feel the cool breezes that surround it.

From Hagerstown the drive rambles south on Rte. 65 past farms, hollows, and waving fields of corn to Sharpsburg, a friendly village today that abuts a grim reminder of the Civil War.

Dutchman's breeches supply whimsical accents along the banks of the old Chesapeake and Ohio Canal.

12 Antietam National Battlefield

Wooded hilltops and murmuring streams belie the horrors that unfolded on this notorious battlefield throughout the hours of September 17, 1862—the bloodiest day of conflict in any American war. On that fateful day, during the first Confederate invasion of the North, forces of the North and South clashed at three different sites: in a cornfield, along a sunken road (later dubbed Bloody Lane), and on a graceful bridge. The confrontations resulted in no tactical gain or loss for either side—no loss, that is, except for the 23,000 men who lay dead or wounded around the smoldering, smoking battleground. You can learn all about the somber event at the modern visitor center and perhaps take a driving tour of the historic battlefield.

From Sharpsburg follow Rte. 34 northeast to Crystal Grottoes, a cavern with walkways that snake through intriguing underground limestone formations. Boonsboro, a bit farther along Rte. 34, is said to have been founded by relatives of Daniel Boone. From the center of town, Rte. 40A leads southeast to Washington Monument State Park.

13 Washington Monument State Park

Somewhat obscured by foliage and squat in shape, this Washington Monument looks to some like an ugly stepsister of the tall, sleek obelisk that graces the National Mall in Washington, D.C. But the juglike stone structure that sits atop South Mountain in Washington Monument State Park nonetheless boasts a distinction: it was the first memorial ever built to honor the nation's first president, and it embodies the pride and patriotism of an entire town and its surrounding region. On the Fourth of July in 1827—51 years after the signing of the Declaration of Independence—nearly every citizen of Boonsboro marched two miles up the mountainside and, one by one, laid each stone in its proper place. An inner staircase climbs the 34-foot tower to a marvelous perch that takes in miles of gentle hills and valleys. You can enjoy a picnic in the park or hike on one of its trails before continuing east on Rte. 40A into the historic city of Frederick; the Appalachian Trail passes through the park, part of a path through many of the Eastern states.

14 Frederick

Rolling farmland surrounds the city of Frederick, a bustling commercial hub and college town with gracious Federal town houses and spired churches that exude an appealing, old-fashioned charm.

On tree-shaded West Patrick Street, you'll find the old red-brick home of Barbara Fritchie, the fiery, then-95-year-old patriot who, legend says, defiantly flew the Stars and Stripes in the face of the invading Southern general Stonewall Jackson and his rebel horde in 1862. Her actions on that day were imortalized in verse, according to poet John Greenleaf Whittier, who gave voice to Fritchie's fervent exclamation:

"'Shoot if you must
      this old gray head,
   But spare your country's flag,'
      she said."

Visibly shamed, Jackson then shouted to his soldiers:

"Who touches a hair
      on yon gray head
   Dies like a dog!
      March on!"

Today Barbara Fritchie's spirit is also memorialized in a museum displaying her furniture, quilts, china, and other relics that evoke life in 19th-century Maryland.

Eastern Shore Sampler

Sprinkled with farms, fishing villages, plantations, and marinas, Maryland's Eastern Shore is a landscape perfectly wedded to the waters of the Chesapeake Bay.

An aerial view of the village of Oxford, with its many sailboats on Chesapeake Bay.

So named because it abuts the Eastern margin of the Chesapeake Bay, Maryland's Eastern Shore is endowed with scores of inlets, bays, rivers, and canals. Even the livelihoods (farming and fishing) and pastimes (hunting and sailing) of those who live here reflect the Eastern Shore's age-old interplay between land and water.

1 Chesapeake City

Beginning at the town of Elkton, the drive cruises south on Rte. 213 toward Chesapeake City, or Canal Town, as it is known locally. There the highway soars across a bridge high above the Chesapeake and Delaware Canal, which connects the Chesapeake Bay with the Delaware Bay—a shortcut to the Atlantic Ocean. Completed in 1829, the waterway saves ocean-going vessels a 300-mile journey south, then north, around the tip of the Delmarva Peninsula.

Chesapeake City itself consists of a restored tavern, general store, and pastel saltbox houses where canal builders once lived. At the edge of town, near an inlet dotted with sailboats, the Chesapeake & Delaware Canal Museum houses a fine collection of canal memorabilia. The museum is perched right on the bank of the canal, and visitors can watch giant barges led by tugboats and ocean freighters ply the placid waters.

2 Chestertown

Continuing south, Rte. 213 swings through cool woods and rolling hills, past farmhouses and fields of wheat and corn. As far back as the 17th century, English planters tended tobacco plantations here, using their profits to build gracious mansions and spending their leisure hours caring for their race-horses and hunting foxes.

Even today, racehorses are an ongoing "industry" in this part of Maryland. The 10,000-acre Maryland Lands Trust, one of the largest land preservation areas on the Eastern Shore, is home to a number of horse farms (as well as agricultural farms) and more than 1,000 of the nation's most prized Thoroughbreds. They have included such equine luminaries as Kelso, Northern Dancer, Bet Twice, and other world-class equestrian champions.

The drive glides along Rte. 213 through Colonial villages such as Georgetown, Locust Grove, and Kennedyville, passing over tidal streams that feed the Chesapeake Bay to the west. Farther along, the entrance to Chestertown is signaled by a compound of brick edifices known as Washington College (named for the first president, who visited here in 1784 and donated 50 guineas towards its establishment). The handsome 18th-century village features sycamore-shaded streets, gardens trimmed with boxwood, and an inn more than two centuries old. Pre-Revolutionary houses built by well-to-do merchants face the Chester River, best viewed by walking across the Chester River Bridge. Down by the waterfront near the customs house, a historic moment took place in 1774 when townsfolk, disgusted with the British tax on tea, dumped a large shipment into the water. This patriotic act (reminiscent of the Boston Tea Party of 1773) is commemorated by residents each May with a Colonial-style parade.

3 Wye Mills

Traffic often crowds Rte. 213 as it nears the turnoff for the Chesapeake Bay Bridge, which links the Eastern Shore with Annapolis and Washington, D.C. After gliding by thickets of pine interspersed with wetlands, the drive crosses Rte. 50 and joins up with narrow Rte. 662.

Driving south, you'll soon enter the crossroads of Wye Mills, where visitors can tour the 18th-century Wye Mill that lent the town its name. The mill once supplied cornmeal to George Washington's hungry troops at Valley Forge during the frigid winter of 1778.

4 Wye Island Natural Resources Management Area

As a side trip, drive west on Rte. 50 a few miles, then follow signs to the turnoff south to Wye Island Natural Resources Management area, located in the tidal rescesses of the Chesapeake Bay between the Wye and the Wye East rivers. It is a prime spot to observe migratory waterfowl and shore birds in their native habitats.

Returning to Rte. 662, the drive takes what seems to be an indecisive course, weaving its way back and forth across Rte. 50—the Main Street of the Eastern Shore, with the traffic to prove it—on its way south to the town of Easton, which dates to Revolutionary times.

A great blue heron at Blackwater National Wildlife Refuge.

5 Easton

Clapboard houses and white picket fences line narrow, shady streets in Easton, gateway to the Chesapeake Bay. For a scenic detour that offers a wind-in-the-hair view of the bay, ramble down Rte. 333 to Oxford.

Once rivaling Annapolis among pre-Revolutionary ports, Oxford saw many tons of tobacco and grain (and, on a somber note, slaves and convicts) pass through its customs house. A replica of the original building stands down by the Tred Avon River, where the landing for the Oxford–Bellevue Ferry (nine-car limit) beckons to travelers. (A ferry has operated here since 1683; the first owner accepted tobacco for fares.) On the other side, motor up to the picturesque village of St. Michaels, whose harbor on the Miles River is crowded with sleek yachts. For a detailed view of the town's seagoing legacy, visit the famed Chesapeake Bay Maritime Museum; it features everything from an old lighthouse and waterfowl decoys to historic bay boats.

Follow Rte. 33 down the narrow neck of land known locally as Bay Hundred Peninsula to Tilghman Island, connected to the mainland by a tiny drawbridge. Here you get a wide-angle view of the vast blue-gray waters of the Chesapeake Bay, America's largest estuary. Crab huts are scattered here and there on the windblown island's shores, home to hardy fishermen who for generations have sought blue crabs, oysters, clams, and other treasures in the bay's salty depths. After sampling the local harvest transformed into such succulent delights as crab cakes and soft-shell crab sandwiches (or eaten steamed), backtrack to East-

Trip Tips

Length: About 110 miles, plus side trips.

When to go: Popular year-round.

Words to the wise: The Oxford-Bellevue Ferry is closed from mid-December until late February.

Not to be missed: Waterfowl Festival (early November), Easton.

Nearby attractions: Annapolis. Ocean City. Assateague Island National Seashore (inhabited by wild ponies), south of Ocean City.

Further information: Maryland Office of Tourism, 217 East Redwood St., Baltimore, MD 21202; tel. 800-634-7386, www.mdwelcome.org.

on on Rte. 33 and head south on Rte. 50 into Cambridge.

6 Cambridge

This old port dates from the 1680s, but the earliest buildings that survive here are the elegant Georgian- and Federal-style homes that line High Street. The street slopes down to the town wharf, which commands a beautiful view of the Choptank River. Eight miles southwest of town, poised serenely on the banks of Church Creek, lies the Old Trinity Episcopal Church, erected in the late 1600s. Built with money from the royal pocketbook, this brick chapel (one of the nation's oldest in continuous use) is surrounded by a fascinating old graveyard.

7 Blackwater National Wildlife Refuge

In a land obsessed with goose hunting, where marksmanship is highly esteemed and decoys

decorate mailboxes, migrating geese are in need of a safe haven. Consequently, each year legions of these birds flock to the enormous Blackwater National Wildlife Refuge, where they can hide out in peace. The maze of marshy channels and woodlands provides a year-round home for many other birds as well. For a close-up view, take the sinuous five-mile Wildlife Drive into the heart of the preserve, which recalls the tidewater scenery witnessed by Eastern Shore settlers some three centuries ago.

Brandywine Valley

Cultivated by one family—the Du Ponts—and immortalized by another—the Wyeths—this lush and lovely landscape seems like a painting come to life.

The stately and formal grounds of the Nemours Mansion north of Wilmington.

Named for a river that in its upper reaches could pass for a creek, the Brandywine Valley stretches 35 miles from the rolling hills of southeastern Pennsylvania to the northern part of Wilmington, Delaware. And almost every acre is rich with romance, history, or just plain beauty.

1 Nemours Mansion

Go almost anywhere in Brandywine country, and you're likely to encounter the name Du Pont. The first member of this notable clan to arrive in America, Pierre Samuel du Pont de Nemours, emigrated from France with his family in 1799. Three years later one of his sons, Éleuthère Irénée, established a gunpowder plant beside the Brandywine River in Delaware. By the early 20th century, the family business had grown into the world's largest chemical company. The Du Ponts eventually became one of the richest families in America, and they poured a good deal of their wealth into their properties.

The first of several monuments to the Du Pont dynasty to be seen here is the Nemours Mansion, located on Rockland Road between Rtes. 202 and 141 north of Wilmington. A modified Louis XVI–style château, this 102-room masterpiece was built in 1910 by Pierre Du Pont's great-grandson Alfred, who used it as a refuge from scorning relatives after his divorce. Antique furnishings, tapestries, and a fine collection of 17th-century Dutch paintings are among the items on exhibit here. Visitors to the 300-acre estate can cap a house tour with a stroll through gardens that some say rival those found at the Palace of Versailles.

2 Hagley Museum

Turning south on Rte. 141, the drive reaches the Hagley Museum, site of the Du Pont Company's early gunpowder mills. In use from 1802 until 1921, when the mills closed, these works made the Du Pont family the largest manufacturer of gunpowder and construction explosives in America. Much of the original machinery has been carefully restored and can be toured in the Hagley Yards, part of the indoor-outdoor museum that traces the long history of powder making. Also found on these 240 wooded acres are several interesting buildings—including a furnished cottage and school—that vividly evoke the lifestyle of Du Pont workers and their families. Farther upstream, overlooking the original powder mills, sits Eleutherian Mills, an 1803 Georgian-style residence whose furnishings reflect the tastes of five generations of Du Ponts.

:::::: Trip Tips ::::::

Length: About 20 miles.

When to go: Pleasant year-round, but best in spring and fall.

Nearby attractions: Phillips Mushroom Museum, Kennett Square, PA; Franklin Mint Museum, Franklin Center, PA; Valley Forge National Historical Park, King of Prussia, PA; Colonial New Castle, Delaware's first capital.

Further information: Brandywine Valley Tourist Information Center, P.O. Box 910, Kennett Square, PA 19348; tel. 800-228-9933, www.visitdelaware.com.

3 Winterthur

The rolling countryside near Centerville, Delaware, is a cornucopia of palatial estates. But no piece of real estate here can quite compare with Winterthur (pronounced *WIN-ter-toor*), the ancestral home of Henry Francis Du Pont. This 983-acre compound—which explodes with lyrically beautiful combinations of flowers from February until November—was lovingly landscaped by its owner, whose passion for his property led him to eventually become an expert in horticulture.

The magnificence of the grounds at Winterthur is perhaps exceeded only by that of its centerpiece, a nine-story museum housing some 90,000 examples of American decorative arts dating from 1640 to 1860. Installed in nearly 175 meticulously restored, period-accurate rooms, these rare objects —including silver tankards crafted by Paul Revere and a dinner service made for George Washington— form one of the largest treasuries of its kind in America.

4 Longwood Gardens

In 1906 Pierre S. Du Pont, following in the tradition of his nature-loving ancestors, bought land in the Brandywine Valley to rescue an arboretum in danger of being destroyed for timber. With time— and the help of the Du Pont fortune—his investment evolved into Longwood Gardens, one of the grandest gardens in the world.

Located just west of the intersection of Rtes. 1 and 52, this paradise of plants boasts more than 11,000 different species in two types of settings: outdoors on 350 exquisitely manicured acres, and indoors in conservatories that shelter 20 indoor gardens. Among the most notable attractions here are the Flower Garden Walk, the Italian Water Garden, the Main Fountain Garden, the indoor Children's Garden, the Orchid Display, and the Silver Garden, featuring plants that flourish in some of the world's harshest environments. On summer evenings you can spread a blanket beside one of the three Fountain Gardens and enjoy a concert, a play, or a fireworks display.

5 Chadds Ford

Just south of the intersection of Rtes. 1 and 100 lies another institution that inspires deep pride among area residents, the Brandywine River Museum. Displayed on its walls are works by Howard Pyle, Rockwell Kent, and some 300 other artists. But it is the Wyeths—America's so-called First Family of Art— who give the place its special éclat. Three generations are represented here: N. C. Wyeth, one of the most popular and prolific illustrators of his day; his son Andrew, the celebrated realist painter; and Andrew's son, Jamie, who carries on the family's tradition of richly textured landscapes that capture the quiet splendor of their beloved Brandywine Valley.

The building that houses this unique collection of Americana—a converted 19th-century gristmill—is something of a work of art in itself. The galleries (including one illuminated solely by natural light) are graced by the original hand-hewn beams and wide-board pine floors. The lobbies, walled with glass, look out onto gardens of wildflowers and, beyond, the Brandywine River, where herons can sometimes be seen nabbing fish in the shallows.

Heading north on Rte. 1, the drive passes through Chadds Ford. The town is named for John Chad, a farmer who ran a ferry back and forth across the Brandywine River in the early 1700s. At the intersection of Rtes. 1 and 100, head north on Rte. 100. About half a mile up the road you'll find Chad's carefully preserved two-story house, now a museum.

Hagley Mill provided power to the Du Pont's gunpowder plant near Westover Hills.

Hagley Yards, part of the Hagley Museum, traces the history of gunpowder-making on Brandywine Creek.

6 Brandywine Battlefield

On September 11, 1777, British troops marched past the site of the Brandywine River Museum and, less than a mile to the east, handed a defeat to those of General George Washington. The future president then met the greatest test of his leadership by pulling the Continental Army through a brutal winter encampment at Valley Forge. The clash is recounted at the visitor center and reenacted each September. Nearby are the headquarters of Washington and his French ally, the marquis de Lafayette. Just east of the park, a turn either north or south on Rte. 100 leads through a lush green landscape where, on one side of the road, you may spot a herd of Holsteins grazing in their pasture and, on the other, thoroughbreds leaping over split-rail fences and standardbreds trotting with dapper riders at their reins.

Indiana, Hill and Dale

Backwoods charm blends with worldly sophistication in south-central Indiana, a hilly hinterland rich with pioneer history.

Red barns and rolling pastures punctuate valleys amid Brown County's rolling hills.

Life slows to a relaxed pace amid these rolling hills, where people still take time to spin a yarn, tune a fiddle, and sit on the porch with a glass of lemonade. But Indiana also has a certain cosmopolitan flair. Artists and scholars have long made the region their home, and Bloomington, a booming college town, offers many of the attractions of big-city life. Yet it manages at the same time to remain friendly and unpretentious —welcome Hoosier hallmarks.

1 Bloomington

Tree-lined avenues with a wide selection of shops and restaurants crisscross Bloomington, a pretty town known for its limestone buildings. The downtown historic district features such stately gems as the 1906 Monroe County Courthouse, an ornate structure crowned with a cupola.

The town's centerpiece, though, must surely be its college, Indiana University. The campus boasts ivy-draped halls and dormitories, and many trees grow on its grounds. Of note too are the Auditorium Hall of Murals, with paintings by Thomas Hart Benton, and the Indiana University Art Museum, which displays works by Picasso, Rodin, Warhol, and other artists.

An artistry of another stripe is required for the Little 500, a bicycle race that takes place each April at Indiana University. In the grueling event, riders work as teams, substituting for one another as they race around an oval track. Or try the Annual Hilly Hundred Weekend, a three-day classic for bicycle tourists with more than 5,500 riders.

After sampling Bloomington's attractions, including Indiana's oldest winery—the Bloomington Oliver Winery on Rte. 36—follow Rte. 46 east as it dips and bobs through the hills and hollows of rural Brown County. At Belmont, turn onto T. C. Steele Road, a country lane winding through hickory and oak groves and meadows colored with patches of sun-flecked goldenrod.

2 T. C. Steele State Historic Site

The painter Theodore Clement Steele purchased 171 acres here in 1907. His home, known as the House of the Singing Wind, holds an abundance of fine furniture and decorative objects; the nearby barn, which Steele built for use as a studio, displays his colorful paintings. Visitors can walk along trails to see the woods and fields that inspired him and wander to Selma N. Steele State Nature Preserve, named for the artist's wife. Riotous drifts of summer wildflowers in the preserve contrast with the carefully cultivated beauty of daffodils and irises found in other areas of the Historic Site's property.

Just to the south lies Monroe Lake, a large reservoir that extends its watery tentacles between forest-clad hills. Hardin Ridge, a popular spot for enjoying the lake, is situated in Hoosier National Forest and offers swimming, camping, and boat launches. Bald eagles, their nests high up in the trees, are fairly common here.

3 Nashville

The folksy charm of Gnaw Bone, Bean Blossom, and other rural communities is a Brown County stock in trade. But when people mention local color, they are probably referring to the hillsides, where showtime takes place every spring and fall. First onstage are dogwood and redbud trees costumed in white and pink. Then comes a rainbow of wildflowers that slowly fades as autumn ushers in the finale: a blazing display of maples and oaks glowing like embers at the edge of winter.

The town of Nashville complements all this natural beauty. A gathering place for artists, it has antique shops, art galleries, and

A dogwood tree bursts with blooms, boasting the beautiful bounty of spring.

craft stores. Taste the famous fried biscuits at Nashville House, listen to the spinners of tall tales on Liar's Bench outside the old courthouse, or, in June, attend the Bill Monroe Memorial Bean Blossom Bluegrass Festival, the oldest festival in the world dedicated to Monroe's "high lonesome" bluegrass songs.

A few miles east of town, Rte. 46 leads to Brown County State Park. Once across the covered bridge at its entrance, visitors can explore nearly 16,000 acres of pristine woodland. Lakes and streams are plentiful here, and you can always find a place to paddle a canoe, hike a shady trail, or catch a glimpse of migrating teal or other waterfowl.

4 Story

The drive turns southward on Rte. 135, following a twisting course lined with thick stands of trees and daisy-dotted meadows. Soon you will come to the resurrected ghost town of Story, founded in 1851. Riders in horse-drawn carts once stopped at Story to buy supplies and swap tales. Now visitors come to take in the old-time ambience of the village and its Story

Inn, an early country store that has been converted into a gourmet restaurant—call for reservations.

5 Starve Hollow State Recreation Area

Wild turkeys, ruffed grouse, deer, and raccoons are among the denizens of this recreation area. To learn about the animals, stop at the Driftwood Nature Center; then you might spot some of them in the wild as you walk along the nature trails. Starve Hollow Lake, the area's centerpiece, is stocked with catfish, bluegills, and bass, while dozens of prime campsites nestle along the shores. Back on Rte. 135, the drive curves past small fields and hills decked with oak, poplar, maple, and hickory trees. Along the way, it passes through Salem, a quiet town with a public square and historic courthouse.

6 Corydon

When Indiana became a state in 1816, the tiny town of Corydon was made its first capital. Here the constitutional convention drew up a blueprint for government in the limestone capitol, which still

stands near the town square. Nearby are the 1817 Thomas Posey House and the oldest building in Corydon, the 1800 Branham Tavern, which is constructed of logs. Other must-see stops in Corydon include Turtle Run Winery, glass-making artisans, Cave Country Canoes, Corydon Jamboree—a favorite for devotees of country and gospel music—and Wyandotte Caves off Rte 62 about eight miles outside of town; reach the caves by taking exit 105 on I-64.

To the south the Battle of Corydon Memorial Park honors yet another era. Indiana's only Civil War battle took place at the site, where the state's home guard surrendered to a much larger force of Confederate soldiers after a brief skirmish. The occupation did not last long: the Southern army commandeered all the fresh horses they could find, then marched off to their next encounter.

7 Squire Boone Caverns

The drive continues southward on Rte. 135 as it heads for the access road to Squire Boone Caverns. A brother of the famed frontiersman, Squire Boone built a log house and a gristmill here in 1804. Years earlier he had eluded pursuing Indians by taking shelter in a nearby cavern—a stroke of good fortune that inspired him to return and settle in the region with his family.

Today visitors find on the site a small theme park with pioneer-era buildings, hayrides, and other bucolic amusements. The caverns, a complex of rooms and passageways hollowed into the limestone by underground streams, can be seen on guided tours. The distinctly cool, dark realm contains milky rimstone dams, impressive stalactites and stalagmites, and limpid pools populated by blind crayfish—their eyes unneeded in a world without light.

Scenic Southeastern Ohio

Ohio's southland offers a full slate of pleasing sights—streams and rivers, tidy apple orchards, sprawling forests, modest pioneer towns, and mysterious Indian monuments fashioned from the earth itself.

Conkle's Hollow, with its sandstone ledges and wooded slopes, is a unit of Hocking Hills State Park.

Ohio sheds its urbane modern mask and reveals some of its old-time pioneer spirit along this drive, which threads through a region as varied and colorful as an antique mosaic. History is part of the landscape here, where covered bridges and mellow old buildings nestle in valleys that once echoed with the blasts of steamboat whistles. But the area's past goes deeper still, back to a time when long-vanished Native American civilizations were a flourishing presence in these rugged hills.

1 Chillicothe

Named with a Shawnee tribal word that means "town," Chillicothe first became the capital of the Northwest Territory, then the state of Ohio in 1803. It has since grown into a manufacturing center, with many reminders of its past still standing, including a number of stately 19th-century Greek Revival mansions. You'll also find the home of Thomas Worthington, one of Ohio's founding fathers. The lush grounds surrounding his 18-room mansion, known today as Adena State Memorial, overlook the Scioto River valley.

Only three miles separate Adena from Mound City at Hopewell Culture National Historical Park. In terms of time, though, the distance is actually some 2,000 years. The grassy mounds, surrounded by an earthen wall, were built by Hopewell Indians for burials and other ceremonies. Excavations have unearthed a treasure trove of artifacts, yet no one knows for certain where the Hopewells came from or to whence they disappeared.

2 Hocking Hills State Park

From Chillicothe the drive heads east on Rte. 50, then follows Rte. 327 north to the access road for Tar Hollow State Park, named for the tar that pioneers collected from the shortleaf and pitch pines that grow on the ridges. Motorists can pause to sample the area's mix of

Trip Tips

Length: About 170 miles.

When to go: Pleasant year-round.

Nearby attractions: Serpent Mound State Memorial, featuring an Indian mound built in the form of a huge snake, about 50 miles southwest of Chillicothe. The Wilds, a 9,100-acre conservation center with rare and endangered animals, about 20 miles north of McConnelsville on Rte. 284.

Further information: Ohio Division of Travel and Tourism, 77 South High St., P.O. Box 1001, Columbus, OH 43216; tel. 800-282-5393, www.ohiotourism.com.

Star Route

⭐ Covered Bridge Scenic Byway

A surplus of rural charms enhance the rolling terrain of the easternmost sector of Wayne National Forest, where the Covered Bridge Scenic Byway—Rte. 26—winds northward from Marietta. Tracking the Little Muskingum River, the drive passes family farms, small towns, and four of the old-time spans, one of which you can drive across. Here and there the road climbs ridges that provide sweeping views until, 44 miles later, the drive reaches its end in lovely Woodsfield.

lakes and forests or continue north to Laurelville and Rte. 180 in quest of other treasures of the region.

A turn southeast on Rte. 374 leads to Hocking Hills State Park, 2,000 acres filled with waterfalls, deep gorges, and unusual caves and sandstone formations that give this part of Ohio a grandeur as dramatic as it is unexpected. Eastern hemlocks, mountain laurels, ferns, and rare wildflowers thrive in the moist, wooded hollows—the haunts of both red and gray foxes and more than 100 species of birds.

The park is divided into six separate areas, each named for a distinguishing landmark—Rock House, for example, or Conkle's Hollow. At Old Man's Cave the visitor center overlooks a creek, whose racing water has carved a gorge two miles long, with several waterfalls. From the Lower Falls hikers can traverse the Buckeye Trail through a series of rugged, hemlock-shaded valleys. At

trail's end the view takes in the 50-foot-high veil of Cedar Falls.

3 Lake Hope State Park

The drive slices into the wooded valley of Big Sandy Run on Rte. 56, then dips southward on Rte. 278 to reach Lake Hope. Cradled amid low, rounded hills, the lake is a favorite with swimmers and boaters. Birders also flock to the surrounding parkland, where cardinals (Ohio's state bird) flash through foliage, wild turkeys gobble in the underbrush, and the hollow tappings of pileated woodpeckers, largest of their genus, reverberate through the forest.

4 Nelsonville

The drive turns around and climbs northward along Rte. 278, entering Wayne National Forest. Rolling up and down hills and valleys, it leads to Nelsonville, a place where the 1800s are very much alive and well. Its fine Victorian homes, historic public square, Stuart's Opera House, and the Dew Hotel still look much as they did in the 19th century. On summer weekends the Hocking Valley Scenic Railway, located just off Rte. 33, chugs into the surrounding hills. Robbins' Crossing, one of the train's stops, operates as a museum, re-creating life in a rural Ohio community of the 1850s.

5 Muskingum River Parkway

Living history of another kind, but from the same era, can be found at McConnelsville, a former steamboat town. Boats on the Muskingum River still sound their horns as they approach the McConnelsville lock. Built more than 150 years ago and operated by hand, it is one of 10 similar locks that were built from 1837 to 1841 in order to tame the unpredictable river and accommodate the crush of steamboat traffic traveling between the towns of Dresden and Marietta.

The river and its historic lock system can be toured via the Muskingum River Parkway (Rtes. 376, 266, and 60). Six of the early marvels of engineering, counting the one in McConnelsville, are situated at intervals along the way. From bankside picnic areas you will likely watch the passing procession of cruisers, houseboats, motorboats, and other craft as they glide across waters that once were churned by smoke-belching paddle wheelers.

6 Marietta

On the approach to Marietta, you will be following in the footsteps of John Chapman, who adopted the name Johnny Appleseed to

honor his life's ambition. The legendary figure—according to most accounts, a true eccentric in ways more than horticultural—was a tireless planter of apple trees in the early 19th century.

The Muskingum River empties into the Ohio River at Marietta. Founded in 1788 by veterans of the Revolutionary War, this appealing riverfront city was the first American settlement in the Northwest Territory, and in the steamboat era it became a major port and shipbuilding center. A vintage steamboat is on display at the Ohio River Museum, and a stern-wheeler at the waterfront offers regular excursions up and down the Ohio and Muskingum rivers.

A male cardinal takes shelter in a tangle of branches.

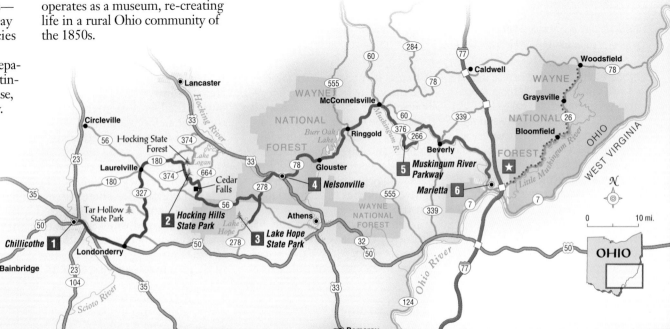

Amish Byways

Like the delicate needlework of a handmade quilt,
the rustic lanes of eastern Ohio stitch the colors of the
countryside into a richly textured whole.

*With its tidy arrangement of unadorned buildings, this farm near Fredricksburg is
a classic example of an Amish homestead.*

The sights along this scenic journey are, quite literally, nothing fancy. The Amish, sometimes called the Plain People, live a life of modesty and simplicity, shunning modern conveniences. Governed by ancient rhythms of planting and harvesting, their customs—as pure as apple butter, as practical as a straw hat in summer—offer fascinating glimpses into days gone by.

1 Malabar Farm State Park

Within its first few miles, this drive will dispel any notions that Ohio is flat: as it runs southeast alongside the Clear Fork River, Rte. 97 bounces over hill after wooded hill. Indeed, one reason why many early settlers were attracted to this lush, rolling landscape was its uncanny resemblance to the rural alpine valleys they had left behind in their native countries of Switzerland, Austria, and Germany.

Turning northward on Rte. 95 at Butler, the drive continues to Malabar Farm State Park, once the country estate of Pulitzer prizewinning author Louis Bromfield. Named for the India subcontinent's Malabar Coast, a spot where Bromfield had once spent time, the farm encompasses more the 900 acres of fields and forests.

Among the many celebrities who visited Bromfield were Humphrey Bogart and Lauren Bacall, who spent their honeymoon here in 1945. Bromfield's 32-room mansion, which seems all the more lavish in contrast to the nearby Amish country, is open year-round, and tours of the grounds—the only working farm in the Ohio State Park system—are conducted by tractor-drawn wagon. A few miles farther on, Pleasant Hill Lake Park draws boaters, anglers, and anyone else in search of a cooling dip.

2 Mohican Memorial State Forest

Back on Rte. 97 the drive continues east through rolling hills as it approaches Mohican Memorial State Forest. Embracing a total of some 5,000 acres, the preserve straddles the Clear Fork–Mohican River. Though 22 miles of trails and old logging roads beckon visitors into the wilds, you can also see a great deal by car. For a quick tour follow the park road north to the covered bridge that spans the river, then venture on foot along the water's edge to Big and Little Lyons Falls and plunging Clear Fork Gorge, just below the Pleasant Hill Dam. It's hard to tell, but most of this area was once cleared for farming; during the Depression-era 1930s the Civilian Conservation Corps helped in reforestation efforts.

3 Millersburg

Amish country begins somewhere east of Loudonville. There's no official boundary; you'll know that you have arrived when you find yourself sharing the road with a horse-drawn buggy or spot a team of Belgian horses pulling a plow

or wagon through a field. Some 35,000 Amish—the largest community of its kind in the world—reside in the gently folded farmlands that roll eastward from this point, the 400 square miles of very special land known throughout the region as Amish Country.

Millersburg, like many towns in the region, is a busy crafts center where visitors can rub elbows with the Amish who come to buy supplies and sell their wares. Prowl the shops for leather goods, furniture, woolens, and handmade quilts (true treasures). Then visit Victorian House, an opulent Queen Anne home turned museum, whose 28 antique-filled rooms are a far cry from the sparse-yet-appealing Amish austerity that otherwise prevails in these parts.

4 Berlin

About five miles east of Millersburg, a turnoff on Rte. 557 leads south to the aptly named village of Charm. Surrounded by lush, rolling farmland, Charm makes you feel as if you've wandered into a Grant Wood painting. Amish

farms are limited in size to the amount of land that a single family can work without modern machinery, and each rise in the road will reveal as many as a dozen farmsteads, their simple white houses, huge dairy barns, and neatly furrowed fields laid out as precisely as the squares on a checkerboard.

Returning to Rte. 39 east, the drive soon reaches another farming town, Berlin, where visitors can learn about the Amish and their Anabaptist kin, the Mennonites. Stop at the Mennonite Information Center, located on County Road 77, just off Rte. 39. Its chief attraction is a grand cyclorama, or circular painting. Measuring 10 feet high by 265 feet long, this magnificent mural depicts the heritage of the Amish and Mennonite people from their mutual origins in medieval Zurich, Switzerland, in 1525 to the present.

About one mile east of town, a former Amish farm offers tours, buggy rides, quilt-making demonstrations, and a pondside that makes a great spot for a picnic.

5 Sugarcreek

Of all the picturesque towns that can be seen along the drive, perhaps none is as distinctive as Sugarcreek. Nicknamed The Little Switzerland of Ohio, Sugarcreek really does conjure up the flavor of a Swiss village. Here you may find yourself bobbing to the beat of polka music that drifts out from

Covered bridge at Mohican Memorial State Forest.

the town's storefronts, all colorfully decorated with appealing alpine scenes.

Sugarcreek is also the departure point for the Ohio Central Railroad, which offers tours of Amish country. The depot is on Factory Street, not far from the local McDonald's—equipped with hitching posts to accommodate Amish horse-drawn buggies.

6 Schoenbrunn Village State Memorial

At New Philadelphia head southeast on Rte. 259 (High Avenue) to Schoenbrunn Village State Memorial, site of Ohio's earliest Christian settlement. Founded in 1772 as a Moravian mission to the Delaware Indians, Schoenbrunn (German for "beautiful spring") lasted only five years, but today its 17 reconstructed log buildings evoke life on the Ohio frontier. The original cemetery endures as a mute memorial to the heroic men and women who braved wilderness and war to make their homes here.

Continue east on Rte. 39 east until you reach Sherrodsville; then follow Rte. 212 northwest to the sandy beach at 1,540-acre Atwood Lake, a crescent of blue amid green forest and farmland. To finish the drive, return to Rte. 39 and continue east for 40 miles on this long, rolling straightaway to Wellsville, the mighty Ohio River, and the West Virginia border.

Bluegrass to Pennyroyal

This richly endowed landscape in the heart of rural Kentucky is famed worldwide
for its champion racehorses, velvet-smooth bourbon, and colossal caverns.

Bluegrass means a seemingly endless sea of green pastures, white rail fences, and thoroughbred horses near Lexington.

Trod by Daniel Boone in the 1700s, central Kentucky evolved from raw wilderness to a land of gentility, where local folk became wealthy by raising thoroughbred horses and producing fine whiskey. Indeed, Kentucky was virtually made for these two treasures: its ancient beds of limestone enrich the native bluegrass (making the bones of the horses that graze on it especially strong) and sweeten the waters of the pristine streams used to produce prized Kentucky bourbon.

1 Lexington

This gracious city is bedecked with such antebellum gems as Ashland, a Federal-style mansion built by statesman Henry Clay, and the Hunt-Morgan House, dating from the early 1800s. But the main delight here is the countryside, where the fastest thoroughbreds and standardbreds in America graze contentedly on meadows of bluegrass behind white wooden fences. For a firsthand look at the business of horses, stop at Keeneland Race Course, a traditional track complete with shade trees and grand-stand. Or spend an afternoon at Kentucky Horse Park, where displays on 1,200 sprawling acres celebrate the noble *equus*.

Head out of town on Rte. 68, a charming road edged with ancient stone walls, gabled horse barns (some as fancy as French châteaus), and seemingly endless fields of burley tobacco. The road crosses the Kentucky River Gorge, where the olive-green river flows between palisades of white limestone. Farther along, the route passes through lush, rolling farmland punctuated by stands of walnuts and oaks.

2 Shaker Village of Pleasant Hill

The plain yellow and white buildings of Shaker Village (also known as Shakertown) are set on verdant, oak-studded hills in the little town of Pleasant Hill. This was once home to some 500 Shakers, a 19th-century religious order and community known for its agricultural skills, ritualistic dancing, and dedication to a simple life apart from the bustle of the world. Though the Shakers are long gone (the last died in 1923), their spirit lives on at this former home—now a museum complete with crafts demonstrations, guides in Shaker dress, and such examples of their handiwork as flat brooms and wooden clothespins (original Shaker inventions). Visitors are welcome to spend the night in one of the old communal buildings, where the clean, bright rooms are sparsely decorated with handwoven rugs and simple wooden furniture.

3 Harrodsburg

Virgin forests and abundant game lured James Harrod to this area in 1774. Here, some 250 miles from the nearest town, he built the first permanent white settlement west of the Alleghenies. The original fort is gone, but a replica with two-story blockhouses and dirt floors conveys a vivid sense of frontier housing. In summer people in pioneer-style costumes (women wear gathered skirts and white pin-on aprons) demonstrate such frontier crafts as rug weaving, blacksmithing, and broom making. Next to the fort, the fieldstone markers of the original graveyard are scattered in a grove of trees.

To view another side of Harrodsburg, visit the venerable Beaumont Inn (originally built as a finishing school for girls). Here, amid flowered carpets, antique furniture, and curtains of Brussels lace, you can sample such local culinary delights as hickory-smoked country ham, spoon bread, and General Robert E. Lee orange-lemon cake.

4 Danville

In Danville, a short jaunt down Rte. 127, you'll find the state's first

college, first log post office, and first law school—hence the sobriquet City of Firsts. West of town Kentucky's bloodiest battle in the entire Civil War unfolded on a hot autumn day in 1862, when thirsty Confederate troops came across Union soldiers who were guarding a nearly dry creek. Cannonfire and screams filled the air as 40,000 men played out a gory battle that, when the smoke cleared, left some 7,500 dead and marked a fatal loss of initiative for the South. A trail winds across the battlefield (now a serene parkland), and a museum showcases rifles, cannons, musket balls, uniforms, canteens, and other Civil War memorabilia.

5 Springfield

The drive rolls west on Rte. 150, past fields of hay and corn and

farmhouse gardens overflowing with lilies, and jogs into the handsome village of Springfield. Southwest of Springfield, a scenic detour via Rtes. 152 and 49 passes through picturesque fields to the village of Loretto. Here a cluster of rustic red-shuttered buildings perched along the banks of a crystal-clear stream comprise the family-run Maker's Mark Distillery. For nearly two centuries it has made some of the finest, smoothest bourbon in the world. Inside the stillhouse, where the pungent smell of sour mash fills the air, you can dip your finger into the cypress vat and taste the bubbling brew, then watch as the copper still transforms the mix into bourbon. Local law forbids sampling the finished product, though other tippling opportunities abound at the many inns

that line the streets of Bardstown, the next stop on the drive, located in a nearby "wet" county.

6 Bardstown

Visiting Bardstown on a tour of the Western Frontier in 1797, the French king Louis Philippe found a city replete with elegant homes, posh inns, and reputable learning institutions—a description that still rings true. A less regal visitor—but no less esteemed—was young composer Stephen Foster, who came in 1852 to vacation with his relatives at Federal Hill, a gracious plantation house that inspired him to write the ballad *My Old Kentucky Home.* Today visitors are guided by women in hoop skirts who call attention to priceless heirlooms, rare old portraits—and the patriotism of Foster's uncle. The mansion's ceilings are 13 feet high, its brick walls are 13 inches thick, and each flight of stairs has 13 steps

Get a look behind the scenes at the exciting pounding hooves of racehorses at Keeneland Race Course, near Lexington.

—all in zealous tribute to the numerical count of America's original states.

Before heading south on Rte. 31E, explore the charming downtown district, where you'll find weathered brick houses on tree-shaded streets, the first cathedral built west of the Alleghenies (it was dedicated in 1819), and the Oscar Getz Museum of Whiskey History.

7 Hodgenville

Rte. 31E meanders through deep woods and past the boyhood home of Abraham Lincoln: a reconstructed log cabin beside rippling Knob Creek marks the site. A few miles farther the drive enters the town of Hodgenville, a virtual

Hodgensville celebrates the nearby 1809 birthplace of Abraham Lincoln.

theme park celebrating Lincoln. A bronze statue overlooks the town square; the Lincoln Museum is brimming with exhibits and memorabilia; and on Saturdays a "Lincoln Jamboree" is held. South of town, at the Abraham Lincoln Birthplace National Historic Site,

you can visit the templelike monument of granite and pink marble that enshrines the crumbling log cabin in which the great president is said to have been born in 1809.

8 Crystal Onyx Cave

Rambling south on Rte. 31E, the drive enters the region called the Pennyroyal—named for an herb but renowned as the locale of some of the world's most amazing caves. Beyond tourist-oriented Cave City, which is full of flashing neon signs, two stops in particular are worth your while: Crystal Onyx Cave, a labyrinth of rare onyx columns; and Horse Cave (also known as Hidden River Cave) in the city of Horse Cave. John Muir noted that in hot weather "the cold air that issues from its fern-clad lips" could cool everyone in town.

9 Mammoth Cave National Park

Follow signs to the East Entrance of Mammoth Cave National Park, where some 4,000 years ago woodland Indians discovered the fern-draped mouth of Mammoth Cave. Exploring its mazelike depths with flaming torches held high above their heads, they must have been astonished by the gigantic chambers whose ceilings sparkle with delicate white gypsum crystals. What must have amazed the Indians most of all was the cavern's sheer enormity: rooms as large as modern-day concert halls and wide corridors that go on underground for miles and miles.

Little did these Indians know that they were the first to explore one of the most extensive cave systems in the world. (Its charted passages meander more than 350 miles in darkness beneath the forest-covered hills, and countless others remain unexplored.) Sometime around the birth of Christ, for reasons that experts have yet to determine, the Indians abandoned Mammoth Cave, and it fell into

Kentucky Horse Park's tours are conducted by Clydesdale-drawn wagons.

obscurity until 1797. Then, according to legend, a lone hunter tracking a wounded bear he had shot stumbled across the cool, damp opening. After this serendipitous discovery, stories spread around the globe about the behemoth natural caverns, and soon its corridors were filled with exclamations of wonder called out by curious visitors. Weddings were held in the cave's enormous, high-ceilinged rooms, as were fancy balls.

Today a variety of tours are offered by the National Park Service, ranging from a quarter-mile stroll to a five-mile belly-crawling, body-squeezing trek (a warm coat is

recommended for the former, and kneepads are required for the latter). One tour includes a stop at the Snowball Room, where the lofty ceiling dazzles the eye with frostlike nodules of gypsum.

Among the cave's permanent residents are an assortment of creatures that have over the millennia adapted to the midnight environment of this netherworld. Colorless, eyeless fish haunt the cool waters of Echo River, as do similarly blind crayfish. Other native cave dwellers include spiders, beetles, and cave crickets. That any creature can survive in this sunless realm is astounding; so is the fact that the cave itself is constantly expanding in size as its dripping and flowing water dissolves the stone and carves the caverns ever deeper down into the bowels of the earth.

10 Duncan Hines Scenic Byway

Continuing through Mammoth Cave National Park, the drive hops across the Green River by ferry, entering an area of wild backcountry—a veritable Garden of Eden compared to the darkness and silence of the caves beneath the ground. Sunlight filters to the forest floor through a thick canopy of maples, beeches, sycamores, oaks, and hickories, and the forest is filled with chirping songbirds. Here the seasons are exquisitely portrayed, beginning in spring and summer with a colorful procession of blooming dogwoods, redbud trees, and wildflowers. In the fall blazing reds and golds ignite the foliage. But only in winter, when the ground is barren and brown and all the leaves are gone, can you see the craggy layers of limestone—along with all their sinkholes, streams, and fissures oozing with icy water—that tell of the deep bond between the land above and the dark world below.

Continuing north out of Mammoth Cave National Park, the drive follows the well-marked Duncan Hines Scenic Byway past lofty ridges, deep valleys, and outcroppings that look like ancient weathered castles. At the southern tip of Nolin River Lake, the byway veers north to Bee Spring, then west and south through such charmingly named villages as Sunfish, Sweeden, and Windyville. As you continue along

this series of country lanes edged with fieldstone fences, follow the scenic byway signs all the way into the town of Bowling Green.

11 Bowling Green

George and Robert Moore, two brothers, donated land to found this town on a bend in the Barren River in 1798. According to lore, it was named in honor of Bowling Green Square in New York City. Today Bowling Green is a blend of the old and the new, from the elegant 1872 Italianate home known as River View at Hobson Grove, to the recently founded National Corvette Museum, a high-tech tribute to the quintessentially American sports car, manufactured here in Bowling Green by General Motors. The museum features classic Corvettes spanning the years since 1953, when the first model rolled off the assembly line.

12 Jefferson Davis Monument

The drive follows Rte. 68 through the town of Russellville, whose collection of historic edifices includes the old Southern Bank Building, robbed by outlaw Jesse James in 1868. A few miles farther, a tall white obelisk—bearing a remarkable resemblance to the Washington Monument in the

nation's capital—towers 351 feet above the surrounding farmland. Located in the little town of Fairview, the structure signals local sympathy for Jefferson Davis, first and only president of the Confederate States of America, who was born here in 1808 and stayed loyal to the Southern cause all his life. An elevator to the top of the monument takes you to a sweeping vista of barns, silos, and farmhouses scattered across an appealing patchwork of fertile fields.

Farther along on Rte. 68, the road enters the old-time world of the Amish (watch for their horse-drawn carriages), where fields of golden corn sway gently in the breeze and roadside stands offer freshly harvested beans, peaches, tomatoes, and corn.

13 Hopkinsville

One of Kentucky's larger cities, with a population of some 30,000, Hopkinsville has long been a leading

market for tobacco. In recent years factories have thrived here as well, producing everything from truck frames, textiles, and flour to springs and bowling balls.

In its distant past Hopkinsville was a stop on the infamous Trail of Tears. Cherokee Indians who did not survive the grueling trek are memorialized at the Trail of Tears Commemorative Park.

For a diverting look at more of the town's past, stop by the Pennyroyal Area Museum on East Ninth Street. Its eclectic exhibits (including Edgar Cayce, known even after death as one of the world's greatest psychics; Indian lore; Civil War mementos; pioneer furnishings; and old farm tools) seem to be borrowings from the most intriguing attics in southwestern Kentucky.

The Trail of Tears Commemorative Park reminds Cherokees of a sad time in their history.

Midland Trail

In the rugged mountains of lower West Virginia, where wild rivers race between towering cliffs, the twists and turns along this drive offer irresistible temptations to slow down and savor the views.

Glade Creek Gristmill in Babcock State Park is a reconstruction that faithfully evokes the past.

Climbing beside the Kanawha River to wooded hills and ridgetops, the narrow ribbon of Rte. 60—the Midland Trail—unfurls across the heart of West Virginia. Here in a region where Civil War battles were fought and generations of miners dug for coal, the bittersweet sound of the folk ballads of another era still lingers in the air. But today it is nature's music that dominates, breaking the silence with songs as graceful as the hills and as entrancing as a rushing river.

1 Charleston

Though the Midland Trail's official route was expanded a few years ago and now starts in Huntington, we will begin the drive in Charleston. (Purists may want to visit Huntington to see the B & O Railway Station, Old Central City, Huntington Museum of Art, and the old-time amusements of Camden Park.)

The old James River–Kanawha Turnpike, built to link Richmond, Virginia, with Charleston, West Virginia, followed the course of an old bison path that later became an Indian trail across the Alleghenies. Today the two-lane road (Rte. 60) is known as the Midland Trail.

Start at Charleston's most impressive landmark: the mammoth marble state capitol building, completed in 1932. Facing the Kanawha River—long the economic lifeline of the city—the capitol boasts a golden dome that serves as a beacon for miles around. The red brick governor's mansion and the contemporary Cultural Center are among the adjoining features of the lively Capitol Complex.

As you depart the Mountain State's largest city, traveling east on Rte. 60, you might want to pause at Daniel Boone Park. The riverfront oasis commemorates the renowned woodsman, who lived for a time in the area. A log house and the 1834 Craik-Patton House, both furnished with period antiques, are open for tours.

2 Kanawha Falls

For the first several miles, Rte. 60 passes through a drab industrial corridor. The factories, important in the state's growth and history, were built to refine the minerals and fuels that were discovered in this part of the Kanawha Valley. By the early 1800s the town of Malden, for example, was a major producer of salt, a commodity that at the time was literally worth its weight in gold.

Farther along, the factories disappear, the air clears, and the drive begins its ascent into the Alleghenies. The road winds atop ridges cloaked with beeches, oaks, and hickories, while stands of pines add year-round dabs of dark green. In places you'll drop into fertile valleys where the sap of the sugar maples, known locally as sweetwater, is tapped in springtime and boiled down into syrup. Just before Gauley Bridge, pretty Kana-

Forest views at Hawks Nest State Park.

wha Falls pours down a natural staircase of succeeding and massive sandstone ledges. Farther upstream, the Gauley and New rivers unite to form the Kanawha.

3 Hawks Nest State Park

The terrain turns intensely rugged as the drive, looping around a succession of hairpin turns, climbs to Hawks Nest State Park. Perched on a clifftop 585 feet above the sinuous curves of the New River, the area offers bird's-eye views that extend for miles. A park gondola carries passengers down into the depths of the gorge. Wildflowers

stud the slopes in spring; come fall, the region is a golden blaze of fluttering foliage. At the water's edge, visitors can boat and picnic.

4 New River Gorge National River

Pioneers called it the New River, but geologists say that this waterway, which has barreled down the same course for about 65 million years, is one of America's oldest. As rafters who sweep down the New's white-water are the first to attest, its venerable age hasn't diminished the river's free-flowing vigor. In fact, its roiling rapids are judged the most difficult east of the Rockies.

Although Rte. 60 has several overlooks along the northern end of the New River Gorge, an even better place to glimpse the chasm is at the Canyon Rim visitor center on Rte. 19. Awesome cliffs—some nearly 1,000 feet high—vault into view, and far below, the New River sparkles in the sun as it races northward. New River Gorge Bridge, just west of the visitor center, soars 876 feet above the water, making it the second-

highest single-arch span in the country. Throwing caution to the winds, parachuting daredevils come once a year to leap from the bridge's vertigo-producing heights, from whence they gently float downward to land on sandbars in the river.

Now a semiwilderness of tree-covered ridges and sandstone outcrops, the river corridor was until fairly recently one of the busiest coal-mining centers in the country. To this day miners and other long-time locals gather at the visitor center to recount their experiences in conversations that help to keep alive West Virginia's time-honored tradition of storytelling.

5 Babcock State Park

Most of the old mines were abandoned by the 1930s, and nature ever since has been reclaiming the ground under towns on which they stood. This regrowth is apparent at Babcock State Park. The 4,127-acre tract, lying to the south along Rte. 41, earns special renown for its two different kinds of wild rhododendrons—one bedecked with purple flowers, the other with white blooms—that enliven the hillsides from May until July. Birds carol in the canopy of hardwoods, and trout fight the currents of Glade Creek. Also of note are a reconstructed gristmill that stands at the stream's edge, and some 20 miles of trails tempting hikers to explore the parklands.

6 Big Sewell Mountain

Zigzagging across the Allegheny Plateau, the Midland Trail crests as it rolls across the summit of Big Sewell Mountain. The peak, which climbs to 3,170 feet, served as a camp for Robert E. Lee and his Confederate troops during an 1861 Civil War campaign.

Many other parts of this rumpled region—a strategic link between North and South—were fought for and occupied during the war. As the drive rolls onward through rural hamlets, you'll come to Lewisburg, once a Confederate outpost, where some buildings still bear the scars of battle. Yet Lewisburg's past goes back even further. One stone church, complete with the original pews, was erected by settlers in 1796. Several historic houses, inns, a library, and a courthouse also were built in the decades before the Civil War.

7 White Sulphur Springs

A steady supply of spring water, tinged with smelly sulphur and other minerals, has been drawing health seekers—presidents and politicians among them—to this fashionable retreat since the 18th century. At the town's edge, tucked amid forested hills and lush green pastures, stands the venerable Greenbrier Resort, looking like the White House—only bigger—and evoking the elegance of the Old South that typifies this glorious region.

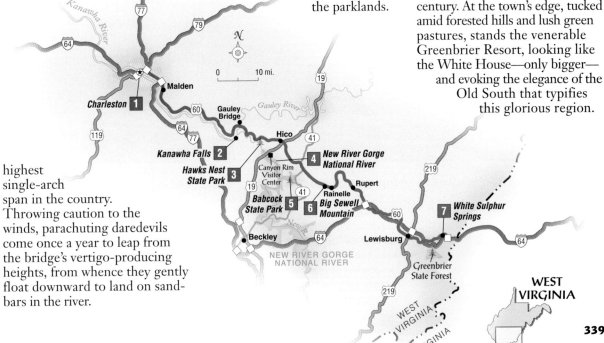

Potomac Highlands

If West Virginia is, as its residents rhapsodize, "almost heaven,"
then the hills and hollows of the Potomac Highlands are surely on the outskirts of Eden.

Blackwater Falls are the namesake for a state park west of Davis, with clear, tannin-stained waters the color of root beer.

"Here's to West Virginia," a local toast proclaims, "the most northern of the southern states, the most southern of the northern states, the most western of the eastern states, and the most eastern of the western states." Yet for all the diversity and centrality of the state itself, the region known as the Potomac Highlands (named for the river whose headwaters rise here) is remarkably remote. Isolated by rugged mountainous terrain, this eastern side of West Virginia, which is not only high in elevation but remarkably wild amidst large population centers and farmland, rewards visitors with mile after mile of pastoral beauty. Its towns are few and far between, and its roadways—as twisted as tangled twine—are tailor-made for wandering.

1 Monongahela National Forest

Soon after crossing the Maryland–West Virginia border, Rte. 219 ventures southwest into the Monongahela National Forest. So vast is this forest—it spreads over more than 900,000 acres—that for all but a few miles, this drive stays within or near its borders. Reclaimed from once overharvested timberland, the forest boasts three swimming beaches, 19 campgrounds, more than 700 miles of hiking trails, and over 600 miles of trout-inhabited and angler-inviting coldwater streams.

West Virginia has been dubbed the Mountain State, and perhaps nowhere does that nickname seem more apt than in Monongahela National Forest, where over 100 peaks soar to 4,000 feet or more. Together they make up the Allegheny Front of the Appalachian Mountains, which forms a natural barrier to passing weather systems. The mountains divide the forest into two distinct climates: on the

When Ramps Grow Rampant

In early March some West Virginians head for the hills, driven not by spring fever but by a craving for ramps, or wild leeks. These local delicacies, which thrive in the cool climate of high elevations, look like lilies of the valley but taste like nothing else on earth. More pungent than garlic or onions, ramps have such an overpowering aroma that the only way to tolerate ramp eaters is to join them. Visitors can do just that at any of a number of ramp festivals held in the Highlands in April, including those at Elkins and Richwood.

wetter, western side of the front, northern hardwoods such as cherry and maple mingle with oak and tulip trees, while to the east look for oak, cedar, and even cactus. No fewer than five major river systems originate within the forest, giving rise to hundreds of miles of waterways. East of the divide you'll find the Potomac and James rivers, while the Ohio River and its tributaries wind to the west.

2 Blackwater Falls State Park

Where rivers and mountains meet, waterfalls are certain to result, and the Potomac Highlands are blessed with cascades aplenty. One of the most picturesque spots in the state is Blackwater Falls, the crown jewel of 1,688-acre Blackwater Falls State Park, located just west of Davis off Rte. 32.

Looking at the glassy Blackwater River as it lazes through a deep, half-mile-wide crevice, you would never know that it's about to make a six-story plunge to the riotous

gorge below. The river's name has more to do with science than with poetry: darkened by tannic acid from the fallen needles of red spruces and hemlocks, the water glows with a distinct amber tint as it pours over the falls, echoing the autumnal display of the surrounding hills. A staircase leads visitors to the base of the falls. The park also features a network of trails and overlooks offering glorious vistas of the upper and lower gorges and the hills beyond. A second cataract, Pendleton Falls, connects the river with Pendleton Lake, a popular spot for fishing, boating, and swimming.

3 Canaan Valley Resort State Park

When George Casey Harness first beheld this beautiful valley, he declared, "Behold! I have found the land of Canaan"—and the name stuck. Tucked inside a deep bowl ringed by several of the Alleghenies' highest peaks, the park boasts some 6,000 acres of the most diverse and unspoiled terrain in the highlands, including lush meadows, misty evergreen forests, and America's second-largest inland wetland, an area called the Canaan Valley Wetlands.

Like its namesake, Canaan Valley teems with critters of every kind—coyotes, wild turkeys, beavers, black bears, foxes, and deer so tame and plentiful that they practically pose for admiring photographers. At an elevation of over 3,000 feet, the valley enjoys cool summer temperatures, and an average annual snowfall exceeding 150 inches makes it a mecca for skiing enthusiasts. In any season the summit of Weiss Knob (accessible by chairlift) offers a sensational panorama of the highlands.

4 Dolly Sods Scenic Area

Ranging in elevation from 2,600 to over 4,000 feet, the tundralike

Autumnal colors glow when frosts settle on the maples and birches of Blackwater.

terrain of Dolly Sods has a barren beauty that is more like northern Canada than the mid-Atlantic. After much of the plateau's hemlock and red spruce forests were cleared in the 1880s, fires and erosion stripped away the topsoil, right down to the bedrock in some places. Despite the devastation, Dolly Sods abounds with vegetation—upland wildflower meadows, blueberry and huckleberry thickets, cranberry bogs, and patches of dwarf red spruce. These areas support numerous foxes and beavers, and in summer a symphony of songbirds.

Dolly Sods is also one of the great hawk-watching spots in the Appalachians, because winds bouncing up and over the Allegheny Front create a natural airborne highway for migrating

raptors and other birds. For the best viewing during the spring and fall migration seasons, follow Rte. 75 all the way to its terminus at Bear Rocks.

5 Elkins

Backtracking from Dolly Sods to Rte. 32, continue south to Harman, then head west on Rte. 33 to the Bear Heaven Recreation Area, named for its black bear population. From there the highway leads into Stuart Memorial Drive, a winding mountain road that passes some of the region's most spectacular alpine scenery, including 4,020-foot-tall Bickle Knob, just to the north. For a closer look at this rocky giant, take the turnoff for the Stuart Recreation Area to the Bickle Knob Picnic Area, where a lookout tower four stories

Star Route

★ Highland Scenic Highway

Cutting across Monongahela National Forest, this 43-mile route—much of which follows Rte. 150, the highest major road in the state—provides dramatic views of the Allegheny Highlands. The side trip, accessible from April through November (weather permitting), begins just north of Marlinton and travels through hardwood forests to Richwood. Along the way, you'll find waterfalls, 150 miles of trails, and the 36,000-acre Cranberry Wilderness Area.

high affords unforgettable 360-degree views. From its observation deck, you can see the front range of the Cheat Mountains, the rim of nearby Otter Creek Wilderness, the summit of Spruce Knob—at 4,861 feet, the highest point in West Virginia—and the town of Elkins, which sits astride the Tygart Valley River.

In addition to being the headquarters for the Monongahela National Forest (the town serves as a base camp for many recreational activities), Elkins is home to Davis and Elkins College. Its campus features two of the most meticulously restored Victorian structures in the state, the Halliehurst Mansion and Graceland Inn. Formerly the home of Stephen Elkins, cofounder of the college and onetime Secretary of War, the baronial mansion (named in honor of his wife, Hallie) is replete with turrets, Tiffany stained-glass windows, and elaborate interior trim fashioned from native hardwoods. The campus also houses the Augusta Heritage Center, which hosts a variety of workshops and events celebrating traditional

music, crafts, and customs of the highlands. Continue south on Rte. 219 to Huttonsville, then follow Rtes. 92 and 250 to the Gaudineer Scenic Area.

6 Gaudineer Scenic Area

Nearly half a million acres of West Virginia mountains were once blanketed by hemlocks. In only a few decades, timber barons devastated these rich woods, but on the slopes below Gaudineer Knob, 140 acres of virgin forest escaped the axe by a fluke of fate: they were simply overlooked by a surveyor.

Stretching 100 feet skyward, this stand of trees is estimated to be three centuries old and forms a cluttered canopy of limbs above the silent mosses of the forest floor. Skirting the region's western border, the Shavers Fork River is one of the most abundantly stocked trout streams in the region.

7 Snowshoe Mountain

Scraping the heavens at 4,863 feet, Snowshoe Mountain, just north of Rte. 66, is one of West Virginia's most popular four-season resorts. It's a haven in winter for skiers, of course, but when spring turns its white slopes green with grass, mountain biking becomes the sport of choice. Those who prefer a more leisurely form of sightseeing can hike along the resort's 100 miles of trails and old logging roads, which crisscross an enchanted countryside of hardwood forest, burbling mountain streams, and meadows spangled with wildflowers.

8 Cass Scenic Railroad State Park

By 1911 West Virginia had over 3,000 miles of logging rail lines, more than any other state in the Union. Powered by mighty locomotives, the trains hauled tons of timber up and down the steepest mountain grades, and in places the lines seem to defy not just

gravity, but common sense as well. The logging lines are long since gone—abandoned, forgotten, and buried beneath the detritus of the forest floor—but at the town of Cass (located several miles farther east on Rte. 66), 11 miles of track remain to give visitors a taste of the past.

Puffing black smoke and

chugging along at a hard-won speed of five miles per hour, some of the last remaining Shay and Heisler engines tote not wood but sightseers up two steep switchbacks to the windswept summit of

Cass Scenic Railroad huffs and puffs with steam.

Bald Knob (the second-highest point in the state), where the views extend well into neighboring Virginia. Allow 4½ hours for the round-trip train ride and enough time to tour the town itself, which has been converted into a living museum of West Virginia logging life.

9 Greenbrier River Trail

Returning to Rte. 219, the drive jogs west to the town of Slatyfork, where Sharp's Country Store provides a perfect opportunity to stretch your legs as you rummage through its wares. Run by the same family for three generations, Sharp's is the quintessential small-town general store. Crammed to the rafters with everything from laundry soap to antique gramophones, it is as much a repository

The loop road in Canaan Valley Resort State Park passes under a leafy bower.

of local culture as it is a place of commerce.

Continue south on Rte. 219 for about 15 miles to Marlinton. There you can stop at the old train station (now occupied by an information center), which is located on the Greenbrier River Trail. Running alongside the Greenbrier River from Caldwell to Cass, the 75-mile trail follows an old rail bed of the Chesapeake and Ohio Railroad through some of the highland's most picturesque countryside. The scenery is at its best in spring, when violets, trilliums, lilies, and a host of other wildflowers are in full bloom and returning songbirds fill the air with their melodies. Best of all, because the grade is virtually flat, anyone can hike, bike, or ski a favorite stretch.

10 Watoga State Park

Both the oldest and largest of West Virginia's state parks, 10,100-acre Watoga takes its name from the Cherokee word *watauga*, meaning "river of islands"—a reference to the wide, sandy Greenbrier River, which forms the park's western border. For a delightful view of the river and the park's rugged jumble of ridges, hollows, and thick second-growth forest, try Arrowhead Trail, a steep but rewarding one-mile trek climbing from the Riverside Campground area to the old log lookout tower. Or drive the park road up to the T. M. Cheek Memorial, one of the highest spots in the park, for a sunset picnic.

Tiny Hillsboro, a mile farther south on Rte. 219, might seem like an ordinary West Virginia mountain town, but literary pilgrims know it as something far more significant—the birthplace of Pearl S. Buck, author of *The Good Earth* and the first American woman to win both the Nobel and

Pulitzer prizes. Buck spent most of her childhood in China with her missionary parents but fondly remembered her grandparents' spacious West Virginia farmhouse as her "gateway to America." You will find it open from May through October; the house represents an intriguing mix of Oriental and Occidental, with furnishings that range from handcrafted walnut pieces crafted by Buck's own grandfather to a small collection of Oriental memorabilia.

11 Droop Mountain Battlefield State Park

In no state did the Civil War create such sharp divisions of loyalty as it did in West Virginia. While 30,000 men from the hills took up arms for the Union cause, some 7,500 others traveled south to don Confederate gray. So when the Battle of Droop Mountain took place on November 6, 1863, the fighting—quite literally—pitted brother against brother.

The clash would also signal an end to the conflict on West Virginia soil; Union forces outflanked Confederate troops on the peak and sent them heading south for good. Some 7,000 men fought that day, and a few of the 400 who lost their lives are buried here. Three and a half miles of trails lead from the Battlefield Museum and cemetery through the 287-acre grounds to majestic ridgetop views of the Greenbrier Valley to the north.

12 Beartown State Park

A few miles southwest of Hillsboro, a spur road leads to Beartown State Park, a 107-acre preserve on the eastern slope of Droop Mountain. Erosion has gnawed away at the ancient sandstone that forms the mountain's crest, leaving behind massive boulders, deep crevices, towering cliffs, and sandstone corridors—a giant three-dimensional maze so thick with vegetation that you'll feel as if you've stumbled upon a natural greenhouse. In the

cool, damp recesses, pockets of ice sometimes linger until late summer.

13 Lewisburg

Following in the footsteps of retreating Confederate forces, the drive descends the back of Droop Mountain, making a long glide down to Lewisburg, 1,000 feet lower in elevation and some 24 miles to the south. A 236-acre parcel of the town has been designated a National Historic District; it's easily explored on foot with the aid of a map from the visitor center at Carnegie Hall, which also serves as the town's cultural hub. Other stops on the tour include the Old Stone Church (the oldest continuously operated church west of the Alleghenies), the Museum of the Greenbrier Historical Society, the Greenbrier County Courthouse, and the Confederate Cemetery. A wander among historic tombstones will lead you to the common grave of 95 unidentified soldiers, casualties of the Battle of Lewisburg.

Skyline Drive

Weaving through Shenandoah National Park,
the Skyline Drive confirms its reputation, mile after glorious mile,
as one of the loveliest roads in America.

:::::: Trip Tips ::::::

Length: 105 miles.

When to go: Popular year-round, but best from mid-April through October.

Lodging: Available at Skyland and Big Meadows lodges and Lewis Mountain cabins.

Nearby attractions: Skyline Caverns, in Front Royal. Luray Caverns, in Luray. Monticello, President Thomas Jefferson's home, Charlottesville.

Words to the wise: Since the drive is two lanes wide and the speed limit is 35 m.p.h., traffic may be slow in peak seasons. On trails, wear hiking shoes and avoid unprotected ledges. The drive may be closed after snow or ice storms.

Visitor centers: Dickey Ridge, Big Meadows.

Further information: Shenandoah National Park, 3655 U.S. Hwy. 211 East, Luray, VA 222835; tel. 540-999-3500, www.nps.gov /shen.

Skyland Lodge in Shenandoah National Park captures sunset views of autumn's colors in the nearby forest.

High in the misty mountains of Virginia is a highway to heaven, a gracefully winding road that reigns over a picturesque patchwork of lush valleys, rounded peaks, and gently rolling pastures. Best of all, this wonderful wilderness lies within a two-hour drive of Washington, D.C., and is a one-day trip from New York.

1 Shenandoah Valley Overlook
Winding 105 miles along the crests of the Blue Ridge Mountains, the Skyline Drive is truly a feast for the eyes: more than 75 overlooks and 500 miles of nearby trails treat visitors to some of the most splendid and serene scenery found anywhere. Shenandoah Valley Overlook, one of the first points of interest along the two-lane highway as you travel south from Front Royal, provides a sweeping view of the valley, the Shenandoah River, and 40-mile-long Massanutten Mountain, which rises between the river's two forks. History buffs will be intrigued to learn that Signal Knob, a peak at the right-hand side of the mountain, was used at various times during the protracted Civil War as a communications base by both the blue-coat Union and gray-uniformed Confederate troops.

2 Range View Overlook
Perched 2,800 feet above sea level, this overlook has perhaps the best vistas in the northern part of the drive. To the south, running as far as the eye can see, are the Blue Ridge Mountains, named for the haze (a combination of tree vapors and, nowadays, smog) that constantly hovers over their slopes.

344

3 Hogback Overlook

To get a full view from this overlook (the longest one in the park), you will have to stop near the middle or once at each end. Either way, the scenery is sensational. On a clear day, as many as six or more bends of the serpentine Shenandoah River can be seen.

4 Marys Rock Tunnel

At mile 32.2 you reach Marys Rock Tunnel, a 600-foot-long corridor carved through a granite ridge. No one knows for sure how Marys Rock got its name, but legend has it that when Francis Thornton, a local landowner, brought his new young bride to this summit to show her the vastness of his property, he christened it Marys Rock. At Meadow Spring parking area, a two-mile trail of moderate difficulty leads to the summit, which is one of the few places in the park that affords a 360-degree panorama.

5 Pinnacles Overlook

The drive overlooks Virginia's rolling piedmont country as it snakes along the crest of the Blue Ridge Mountains on its way to Pinnacles Overlook. The view of Old Rag Mountain, to the south, is a bold reminder that nature favors constant change. When it was formed a billion years ago, this mass of granite was bare. Later it was covered with lava and ocean sediment, which have since worn away to reveal, once again, the stone's original surface.

In a similar way, the Shenandoah region has made a comeback of its own. Not so long ago the land was largely deforested by farmers, loggers, and hunters. In the early part of this century, more and more mountaineers left to seek

Rustic barns, horses, and croplands extend for miles outside Shenandoah National Park and the Shenandoah Valley.

their fortunes elsewhere, and in the 1920s a movement began to set aside land for a national park with a ridgetop road. Shenandoah National Park was authorized by Congress in 1926. In 1931 President Herbert Hoover, hoping to spur economic growth in the depressed area, approved the construction of the Skyline Drive; it was completed in 1939, four years after the park was established. Today an astonishing 95 percent of the area is completely reforested.

Countless roadside bouquets of mountain laurel greet visitors along the Skyline Drive during the springtime.

6 Stony Man Overlook

As you enter the overlook here from the north, 4,011-foot-tall Stony Man Mountain will loom straight ahead. Look closely at its rugged profile—and use a little imagination—and you can make out the old fellow's eye, nose, mustache, and beard. For an even better view of the summit, take a short hike up the Little Stony Man Trail, which leads past cliffs com-

posed of greenstone, a gray-green rock formed during ancient volcanic eruptions. At night the lights of Luray and other nearby towns twinkle below in the distance.

7 Skyland

In 1894 George Freeman Pollock, a pioneer conservationist who was later instrumental in establishing Shenandoah National Park, also founded a rustic resort in the Blue Ridge Mountains that he loved so deeply. He called it Skyland—a reminder of its lofty location near the highest point on the Skyline Drive. Today this popular lodge provides peerless views of the valley below and the mountains beyond. In addition to varied accommodations (ranging from quaint cabins to modern suites), Skyland offers horseback riding, pony rides for children, and the Stony Man Nature Trail, a 1.6-mile round-trip that ascends the slopes of Stony

Man Mountain. Leading visitors on a self-guided hike, the scenic trail passes a wide assortment of the 100 or so types of trees found in Shenandoah National Park.

Step back in time by visiting Massanutten Lodge, the recently renovated former residence of Addie Pollock, wife of George Freeman Pollock.

8 Whiteoak Canyon

Near the south entrance to Skyland resort is a 4.6-mile round-trip trail that leads to the first fall in Whiteoak Canyon, a shady mountain glen that has been called "the scenic gem" of Shenandoah National Park. A meandering stream, towering oaks and hemlocks, giant boulders, and a steep gorge with six waterfalls (the tallest of which drops 86 feet) make this a place of wild, idyllic beauty.

A nearby trail leads through part of Limberlost, a grove of stately hemlocks that are centuries old. The trees, according to one tale, owe their lives to Skyland founder George Pollock, who paid loggers $10 apiece to leave them standing. With its damp coolness, eerie stillness, and shimmering shafts of sunlight that filter through the delicate foliage, Limberlost evokes the mood of a great Gothic cathedral. The Limberlost Trail leads past an old apple orchard to the Crescent Rock Trail, which climbs 325 feet to Crescent Rock Overlook.

9 Crescent Rock Overlook

An easier way to reach Crescent Rock Overlook is to take Skyline Drive to mile 44.4. As the drive continues south, Hawksbill Mountain, the highest point in the park, looms to the west. At mile 46.7 (the Upper Hawksbill parking area), a one-mile trail leads to the 4,051-foot-tall summit. The reward that awaits visitors there is threefold: a panoramic view of the Blue Ridge Mountains, which

fade into rolling farmland to the west and green hills to the east; a glimpse of a high-elevation forest dominated by balsam firs and rare red spruces; and the best vantage point in the park for spotting broad-winged hawks and other birds of prey during their annual fall migration.

10 Dark Hollow Falls

Continuing south on Skyline Drive, the road winds through a hardwood forest before reaching the Dark Hollow Falls parking area at mile 50.7. There a short but steep trail leads to the head of the falls—a series of gurgling cascades that drop 70 feet through a wooded ravine. Among the falls' admirers was Thomas Jefferson, who was so fond of this region that when he built his home, Monticello (located a bit to the east of the park near Charlottesville), he was careful not to let any of its outbuildings block his view of the mountains.

11 Big Meadows

Wide-open spaces are rare in this densely forested region, so this 150-acre clearing—a grassy tableland of meadows, pastures, and gardens—offers a surprising change of scenery. Situated high on the ridges of the Blue Ridge Mountains, Big Meadows has been level for several centuries. Indians and, later, settlers are believed to have burned the area regularly (perhaps after it was already cleared by a lightning-ignited fire) to make it a better hunting ground and pastureland. The National Park Service has adopted a similar strategy—a combination of mowing and controlled burning—to preserve the historic site and provide wildlife habitat.

While tall trees are conspicuously absent from the landscape, several hundred types of wildflowers thrive in the area's swampy wetlands and surrounding fields—in fact, Big Meadows has the greatest concentration of wildflowers in Shenandoah National Park. Guided tours of this botanical bounty are usually offered on the second weekend in May, when the park hosts its annual Wildflower Weekend. Violets, trilliums, geraniums, azaleas, pink-and-yellow lady's slippers, and jack-in-the-pulpits are just of few of the springtime blooms to be savored.

Although the big meadow has no designated trails, visitors are free to explore. As you wander about, you may spot white-tailed deer (about 6,000 live in the park), groundhogs, gray foxes, and numerous other critters. On spring evenings male woodcocks perform flamboyant feats of aerobatics during their courtship flights.

12 South River Overlook

On the way to South River Falls, the big blue sky suddenly seems much smaller as it plays hide-and-seek through a canopy of oaks and hickories. Each season, this area—like the rest of the park—stages a brand-new extravaganza. In springtime the air is sweetened by the scent of azaleas and other flowers and by the melodies of woodland birds, including warblers, wrens, thrushes, and seven kinds of woodpeckers. By summer, nature's canvas is no longer speckled with soft pastels but covered by a great green blanket. Come autumn, the canvas is ablaze with dazzling hues of orange, yellow, and red. When winter finally arrives, Shenandoah becomes a virtual still life, its rhythms as slow as the icy waterfalls that whisper from afar.

13 Swift Run Overlook

From this overlook you can gaze back over Swift Run Gap, one of many spots where Skyline Drive

intersects the Appalachian Trail. Stretching some 2,000 miles from Maine to Georgia, the trail is the longest continuous footpath in North America. It roughly parallels the drive, following the mountain crest for 94 miles through the park. Numerous spurs branch off the main path, some leading up to high peaks, others winding down into deep ravines.

14 Big Run Overlook

The secret to Skyline Drive's appeal is its contrasting perspectives —short-range views of forests juxtaposed with long-range vistas of the distant mountains and valleys. At this overlook, for example, nearby trees frame panoramas of far-off peaks, creating scenes that are postcard perfect. For the more adventurous, a steep trail descends into Big Run Valley, where a fish-filled stream leads to a small waterfall and several pools large enough for a dip.

15 Blackrock

This summit, and the talus slopes below it, may seem black from a distance, but they are actually dark brown—the color of the coarse lichen that covers them. Since no trail leads to the top of Blackrock, visitors must clamber up a slope littered with fallen rocks. The view atop the summit is well worth the effort: a sweeping survey of forested mountains and the valley beyond.

16 Crimora Lake Overlook

Near mile 92.6 is Crimora Lake, one of the few lakes visible from the drive. Crimora is more notable for what stands beside it than for the lake itself: to its left is an abandoned manganese mine—once the largest source of this rare mineral in America. The overlook also provides a scenic vista that includes several different mountains.

17 Sawmill Run Overlook

From the middle of this overlook, visitors can see several mountains stretching toward the horizon—a farewell glimpse of Shenandoah's unforgettable beauty. The Skyline Drive comes to an end at Rockfish Gap, but still the magnificent scenery goes on. Picking up where the drive leaves off, the Blue Ridge Parkway continues southwest for another 469 miles all the way through the George Washington National Forest to Great Smoky Mountains National Park. It's a drive well worth taking on your own.

Blue Ridge Parkway

Soaring to the crests of the ancient Appalachians, America's longest scenic drive
entices travelers with views of misty mountains and verdant valleys
that have scarcely changed since the days of Daniel Boone.

By mid-June Catawba rhododendrons explode with color on the slopes of Craggy Dome at Craggy Gardens.

Born as a "make-work" road-building project in the hard times of the Great Depression, the Blue Ridge Parkway endures today as one of America's most famous and beloved highways. Winding through Virginia and North Carolina, across some of the East's highest peaks, the route is bookended by two national parks—Shenandoah to the north and Great Smoky Mountains to the south. In every season of the year, each of the parkway's 469 miles abounds with scenic and cultural delights.

◼ Humpback Rocks

In contrast to the bustle of I-64 at Rockfish Gap, where the drive begins, the Blue Ridge Parkway is nothing less than soothing. As welcoming as a rolled-out carpet, the drive ushers motorists into a lush, high-country forest of oaks and maples—a passageway to a different world. As you enter, you may well be greeted by a white-tailed deer or two pausing along the roadside before skittishly disappearing into the woods.

Just six miles from the parkway's start lies Humpback Rocks, named for the humped shape of the nearby outcrops. Here a reconstructed farm museum depicts life as it was in the 1700s, when white settlers first came to these remote mountains. A number of pioneer structures have been imported to the farm from other places as examples of the local architecture. One cabin's skillfully constructed stone fireplace and hand-split log floors testify to the varied skills needed by settlers, and a bear-proof pigpen is a reminder that wild animals once were serious competitors to survival on the American frontier.

Humpback Rocks is the first of a long and rewarding series of recreational areas operated by the National Park Service along the parkway. The public is also served by an inviting array of fine campgrounds, picnicking sites, visitor centers that debunk misconceptions about the culture of the region, and interpretive displays.

◼ Whetstone Ridge

After climbing toward Bald Mountain to the west, the route traverses aptly named Whetstone Ridge; long ago hunters and homesteaders came here to quarry fine-grained sandstone they used to sharpen their knives and axes.

At least a few of those freshly honed axes may have been used to cut firewood for a business of a different sort: two miles farther along is a spring where moonshiners once brewed homemade corn whiskey, known to those whose pounding heads attested to overindulgence as white lightnin'.

Atop Grandfather Mountain, south of Moses H. Cone Memorial Park.

3 Buena Vista Overlook

The northern section of the Blue Ridge Parkway follows a narrow crest with views both east, to the Virginia Piedmont, and west, over the Shenandoah Valley toward the Allegheny Mountains. The Buena Vista Overlook (one of 275 along the drive) is well worth a pause to see its grand panorama of endless wooded ridges and hills—bringing to mind a waving green sea.

Take a moment here, too, to contemplate the geological processes that created these scenic marvels. Among the earth's oldest mountains, the Appalachians once were as tall and sharply peaked as the far younger Alps and Rockies. Since their uplift hundreds of millions of years ago, erosion—that most patient and persistent of sculptors —has smoothed their shapes into the gently rounded contours you see today. The resulting profile may be less spectacular than those elsewhere, but like a venerable family patriarch, the ancient Appalachian Range is dignified by its worn and weathered countenance.

4 James River

In a looping descent, the parkway reaches its lowest elevation (649 feet) near the James River, a placid ribbon of blue flowing through a densely wooded gorge. In the mid-1800s a canal was dug along 200 miles of the James, the beginning of a proposed waterway intended to link the Ohio River with the Atlantic Ocean. (The original plan, some historians say, was conceived by none other than George Washington.) Modern travelers can see a restored portion of the project via a footbridge from the James River Visitor Center. Mules and draft horses laboriously pulled barges along the canal, pausing now and then while a lock raised or lowered the vessel (at this lock, for instance, the vertical distance is 13 feet). It's no wonder that the freight-hauling efficiency of railroads eventually doomed the ambitious scheme to extend the canal.

5 Peaks of Otter

Climbing again, the road reaches an elevation of 3,950 feet at Apple Orchard Mountain, its highest point in Virginia. The "orchard" that gave the mountain its name is really a forest of low, gnarled oaks, stunted by bitter winter winds on these exposed heights (the dwarfed woodland reminded early settlers of an old, neglected apple orchard).

Ten miles south, the drive reaches the valley between Sharp Top and Flat Top—the twin Peaks of Otter that mark the headwaters of the Otter River. Since the days of the Indians, the valley has been a favored stopping place for travelers. They are drawn not just by the refreshing water of a nearby spring, but by the beauty and serenity of the entire scene. Wagonmasters camped here in Revolutionary War times, and an inn was established on the site as early as 1830. Today the Peaks of Otter Lodge is a favorite among parkway regulars for its hospitality and cuisine—and for the vista across Abbott Lake to Sharp Top, so named because its summit tapers to a rocky point.

Along the Elk Run Trail, a short loop behind the Peaks of Otter visitor center, the loudest sounds are likely to be the excited squeaks of chipmunks or the cackling "laugh" of a pileated woodpecker clinging to a tall tree. Nearby Fallingwater Cascades Trail is more strenuous, but its exquisite

waterfall is an enticement to hikers. Along the trail in spring, legions of purplish-pink rhododendron blooms create a striking contrast with the dark foliage of the stately, towering hemlocks.

6 Roanoke Mountain

Theoretically, given the time and the stamina, you could hike more than 2,000 miles on the famed Appalachian Trail. Winding along mountain crests from Maine to Georgia, it is the world's longest, continuous, marked hiking path. In some northern sections of the Blue Ridge Parkway, the trail nears the road frequently, making it easy for anyone to sample the solitary pleasures of the ancient path for a short-distance trek. One such opportunity is at Bearwallow Gap, near milepost 90; for the next 10 miles, the trail never strays far from the parkway, providing stretches where hikers can be alone with the chirps of birds and the soothing sound of the wind in the treetops. Near milepost 115, you'll find

The Linn Cove Viaduct winds past the slopes of Grandfather Mountain.

Sunsets are often colored deep purple in the Blue Ridge Mountains.

Virginia's Explore Park with interpretive exhibits and demonstrations, as well as access for biking along the Roanoke River.

Farther along, at milepost 120, the drive takes a short side trip to the summit of Roanoke Mountain. From the overlook the city of Roanoke, nestled amid forested hills, looks like a toy town taken from a model railroader's layout.

7 Smart View

Among the parkway's delights are the old-fashioned names a traveler encounters along the way. Devils Backbone, Air Bellows Gap, Headforemost Mountain, Rough Butt Bald, and Bee Tree Gap may sound quaintly funny to the modern ear. But they were perfectly apt and descriptive to the mountain folk who applied them generations ago. One example is the picnic ground near milepost 154, which offers a panorama that settlers dubbed "a right smart view"—understatement, indeed, for a dazzling vista that takes in miles of hills and

valleys undulating to the hazy horizon. Be sure to walk to the one-room log cabin nearby. Occupied until 1925, the house may not have provided much in the way of material comforts, but even kings or millionaires couldn't complain about its "picture window."

In mid-May this section of the parkway blazes with the crimson-orange blooms of wild azaleas—the brightest of all the many flowers in these parts—which erupt in eye-popping displays along the roadside.

8 Mabry Mill

Although the story is probably exaggerated, folks who needed hardware, corn ground into meal, logs milled, or horses shod once went to see Ed Mabry. He ran a combination sawmill, gristmill, and blacksmith shop from 1910 to 1935. Today, local craftsmen honor his spirit with demonstrations of mountain skills, even as the smell of fresh apple butter wafts through the air. The old mill, one of the

parkway's most photographed sights, stands serenely on the bank of a small pond—oblivious, it seems, to the passage of time since Uncle Ed stood by the fire at his forge in a building separate from the store, pounding red-hot iron into equine footwear.

9 Groundhog Mountain

While you may spy a groundhog (or woodchuck) in the meadow here, the chubby little critter isn't this spot's main attraction. Rather, it's an exhibit of three of the most popular types of split-rail fence, the rustic enclosure that once graced so many farmsteads in the Appalachians. Snake, buck, and post-and-rail fences border an observation tower that was built to resemble a tobacco barn; they're part of more than 300 miles of wooden fences along the length of the parkway.

Just a mile down the road is the log cabin of Aunt Orelena Puckett, one of the legendary characters of the Blue Ridge. She bore 24 children, but tragically, none lived beyond the age of two. Later in life she devoted herself to helping others secure what she couldn't have: she became a midwife and delivered more than 1,000 babies in the area around Groundhog Mountain, venturing out in all kinds of weather whenever the call for help came, and never charging more than six dollars. Her last "bornin'" was her own great-grandnephew in 1939—the year she died, at an age of nearly 100 years. Continuing along the route, drive southwest from Groundhog mountain a few more miles and you'll come to the Blue Ridge Music Center.

10 Blue Ridge Music Center

Throughout the summer months, the warm air of the Blue Ridge Mountains echoes to the sounds of outdoor summer concerts featuring old-time and contemporary mountain music. A new music interpretive center is slated to open in summer 2005, and it will expand the already enjoyable offerings by sharing the history of mountain music in the region.

11 Cumberland Knob

The parkway crosses the Virginia–North Carolina state line just before milepost 217 in a rolling pastoral landscape of farms, fields, and forests. Among those who surveyed this boundary back in 1749 was Peter Jefferson, father of our third (and, Virginia is proud to claim, our most scholarly) president.

Just beyond the visitor center at the Cumberland Knob Recreation Area, you'll find the intriguingly named overlook known as Fox Hunters Paradise. Here, ac-

---

:::::: Trip Tips ::::::

Length: 469 miles.

When to go: Popular year-round, but loveliest in spring and fall.

Words to the wise: Some sections of the parkway may be closed in winter due to snow and ice.

Nearby attractions: Biltmore Estate, Asheville, NC. Blue Ridge Music Center, Cumberland Knob, NC (to open summer, 2005).

Visitor centers: Humpback Rocks; James River; Peaks of Otter, Rocky Knob; Cumberland Knob; Moses H. Cone, Linn Cove Viaduct; Linville Falls; Craggy Gardens.

Further information: Blue Ridge Parkway, 199 Hemphill Knob, Asheville, NC 28803; tel. 828-298-0398, www.nps.gov/blri/.

Linville Falls tumbles through a gap in the bedrock.

12 Doughton Park

South of Cumberland Knob the parkway curves gently through lovely meadows and passes into blustery (especially in winter) Air Bellows Gap. Farther ahead lies the serene and grassy Doughton Park area, where a restaurant, lodge, and campground welcome visitors. At dawn and dusk deer come to feed in these rolling fields, always alert and quick to bound back into the safety of the surrounding forest. Less shy are the tuneful juncos that hop and flit around the lodge.

13 Jumpinoff Rocks

Another of the drive's whimsically named spots, Jumpinoff Rocks (dubbed by local folks) lies at the end

of a half-mile path fringed with trailing arbutus and cinnamonbush. Once you get there, don't jump off the rocks; just enjoy the lofty Blue Ridge Mountain panorama. Farther along the drive, past E. B. Jeffress Park and Deep Gap, the parkway crosses Daniel Boone's Trace (near milepost 285), a path once scouted by the legendary frontiersman, mountain man, and farmer himself.

companied by the doleful baying of hounds, hunters once galloped through the woods below in pursuit of the elusive red fox. This magnificent viewpoint looks out over steep tree-covered bluffs toward the gentler slopes of the Piedmont country to the east.

14 Moses H. Cone Memorial Park

Just before the turn of the century, Moses Cone, a textile magnate who was known as the Denim King, chose this site for his country estate he called Flat Top Manor. Building this mountaintop hide-

away was not easy; materials had to be hauled up by oxcart. Once Cone was settled here, he planted several apple orchards and built 25 miles of carriage roads on his property; today, these shady lanes

induce visitors to explore the nearby hills and lakes. Cone's mansion, with its impressive columned entryway, is now a parkway crafts center and gift shop.

On the ancient slopes of Grandfather Mountain, a few miles farther along, the first signs of the spruce-fir forest of the North Carolina high country begin to appear as dark green swatches in the blanket of forest. Here, too, is the amazing Linn Cove Viaduct, bending gracefully around the eastern slope of the peak. Elevated on seven pillars to avoid environmental damage, the quarter-mile-long viaduct was formed of 153 individually designed segments. The bridge was dedicated in 1987 and marked the official completion of the Blue Ridge Parkway, 52 years after it was begun.

GEORGE WASHINGTON NATIONAL FOREST

WEST VIRGINIA

JEFFERSON NATIONAL FOREST

Rockfish Gap
Charlottesville
1 Humpback Rocks
2 Whetstone Ridge
3 Buena Vista Overlook
4 James River
Lynchburg
Explore Park
Peaks of Otter 5
Roanoke
6 Roanoke Mountain
Smith Mountain Lake

Rocky Knob
7 Smart View
8 Mabry Mill
Danville
Blue Ridge Music Center 10
Cumberland Knob 11
9 Groundhog Mountain
VIRGINIA
NORTH CAROLINA

TENNESSEE

Blue Ridge Parkway
12 Doughton Park
13 Jumpinoff Rocks
14 Moses H. Cone Memorial Park
Winston-Salem

Crabtree Meadows 16
Mt. Mitchell State Park 17
15 Linville Falls
Heintooga Ridge Spur Road 23
Craggy Gardens 18
Asheville
Lake James
FOREST
Statesville

CHEROKEE NATIONAL FOREST
PISGAH NATIONAL FOREST

GREAT SMOKY MTNS NAT'L PARK
Waterrock Knob 22
Waynesville
Richland Balsam 21
Devils Courthouse 20
19 Mt. Pisgah
NANTAHALA NATIONAL FOREST

VIRGINIA

NORTH CAROLINA

SOUTH CAROLINA

N

0   20 mi.

15 Linville Falls

The earliest settlers who stepped ashore in eastern North America found a magnificent forest stretching across half the continent. In those days, it's been said, a squirrel could travel treetop-to-treetop from the Atlantic Coast to the Mississippi River and never have to touch the ground. Thanks to landowners who refused to harvest timber here, and John D. Rockefeller, Jr., who bought the land and donated it to the public, Linville Gorge is among the few places left to still resemble America's vanished virgin woodland. In this pristine valley, massive white pines tower skyward beside lacy hemlocks, ruler-straight tulip trees, and exotic-looking Fraser magnolias with leaves up to a foot long.

Jewels worthy of this gorgeous setting, Upper and Lower Linville Falls cascade into the deep gorge like shimmering silver curtains. The broad trails that lead to the canyon overlooks here are among the most picturesque anywhere on the drive. In fact, if parkway travelers were allowed to visit only one stop along the route, most would mention wild and lovely Linville Gorge as their first choice.

16 Crabtree Meadows

Farther south lies McKinney Gap, most memorable for the lifestyle of its namesake—an 1800s homesteader who lived with four women and sired 42 children. The family traded produce for such items as shoes, which were bought by the wagonload to people more accustomed to buying shoes from itinerant peddlers, country stores, and their mail-order catalogues.

At Crabtree Meadows, the spring flowers—from wild irises and columbines to lilies and mountain laurels—are especially bountiful, but the main attraction here is the famed Crabtree Falls, a steep but breezy hike downhill

Sunflowers in North Carolina fields turn their faces as the day progresses, following the solar orb's path in the sky.

from the campground. The lacy veil of water cascading down the ledges of a high rock wall creates one of the parkway's most memorable scenes.

17 Mt. Mitchell State Park

Near milepost 354 the parkway leaves the Blue Ridge Range and loops past the southern end of the Black Mountains. Named for the dark hues of their spruce and fir forests, the Blacks are the highest peaks east of the Mississippi River, reaching their zenith at 6,684-foot Mt. Mitchell. Be sure to take the short side road to the state park at Mitchell's summit, a delightfully cool retreat even in midsummer. In winter, however, only the hardiest visit this harshly arctic site: temperatures can reach 25°F below zero, with the winds exceeding 100 miles per hour.

18 Craggy Gardens

Of all the parkway's glorious displays of color, none can match the blossoming of Catawba rhododendrons at Craggy Gardens in June. These elegant shrubs (members of the heath family, as are mountain laurels and azaleas) prefer lots of sunlight, unlike their relatives, rosebay rhododendrons, which prefer shade. The shrubs blanket the windy ridge like a vast, verdant overcoat, and in late spring clumps of their pale purple blossoms seem to float atop the green slopes.

Treeless highlands like Craggy Gardens are traditionally called balds because of their smooth appearance (resembling bald spots) when observed from a distance; the shiny leaves of shrubs such as rhododendron and laurel also led to the name heath slick. But early travelers who had to push their way on foot through the dense, tangled vegetation came up with a much more graphic epithet: laurel hell.

19 Mt. Pisgah

After arcing to the east of Asheville, the drive (at milepost 399) threads through the quarter-mile Pine Mountain tunnel, the longest on the parkway. A total of 26 tunnels were blasted through hills and ridges during parkway construction; 25 are located in North Carolina, while the route through Virginia required only one.

Imposing Mt. Pisgah (named for the biblical peak from which Moses saw the Promised Land) boasts one of the parkway's most popular recreation areas, featuring a lodge, campground, restaurant, hiking trails, and seasonal ranger programs. The area is popular not only with people but also with black bears, which from time to time wander onto the campground. While bears might be seen by motorists almost anywhere along the parkway, this thickly wooded upland is particularly noted for sightings of the shaggy, shambling mammals. In the 18th and 19th centuries and before, the black bears that lived here had a number of notable neighbors, including migrating elk and bison, beavers, wolves, and mountain lions.

Near milepost 417 the view to the east is dominated by Looking Glass Rock's 600-foot-high granite cliff, rising from the luxuriant forest like a fortress of stone. The cliff got its name because water (and in winter, ice) on the sheer rock face sometimes reflects light as though the mountainside were one gigantic shining mirror.

20 Devils Courthouse

Cherokees and settlers alike believed that this rocky summit was haunted by demons. (Its outcrops conceal a cave where the devil himself was believed to hold court.) The only mystical force a modern traveler is likely to experience is a sense of awe when beholding the view from the top of the steep trail, where you can see as far as South Carolina, Georgia, and Tennessee. Remember that alpine plants are fragile—stay on the marked trail.

21 Richland Balsam

The name of this stop is short for Richland Mountain of the Balsam Range. Because of its elevation— the highest point on the parkway at 6,047 feet—the spruce-fir forest here seems like a piece of Canada transported south. Birds associated with more northern regions are often found along the Richland Balsam nature trail, among them veeries, winter wrens, and dark-eyed juncos. Ravens tumble and soar overhead, voicing their characteristically hoarse, croaking call.

The dead Fraser firs in this forest, which stand out like ghostly sentinels, were killed by a tiny insect called the balsam woolly adelgid. Accidentally imported to the United States from Europe around 1908, the insect has destroyed an enormous number of the adult firs in places along the parkway. Scientists have been unable to develop a practical control method; the hope is that surviving trees will develop a natural resistance to the pest.

22 Waterrock Knob

Descending steadily as it nears its southern terminus, the parkway snakes past Waterrock Knob, a landmark valued since pioneer days for its mountainside spring. Six miles beyond, the drive enters the Cherokee Indian Reservation. Cherokees have lived in these highlands for untold generations, and their heritage is evident in the names of dozens of local places, including nearby Lake Junaluska, the Tuckaseigee River, and the Nantahala National Forest.

23 Heintooga Ridge Spur Road

Turning north off the Blue Ridge Parkway at milepost 458, this short spur road takes visitors on a side trip to famed Mile-High Overlook, which, true to its name, is perched at an elevation of 5,280 feet. Commanding the horizon are the tall peaks of the Great Smoky Mountains—most notably Clingmans Dome, Mt. LeConte, and Mt. Guyot. The spur road continues to Balsam Mountain Campground and Heintooga Overlook.

Backtracking to the main parkway, the drive winds ever downward along wooded ridges, passing through five more tunnels before crossing the Oconaluftee River and reaching its end point near the Oconaluftee Visitor Center in Great Smoky Mountains National Park. The vast wilderness preserve, one of America's loveliest showcases of natural beauty, serves as an apt climax to this long journey on the venerable—and memorable —Blue Ridge Parkway.

One of the parkway's gems is Linville Falls, here accented by daubs of autumn color.

James River Plantations

Some of time's finest treasures can be found along this drive,
which starts in the modern city of Richmond, passes centuries-old plantations,
then ends in one of the places where America began.

A perfectly proportioned Georgian Colonial mansion is the masterwork of Shirley Plantation, in Charles City, Virginia.

On its twisting journey across southeastern Virginia to Chesapeake Bay, the James River flows with subdued yet stately grace through a landscape that would still be recognizable to the families who built their plantation-style homes along its banks in the 17th and 18th centuries. Today their grand houses still stand as dramatic summations testifying to a vanished era, and Rte. 5, the road that links them, serves as a virtual time line through that sometimes turbulent past.

1 Richmond

Nowadays modern skyscrapers cast their reflections on the James River in Richmond, where the streets were originally laid out in 1737. Down through the centuries, those streets have witnessed more than their share of history. The British plundered Richmond during the Revolutionary War, and as capital of the Confederacy during the Civil War, it was bitterly contested. Many buildings were destroyed by fire when Richmond was evacuated as Union troops approached in 1865. Fortunately, the state capitol, a graceful 18th-century building designed by Thomas Jefferson, survived, as did many other historic structures, with the result that the city enjoys a pleasing mix of the old and the new.

For a journey into the past, take a drive on Rte. 5, which begins near the capitol and heads to the southeast out of the city. Before long, in Charles City County, the 20th century seems to melt away, replaced by an agricultural landscape—corn, winter wheat, soybeans, and cotton are the principal crops—that has neither traffic lights nor large towns to interfere with its idyllic calm. Weaving through this rural region, Rte. 5 leads to plantation houses that sit, one after another, like a string of pearls along the banks of the James River. Shirley, the first of them, is located off Rte. 5 about 18 miles from Richmond.

2 Shirley

Motorists approach the mansion here by driving down Shirley Plantation Road, which becomes a dirt lane that ends at a cluster of 18th-century brick outbuildings, called dependencies. In earlier times guests arrived by boat along the James River, where they looked up to see the front of this perfectly proportioned Georgian Colonial house. The plantation itself was begun in 1613, making it the oldest in Virginia, and to this day its 700 acres are sown with seeds each spring.

Owned by the same family for 10 generations (Robert E. Lee was a member of the clan), the house has an outstanding portrait collection and a stunning three-story staircase that seems to float unsupported in the hallway. Also noteworthy is the wooden pineapple—a symbol of hospitality—perched atop its mansard roof.

3 Berkeley

Found in the Union troops that bivouacked on the grounds of the elegant brick manor house at Berkeley during the Civil War was a young Scottish drummer boy; some 45 years later he returned to purchase the property, which by then had become an uninhabitable ruin surrounded only by forlorn, neglected lawns.

After decades of restoration, the birthplace of President William Henry Harrison, which was completed in 1726, regained its standing as one of America's most distinguished landmarks. The rooms feature handsome woodwork and are furnished with a magnificent collection of 18th-century antiques. The grounds, at their best in late spring, also have been nursed back to health, with roses, azaleas, daffodils, and dogwoods growing on five beautifully groomed terraces that stairstep to the James River.

4 Westover

One of the finest Georgian-style houses in America, Westover, unfortunately, opens its famous pineapple-topped door to visitors only during Garden Week in April. The rest of the year, you'll have to be content with admiring its magnificent exterior as you stroll around the landscaped grounds. They boast 150-year-old tulip trees, a formal garden, and a sweep of lawn that unfurls like a carpet down to the ever-present river.

5 Sherwood Forest Plantation

Three miles beyond Charles City's 1730s courthouse, which still serves as the civic heart of the community, is America's longest frame house—at 301 feet—and forms the centerpiece of this plantation. Once owned by U.S. President John Tyler and still occupied by Tyler family members today, the

white clapboard house at Sherwood Forest can be seen on guided tours by appointment only. (To see the house, call 804-829-5377.) The grounds—29 acres of lawns, terraced gardens, and woods containing more than 80 kinds of trees—also are open to the public. Included among the outbuildings are the servent's quarters, a 17th-century tobacco barn, and President Tyler's law office.

6 Colonial Parkway

After crossing a swing-span bridge over the Chickahominy River, Rte. 5 meets Rte. 614, which takes you to Jamestown Island. A five-mile auto tour loops through the island's marshes and the pine forests where the English began their first permanent settlement in America.

An allée of hardwoods leads to Berkeley Plantation.

Colonial Parkway, a leisurely 23-mile drive threading amid dogwood and redbud trees, links Jamestown to Williamsburg and Yorktown. The parkway is punctuated with scenic turnouts and historical markers. At Colonial Williamsburg visitors can stroll the streets of the superbly re-created 18th-century capital of Virginia. At Yorktown they will be walking in the footsteps of George Washington, whose army triumphed here in the last major battle of the Revolution, thus assuring American independence.

·:·:·: Trip Tips ·:·:·:

Length: About 75 miles, plus side trips.

When to go: Pleasant year-round.

Nearby attractions: Busch Gardens, a theme park and re-created European villages, southeast of Williamsburg via Rte. 60. Colonial National Historical Park and Jamestown Settlement, in Jamestown.

Not to be missed: Historic Garden Week, when many private properties in Virginia—the James River area included—are open to the public. Held the last full week in April. For information, contact the Garden Club of Virginia; tel. 804-644-7776.

Further information: Virginia Tourism Corporation, 901 East Byrd St., Richmond, VA 23219; tel. 800-932-5827, www.virgina.org.

East Tennessee Border Tour

Along the rugged eastern border of Tennessee lies one of America's original frontiers,
a realm of towering trees, shadowy hollows, and sparkling waterfalls.
Traversed long ago by hardy pioneers, much of this land remains wild today.

A blue haze over the forests of the Great Smoky Mountains National Park will soon reflect the fiery reds and golds of autumn.

The name Great Smoky Mountains was inspired by the bluish haze that hovers over the forest—the result of vapors exhaled by millions of trees. But history, too, imbues these ancient peaks, among the highest in the Appalachian range. This territory was sacred to the Cherokee Indians, and among the Europeans that followed, the land inspired a fiercely dedicated pride of place. It has yielded more than its share of statesmen and scalawags, fighters and frontiersmen, whose lives have been immortalized (and embellished) by front-porch raconteurs. The art of storytelling, in fact, has long been a favored pastime in the hills of eastern Tennessee.

1 Hiwassee State Scenic River

After tooling north from Ocoee on Rte. 411, the drive veers east onto Rte. 30 and parallels the Hiwassee River as far as the town of Reliance. From here you can ride the waters in a raft or canoe, or you can continue east into the wilderness on the hiking trails that wind along the river's forested banks. Look for great blue herons stilting through the sun-dappled backwaters, and ospreys making high-speed dives in an effort to snatch trout.

2 Tellico Lake

Rte. 411 follows the contours of the mountains north and east to Tellico Lake, which fingers its way into valleys flooded by the damming of the Little Tennessee River. Along the lake—and beneath it—lie ancestral lands of the Cherokee Indians. Their capital, Tanasi (the word that evolved into "Tennessee"), stood on a site just offshore from the Chota Peninsula, where a stark memorial of eight stone pillars commemorates the eight posts that once supported

Star Route

⭐ Ocoee Scenic Byway

This venerable byway follows Rte. 64 through the Cherokee National Forest for 26 miles between Ocoee and Ducktown. Highlights along the journey include views of Chilhowee, Sugarloaf, and Big Frog mountains; the overlook by the dam at Parksville Lake; a scenic seven-mile spur (Forest Road 77) whose leaf-canopied corridor yields to wide-open vistas at the summit of Chilhowee Mountain; and a six-mile stretch of gorge, where rafters brave the roaring white water of the Ocoee River as it rushes beneath towering cliffs.

the tribe's meeting house. A short drive away is the Sequoyah Birthplace Museum, honoring the life of the man who, inspired by the white man's "talking leaves," created the Cherokee alphabet.

As a diversion, climb to the clouds on the Cherohala Skyway, which follows old wagon-trail routes from its start at the Tellico Plains, Tennessee, on Rte 165, reaching altitudes of more than 5,000 feet as it travels 52 miles to Robbinsville, North Carolina. Other attractions of the route include Whigg Meadows near Haw Knob—the highest point in Monroe County—and Indian Boundary Lake, a popular place for swimming, fishing, picnicking, and camping.

3 Foothills Parkway

Just beyond Tellico Lake, head east on Rtes. 72 and 129 to reach the Foothills Parkway, a development-free national park road that runs for 17 miles along the azalea-strewn Chilhowee ridgeline. The Parkway and its numerous scenic overlooks provide catbird seats that preview the Great Smoky Mountains to the east. From the observation tower at Look Rock, just half a mile off the road, you can spy the fabled, misty peaks and—in the other direction—see all the way to the city of Knoxville.

Or you can gaze up into the sky, where large numbers of raptors (including broad-winged hawks and red-tailed hawks) are easily spotted as they soar and dive for aerial prey during their spring and fall migrations.

4 Cades Cove

Heading east on Rte. 321, the drive swings past Townsend and veers deep into Great Smoky Mountains National Park. Here,

A mantle of mist blankets the ridges of Great Smoky Mountains National Park.

Twin fawns pause for a look at visitors along a Cades Cove walking trail in the Great Smoky Mountains National Park.

in this half-million-acre Eden, which harbors 90 percent of the old-growth forest in the eastern United States, a distinctive man-made environment survives as well—in a place called Cades Cove.

First settled in 1818, Cades Cove grew within its first four decades into a self-sufficient community of nearly 700 souls, then sank into a secluded decline before its absorption by the park. An 11-mile loop leads through the old community, past sturdy, mud-mortared log cabins; stout old churches hand-built by their congregations; a number of barns; a blacksmith shop; and a water-powered mill where stone still grinds corn into meal. Visitors to Cades Cove get a vivid sense of how these folks made their way in the world a century and a half ago.

5 Newfound Gap Road

The 34-mile Newfound Gap Road (Rte. 441) crosses Great Smoky Mountains National Park between Gatlinburg, Tennessee, and Cherokee, North Carolina. A virtual byway in the sky, the road follows a mountain path so tortuous that at one point it has to loop back over itself to gain altitude. Beginning in a lowland Smokies environment of tulip trees, basswoods, magnolias, and sycamores, the road climbs through a typical northern hardwood forest of yellow birch, American beech, and sugar maple. By the time it reaches the top of the nearly mile-high gap, the trees consist mainly of red spruce and Fraser fir, suggesting the forests of Canada. In this alpine clime a seven-mile spur road, followed by a short footpath, leads to the top of Clingmans Dome, the park's highest point.

6 Roaring Fork Motor Nature Trail

One of the highlights of the looping Roaring Fork Motor Nature Trail (a calming contrast to the touristy hubbub of nearby Gatlinburg) is the cool curtain of water known as Grotto Falls, hidden within a hemlock forest a half hour's walk from one of the loop's parking areas. If you like,

357

Autumn sweeps across the Cherokee National Forest near the Cherohala Skyway.

he paid a boy to read to him while he sewed. His shop soon became a gathering place for anyone who wanted to talk politics. The tailor's name was Andrew Johnson, and Greeneville set him off on the path to public life, which led—upon the assassination of Abraham Lincoln—to the presidency of the United States.

Greeneville's Andrew Johnson National Historic Site includes two of Johnson's homes and his eagle-topped gravesite. Most poignant of all, though, is the little tailor shop with its shears, thimble, and flatiron, symbols of the fact that our democracy draws deeply from the populace for its leaders.

hunter, congressman, and Alamo martyr—first saw daylight in 1786. In honoring Crockett, the little cabin serves also as a tribute to the hardiness and flint of that first generation of settlers born west of the Appalachians.

9 Jonesborough

Jonesborough looks like the town that time forgot—in fact, it was once the capital of a state all but forgotten by history. In 1784, when North Carolina gave the

follow the trail past the falls for four strenuous miles to the top of Mt. LeConte. One of the loftiest of the Great Smoky Mountains, LeConte offers vistas that amply reward those who make the climb.

7 Greeneville

Wending north and east of Gatlinburg, the drive follows Rte. 321 and another short stretch of the Foothills Parkway to the small city of Greeneville. Back in

1826, Greeneville offered a fresh start in life for a young tailor so intent on self-improvement that

8 Davy Crockett Birthplace State Park

The frontier hero wasn't "born on a mountaintop in Tennessee," as the song would have it, but at no less beautiful a spot, where Limestone Creek meets the Nolichucky River. Today's park features a replica of the log cabin where Davy Crockett—bear

Trip Tips

Length: About 400 miles in all, plus side trips.

When to go: Year-round, but best in spring, summer, and fall.

Words to the wise: Some roads may be closed in winter due to snow and ice.

Nearby attractions: Knoxville Museum of Art, Knoxville. Dollywood, Pigeon Forge. Museum of Appalachia, Norris. Forbidden Caverns, Sevierville.

Visitor centers: Oconaluftee, Cades Cove, and Sugarlands, located in Great Smoky Mountains National Park.

Further information: Great Smoky Mountains National Park, 107 Park Headquarters Rd., Gatlinburg, TN 37738; tel. 865-436-1200, www.nps.gov/grsm/.

Catawaba rhododendrons blanket Roan Mountain in Cherokee National Forest.

federal government all its lands west of the Appalachians, the local yeomen, left without a government, met at Jonesborough to organize the state of Franklin. Never recognized by Congress, Franklin struggled along for less than five years and ultimately became part of the new state of Tennessee. Jonesborough is Tennessee's oldest town, and it certainly looks the part—not through neglect, but because of its conscientious program of historic preservation. You can take a walking tour of the downtown historic district—a living scrapbook of American architectural styles, studded with gems such as step-gabled brick houses, venerable Victorian homes, and an old inn that once provided board for a young law student named Andrew Jackson. In 1788 the hot-tempered Jackson faced another lawyer in a duel here—a tale that might provide grist for a participant in the National Storytelling Festival, held in Jonesborough each October.

10 Elizabethton

At Sycamore Shoals State Historic Area near Elizabethton, you can visit reconstructed Fort Watauga, one of the first white settlements to be found west of the thirteen British colonies. Here, in 1775, the future of westward expansion was sealed when speculators bought 20 million acres of land from the Cherokee Indians.

At Elizabethton's John and Landon Carter Mansion, built in the 1770s, visitors can stroll around the grounds and tour the home's elegant interior, much of it original. Nearby, at the Doe River, you can visit an old covered bridge—a cool, dark tunnel into the 1880s—that is still open to traffic.

11 Cherokee National Forest

Stretching along most of Tennessee's eastern border—interrupted only by Great Smoky Mountains National Park—Cherokee National Forest is laced with enticing trails. In autumn huge numbers of nut-bearing trees release a slow-motion hail of black walnuts, butternuts, beechnuts, hickory nuts, pecans, and acorns to the forest floor, where wild boar—rarely seen—vie with bear and squirrels for nature's feast. The national forest covers 633,000 acres in ten counties of east Tennessee and is home to a wide variety of wildlife and wildflowers. Mountain trout fill its cold streams, and footpaths garnished with tiny white and yellow flowers lead to a myriad of hidden waterfalls as they crisscross the ancient Appalachian Trail that traverses the forest's high ridges. Stop at ranger stations for hiking, kayaking, biking, and fly-fishing information.

12 Watauga Lake

Jutting away from Rte. 321 at the hamlet of Hampton, the drive follows Rte. 19E to Roan Mountain State Park. You can drive to the 6,285-foot summit, where Catawba rhododendrons form a 600-acre natural garden. In late June, during the Roan Mountain Rhododendron Festival, the road to the top is like a storybook path to a crimson-and-purple sea of blossoms.

Once you return to earth, backtrack to Rte. 321 and head east to Watauga Lake. In the 1940s the entire town of Butler had to move when the Tennessee Valley Authority built 331-foot-high Watauga Dam, creating the 16-mile-long lake. Watauga, bordered by forests and campsites and filled with bass, serves as the gateway to the Doe Valley, where century-old homesteads are surrounded by rich family farms. Tennessee, Virginia, and North Carolina huddle around this serenely uncrowded corner of the Appalachians, where the drive terminates at the aptly named community of Mountain City.

High-country wildflowers blanket the Appalachian Trail.

Carolina Countryside

The sounds of songbirds, waterfalls, and dulcimers waft through this Smoky Mountain wonderland, where slopes and hollows are spangled with the blooms of azaleas, mountain laurels, and rhododendrons.

This idyllic cabin is part of the Cradle of Forestry in Pisgah National Forest.

The misty mountains and shaded valleys of western North Carolina, once a heartland of the Cherokee Indians, later became home to hard-scrabble farmers whose descendants are still given to storytelling, feuding, and fiddle playing. As this drive journeys west from the city of Asheville, much of the landscape sheds its look of 20th-century civilization. In fact, if it weren't for such reminders as paved roads and power lines, you might easily believe you were driving back through time.

1 Cherokee

It's sad but true that places of sublime natural beauty, such as Great Smoky Mountains National Park, often seem to spawn more than their share of commercial ventures. That's certainly the case as Rte. 19 tools west from Asheville and I-40, heading toward the town of Maggie Valley. There the road passes innumerable "Authentic Indian Trading Posts," and if you're so disposed, you can take a chairlift, incline railway, or shuttle bus to a mountaintop where the Ghost Town in the Sky offers staged gunfights, roller-coaster rides, and country music shows.

For more scenic views, ignore the tourist areas and continue west through a domain of rolling hills and sparkling streams, whose Cherokee name means the "Land of the Blue Mist" (a reference to the haze that hovers over the forest). The once-vast Cherokee lands were ultimately reduced to some 56,000 acres—the Cherokee Indian Reservation, which is nestled between the national park and the northern edge of Nanta-hala National Forest. The town of Cherokee, the heart of the reservation, features several fine

⭐ Indian Lakes Scenic Byway

Winding through one of the most remote corners of the state, the byway begins in Almond and heads northwest on Rte. 28 to Fontana Village, a year-round resort where a 480-foot-high dam holds back serpentine Fontana Lake. A series of hairpin turns zigzags to the junction with Rte. 129, where the drive swings south along the blue waters of Santeetlah Lake and trail-laced Joyce Kilmer Memorial Forest (named for the poet), ending in the tiny town of Topton.

museums on Cherokee history, and north of town on Rte. 441, the resident docents at the Oconaluftee Indian Village demonstrate the skills and crafts of a centuries-old Cherokee community.

2 Bryson City

Where the Smokies meet Nantahala National Forest, Rte. 19 curves southwest around gently swelling hills and the purling waters of the Oconaluftee and Tuckasegee rivers. At Bryson City the great outdoors is the main attraction, as evidenced by the sheer number of fishing, boating, rafting, hiking, and camping outfitters.

To experience the countryside, follow the Road to Nowhere, a scenic route that traces the north shore of Fontana Lake into Great Smoky Mountains National Park and ends at a 1,200-foot tunnel. You can also head for the near-

by Noland Creek Trail, a six-mile path that captures the essence of springtime: magenta rhododendrons, blazing azaleas, and peppermint-streaked mountain laurels erupt from rocky dells and shade the dappled stream. Autumn's charms are equally engaging: as you look north, the mountains hunch over the narrowing creek bed, and flame-colored leaves shine through shawls of gauzy mist.

3 Nantahala Gorge

About 13 miles southwest of Bryson City, Rte. 19 plunges into the dramatic 8½-mile-long Nantahala Gorge. Formed by the Nantahala River as it sliced through the hills between Nantahala Lake and Fontana Lake, the canyon is so deep in places that the sun doesn't touch the river's foaming waters until noon, leading the Cherokees to dub it with a name meaning "Land of the Noonday Sun." Rafting and kayaking enthusiasts, however, call it white-water heaven: dam-controlled releases make for

some of the most consistently exciting paddling east of the Mississippi. To sample the thrill of a particularly rough stretch without getting your feet wet, hike the trail to the river's edge at Patton's Run Overlook, where the joyful yells of the paddlers harmonize with the thunderous roil of the rapids. Sometimes adding to the din is the piercing whistle of trains on the Great Smoky Mountains Railway, a passenger-and-freight line that you can board at Bryson City to take a scenic excursion through the Nantahala Gorge and beyond. As you stroll back along the trail from Patton's Run Overlook, listen for the melodious warble of the Eastern bluebird.

Once the road and the railway emerge from the gorge near the town of Nantahala, the two routes parallel each other into a broad green valley, passing through the towns of Topton, Andrews, and Marble. Barely touched by

The Biltmore Estate in Asheville is considered the birthplace of modern forest management.

⋮⋮⋮⋮⋮ Trip Tips ⋮⋮⋮⋮⋮

Length: About 240 miles, plus side trips.

When to go: Popular year-round.

Words to the wise: Some roads are not suitable for recreational vehicles due to weight limits and sharp curves.

Nearby attractions: Mt. Mitchell State Park, Rte. 128, northeast of Asheville. Biltmore Estate, Asheville. Museum of the Cherokee Indian, Cherokee. Great Smoky Mountains National Park, north of Cherokee. Mountain Heritage Center, Cullowhee.

Visitor center: Oconaluftee, in Great Smoky Mountains National Park.

Further information: Supervisor's Office, National Forests in North Carolina, 160A Zillicoa St., Asheville, NC 28801; tel. 828-257-4200, www.cs.unca.edu/nfsnc.

the 20th century, these communities are home to families who have lived here for generations.

▣ Lake Hiwassee

The scenic railway ends at Murphy, located at the confluence of the Hiwassee and Valley rivers and at the eastern tip of Lake Hiwassee. Like many of the lakes in this land of fast-running streams and wrinkled hills, Hiwassee was formed by a dam built when the Tennessee Valley Authority sought to bring flood control and electricity to rural communities in the 1930s and 1940s. At the lake's Hanging Dog Recreation Area, visitors can pitch tents, launch boats, and hike on backcountry trails.

About 12 miles east of Murphy on Rte. 64, you'll find beautiful Chatuge Lake, considered by some to be the crown jewel of the TVA reservoirs. From here Rte. 64 skips along the ridges and crests of the Chunky Gal Mountains (named, according to lore, for a chubby Cherokee lass who ran away with her lover without her father's permission). Unlike the jaggedly spectacular Rockies, the Smokies —no less beautiful—have been softened by time and circumstance. Too far south to have been gouged by glaciers, too old to show signs of violent uplift, the land has been slowly smoothed by wind and water over countless millennia.

On its way east the drive passes one bucolic scene after another: the flanks of rounded peaks where

Whitewater Falls near Cashiers changes character as runoffs increase or decrease.

cattle graze behind split-rail fences; rusty farm machinery standing beside ramshackle barns of rough-hewn lumber; and rustic farmhouse chimneys adding their own rising smoke to join with the ever-present blue haze. After breezing through the hamlet of Rainbow Springs, the highway's route crosses through Winding Stair Gap and then heads in an easterly direction toward Franklin.

▤ Franklin

The hills around Franklin may lack gold, but the valley town where two rivers and a number of streams converge has its share of jewels. Rte. 28 leads north through the Cowee Valley, where precious stones such as sapphires, rubies, and garnets used to be mined commercially. The numerous mines hereabouts now cater to rockhounds, who sieve through the muck hoping to find treasure.

Nature lovers and vista viewers have an easier time of it, especially a few miles west of town at Wayah Bald, which stands sentinel at 5,385 feet above sea level. On the road up to the unusually treeless (bald) summit, wildflowers signal the changes in elevation: butterfly weeds, fireweeds, bluets, and Indian paintbrushes give way to flame azaleas, whose June fireworks draw hundreds of awestruck shutterbugs. Higher still, white azaleas and mountain laurels drop their snowy petals to carpet the ground. A rock tower at the very top, built by the Civilian Conservation Corps in 1933, provides a spectacular 360-degree view of the Nantahala and Cowee mountains; the peaks drift in the mist-like islands rising from a pearl-colored sea. The area is criss-crossed by numerous hiking trails, many branching off from the Bartram and Appalachian trails, which intersect on the shrubby summit of Wayah Bald.

6 Cullasaja River Gorge

The stretch of Rte. 64 that follows the Cullasaja River southeast from Franklin is known as the Waterfall Byway, and for good reason: about a dozen silvery cascades spill down the hills on either side of the road, and after a thunderstorm countless trout streams in the area are transformed into unfishable torrents.

Just past the tiny community of Cullasaja, the road swoops into the Cullasaja River Gorge, whose dramatic twists and drops are occasionally counterpointed by the aerial antics of birds of prey soaring and then plummeting overhead. After tunneling through a dense hardwood and hemlock forest, past tangles of rhododendron camouflaging the riverbanks, the road bursts out onto a bare shelf of rock high above the river. Far below, the series of cascades that make up Cullasaja Falls crash down 250 feet in barely half a mile —a dramatic display of raw natural beauty. Six miles farther the oddly named Dry Falls spills over an outthrust lip of rock into a pool 75 feet below. The water is anything but dry; the falls was so named because visitors can walk behind the waterfall and remain dry. One mile farther down the road, you'll come to Bridal Veil Falls, which unfurls a 120-foot ribbon of white and is even "drier" than Dry Falls. A spur road lets you drive behind the cascading water and glimpse rainbows in the morning sunlight.

7 Highlands

Once it leaves Bridal Veil Falls behind, the drive traces the shoreline of Lake Sequoyah on the way into Highlands. Built near 4,635-foot-high Satulah Mountain, this aptly named town is one of the highest incorporated communities in the East. After subsisting on a diet of hamlets barely large enough to support a single gasoline pump, travelers who tool into Highlands find a refreshing array of treats: spruced-up houses, bed-and-breakfast inns with lace curtains and overflowing window boxes, and shops stocked with the sorts of frippery that appeal to visitors with large disposable incomes.

East of town a two-mile loop trail leads off Rte. 64 to the top of massive Whiteside Mountain, a sheer 2,000-foot wall of white granite. The mountain contains a fascinating bit of graffiti—an inscription carved in old Spanish that might have been cut by one of Hernando De Soto's gold-hunting conquistadors in 1540.

8 Cashiers

Not many dogtrot farm cabins can be seen along Rte. 64 from Highlands to Cashiers (pronounced "*CASH-ers*"); this is summer resort country, catering to well-to-do Southerners who flee from the sweltering lowlands to posh country clubs, groomed golf courses, and exclusive mountain retreats.

Even so, nature still holds sway in a few locales away from the main roads. The headwaters of the Chattooga River (the movie *Deliverance* was filmed a bit farther south on the Chattooga) offer some of the wildest white water in the country. Southeast of Cashiers, off Rte. 281, lies Whitewater Falls, one of the highest falls in the eastern United States, with curtains of water that tumble 411 feet over boulders and cliffs. The falls is not, however, for those who like to wipe the spray off their brow; the main vantage point, an overlook reached by a paved path, is the closest you'll get. Still, the sight of the river thundering downward in a spray-wrapped cataract is awe-inspiring, and your senses will be inundated by the sounds of the roaring torrent plunging into the ravine.

Fall colors cloak North Carolina's ridgetops as days shorten and the air becomes crisp.

9 Lake Toxaway

A few miles to the east of Whitewater Falls, Rte. 64 glides onto a concrete bridge above the Toxaway River, which flows from Toxaway Falls, on the south side of the road, into Lake Toxaway, to the north.

About 18 miles farther east lies the resort town of Brevard, home of the Brevard Music Center, which sponsors summer concerts ranging from classical to pop. For those driving west, Brevard is the gateway to waterfall country; for those driving east, it's the gateway to Pisgah National Forest, which is just north of town on Rte. 276.

10 Forest Heritage Scenic Byway

The last leg of the drive follows Rte. 276 along a portion of the Forest Heritage Scenic Byway. North of Brevard, you will pass between a pair of stone columns marking the entryway to Pisgah National Forest, where, by careful nurturing, forest logged down to stumps and bare ground has been replaced with lushly variegated groves of pines, hemlocks, birches, sycamores, tulip trees, and oaks.

Heading north along the Davidson River (one of the country's top trout streams), the byway skirts a picnic area and campground be- fore arriving at Looking Glass Falls, named for nearby Looking Glass Rock, whose dampened granite face gleams like a mirror. A short distance beyond, at Sliding Rock, bathers can glide down a glassy, water-smoothed, natural rock slide that descends into an enormous pool. Complete with observation platforms, handrails, ropes, and lifeguards, Sliding Rock is often as crowded as it is thrilling.

A bit farther north on the byway lies the Cradle of Forestry, where multiple exhibits highlight various methods of forest conservation— especially those developed by Dr. Carl A. Schenck. Schenck, who immigrated from Germany to succeed Gifford Pinchot in supervising the 100,000-acre forest attached to George Vanderbilt's palatial Biltmore Estate in Asheville, helped usher U.S. forest management practices into the 20th century.

The drive continues north past the Pink Beds (home to acres of blossoming swamp pinks, azaleas, and laurels), across the Blue Ridge Parkway, and along the East Fork of the Pigeon River, where it passes through rural mountain villages and colorful orchards as it nears its final stop at Waynesville.

Outer Banks Highway

Breezy and beautiful, North Carolina's barrier islands are imbued
with the spirits of the Wright Brothers,
sailors lost at sea, and the mysterious Virginia Dare.

The Ocracoke Ferry pulls out of harbor on its way back to Hatteras or the mainland.

It's not for nothing that the Outer Banks coastline is nicknamed the Graveyard of the Atlantic. Buffeted by winds and crosscurrents, the waters off this fragile finger of land jutting far out to sea are littered with more than 500 shipwrecks. But for vacationers these shores are a delight; sun-kissed breezes, rolling blue waves, undulating dunes, and seafood feasts keep folks coming back year after year.

1 Wright Memorial Bridge

Rte. 158, the northern approach to the slender thread of barrier islands known as the Outer Banks, can be heavily trafficked on summer weekends, so it's a good thing that the drive through rural Currituck County can be so pleasant. As the highway drifts past farmland and salt

marshes along the shallow waters of Currituck Sound, seductive roadside vegetable stands and barbecue joints vie for motorists' attention.

All that changes abruptly at Point Harbor, where the Wright Memorial Bridge, a low-lying two-laner, carries visitors across the silver-blue sound to a bustling resort playground. After miles of clapboard farmhouses and soybean fields, the sparkling blue ocean looms ahead, edged by a glorious expanse of beach.

2 Kill Devil Hills

It was the weather that lured Wilbur and Orville Wright to these islands in 1900. But the Ohio bicycle makers didn't come for the

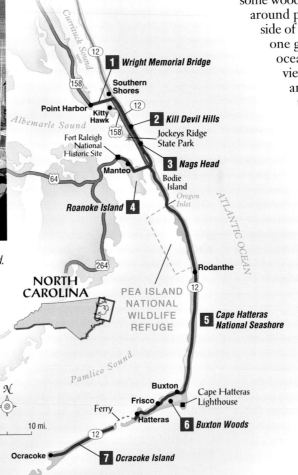

sun; they came for the wind, which was needed for their pioneering experiments in aviation. From atop a huge sand hill in what is now Kill Devil Hills, the brothers took their homemade craft on the first powered flight in history—120 feet in 12 seconds. Today, at the Wright Brothers National Memorial, a mighty granite pylon on Big Kill Devil Hill commemorates their feats. You can view two replicas of Wright aircraft at the exhibit center, and outdoors the park has markers that show the distances and durations of four historic flights the Wright brothers made among these windy dunes.

3 Nags Head

More than a century ago, summer resorters hereabouts built handsome wooden cottages with wraparound porches on the sound side of the island. Then someone got the idea that the ocean side had better views, better swimming, and a salt-air breeze that discouraged mosquitoes. So the homeowners placed logs beneath their cottages and rolled them over marshlands and dunes to the oceanfront at present-day Nags Head, where they raised the cottages on stilts to let storm waters surge harmlessly underneath. The homes, known as the Unpainted Aristocracy, still stand on the beach road between mileposts 11 and 15, but today they are flanked by a clutter of souvenir shops. Across the highway, in startling contrast, stand huge mounds of white sand, the dune system that makes up Jockeys Ridge State Park. You can climb 125-foot Jockeys Ridge, the highest single sand dune on the East Coast, and watch hang gliders leap from the top.

Jockeys Ridge is part of a system of sand dunes that shelter an ancient maritime forest, the Nags Head Woods Preserve. This idyllic stand of oaks (some of them 500 years old) and rare wildlife was salvaged by the Nature Conservancy in the 1980s. Although the woods are linked to Jockeys Ridge, you'll have to backtrack to milepost 10 on the Rte. 158 bypass to reach the forest and the visitor center. Trails lead through the moss-draped woodland past crystal-clear freshwater ponds and flowering dogwoods. Be sure to call ahead before visiting.

4 Roanoke Island

In 1587 English settlers attempted to colonize Roanoke Island. But by 1590 the community had inexplicably vanished, along with the first child born of English parents in the New World—Virginia Dare. All that remained was the word CROATOAN, carved into a tree for subsequent voyagers to discover and for theorists to ponder for centuries to come. At Fort Raleigh National Historic Site, you can see the community's reconstructed fort, which lends a poignant resonance to the mysterious story of the Lost Colony.

Next door to Fort Raleigh, you'll find another memorial to the lost colonists: the Elizabethan Gardens, 10 acres of carefully tended native and exotic plants, garden statuary, and a sunken garden.

Brown pelicans are a common sight on the Cape Hatteras shore, where they sunbathe.

On your way back to Rte. 158, drop in at Manteo, a charming village on Shallowbag Bay. Here you can tour the *Elizabeth II*, a reproduction of a 16th-century sailing ship, built in 1984 to commemorate the 400th anniversary of the first voyage to Roanoke Island.

5 Cape Hatteras National Seashore

The drive pushes south on Rte. 12 into Cape Hatteras National Seashore—an expanse of undeveloped shoreline. In places the barrier island is so slender that you can see the Atlantic on one side of the road and Pamlico Sound on the other.

Across the Herbert C. Bonner Bridge, a long, arched span over the sparkling blue waters of Oregon Inlet, lies Pea Island

National Wildlife Refuge. The vast numbers of snow geese and egrets in its salt marshes can be viewed from observation platforms. A few miles to the south, stop at the Chicamacomico Lifesaving Station, built in 1874. In this handsome structure exhibits recall the plucky lifesavers who used to rescue mariners from the Graveyard of the Atlantic.

For over a century sailors were warned away from the dangerous shoals by the towering striped lighthouse at Cape Hatteras. The 208-foot beacon, the tallest brick lighthouse in the country, comes into view as you approach Buxton. At its feet surfers test the rolling swells that threaten to devour the old tower, whose base is being eroded by the pounding surf.

6 Buxton Woods

On the sound side north of Buxton, windsurfers flock to Canadian Hole, where conditions are said to be perfect. Here you can watch dozens of colorful, billowing sails waltz across the cobalt sea.

Between Buxton and the town of Frisco, take a hike on the Buxton Woods Nature Trail, a well-marked loop that winds past stands of gnarled live oaks, blue beech trees, and unusual dwarf palmettos.

At the end of Hatteras Island, board the free ferry to Ocracoke Island for a 30-minute ride. As the boat chugs out of port, note the swirling body of water that separates the two islands. Hatteras Inlet was formed when a hurricane ripped through the island in 1846; the same storm created Oregon Inlet to the north.

7 Ocracoke Island

Picturesque Ocracoke Island is a relatively isolated place, with gentler surf and finer sand than can be found at points north. Here one can cast for bluefish in the ceaseless rolling surf, go crabbing in the waters of the sound, or simply beachcomb for sea snails, Scotch bonnets, whelks, or interesting pieces of flotsam driftwood or jetsam washed up by the tides.

For a change of pace, drive to the Ocracoke Pony Pens to visit the remnants of a herd of wild ponies that have lived on these shores for ages. Or take a stroll through the quaint village of Ocracoke, which arcs around a tidal harbor called Silver Lake. Here you can rent a bike, grab some fresh crab cakes or Hatteras clam chowder, and perhaps (depending on your itinerary) board one of the ferries leading to points on the mainland. More likely you'll choose to retrace your steps northward along the Outer Banks, once again savoring each gorgeous mile of sand, sea, and sky.

Cherokee Foothills Scenic Highway

Threading along the slopes of the southern Appalachians, this drive crosses
an ancient Indian path as it winds past orchards and a historic battlefield
to a land of forests, lakes, and a legendary white-water river.

The shimmering sky-blue waters of Lake Jocassee are home to adjacent Devils Fork State Park.

::::: **Trip Tips** :::::

Length: About 130 miles, plus side trips.

When to go: Fine scenery year-round; icy conditions may close roads in winter.

Nearby attractions: Kings Mountain State Park, with a re-created homestead, and Kings Mountain National Military Park, an American Revolution battleground, northeast of Gaffney via Rte. 29. Oconee State Park, with camping and hiking, north of Walhalla via Rte. 107.

Further information: Discover Upcountry Carolina, P.O. Box 3116, Greenville, SC 29602; tel. 800-849-4766, www.theupcountry.com.

Like ivy clinging to an old stone wall, the Cherokee Foothills National Scenic Highway climbs over the slopes of the Blue Ridge foothills, forming a 130-mile arc in northwestern South Carolina. Along the way, the drive invites travelers to walk woodland trails to tumbling waterfalls, enjoy the solitude of mountain brooks, and gaze at highlands rolling to the horizon. Sample all of these delights, and you'll see why members of the Cherokee tribes called this land *Sah-ka-na-ga,* or "Great Blue Hills of God."

1 Gaffney

Every spring the rosy blush of peach blossoms welcomes motorists to Rte. 11, Cherokee Foothills National Scenic Highway. Come summer, roadside stands fill with the luscious fruits, which make for big business in these parts—a fact emphasized by Peachoid, Gaffney's million-gallon water tower, painted to look like a gigantic peach.

Just west of Gaffney the byway passes Cowpens National Battlefield, where a ragtag band of patriots met a much larger force of elite British troops in 1781. Despite the seeming mismatch, the skilled tactics of General Daniel Morgan earned the Americans a resounding victory—one in a series of triumphs in the South that helped pave the fledgling nation's road to independence. Today an interpretive walk guides visitors through the now-peaceful meadow that in Revolutionary times once rang with musket fire and the clang of clashing sabers.

2 Caesars Head State Park

Winding westward, the drive goes past Jones Gap State Park on the way to Caesars Head State Park, situated just to the north via Rte. 276. The two parklands, linked by a five-mile trail along the Middle Fork of the Saluda River, rank among South Carolina's finest wild places. The road up to Caesars Head, a mountaintop monolith, rewards visitors with a panorama of the Blue Ridge foothills, their green crests disappearing in the distance. At the overlook's edge, sheer cliffs drop a total of 1,200 feet.

More than 50 waterfalls—among them some of the tallest in the East—splash down from the heights of the Upcountry, as South Carolinians call these western mountains. Raven Cliff Falls, a bit north of Caesars Head, can be reached by a moderately strenuous two-mile hike. At trail's end visitors look up to see a series of cascades that plunge more than 400 feet through a narrow gorge. In autumn, when the foliage of oaks, hickories, and maples achieves its peak, Raven Cliff affords one of the state's most splendid scenes:

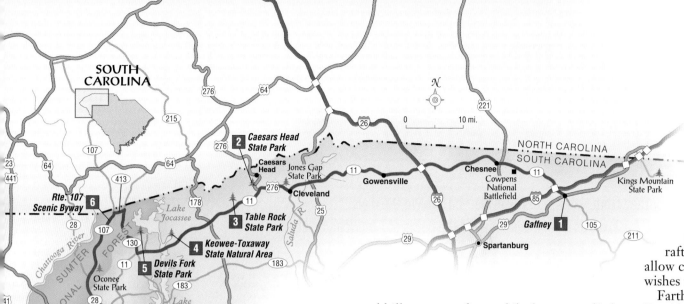

SOUTH CAROLINA

a misty tableau of yellows, reds, and oranges enlivened by the dancing silver water of the falls.

3 Table Rock State Park

The Great Spirit, according to the Cherokees, dined atop this park's granite summit, giving basis to the name—Table Rock—that has endured to modern times. Table Rock Lodge, built by the Civilian Conservation Corps, sits at the edge of PinnacleLake and offers views of the peak. Challenging trails climb to the summit; an easier hour-long hike crisscrosses Carrick Creek, where blossoming mountain laurels and rhododendrons grace the woods in spring with clouds of rose-pink, purple, and white.

4 Keowee–Toxaway State Natural Area

European pioneers encountered a thriving Cherokee culture in these rugged hills. For a time the two peoples lived in peace, but as more and more settlers came, the Cherokees, like other eastern tribes, were forced to leave their homeland for points west. To learn about this sad chapter in history, stop at Keowee–Toxaway State Natural Area's Interpretive Center, where a museum and kiosks display such artifacts as arrowheads and pottery. Also be sure to sample the nearby woodlands, which envelope the shores of man-made Lake Keowee. The sprawling reservoir has inundated the onetime capital of the Lower Cherokees—a village also called Keowee, or "Land of the Mulberry Groves."

5 Devils Fork State Park

After crossing Lake Keowee, turn north on Rte. 25 to reach Devils Fork State Park, located on the shores of Lake Jocassee. Though it might be difficult to shift your gaze from the sparkling water of the lake or to interrupt your search for such wildflowers as trout lilies and Oconee bells, a skyward glance may be rewarded by a glimpse of a peregrine falcon, one of America's most majestic birds of prey. Other denizens of the park include wild turkeys, white-tailed deer, and gray foxes, while the waters of Lake Jocassee teem with bass, sunfish, and trout.

Back on Rte. 11, the drive splits northward in another side trip, Rte. 130, for a visit to Lower Whitewater Falls, part of the tallest series of waterfalls in the East. To view the cascade—its wide veil of water leaps for more than 400 feet—stop at the Bad Creek Hydroelectric Project for a hike along Foothills Trail or a drive to an overlook.

6 Rte. 107 Scenic Byway

The tour parallels the state border as it follows Rte. 413 west, then takes Rte. 107 south through the mountains of Sumter National Forest. Meandering through pines, oaks, hickories, and hemlocks, the highway is the gateway to many of the Upcountry's most appealing sites. First you'll pass the Walhalla National Fish Hatchery, which raises about a million trout each year. The hatchery also marks the entry to the Ellicott Rock Wilderness, a rugged realm of waterfalls and woodlands that boasts one of America's most renowned— and most remote— white-water rivers: the Chattooga. Although many of its rapid-choked stretches are rated strictly for experts, raft trips on gentler sections allow chances for anyone who wishes to try them.

Farther south, Rte. 107 meets Rte. 28, which leads to the Stumphouse Tunnel Park. The preserve has several trails, complete with interpretive displays, and a picnic area that affords a view of 200-foot Issaqueena Falls. The drive then heads to Walhalla, a pretty town amid orchards, and rejoins Rte. 11, which rolls south to the expansive waters of Hartwell Lake.

Raven Creek Falls at Caesars Head State Park tumble over stairstep after stairstep.

DRIVE 114

Natchez Trace Parkway

On this journey from Natchez to Nashville, you'll relive the days
when riverboat men and backwoods adventurers braved the perils of America's frontier.

::::::: Trip Tips :::::::

Length: About 450 miles, plus side trips.

When to go: Spring and fall.

Lodging: Available in nearby towns and cities. During pilgrimage seasons (spring and fall), make reservations well in advance.

Words to the wise: Observe the 50 m.p.h. speed limit, which is strictly enforced. When driving, be on the lookout for bicyclists and deer; when hiking, beware of ticks, snakes, and poison ivy.

Nearby attractions: Vicksburg National Military Park, Vicksburg, MS; Mississippi Petrified Forest, near Flora, MS; Country Music Hall of Fame, Nashville, TN.

Visitor centers: Mt. Locust, Tupelo, Kosciusko, Colbert Ferry.

Further information: Natchez Trace Parkway, RR1, NT-143, Tupelo, MS 38801; tel. 800-305-7417, www.nps.gov/natt/.

Windsor Ruins, at Port Gibson, are stark and skeletal testimony to what was once the grandest antebellum home in Mississippi.

If roads could share their stories, few would have a better tale to tell than the Natchez Trace Parkway. Stretching diagonally from the Mississippi River into the Tennessee Valley, this 8,000-year-old pathway has felt the tread of early Indians, marching armies, intrepid pioneers, and Spanish conquistadors. Today the historic route is roughly paralleled by a national parkway administered by the National Park Service, whose low speed limit and lack of commercial traffic make for a wonderfully lazy Southern sojourn.

1 Natchez

The romantic Mississippi River town that lent its name to both the old trail and the modern parkway is one of the loveliest and most historic communities in the South. Founded in 1716, Natchez—the name comes from an Indian tribe that settled here in the 1500s—was at that time the only port on the Mississippi between bustling New Orleans and the mouth of the Ohio River.

During the steamboat era the town's strategic location enriched so many of its citizens that more than half the millionaires in America lived here. Many of their lavish homes, like Natchez itself, went virtually untouched by the Civil War and are among the town's 500-odd carefully preserved antebellum structures. Some of these magnificent mansions are open to visitors year-round, including such favorites as Stanton Hall, a structure that covers an

368

entire city block; Magnolia Hall, which was shelled by a Union gunboat in 1862; Longwood, the largest octagonal house in America; red brick Rosalie, perched on a bluff beside the broad, muddy Mississippi; and Melrose, known for its unique Greek Revival style and distinctive outbuildings. Other homes may be visited only in the spring and fall, when the famed Natchez Pilgrimage Tours attract thousands of visitors, who stroll beneath live oaks draped with Spanish moss to relive the glory of a bygone era.

2 Emerald Mound

Heading northeast from Natchez, the drive follows Rte. 61, which joins the beginning of the parkway a few miles outside the city. Once on the Natchez Trace, the route winds through rolling hill country so dense with oaks, pines, beeches, and magnolias that their overhanging limbs in places seem clasped together like fingers. The first travelers along the original trace (from a French word meaning "track" or "path") were no doubt wild buffalo seeking the easiest path south. Tracking their hoofprints, Indians blazed the trail farther, connecting villages with an intersecting series of game trails through the unbroken woodland.

At milepost 10 the region's Indian heritage is highlighted by an ancient ceremonial site known as Emerald Mound. Built about 700 years ago by the Mississippians (ancestors of the now-extinct Natchez tribe), the flat-topped, 35-foot-high earthen structure covers eight acres, making it the second-largest ceremonial mound in America. Emerald Mound was once surmounted by smaller secondary mounds and temples, but

Rosalie, one of the many southern belles that grace the city of Natchez.

most vestiges of these have long since disappeared as completely as their builders. Nearby is the entrance to Natchez State Park, a good spot for camping and fishing.

3 Mt. Locust

Throughout its long history the Natchez Trace has shown the way for an incredible caravan of travelers: trappers and traders, pioneers and preachers, soldiers and scoundrels. But of all those who have trodden here, the group that is perhaps most identified with the

A traveler on Natchez Trace follows in the footsteps of history.

trace are the riverboat men who, starting in the late 18th century, began a regular trading routine with cities on the lower Mississippi.

Known as Kaintucks (though they came from many states besides Kentucky), these rough-and-ready entrepreneurs guided their flatboats and rafts down the Mississippi to deliver goods at Natchez or New Orleans. Once their business had been completed, they sold their boats for lumber and trekked home on foot rather than push upstream against the current. Darkened by the sun and often dressed in tatters, they had, according to one observer, "beards eighteen days old, adding to the singularity of their appearance, which was altogether savage."

By 1810 as many as 10,000 Kaintucks a year were trudging northward toward Nashville on the trace. Before long, such heavy traffic had turned a crude, narrow wilderness trail into a clearly defined route. (In 1806 the trace was broadened to 12 feet by order of Thomas Jefferson to make it passable for wagons.) To serve the boatless boatmen who faced a long journey home, a series of inns, called stands, sprang up along the route, spaced about one day's walk apart. Of the 50 original stands, only Mt. Locust remains. Restored to its 1820 appearance, the simple wooden house is built on pilings to keep the interior cool during summer; the design also features a long front

gallery, or porch. Most of these primitive shelters provided little more than a plate of cornmeal mush and a spot to sleep on a wooden floor, but to weary travelers making their way on a journey of nearly 500 miles, they must have seemed as inviting as any posh New Orleans hotel.

4 Windsor Ruins

A turn west off the parkway onto Rte. 552 leads along a quiet back-country road to Windsor Ruins, the haunting skeleton of what was once the largest and most impressive antebellum home in Mississippi. Completed in 1861 at the then-staggering cost of $175,000, Windsor served as an observation post for Confederate troops and, later, as a hospital for the Union Army. Ironically, the building survived the Civil War intact, only to be destroyed in 1890 by a fire ignited by a careless smoker. Today, all that remains of the once-magnificent mansion is 23 weathered Corinthian columns, their ornate iron capitals touching nothing but the deep blue southern sky.

5 Port Gibson

From Windsor Ruins the drive curves northeastward to rejoin the parkway, via Rte. 18, near milepost 40. Just before the junction, you pass through historic Port Gibson, the town General Ulysses S. Grant reportedly decreed was "too beautiful to burn" during his march to Vicksburg in 1863. Among the antebellum structures that inspired his benevolence are Oak Square, a 30-room Greek Revival mansion (now a bed-and-breakfast inn) and the 1859 First Presbyterian Church. Its soaring steeple is topped with a gilded 10-foot-tall metal hand pointing skyward, and its interior features chandeliers from the Robert E. Lee, one of the most majestic steamboats ever to ply the Mississippi.

The dawn of the steamboat era, around 1812, marked the beginning of the end for the Natchez Trace: river travel was so much easier and safer than the overland journey that, by the 1820s, the pathway was virtually abandoned and forgotten. Not until the early 20th century were efforts made to locate and mark the historic route.

6 Rocky Springs

Even at the peak of its popularity, the Natchez Trace was frighteningly lonely and remote, a jungle-like place where a traveler might walk or ride for hours without seeing a single soul. Poisonous snakes, ruthless bandits, Indian warriors, treacherous terrain—these were just some of the hazards that earned the trail its ominous nickname: the Devil's Backbone.

At mile 41.5 a portion of the original trace (one of a dozen sections that are accessible) gives visitors a taste of what early travelers must have experienced. Worn deep into the earth by countless footsteps and hoofbeats, this eroded tunnel is as spooky as ever. Spanish moss drips from tall trees, a chorus of crickets issues an almost deafening trill, and the forest is often shrouded in a steamy haze. Up ahead lies another eerie place, the ghost town known as Rocky Springs, where you'll find the southernmost campground on the parkway.

7 Mississippi Crafts Center

At milepost 87 the drive detours around an incomplete section of the Natchez Trace Parkway (via I-20, I-220, and I-55) through the capital city of Jackson. Just a mile after returning to the parkway, you'll reach the Mississippi Crafts Center, housed in a dogtrot log cabin. All of the objects on display here were created by members of the Mississippi Craftsmen's Guild. On weekends from

March through October, artisans demonstrate their homespun skills in pottery, quilting, basket weaving, and many other crafts, both traditional and contemporary.

8 Cypress Swamp

For several miles the parkway hugs the western border of Ross Barnett Reservoir, whose shimmering blue waters attract waterskiers in summer and anglers year-round (bass and catfish are common). Near the reservoir's north end lies Cypress Swamp, an abandoned river channel that abounds with two types of water-loving trees, tupelos and bald cypresses. A 20-minute nature trail begins on an elevated boardwalk, which leads through a wetland full of natural wonders. Turtles sunning themselves on logs plop into the still water as walkers approach, lazy alligators drift by like floating logs, and great blue herons spear fish with remarkable skill. About 40 miles

ahead, just north of Kosciusko, you'll find a visitor information center with exhibits on the colorful history of the parkway.

9 French Camp

Louis LeFleur, a French Canadian married to a Choctaw woman, established a stand serving Natchez Trace travelers here in 1812.

Today visitors can browse over French and Indian artifacts in a restored 1840 log cabin and inspect a sorghum mill, where a favorite Southern treat, molasses, is made on weekends from late September through October.

10 Jeff Busby Site

Winding its way northeastward, the drive soon arrives at Jeff Busby Site, named for a congressman who played a key role in the preservation of the trace. This recreation area offers camping, picnicking, and the only fuel station located directly on the parkway. A nature trail, identifying native plants and

the ways pioneers used them, leads to Little Mountain, which, despite its name, is one of the highest points found in the state of Mississippi. From its 603-foot summit, you can see as far as 20 miles on a clear day.

In the pine and hardwood forest near milepost 203 is a reminder of a tragic chapter in the natural history of America. The Pigeon Roost roadside exhibit marks the spot where millions of migrating passenger pigeons once rested. Thought to have been the most abundant bird species in the world in Colonial times, the passenger pigeon, flocks of which would blacken the sky for hours at a time, was wantonly slaughtered for food and sport. Its numbers declined precipitously toward the end of the late 19th century, and the last known member of the species died in the Cincinnati Zoo in 1914.

11 Tombigbee National Forest

Curving gently through rolling countryside, the parkway traverses 66,000-acre Tombigbee National Forest, which offers a different treat in every season. In spring, as jack-in-the-pulpits hide beneath their hoods, redbuds burst forth with pink blossoms, and flowering dogwoods dot the forest with clouds of white. Come late autumn, the colors of the forest are even more vibrant, as oaks, hickories, maples, and sweetgums go out in glory. Thanks to its abundance of shortleaf and loblolly pines, the forest remains green in winter and shady on sultry summer days.

The Witch Dance Horse Trail, at milepost 233, takes its intriguing name from a local legend about mysterious bare spots on the forest floor. Witches once gathered here to dance, the story goes, and wherever their black-slippered feet touched the ground, the plants withered and died, never to grow back again. A few miles ahead, a spur road leads west to 200-acre Davis Lake, a good spot for swimming and boating.

12 Tupelo

This part of Mississippi was once the floor of an ancient sea, yielding a limy black soil that, centuries later, would prove ideal for growing cotton. Cattle now graze on many of the prairies near the parkway as it approaches Tupelo, the largest city in the northeastern part of the state. Although Tupelo's history is as rich as its cropland—a Chickasaw Indian village was located nearby, and the town is the site of the last major Civil War battle fought in Mississippi—people now flock here from all over the world because of an everyday event that occurred on January 8, 1935. On that date, in a tiny two-room house built with $180 worth of materials, twin sons were born to Gladys and Vernon Presley. One boy, Jesse Garon, died at birth; but the other, Elvis Aaron, grew up to become the King of Rock 'n' Roll. His fans, whose worship has never waned in the years since his death in 1977, visit Tupelo by the thousands each year to glimpse his boyhood home, his elementary and junior high schools, and the hardware store where he bought his first guitar.

The Natchez Trace Parkway has its headquarters about five miles north of town at the Tupelo visitor center, where travelers will find a scenic nature trail and a museum chronicling the history of both the old Natchez Trace and the modern parkway.

13 Donivan Slough

The 20 minutes it takes to walk the trail at this imposing bottomland forest (located at milepost 283) are well rewarded. Water oaks, sycamores, sweetgums, bald cypresses, beeches, and river birches thrive here, but among the most splendid specimens are the tulip trees, tall and arrow-straight. Often called yellow poplars—though they're more closely related to magnolias—these woodland giants flaunt beautiful greenish-orange tulip-like flowers in spring. Farther north, at milepost 287, sprawl the Pharr Mounds, the largest archeological site in Mississippi. Built around 100 B.C., these earthworks cover some 90 acres.

14 Tishomingo State Park

Just beyond Donivan Slough, the parkway crosses the Tennessee-Tombigbee Waterway, a shortcut for commercial shipping between the Tennessee River and the Gulf of Mexico. Farther ahead, the route bisects 1,500-acre Tishomingo State Park, one of the loveliest spots in Mississippi. The park's steep hills, which are in fact the westernmost extension of the Appalachian Mountains, make for so many bluffs, waterfalls, and rocky ridges that one feels a world away from the flatlands of the Mississippi River Delta. Except in winter the park offers an eight-mile canoe trip along Bear Creek, past high sandstone bluffs and over rocky rapids.

15 Freedom Hills Overlook

After spending three-quarters of its journey in Mississippi, the drive crosses into Alabama for a brief

Unfurling its emerald splendor, Water Valley, southwest of Tupelo, affords one of the grandest views from Natchez Trace Parkway.

visit—just 33 miles. At Freedom Hills Overlook (milepost 317), a short but steep trail leads to a view of tree-covered highlands along the western edge of the Cumberland Plateau. The drive then breezes on past lush rolling hills that are especially pretty in the late afternoon, when long shadows cast a bluish tint on the gently folded landscape.

16 Colbert Ferry

At Colbert Ferry the parkway crosses Pickwick Lake via the mile-long John Coffee Memorial Bridge. Well over a century before the bridge was built, the site's name-sake, a mixed-blood Chickasaw chief named George Colbert, operated an inn and ferry here for Natchez Trace travelers. A shrewd businessman, Colbert reportedly charged Major General Andrew Jackson $75,000 to ferry his troops across the Tennessee River on their return from the Battle of New Orleans in 1815. A section of the old trace leads past the site of Colbert's house. At the north end of the bridge, near milepost 329, is a picnic area and a boat ramp.

17 Sunken Trace

Rather than following one un-varying line, the original Natchez Trace had paths that often shifted —the result of changes in terrain, weather, or the whims of Spanish Colonial rule. At Sunken Trace, located at a spot just nine miles beyond the Alabama-Tennessee border at milepost 350, visitors can spot three distinct trails, evidence that early travelers changed course at various times to skirt miring mudholes.

18 David Crockett State Park

Just past milepost 370, Rte. 64 leads eastward from the Natchez Trace to David Crockett State Park, named for the legendary Tennessee pioneer who died at the siege of the Alamo in 1836. (Despite the words of a popular song about the "king of the wild frontier," he was known in his time as David, not Davy.) Crock-ett established a powder mill, gristmill, and distillery here on the bank of Shoal Creek in 1817; all were washed away by a flood in 1821. Today campers can catch a bass for supper on Lindsey Lake, and hikers on the park nature trail can pause to enjoy the delight-ful scene at Crockett Falls, a series of cascades on Shoal Creek. Back on the parkway continue to mile-post 375, where an unpaved, for-est-fringed section of the old trace —unsuitable for large trailers and recreational vehicles—climbs to a high ridgeline with fine views of the surrounding hills and valleys.

19 Meriwether Lewis Site

As the drive winds northward past the Buffalo River, keep an eye peeled for woodchucks, foxes, coy-otes, and—where the road passes through fields and pastures— bluebirds perched on roadside fence wires. The Meriwether Lewis Site, at the junction with Rte. 20, is one of the region's most popular recreation areas, with camping, hiking trails, and a section of the old trace leading down to Little Swan Creek. Lewis, co-leader of the historic Lewis and Clark expedition to the Pacific Northwest, was only 35 when he died of gunshot wounds at an inn here in 1809. Though believed to have been a suicide from the out-set, murder and conspiracy theo-ries have circulated since soon after his death. His gravesite is marked with a broken stone col-umn, symbolic of a life cut short by tragedy.

20 Jackson Falls

At milepost 404 a precipitous trail descends from the parkway to the base of a waterfall on Jack-

Rising from the murky waters of Cypress Swamp, some bald cypresses are centuries old.

son Branch, where springtime freshets create a shimmering sil-very cascade that splashes down glistening dark rocks. The falls are named for Andrew Jackson, the renowned general who be-came the seventh president of the United States. At the parkway's northern terminus in Nashville, you'll find the Hermitage, Jack-son's white-columned home and the site of his tomb.

About 20 miles past the falls, the Natchez Trace reaches its highest point—1,100 feet above sea level. This long ridge, the Tennessee Valley Divide, once marked the boundary between the United States and the Chickasaw Nation, its neighbor to the south.

21 Garrison Creek

Named for an army garrison that was established nearby in 1801, the parkway's northernmost picnic site is the trailhead (at mile 427.6) for a 24½-mile hiking and bridle path that meanders across the Ten-nessee highlands. The old trace was designated an official postal route at the beginning of the 19th century; as a result, army troops made improvements to the road-bed in this area—at mile 426.3, just over a mile to the south—to try to speed up the pace at which mail was delivered between Nash-ville and Natchez. Trusting that the mail carriers would know the shortest and easiest way and would provide companionship in case of danger, newcomers often accom-panied these seasoned riders on their journeys. The post rider was adopted by the National Park Ser-vice as the official symbol of the Natchez Trace Parkway, and today you'll find the silhouette of a horse and rider adorns the signposts along the entire route, a recur-ring reminder of the roadway's frontier heritage.

Lookout Mountain Parkway

On a clear day you may not be able to see forever,
but you can come mighty close from the summit of Lookout Mountain,
where panoramic vistas overlook seven states.

:::::: **Trip Tips** ::::::

Length: About 120 miles, plus side trips.

When to go: Pleasant year-round.

Nearby attractions: Rock City Gardens, a 10-acre tract that contains rare vegetation and unusual sandstone formations, off Rte. 157 in Georgia, just south of Tennessee. Chattanooga Nature Center, with marked roads and trails that pass through areas lush with wildflowers, shrubs, and trees, off Rte. 11 in Chattanooga, TN.

Further information: Lookout Mountain Parkway Association, P.O. Box 681165, Fort Payne, AL 35968; tel. 888-805-4740, www.tourdekalb.com.

Visitors of all ages will enjoy the views of the canyon's clefts from the picnic area in Cloudland Canyon State Park.

The sturdy ridge of Lookout Mountain angles for about 80 miles across parts of three states: Alabama, Georgia, and Tennessee. Nowhere more than 10 miles wide, the mountain seems a world unto itself, featuring a diverse display of plant life. Oaks and maples intermingle with poplars and dogwoods, while bouquets of sunflowers, lobelias, and black-eyed Susans spangle the fields. The parkway itself, marked by green signs, cobbles together a dozen rural byways to fashion a 120-mile-long paradise that includes cascades, canyons, and even caverns.

1 Noccalula Falls Park
Alabama's natural beauty shares the stage with Indian lore at this 250-acre park to the north of Gadsden. Once called Black Creek Falls, the 90-foot waterfall here now bears the name of the Cherokee princess Noccalula, who is said to have hurled herself to a watery death rather than marry a man she did not love. A bronze statue of the lovelorn maiden, poised to leap into the thundering cascade, looks out endlessly on the falls.

Nearby, a stairway descends into Black Creek Gorge, a snaking chasm carved into the rocks just downstream from the falls. A 1½-mile trail shadows the waterway as it races between towering sandstone bluffs. Another pathway, the Lookout Mountain Hiking Trail, which one day will lead all the way to Chattanooga, also can be sampled at Noccalula Falls Park.

2 Little River Canyon
The green signs along Tabor Road, Rte. 89, the first leg of the Lookout Mountain Parkway, will guide you north to State Rte. 68, where the parkway becomes Rte. 176 with Leesburg on the left and Collonsville to the right. Farther along, at a community called Dogtown, the drive makes a brief, beautiful detour from the parkway itself, taking Rte. 176A northeast along the western rim of Little River Canyon.

The roadway parallels the steepwalled rift, one of the deepest to be found east of the Mississippi River. Turnouts are sprinkled along the route; stand at the canyon's edge, if you dare, and listen for the distant music of the Little River, rushing along some 700 feet below. You can even follow one of several trails that lead down the sandstone cliffs to the cloistered canyon floor and reward yourself with a refreshing summertime dip in one of the Little River's sheltered swimming holes. After you enjoy this side trip, return to the parkway by following Rte. 35 westward to Rte. 89.

3 DeSoto State Park

Although the Spaniard Hernando De Soto found no gold when he explored this region in 1540, modern seekers of nature's treasures will find prizes aplenty: 20 miles of trails lined with uncountable riches. Famed for its springtime display of flowering shrubs, this wooded preserve is equally stunning in autumn, when hardwoods put on a show of foliage as colorful as a painter's palette. Be sure to catch each season in all its glory from the overlook at nearby 120-foot DeSoto Falls, the highest cascade in the area. The reservoir above the falls makes for a lovely picnic spot—and a tempting find for anglers.

4 Sequoyah Caverns

The drive detours again, heading west to Rte. 11, where signs will direct you to the underground world of Sequoyah Caverns, with caves and passageways that honeycomb the rock. Thousands of fossils are forever frozen in time on the walls and ceilings, while underground lakes—silent, clear, and still —double every image like natural funhouse mirrors. Above ground the park has a small collection of animals—including fallow deer, goats, ducks, and peacocks.

5 Cloudland Canyon State Park

Back on Lookout Mountain Parkway, you'll traverse the spine of Lookout Mountain along Rte. 117, which zigzags eastward through woodlands on the way to Georgia. Beyond the town of Cloudland, the

Point Park, a Civil War memorial atop Lookout Mountain, offers views of Chattanooga.

parkway continues to press northward along Rte. 157, then turns onto Rte. 136 for a short jaunt to Cloudland Canyon State Park. One of the region's finest preserves, its 2,200 or so acres embrace a cluster of ravines and waterfalls. With elevations that range from 800 to 1,900 feet, this is rugged terrain but well worth exploring. Exhilarating panoramas of the hills and hollows will prepare sightseers for the grandeur that awaits at Cloudland Canyon itself, a deep cleft slashed into shale and sandstone by Sitton Gulch Creek. For a front-row seat, stop at the park's main picnic area.

6 Point Park

The parkway heads northward along Rte. 189, which returns you to Rte. 157 a few miles south of the Tennessee border. Once across the state line, the drive follows

Rte. 210 to the scenic loop that passes Point Park—a fitting climax to this journey along the length of Lookout Mountain. The ridge reaches its highest point here, cresting at 2,126 feet, and boasts a view to match, with vistas of the Tennessee River gliding slowly past the city of Chattanooga. On clear days you can also see portions of six other states: Alabama, Georgia, North Carolina, South Carolina, Kentucky, and even Virginia. For a glimpse of the mountain's interior, visit Ruby Falls, a watery plume that splashes down through a cave located more than 1,000 feet underground. The hidden realm— an elevator will whisk you there— also claims among its charms several subterranean chambers that are bejeweled with onyx as well as with dripstone; when illuminated, the cave's walls shimmer with rainbowlike colors.

North Georgia Highroads

Just a short hop from the gleaming glass towers of Atlanta lies a mountainous getaway little touched by any but nature's hand.

Pink lady's slippers dot the forest floor in Chattahoochee National Forest.

Once part of Cherokee country, this rocky edge of the Appalachian Mountains has at points in time attracted prospecting pioneers in search of gold. The treasure proved fleeting, but northern Georgia continues to reward with its unforgettable sights and sounds—towering waterfalls, secluded gorges, orchards and farms wedged among the mountains, and remote little towns that keep watch over timeless folkways.

1 Toccoa

Leaving behind the high-speed traffic of I-85, the drive begins by following Rte. 17 northwest to the town of Toccoa, which takes its name from the Cherokee word for "beautiful"—an apt description for this place at the southeastern edge of Chattahoochee National Forest. Ranging across most of the state's northern tier, the forest abounds with ferns, wildflowers, shrubs, pines, and stands of long-lived oak and hickory trees. The mountainous terrain is laced by rivers and creeks, their downhill journeys punctuated by an abundance of waterfalls. The first, Toccoa Falls, drops about 186 feet. To reach it, follow the signs from Rte. 17 to Toccoa Falls College a few miles outside of Toccoa, where a creekside trail leads to the deep pool at the base of the cascade, whose nonstop melody grows louder as you approach.

2 Tallulah Gorge State Park

The drive follows Rte. 441 north, then turns eastward for a short stretch along Old Rte. 441 (Scenic Loop 15), which clings to the rim of Tallulah Gorge. Drivers will have to keep their eyes on the road, but turnouts along the way let everyone else enjoy the vistas, though all can enjoy the view from the suspension bridge over the gorge. The cleft's walls plummet to the Tallulah River, which races along about 1,000 feet below. For more views stop at Tallulah Gorge State Park, where a trail overlooks three waterfalls and outcrops known as Lion Rock and Lover's Leap.

Farther ahead in Clayton, once a trading post for Cherokee Indians, you'll find a bustling downtown area that brims with stores offering antiques, traditional crafts, and other homespun keepsakes. Whitewater enthusiasts also can be seen in the streets of Clayton, where three outfitters have set up shop in order to guide adventurous visitors on the nearby Chattooga River down rapids that vary in difficulty from Class III to V. You can visit the waterway via Rte. 76 east, one of only a few roads that lead to the notorious wild and scenic river.

3 Black Rock Mountain State Park

Black Rock Mountain State Park combines history with some of the boldest ridges in the lower Blue Ridge Mountains. Located on Foxfire Lane under Black Rock Mountain, the Foxfire Museum features exhibits that highlight the region's traditional mountain culture. Black Rock itself, named for a black cliff composed of the mineral biotite, bestrides what some call the Eastern Continental Divide: water falling on its flanks will flow to either the Atlantic or the Gulf of Mexico. Perched above 3,640 feet, the area has overlooks commanding views that on clear days extend for 80 miles or so.

4 Moccasin Creek State Park

The drive backtracks to Clayton, then follows Rte. 76 westward to Rte. 197 and Moccasin Creek State Park, a pint-size playground that hugs the western shore of Lake Burton. Anglers come here to cast for trout, bass, panfish, and bluegills. Others visit simply to enjoy leisurely walks along the lake's shoreline and up the nearby slopes, a pastime that is especially appealing during the hot summer months, when the high elevation

::::: Trip Tips :::::

Length: About 170 miles, plus side trips.

When to go: Fine scenery year-round, though the fall can be crowded on weekends and winter's are sometimes icy.

Nearby attractions: Amicalola Falls State Park, where a series of cascades tumble a total of 729 feet, off Rte. 52 west of Dahlonega. Lake Winfield Scott, a clear lake high in the mountains, Rte. 180 west of Vogel State Park.

Further information: Georgia Tourism Division, P.O. Box 1776, Atlanta, GA 30301-1776; tel. 800-847-4842, www.georgiaonmymind.org.

and deep shade of the forest offer relief from the heat—so much so, in fact, that Moccasin Creek is known as "the park where spring spends the summer."

Once back on Rte. 76, you'll quickly come to the Popcorn overlook, which takes in the rumpled ridges that rise from Lake Burton. Farther along, the highway crosses the Appalachian Trail at Dicks Creek Gap, a slender notch that has yet another inviting

ing, and fishing are popular here, and in the lakeside town of Hiawassee, the trails at Hamilton Gardens traverse a paradise filled with tulip trees, dogwoods, azaleas, and rhododendrons.

After taking a walk through the gardens, follow Rte. 76 past the blue bulk of sturdy ridges to the town of Young Harris. From there you'll descend beside Butternut Creek, which twists and turns amid a valley graced with apple orchards, cultivated fields, and wind-rippled meadows.

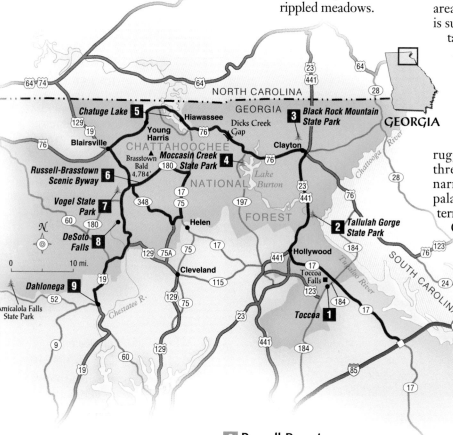

can reach the visitor center on top by trail or, for a fee, by shuttle bus. Descending from the mountain's flanks, the byway continues past forests and wilderness areas along what is often for first-timers a white-knuckle course.

7 Vogel State Park

After completing the scenic loop, the drive heads south on Rte. 19/129, where you'll be greeted by a cascade on the approach to 223-acre Vogel State Park. The area's centerpiece, Lake Trahlyta, is surrounded by a ring of mountains cloaked with dense forests. A Civilian Conservation Corps museum also commemorates that Depression- and New Deal–era work program.

8 DeSoto Falls

As Rte. 19/129 arcs past the rugged Blue Ridge foothills, it threads through Neel's Gap, a narrow pass shared with the Appalachian Trail, whose southern terminus is just a few ridges away. Called Mountain Crossings, it's the only spot on the trail that is covered with a man-made structure. Visitors to DeSoto Falls are treated to a trio of tumblers, which can be viewed along a three-mile stretch of trail. Known as Upper, Middle, and Lower DeSoto Falls, they drop, respectively, 200, 80, and 20 feet. As a historical footnote, the falls, like many places in the South, take their name from Spanish explorer Hernando De Soto. According to one local legend, a piece of armor that was found here is said to have belonged to the conquistador, who trudged through this region in the early 1500s searching for riches.

Natural waterslides at Tallulah Gorge State Park.

9 Dahlonega

A horde of dreamers and schemers under the spell of gold fever came to comb the hills here in 1828. Dahlonega, a Cherokee word that translates as "precious yellow," was in fact named for the treasured metal. Even the federal government had a stake, establishing a mint that was pressing coins until the outbreak of the Civil War. Today Dahlonega wears several hats: gracious southern mountain town, busy county seat, and jumping-off point for wilderness adventures. Visitors can relive prospector days at the Gold Museum State Historic Site; some even try their luck panning for gold on the Chestatee River or at Crisson's and Consolidated Gold Mines.

rest area with picnic sites and far-reaching views.

5 Chatuge Lake

The drive soon nears the glittering expanse of Chatuge Lake, a reservoir that extends into North Carolina, where the lake's glassy surface mirrors the mountains that slant down to its shores. Camping, boat-

6 Russell-Brasstown Scenic Byway

Blairsville, an old-fashioned mountain town, was settled in the shadow of 4,784-foot Brasstown Bald, Georgia's highest mountain. The Russell-Brasstown Scenic Byway, a 41-mile loop along State Rtes. 180, 17/75, and 348, climbs to just below the peak's crest. You

Georgia's Pristine Coast

Along the coast of Georgia, no sharp boundary separates land and sea: amid countless creeks, estuaries, and lazy rivers, dry land dissolves into tidewater in a graceful mélange of marsh, sea, sand, and sky.

The sand dunes of Cumberland Island stretch for 15 miles along a picturesque Atlantic beach.

For 120 miles, from serene Savannah to the St. Marys River at the Florida border, nearly half a million acres of salt marsh define Georgia's Atlantic Seaboard. This coast, however, is not a place that surrenders easily to a straightforward drive: there's always another side trip to take, always another jaunt onto an island causeway or down an alluring byway.

1 Savannah

A mid-1700s capital of the Georgia colony, the city of Savannah remains the elegant legacy of its original planners. Its streets are gracefully punctuated by more than 20 squares, beautified in turn with fountains, statues, and flowering shrubs. Savannah is best seen on foot, one where a stroll in most any direction rewards you with charming discoveries: elaborate cornices that adorn old mansions, marble heroes surrounded by azalea blooms and bright green lawns, the picturesque iron bridges of Factors Walk, the live oak alley leading to the fountain in Forsyth Park, and Skidaway Island—a beautiful mix of state park and residences. Amble through Savannah's historic district, where more than 1,000 meticulously restored homes and commercial buildings reflect the antebellum years when cotton was king and this genteel city was in its prime.

2 Tybee Island

As you head east out of Savannah, follow palmetto-lined Rte. 80 over the Bull River and into a salt marsh wilderness, where the languid feeder streams of a vast estuary rise and fall to a tidal pulse and pelicans angle through the sky.

Just off the road on Cockspur Island stands Fort Pulaski National Monument, built in 1829 to defend Savannah's sea approaches; it was pummeled into submission by Union guns in the desperate siege of 1862. The road ends at Tybee Island, where summering Savannahians recline on broad beaches, bike down sandy lanes, and sate their hunger with steamed blue crabs. Tybee's lighthouse is Georgia's oldest and tallest; rising from foundations that predate the Revolutionary War, it casts its

---

::::: Trip Tips :::::

Length: About 170 miles, plus side trips.

When to go: Popular year-round.

Words to the wise: The number of daily visitors to Cumberland Island is limited, so phone ahead for information and to make reservations.

Nearby attractions: Hilton Head Island, South Carolina, via Rte. 278 north of Savannah. Okefenokee Swamp Park, near Waycross. Mary Miller Doll Museum, Brunswick.

Further information: Georgia Tourism Division, P.O. Box 1776, Atlanta, GA 30301; tel. 404-656-3590, www.georgiaonmymind.org.

The Savannah waterfront is best enjoyed on a warm summer evening.

beam across the harbor that long ago ensured Savannah's prosperity.

3 Fort McAllister State Historic Park

After backtracking to the mainland, the drive heads south from Savannah on Rte. 17 past dense coastal pine forests and Melon Bluff, a private preserve of sweeping river views and moss-draped oaks. At the town of Richmond Hill, it turns east on Rte. 144 toward lovely Fort McAllister State Park near the mouth of the Ogeechee River. An intriguing nature trail and a choice scattering of sylvan campsites invite visitors to share the tranquil riverbanks with an avian population that includes strutting gallinules and rails, barred owls, and the painted bunting, the most extravagantly hued of all North American birds.

Fort McAllister was the scene of a grim encampment during the Civil War. Here Confederate troops dug massive walls of earth to block horrific Union bombardments from the sea, only to fall to Sherman's land attack as Savannah's fate was sealed in the waning days of 1864. Now fully restored and surrounded by green, Fort

McAllister stands guard against nothing more than the sea breeze wafting in across the wildlife haven of Ossabaw Island to the east.

4 Harris Neck National Wildlife Refuge

As you continue south on Rte. 17 through Midway, consider stops at Fort Stewart Museum, the Historical Liberty Trail, and Fort Morris Historic Park. Further, at South Newport, look on your left for the sign that marks the site of the "Smallest Church in America"— a 10- by 13-foot chapel with a modest 12 seats. Nestled in a mossy glade, the church is open to wayfarers of all denominations 24 hours a day.

There is no sign on Rte. 17 pointing the way to the Harris Neck National Wildlife Refuge. But it's easy enough to get there: just take the next left after the church, turning onto Rte. 131 at the tiny hamlet of South Newport, and drive for some seven miles. At this extensive refuge, nature has been carefully cajoled by conservationists, creating a quiltwork of wildlife habitats. Nearly two-thirds of Harris Neck's 2,700 acres consists of salt marsh, which is

The Altamaha river inlet is dotted with boat anchorages and shrimp restaurants.

complemented by freshwater impoundments that attract herons, ibises, and migrant waterfowl such as widgeons and delicately patterned gadwalls. Deer, raccoons, opossums, and minks live here as well. Fifteen miles of paved roads snake through the refuge, including a well-marked eight-mile driving trail that leads from upland stands of live oaks garlanded with Spanish moss to shadowy swamps, where green-backed herons stalk their prey among the buttresslike roots of old cypresses.

5 Altamaha Historic Byway

Near the town of Darien, Rte. 17 passes through miles of pine forest harvested for the paper industry. For a distance, it also parallels the Colonial Coast Birding Trail—each site is marked and worth visiting. If you are hungry, stop for pork barbeque served at many local gas stations, or sample the seafood in Darien. Its wharf is crowded with shrimp boats and other fishing vessels, their salty nets drying in the sun amid the swoops and cries of gulls. A mile east of Darien stands restored Fort King George, built by the British in 1721 as a bulwark against the Spanish in Florida.

The seven-mile Altamaha Historic Byway, as Rte. 17 south of Darien is often called, weaves a long skein of social and natural history. Exhibits at the Hofwyl-Broadfield Plantation, for example, hark back to the days when rice—not cotton—was king in this part of the South.

Centuries of fortification and agriculture seem to melt away as you enter the Altamaha Waterfowl Management Area, 26,000 timeless acres of hummocky marshland where the booming of an old bull alligator is as likely to pierce the air as any human sound.

6 Marshes of Glynn

Farther south, Rte. 17 swings into Brunswick, the second-largest city on the Georgia coast and the gateway to the Golden Isles, as they are known locally. Once you turn east at Brunswick onto the causeway that heads out to St. Simons Island, you are surrounded by the vast and magnificent expanse of salt grasses dubbed the Marshes of Glynn. In the words of the 19th-century poet Sidney Lanier, the marshes make up a domain where "all is still and the currents cease to run, / And the sea and the marsh are one." The poet affectionately characterized the great marshland as "candid and simple / and nothing-withholding and free."

The marshes simply surround you, stretching from one horizon to the other. Besides their seeming infinitude, and apart from their marvelous productivity as a foundation link in Georgia's coastal food chain, the single most impressive aspect of this ocean of salt grasses is its color. Deeply verdant in summer, dormant brown in winter, the Marshes of Glynn span the gamut of greens when they are brought to life by the warm spring rains. Pea green, lime green, chartreuse, pastel greens shading almost to violet in the afternoon light—the spring marshes are the color green made alive and infinitely changeable.

7 St. Simons Island

At the causeway's eastern end lie St. Simons, Little St. Simons, and Sea islands, which seem to fit together into a rounded whole like pieces of a jigsaw puzzle. Here ongoing development and the wild coastline mix to create a manicured middle ground. For all of their golf courses and comfortable homes on rambling lanes, these islands manage to preserve stretches of shoreline and the stands of live oaks that captivated the American naturalist William Bartram in 1774.

Near the middle of St. Simons, largest of the Golden Isles, lies Fort Frederica National Monument. Here the ruins of a fortified town, along with a film and exhibits at the visitor center, memorialize the earliest days of the Georgia Colony. At nearby Couper's Point, a historic lighthouse is the centerpiece of the Museum of Coastal History, where maritime artifacts cast a spotlight on the area's past.

Visitors can drive across a bridge to Sea Island, St. Simons' neighbor to the east. This lush, green, carefully tended isle is a favorite of the well-to-do; its five-star resort, the Cloister, is visited by everyone from movie stars to presidents.

Reachable by ferry, the third island, Little St. Simons, contains

Visitors from the Sea

On warm nights the beaches of Jekyll Island, Cumberland Island, and other spots along Georgia's coast are visited by fleets of lumbering giants known as loggerhead turtles. Weighing from 300 to 800 pounds and measuring more than a yard long, the loggerheads crawl onto the beach, dig deep holes, and each deposit more than 100 leathery shelled eggs. When the young turtles hatch two months later, they scramble down the beach into the sea.

another resort, where guests can ride horseback, hike through acres of virgin pine, canoe across quiet marshes that teem with wildlife, and go surf-casting for redfish.

8 Jekyll Island

You'll have to backtrack to the mainland and cross the marshes yet again to reach storied Jekyll Island, a link with the Gilded Age. In 1886 a few dozen captains of industry—familiar names such as Morgan, Rockefeller, Lorillard, Pulitzer, Vanderbilt, and Goodyear—bought the island and built the elegant Jekyll Island Clubhouse; it survives today as a hotel with posh sitting

rooms and croquet on the lawn. They also built family "cottages" with up to 31 rooms (one had an astonishing 17 bathrooms).

The scenic island is laced with paved bicycle trails that lead to lovely picnic spots, broad sandy beaches, and secluded wildlife areas where a host of wading birds keep cautious company with the ever-watching alligators.

From Jekyll Island the drive returns to Rte. 17 and breezes through the tiny villages of Spring Bluff, White Oak, and Woodbine. At Kingsland, a turn onto Rte. 40 leads to St. Marys, where you can catch a ferry for a 45-minute voy-

age to serenely gorgeous environs of Cumberland Island.

9 Cumberland Island National Seashore

No vehicles are permitted on the ferry from St. Marys to Cumberland Island, where human activity is largely limited to camping and day visits, so you'll have to get around on foot (unless you stay at the private Greyfield Inn, which is equipped with bicycles). Trails canopied with live oaks, cabbage palms, and holly lead through this pristine wilderness, roamed by such creatures as armadillos, wild pigs, wild turkeys, even wild

Time stands still in the Jekyll Island Historic District, built in the 1880s.

horses. Ospreys wheel above Cumberland's tidal creeks, alligators doze in its freshwater ponds, and loggerhead turtles lay their eggs on the sandy beaches. Among the few signs of civilization are the Dungeness Ruins, the overgrown skeleton of an 1880s Carnegie mansion located about a mile south of the ferry dock. Remember that the last boat back to the mainland leaves at 4:45—unless you're staying here and can spend a leisurely evening lulled by the wildlife serenade.

Gulf Coast Drive

Not quite the Deep South, yet a far cry from the
resort meccas of the Florida Peninsula, the state's panhandle
moves to the modest rhythm of a soft gulf breeze.

Restored buildings that house inns, antique stores, and restaurants, which feature fresh-caught seafood, dot central Apalachicola.

Between Panama City and Tallahassee, Florida's Gulf Coast is sheltered by sandy barrier islands and isolated from points north by vast forests. The Florida boom has for the most part left this stretch of coast alone—left it to migrating shorebirds that find first landfall here in spring, to drowsy alligators, and to folks who'd rather enjoy an Apalachicola oyster than a night on the town.

Star Route

⭐ **Apalachee Savannahs Scenic Byway**
Beginning on Rte. 65 at the southern border of Apalachicola National Forest, the drive pauses at Fort Gadsden Historic Site, where an outdoor museum highlights the fort's role in the Civil War. Swinging northwest on Rte. 379 at Sumatra, the byway passes cypress bogs, longleaf pine flats, and the grassy savannahs that give the route its name. Paralleling the Apalachicola River north to Rte. 12, the byway is garnished with a spectacular array of wildflowers.

1 St. Andrews State Park

Reached via Thomas Drive, which turns off Rte. 98 three miles west of Panama City, St. Andrews State Park is tucked between the Gulf of Mexico and a calm saltwater lagoon, gathering the diverse flavors of Northwest Florida into a single 1,000-acre package. Campers and day-trippers can explore steep sand dunes and immaculate beaches, dense pine woods, a freshwater lake, marshes teeming with herons and alligators, and a nature trail that snakes through a fascinating variety of wildlife habitats. Anglers who come to St. Andrews, whether for surf casting or fishing from the jetty, will be rewarded with an abundance of bluefish, bonito, redfish, dorado, flounder, perch, and Spanish mackerel.

For an escape even farther into the languid life of the Gulf Coast, visitors can travel by boat to nearby Shell Island. Awash with seashells—and refreshingly free of development—this barrier island, some seven miles of white sand and scrub forest, is a serene oasis where gentle breezes rustle the tawny-topped sea oats that anchor the shifting sands of the ever-shifting sand dunes.

2 St. Joseph Peninsula State Park

Return to Panama City and then head southeast on Rte. 98 to Rte. 30E and the St. Joseph Peninsula. Civilization seems to run out as the road crooks north from Cape San Blas toward St. Joseph Peninsula State Park. Some two-thirds of this sanctuary is preserved as a wilderness area, where the brown pelicans swoop seaward and the beach belongs to horseshoe crabs and nesting sea turtles.

To the south and east of the peninsula, you'll find St. Vincent Island (accessible by private boat), a fine place for savoring the music of windblown cabbage palms or viewing the great gangling wood storks that visit in summer.

3 Apalachicola

Returning to Rte. 98, the drive tools east into Apalachicola, where the law dictates that no building can be higher than three stories, making for a pleasantly human-scale town. The cotton business once reigned supreme here, and a pair of partially restored warehouses from that era still stand. Numerous other buildings have already been restored and now host antique shops and seafood restaurants serving the day's catch from the bay. The town's life today centers around its harbor, where oystermen haul in enormous harvests from the rich beds out in the bay. Along the old streets behind the waterfront, handsome Greek Revival homes eloquently recall prosperous Antebellum days. Some are now bed-and-breakfast inns, spots where visitors can stay.

Also here is the John Gorrie State Museum, where exhibits tell of a young doctor who, trying to

St. Vincent's Island retains as its prime attraction the remote flavor of an earlier Florida, at one with nature.

keep yellow fever patients cool in the 1840s, invented the first mechanical icemaker and so laid the foundation for artificial cooling of the air. The air conditioner, of course, is now a Florida icon.

4 St. George Island State Park

Continue east over the Gorrie Bridge from Apalachicola to Eastpoint, then angles south onto a bridge leading to St. George Island. The easternmost 2,000 acres of this spit of dunes and marshes that separates Apalachicola Bay from the Gulf of Mexico has been set aside as a park—a boon not only to hikers, campers, anglers, and beach lovers, but to the shorebirds that depend on the undeveloped

coastline as a resting place for their migration stopovers.

Willets, snowy plovers, least terns, and black skimmers are among the many kinds of birds that gather along the St. George beaches in spring and fall. The migration routes of some species extend all the way from Argentina and Brazil to the Arctic tundra of North America. The shorebirds that you see feeding on minute crustaceans and other tiny sea creatures can survive only if development-free way stations such as St. George Island survive as well.

5 Carrabelle

From its southernmost thrust into the Gulf at Apalachicola, the

northwest Florida coastline arcs to the northeast. At easygoing Carrabelle, a celebrated local attraction is a telephone booth billed as the world's smallest police station.

From Carrabelle's impressive marina, charter boats head out into the gulf in search of tarpons, groupers, amberjacks, and red snappers. A little ferry also motors out to Dog Island, where 100 or so householders and an eight-room inn (bring your own food) share sand and serenity with a vast Nature Conservancy preserve.

6 Ochlockonee River State Park

Northeast of Carrabelle and some 10 miles inland from the Gulf on

Rte. 319, you'll arrive at the pine woods and oak thickets of Ochlockonee River State Park. The park provides a habitat for gray foxes, which, unlike their red cousins, can climb trees to get at fruit, nuts, and the occasional unlucky bird. Sharing the forests along the banks of the Ochlockonee River are bobcats, deer, alligators, and rare red-cockaded woodpeckers.

7 Apalachicola National Forest

Much of the inland sections of the region are forests dominated by longleaf pines, turkey oaks, and palmettos. In addition to woodland, the half-million-plus acres of Apalachicola National Forest contain a wealth of freshwater swamps and marshes, creating a habitat quite different from that of the coast. At the forest's heart lie some 22,000 acres of the Bradwell Bay Wilderness, where black bears shoulder their way through azalea thickets and sweet-bay magnolia swamps, and pitcher plants lure insects to a nectary doom.

The best route through the Apalachicola hinterlands is by water: the 67-mile canoe trail that follows the lazy curves of the Ochlockonee and Sopchoppy rivers, where paddlers glide along in the blissfully cool shade of bald cypresses and water oaks.

8 St. Marks National Wildlife Refuge

After reconnecting with Rte. 98 and continuing east, the drive noses south on Rte. 59 to the St. Marks National Wildlife Refuge. From observation decks overlooking dense woods and swampland,

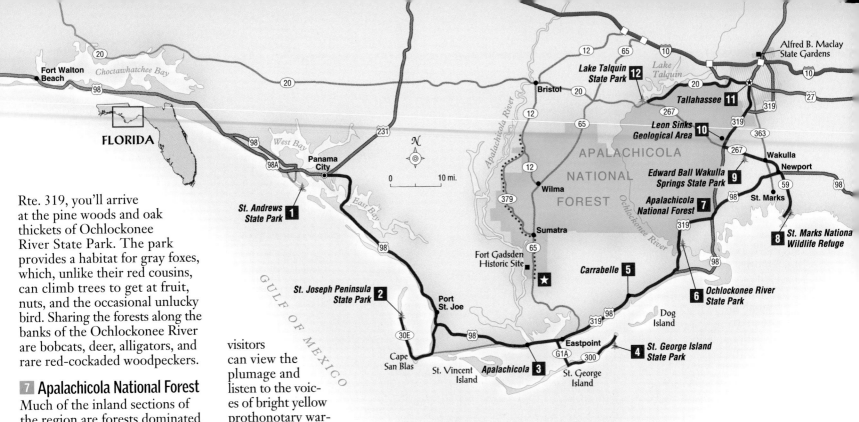

visitors can view the plumage and listen to the voices of bright yellow prothonotary warblers, Acadian flycatchers, eastern meadowlarks, and some 200 other kinds of birds.

Nearby, at the head of Apalachee Bay, stands the 80-foot St. Marks Lighthouse, fashioned of limestone blocks taken from the ruins of a 17th-century fort. The light has cast its beam into the night skies above the Gulf of Mexico since the early 1830s.

Tunnels of Tallahassee

Radiating from the center of Tallahassee to its rural outskirts are five delightful, officially designated Canopy Roads. The routes are so named because they are lined on both sides with live oaks whose branches, garlanded with Spanish moss, meet overhead to form virtual tunnels of foliage. The five Canopy Roads (Old Bainbridge, Centerville, Meridian, Miccousukee, and Old St. Augustine) wind by old plantations, Indian mounds, manicured picnic areas, tranquil lakes, and resplendent flower gardens.

9 Edward Ball Wakulla Springs State Park

Hollywood filmed its early Tarzan movies at Wakulla Springs (on Rte. 267), a pristine riverbank environment preserved by the farsighted efforts of financier Edward Ball. You can enjoy this watery realm—vibrant with snakes, alligators, and waterfowl—from the safety of a riverboat or hike the hospitable trails of the park's magnificent virgin upland hardwood forest.

The spring itself was discovered long ago by Indians, and according to legend it was also visited by the Spanish explorer Ponce de Leon, seeker of the Fountain of Youth, who is said to have wintered here. The crystal-clear pool, nearly 125 feet deep,

is fed by an underground river that discharges some 600,000 gallons per minute into the spring's basin and then into the Wakulla River. With the aid of a glass-bottomed excursion boat, visitors to the spring can look down to the entrance of a cave where mastodon bones are lodged—and from which a complete skeleton of one of the prehistoric creatures was retrieved by paleontologists in 1935.

10 Leon Sinks Geological Area

Just off Rte. 319, not far from Tallahassee, a corner of the Apalachicola National Forest harbors another unusual aspect of the region's geology. The Leon Sinks are a collection of five enormous holes in the forest floor, places where the bottom seems to have dropped out of terra firma. They were created when rainwater percolating through sandy soil dissolved segments of the weak, porous limestone below, causing the substructure to collapse. At Big Dismal Sink, the largest of the holes, the rim above the void measures 200 feet across. Seventy-five feet below—beneath steep walls overgrown with magnolias, laurel oaks, and more than 70 other kinds of plants—lies the surface of a deep, placid pool.

11 Tallahassee

Courtly by nature and modest in size, this panhandle city has more in common with its Deep South sisters, Savannah and Charleston, than with the metropolises of the Florida Peninsula. Tallahassee has been the state capital since 1824, when its promoters pointed to its "central" location—halfway between Pensacola and St. Augustine (back then, folks discounted the hot, malarial reaches to the south).

Tallahassee nestles amid gentle green hills, the southernmost outriders of the Appalachians.

Easy-access walkways invite visitors to Apalachicola National Forest's many trails.

Trip Tips

Length: About 230 miles.

When to go: Best between March and October.

Words to the wise: Destructive hurricanes struck Florida's Gulf Coast in 2004, and the damage was still being assessed as this book went to print; check the Visit Florida website or call before you travel.

Not to be missed: Deep-Sea Fishing Rodeo (October), Destin.

Nearby attractions: Florida Caverns State Park, near Marianna. Torreya State Park, near Greensboro. City of Pensacola.

Visitor center: St. Marks National Wildlife Refuge.

Further information: Visit Florida, P.O. Box 1100, Tallahassee, FL 32302; tel. 888-735-2872, www.visitflorida.com.

The view from the observation deck atop the 22-story New State Capitol makes the city seem a virtual island in a piney gulf, with the real Gulf, marked by the just-visible St. Marks Lighthouse, a scant 25 miles distant.

Nearby is the majestically domed Old Capitol, built in 1845 and now beautifully restored inside and out. White columns and resplendent red-and-white-striped awnings greet visitors, who can step inside to view exhibits on Florida's past.

Another way to experience the past is to take a stroll through one of Tallahassee's historic districts. Adams Street Commons occupies one city block of restored 19th-century buildings and exudes an old-fashioned, southern town-square ambience. The Calhoun Street and Park Avenue historic districts show off elaborate homes (the Bloxham, Cobb, Randall-Lewis, Knott, Murphy, Bowen, and Shine-Chittenden houses, for example) built by Tallahassee's well-to-do in the 1800s.

Located just north of town on Thomasville Road (Rte. 319) is the Alfred B. Maclay Gardens State Park, Tallahassee's most glorious outdoor attraction. Legions of azaleas, redbuds, dogwoods, magnolias, amaryllises, and other native flora grace the landscape here, along with the specialty of onetime owner Alfred Maclay: 150 varieties of fall- and winter-blooming red, white, and pink camellias.

12 Lake Talquin State Park

In 1927 the newly built Jackson Bluff Dam harnessed the powerful Ochlockonee River, forming sinuous Lake Talquin in its river valley. The lake meanders along the borders of the Apalachicola National Forest to the west of Tallahassee. Here anglers compete with bald eagles and ospreys for speckled perch and largemouth bass, while hikers wind along pine-scented trails in a dense woodland that seems almost a world apart from the panhandle's salty, wind-swept coast.

Road to Flamingo

Nowhere in all of America does water so define a place
as it does in the magnificent Florida Everglades, a "river of grass"
so shallow and slow-moving that it provides proof positive:
still waters don't always run deep.

*Knobby cypress knees protrude
from sunset-colored waters in
the Everglades National Park.*

The road to Flamingo, the southernmost town on the Florida mainland, begins barely an hour's drive south of downtown Miami. Yet this route through the heart of the Everglades makes civilization seem a good deal farther away.

1 Everglades National Park

"There are no other Everglades in the world," wrote conservationist Marjory Stoneman Douglas in 1947. She was referring, of course, to the unique natural character of these wetlands: the several distinct environments that combine to form a highly complex ecosystem; the web of life that is as fragile as it is fertile; and the "river of grass" whose original 50-mile breadth made it the widest river in the world. But perhaps what most impresses visitors to this lush, liquid realm is its incredible flatness. Indeed, the highest point in the park stands only 10 feet above sea level. Looking more like an African savanna than a wetland, this sea of saw grass, its tall stalks barely ruffled by the passing breeze, stretches from horizon to horizon, broken only by an occasional tree island, or hammock. Embracing some 4,000 square miles, the region is so vast that even 1.5-million-acre Everglades National Park (the second-largest national park in the lower 48 states) occupies a mere one-fifth of its total area.

2 Main Visitor Center

The remarkably diverse habitats and wildlife of the Everglades make it one of America's most precious natural wonders. Mangrove forests, freshwater sloughs, cypress stands, pinelands, coastal prairies, freshwater marl prairies, hardwood hammocks, estuaries—all can be seen here. The park is also home to an astonishing array of animals, including more than 600 species of fish, some 300 types of birds, and at least 67 kinds of mosquitoes. Among the threatened or endangered creatures that find sanctuary here are the Florida panther, the American alligator, the southern bald eagle, and the Key Largo cotton mouse.

The park's entrance is located 12 miles southwest of Homestead on Rte. 9336. Through a cluster of stately West Indian mahogany trees, you can glimpse the gabled roof of the main visitor center. Built to replace the one shattered by Hurricane Andrew in 1992, the structure houses exhibits on the park's history, habitats, and the hurricane itself.

Though it certainly wounded the Everglades—damage is most visible in the high, headless palms and the tall pines with missing limbs—Andrew, like all hurricanes, was part of the park's natural cycle. These storms' rains are critical, and while the fierce winds often topple trees, they also distribute

Park visitor-center huts with palm-thatched roofs go native in the Everglades.

FLORIDA

3 Royal Palm Visitor Center

As you head west toward the Royal Palm visitor center (located off a spur road leading south), you may encounter sunbathing turtles, great egrets, and hordes of butterflies. The visitor center, a concrete oasis tucked beneath palms, serves as the starting point for two short but exciting nature trails, each one providing a chance to see wildlife up close. From the Anhinga Trail you might spy alligators, marsh rabbits, and of course, the animal that gives the path its name, a bird with a razor-sharp bill that it uses to spear fish. While walking the Gumbo Limbo Trail, you can study a wide variety of aerial orchids and ferns, along with the gumbo limbo itself, a graceful smooth-barked red tree once used for making carousel horses.

4 Pa-hay-okee Overlook

When the waters are high and the air is still, the shimmering saw grass looks as if it's growing from glass. The tranquil glades then become an aquatic mirror, with clusters of green extending above and below the surface. In reality, of course, the mirror is moving. Flowing southward from Lake Okeechobee to Florida Bay, the water of the Everglades—only six inches deep in many spots—glide at the rate of less than one mile per day across porous limestone bedrock. At the Pa-hay-okee Overlook, some 10 miles west of Royal Palm, you can appreciate the sheer immensity of this expanse, a massive sheet of water whose movement to the ocean is all but imperceptible on most occasions.

5 Mahogany Hammock

Within minutes you'll reach Mahogany Hammock, a thick jungle alive with the strains of animal music: the bellowing of alligators, the dizzying buzz of mosquitoes, and the unmistakable ribbits of frogs. A boardwalk winds through the area, which contains one of the oldest and largest mahoganies in America, a towering tree dating back some 300 years.

6 West Lake

As the drive heads farther south, it reaches a transition zone where fresh water from sloughs and wet prairies mixes with salt water from Florida Bay and the Gulf of Mexico. The resulting nutrient-rich "soup" nourishes not only many types of fish, but salt-tolerant mangrove trees as well. Those that surround West Lake (red, black, and white mangroves) are part of an impenetrable labyrinth, a web of tangled branches and high knotty roots that protect inland areas by forming a buffer against high winds.

West Lake is one of the best places here for observing the park's premier predators—alligators. Kin to animals that lived alongside the dinosaurs, the are cold-blooded creatures who conserve energy by spending most of their time motionless. But when they pursue their prey, they can become sprinters, able to outrun even humans for short distances.

After alligators, the park's most popular inhabitants are birds, and more than 400 species live here. One of the best bird-watching sites is just south of the mangrove forest at Mrazek Pond, which attracts, among other species, the rare roseate spoonbill. On winter mornings and evenings, listen for wood storks, pelicans, and pig frogs.

The key-strewn waters of nearby Florida Bay—40 miles wide and 25 miles long—appear more green than blue. As the drive approaches Flamingo, that color continues to dominate the scenery, which includes more than 100 different plant species.

7 Flamingo

The southernmost headquarters of Everglades National Park, this town—named for the pink long-legged birds that once frequented the area but now are seen only rarely—serves as a base for excursions to nearby bays, lakes, rivers, and tropical beaches. Its shore is anchored by a marina, a visitor center, and a utilitarian lodge. Flamingo is also the launching point for canoe trips along the 99-mile Wilderness Waterway, a well-marked backcountry route that provides an unrivaled tour of the region's richly varied wildlife.

Overseas Highway

Island-hopping to land's end, this one-of-a-kind highway offers the promise of radiant seascapes, exotic underwater worlds, and animals found nowhere else in America.

Spanning land and sea, Seven-Mile Bridge on Rte. 1 wends its way from mainland Florida to Key West.

Completed in 1938 along the course of an ill-fated railroad that had been destroyed by a hurricane, the Overseas Highway (Rte. 1) leaps from island to island across 42 bridges as it arcs southwestward through the Florida Keys. The islands were first seen by Europeans in the 16th century, when Spanish flotillas were carting off the riches of the New World. Today visitors come for different kinds of treasure—sunshine, escape, and clear, warm waters that teem with life.

1 North Key Largo

Instead of heading south from Florida City on the first leg of Rte. 1, take Card Sound Road to the northern end of Key Largo for a glimpse of what the islands looked like before this area's commercial boom. Beyond the toll bridge, this sparsely populated sector boasts a stand of virgin forest in which exposed coral formations dot the landscape, along with palms, marshes, mangrove swamps, and the occasional wild orchid. Among the rare animals found in this wilderness are saltwater crocodiles, scarlet ibis, pelicans, and roseate spoonbills; even the endangered Florida panther has been spotted here.

2 Key Largo

Some 30 miles long but averaging only about 2 miles in width, Key Largo is the largest of the Florida Keys. For a revealing look at its geologic underpinnings, slow down near mile marker 103 on Rte. 1, where an exceptionally fine expanse of coral has been exposed on the bank of a man-made channel.

Though tourist facilities and commercial development are much in evidence along the highway, here as elsewhere in the keys the sea is never very far away. At Key Largo the most notable marine attraction is John Pennekamp Coral Reef State Park, an undersea wildlife preserve. In addition to hordes of brightly colored fish, the reef is home to throngs of sea stars, sand dollars, sea anemones, crabs, and sponges. Tours by glass-bottom boat are available, and the more adventurous can snorkel and scuba dive in the seas of this underwater wonderland.

3 Islamorada

Stretching from Windley Key to Long Key, the Islamorada area is renowned as a center for sportfishing. Among its other attractions is the Theater of the Sea, a marine park at mile 84.5 that features performing dolphins and seals.

From the docks near mile 78.5, boats depart for excursions to the wilds of nearby Lignumvitae Key State Botanical Site, where the virgin forest includes such exotic species as strangler figs, pigeon plums, and gumbo-limbo trees. Boat tours also are available for visits to Indian Key State Historic Site, a lonely 10-acre islet that served as a bustling county seat until it was devastated during an Indian rebellion in 1840. Self-guiding walks lead through the ruins of the town, where tropical plants now flourish.

To the south of Indian Key, visitors can explore San Pedro Underwater Archaeological Preserve. The site of a 1733 Spanish shipwreck, it is now a mecca for skin divers and snorkelers.

4 Long Key State Park

Wending among the tropical hammocks and mangrove-fringed lagoons in this 1,100-acre park are a variety of self-guiding nature trails, including one that was designed for exploration by canoe. The staff offers interpretive programs, with an emphasis on birds, sea turtles, and the fragile environ-

Hemingway House, the famous writer's residence, on Key West.

horizons—the bridge is perhaps the most astonishing stretch on the entire Overseas Highway.

6 Bahia Honda State Park

Although the Keys are not noted for large sandy beaches, the ones bordering the Atlantic Ocean at Bahia Honda are some of the island chain's finest. Charter boats ply offshore waters in search of game fish—including the spunky tarpon, a favorite among sportsmen. Hikers along the area's nature trail should be on the lookout for the endangered small-flowered lily thorn and one of America's largest remaining stands of silver palms. Many wild animals—tree frogs, falcons, pelicans, loggerheads, and geckos, for example—also live within or just outside the park's borders.

7 National Key Deer Refuge

The key deer, found in the Florida Keys and nowhere else, is a subspecies of the larger, more common white-tailed deer. The main difference between the two is their size; an adult key buck stands only about 2½ feet

tall at the shoulder. After near extinction the animals are slowly repopulating their 7,900-acre refuge.

Great White Heron National Wildlife Refuge and Key West National Wildlife Refuge also are located in the Lower Keys region. Although the shoals, reefs, and low-lying islands that make up these sprawling sanctuaries are reached mainly by boat, they reward visitors with solitude and miles of pristine wilderness.

8 Key West

Once a hideaway for pirates, Key West today is a colorful patchwork of gardens, alleyways, historic buildings, shops, museums, and lively marinas. The southernmost city in the continental United States, it attracts a heady mix of fishermen, shopkeepers, navy personnel, Cuban refugees, artists, and assorted eccentrics with alternative lifestyles. Two greats, Ernest Hemingway and John James Audubon, are among those who once chose to live and work here.

But what really separates Key West from most other cities is its island charm. Perhaps the best way to experience its unique flavor is to visit Mallory Square, where locals and sightseers congregate each evening, amid a carnival-like atmosphere complete with street performers, to celebrate and toast the glowing sun as it sets beneath the sea.

ments in which they live. The area's seaside campsites offer clear views of the ocean, making this a popular spot for swimming.

5 Marathon

For a tranquil contrast to the hustle and bustle you'll find in touristy Marathon, seek out the solitude of Crane Point Hammock. In addition to its wetlands and exotic hardwoods, the 64-acre preserve contains a few remnants from pre-Columbian times. The Museum of Natural History of the Florida Keys, situated at the hammock's entrance by mile marker 50, has a wide range of exhibits, from ancient artifacts to pictures taken from outer space. There's even a re-created coral reef—an excellent place to explore undersea life and still stay dry.

As you leave Marathon to visit points south, you'll come to the famed Seven-Mile Bridge. Traversing the blue waters of Moser Channel—where only the merest specks of land intrude upon far-off

389

Photo Credits

Cover *(main)* Photo courtesy of SCPRT; *(bottom, left to right)* Courtesy of Rhode Island Tourism Division/Kindra Clineff; Kurt E. Asplind; Travel Montana/Donnie Sexton.

2–3 John M. Rickard. **10** Chuck Place. **12, 13** Courtesy of Washington State Tourism/ Sunny Walter. **14, 16** Courtesy of Washington State Tourism. **17** *(left)* Courtesy of Washington State Tourism; *(left insert)* Courtesy of Washington State Tourism/Walter Hodges; *(right)* Courtesy of Washington State Tourism/Cynthia Hunter. **18** Courtesy of Washington State Tourism/ Sunny Walter. **19** Courtesy of Washington State Tourism. **20** Courtesy of Washington State Tourism/Sunny Walter. **21** Courtesy of Washington State Tourism/J. Poth. **22, 23, 24, 25** Courtesy of Washington State Tourism/Sunny Walter. **26** *(left)* Central Oregon Coast Association; *(right)* Gerry Ellis/Ellis Nature Photography. **27** Larry Ulrich. **28** Central Oregon Coast Association. **30** *(insert)* James D. Watt/ Animals Animals/Earth Scenes. **31** David Muench. **32** Oregon's Mt. Hood Territory/ Larry Geddis. **33, 34** Peter Marbach courtesy Hood River County Chamber of Commerce. **35** Dan Sherwood. **36** Gregg Morgan/BLM. **37** *(left)* Ron Murphy/BLM; *(right)* Robert J. Dolezal. **38** *(top)* Ron Murphy/BLM; *(bottom)* Terry Tuttle **39** Gregg Morgan/BLM. **40** David Muench. **41** Ric Ergenbright. **42** Kurt E. Asplind. **43** Jack Hopkins: Courtesy Humboldt County CVB, www.redwoodvisitor.org. **44** Photo by Don Leonard: Courtesy Humboldt County CVB, www.redwoodvisitor.org. **45**

Photo by Don Forthuber: Courtesy Humboldt County CVB, www.redwoodvisitor.org. **46, 48** Shasta Cascade Wonderland Association. **49** Sandi Mehler. **50** John M. Rickard. **52** Chuck Place. **53** John M. Rickard. **54** Kurt E. Asplind. **56** John M. Rickard. **57** Kurt E. Asplind. **58** Larry Ulrich. **59** Kurt E. Asplind. **60** San Luis Obispo County VCB. **61** *(left)* Larry Ulrich; *(right)* San Luis Obispo County VCB. **62** San Luis Obispo County VCB. **63** *(top)* San Luis Obispo County VCB/Aaron Culp; *(bottom)* San Luis Obispo County VCB. **64, 65, 66, 67, 68** Kurt E. Asplind. **70** Blaine Harrinton III. **71, 72, 73** Nevada Commission on Tourism. **74, 75, 77** Kurt E. Asplind. **78, 79** Robert J. Dolezal. **80** *(insert)* Wayne Lynch/DRK photo. **81** Kurt E. Asplind. **82** Robert J. Dolezal. **83** Kurt E. Asplind. **84, 85** Kaua'i Visitors Bureau. **86, 87** Oahu Visitors Bureau. **88, 89** ©1996 Ron Dalquist. **90** *(top)* Big Island Visitors Bureau/Thomas Peter Widman; *(bottom)* David Muench. **91** David Muench. **92** ©Greg Vaughn/Pacific Stock. **93** Robert J. Dolezal. **94** Kurt E. Asplind. **96** Idaho Parks. **97,98** Peg Owens/Idaho Travel Council. **99** Ron Row/Idaho Travel Council. **100** Chris Ramsdell/Idaho Travel Council. **101** Travel Montana/Donnie Sexton. **102, 103** Peg Owens/Idaho Travel Council. **104** Travel Montana/Rick & Suzi Graetz. **105** Travel Montana/Susan Albrecht. **106, 108, 109,110** Travel Montana/Donnie Sexton. **111** C.M.Russell painting, "The Lookout," watercolor, 1898; courtesy C.M.Russell Museum, Great Falls, Montana. **112, 113** Travel Montana/Donnie Sexton. **114** Fred

Pflughoft. **115** Wyoming Travel & Tourism. **116** Fred Pflughoft. **117** Egret Communications. **119** Pete Saloutos. **120** Egret Communications. **121** *(left)* Pete Saloutos; *(right)* John M. Rickard. **122** John M. Rickard. **123** Wyoming Travel & Tourism. **124, 125** Fred Pflughoft. **126, 127** The Wagner Perspective. **128** Wyoming Travel & Tourism. **130, 131, 133, 134, 136, 137** Photo courtesy Utah Division of Travel Development/Frank Jensen, photographer. **138** Kurt E. Asplind. **139** Tom Bean. **141** Photo courtesy Utah Division of Travel Development/Frank Jensen, photographer. **142, 143, 145** Rocky Mountain State Park. **146** Glenn Randall. **147** Glenn Randall. **148** Terry Donnelly. **149** Jeff Gnass. **151** David Muench. **152, 154** Sally Pearce/Colorado Scenic and Historic Byways Program. **155** *(top)* Kurt E. Asplind; *(bottom)* Sally Pearce/ Colorado Scenic and Historic Byways Program. **156** David Muench. **157** Kim Tune. **158** Photo courtesy Utah Division of Travel Development/Frank Jensen, photographer. **159** Larry Ulrich. **160** Tom Bean. **161** T. A. Wiewandt/DRK Photo. **162** Bob Willis. **163** Prewitt Company. **164** Tom Till. **165** Wayne Schroeter. **166** Chris Coe. **167** Larry D Fellows. **168** Larry D Fellows. **169** Larry Ulrich. **170** Larry D Fellows. **171** Prescott Area Coalition for Tourism. **172** Jerry Sieve. **173** Wayne Schroeter. **174** Larry Ulrich. **175** Dale Schicketanz. **176** Courtesy: New Mexico Department of Tourism/Mark Nohl. **177** Courtesy: New Mexico Department of Tourism. **178** Rod Planck/ Tom Stack & Associates. **179** Courtesy: New Mexico Department of Tourism.

Index

*Page numbers in **bold type** refer to illustrations.*

*Page numbers in **bold type** refer to illustrations.*

*Page numbers in **bold type** refer to illustrations.*